Encyclopedia of

AMERICAN JEWISH HISTORY

Encyclopedia of

AMERICAN JEWISH HISTORY

Volume 2

**Stephen H. Norwood and
Eunice G. Pollack, Editors**

A B C · CLIO

Santa Barbara, California   Denver, Colorado   Oxford, United Kingdom

Library of Congress Cataloging-in-Publication Data
Encyclopedia of American Jewish history / Stephen H. Norwood and Eunice G. Pollack, editors.
  p. cm.
  Includes bibliographical references and index.
  ISBN-13: 978-1-85109-638-1 (hard copy : alk. paper)
  ISBN-13: 978-1-85109-643-5 (ebook)
  1. Jews—United States—History—Encyclopedias. 2. Jews—United States—History. I. Norwood, Stephen H. (Stephen Harlan), 1951– II. Pollack, Eunice G.
E184.35.E53 2008
973'.04924--dc22

2007013889

12 11 10 09 08   1 2 3 4 5 6 7 8 9 10

Production Editor: Anna A. Moore
Editorial Assistant: Sara Springer
Production Manager: Don Schmidt
Media Editor: Jason Kniser
Media Resources Coordinator: Ellen Brenna Dougherty
Media Resources Manager: Caroline Price
File Manager: Paula Gerard

ABC-CLIO, Inc.
130 Cremona Drive, P.O. Box 1911
Santa Barbara, California 93116–1911

This book is also available on the World Wide Web as an ebook. Visit http://www.abc-clio.com for details.

This book is printed on acid-free paper. ∞

Manufactured in the United States of America

Contents

VOLUME 1

Preface xiii
Maps xvii

1
Immigration and Settlement

Sephardic Jews in America, *Aviva Ben-Ur*   1

American Jews in the Colonial Period,
   William Pencak   9

American Jews in the Revolutionary and Early
   National Periods, *Frederic Cople Jaher*   15

German Jews in America, *Stanley Nadel*   24

East European Jewish Immigration, *Gerald Sorin*   36

Jewish Immigration to Galveston,
   Elizabeth Hayes Turner   43

Soviet Jewish Immigration, *Annelise Orleck*   47

Jewish Identity in America, *Edward S. Shapiro*   50

2
Demographic and Economic Profiles of Twentieth-Century American Jewry

The Demography of Jews in Twentieth-Century
   America, *Calvin Goldscheider*   57

The Economic Status of American Jews in the
   Twentieth Century, *Barry R. Chiswick and*
   Carmel U. Chiswick   62

3
Judaism in America

Orthodox Judaism, *Jeffrey S. Gurock*   67

Reform Judaism, *Lance J. Sussman*   74

Conservative Judaism, *Lawrence Grossman*   82

Reconstructionist Judaism, *Jacob J. Staub*   89

Hasidic Judaism, *Allan Nadler*   97

Women in the Development of American Judaism,
   Karla Goldman   106

Isaac Leeser (1806–1868), *Lance J. Sussman*   110

David Einhorn (1809–1879), *Lance J. Sussman*   112

4
Jewish Communities

The Lower East Side, *Gerald Sorin*   115

Brownsville, *Gerald Sorin*   122

South Florida, *Henry A. Green*   127

Los Angeles, *Gil Graff and Stephen J. Sass*   132

Chicago, *Irving Cutler*   134

Philadelphia, *Jonathan Rosenbaum*   140

Jews in the South, *Leonard Rogoff*   145

Jews in the West, *Ava F. Kahn*   149

New Mexico, *Ava F. Kahn*   155

Jews in Small Towns in America, *Ewa Morawska*   156

Jewish Agricultural Colonies, *Ellen Eisenberg*   162

Jews in Suburbia, *Etan Diamond*   165

5
Antisemitism in America

Antisemitism in American Literature before 1960,
  Robert Michael   169

Leo Max Frank (1884–1915), *Stephen J. Goldfarb*   175

Henry Ford and the Jews, *Neil Baldwin*   180

Antisemitic Violence in Boston and New York during
  World War II, *Stephen H. Norwood*   187

Antisemitism and Right-Wing Extremist Groups
  after 1960, *John George*   189

African American Antisemitism in the 1990s,
  Eunice G. Pollack   195

The Crown Heights Riot, *Edward S. Shapiro*   200

6
Zionism in America

American Zionism to the Founding of the
  State of Israel, *Melvin I. Urofsky*   203

Revisionist Zionism in America, *Rafael Medoff*   208

Golda Meir (1898–1978), *Michael Alexander*   212

Marie Syrkin (1899–1989), *Ranen Omer-Sherman*   214

7
The Holocaust and America

America's Response to Nazism and the Holocaust,
  David S. Wyman and Rafael Medoff   217

Holocaust Survivors and Their Children in
  America, *Eva Fogelman*   224

The Making of the United States Holocaust
  Memorial Museum, *Edward T. Linenthal*   228

Meyer Levin (1905–1981), *Ralph Melnick*   231

8
Jewish Organizations

The Workmen's Circle, *Jack Jacobs*   235

The Jewish War Veterans of the United States of
  America, *Stephen H. Norwood*   238

The American Jewish Committee, *Jerome A. Chanes*   240

The Anti-Defamation League, *Abraham H. Foxman*   242

The American Jewish Congress, *Jerome A. Chanes*   248

The Jewish Labor Committee, *Gail Malmgreen*   251

The Simon Wiesenthal Center, *Harold Brackman*   256

9
Jews and the Press

The Early Yiddish Press in the United States,
  Tony Michels   261

Abraham Cahan (1860–1951), *Gerald Sorin*   268

The American Jewish Press, *Donald Altschiller*   271

10
American Jews in Political
and Social Movements

American Jews in Politics in the Twentieth Century,
  Benjamin Ginsberg   277

American Jewish Involvement in Public Affairs,
  Jerome A. Chanes   281

American Jews in the Socialist and Communist
  Movements, *Gerald Sorin*   283

The Rosenberg Case, *Henry D. Fetter*   290

Jewish Anarchism in America, *Ori Kritz*   297

Commentary and the Origins of Neoconservatism,
  Henry D. Fetter   300

Jewish Women in the American Feminist
  Movement, *June Sochen*   307

Emma Goldman (1869–1940), *Candace Falk*   310

Meyer London (1871–1926), *Gerald Sorin*   313

Henry Kissinger (b. 1923), *Michael Alexander*   316

11
Jews in Wars
and the Military

Jews and the Civil War, *Larry M. Logue*   321

American Jews and World War I,
  Christopher M. Sterba   326

American Jews in the Spanish Civil War (1936–1939),
    Fraser M. Ottanelli   327

American Jewish Soldiers in World War II,
    Deborah Dash Moore   329

12
American Jews and the Law

The Jewish Justices of the Supreme Court,
    Henry D. Fetter   335

13
American Jews and Crime

American Jewish Gangsters, *Robert A. Rockaway*   349

14
American Jews and Labor

Jews and the International Ladies' Garment
    Workers' Union, *Gus Tyler*   359

Jews and the International Fur Workers' Union,
    Sandra Spingarn   362

David Dubinsky (1892–1982), *Robert D. Parmet*   365

Samuel Gompers (1850–1924), *Grace Palladino*   367

Sidney Hillman (1887–1946), *Gerd Korman*   370

Pauline M. Newman (1890–1986), *Annelise Orleck*   374

Selig Perlman (1888–1959), *Mark Perlman*   378

Rose Pesotta (1896–1965), *Elaine Leeder*   381

Rose Schneiderman (1882–1972), *Annelise Orleck*   383

Toni Sender (1888–1964), *Stephen H. Norwood*   388

Albert Shanker (1928–1997), *Richard D. Kahlenberg*   390

Index I-1

VOLUME 2

Preface xi
Maps xv

15
American Jews in Business and Philanthropy

Jewish Department Store Magnates, *Kenneth Libo*   395

Southern Jewish Retailers (1840–2000),
    Sarah S. Malino   400

American Jews and the Diamond Business,
    Renée Rose Shield   404

Julius Rosenwald (1862–1932), *Peter M. Ascoli*   406

Jacob H. Schiff (1847–1920), *Naomi W. Cohen*   407

16
Intergroup Relations

Jews and the Slave Trade, *Seymour Drescher*   411

Black–Jewish Relations in the Nineteenth Century,
    Harold Brackman   417

Jews and Black Rights (1900–1950),
    Stephen H. Norwood   424

Black–Jewish Relations since 1950, *Murray Friedman*   428

Jews and Affirmative Action/Preferences,
    Jerome A. Chanes   432

Jewish–Christian Relations in the United States in the
    Twentieth Century, *George R. Wilkes*   435

Joseph Dov Soloveitchik (1903–1993),
    George R. Wilkes   438

Leon Kronish (1917–1996), *Henry A. Green*   440

Jewish–Muslim Relations, *Yehudit Barsky*   442

17
American Jews in Entertainment and Popular Culture

Yiddish Theater in America, *Edna Nahshon*   449

Jews and Broadway, *Stephen J. Whitfield*   455

Jews and Hollywood, *Robert Sklar* 460

American Jews and the Catskills, *Phil Brown* 467

American Jews and the Comics,
 Stephen E. Tabachnick 469

American Jews and Television, *Vincent Brook* 474

The Marx Brothers, *Harold Brackman* 481

American Jewish Comedians, *Lawrence J. Epstein* 483

Woody Allen (b. 1935), *Harold Brackman* 491

American Jewish Women Entertainers, *June Sochen* 494

Harry Houdini (1874–1926), *Bette Howland* 498

Al Jolson (1886–1950), *Michael Alexander* 499

Samuel "Roxy" Rothafel (1882–1936), *Ross Melnick* 503

Sammy Davis Jr. (1925–1990), *Michael Alexander* 506

American Jews and Science Fiction, *Steven H. Silver* 507

Isaac Asimov (1920–1992), *Michael Levy* 510

Emma Lazarus (1849–1887), *Ranen Omer-Sherman* 571

Ludwig Lewisohn (1882–1955), *Ralph Melnick* 573

Bernard Malamud (1914–1986),
 Edward A. Abramson 577

David Mamet (b. 1947), *Ira Nadel* 581

Donald Margulies (b. 1954), *Donald Weber* 584

Arthur Miller (1915–2005), *Terry Otten* 586

Chaim Potok (1929–2002), *Edward A. Abramson* 590

Morris Rosenfeld (1862–1923), *Ori Kritz* 594

Leo Calvin Rosten (1908–1997), *David Mesher* 595

Henry Roth (1906–1995), *Hana Wirth-Nesher* 598

Philip Roth (b. 1933), *Debra Shostak* 601

Isaac Bashevis Singer (1904–1991), *Edward Alexander* 606

Leon Uris (1924–2003), *Kathleen Shine Cain* 611

Morris Winchevsky (1856–1932), *Ori Kritz* 614

Herman Wouk (b. 1915), *Edward S. Shapiro* 615

18
American Jews in Sports

American Jewish Men in Sports,
 Stephen H. Norwood 513

American Jewish Women in Sports, *Linda J. Borish* 522

Senda Berenson (1868–1954), *Ralph Melnick* 527

Hank Greenberg (1911–1986), *Henry D. Fetter* 529

Sandy Koufax (b. 1935), *Henry D. Fetter* 531

Marvin Miller (b. 1917), *Roger I. Abrams* 533

20
American Jewish Literary Critics

Irving Howe (1920–1993), *Edward Alexander* 621

Alfred Kazin (1915–1998), *Richard M. Cook* 623

William Phillips (1907–2002), *Alan M. Wald* 625

Philip Rahv (1908–1973), *Alan M. Wald* 628

Lionel Trilling (1905–1975), *Mark Shechner* 630

19
American Jewish Novelists, Essayists, Poets, and Playwrights

Early Jewish Writers in America, *Michael P. Kramer* 537

New Jewish Immigrant Writing, *Donald Weber* 545

Jewish American Women Fiction Writers, *June Sochen* 550

Sholem Asch (1880–1957), *Jeremy Dauber* 554

Saul Bellow (1915–2005), *Ben Siegel* 557

Joseph Bovshover (1873–1915), *Ori Kritz* 563

David Edelshtat (1866–1892), *Ori Kritz* 565

Daniel Fuchs (1909–1993), *David Mesher* 566

Michael Gold (1894–1967), *Alan M. Wald* 568

21
American Jews and Art

Jewish American Artists and Their Themes in the
 Twentieth Century, *Ori Z. Soltes* 635

Jewish American Artists and the Holocaust,
 Matthew Baigell 640

Jewish and Christian Symbols in the Work of Jewish
 American Artists, *Ori Z. Soltes* 645

Clement Greenberg (1909–1994), *Matthew Baigell* 649

Harold Rosenberg (1906–1978), *Matthew Baigell* 650

Meyer Schapiro (1904–1996), *Donald Kuspit* 652

Jack Levine (b. 1915), *Samantha Baskind* 654

Man Ray (1890–1976), *Milly Heyd* 655

Larry Rivers (1923–2002), *Samantha Baskind*   658

George Segal (1924–2000), *Milly Heyd*   659

Raphael Soyer (1899–1987), *Samantha Baskind*   662

22
American Jews and Music

The Cantorate in America, *Mark Kligman*   665

Jews in Rock 'n' Roll, *Glenn C. Altschuler*   670

Contemporary Jewish Music in America,
    Mark Kligman   679

Irving Berlin (1888–1989), *David M. Schiller*   683

Leonard Bernstein (1918–1990), *David M. Schiller*   686

Marc Blitzstein (1905–1964), *David Z. Kushner*   691

Ernest Bloch (1880–1959), *David Z. Kushner*   693

George Gershwin (1898–1937), *David M. Schiller*   696

Benny Goodman (1909–1986), *David M. Schiller*   699

Steve Reich (b. 1936), *David Z. Kushner*   702

Arnold Schoenberg (1874–1951), *David M. Schiller*   704

23
American Jews and the Social Sciences

American Jews and Psychology,
    Nicole B. Barenbaum   707

Jews in the Development of American
    Psychoanalysis: The First Fifty Years,
    Arnold Richards   710

Jewish Emigrés of the Frankfurt School,
    Stephen Eric Bronner   713

American Jews in Economics, *Robert Solomon*   717

Hannah Arendt (1906–1975), *Stephen J. Whitfield*   722

Franz Boas (1858–1942), *Matti Bunzl*   724

Horace Kallen (1882–1974), *Samuel Haber*   727

Paul Lazarsfeld (1901–1976), *Terry Nichols Clark*   730

Max Lerner (1902–1992), *Sanford Lakoff*   732

Robert Merton (1910–2003), *Samuel Haber*   734

24
American Jews in Science

American Jews in the Physical Sciences,
    Yakov M. Rabkin   739

Albert Einstein (1879–1955), *John Stachel*   742

American Jews and the Ideology of Modern Science,
    Stephen P. Weldon   745

25
American Jews and Education

Jewish Education in America, *Jonathan B. Krasner*   749

Brandeis University, *Clifford D. Hauptman and
    John R. Hose*   755

26
Jewish History and American Jewish Historians

Salo Baron (1895–1989), *Frederic Krome*   763

Jacob Rader Marcus (1896–1995), *Gary P. Zola*   764

Bertram W. Korn (1918–1979), *Gary P. Zola*   767

YIVO Institute for Jewish Research in the
    United States, *Cecile Esther Kuznitz*   768

The American Jewish Archives, *Gary P. Zola*   770

List of Contributors   773
Index   I-1

Preface

The *Encyclopedia of American Jewish History* records and analyzes the American Jewish experience from its beginnings in the mid-seventeenth century to the present. It examines the encounters with, and impact on, America of successive waves of Jewish immigrants and their descendants, including Sephardim, Ashkenazim, Holocaust survivors, Soviet Jews, and Mizrahim.

The *Encyclopedia* considers American Jews both as a religious and an ethnic group. Articles trace the continuity and the changes that Judaism underwent in America, covering all the major branches and religious movements: Orthodox, Reform, Conservative, Hasidic, Reconstructionist. Authors explore the identities Jews forged in America. Reflecting Jews' varying degrees and rates of acculturation and assimilation, these identities are arrayed along a wide continuum.

Several articles provide overviews of the transformation of the Jewish ethnic community in America. They analyze demographic patterns, occupational structures, and social and economic mobility, tracing changes over time. Authors assess what was unique about the American Jewish experience. Other articles analyze American Jews' voting behavior, political alignments, and general involvement in public affairs.

The *Encyclopedia* examines a multiplicity of Jewish communities in America. These range from small settlements in early colonial cities to large, heavily Jewish neighborhoods in major late nineteenth- and twentieth-century metropolises, to concentrations in post–World War II suburbia. Authors assess what was distinctive about Jewish life in regions such as the South and the West, as well as in small towns and agricultural communities.

Although American historians and textbooks have generally marginalized and even ignored the Jewish experience, Jews have profoundly influenced American society. The *Encyclopedia* demonstrates that, despite the numerous barriers confronting them, Jews significantly shaped American culture. Jews have had a major impact on American literature, theater, film, and television. For significant periods they dominated comedy, and were of critical importance in the comic strip and comic book industries. Superman, Batman, and Spider-Man were Jewish creations. There were periods when Jews were heavily overrepresented in important sports, notably boxing and basketball, and in sportswriting. Their imprint on American art and music has been far-reaching.

Although Jews long encountered severe restrictions in American academia, their impact on many disciplines is striking. The *Encyclopedia* explores the Jewish role in such fields as psychoanalysis and psychology; the physical sciences and economics, in which American Jewish Nobelists have figured prominently; anthropology and sociology, and even African American history. Articles consider such social scientists as Franz Boas and Horace

Kallen, who pioneered in configuring a multicultural American identity.

Jews have been especially prominent in the American labor movement and in some sectors of American business, including department stores. Many Jews, such as Jacob Schiff and Julius Rosenwald, ranked among the nation's leading philanthropists. Many articles explore how Jewish men and women built thriving trade unions from the ground up, sparked some of the most important strikes and organizing campaigns in American history, and led national labor bodies, like the American Federation of Labor and the National Women's Trade Union League.

Jews were critical in molding important American political and social movements. These ranged from various forms of socialism on the Left to neoconservatism on the Right, all of which the *Encyclopedia* details. Jews played very significant roles in the twentieth-century civil rights movement, as frontline activists, advisors, lawyers, and financial supporters. Martin Luther King Jr. credited Jews with a massive contribution to the struggle for black advancement. Jewish women played decisive parts in initiating and leading the American feminist movement that resurfaced in the 1960s and 1970s.

As a minority, Jews have had complex and extensive relations with other religious and ethnic groups in America. Articles assess the nature, extent, and limitations of intergroup cooperation. The *Encyclopedia* examines the Christian majority's attitudes toward Judaism and treatment of Jews from the colonial period to the present. American Jews have been at the center of efforts to expand religious and civil liberties and to strengthen and maintain the separation between church and state. The work traces the relations between Jewish and Muslim associations in the United States, a subject of increasing importance. Several articles chronicle Jews' extensive contacts with African Americans, illuminating the significant commonalities and differences in the groups' experiences. Authors address black–Jewish cooperation as well as tensions between the groups, including the Crown Heights riot. Other essays highlight American Jewish social scientists' pioneering work on cultural diversity, recognizing America as the dynamic product of multiple ethnic influences.

Although often overlooked, the contribution of Jews to America's military endeavors has been significant. Articles detail Jews' participation in wartime service, often at rates higher than their percentages in the American population. Authors address antisemitism in the U.S. armed forces and Jews' efforts to combat it. Particular attention is devoted to Jews' experience in the Civil War, Spanish-American War, World War I, the Spanish Civil War, World War II, and the Jewish veterans' organizations.

The *Encyclopedia* examines the wide range of Jewish women's activities in America, including their experience in, and impact on, religious life inside and outside the synagogue and temple. Several authors address the unprecedented expansion of Jewish women's roles in Judaism in recent decades. Significant attention is also given to Jewish women's very prominent role in the American labor movement, with articles profiling several leaders and activists. Essays explore the roles of Jewish women entertainers in Yiddish theater, on Broadway, in film, and on television. Authors discuss American Jewish women writers, poets, and artists. Articles assess Jewish women's major impact on the shaping of women's sport in America.

Antisemitism, while less virulent than in Europe and the Middle East, significantly constricted Jews' lives in America. Jews encountered Christian theological antisemitism and discrimination from the time of their first arrival in North America in 1654. Throughout the *Encyclopedia,* authors assess the changes in severity and the impact of antisemitic prejudice, examining the roles of churches, federal, state, and local government, corporate business, higher education, social organizations, and other institutions. One author underscores the antisemitism of many of America's eminent literary figures, a subject often accorded little attention in works about them.

Particularly intense outbreaks of antisemitism receive close scrutiny, such as the Leo Frank case, the waves of physical assaults on Jews during World War II in Boston and New York, and the 1991 Crown Heights riot. Attention is also given to such antisemitic episodes as General Ulysses S. Grant's General Order No. 11 during the Civil War. Several articles analyze twentieth-century antisemitic movements, including those stimulated by Henry Ford's concerted campaign against the Jews, Coughlinism and the Christian Front, and post-1960 right-wing extremist groups, like the Liberty Lobby, Holocaust deniers, and Christian Identity. Other articles focus on various strains of African American antisemitism, including that of the Nation of Islam, as well as Muslim antisemitism.

Authors explore the impact of the Holocaust on American society and on American Jews. One article analyzes the causes of the U.S. government's limited response to the Nazis' annihilation of Europe's Jews. Others concentrate on literary and artistic attempts to grapple with the horrors and implications of the Holocaust, a genocide unprecedented in history. The U.S. Holocaust Memorial Museum, embodying a commitment to educate about the Shoah and to preserve the memory of the lives destroyed, also receives attention. One author focuses on the responses to Holocaust survivors who settled in America and on the experiences of their children.

American Jews were significant in the development of Zionism. Articles examine the origin and growth of the American Zionist movement and its relations with European Zionism, exploring the debates and divisions over strategies and goals. Attention is given to prominent Zionist leaders and activists in America, such as Louis Brandeis, Golda Meir (Meyerson), and Marie Syrkin.

American Jews have established numerous national organizations that address and express the needs of the Jewish community, defending the rights of Jews and combating antisemitism and other forms of prejudice and discrimination. The *Encyclopedia* traces the formation and evolution of many of these groups, and assesses their impact on American society and Jewish life. The organizations considered include the American Jewish Committee, the American Jewish Congress, the Anti-Defamation League, the Simon Wiesenthal Center, the Jewish War Veterans, the Workmen's Circle, and the Jewish Labor Committee.

The efforts of the American Jewish community to shape and sustain American Jewish identity found expression in Jewish education and journalism. Articles assess all levels and forms of Jewish education, covering the great variety of Jewish schools, including yeshivas, Talmud Torahs, day schools, Sunday schools, summer camps, seminaries for the training of Jewish teachers, and Jewish studies in universities. Authors explore the rich and diverse heritage of Jewish journalism, examining the proliferation of both Yiddish- and English-language newspapers in America. Jews have established major archival collections in the United States to preserve the record of Jewish life and culture in both pre-Holocaust Europe and America. The *Encyclopedia* contains articles on major Jewish archives in this country and on the scholars who first established the field of American Jewish history.

In formulating this *Encyclopedia*, we sought to provide a resource readily accessible to many audiences: to scholars across the humanities, the arts, and social sciences; to students and faculty in colleges, universities, and high schools; and to the general public. Articles both chronicle and analyze the American Jewish experience. In addition to offering a wealth of information, essays develop themes that give shape to American Jewish history, culture, community, and individual lives. The *Encyclopedia* brings together in one place multiple perspectives on the American Jewish experience, presented by eminent scholars in a wide range of fields, from the United States, Israel, England, and Canada.

Eunice G. Pollack
Stephen H. Norwood

Maps

By Sir Martin Gilbert

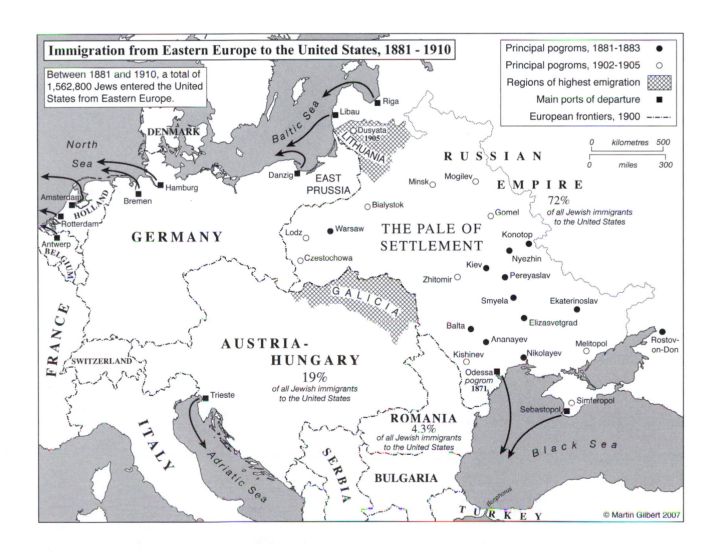

Immigration from Eastern Europe to the United States, 1881 - 1910

Between 1881 and 1910, a total of 1,562,800 Jews entered the United States from Eastern Europe.

Principal pogroms, 1881-1883 ●
Principal pogroms, 1902-1905 ○
Regions of highest emigration
Main ports of departure ■
European frontiers, 1900 —·—·—·—

0 kilometres 500
0 miles 300

DENMARK
North Sea
Baltic Sea
Riga
Libau
Danzig
EAST PRUSSIA
Dusyata 1905
LITHUANIA
RUSSIAN EMPIRE
72% of all Jewish immigrants to the United States
Hamburg
Bremen
Amsterdam
HOLLAND
Rotterdam
Antwerp
BELGIUM
GERMANY
Minsk
Mogilev
Bialystok
Gomel
Lodz
Warsaw
Czestochowa
THE PALE OF SETTLEMENT
Konotop
Nyezhin
Kiev
Pereyaslav
Zhitomir
Smyela
Ekaterinoslav
Elizasvetgrad
Balta
Ananayev
Melitopol
Rostov-on-Don
FRANCE
SWITZERLAND
AUSTRIA-HUNGARY
19% of all Jewish immigrants to the United States
GALICIA
Kishinev
Nikolayev
Odessa pogrom 1871
Sebastopol
Simferopol
Trieste
ITALY
Adriatic Sea
ROMANIA
4.3% of all Jewish immigrants to the United States
SERBIA
BULGARIA
Black Sea
Bosphorus
TURKEY

© Martin Gilbert 2007

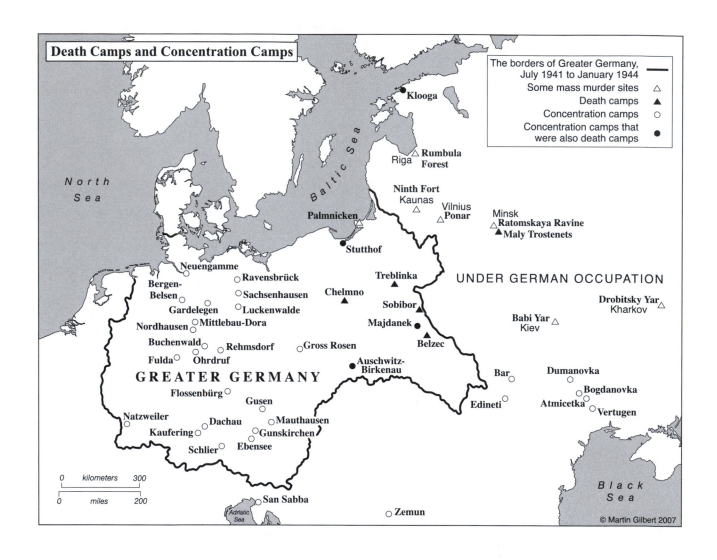

Death Camps and Concentration Camps

The borders of Greater Germany,
July 1941 to January 1944 ▬
Some mass murder sites △
Death camps ▲
Concentration camps ○
Concentration camps that
were also death camps ●

*North
Sea*

Baltic Sea

Klooga ●

Riga △ **Rumbula
Forest**

**Ninth Fort
Kaunas** △

Vilnius
Ponar △

Minsk
△ **Ratomskaya Ravine**
▲ **Maly Trostenets**

Palmnicken △

Stutthof ●

Neuengamme ○

**Bergen-
Belsen** ○

○ **Ravensbrück**

○ **Sachsenhausen**

Treblinka ▲

Chelmno ▲

UNDER GERMAN OCCUPATION

Gardelegen ○

○ **Luckenwalde**

Sobibor ▲

Drobitsky Yar △
Kharkov

Nordhausen ○
○ **Mittlebau-Dora**

Majdanek ●

Babi Yar △
Kiev

Buchenwald ○
○ **Rehmsdorf**

○ **Gross Rosen**

Belzec ▲

Fulda ○
○ **Ohrdruf**

● **Auschwitz-
Birkenau**

Bar ○

Dumanovka
○

GREATER GERMANY

○ **Bogdanovka**

Edineti ○

Atmicetka ○
○ **Vertugen**

Flossenbürg ○

Gusen
○

Natzweiler ○

○ **Mauthausen**

Dachau
○

Kaufering ○

○ **Gunskirchen**

Schlier ○
○ **Ebensee**

0 kilometers 300

0 miles 200

○ **San Sabba**

*Adriatic
Sea*

○ **Zemun**

*Black
Sea*

© Martin Gilbert 2007

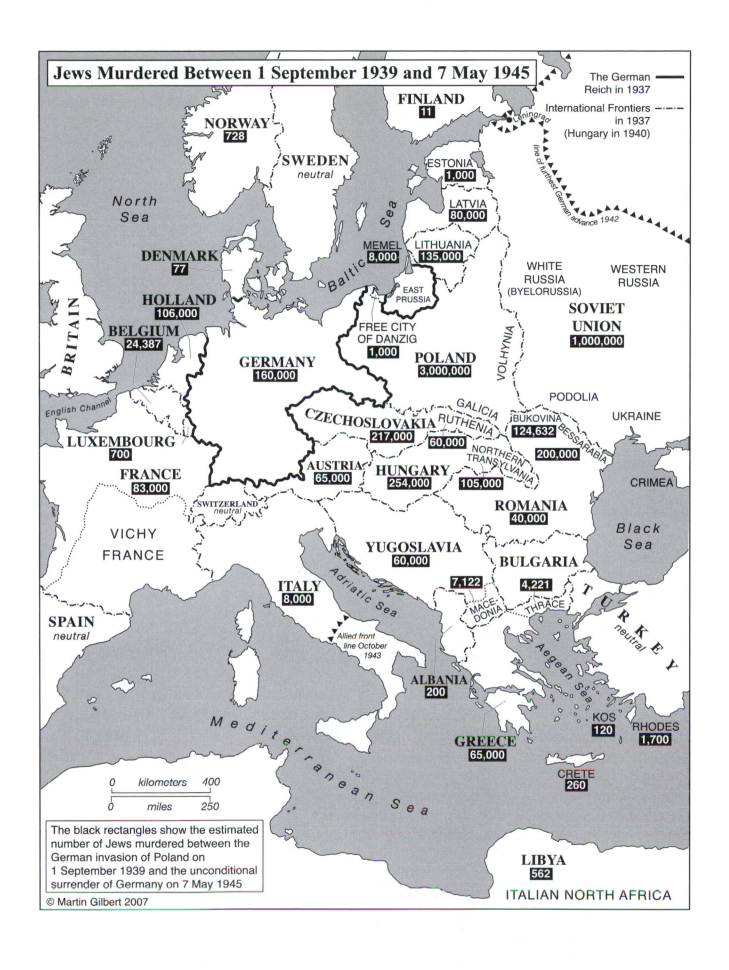

Jews Murdered Between 1 September 1939 and 7 May 1945

The German Reich in 1937 ——

International Frontiers in 1937 (Hungary in 1940) ——·——

FINLAND 11

NORWAY 728

SWEDEN neutral

North Sea

Baltic Sea

Leningrad

line of furthest German advance 1942

ESTONIA 1,000

LATVIA 80,000

DENMARK 77

MEMEL 8,000

LITHUANIA 135,000

EAST PRUSSIA

WHITE RUSSIA (BYELORUSSIA)

WESTERN RUSSIA

HOLLAND 106,000

BELGIUM 24,387

FREE CITY OF DANZIG 1,000

SOVIET UNION 1,000,000

English Channel

BRITAIN

GERMANY 160,000

POLAND 3,000,000

VOLHYNIA

PODOLIA

CZECHOSLOVAKIA 217,000

RUTHENIA

GALICIA

BUKOVINA 124,632

BESSARABIA

UKRAINE

LUXEMBOURG 700

AUSTRIA 65,000

HUNGARY 254,000

NORTHERN TRANSYLVANIA 105,000

60,000

200,000

FRANCE 83,000

SWITZERLAND neutral

ROMANIA 40,000

CRIMEA

Black Sea

VICHY FRANCE

YUGOSLAVIA 60,000

BULGARIA 4,221

7,122

SPAIN neutral

ITALY 8,000

Adriatic Sea

MACE-DONIA

THRACE

T U R K E Y neutral

Aegean Sea

Allied front line October 1943

ALBANIA 200

KOS 120

RHODES 1,700

Mediterranean Sea

GREECE 65,000

CRETE 260

0 kilometers 400

0 miles 250

The black rectangles show the estimated number of Jews murdered between the German invasion of Poland on 1 September 1939 and the unconditional surrender of Germany on 7 May 1945

LIBYA 562

ITALIAN NORTH AFRICA

© Martin Gilbert 2007

Encyclopedia of

AMERICAN JEWISH HISTORY

American Jews in Business and Philanthropy

Jewish Department Store Magnates

By 1880 for shoppers across America, the department store, the fullest realization of the nation's retailing prowess, offered under one roof a panoply of goods, ranging from ordinary clothing and household goods to party dresses and luxury items. Legions of such stores were established by German Jewish entrepreneurs who immigrated to America in the mid-nineteenth century and started out invariably as peddlers. Such were the origins of a long and venerable procession of recognizable names including Bloomingdale's, Abraham & Straus, Macy's, Gimbel's, Altman's, Stern's, and Bergdorf Goodman in New York alone.

While some future department store magnates settled in New York, others settled elsewhere, like the Filenes of Boston, the Kaufmanns of Pittsburgh, the Lazaruses of Columbus, the Garfinkels of Washington, D.C., the Riches of Atlanta, the Goldsmiths of Memphis, the Neimans and Marcuses of Dallas, the Goldwaters of Arizona, the Gumps and Magnins of California, the Maiers and Franks of Oregon, and many others. Fundamentally altering the fabric of the nation's urban and suburban landscape, collectively they transformed the very scope and definition of shopping. By the early part of the twentieth century, department stores run by German Jewish entrepreneurs existed in practically every city and town of any significance in America.

Though Jews cannot say they invented the department store—Lord & Taylor, A. T. Stewart, Jordan Marsh, and other Yankee entrepreneurs deserve credit for that—they can lay claim to its development from an oasis for the well-heeled into a far more democratic institution where, in tasteful surroundings, a wide variety of commodities reflecting taste, style, and practicality were made accessible to rich and poor alike. Their success arose in no small measure due to well-conceived advertising and marketing campaigns that eventually became the industrial norm. Excelling not only as businessmen who perfected competitive, one-stop shopping, but also as philanthropists and civic leaders who cultivated social responsibility, the German Jewish entrepreneurial elite and their descendants occupied positions of honor and trust, both in the Jewish community and in society at large.

The immigrant "founding fathers" were part of a mass migration of German Jews to America that began in the wake of the Napoleonic Wars and continued into the late nineteenth century. The migration was precipitated by the defeat of Napoleon, whose progressive policies toward Jews were replaced in Germany by harsh reactionary laws, such as barring Jews from holding land or confining them to specific crafts and trades. In addition, Jews were subject to capricious taxation designed to keep them poor and harsh legislation that prevented younger sons from marrying. All this was a throwback to pre-Napoleonic times. To survive, Jews were willing to make a greater effort, to put up with more, to take chances, whether this meant accepting a lower rate of profit, entering territories eschewed by others as too dangerous, or taking risks with new methods and ideas. Although the future magnate did not come to America with much ready capital, "unlike the peasant, he appreciated the significance of income as a potential source of further income" (Supple 1997).

As Europe grew increasingly inhospitable to Jewish life, a rapidly expanding United States encouraged the migration of European settlers, regardless of their religious backgrounds. "We hold out to the people of other countries an invitation to come and settle among us as members of our rapidly expanding family," President John Tyler declared to Jews and Gentiles alike in an 1841 message to Congress, "and for the blessings which we offer them we require of them to look upon our country as their country, and to unite with us in the great task of preserving our institutions, and thereby perpetuating our liberties." These words and others like them signaled a new chapter in the history of the Jewish people. Here was a place where no official distinctions were made between Jews and Christians. Tyler's thoughts were in the air and word traveled fast to Germany. By the Civil War, the population of German Jews in America, fewer than ten thousand in 1830, had mushroomed to over a hundred thousand.

Future department-store magnates were part of a migration of tens of thousands of German Jews who came to America in the middle of the nineteenth century and fanned out across the nation as peddlers. Often Jewish wholesalers who had arrived earlier got them started by providing them, on credit, with dry goods, notions, clothing, tinware, toys—whatever they could carry—to find new markets for their merchandise. Adam Gimbel, Lazarus Straus, Isaac Sanger, Isaac Magnin, and other immigrant budding entrepreneurs discovered in their peddlers' packs the ingredients for future department stores. By 1860, a majority of America's peddlers were of German Jewish origin. Accompanying other settlers by covered wagon, on riverboats, or on foot, Jews ventured where none had gone before. Wherever business proved profitable, a Jewish wife and family were likely to follow. In a matter of a few years a Jewish community would form out of a cluster of downtown enterprises, one or more of which would develop into a full-fledged department store. So it was in countless cities up and down the Atlantic seaboard, along the Great Lakes, and on the major tributaries of the South, the Southwest, and the far West. Wherever a distribution point of any consequence existed from Portland, Maine, to Portland, Oregon, a German Jewish department store was sure to follow.

As it was for Lazarus Straus, peddling was invariably the first step. Leaving behind a wife (who was also his first cousin) and four children, Lazarus departed his native Bavaria for the United States in 1852 to become a pack peddler in rural Georgia. In less than two years Lazarus owned his own store in the town of Talbotton, where his family joined him in August 1854. Everyone contributed to the family's survival. "The children made candles, helped in the vegetable garden, and at the store, which was open until 9:30 every night" (Harris 1994).

Lazarus and his sons prospered by exchanging agricultural products for manufactured items such as clothing, household wares, and tools, as their forefathers had done in Germany for generations. During the Civil War Lazarus's eighteen-year-old son Isidor served as a Civil War agent in Europe, where he labored at selling Confederate bonds while arranging for ships to break through the increasingly effective Yankee blockade. Returning after the war with $10,000 in gold, Isidor encouraged his parents to move to New York by buying them a townhouse on West 49th Street, where they lived comfortably while pursuing economic prospects. On Chambers Street one day Lazarus noticed a sign reading "Cauldwell's Crockery." Recognizing the name of a former supplier, Lazarus went in, introduced himself, and established a rapport with Cauldwell that led to Lazarus's buying the business and taking a three-year lease on the building at $3,000 a year.

In 1866, with the help of Isidor, the crockery firm of L. Straus and Son came into being. It soon expanded to include wholesale and retail operations in crockery as well as pottery, glass, and bric-a-brac. In 1874, the Strauses leased a 25-by-100-foot space in the basement of the store of one of their customers, Captain Rowland Hussey Macy, founder in 1857 of R. H. Macy & Co. By 1874 Macy's had become indistinguishable from other multifloor retail stores specializing in "fancy" and imported dry goods. Before the year was out, the Strauses had introduced Christmas displays and a bearded Santa. In less than a decade the Strauses were partners in the business. In 1888 Isidor and his brother Nathan took over the store.

F. & R. Lazarus & Co., Columbus, Ohio. (American Jewish Historical Society)

Captain Macy's business rested on two principles: "one price only" and "only cash." The Strauses continued these policies but added others of their own that were considered quite radical in their day. These included depositor accounts (DAs), a precursor of American Express, for customers who did not want to carry cash; competitive pricing; and money-back guarantees. (Macy's reputation for cheaper prices became so prevalent that it led its chief competitor to protest for years that "Nobody but nobody undersells Gimbel's.") The success of the Strauses after they took over Macy's was remarkable. In 1893 they joined forces with Abraham of Abraham & Straus. In 1902, four years after Lazarus's death, they opened what was billed as the largest department store in the world on Herald Square, where it has remained for over a century. Isidor

and his wife Ida went down on the *Titanic*, after which Nathan sold his half share in Macy's to Isidor's children, Jesse, Percy, and Herbert, who are credited with adding Macy's Window and Macy's Basement to a litany of Macy's innovations.

While Isidor's role was that of storekeeper, Nathan established the family's reputation for philanthropy. For years his chief concern was public health. Whether by campaigning for the compulsory pasteurization of milk as president of the New York Board of Health, by establishing almost three hundred milk stations throughout America, by financing Hadassah-run child welfare stations and health centers in Palestine, or by giving away almost two-thirds of his fortune during his lifetime, Nathan Straus set a high example of civic responsibility for Jewish Americans throughout the country. "He's a great Jew," declared President William Howard Taft, "and the greatest Christian of them all."

Like Macy's, Sears, Roebuck was not founded by Jews. Rather, it was founded as a small Midwestern mail-order firm by Richard Sears, who sold half the business to Aaron Nusbaum who, in turn, sold half of his half interest to Julius Rosenwald. The son of German Jewish immigrants, Rosenwald was born in Springfield, Illinois, when Lincoln was president. After purchasing the remaining half of Nusbaum's share, Rosenwald, in collaboration with his boyhood friend Henry Goldman of the investment firm Goldman, Sachs & Co., turned Sears into a public corporation, which he headed.

By now Jewish department store families were consolidating their impressive prewar role in mass merchandising. "By the post–[World War I] era, Macy's, Gimbel's, Abraham & Straus, . . . Ohrbach's, Bergdorf Goodman, Franklin Simon, and Bloomingdale's dominated the New York market. By then, too, Macy's had become the largest department store in the world; Rich's in Atlanta, the largest department store in the South; . . . Neiman-Marcus the largest and most prestigious . . . in the Southwest" (Sachar 1992). Moving vigorously to open scores of retail outlets, by 1931 Rosenwald had advanced Sears into first place among the nation's mass-merchandising operations and among the most respected in American retail business. Like Nathan Straus, Julius Rosenwald was also a major American philanthropist, having provided more money than any other individual for the education of blacks in America, for establishing Jewish farm colonies in the Soviet Union, for interest-free loans to the International Ladies' Garment Workers' Union, and for the antecedents of Blue Cross.

Isaac Sanger was one of hundreds of German Jews who came to New York in the early 1850s and then went on to Texas to cash in on the cattle boom. In no time Sanger was operating a general merchandise store in McKinney, a tiny settlement four weeks by wagon from Houston. After a younger brother, Lehman, arrived to take charge of the McKinney operation, Isaac opened another store at Weatherford. After receiving a few antisemitic threats, Isaac responded generously to the fund-raising efforts of various churches in the area. After Isaac (along with his brothers Lehman and Philip) served in the Confederate Army, he and Lehman opened a store in Millican.

At the time, the economy of Texas rested largely on barter, as did the German economy of Sanger's youth. Thus, women would come to Sanger Brothers with eggs, butter, or whatever else they had to trade, while men would bring in hides, wool, or vegetables. After making a fair exchange in manufactured items for whatever was brought in, the Sanger brothers transported what they had bartered for to New Orleans to sell to a wholesaler for cash, thus making a double sale. Using their savings, the Sangers established a chain of stores, with another Sanger brother taking charge of each new venture. This was typical among emerging department-store magnates with large families.

When Dallas showed signs of becoming a major center of commerce and trade, the Sangers consolidated their operations there. Except for a store in Waco, all other establishments were closed. The Sangers had no reason to regret this move, for as Dallas prospered, so did Sanger Brothers.

Neiman-Marcus, a Dallas department store with a reputation for class, was established by two Sanger Brothers' employees. Herbert Marcus began his career as a shoe clerk at Sanger Brothers. Born in Louisville of recently arrived immigrants in 1878, at fifteen he followed his brother to Texas. At Sanger's, Herbert got to know another budding entrepreneur, Abraham Lincoln Neiman, known as Al, who promoted sales for local merchants with banners promising unbelievable bargains, brass bands, fire department parades—anything to attract attention. After marrying Herbert's sister Carrie, Al opened Neiman-Marcus in 1907 with his brother-in-law. Unlike their competitors, they opened a frankly expensive store in a cattle town well before an oil boom enriched the city. In effect, they brought a level of affluence to Texas that it had not known before. Even riskier was their insistence that their ready-made apparel would be even finer than tailor-made clothing. That they succeeded in convincing their wealthier customers of this, at the same time "attracting and keeping a large trade of middle class and working women without whom [Neiman-Marcus] could not have survived and grown" (Harris 1994), is all to their credit. They did this by buying only the most fashionable and best-quality clothing and then explaining to customers, sometimes in great detail, what made it more fashionable and better made and therefore worth every penny.

I. Magnin was a precursor of Neiman-Marcus. The store was named after Isaac Magnin, a Dutch Jew who came to San Francisco in the 1870s with his wife Mary Ann and six children. Mary Ann, the power behind the throne, excelled at making lace-trimmed lingerie for brides. Attracting a procession of ladies, as well as some women who were not, to their humble home, Mary Ann planned, skimped, and scraped until she and her husband opened I. Magnin & Co. on Market Street, which became the carriage trade store of the city.

Economic success brought respect but not inclusion in WASP social circles. This encouraged the magnates all the more to take the lead, along with successful German Jewish financiers, in forming a German Jewish elite differentiated in background, culture, religious observance, social outlook, and activities from both middle- and working-class Jews and socially conscious gentiles. Together with their families, which were often quite large, Jewish magnates were instrumental in establishing and supporting Reform temples and ornate social clubs, philanthropic organizations, such as United Hebrew Charities and the Federation of Jewish Philanthropies, and fraternal and protective societies, such as B'nai B'rith, the American Jewish Committee, and the Anti-Defamation League. All of these organizations benefited greatly from the largesse of the local department-store magnate.

Pioneer magnates as a rule occupied honored positions in the local Reform Temple, which conformed to their needs, wants, and values. The founder of American Reform Judaism, Isaac Mayer Wise, saw eye to eye with them. If the service is too long, he counseled, shorten it. If it is too foreign, change it to conform more to Protestant norms. For a people who had left Germany as pariahs to become Americans, Wise's appeal was enormous. By the end of the Civil War practically every city in the country that was blessed with a department store also boasted a Reform temple.

Being a good husband and father and raising a large family in a commodious house constituted an important part of a magnate's life. An extension of this life was the German Jewish social club. Whether it was the Harmonie in New York, the Standard in Chicago, or the Concordia in San Francisco, the social club was the place to go to smoke a good cigar and arrange everything from marriages to musicales, perhaps with a budding Richard Rodgers or Oscar Hammerstein at the piano. Every social club had a hall, and the Standard Club of Denver was no exception: "The hall provides the best appointed stage in Denver out-

side of the Tabor Opera House, and will be used for private theatricals. The reading room will be provided with all the leading papers of the country. A library fund has already been started and a large amount raised" (*Rocky Mountain News,* October 31, 1881). That by now there were scores of cities throughout America with German Jewish social clubs of this caliber or better is a testimony to the relatively high quality of life enjoyed by the magnate and his family wherever he happened to settle.

Just as the magnate's lifestyle often set a standard for his gentile peers, so did his department store set civilized standards of style and taste for his customers. In 1880 Charles Ilfeld of Santa Fe opened a western version of Wanamaker's "at a point on San Francisco Street which makes it the most prominent house on the street. Its front is handsome and imposing. Pendant from the ceiling are four elegant chandeliers supplied with handsome lamps until gas can be secured. . . . Messrs. Ilfeld & Co. have just received large quantities of dry goods, clothing, gents furnishing goods, hats, caps, boots, shoes, native wines, tobacco, cigars, staple and fancy groceries, wool and hides, country produce, hardware, plated ware, glass and chinaware, saddlery and leather, musical instruments, patent medicines, drugs, miners supplies, etc. etc." (*The Daily New Mexican,* October 18, 1880). By now there was not a single urban center of any significance in America that did not have a German Jewish–owned department store adding a touch of class, a bit of style, to an otherwise raw and colorless urban landscape. So the stores would last until the late twentieth century, by which time most of them had closed or had been bought out at a handsome profit by a local competitor or by a department store chain with a New York Stock Exchange listing, such as Associated, Federated, Allied, or Independent.

The Jewish magnates exhibited a degree of civic mindedness unique in business circles. No one, however, outdid Rich's of Atlanta. Year after year Rich's supplied uniforms for the baseball team, musical instruments for the marching band, floats, bunting, flags, and Japanese lanterns for the parades, not to mention special equipment for "the Masonic picnic, the firemen's ball, the pig, sheep, cattle, horse, or flower show, . . . the gift of door prizes and the purchase of raffle tickets or baked goods, . . . and at least one printed program advertisement from every church, grade school, high school, ladies' book club, poetry reading society, barbershop quartet, debating league, sewing circle, and china-painting club in Atlanta" (Harris 1994).

Why did the Riches and a legion of German Jewish department store magnates do so much for their respective communities? In large part, these immigrants who had made good possessed an ancestral tradition that underscored social conscience and moral imperative. Performing acts of civic goodwill was good business and an effective way of eroding social and political barriers, as well as blurring class lines. It was also a way for the descendants of a much oppressed people to express their gratitude for the opportunity to leave their mark in the annals of American economic and social history by forever transforming the definition of shopping and by altering the very fabric of the nation's landscape.

Kenneth Libo

References and Further Reading
Ashkenazi, Elliott. 1998. *The Business of Jews in Louisiana 1940–1875.* Tuscaloosa: University of Alabama Press.
Becker, Peter R. 1979. "Jewish Merchants in San Francisco: Social Mobility on the Urban Frontier." *American Jewish History* (June): 201–223.
Birmingham, Stephen. 1967. *"Our Crowd": The Great Jewish Families of New York.* New York: Harper & Row.
Cohen, Naomi W. 1984. *Encounter with Emancipation: The German Jews in the United States, 1830–1914.* Philadelphia: Jewish Publication Society.
Feingold, Henry L. 1981. *Zion in America.* New York: Hippocrene Books.
Harris, Leon. 1994. *Merchant Princes.* New York: Kodansha.
Hertzberg, Arthur. 1997. *The Jews in America.* New York: Columbia University Press.
Libo, Kenneth, and Irving Howe. 1984. *We Lived There Too.* New York: St. Martin's Press.
Newmark, Harris. 1972. *Sixty Years in Southern California.* Los Angeles: The General Alumni Association, University of Southern California.
Sachar, Howard M. 1992. *A History of the Jews in America.* New York: Alfred A. Knopf.
Simonhoff, Harry, 1959. *The Saga of American Jewry, 1865–1914.* New York: Arco.
Supple, Barry. 1997. "A Business Elite: German Jewish Financiers in Nineteenth-Century New York." In *The American Jewish Experience,* edited by Jonathan D. Sarna, 99–112. New York: Holmes & Meier Publishers.

Southern Jewish Retailers (1840–2000)

As Jewish merchants opened shops in small Southern towns and built elegant department stores in growing Southern cities in the late nineteenth and early twentieth centuries, they encountered the racialized Southern culture. Their diverse clientele consisted of rural and urban folk from all social classes, black and white farmers, as well as city dwellers. Though eager to buy, many native-born Southern whites, steeped in Southern Protestantism, considered Jews an alien people, at once living examples of "Old Testament" figures and "Christ killers." Most rural Southerners had never met a Jew, until an immigrant Jewish peddler traveled along the back roads where their farms were located or a Jewish family arrived in town to open a store. Successful Southern Jewish retailers negotiated a place for themselves in their business communities, yet they were aware of their social marginality.

Even the wealthiest Jews experienced social exclusion and recurring antisemitism. During the 1950s and 1960s, as civil rights activism spread through the Deep South, high-profile downtown Jewish store owners who had welcomed black customers while adhering to common segregation practices, were among those targeted by economic boycotts. Rabid segregationists labeled the movement a "Jewish–Communist conspiracy," creating a significant dilemma for Jewish Southerners. White Citizens Councils mobilized resistance and even attracted a few Jewish members. By contrast, several Southern rabbis passionately advocated racial justice, marched, and negotiated for social change, while some groups of Jewish women worked for school desegregation. Yet most Southern Jews remained silent during the struggle—retailers were among those most vulnerable. Some of their businesses never recovered.

Jewish retailing took several forms in the segregated South: small general stores located in rural areas stocked with farmers' supplies (furnishing merchants); expanded dry goods, hardware, and supply stores in small towns; specialized, moderately priced stores in the working-class neighborhoods of Southern cities; and the elegant multifloor department stores, rivaling New York's Macy's or Philadelphia's Wanamaker's. Both German and Eastern European Jews became proprietors of these family-owned businesses; many of their stores withstood the economic challenges of the Great Depression and the World Wars, lasting as independent institutions until the late twentieth century when many full-service department stores were systematically sold to national retailing conglomerates, such as Federated Department Stores. Smaller businesses often just closed.

Until then, the Jewish retailer had long remained a familiar figure in the Southern history narrative. A journalist recently interviewed Maurice Krawcheck, owner of Max's Clothing Shop in Charleston, South Carolina, as he held his Going Out of Business Sale. He had expected his sons to take over the business that his immigrant father had opened seventy years earlier, but neither was interested. Historian Stuart Rockhoff explained, "The story of Jews in the South is a story of parents who built businesses for children who did not want them. . . . the decline of the Southern Jewish retailer is part of the larger story of the decline of rural America" (Glanton 2005).

At the turn of the twentieth century, Southern retailing prospects looked promising to acculturated German Jews and to more recent immigrants from Eastern Europe, as they participated in revitalizing the Southern economy after the Civil War. Historian Lee Shai Weissbach discovered evidence of Jewish-owned department stores in small towns across the South in this era, such as S. Waxelbaum and Son in Macon, Georgia, J. Weisman and Company in Marshall, Texas, Weil Brothers and Bauer in Alexandria, Louisiana, Heinemann's Department Store in Jonesboro, Arkansas, M. Ullman and Company in Natchez, Mississippi, Simon Switzer's The Valley in Vicksburg, Mississippi, and Winner and Klein in Meridian, Mississippi. These stores prospered in towns with populations fewer than 50,000 and with Jewish populations less than 1,000, but large enough to support Jewish communal life. In her fictionalized family memoir, *The Jew Store,* Stella Suberman recalls her childhood in a small town in northwestern Tennessee where her immigrant father opened Bronson's Low-Priced Store in 1920 with credit extended by St. Louis wholesalers. As the only Jewish family in town, their success depended on the Klan's approval, though farmers and workers, black and white, enthusiastically awaited its opening.

In *The Peddler's Grandson: Growing Up Jewish in Mississippi* (1999), Edward Cohen explains how his grandfather and his brother, Rumanian immigrants, opened Cohen Brothers in Jackson, Mississippi, in 1898. They employed an aunt as the bookkeeper, and his father and two uncles worked in Cohen Brothers for the rest of their lives. Family lore claimed that during tense, antisemitic years, the elder Cohens told neighbors and customers only that they were from New York. With a vivid sense of being an outsider as a Jew, Mississippi-born Cohen relates a story repeated in several accounts of Southern Jewish merchant families: when the Klan marched down Main Street of their towns in full regalia, Jewish merchants could often identify the members by the shoes they had sold them. In the days before shopping centers and black-owned stores, Cohen Brothers became a gathering spot for white working-class and black families, he explained, because its merchandise was moderately priced. Most customers purchased goods on credit negotiated with Cohen's father, based on carefully recorded credit histories.

Although neither Cohen's nor Suberman's mother regularly worked in the store, many wives and daughters shared the hard work of storekeeping. "Jewish women could . . . be found behind the counter far more often than on the pedestal," observed James Hagy, historian of early Charleston's Jewish community (Rosengarten 2002). David Polikoff opened a dry goods store in Abbeville, South Carolina, in 1900. As the store expanded, it became a full-fledged department store with saleswomen trained by Polikoff women. Polikoff's served generations of farmers in rural South Carolina and Georgia. When David Polikoff's son and business heir, Myer, died in 1986, his wife Rosa managed their store until her death in 2000. When Richmond's store magnate William Thalheimer opened his first store in 1842, his wife Mary became the buyer. Eli Evans recounted that he worked in Evans' United Dollar Store in Durham, North Carolina, during busy times from age nine on and that his parents shared the responsibilities for managing the store. Durham historian Leonard Rogoff discovered records of several other multigenerational family stores and evidence of women's employment in retailing in the early twentieth century. The local newspaper described Carry Levy, a widow, who owned a notions store as a "woman of fine taste and an expert buyer." Carrie Kronheimer and Birdie Lehman worked as buyers and managers at their brother's department store.

According to Durham city directories, in 1902 approximately 70 percent of Durham's Jews were employed in retail trades, although by 1938 the number had dropped to 54 percent, as Jews branched out into manufacturing and the professions (Rogoff 2001). By the 1960s Durham's new suburban malls undercut the Main Street Jewish merchants. Some reestablished themselves in the new malls, while others sold their stores and found new ways to earn a living or moved away.

As they built grand department stores in larger Southern cities, Jewish merchants utilized the most innovative technology, selling strategies, and techniques for maintaining a loyal sales force. They advertised widely in local newspapers, including black community newspapers. Birmingham department store owner Louis Pizitz, for example, introduced a one-price policy in his grand store, so that salespeople and customers were not required to bargain. At his Grand Opening in 1900, newspaper ads proclaimed "Our Ready-Made Department is one of the handsomest in the city and comprises everything that is nobby and stylish." By 1937, Pizitz had seventy-four departments and 750 employees (Elowitz 1974).

Sanger Brothers in Dallas opened in 1872 with a doorman who greeted customers and with gaslights blazing. They installed electricity in 1883 as soon as electrical power came to Dallas. They provided free home delivery, an economy basement, and an escalator by 1912. As one of the first stores in Dallas to hire women as salesclerks, they introduced a sales training program, a night school for employees, and an employee savings and loan program. Because the Sanger Brothers were sensitive to employment discrimination against Jews, they never turned away a Jewish applicant for a job. Goldsmith Brothers Department Store in Memphis, which opened in the 1870s, was also known for boldness in merchandising, careful supervision of employees in manners and skillful selling, basement sales, and the Spirit of Christmas parade, a local tradition that lasted until the 1960s.

Rich's of Atlanta, founded in 1867, part of the rebuilding of the city, consciously cultivated a reputation as a "Southern Institution." In addition to its elaborate variety of merchandise, its distinctive trademark was its special treatment of customers, making sure that they were satisfied, no matter how outrageous a customer's demand. Store policy dictated that credit be extended liberally, that refunds be given at full price, or that exchanges be made for all merchandise, even for items not purchased at Rich's. They offered free classes in knitting, embroidery, crocheting, sewing, cooking, canning, and contract bridge. They also employed a registered nurse for employees and customers.

Nurturing Rich's Southern identity, their newspaper ads and store windows displayed appropriate attire for Atlanta's yearly horse show and debutante balls. Although the Jewish Rich family members were never invited to these exclusive affairs, they indicated their interest in and connection to Atlanta's elite society's celebrations through

these imaginative advertising strategies. They also initiated the ceremonial lighting of a fully decorated sixty-foot Christmas tree set atop the store on Thanksgiving evening, complete with local choirs singing Christmas carols.

Opening its doors in Dallas in 1907, Neiman-Marcus remains a national institution today, although it is no longer family owned. Originally the store defined itself as a high fashion specialty store with wide variety and the most exclusive lines in women's clothing, but Herbert Marcus, his sister Carrie Marcus, and her husband Al Neiman gradually added accessories, children's clothing, and menswear. The Neiman-Marcus family built unique personal relationships with customers. Each salesperson was required to keep a clientele book. As the main buyer, Carrie Marcus had an unusual sense of style and wanted the store to attract trade from middle-class and working-class women as well as the wealthy. Carrie, Herbert, and Al trained salespeople in proper language and manners to work with a variety of customers. They organized parades, introduced a nationally distributed catalogue and mail-order business, and advertised in *Harper's Bazaar* and *Vogue*. They introduced fashion shows and art exhibits, and raised money for charity at gala events open to the public.

Many Jewish merchants across the South were keenly aware that antisemitic sentiment often lay just beneath the surface of their non-Jewish friends and colleagues. To demonstrate their respectability and commitment to their home communities, Jewish merchants frequently assumed leadership in civic affairs and joined multifaith fraternal organizations such as the Masonic lodges. "To ensure the success of both Dallas and his store," Alex Sanger, for example, was elected as an alderman, became president of the fire department, donated money to help construct a public library, and joined other prominent businessmen in organizing a state fair and exposition (Biderman 2002). Store owners also responded to public crises generously. Birmingham merchant Louis Pizitz sent truckloads of food and clothing to miners on strike in 1908. During the Depression, he turned the store into a restaurant and served Thanksgiving dinner to anyone in need.

In Atlanta, Rich's made a substantial effort to sustain Atlanta's economy in hard times. When the price of cotton dropped significantly in 1914 and 1920, the store bought bales of cotton above market prices. After World War I, they redeemed Liberty Bonds at face value, so that consumers could buy. In 1930, when the city had no money to pay its schoolteachers, store president Walter Rich called the mayor and suggested that the city issue scrip that could be used as cash, with no obligation to the store. Rich's paid $645,000 for the scrip and held the debt until the city raised enough money to repay it.

Leo Frank's lynching in Atlanta in 1915 haunted Southern Jews for many years. Representing the outsider, the Northern capitalist who had the power to monopolize the new South's wealth and women, the Frank case captured press attention for two years. During his trial, crowds gathered on rooftops near the courtroom and shouted, "Hang the Jew." When Frank was lynched in 1915, a photo of his lynched body became a popular souvenir postcard. Consequently, many twentieth-century Southern Jews encouraged their children to "blend" into Southern white society, to be silent on controversial issues, and to accept the values of Southern culture, including the racial status quo. They were to be Jewish, but not "too Jewish." When Rabbi Jacob Rothschild at Atlanta's famous temple, the Hebrew Benevolent Congregation, urged his congregants to support desegregation of Atlanta's schools, one of his young congregants, much too young to remember the case, asked, "What, and start the Frank Case all over again?" (Rothschild 1967).

Within the segregated South, Jews had a reputation among some black leaders for treating black employees better than other Southern whites did. Jewish merchants extended credit to black people, addressed them as Mr. and Mrs., and often paid them somewhat higher wages than other whites did. Yet when the Supreme Court handed down the *Brown v. Board of Education* decision (1954) desegregating public schools, it precipitated a significant crisis for many Southern Jews, especially for Jewish merchants. Black civil rights leaders expected support from local Jewish communities, but most Southern Jews refused to speak out against racial injustice, despite considerable Jewish support for the movement in other regions of the country. Black leaders expressed frustration. As Aaron Henry, NAACP president in Clarksdale, Mississippi, remarked, "In the fight for human dignity, we have never underestimated our opposition, but we have overestimated our support. We thought that naturally we would have the Jews on our side, because the enemies of the Jews were usually found in the same group that opposes us. But we don't have the Jews supporting us" (Webb 2001). A rash of synagogue bombings in the late 1950s exacerbated Jewish

fears of growing antisemitism, associated with racial unrest. Unexploded bombs were found near Reform temples in Charlotte, North Carolina, Gastonia, North Carolina, and Birmingham, Alabama. Bombs damaged an Orthodox synagogue in Miami, the Jewish community centers in Nashville, Tennessee, and Jacksonville, Florida, and the Reform Temple on Peachtree Street in Atlanta. In addition, some segregationists explicitly accused Jews of instigating and financing the black freedom struggle.

As sit-ins at segregated public facilities spread across Southern towns and cities in 1960, Atlanta University students staged a sit-in at a drugstore near the university. Despite efforts of Mayor William Hartsfield, demonstrations continued into the summer, targeting Rich's department store. Richard Rich, the store's owner, had responded quickly to requests from black customers to install more restroom facilities for them in the 1950s and had been personally generous to black institutions. Consequently, activists believed that, because Rich was Jewish, he would be most amenable to change, yet he refused to yield to demonstrators' demands. Rich admitted to civil rights leader Julian Bond that he feared that a "large cadre of anti-Semites and racists would descend upon him" (Webb 2001). As boycotts continued, Rich's black clientele returned their credit cards, and Rich's profits plummeted. Finally, after several months Rich's agreed to desegregate, and Atlanta's downtown began to flourish again.

Jewish storeowners across the South faced similar conflicts. Edward Cohen explained that his father's successful Jackson store, despite its policy of serving blacks, was on Capitol Street, the street identified by the NAACP as the street to boycott. Though his family pleaded with the NAACP not to boycott their store, it refused. After two years of boycotting, the store never regained its former profits. Cohen characterized his feelings about the civil rights movement as "tortured ambivalence," as he listened to his rabbi, Perry Nussbaum, chastise his congregants for their complacency and unwillingness to champion the black freedom struggle. Cohen's congregation sensed their own vulnerability, while his family worried about a race war in the streets of Jackson (Cohen 1999). Most Southern Jews who were at all sympathetic to the movement were "moderates" or "gradualists," according to the terminology of the era. The young northern Jews who traveled south for Freedom Summer in 1964 could not understand Southern Jews' dilemma at all, perceiving them as racists and cowards. Cohen's sensibilities, echoed by other Southern Jewish writers, reveal the evolving historical complexity of Southern Jewish identity, politics, and lived experience that deserves further study.

Sarah S. Malino

References and Further Reading
Biderman, Rose G. 2002. *They Came to Stay: The Story of the Jews of Dallas, 1870–1997.* Austin, TX: Eakin Press.
Cohen, Edward. 1999. *The Peddler's Grandson: Growing Up Jewish in Mississippi.* New York: Random House.
Elowitz, Mark H. 1974. *A Century of Jewish Life in Dixie: The Birmingham Experience.* Tuscaloosa: University of Alabama Press.
Evans, Eli. 2005. (orig. 1973). *The Provincials: A Personal History of Jews in the South.* Chapel Hill: University of North Carolina Press.
Glanton, Dahleen. 2005. "The Tradition of the Southern Jewish Retailer Winds Down." *Chicago Tribune* (January 16).
Harris, Leon. 1979. *Merchant Princes: An Intimate History of Jewish Families Who Built Great Department Stores.* New York: HarperCollins.
McMaster, Carolyn. 1994. *A Corner of the Tapestry: A History of the Jewish Experience in Arkansas, 1820s–1990s.* Fayetteville: University of Arkansas Press.
Rogoff, Leonard. 2001. *Homelands: Southern Jewish Identity in Durham and Chapel Hill, North Carolina.* Tuscaloosa: University of Alabama Press.
Rosengarten, Theodore, and Dale Rosengarten, eds. 2002. *A Portion of the People: Three Hundred Years of Jewish Life.* Columbia: University of South Carolina Press.
Rothschild, Janice. 1967. *As But a Day: The First 100 Years: 1867–1967.* Atlanta, GA: Hebrew Benevolent Congregation.
Suberman, Stella. 1998. *The Jew Store.* Chapel Hill, NC: Algonquin Books.
Webb, Clive. 2001. *Fight against Fear: Southern Jews and Black Civil Rights.* Athens: University of Georgia Press.
Weissbach, Lee Shai. 1997. "Eastern European Immigrants and the Image of the Jews in the Small-Town South." *American Jewish History* 85,3: 231–262.

American Jews and the Diamond Business

In the twentieth century, European Jews extended the ancient and worldwide diamond business to New York City, where they made it flourish as the largest diamond market in the world. Although some Jews who knew the diamond trade came to New York early in the twentieth century, other Western European Jews who were able to flee persecution during and after World War II came to America to begin again. Equipped with their knowledge of the industry, they established small manufacturing shops in Manhattan, where the trade is still centered today. While diamond activity expanded to numerous centers in the United States, New York's 47th Street has persisted as the hub of the trade in this country.

Diamonds were important to Jewish rituals and beliefs long before Jews became involved in diamond trading in the first millennium. Like people everywhere, Jews were enthralled with the hard and glittery stones. Since the biblical era, wisdom and sacred texts such as the Torah were compared to diamonds and precious stones, gems were used to adorn the texts, and halachic (legal) writings documented the procedures to resolve disputes over diamonds.

Although European Jews since the Middle Ages were excluded from large numbers of occupations, many found work in the jewelry and diamond trade. While the church forbade Christians to lend money, this remained a role open to Jews, as were positions as merchants, traders, and jewelers, and other professions associated with money. Jewish jewelers and precious gem traders could use their connections with the wealthy to be successful. Although they benefited from being brokers between foreign groups, as traders in an ethnically distinct minority, their position always remained precarious (Zenner 1991).

When the first diamonds mined in the riverbeds of India in the seventeenth century reached Europe, they were so rare that they were reserved for royalty. When Jews were expelled from Spain in the Inquisition of 1492 and from Portugal in 1497, Jewish traders took their expertise to Amsterdam and helped increase the trade between India and Europe. Jews polished and traded diamonds in England, the Netherlands, and Belgium. By the nineteenth century, when Antwerp became a prime diamond center, a number of Eastern European Jews, eager to leave the *shtetl* and carve out a better life, migrated there to launch fledgling businesses. For generations, Jewish sons followed fathers into these small family firms. The predominantly Jewish trade was devastated by World War II. With the help of diamonds and other jewels to buy safe passage, Jews who were able to escape the genocide fled mainly to the United States, Palestine, South America, South Africa, Cuba, and Puerto Rico. The immigrants' commercial experience, their contacts with diamond merchants in other

American Jews sorting diamonds. (Renée Rose Shield, Ph.D.)

countries, and the aid of family members already settled in the United States proved invaluable in helping them establish their businesses.

Diamond trading is organized through the umbrella organization of the World Federation of Diamond Bourses (WFDB), which shares information about members, ensures uniformity of trading rules, and facilitates trading. In the United States and elsewhere, disputes are settled by elected, highly respected arbitrators who base their decisions on Talmudic principles of fairness. Each diamond bourse functions like a marketplace bazaar in which traders haggle about price and quality and come to an agreement through a handshake and the words, *mazal und brucha* (luck and blessing). Trust and personal reputation—rather than contracts—remain hallmarks of the trade.

The United States is the largest diamond market in the world, and most of the supply enters the country through New York. While India and Israel dominate the manufacture of the smallest diamonds and Antwerp is the major distribution center, New York reigns supreme for its skilled manufacture of the finest and largest stones.

Although the New York diamond trade is more than 95 percent Jewish, it is a boisterous ethnic mix. The 47th Street diamond district includes European- and American-born Jews, as well as Jews from Iran, Israel, India, and elsewhere. They are also diverse in their degrees of religiosity, individual histories, and personalities. Though many children of the original generations of American Jewish traders chose not to enter the business, in the last few generations large numbers of younger Hasidic Jews have flocked to the trade, where they enjoy the insular work setting that respects and protects their religious beliefs. The "club" closes before sundown on Fridays, is closed on Saturdays and Jewish holidays, and contains a *shul* and a kosher restaurant. Although to outsiders, the traditionally garbed and religiously fundamentalist Hasidim—which include both Satmars and Lubavitchers—appear to dominate the trade, they do not constitute a majority. Indeed, the last few decades have also seen the introduction of non-Jewish traders from East Asia. With the significant increase in diamond purchases by Asian consumers, larger numbers of traders are from China, Malaysia, Korea, Japan, and Thailand. Still, despite the cultural mix and the cacophony of languages, Yiddish persists as an important language of the trade. The primary guarantors of success—with those of one's own or another culture—are to be shrewd, to be considered honest, and to have the right goods at the right price.

Although a minority, women have made impressive inroads into the American trade in recent years, sometimes serving as arbitrators and frequently enjoying commercial success. The New York trade remains dominated by small family firms that often persist for generations. Older diamond traders in these families typically work into advanced old age, in part because they are cushioned by the supportive, albeit competitive, social milieu. They trade every day with people they have known intimately for many decades.

Renée Rose Shield

References and Further Reading
Kanfer, Stefan. 1993. *The Last Empire: De Beers, Diamonds, and the World.* New York: Farrar Straus Giroux.
Mintz, Jerome R. 1992. *Hasidic People: A Place in the New World.* Cambridge, MA: Harvard University Press.
Shield, Renée Rose. 2002. *Diamond Stories: Enduring Change on 47th Street.* Ithaca, NY: Cornell University Press.
Zenner, Walter P. 1991. *Minorities in the Middle: A Cross-Cultural Analysis.* Albany: State University of New York Press.

Julius Rosenwald took the mail-order business founded by Richard Sears, modernized it, and with the fortune he made engaged in extensive philanthropy. (Library of Congress)

Julius Rosenwald (1862–1932)

Business Leader and Philanthropist

Julius Rosenwald was one of the most prominent business leaders and philanthropists of early twentieth-century America. He was president of Sears, Roebuck from 1908 to 1924 and before the Depression amassed a fortune estimated at $200 million. He gave away $63 million during his lifetime and through the foundation he established in 1917 (an amount close to $1 billion in 2006 dollars).

Rosenwald bought one-quarter of Sears, Roebuck for $37,500 in 1895 and began work there as a vice president

in 1896. He brought system and order to the mail-order company, which, when he arrived, was in a chaotic state. He oversaw the construction of a large and state-of-the art facility west of Chicago's Loop, and, with others, developed a system whereby an order was shipped out within twenty-four hours of its receipt. In 1908, when Richard Sears resigned from the business he had founded, Rosenwald became the president of the largest retail company in the world. His management style was marked by an unusual form of governance by committee. Rosenwald and a few trusted associates, including Albert Loeb and Max Adler, made the key decisions that kept Sears at the forefront of the mail-order world. Rosenwald also showed great concern for the welfare of his workers, and in 1917 he instituted the generous profit-sharing plan that benefited millions of Sears employees throughout the twentieth century. After World War I, Rosenwald rescued Sears, Roebuck from financial ruin by donating $5 million of his own money to the company and by buying the land on which the Sears plant stood.

Julius Rosenwald was introduced to philanthropy by his rabbi, the noted Emil G. Hirsch, whose vision of social justice strongly appealed to him. Starting in 1904, Rosenwald began contributing to primarily local Jewish causes. In 1908, he became president of the Associated Jewish Charities, the German Jewish umbrella organization that doled out funds to a variety of organizations. One of Rosenwald's most notable achievements in Chicago was to bring about the union of the Associated Charities with a similar organization founded by Eastern European Jewish immigrants. The Jewish Charities of Chicago, founded in 1922, united these two sometimes antagonistic strands of Jewish immigration, and Rosenwald was instrumental in its creation and served as the organization's first president.

A founder of the American Jewish Committee, Rosenwald galvanized the Jewish community by a challenge grant in 1917 to aid the Jewish victims of World War I in Europe. Asked to make a lead gift to such a campaign, he pledged to donate $1 million if an additional $10 million could be raised. The resulting campaign, which lasted nine months, electrified not only Jews but also other groups and individuals across the nation. On an international level, Rosenwald was not a Zionist, though he once declared, quoting Jacob Schiff, that he was not an anti-Zionist but a non-Zionist. Rosenwald contributed to organizations in Israel, including an Agricultural Experiment Station near Haifa and the Technion, but he was not in favor of sending large numbers of Eastern European Jews to Palestine. He was, however, strongly attracted by a Joint Distribution Committee program to resettle Russian Jews in agricultural colonies similar to kibbutzim in the Crimea and Ukraine, and in 1926 Rosenwald pledged $6 million toward this effort.

In addition to funding Jewish causes, Rosenwald was a notable funder of African American projects and was a major part of the movement to better relations between blacks and Jews in the early twentieth century. Through his friendship with Booker T. Washington, he assisted in funding the construction of 5,357 schools, shops, and teachers' homes throughout the rural South from 1913 to 1932. Designed as primary schools for black children, these "Rosenwald" schools lasted until integration in the 1960s. Rosenwald was inspired to assist African Americans be-

cause of what he perceived as similarities in the prejudicial treatment accorded both blacks and Jews. He came to believe that blacks were the equal of whites and should be treated as equals, a radical concept in the Jim Crow era.

The Julius Rosenwald Fund, established in 1917, was the first major American foundation to go out of existence voluntarily in accordance with the belief of its founder that each generation should give away its own money. He was opposed to what he called perpetuities—foundations that exist forever, and in 1912, with a great show of publicity, he gave away $687,500 to a variety of causes with the slogan "Give While You Live."

Peter M. Ascoli

References and Further Reading
Ascoli, Peter M. 2006. *Julius Rosenwald: The Man Who Built Sears, Roebuck and Advanced the Cause of Black Education in the American South.* Bloomington: Indiana University Press.
Werner, M. R. 1939. *Julius Rosenwald: The Life of a Practical Humanitarian.* New York: Harper and Brothers.

Jacob H. Schiff (1847–1920)

Wealthy Investment Banker and Philanthropist

Jacob Henry Schiff was recognized internationally as the foremost leader of the American Jewish community. He owed his position to a confluence of factors: a Midas-like touch in the financing of railroads, a hypersensitivity to the Jewish image and Jewish cultural interests, and a fearless and aggressive nature that drove him to attack a host of problems, from the medical needs of new immigrants to the struggle for Jewish emancipation in Russia. Fast becoming the linchpin of the small elite who constituted the American Jewish establishment, he earned the respect and admiration of fellow Jews, Christians, and American and foreign government officials.

Born to an upper-middle-class and highly respected family in Frankfurt-am-Main, Jacob Schiff attended the modern Orthodox school of Rabbi Samson Raphael Hirsch until age fourteen. Grounded in secular and Jewish studies, he supplemented his education by reading extensively throughout his life. Although he later broke with the

Investment banker and philanthropist Jacob Schiff walks with his wife. (Library of Congress)

Orthodox discipline of his home and school, his boyhood instilled in him an abiding love of Judaism and of things German, and an ingrained sense of *noblesse oblige*.

Against his father's better judgment, Schiff came to the United States when he turned eighteen. He settled in New York City and immediately sought a place in the expanding post–Civil War banking circles. Like all immigrants who relied on ties of kinship and friendship to ease their adjustment, he looked for and received aid from German Jews who had preceded him to the country. In 1875 he married Therese Loeb, daughter of Solomon Loeb, and became a partner in Kuhn, Loeb, her father's small banking firm, which had evolved from a successful clothing business in the Midwest.

The Schiffs readily found their place in the Jewish socioeconomic elite of the city, a group anxious for acceptance in the larger society, who patterned their manners and institutions on those of the Protestant upper-middle and upper classes. A close-knit circle, the members spoke German at home and to each other, they worshiped at the same synagogues, they sent their children to the same schools, and they supported the same Jewish institutions. They acculturated rapidly but stopped short of converting to Christianity.

Schiff's financial acumen and his aggressive approach turned Kuhn, Loeb into a major investment firm that specialized in the financing of railroads and industrial corporations. Cooperating with European Jewish bankers—principally Ernest Cassel and the Rothschilds of London and the Warburgs of Hamburg—Schiff was a notable success during America's age of industrialization. A major player in the Union Pacific affair that pitted railroad giants Edward Harriman (and Schiff) against James Hill (and J. P. Morgan), respect for Kuhn, Loeb soared. By then, it ranked publicly as equal to, or at least second only to, the Morgan firm, and on Wall Street the names of "Schiff," "Kuhn, Loeb," and "52 William Street" (the home of the firm from 1903 on) were interchangeable. Schiff's prestige and fortune remained virtually unscathed by the Equitable Life Assurance scandal and by the antibusiness mood of the Progressive Era. The firm's international interests continued to expand, particularly in the Far East, and in 1904–1905 Kuhn, Loeb successfully financed Japan's war against Russia. Not only did his financial coups enrich Schiff personally, but they underlay his influence in American society and his clout in the Jewish community.

At the same time that Schiff was building an international banking empire, he established his position as the foremost leader of American Jewry. He entered Jewish communal affairs by way of philanthropy. Although he contributed sizable funds to civic and nondenominational causes as well, he was most concerned with his fellow Jews. At a time when charity was mainly in the hands of the private sector, his principles for giving were very much like those of Andrew Carnegie. He believed in the unfettered right to accumulate wealth, but the wealthy, who had proved their ability by their economic achievements, were stewards for the needy. Upon them lay the responsibility to disburse their excess wealth during their lifetimes and to relieve the deserving poor by providing them with opportunities to pursue productive lives.

Virtually no bona fide Jewish relief or educational institution was denied Schiff's help. Help according to Schiff meant more than signing checks; it involved regular visits to the institution, frequent meetings, and even time spent with those served by the institution. He especially enjoyed the chance to shape policy and exert control over his pet philanthropies. The Montefiore Home and Hospital for Chronic Diseases was his favorite, and, as both its president and financial angel from 1885 until his resignation in 1920, Schiff ruled it—directors, staff, and patients—like a virtual fiefdom. His successor at Montefiore paid tribute to the banker's years of service when he called the period of 1880–1920 the "Schiff era in Jewish philanthropy."

Philanthropy, like all social affairs, was shaped by Schiff's views of Jewish–Christian relations. A staunch defender of Jews and Judaism against any form of discrimination, he demanded equality for Jews from the government in matters of political appointments and services as well as from private agencies in matters of benefits and privileges. The private agencies understood that noncompliance meant the forfeiture of contributions from Schiff, and the government recognized the banker's influence on Jewish voters. Schiff repaid the favors he incurred, while he simultaneously insisted that the Jewish institutions he supported be open to members of all faiths. Proper Jewish behavior, he believed, enhanced the Jewish image, which in turn would further the goal of full acceptance by the gentile society.

A proud Jew, he actively sought ways to disseminate public knowledge of the Jewish cultural heritage that had so importantly enriched Western civilization. For example, toward that end he generously endowed the Semitics Museum at Harvard University and its acquisition of ancient Hebrew artifacts. That, like his gifts of books about Judaism to libraries and Christian clergymen, would lead, he hoped, to greater acceptance of the Jew. Charles Eliot, Harvard's president and personal friend, agreed that the museum would serve as a counterweight to Christian antisemitism.

From the turn of the century until the outbreak of World War I, Schiff focused primarily on the plight of the 5–6 million Jews in czarist Russia. Pogroms, expulsions, and economic privation were hardly new, but they persisted with greater intensity. The problem for American Jewish communal leaders was multifaceted. The immediate need, to ameliorate the plight of the victims, gave rise to new relief agencies, and Schiff, because of his wealth and his ties to Jewish leaders in Western Europe, was at the hub of the activity.

For those who made their way to America—some 2 million by 1914 (Cohen 1999)—the tasks involved in easing their adjustment required even more planning. For example, the Baron de Hirsch Fund, of which Schiff was one of the nine original trustees, provided the new arrivals with classes in English and civics, training in manual arts, and practical aid for agricultural settlement. To solve some health problems on New York's Lower East Side, the Schiff family sponsored Lillian Wald's visiting nurses service and her settlement house on Henry Street. Schiff especially favored schemes to disperse the immigrants; he supported the Industrial Removal Office of the Hirsch Fund, and he toyed with similar ideas for moving immigrants to outlying areas and to other countries. Most original of all was his short-lived Galveston plan that landed the new arrivals in Texas and settled them in the Midwest. It thereby avoided the social problems of the crowded ghettos on the Atlantic coast. On another level entirely, the banker and his associates dreaded the spread of socialism and atheism—"un-American" doctrines—among the immigrants. Schiff and most of his associates were Reform Jews, but for rabbis and teachers to reach and properly train the new arrivals, they supported a Conservative institution, the Jewish Theological Seminary. By such means they sought to change the prevalent image of the undesirable Russian Jew and, even more important to Schiff, to preserve the country's tradition of unrestricted immigration.

No matter how well intentioned the institutions and plans for the new immigrants, the stewards frequently evoked the resentment of their intended beneficiaries. They neither consulted the new arrivals for *their* opinions, nor did they successfully mask their own dislike of the less-cultured newcomers. The stewards knew that their control of the community would ultimately be challenged by the far more numerous Russians, so it behooved them to train the latter appropriately, setting them on the proper path of acculturation and acceptance by Americans. Schiff, who sought the approval of the immigrants and who favored the empowerment of the acculturated Eastern Europeans under the direction of the stewards, was less high-handed than the others. Only when the new arrivals mounted a serious campaign for a democratically elected American Jewish Congress that would wrest control from the established stewards did he rant against the so-called agitators.

The long-range aim of the elitist communal leaders was to end persecution by securing equal rights for the

Jews in the czarist domain. As a group they operated through their newly organized defense agency, the American Jewish Committee (1906), which generally deferred to Schiff. But, short of obtaining intervention by the American government or building up the public's sympathy, there was little they could do. Schiff, however, was in a unique position. Government officials, including the secretary of state and the president, could not ignore the powerful banker. The stewards of the American Jewish Committee, led by Schiff and his lieutenant, Louis Marshall, forced the abrogation of a Russo-American treaty despite President William Howard Taft's opposition, but their underlying objective remained elusive. St. Petersburg was far more impressed, however, with Schiff alone. He had financed Japan's defeat of Russia, and he persisted in using his influence with American and European banking houses to block Russia's access to loans. When Schiff was invited several times to St. Petersburg as a guest of the government—he never went—he let it be known that he would trade loans for Jewish rights. His hatred of Russian discrimination figured importantly in keeping him pro-Germany and anti-Allies until the Russian Revolution of March 1917.

The fortunes of Kuhn, Loeb suffered during the war. Its international activity was perforce curtailed, and Schiff's refusal to participate in a major loan to the Allies as long as it could benefit Russia—an issue that divided his usually compliant partners—triggered an outburst of suspicion and antisemitism against Schiff and Kuhn, Loeb on the part of the Anglophile bankers headed by Morgan. According to conclusions of a Justice Department probe, neither Schiff nor Kuhn, Loeb was found guilty of unpatriotic behavior; the firm did not advance the sums of money that German agents in the country expected, nor did it propagandize on Germany's behalf. Although Schiff's name was blackened in the *German* press, the stigma of being a German sympathizer dogged him in *America* throughout the war.

Wartime sentiment and a resurgence of popular antisemitism increased Schiff's activities in the Jewish community. Even as they coped with the relief needs of Jews abroad, Schiff and his associates were called upon to rebut the charges against the un-American draft-dodging Jews. Simultaneously, they defended their fellow Jews against slurs by the military, government agencies, and private institutions. (Schiff himself took on discrimination by the powerful American Red Cross.) They preached incessantly to their fellow Jews against Socialist pacifism and against ideas like Jewish military units or all-Jewish liberty loans. A dread of Jewish separatism also underlay their bitter opposition to the Zionist-controlled American Jewish Congress. To be sure, Schiff modified his Reform anti-Zionist stand during the war. Acknowledging now that Jews were a people as well as a religious group, he explained that the reservoir of Jewish culture in Eastern Europe had evaporated with the Russian revolutions of 1917 and that he therefore supported the idea of a Jewish cultural and religious center in Palestine. But he continued to oppose political Zionism, which, he charged, separated the Jews from the Western societies in which they lived.

Schiff's style of leadership did not long survive the war. Few could match his wealth or philanthropic gifts, and the postwar managerial revolution largely depersonalized the governance of Jewish communal institutions. Nevertheless, he left a permanent stamp on the history of American Jewry.

Naomi W. Cohen

References and Further Reading
Adler, Cyrus. 1929. *Jacob H. Schiff: His Life and Letters.* 2 Vols. Garden City, NY: Doubleday.
Carosso, Vincent P. 1976. "A Financial Elite: New York's German-Jewish Investment Bankers." *American Jewish Historical Quarterly* 66,1: 67–88.
Cohen, Naomi W. 1999. *Jacob H. Schiff: A Study in American Jewish Leadership.* Hanover, NH: Brandeis University Press.

Intergroup Relations

Jews and the Slave Trade

The Atlantic slave trade has been the object of enormous scholarly and public attention for more than a generation. Its significance for the history of Jewry has been muted by modern liberal Jewish sensibilities and distorted by modern antisemitic exaggeration. One of the unfortunate results of the bitter debates over black–Jewish relations at the close of the twentieth century was to concentrate scholarly attention on the need to refute allegations by the Nation of Islam and others concerning the supposed Jewish domination of the transatlantic slave trade. A truly scholarly consideration of Jewish history in relation to the African slave trade must be based on an accurate assessment of the dimensions of Jewish participation within the context of the Atlantic slave trade history.

During three and a half centuries after 1500, more than 11 million Africans were loaded and transported in dreadful conditions to the tropical and subtropical zones of the Americas. This massive coerced transoceanic transportation system was only one element of a still broader process of migration. The coerced movement of Africans long exceeded the combined voluntary and involuntary migrations of Europeans. By the beginning of the nineteenth century, up to three Africans had been landed in the Americas for every European who crossed the Atlantic. Six percent of these Africans were landed in continental North America, compared with 49 percent delivered to the Caribbean and 45 percent to mainland Latin America.

The slave trade is usually presented in terms of a triangular trade: Europeans provided the capital, organization, trade goods and the means of transportation; Africans provided the initial captives and the means of intracontinental movement; and Europeans in the Americas provided the means for redistributing transported captives to productive occupations in various regions of the New World. Viewing the role of religious or ethno-religious groups in the African slave trade within this more familiar framework presents unusual methodological difficulties. The trade involved tens of thousands of perpetrators. Among them were pagans, Muslims, Catholics, Protestants, and Jews. Those who participated may be further divided into scores of groups by ethnic designation. The trade in humans flowed easily from one religious and commercial entity to another. Culturally defined identities had some impact on individual or group practices, but over the whole period of its existence the transatlantic slave trade appears to have been an activity rigorously driven by cost-benefit calculations.

Analyzing the specific relation of Jews to the Atlantic slave trade is warranted by a peculiar historiographical tradition. "Scarcely were the doors of the New World opened to Europeans," declared the economist and sociologist Werner Sombart a century ago, "than crowds of Jews came swarming in. . . . European Jewry was like an ant-heap into which a stick [expulsion from Spain] had been thrust. Little wonder, therefore, that a great part of this heap betook itself to the New World. . . . The first traders in America were Jews," as well as "the first plantation owners" in African São Tomé, and the first transplanters of sugar and slaves across the Atlantic. Jews were the "dominant social class [*die herrschende Kaste*]" of Brazil. Along with Portuguese criminals, they constituted almost the entire population of that colony, which reached its peak of prosperity only with "the influx of rich Jews from Holland" (Sombart 1951). In support of his interpretation, Sombart drew heavily on accounts by Jewish historians and encyclopedists. As Jewish migration to the Americas swelled at the end of the nineteenth century, writers sought to establish the earliest possible Jewish presence of their ancestors in the New World and to magnify their role in the grand narrative of European westward expansion. The search for a Jewish foundational presence in Atlantic development continues to find supporters among authors with dramatically contrasting motives.

Sombart grossly exaggerated in two respects. Jews were not legally permitted to live anywhere in the Iberian Americas for more than three centuries after Columbus's voyages of exploration. The "influx" of Jews to Brazil during the period of Dutch occupancy amounted to fewer than 1,500 settlers and lasted for less than a single generation. But Sombart's hyperbolic account was correct in one respect. Three centuries of cumulative expulsions of Jews from the Atlantic maritime states reached their climax as Europe's great westward expansion began in the late fifteenth century. The simultaneous departure of both the Columbian expedition and of Jewry from Spain in 1492 was emblematic of a broader movement in European history. By 1500, Jews had been expelled from the kingdoms of England, France, Spain, and Portugal. Within two more generations they had been excluded from most of the Habsburg Netherlands, from the Baltic seacoast, and from large parts of Italy. Except for areas directly under the authority of the Holy Roman emperors (the Habsburgs), the collapse of Jewish life in both Catholic and Protestant Europe was virtually complete by 1570. Open allegiance to Judaism was entirely extinguished in Spain, Portugal, Italy south of Rome, the Netherlands, England, France, and most of the Germanies. In isolated areas where Jews were not physically expelled, the Jewish presence in Western and Central Europe had become altogether marginal.

The age of European exploration was therefore also initially the age of "the most fundamental restructuring of Jewish life in Europe" (Israel 1989), between the Roman destruction of the Jewish nation and the later German annihilation of the twentieth century. By the time Africans began to be exported to the Americas in significant numbers (ca. 1570), Europe's rulers had forced the overwhelming mass of European Jewry eastward to Poland, Lithuania, and the Ottoman empire or southward to North Africa. Neither the rulers nor the merchants (including the Jewish merchants) of those new regions of settlement were involved in the Atlantic slave trade. Jews could not live securely anywhere along the European Atlantic seaboard during the century after the Columbian expedition, the century in which the Euro-African coastal supply systems and the Iberian American slave systems were created in the New World. Jews were consequently prohibited from openly participating in cofounding the institutions of the slave trade at any African terminus of the triangular trade or in the transoceanic Middle Passage. Success in such long-distance voyages, Europeans discovered, was initially enhanced by access to politically privileged monopolies in Europe, to trade enclaves on the African coast, and to colonial settlements in the Americas.

Until the end of the seventeenth century, governmental agencies or quasi-public trading companies were primarily monopolistic enterprises. In a confessionally intolerant Europe and its overseas extensions, it was virtually impossible for Jews to hold the principal managerial positions in these official slave-trading companies. For three centuries after 1500, Spanish slave trade licenses and *asientos* (monopoly contracts for the delivery of slaves to the Spanish colonies) were never awarded to Jews. This was equally true for the Portuguese, Dutch, English, and French trades. Jews could at most exercise influence at the margins of these enterprises as negotiators and consular intermediaries. Even subcontracting to Jewish merchants for the delivery of slaves contributed to the Spanish government's refusal to renew the *asiento* to the Portuguese Royal Guinea Company at the beginning of the eighteenth century.

If Jews could play no role in the initial political and legal foundations of the European transatlantic slave trade, the elimination of Jewry from the Iberian peninsula did create a major economic niche for some descendants of the forcibly converted Jews in Iberia. In 1497, the forced mass conversion of 100,000 Iberian Jews residing in Portugal created a novel situation. As "New Christians," descendants of ex-Jews were free to take advantage of the expanding Portuguese seaborne empire. During the sixteenth century the Portuguese trading network dramatically expanded along the coasts of Africa, the Indian Ocean basin, and on the east coast of South America. For more than a century after the 1490s, the Portuguese held a virtual monopoly in the trades flowing from these areas.

At the same time Portugal's stigmatization of New Christians as members of a legally tainted and inherited status group also subjected them to genealogical scrutiny, humiliation, confiscation, and violence from generation to generation. The volatile situation of the New Christians was symbolized by the first, and only, mass deportation of European children to the tropics. Following the flight of Jews from Spain to Portugal after the expulsion of 1492, the Portuguese monarch had 2,000 children abducted from their Jewish families. They were forcibly baptized and deported to São Tomé, an uninhabited island off the coast of Africa. The survivors of this first cohort of New Christians in Africa were mated at maturity with imported Africans. Their descendants, joined by further voluntary and involuntary migrations of New and Old Christians from Portugal, became São Tomé's principal inhabitants and traders.

In comparative terms the Early Modern Iberian empires allowed New Christians to play a role in the Atlantic slave trade that was never to be matched by Jews in any part of the world. The slave trade opened up transoceanic niches of entree and refuge that gave New Christians an initial advantage in human capital over other merchants. If their quasi-pariah religious status kept them at least once removed from institutional power, that same status tended to make them most effective in a world where opportunities for long-term credit were dependent on kinship and trust. Rulers considered slaving so valuable an activity that its New Christian practitioners might hope to be exempted from periodic group expulsions. In one purge, New Christians were allowed to remain in Angola only if they were merchants. As commodities, slaves opened doors into the American empires at times when other types of goods were restricted or excluded. Slaving was long a privileged means of gaining a foothold in Spanish as well as in Portuguese America.

New Christians were, of course, legally denied the opportunity to openly transmit Jewish culture and rituals. The Inquisition's premise of "impure blood," as well as an alleged collective propensity of such Christians to heresy and "Judaization," made kinship linkages perilous. Most of those who remained within the Iberian orbit in fact attempted to assimilate as rapidly as possible. Historians of Portuguese and overseas New Christians have concluded that consecutive generations became culturally and religiously indistinguishable from, and intermarried with, "Old Christians."

One must therefore be extremely cautious about conflating New Christians and Jews, or "Crypto-Jews." Neither in their social aspirations nor in their approach to economic activity can one differentiate significantly between New and Old Christians in the slave trade. In discussing economic activity in the early modern Iberian empire, nothing is to be gained by linking New Christians more closely with Jewish merchants, with whom they traded at long distance, than with Old Christian merchants, with whom they traded and lived. Denied full legitimacy in the community of the faithful, however, New Christian merchants might develop trading networks that were based on trusted family connections and might restrict their loyalties to kinsmen or to other familiar New Christians. Given this balance of negative institutional, social, and legal coercion, along with these familial advantages, New Christian merchants managed to gain control of a sizable share of all segments of the Portuguese Atlantic slave trade during the Iberian-dominated phase of the Atlantic system (1450–1630).

During the formation of the "second Atlantic system" (ca. 1640–1700), the Iberian slaving monopoly was definitively broken. The locus of the slave trade shifted northward from Portuguese Brazil to the Caribbean. Most Northwestern European and Baltic states attempted to enter the transatlantic commercial system: the Netherlands, England, France, Denmark, Sweden, Brandenburg, and Courland. In the second half of the seventeenth century the number of separate state-sponsored companies engaged in the transportation of African laborers reached its peak. For the first time, Jews openly participated in this more competitive environment and played their most tangible role in the Atlantic slave trade.

The first reappearance of a Jewish merchant community in Europe's Atlantic states occurred in Amsterdam, just a century after the Spanish expulsion. During the following century, the Dutch transatlantic trade was conducted from Europe primarily by means of a chartered monopoly given to the West India Company. Jewish merchants could enter the Dutch slave trade in only two ways: as passive investors in the company or as illegal private traders. With regard to the first, Jewish investment in the West India Company was remarkably small. It amounted to only a 1.3-percent share of the founding capital. Jews represented a minuscule segment of the Dutch slaving compared with the New Christians' role in the Portuguese trade. The Netherlands was also far better endowed with capital, commercial skills, and entrepreneurs than the Portuguese had been a century before. In the transportation of slaves from Africa, Jews were scarcely involved during the century of the West India Company's slave trade monopoly (1630–1735). Only one Jewish merchant is recorded as obtaining permission to sail directly to the African coast and to complete the Middle Passage. The expansion of the Dutch seaborne empire along the African coast also seems to have contributed little to the establishment of any Jewish presence there. The Dutch seizure of many important Portuguese African trading centers in the 1630s and 1640s resulted neither in a great influx of European Jews nor in the reconversion of resident Portuguese New Christians.

The main Jewish link with the Dutch slave trade came at its New World terminus. The Dutch were fully launched as a slaving power after their conquests in Brazil and Africa during the 1630s and early 1640s. However, they lacked a metropolitan Dutch population eager or desperate enough to relocate to the Americas. The West India Company welcomed Jews as colonizers and as onshore middlemen in newly conquered Brazil. It was at this western margin of the early Dutch transatlantic venture that Jews played their largest role. In the 1640s, the Dutch briefly became Europe's principal slave traders. During the eight years between 1637 and 1644, Jewish merchants accounted for between 8 and 63 percent of annual onshore purchasers of the total of 25,000 slaves landed in Brazil by the West India Company. Upward of a third of these African captives (8,000) may have reached planters through Jewish traders.

The gradual loss of Dutch Brazil to the Portuguese between 1645 and 1654 brought the Jewish presence to an end. Jews then took up a similar activity at another margin of the Dutch empire, its new Caribbean colonies. Refugees from Brazil and Europe were resettled in Dutch-controlled islands and in Suriname on the coast of South America. By the end of the seventeenth century, the island of Curaçao contained the largest Jewish settlement in the Americas. They engaged extensively in a transit trade from Curaçao to the British and French islands and, more significantly, with the Spanish mainland. Over the course of the century between its establishment as a Dutch colony in 1630 and the virtual end of its transit slave trade in the 1760s, Curaçao Jews therefore handled a large proportion of the 85,000 arrivals, about one-sixth of the total Dutch slave trade. The Emmanuels (1970, I) affirm that Jewish participation in the slave trade was largest in the twenty-five years between 1686 and 1710, a period when Postma records 26,364 slaves landed in Curaçao (1990). Comparing the Emmanuels' figures for 1700–1705 (1,108 slaves purchased by Jews) with Postma's total of 6,348 slaves delivered to Curaçao in the same period, Jews accounted for 17 percent of the large-batch purchases of slaves landed. The Emmanuels listed only purchases of obvious "trade" slaves (ten or more) in their individualized list. However, "almost every Jew bought from one to nine slaves for his personal use" (Emmanuel and Emmanuel 1970, I). Non-Jews did likewise. Since Jews were "the second most important element" of Curaçao's population after the Protestants, accounting for 40 percent of the population of Punda around 1715 (Emmanuel and Emmanuel 1970, I), Jewish merchants may have accounted for nearly half of the slaves purchased from the West India Company in Curaçao in the twenty-five years between 1686 and 1710. By 1765, however, Jews owned only 867 (or 16 percent) of the 5,534 slaves on Curaçao.

Less needs to be said about Jewish merchants in the seventeenth-century colonies of other European powers in the Caribbean. Jewish mercantile activity in the English colonies was a modest replication of the pattern set in the Dutch Antilles. In the English case, metropolitan Jews played a minor role as passive investors in the chartered Royal companies. Jewish merchants did not invest in the Royal Adventurers Trading into Africa, or its successor, the Royal African Company, until the 1690s. Eli Faber's carefully researched study of Jewish participation in the British slave system shows that the peak of mercantile investment in the Royal African Company lasted from the mid-1690s to the second decade of the eighteenth century. He calculates that Jews purchased about 7 percent of the Royal African Company slaves landed in Jamaica between 1674 and 1700. A corroborating study, by Trevor Burnard (1996), calculates the Jewish share at 6.5 percent for the slightly longer period 1674–1708. As in the Dutch case, Jews were most prominent at the Caribbean end of the slave trade. However, the Jewish mercantile role in the English islands never approached that of the merchants of Curaçao.

The Jewish share in the French slave trade was even more evanescent. In the French Caribbean colonies, an early Jewish presence, established in the 1660s and 1670s, was virtually eliminated by royal expulsions in the 1680s. As in the English case, Jews in the French colonies never approached the significance of their Dutch counterparts. Jews also played marginal roles in the efforts of Northern Europe's smaller maritime powers to become players in the Atlantic economy. Even in this second phase of the Atlantic slave trade, Jewish mercantile influence remained quite modest. The greatest significance of the Jewish presence in Brazil was that it gave some of them the technological expertise for their successful movement into the Caribbean. In the rest of the Atlantic system, in Europe, along the African Coast, and on the Middle Passage, Jewish participation never approached the significance attained by New Christians in the Iberian Americas.

Although the long eighteenth century (1700–1807) witnessed the absolute peak of the Atlantic slave trade (6.7 million shipped to the Americas), the Jewish mercantile share of the Atlantic slave trade declined. Even on the New World end of the trade, colonies were divided into separate national spheres dominated by non-Jewish settlers and traders. Special investment funds and partnerships allowed metropolitans to invest their capital, including slaving ventures, in the rapidly expanding plantation systems. Intensive research into each of the national trades has failed to turn up more than a handful of Jewish individuals or families in any of these trading circuits. In the Netherlands, well-established families seem to have withdrawn from the transit trade to the New World. In Bordeaux, the center of Jewish mercantile activity in the French colonial trade, Jews accounted for 4.3 percent of the slaves exported by the city's merchants. Only one family, the Gradis, ranked among the major slavers. In England, Jewish investment in the African trade also declined. Jewish wealth accounted for less than 1.6 percent of the original capital of the South Sea Company, launched in 1714. As independent entrepreneurs and ship owners, the metropolitan Jews never ac-

counted for more than 1 percent of ventures during the last fifty years of the British slave trade (1760–1807).

For most of the eighteenth century, Jews remained marginal receivers of consignments of slaves in the colonies. They continued to appear in their initial niche as purchasers of "refuse slaves" for resale. According to British Naval Office records, 6 percent of the 24,000 slaves reexported from Jamaica to other colonies between 1742 and 1769 were carried on Jewish-owned vessels. In British North America, Newport was the leading African slaving port during the eighteenth century and the only port in which Jewish merchants played a significant part. At the peak period of their participation in slaving expeditions (the generation before the American Revolution), Newport's Jewish merchants handled up to 10 percent of the Rhode Island slave trade. Incomplete records for other eighteenth-century ports in which Jews participated in the slave trade in any way show that for a few years they held at least partial shares in up to 8 percent of New York's small number of slaving voyages, usually from African to Caribbean ports. There is no evidence that they played any role in the internal colonial transit trade in a way comparable to that of merchants in Jamaica.

After the United States outlawed the Atlantic slave trade in 1808, an internal, or domestic, slave trade continued to fuel the expansion of slavery to the West. Although the degree of participation of Jewish merchants in slave dealing throughout the South is not fully known, they seem to have been visible as substantial participants in only a few cities. A table of the commissions of fourteen "Prosperous Slave Brokers" of Charleston, South Carolina, shows that the one substantial Jewish brokerage accounted for 4 percent of the commissions (Friedman 1998). According to Bertram Korn, Jews accounted for four of the forty-four slave brokers in Charleston, three of seventy in Richmond, and one of twelve in Memphis (1973). Elsewhere, the anecdotal evidence points to Jews as petty traders, who dealt incidentally in an activity overwhelmingly dominated by non-Jews. Inference from the available records led Korn to estimate that all of the Southern Jewish slave traders probably did not buy and sell as many slaves as did the largest single slave trading firm in the South (1973).

The economic, social, legal, and racial pattern of the Atlantic slave trade was set before Jews made their way back to Northwestern Europe, to the coasts and islands of

Africa, or to European colonies in the Americas. They remained marginal actors in most places and in most periods during the Atlantic slave system: in its political and legal foundations; in its capital formation; in its maritime organization; and in its distribution of coerced migrants from Africa. Jewish slave traders were active only at the western end of the Atlantic, briefly in Brazil, more durably in the Caribbean. At no point during the slave trade were Jews numerous enough, rich enough, or powerful enough to significantly affect the structure and flow of the trade.

The same conclusion does not hold for the New Christian descendants of Jews during the period of Iberian domination (1450–1640). Their importance in the development of the slave trade to the Americas must be given its due. When Portuguese merchants became the first global trading diaspora, New Christians were prominent in its growth. Although distrusted by Old Christian political-religious elites, New Christians found a precarious niche in the Atlantic system. As a loose network of trading families, they pioneered in the formation of the European–Asian–African–American complex that contributed to the New World's first African-based slave economies.

During the next phase of the Atlantic slave trade, when observant Jews entered the system, they found that the comparative advantage of New Christians was sharply reduced. They played insignificant roles in the European, African, and transoceanic components of Northern European slaving. Jewish mercantile communities were far smaller in proportion to Christian networks in Northern Europe than were Iberian New Christians in relation to the Old. Jewish working capital was correspondingly less significant. The advantages of Jewish family networks over their Dutch, English, or French Christian competitors clearly did not match that of "New Christian" merchants over the "Old" in sixteenth-century Iberia.

Only in the Dutch case did Jews play a distinctive, if marginal, part. Their brief prominence after 1640 depended as much on their availability as refugee "risk takers" in tropical frontier colonies as on their talents as entrepreneurs in Europe. They were, as the English essayist Joseph Addison correctly noted, "pegs and nails" in the international capitalist system. During the peak phase of the Atlantic slave trade, from 1700 to 1840, the relative significance of Jews declined still further. By the time the Afro-American slave trade reached its absolute peak near the end of the eighteenth century, both Jews and New Chris-

tians had nearly disappeared from the accounts of the transatlantic slave trade.

A still more intriguing historical question has begun to emerge in scholarly discourse on the role of Jews in the African slave trade. The empirical record makes it relatively easy for historians to demonstrate that Jewish merchants did not dominate this segment of the Atlantic economy. Historians of Jewry might, however, ask why Jews were not involved to a greater degree. The answer clearly cannot be attributed to the distinctive religious or moral traditions of Jewry in early modern Europe. Despite generations of historiographical inference that Jewish tradition encouraged more benign treatment of slaves by Jewish masters, nothing in Jewish law or customs prohibited the purchase or ownership of slaves. The Jewish involvement in Atlantic slavery produced no *responsa* condemning New World slaveholding or slave trading. Jews in the Dutch and English colonies participated in the slave economy without religious condemnation.

If there was no special inhibition against buying and selling human beings by Jews, why didn't merchants turn to better account their presumed diasporic heritage, their transoceanic ethnic network, and their facility with the trading languages of the Atlantic world? From the perspective of the history of the slave trade, these were probably not significant advantages for success in the transatlantic slaving business. In ethnoreligious terms, there certainly was never a Jewish network on the coasts of Africa. Nor did Jewish multilingualism extend to any special competence in the languages of that continent. Success in the African trade depended far more on up-to-date intelligence about the changing tastes of Africans, translatable into rapid business decisions about the optimum assortment of goods for slaving voyages.

Throughout most of the Americas, the available evidence indicates that the Jewish network probably counted for little in Atlantic slaving. The few cases of long-term Jewish participation in the eighteenth-century slave trades offer evidence of cross-religious networks as keys to their success. In case after case, Jews who participated in multiple slaving voyages activities linked themselves to Christian agents or partners. It was not as Jews, but as merchants, that traders ventured into one of the great enterprises of the early modern world.

By the end of the revolutions for independence in the Americas (1770s–1820s), Jewish communities in most slave trading ports had long been in decline. By 1830 the Atlantic slave trade to the British, Dutch, and French colonies and to mainland Spanish America had been abolished. Well before that "Age of Revolution," New Christians had disappeared from the records of the Portuguese-Brazilian slave trade. They were not succeeded by Jews when the Inquisition ceased to function. Jewish merchants played no measurable role in the transportation of well over 2 million Africans to Latin America (mainly Brazil and the Spanish Caribbean) during the nineteenth century before the termination of that traffic in 1867. Nor do Jews appear in the literature on the large-scale internal transit trade of slaves in Brazil before their emancipation in 1888.

Having assayed the modest role played by Jewish merchants in the coerced migration of Africans to the New World, one must also note the impact of that coerced migration on broader Jewish sensibilities. Since early modern Jewry was embedded in the mechanisms of European expansion, trade, migration, and communication, Jews absorbed the racialized perspectives of their Christian and Muslim counterparts in the Old and New Worlds. In the Atlantic world, while few Jews owned slaves and fewer still were engaged in the slave trade, they adopted the prevailing negative images of blacks. This was true even in the Ashkenazic area of Europe least impacted by the economics and institutions of Atlantic slavery. Even in this respect, however, one should be cautious about assigning any special importance to Jewish slavers or slave owners in the formation of Eastern European cultural attitudes. Very few Jews captained slaving voyages from Africa to the Americas, and Jewish discourse in general showed little sustained interest in blacks. Everywhere in the Americas, where Jews were embedded in the institution of slavery, the law of the land, not *halacha* (Jewish law), became their law. The customs of Western Europe, of its colonies, and of the new nations of America became their customs. With the significant exception of the Sabbath, *halacha* and Jewish traditions on slavery were "quietly and conveniently stowed away" (Schorsch 2004). Marginalized themselves, Jewish merchants, like those of every other religious and ethnic group in Western Europe, Africa, and the Americas, availed themselves of the opportunities afforded by the hierarchies of the new Atlantic economy.

Seymour Drescher

References and Further Reading

Brackman, Harold. 1994. *Ministry of Lies: The Truth behind the Nation of Islam's "The Secret Relationship Between Blacks and Jews."* New York and Los Angeles: Four Walls Eight Windows and Simon Wiesenthal Center.

Burnard, Trevor. 1996. "Who Bought Slaves in Early America? Purchasers of Slaves from the Royal African Company in Jamaica, 1674–1708." *Slavery and Abolition* 17: 68–92.

Davis, David Brion. 1984. *Slavery and Human Progress.* New York: Oxford University Press.

Davis, David Brion. 1994. "The Slave Trade and the Jews." *New York Review of Books* 22 (December): 14–16.

Drescher, Seymour. 1999. *From Slavery to Freedom: Comparative Studies in the Rise and Fall of Atlantic Slavery.* New York: New York University Press.

Drescher, Seymour. 2001. "Jews and New Christians in the Atlantic Slave Trade." In *The Jews and the Expansion of Europe to the West, 1500 to 1800,* edited by Paolo Bernardini and Norman Fiering. New York: Berghahn Books.

Eltis, David. 2000. *The Rise of African Slavery in the Americas.* New York: Cambridge University Press.

Emmanuel, Issac S., and Suzanne Emmanuel. 1970. *History of the Jews of the Netherlands Antilles.* 2 Vols. Cincinnati, OH: American Jewish Archives.

Faber, Eli.1998. *Jews, Slaves, and the Slave Trade: Setting the Record Straight.* New York: New York University Press.

Fortune, Stephen Alexander. 1984. *Merchants and Jews: The Struggle for British West Indian Commerce, 1650–1750.* Gainesville: University Press of Florida.

Friedman, Saul S. 1998. *Jews and the American Slave Trade.* New Brunswick, NJ: Transaction Publishers.

Israel, Jonathan I. 1989. *European Jewry in the Age of Mercantilism, 1550–1750.* 2nd rev. ed. Oxford, UK: Clarendon Press.

Korn, Bertram W. 1973. "Jews and Negro Slavery in the Old South." In *Jews in the South,* edited by Leonard Dinnerstein and Mary Palsson. Baton Rouge: Louisiana State University Press.

Postma, Johannes Menne. 1990. *The Dutch in the Atlantic Slave Trade, 1600–1815.* Cambridge, UK: Cambridge University Press.

Schorsch, Jonathan. 2004. *Jews and Blacks in the Early Modern World.* New York: Cambridge University Press.

Sombart, Werner. 1951. *The Jews and Modern Capitalism,* translated by M. Epstein; American edition by Bert F. Hoselitz. Glencoe, IL: Free Press.

Wiznitzer, Arnold. 1960. *Jews in Colonial Brazil.* New York: Columbia University Press.

Black–Jewish Relations in the Nineteenth Century

The encounter between African Americans and Jews occupies a significant place in American Jewish history. Although most studies focus on their interaction in the twentieth-century urban North, black–Jewish relations had a pre-1900 prologue that significantly shaped attitudes and experience.

Overall, Jewish merchants were "accountable for considerably less than 2 percent of the slave imports into the West Indies and North America," according to Jacob Rader Marcus (1970, 2). The Atlantic slave trade was a minor facet of the careers of such prominent eighteenth-century Jewish merchants as Aaron Lopez of Newport, Rhode Island. Over a twenty-year span, Lopez commissioned two hundred international voyages of which fourteen were slave-trading ventures that resulted in the importation of 1,165 slaves, that is, 1 percent of all the slaves imported into Newport during the eighteenth century.

During the early decades of the nineteenth century, as slavery ended in the North but expanded in the South, black–Jewish relations bifurcated along sectional lines. The regional distributions of black and Jewish populations in 1860 were reverse images: 92 percent of all African Americans were Southern, and 80 percent of all American Jews were Northern. The small Southern Jewish community numbered around 30,000, a majority consisting of recent German Jewish immigrants. Its members participated, unevenly, in every facet of Southern life, including the slave system.

After U.S. involvement in the Atlantic slave trade was outlawed in 1808, slave trading persisted in the South. One study found that 8 of 125 professional slave traders—but none of the major traders—were Jews. Bertram W. Korn concluded that all of the Southern Jewish firms specializing in the slave trade combined probably "did not buy and sell as many slaves as did the [non-Jewish] firm of Franklin and Armfield, the largest Negro traders in the South" (1961).

Recent studies of slaveholding by Southern Jews have shown a seeming paradox. An analysis of the 1830 Census found only sixteen Jews among 57,000 Southerners owning twenty or more slaves, and only two Jews among 11,000 owners of fifty or more. Yet in the overall sample, 75 percent of 322 Jewish families were slaveholders, compared to 36 percent of all Southern families. Thus, Jews were negligible in the ranks of the planter class who owned three-fourths of all slaves; yet Jews were about twice as likely to be slave owners as the average white Southerner.

This is because the Southern Jews were concentrated, not in the rural districts where six in seven slaves were held, but in the cities where the norm was diffuse ownership of small numbers of domestic slaves or artisans. In Charleston in 1830, 87 percent of all heads of families owned at least one slave, compared to 83 percent of Jewish family heads; on average, the Jewish householders also owned fewer slaves. The typical Jewish slave owner was an urban smallholder, far removed from the power center of the South's "peculiar institution."

In some Southern cities on the Gulf Coast, patterns in slavery and race relations were carried over from the Caribbean. The institution of *placage*—long-term cohabitation between white men and women of color (both slave and free)—thrived in New Orleans. Daniel Warburg established a lifelong relationship with Marie Rose, a Cuban-born slave whom he freed and maintained in a manner that allowed her to buy slaves of her own. She bore him six children (who were also emancipated), including two who achieved artistic distinction. Eugene Warburg, educated abroad with his father's help, became a renowned sculptor in Europe.

In the 1830s, a French observer visiting Savannah discerned a tendency for Jews to serve as patrons and agents of free people of color. About the same time in New Orleans, philanthropist Judah Touro became known for his benefactions to members of the creole community. Often dependent on Jewish and other white patronage, the antebellum free black elite developed into the leaders of the postbellum African American community.

In the countryside, an enslaved African American's most likely contact with a Jew was not with a slave master but with a peddler or itinerant merchant. In the 1840s and 1850s, German Jewish immigrant peddlers began selling clothes and trinkets to slaves, but they often had to contend with hostile whites who accused them of violating Sunday closing laws, encouraging drunkenness and petty theft among slaves, and generally undermining plantation discipline.

Immediately after the Civil War, freedmen were typically quite friendly toward Jewish peddlers, who treated them courteously and enabled them to become consumers. Earlier, the slaves may have been even more favorably disposed toward these peddlers because subsequent causes of friction—creditor–debtor relations in the context of rural sharecropping and urban merchandising—had not yet developed. It was not until the late nineteenth century that a body of African American folklore emerged reflecting tensions between black customers and Jewish peddlers or storekeepers. W.E.B. DuBois exaggerated the prevalence of economically based black–Jewish tensions in the South in *The Souls of Black Folk* (1903).

Another source of antisemitism among African Americans—religious antipathy to Jews as "Christ killers"—has also been traced to slavery times. White missionaries reputedly used catechisms "especially prepared for colored people" to indoctrinate slaves: "Question: The wicked Jews grew angry with our Savior and what did they do with him? Answer: They crucified him" (Weinberg 1974). White Southerners told stories about how their slaves had absorbed the stereotype of Jews as deicides. In one version, a servant runs away rather than be sold to a Jew because "if the Jews killed the Lord and Master, what won't they do to a poor little nigger like me!" (Glanz 1961).

Some of the slaves' songs also voiced the deicide accusation: "Cruel Jews, jes look at Jesus./ Dey nail Him to de Cross./ Dey rivet His feet./ Dey hanged Him high./ An' dey stretched Him wide./ O de cruel Jews dun took ma Jesus" (McIlhenny 1933). There are a few sermons (including one in Gullah dialect) and folk rhymes and tales expressing the same theme. Most of the evidence of black religious antisemitism, however, such as the reminiscences of James Baldwin and Richard Wright, derives from a period several generations removed from slavery times. Still, African American Christianity—with deeps roots in Southern Methodism and Baptism—shared the explosive ambivalence toward Jews that was characteristic of the evangelical Protestant denominations that were strong throughout the nineteenth-century United States but dominant in the white South. Pictured respectfully as "the people of the Book" destined to return to the Holy Land, Jews were alternatively reviled for their continuing refusal to accept Christ.

Yet the religion of the slaves did not fully replicate their masters'. In the 1790s—a generation before the concerted white campaign to evangelize the slaves—plantation hands were already singing "Let My People Go." Enslaved African Americans developed so intense an identification with the Hebrew children led out of Egyptian bondage that white philosemitism paled in comparison.

Conversely, the crucifixion theme (less prominent in the spirituals than in modern gospel music) was muted. In the classic slave songs, Jesus figured prominently, but on a similar footing with Jacob, Moses, Joshua, Daniel, and Jonah. Moreover, his appearance was often—not as "the

suffering servant" on the cross—but in the garb of an Old Testament "man of war." The Old Testament became a crucible for forging a religion of resistance emphasizing this worldly, collective deliverance. Slave religion affirmed the superiority of Paul's "new covenant" to that of Moses, but it retained a strongly Hebraic cast that inspired generations of slave rebels, culminating in Nat Turner.

There was no consensus among American Jews regarding slavery, and—even if there had been—there were no Jewish national organizations (other than B'nai B'rith) or centralized bodies to express it in a polarizing era when the Catholic Church remained silent and the national Protestant denominations split along sectional lines over the slavery issue. Jews were as deeply divided by geography and conviction as other white Americans.

In the South, where proslavery thinking became required orthodoxy after 1830, one study found "a pattern of almost complete conformity" among Jews (Korn 1961). The two most prominent proslavery politicians of Jewish antecedents—Florida senator David L. Yulee and Louisiana senator and Confederate cabinet member Judah P. Benjamin—married and raised their children outside the faith and displayed no interest in Jews or Judaism. But their political views were widely shared by the small number of Southern rabbis, none of whom south of Maryland spoke out against slavery. The native-born Jewish community of the South produced a handful of dissenters who, typically, left the region for the more ideologically congenial North.

German Jewish immigrants to the South were often horrified by their first sight of a slavemaster's whip. Some maintained a lifelong aversion and refused ever to own slaves, but others adapted quickly and became slave masters. In the border states, Rabbi David Einhorn of Baltimore and journalists Isidore Busch and Moritz Pinner of St. Louis applied the liberal principles of the European Revolution of 1848 to the American slavery issue. But elsewhere in Dixie, German Jewish peddlers and merchants learned to be circumspect, though their friendly treatment of black customers could be read as implicit criticism of white supremacist mores. Two Jewish brothers named Friedman, immigrant storekeepers in rural Georgia, did figure in the annals of the Underground Railroad. They conspired with the slave, Peter Still, to buy his freedom and return him to the North, from which he had been kidnapped decades earlier.

Critics attribute Southern Jews' general acquiescence in "the peculiar institution" to their pervasive desire to succeed in a slave society where white skin conferred superior status. Yet underlying this status drive were well-founded fears that dissent would produce an antisemitic backlash. In fact, during the Civil War, Southern Jews—despite their Confederate loyalties—were specifically scapegoated for the losing war effort.

In the North, Jewish attitudes toward slavery and sectional conflict were much more diverse. Strong antislavery bastions like Philadelphia and Chicago contrasted with New York, with close economic ties to the Cotton Kingdom, and Cincinnati, bordering the upper South, where Rabbi Isaac Mayer Wise harshly criticized abolitionists. Although slavery was legal in Missouri, the St. Louis Jewish community shared the antislavery views of the city's outspoken German American community.

Throughout the North, two factors shaped Jewish opinion. First, minority group insecurities fueled a hunger for political invisibility. The Jewish minority, less than 1 percent of the Northern population, was doubly marginal as a minority made up overwhelmingly of recent immigrants. German Jews drew a cautionary lesson from the contemporary Know-Nothing Movement, which targeted the Irish Catholic immigrants as undesirable. Jewish antislavery activists had to contend with a real concern among their fellow Jews that it would be dangerous to get ahead of public opinion and become identified with a controversial crusade.

The second major factor affecting Jewish attitudes was the antislavery movement's new turn in the 1830s. The earlier freedom societies—led mainly by Quakers, Deists, and Unitarians—had proposed a gradual, compensated approach to ending slavery. Demanding immediate emancipation, the new abolitionist movement was an evangelical crusade. The Jewish merchant community around 1800 had shown an affinity for the elite manumission societies. Antipathy was their more typical reaction a generation later to the evangelical abolitionist crusade.

Ernestine Rose, a rabbi's daughter born in Poland who became a fiery antislavery orator in the United States, was both an atheist and an abolitionist. Yet even she criticized the movement for being tinged with antisemitism. Lewis Tappan, who lamented that more Jews did not rally behind the abolitionist banner, ignored the alienating effects of his fellow leaders in the movement. His brother Arthur, for ex-

ample, wanted to make abolitionism into "a Christian party in politics" and addressed his appeals exclusively to "antislavery Christians," spurning the support of free-thinkers and non-Christians.

The abolitionist press tended to ignore the contributions of antislavery Jews while condemning as "Israelites with Egyptian principles" proslavery politicians with "Jewish names," whether or not they were practicing Jews. In the 1840s, when a Jewish child in Italy was kidnapped and forcibly baptized, an abolitionist newspaper published a vicious satire by a fictitious African American named Sambo criticizing American Jews for protesting such "far-off evils" (Korn 1957).

As the sectional crisis of the 1850s propelled the country toward Civil War, more Jews were drawn into the orbit of abolitionism and antislavery politics. The process was facilitated by the changing ideology of the Garrisonian abolitionists, who repudiated narrow church loyalties and evangelical dogma in favor of universalist religious doctrines that encouraged outreach beyond the Protestant fold. Equally important, antislavery radicals and mainstream Republican politicians embraced the pragmatic view that "side issues" like nativist attacks on non-Protestant immigrants should not be allowed to distract attention from building a coalition against slavery.

Religious prejudices against Jews did not disappear from the antislavery movement, but were muted. Jews became active in Republican politics, and—in the case of three German Jewish immigrants—entered abolitionist legend by fighting alongside antislavery martyr John Brown to keep Kansas free territory. In 1860, when New York rabbi Morris J. Raphall delivered a notorious sermon justifying Old Testament slavery (though not the cruelties of the Slave South), he was quickly isolated on the national scene and, eventually, even in his own city where the Jewish community became strongly pro-Union in 1861. During the Civil War 6,000 Jewish soldiers fought for the Union cause, despite antisemitic incidents on the Northern home front.

Not all Jewish Republican voters and Union soldiers were abolitionists, nor were all Jewish abolitionists free of racial prejudice. Still, the Jewish community moved en masse into the ranks of antislavery Republicanism at the same time as the American Irish, who competed with free blacks for low-end jobs, were becoming ever more staunch antiabolition Democrats.

Abolitionist August Bondi, one of three German Jewish immigrants who fought beside John Brown in Kansas. (American Jewish Historical Society)

German Jews, like other German immigrants, were concentrated in commercial occupations and skilled crafts in which there was less economic friction with African American workers. Free blacks limited their nativist criticisms mostly to the Irish. The African American press occasionally expressed unease about "The German Invasion," yet typically praised German Americans as "our active allies in the struggle against oppression and prejudice" (Smith 1859). German Jews were never singled out for criticism.

Jews also enjoyed some immunity from African American criticism because of their positive religious identification with the Jews as living witnesses to Old Testament truths about deliverance from persecution and bondage. The first manifesto by a black abolitionist, David Walker's *Appeal*, contrasted the religion of resistance of "the Jews, that ancient people of the Lord," with the counsels of passivity and submission taught the slaves by "preachers of the religion of Jesus Christ" (Walker 1829).

While proslavery apologists invoked the (misconstrued) "Noah's Cursing Ham" in the Book of Genesis as proof of white superiority, black abolitionists attached pre-eminent importance to the Old Testament prophecy that "Great men will come from Egypt, and Ethiopia will stretch out her hands to God" (Psalms 68:32). Combined with the Exodus story, this image provided a biblical frame of reference within which African Americans began to speculate that their dispersion to the New World might be part of a divine plan that would end with them helping to redeem or liberate Africa. Thus African American Old Testament bibliolatry nurtured black nationalism.

In response to heightened racism in the North as well as proslavery militancy in the South, African American leaders in the 1840s and 1850s increasingly embraced a nationalist paradigm, emphasizing collective self-help as well as back-to-Africa ventures. Pioneering black nationalists like Martin R. Delany shifted their search for models for African American political action from the biblical Israelites to the modern-day Jews, "scattered throughout . . . almost the habitable globe, [but] maintaining their national characteristics, and looking forward . . . [to] seeing the day when they may return to the former national position of self-government and independence" (Delany 1852).

A frequent visitor to the United States, West Indies–born Edward Wilmot Blyden also drew an analogy between his African improvement program and what he later referred to as "that marvelous movement called Zionism" (Lynch 1967). As early as 1859 black nationalist James T. Holly pointed to continuing political discrimination against Jews in Great Britain to warn African Americans that individual economic success—even by the Rothschilds—was no guarantee of group empowerment. Frederick Douglass and other delegates to the National Negro Convention (1853) adopted a resolution that expressed a widespread sentiment among African Americans: "With the exception of the Jews, under the whole heavens, there is not found a people pursued with a more relentless prejudice and persecution than are the free colored people of the United States" (Moses 1978).

After the Civil War, identification with the Jews as a model for aspiration remained a foundation of African American thought. "Ever since I can remember I have had a special and peculiar interest in the history and progress of the Jewish race," Booker T. Washington wrote in an autobiographical passage that has numerous parallels in the speeches and writings of other late nineteenth-century African American leaders (Washington 1912).

The symbolism of the Exodus from Egypt—slavery followed by forty years in the wilderness—gave the Old Testament story new resonance to freedmen barred from entering "the promised land" by sharecropping and segregation. Constrained by economic and political discrimination, the former slaves shaped a more independent religious life through the new black churches that replaced the underground congregations of slavery.

Ironically, the new institutional autonomy enjoyed by these churches went hand in hand with increasing pressures to conform to the orthodoxies of the white Protestant denominations from the North, whose missionaries trained the first postslavery generation of Southern black ministers and teachers. The missionaries sought to "de-Judaize" the faith of the freedmen, who allegedly did not understand the New Testament. According to one Northern army chaplain, "There is no part of the Bible with which they are so familiar as the story of the deliverance of the children of Israel. Moses is their ideal of all that is high, and noble, and perfect, in man. [They] have been accustomed to regard Christ not so much in the light of a spiritual Deliverer, as that of a second Moses" (Kolchin 1972).

Desiring acceptance from white mentors, African Americans educated in postwar normal schools and colleges often censored their own religious heritage in response to such criticism. Eventually, the Old Testament–oriented spirituals gave way to the new gospel music in which the redemptive Jesus is the overwhelming presence. This was also the period when Protestant Fundamentalism became synonymous with African American Christianity and when theological black antisemitism first crystallized.

In the North, in the years after the Civil War, the increasingly self-confident and socially conscious German Jewish elite became involved in racial betterment efforts even before they took up the cause of Russian Jewish immigrants. The institutional links that Jewish philanthropies and civil rights organizations established with African American counterparts in the early twentieth century built on the initiatives taken a generation earlier by lawyer-politician Simon Wolf, a close political ally of black Republicans Frederick Douglass and John Mercer Langston, and investment banker Jacob Schiff, who spearheaded the movement to end racially separate schools in New York City.

In the South, Jewish politicians were less likely to reach out to the African American community than rabbis such as Aaron S. Bettelheim in Richmond, Benjamin Szold in Baltimore (vilified as the rabbi of Timbuctoo), and later David Marx in Atlanta. But particularly during Reconstruction, Jewish peddlers and merchants put themselves at risk by their willingness to cultivate the freedmen as customers. In 1868 in Franklin, Tennessee—not far from where the Ku Klux Klan was founded two years before—a Jewish storekeeper accused of selling ammunition to freedmen was murdered alongside his African American employee.

The sharecropping and crop lien systems became the Southern norm at the same time that many antebellum Jewish peddlers made the transition to small-town supply merchant. Hostile white observers singled out German Jewish immigrants as the taskmaster, arbiter, and guardian of the depressed rural economy of the postwar South.

In actuality, Jews never dominated the Southern merchant class, though they were a highly visible minority. Before 1880, when the typical Jewish merchant was still a German immigrant, estimates of the foreign-born among the entire merchant class range from 11 to 23 percent. These percentages can serve only as a very rough approximation of the proportion who were Jewish, since all foreign-born merchants were not Jews, nor were all Jewish merchants foreign-born.

More important than numbers was limited economic power. Jonathan M. Wiener has demonstrated that the planters never lost their grip on Southern agriculture, maintaining it by assuming the commercial role themselves or becoming the dominant partner of merchants. In the Alabama Black Belt of the 1870s, merchants often functioned as agents of plantation owners. When Russian Jewish immigrants began arriving in the rural South after 1880, they did business with black tenant farmers under a system that placed ultimate control over credit as well as land tenure in the hands of white planters, almost none of whom were Jews.

Jewish merchants were vulnerable to scapegoating because of their foreign accents and identification with the Shylock stereotype. No matter the actual ethnicity of the owner, "Jew store" became popular shorthand for both country emporiums and urban retailers. Blacks often oscillated between admiration for Jewish merchants and antagonism, emulation, and envy.

African American newspapers in the South regularly carried accounts of the cheating of customers or the eviction of tenants, but "stories about Jews mistreating blacks were infrequent" (Shankman 1982). Wild accusations about "Jewish moneylenders" who held "the purse strings of the world" and were "fast getting control of Southern merchandising, farming, and banking interests" were more often found in Northern black newspapers, the voice of the black elite. Booker T. Washington, whose early speeches contained derogatory references to Jewish merchants, ceased the practice after he began soliciting philanthropists like Julius Rosenwald for contributions to Tuskegee Institute. However, Washington clearly understood the limits of Jewish influence in the South. He supported a Jewish candidate for county sheriff and patronized a Jewish merchant who was a longtime friend of the school, but instructed his business manager not to get "our trade too much centered in the hands of a few Jews" because the real wielders of public opinion were "native Southern white men" (Harlan 1972–1989).

Blacks expressed solidarity with Jews in Mississippi and Louisiana in the early 1890s when white farmers—accusing Jewish merchants of displacing them with black tenants—launched an antisemitic vigilante movement. Over four hundred black Mississippians signed petitions in support of the Jews.

Steven Hertzberg found a "usually amicable" relationship in Atlanta between black customers and Jewish merchants who hired black employees and stayed in the racially mixed neighborhoods in which they did business, living over their stores (Hertzberg 1978). In Atlanta, the more established German Jewish merchants—some emerging as department-store owners—became less dependent on nonwhite trade, but their place at the bottom of the commercial hierarchy was taken by Russian Jewish newcomers who courted an African American clientele.

However, certain trends in Southern cities pointed to a troubled future. Some African American ministers criticized "the cheap Jew" for operating dance halls, movie theaters, and saloons, and for "desecrating the Sabbath," particularly by selling liquor on Sundays. The nascent black business class also began to display competitive resentment toward Jewish merchants.

African Americans who migrated North brought with them a complex and distinctive image of Jews. By 1900 it had crystallized into a motif—Colored Man, Jew, and White Man—that pictured Jews as closer to African Americans than non-Jewish whites, yet prone to get the better of blacks in competitive dealings. Black folklore explained how to distinguish "a cracker from a Jew": "If one of dem is more stingy than he is mean, he's a Jew; and if he's more mean than stingy, he's a cracker" (Dinnerstein 1994).

Yet blacks combined an older religious identification with Jews as the chosen and a newer secular identification with them as a kindred minority. They viewed Jews as a third force, not quite white. Seen as a model worthy of emulation, Jews were distinguished from other immigrant groups, such as the Irish or Italians, who were more likely to be the target of black nativist hostility. The view of the Jews as a special category was sometimes used by African American critics to hold Jews to a higher standard, criticizing them for failings that they tolerated in other groups.

Harold Brackman

References and Further Reading

Delany, Martin R. 1968 (1852). *The Condition, Elevation, Emigration, and Destiny of the Colored People of the United States.* New York: Arno Press.

Dinnerstein, Leonard. 1994. *Antisemitism in America.* New York: Oxford University Press.

Glanz, Rudolf. 1961. *The Jew in Old American Folklore.* New York: Alexander Kohut Memorial Foundation.

Harlan, Louis R, ed. 1972–1989. *The Booker T. Washington Papers.* 10 Vols. Urbana: University of Illinois Press.

Hertzberg, Steven J. 1978. *Strangers within the Gate City: The Jews of Atlanta, 1845–1915.* Philadelphia: Jewish Publication Society of America.

Kolchin, Peter. 1972. *First Freedom: The Responses of America's Blacks to Emancipation and Reconstruction.* Westport, CT: Greenwood Press.

Korn, Bertram W. 1957. *The American Reaction to the Mortara Case: 1858–1859.* Cincinnati, OH: American Jewish Archives.

Korn, Bertram W. 1961. *Jews and Negro Slavery in the Old South, 1789–1865.* Elkins Park, PA: Reform Congregation Keneseth Israel.

Lynch, Hollis R. 1967. *Edward Wilmot Blyden: Pan-Negro Patriot, 1832–1912.* New York: Oxford University Press.

Marcus, Jacob Rader. 1970. *The Colonial American Jew, 1492–1776.* 2 Vols. Detroit, MI: Wayne State University Press.

McIlhenny, Edward A., comp. 1933. *Bef' de War Spirituals.* Boston: Christopher Publishing House.

Moses, Wilson J. 1978. *The Golden Age of Black Nationalism, 1850–1925.* Hamden, CT: Archon Books.

Shankman, Arnold M. 1982. *Ambivalent Friends: Afro-Americans View the Immigrant.* Westport, CT: Greenwood Press.

Smith, James McCune. 1859. "The German Invasion." *Anglo-African Magazine* (February): 42–52.

Walker, David. 1965 (1829). *One Continual Cry,* edited by Herbert Aptheker. New York: Humanities Press.

Washington, Booker T. 1912. *The Man Farthest Down.* Garden City, NY: Doubleday, Page.

Weinberg, Joseph R. 1974. "Black-Jewish Tensions: Their Genesis." *CCAR Journal* 21 (Spring): 31–37.

Jews and Black Rights (1900–1950)

Jews became significantly involved in promoting African American rights during the Progressive period and provided far more support than any other nonblack group in the next several decades. Jews helped organize and finance the leading civil rights organization of the first half of the twentieth century, the National Association for the Advancement of Colored People (NAACP), and comprised a sizable portion of its legal staff. Two Jews, Joel Spingarn and then Arthur Spingarn, served as NAACP president for most of the organization's first forty years. Jews were also prominent financial supporters of the National Urban League, formed to assist Southern black migrants to Northern cities, and served on its executive board. Jewish philanthropists contributed heavily to black education at all levels. Julius Rosenwald alone, by giving any Southern community half the funds to build an African American school if it provided the rest, helped establish over 5,000 of them. Jewish attorneys volunteered their services to the Scottsboro Boys, nine impoverished black youths arrested in 1931 for rapes they did not commit and put on trial for their lives in the most important civil rights case of the early twentieth century. The Jewish-led needle trades unions were critical of labor organizations that remained racially exclusive, and encouraged blacks to join. Jews and blacks forged a coalition to lobby for fair employment and open housing legislation, which persisted into the 1960s.

Both the Jewish and African American press often drew parallels between East European pogroms and American race riots. The Yiddish press equated Southern lynchings of blacks with the Spanish Inquisition's burning Jews at the stake. The *Forverts* (*Forward*) considered the 1917 antiblack riot in East St. Louis, Illinois, similar to the 1903 Kishinev pogrom in Bessarabia. The *Voice of the Negro* in 1906 noted that "in almost every respect the American white man's attitude toward the Negro is that of the Slav toward the Jew" ("The Russian Jew and the American

Negro" 1906). It also warned blacks that the Jews' hard work and upward mobility had not rendered them less vulnerable to prejudice.

American Jews supported African American rights because of similarities in the Jewish and black experiences, and because of idealism and moral conviction rooted in Jewish values, which emphasized the importance of seeking social justice in this world. Every year at Passover, Jews remembered that they were descended from people who had been slaves and who had struggled for freedom. Antisemitism is the world's longest hatred, and, although it was not as virulent in the United States as antiblack prejudice, it intensified and spread during the interwar period, peaking during World War II. Like African Americans, Jews suffered discrimination in jobs and housing, and in access to higher education and facilities like hotels and resorts. Jews were the only white ethnic group in America to suffer frequent physical beatings because they were members of a despised minority.

Jews also shared with African Americans some of their experience of being subjected to police brutality. In many Northeastern cities, police forces were dominated by Irish Americans, many of them strongly prejudiced against both blacks and Jews. In the late 1930s and early 1940s, many police officers in these cities belonged to the virulently antisemitic Christian Front, established by the demagogic radio priest Charles Coughlin. During World War II, when antisemitic violence in America reached its peak, Jews in New York and Boston repeatedly complained that the police did not respond to calls for help when Jews were physically attacked in the streets. In 1943, Boston police refused to pursue or arrest members of a largely Irish American crowd, estimated to number between sixty and three hundred, who had assaulted four Jewish youths, and then arrested the Jews when they protested. While in custody, the police beat them, shouting antisemitic epithets. African American leaders, like New York City councilman Adam Clayton Powell Jr. and Boston NAACP director Julian Steele, noted the similarities between the wartime antisemitic outbreaks in Boston and antiblack riots.

Jews rallied behind the Scottsboro Boys after their arrest in Alabama on a false accusation of raping two white women and helped save their lives. Jews in the International Labor Defense (ILD), the Communist Party (CP) legal front group, were instrumental in providing the defendants their first effective legal support. James Allen (the

Seven of the Scottsboro Boys at the jail in Scottsboro, Alabama, on May 1, 1935. (AP/Wide World Photos)

CP name of Sol Auerbach) had moved from New York to Chattanooga to start up and edit a newspaper called the *Southern Worker*. Allen quickly learned of the defendants' arrest and wired the ILD in New York, which immediately determined to defend the nine black youths. In the *Southern Worker*, Allen denounced the Scottsboro case as a "frame-up from start to finish" (Goodman 1994).

The ILD's chief lawyer, Joseph Brodsky, a Russian Jewish immigrant born in Kiev, visited the defendants, who had been represented by incompetent counsel and quickly found guilty, and promised them that the ILD would vigorously appeal their convictions. Eight of the defendants had received death sentences and one life imprisonment. Brodsky's passionate commitment deeply impressed the youths and their families. Joined by a mostly Jewish staff from New York, Brodsky worked tirelessly investigating the case and preparing appeals, and succeeded in winning new trials from the U.S. Supreme Court.

In 1933, Samuel Leibowitz (1893–1978), a liberal Democrat and one of the nation's leading criminal attorneys, assumed the role of chief defense counsel, without pay. Like Brodsky and his assistants, Leibowitz knew he was risking his life by going to Alabama to represent the black defendants. A Rumanian-born Jew, Leibowitz declared that he had been inspired to join the Scottsboro defense in part by the memory of Leo Frank, a Jew convicted in Georgia twenty years before for a murder he had not committed, in an atmosphere of antisemitic hysteria, and then lynched after the governor had commuted his sentence from death to life imprisonment.

Leibowitz invested enormous energy on behalf of the convicted youths, challenging Alabama's systematic exclusion of African Americans from juries and angering the prosecution by asking that it address black witnesses as "Mister." In his summation at the end of a retrial, prosecutor Wade Wright denounced Leibowitz, Brodsky, and Jews

Samuel Leibowitz (center), defense attorney for the Scottsboro Boys, is flanked by court-appointed bodyguards in 1933. (Library of Congress)

across the nation who clamored for the defendants' exoneration by shouting to the jury, "Show them that Alabama justice cannot be bought and sold with Jew money from New York" (Carter 1979). Throughout the appeals, the Yiddish- and English-language Jewish press strongly supported the accused black youths. Although the intense racism in Alabama made it impossible for Leibowitz to obtain acquittals, his legal skill and passion for racial justice prevented any defendant from being executed and eventually resulted in freedom for all nine.

During the Spanish Civil War (1936–1939), American Jews fought alongside African Americans in the Abraham Lincoln Brigade, a volunteer unit organized in the United States to take part in the first military resistance to fascism in Europe. Like blacks who sought to demonstrate their hatred of racial oppression by clamoring for combat assignments in the Union army during the Civil War, a sizable number of American Jews volunteered to fight fascism in a country that had expelled its entire Jewish population, then Europe's largest, in 1492. The Lincoln Brigade, one-

third Jewish, was the first American military unit to integrate blacks and whites.

Tensions between African Americans and Jews developed in some Northern urban ghettoes during the 1930s, most notably New York's Harlem, where some black nationalists used antisemitic rhetoric in mobilizing against allegedly exploitative neighborhood shopkeepers. The most well-known was the virulently antisemitic Sufi Abdul Hamid, known as Black Hitler, whose followers picketed Harlem Jewish merchants who, they claimed, refused to hire African Americans to work in their stores. The accused shopkeepers often insisted they preferred to employ family members. The picketing peaked in the winter of 1934–1935 and helped precipitate the March 1935 Harlem race riot, marked by widespread looting, a few deaths, and over a hundred injured. There were other contributing factors besides antisemitism, including the district's high unemployment, exacerbated by the Depression and racist hiring barriers in many occupations, and resentment of landlords regardless of background. Rioters also targeted many Italian-owned stores because of Mussolini's designs on Ethiopia.

In 1939, the Negro Improved Benevolent Protective Order of Elks, which had made Samuel Leibowitz a life member in recognition of his heroic defense of the Scottsboro Boys, invited him to Harlem to address 2,000 convention delegates on black–Jewish friction. Concerned that antisemitism was increasing in Harlem, Leibowitz urged black–Jewish dialogue and equated animosity toward Jews with Ku Klux Klanism.

During World War II, both African Americans and Jews complained that defense industries would not hire them and proposed granting the Fair Employment Practices Committee (1941) more power to combat discriminatory hiring practices. Both groups also lobbied for "race libel" bills banning the mailing of literature that defamed an ethnic or racial group.

A Jewish soldier, Sergeant Alton Levy, drew national attention to racism in the U.S. military when in 1943 the army court-martialed, demoted, and imprisoned him for protesting the segregation of black troops at his Nebraska base, including their confinement to separate barracks, mess areas, and recreation centers. Levy, a former labor organizer, also denounced white officers' frequent verbal abuse of black soldiers.

The impact of the Holocaust, Jewish organizations' experience combating intense wartime domestic antisemitism, and expectations that a renewed postwar depression would intensify bigotry all caused the American Jewish Congress, American Jewish Committee, and Anti-Defamation League to step up efforts to combat prejudice after World War II. During the late 1940s, they invested considerable effort in educational work to promote tolerance, emphasizing that defamation of any minority group harmed all of them. Jews and African Americans were alarmed by the rapid postwar growth of the Ku Klux Klan and the emergence of the neo-Nazi Columbians, hate movements that preached violence against both peoples.

Jews provided important support for Jackie Robinson's breaking of baseball's color line, one of the most important civil rights advances of the first half of the twentieth century. Brooklyn's population, where Robinson played, was about 40 percent Jewish, providing a more hospitable environment than probably any other city for the pioneering African American player, who received death threats and vicious taunts from opposing fans. In April 1945, Jewish city councilman Isadore Muchnick, a passionate supporter of civil rights, persuaded the Boston Red Sox to grant a tryout to three black players, including Robinson. Although the Red Sox did not show serious interest in the three, the tryout probably attracted Brooklyn general manager Branch Rickey's attention, influencing his decision to sign Robinson to a minor league contract later that year.

Although most sportswriters remained indifferent to baseball's color bar, or supported it, Jews like Shirley Povich of the *Washington Post*, Roger Kahn of the *New York Herald Tribune*, and broadcaster Walter Winchell denounced it. This had a significant impact, because the African American press did not reach a white mainstream readership, while Povich and Kahn wrote for large-circulation newspapers, and Winchell's Sunday evening radio audience was among the nation's largest. Millions more across the nation read Winchell's syndicated newspaper column. Jewish sportswriters, themselves sometimes barred from hotels as Jews, made a point of bringing to public attention the fact that Robinson was often forced to seek separate accommodations on the road.

The first opposing player to offer Robinson encouragement during his trying rookie year of 1947 was Jewish superstar Hank Greenberg, long harassed by antisemitic fans and opponents. During a game early in the season, Greenberg told Robinson: "Don't pay any attention to these guys who are trying to make it hard for you. Stick in there. . . . I hope you and I can get together for a talk. There are a few things I've learned down through the years that might help you and make it easier." Robinson was deeply moved by this support and told a reporter: "Class tells. It sticks out all over Mr. Greenberg." He noted that the Jewish slugger had also experienced "racial trouble" (Norwood and Brackman 1999).

Jewish scholars did pioneering work in African American history, a field that the established historical profession ignored during the first half of the twentieth century. Recasting African American history was important to the development and reception of the demand that blacks be granted full civil rights. In the late 1930s and early 1940s, historians Harvey Wish and Herbert Aptheker were among the first to conduct significant research on African American slave revolts, and Philip Foner published a sympathetic biography of black abolitionist and civil rights leader Frederick Douglass. All were of East European Jewish, lower-middle-class or working-class backgrounds. James Allen challenged the then-prevailing racist assumptions underlying mainstream scholarship on Reconstruction. Anthropologist Melville Herskovits's *The Myth of the Negro Past* (1941) caused many scholars to take more seriously the notion that African culture had significantly shaped African American identity. Frank Tannenbaum, a Jewish immigrant from Austria-Hungary, published one of the earliest and most influential books on comparative slavery and race relations, *Slave & Citizen* (1946). Branch Rickey, who had worried that public opposition to desegregating major league baseball might render it unfeasible, became persuaded to attempt it by Tannenbaum's argument that increased contacts between blacks and whites would undermine racial prejudice. Rickey credited Tannenbaum with having strongly influenced him to bring Jackie Robinson to the major leagues. In subsequent decades, a very large proportion of scholars of African American history was Jewish.

Stephen H. Norwood

References and Further Reading

Carter, Dan. 1979. *Scottsboro: A Tragedy of the American South.* Baton Rouge: Louisiana State University Press.

Diner, Hasia. 1995. *In the Almost Promised Land: American Jews and Blacks, 1915–1935.* Baltimore, MD: Johns Hopkins University Press.

Goodman, James. 1994. *Stories of Scottsboro*. New York: Pantheon.

Meier, August, and Elliott Rudwick. 1986. *Black History and the Historical Profession, 1915–1980*. Urbana: University of Illinois Press.

Norwood, Stephen H. 2003. "Marauding Youth and the Christian Front: Antisemitic Violence in Boston and New York during World War II." *American Jewish History* 91,2 (June): 233–267.

Norwood, Stephen H., and Harold Brackman. 1999. "Going to Bat for Jackie Robinson: The Jewish Role in Breaking Baseball's Color Line." *Journal of Sport History* 26,1 (Spring): 115–141.

"The Russian Jew and the American Negro." 1906. *Voice of the Negro* (September).

Black–Jewish Relations since 1950

The warm relationship that has existed between blacks and Jews for well over a century has little parallel among the various religious and ethnic groups that make up American society. During the period of slavery, African Americans identified with Jews of the Old Testament, and their hymns and folk music often reflected this attachment. Blacks hoped to emulate the Jewish experience in crossing the river Jordan and entering the promised land of equal citizenship.

In turn, Jews at all social and economic levels viewed harassment and discrimination against blacks as similar to their own experience and reached out to help them. Upper-class German Jewish leaders like Jacob and Mortimer Schiff, James Loeb, and Felix Warburg worked closely with Booker T. Washington at the turn of the twentieth century in the development of his Tuskegee Institute in Alabama. Chicago's Sears, Roebuck department-store tycoon Julius Rosenwald single-handedly established a system of public schools for blacks in the South when Southern states provided few such facilities. Joel Spingarn played a key role in the creation and development of the National Association for the Advancement of Colored People (NAACP) early in the century. And Louis Marshall, the second national president of the American Jewish Committee (AJC), served as its voluntary general counsel at a time when it did not have a professional legal staff. Rebuffed in his effort to win from the Supreme Court a ban on judicial enforcement of restrictive covenants, his posi-

tion was later upheld by the court in the landmark decision of *Shelley v. Kraemer* (1948).

Even poor, immigrant Jews struggling to make a place for themselves in American life at the turn of the twentieth century felt a strong connection to African Americans. At one point, the *Forverts* (*Forward*), the most frequently read newspaper of the new immigrants, compared the East St. Louis race riot of 1917 with the Kishinev pogrom against Jews in 1903.

The black–Jewish alliance continued well into the 1930s and 1940s. Beneath the surface, however, tensions were developing that would fester in subsequent years. Jews often resided in neighborhoods like Harlem, the Bronx, and North Philadelphia, and in other major cities that blacks began to move into after World War I. The latter found, if not a warm welcome, at least little or no violent opposition, as they often experienced elsewhere. Following World War II, Jews, like other Americans, began to move out of these older neighborhoods into tree-lined, outer-city or suburban areas in their upward climb, leaving behind a network of grocery stores and other retail establishments along with rental property.

Economic arrangements between the two groups lent themselves to conflict even as cooperation existed in many areas. The newcomers often needed credit to pay their bills, and this sometimes resulted in misunderstandings or worse. Some landlords were accused of charging exorbitant rents. And even as Jewish civil rights bodies like the American Jewish Congress, Anti-Defamation League, and AJC continued to work closely with the Urban League, NAACP, and other liberal groups after the war, in helping to create a significant body of legislation at city and state levels banning religious and racial discrimination, some African Americans resented what they considered Jewish leaders' patronizing attitude and self-serving role. In fact, far from acting out of self-interest, by aligning with African Americans, Jews hurt their own standing.

The black–Jewish alliance reached a high point with the passage of the Civil Rights Act in 1964 and the Voting Rights Act the following year. Passage of the legislation was aided in no small measure by the disproportionate number of Jews who went into the South in voter registration drives. Their efforts resulted in one of the most memorable events of the civil rights struggle: the murder of two Jews and a black in Philadelphia, Mississippi.

These civil rights gains did not, however, reach deeply enough into the smoldering black ghettos of America.

While some middle-class African Americans were able to take advantage of the new opportunities, many remained mired in poverty, which in some respects grew worse, as an increasingly high-tech economy demanded special training and skills. Many jobs also disappeared overseas where wages were often lower than in the United States.

The situation came to a head in the summer of 1964 when racial rioting broke out in Harlem and Philadelphia following incidents involving the police, and in subsequent summers in the Watts section of Los Angeles, Newark, Detroit, and other cities, reaching an orgy of violence in 1968 after the murder of Martin Luther King Jr. Large numbers of the businesses in the ghettos, many of them owned or run by Jews, were wiped out. Jews directly affected by the rioting tended to be older, more vulnerable, with life savings tied up in their businesses, and unable to move them elsewhere.

In subsequent years, major urban centers witnessed the growth of crime and other disorders, reminding Jews of earlier experiences in Europe when they were victims of pogroms and other forms of mob violence. To be sure, the issue here was less antisemitism than that Jews, like other urban whites, found themselves in the path of the urban storm.

Complicating the situation further, a new class of black leaders arose. They challenged the integration tactics of King, who stood at the center of the black–Jewish alliance in the late 1950s and 1960s. They included militants like Malcolm X, Stokely Carmichael, and H. Rap Brown in the 1960s, and Louis Farrakhan after 1975. The new leaders defined themselves as black nationalists. They considered the civil rights revolution a failure. They argued that blacks must take greater control of their lives and destiny and abandon any reliance on white supporters, who were frequently viewed as simply part of the white power structure that was oppressing African Americans. Carmichael, now known as Kwame Touré, along with political scientist Charles Hamilton, coined the slogan "Black Power," which called for African Americans to take control of schools, the police, and other local institutions that served them directly.

While Black Power seemed threatening to some whites, many Jews who worked with African Americans recognized that, to become part of the society as full and equal partners, African Americans needed to strengthen their communal institutions. What was more worrisome, however, was that some of the new breed of black national-

ists and community activists embraced antisemitism and exhibited hostility to the State of Israel. Malcolm X minimized and even justified the Holocaust. Some black nationalists utilized the notorious forgery *Protocols of the Elders of Zion* in their attacks on Jews. Farrakhan, in a widely disseminated publication, *The Secret Relationship Between Blacks and Jews,* which was prepared by the "Historical Research Department" of the Nation of Islam but listed no authors, charged that Jews had played a dominant role in the slave trade, a claim that has no basis in fact. In the hands of several black academics and intellectuals, including Tony Martin, Franz Fanon, and Harold Cruse, the black struggle in this country was linked to the struggles of darker-skinned peoples all over the world to free themselves from colonial oppression. In this paradigm, Israel came to be seen as an outpost of Western imperialism in the Middle East, the counterpart of alleged Jewish exploitation of blacks in the ghetto.

For the most part Jewish writers during this time clung to the older, universalistic view that had served Jews so well in their own upward rise. They saw their counterparts as following essentially the same path toward fuller integration into American life.

The rise of black nationalism also coincided with the Six Day War in the Middle East in 1967 and the Yom Kippur War six years later. As surrounding Arab nations threatened to drive the Jews of Israel into the Mediterranean Sea, American Jews came to experience a sense of heightened ethnic or group identity. The threat to Israel's safety and security reopened for many the fear that a new Holocaust was impending for their brethren. The successes achieved by the Jewish state in these wars also filled Jews with pride and led to the "Zionization" of American Jewish life. Jews vowed "never again" to react passively to any threat at home or abroad.

Several episodes now caused the rift between blacks and Jews to widen. In 1968, operating under a concept of community control sought by black nationalists, and with the support of the liberal administration of New York mayor John Lindsay and the Ford Foundation, a movement was launched to empower blacks by giving them greater control of public schools in their neighborhoods. Underlying this move was the idea that white teachers could not identify with their student charges and were destructive because they allegedly held low expectations of them.

The situation reached crisis proportions in the Ocean Hill–Brownsville section of Brooklyn in 1968, where a disciple of Malcolm X, Rhody McCoy, was installed as school superintendent. McCoy encouraged, or remained indifferent to, "community activists" who began to use race-based violence and intimidation against both whites and blacks in the area. The new superintendent and local board took the unprecedented step of dismissing nineteen supervisors and teachers, almost all white and Jewish. As the controversy heated up, many teachers walked off the job. Citing antisemitic appeals, Albert Shanker, head of the Jewish-dominated United Federation of Teachers, a union long seen as in the forefront of efforts to improve race relations and an early supporter of community control, launched several city-wide strikes. The strikes disrupted the intricate balance of group relations in New York City. In *The Strike That Changed New York,* historian Jerald Podair suggests that over the years Jews had created "a cosmopolitan influence that helped to blunt the force of more primal passions." Ocean Hill–Brownsville, he writes, ruptured the black–Jewish alliance. It marked the "passage [of Jews] from racial ambivalence to unmistakable 'white' identity," which resulted in greater identification with their white ethnic and largely Roman Catholic fellow citizens (Podair 2002).

Simultaneously, another issue further increased black–Jewish tensions. This was the effort to improve the black condition through affirmative action programs that utilized racial preferences in admissions to universities and professional schools, and in other areas of economic and community life. Jews found themselves divided on the two Supreme Court cases—*DeFunis* in 1974 and *Bakke* in 1978—which ruled certain forms of special treatment of African Americans constitutional and others not. Racial quotas, as Jews and many others came to call such measures, were advanced as a means of dealing with the long history of discrimination and disadvantage experienced by African Americans, but some Jewish agencies felt that their effect was to lock Jews and other whites out of opportunities that should be made available on the principle of merit alone. This, however, ignored the fact that many whites enjoyed preferences in admissions as children of alumni, as did white—and black—athletes. For many Jews, affirmative action programs brought back memories of quotas, a tactic utilized by an older Protestant leadership class in the 1920s and later to keep Jews out of colleges and universities, as well as medical and other professional schools. To most African Americans, the resistance they encountered from Jews was only further evidence of the effort to deny them their rightful place in American life. That some Jews and some Jewish groups were among the opponents of affirmative action programs was frequently seen as hypocritical and an effort to disengage from the civil rights struggle.

A series of incidents and the statements of some black and Jewish leaders further exacerbated the situation. In 1979, it became known that Andrew Young, earlier one of King's chief lieutenants and now U.S. ambassador to the United Nations, had met secretly with an official of the Palestine Liberation Organization (PLO) in New York. This was contrary to the pledge of two presidents of the United States, who took the position that U.S. officials should not meet with the PLO until it recognized the Jewish state. The meeting aroused concern among Jews who saw the PLO as a terrorist organization. Young resigned, to the consternation of many African Americans, who took great pride in one of their numbers reaching so high a position. He was, however, replaced by another African American.

In the early 1980s, Jesse Jackson, another of King's aides, sided with the Palestinians in the struggle in the Middle East and made a number of insensitive remarks. In one highly publicized episode, Jackson, thinking he was speaking off the record to a *Washington Post* reporter who happened to be African American, characterized New York as "Hymietown." When the *Post* reported the remark, Jews and Jewish organizations were outraged and denounced him. Jackson has also refused to distance himself from Louis Farrakhan, who has made antisemitic remarks. This was especially troubling to Jews because the leader of the Nation of Islam proved capable of attracting large numbers of African Americans to his rallies, including a number of black political leaders. More recently, Jackson has reached out to Jews and avoided controversy, but the episode still rankles in the minds of many.

In 1991, a major incident occurred that raised the conflict between the two groups in New York to a fever pitch. After an accident in which a car in a motorcade following the leading Hasidic rabbi in Crown Heights, an ultra-Orthodox area of Brooklyn, took the life of a seven-year-old black youth, blacks from inside and outside the area roamed the streets for several days and nights, shouting antisemitic epithets and smashing windows. The incident culminated in the murder of an Australian Jewish scholar. Many Jews blamed Mayor David Dinkins, an African American, for allegedly failing to respond more aggressively to the violence. The man directly involved in the murder was initially not convicted. Later, following intervention by the federal government, he was tried and convicted, but only on a lesser charge of civil rights violation.

The series of unhappy incidents beginning in the late 1960s has pushed some Jews in more conservative directions and away from their earlier partners. This has occurred primarily at city and state levels. A majority of Jews, for example, voted against liberal John Lindsay when he sought reelection in 1969, following the Ocean Hill–Brownsville strikes, although several issues not pertaining to race were also involved. Ed Koch, a Democrat who over time developed more conservative views, especially on crime, and who publicly denounced "poverty pimps" living off welfare, was subsequently elected mayor of New York City for three terms with strong support from Jews. In 1971, an estimated 50 percent of the Jewish vote was cast for hard-line former police commissioner Frank Rizzo in his successful race for mayor in Philadelphia against a liberal Republican candidate. (Blacks opposed him by a margin of three to one.) Despite this, Jews continue to vote for African American candidates in higher proportions than other whites. On a national level, Jews and blacks remain united in their strong support of the Democratic Party.

This pattern of Jews and blacks diverging politically at local levels has grown in recent years. Following the Crown Heights riot, Rudolph Giuliani won two-thirds of the Jewish vote in his successful race against Dinkins. In his subsequent run against a liberal, but weak, Jewish candidate in 1997, Giuliani received three-quarters of the Jewish vote, an extraordinary development for this prototypical liberal group.

The confrontation of Palestinians and Jews in the Middle East has persisted as a continuing source of friction between blacks and Jews. A majority of the Congressional Black Caucus remains supportive of Israel, but when the U.S. House of Representatives voted 352 to 21, with twenty-nine members voting "present," to back a pro-Israel resolution in May 2002, many of those voting against or "present" were black. Representatives Cynthia McKinney (Georgia) and Earl Hilliard (Alabama) have drawn the most fire from Jews. McKinney charged that a conspiracy of Zionist Jews is responsible for America's pro-Israel foreign policy. In 2002, pro-Israel groups around the country strongly supported challenges to McKinney and Hilliard, who were defeated in Democratic primaries by African American opponents, who went on to triumph in the general elections. In turn, this effort brought out-of-state support for McKinney and Hilliard, primarily from Muslims, Arabs, and others who backed the Palestinian cause. In 2004, after the incumbent gave up the House seat to run for the Senate, McKinney entered the Democratic primary and won easily, going on to regain her seat in the election.

Since the Crown Heights crisis in 1991, a degree of calmness and cooling of the rhetoric has prevailed in black–Jewish relations. Both groups have increasingly turned inward, focusing on issues of more immediate concern to their communities. For Jews, this has meant the continued threat to the safety and security of Israel, along with issues, like assimilation and intermarriage, that threaten the future of Jewry. African Americans, in turn, are living in a post–civil rights era and are struggling more with what the economist Glen Loury has called the "struggle within"—the high percentage of black males in prison, the breakdown of wide segments of the black family, and the high rate of AIDS. In response to these problems, black leaders are strengthening communal institutions, as black militants had urged. These are matters on which Jews can have little impact. At the turn of the twenty-first century, the issue of black–Jewish relations has therefore drifted to the rear as African Americans confront realities less amenable to civil rights solutions and protest marches. For some in both groups, perhaps especially for Jews, the memories of having marched and fought together in a great cause still retain a degree of saliency that continues to spark efforts at cooperation and support in some communities.

Murray Friedman

References and Further Reading
Burdick, Emily Miller. 1998. *Blacks and Jews in Literary Conversation*. Cambridge, UK: Cambridge University Press.
Franklin, V. P., Nancy L. Grant, Harold M. Kletnick, and Genna Rae McNeil. 1998. *African Americans and Jews in the Twentieth Century: Studies in Convergence and Conflict*. Columbia: University of Missouri Press.
Friedman, Murray. 1995. *What Went Wrong? The Creation and Collapse of the Black Jewish Alliance*. New York: Free Press.

Podair, Jerald E. 2002. *The Strike That Changed New York.* New Haven, CT: Yale University Press.

Jews and Affirmative Action/Preferences

Affirmative action has been at the center of numerous debates within and between Jewish groups since the 1960s. The term "affirmative action" covers a wide range of concepts; indeed, its lack of concreteness has led to numerous policy struggles in the history of affirmative action programs. The narrow definition of affirmative action includes any measure or program whose purpose is to correct or compensate for past or present discrimination or to prevent any future discrimination. The elusive term "goals and timetables," often accompanying affirmative action plans, has meant "quotas" to some, and legitimate, benign targets to others. In its strictest sense, the phrase refers to targets set for employing minorities and women, along with time frames for achieving these goals.

Affirmative action was a product not of the 1960s, when it became a national issue, but of an awareness in the early 1940s that eliminating employment discrimination would not be sufficient to overcome the effects of decades in which opportunities had been denied to minority groups, especially blacks. The involvement of the Jewish community in civil rights led to the varied Jewish communal stances on affirmative action. In 1941, to avert a march on Washington threatened by union leader and civil rights activist A. Philip Randolph, President Franklin D. Roosevelt issued Executive Order (EO) 8802, which outlawed discrimination in defense industries (later expanded to include all federal contractors) and created the Fair Employment Practices Committee (FEPC) to oversee enforcement.

Plagued with serious employment discrimination in their own community, Jewish leaders took the opportunity to form the Coordinating Committee of Jewish Organizations Concerned with Discrimination in the War Industries, which was incorporated in 1944 into the newly formed National Community Relations Advisory Council (NCRAC; later the National Jewish Community Relations Advisory Council, NJCRAC; now the Jewish Council for Public Affairs, JCPA). Toward the end of World War II, to counter efforts to abolish the FEPC—the one agency that gave teeth to EO 8802—Jewish groups became involved with the National Council for a Permanent FEPC, started by Randolph in 1943. This coalition marked the beginning of what became known as the civil rights movement, which resulted in landmark judicial decisions and legislative initiatives, notably the Civil Rights Act of 1964 and the Voting Rights Act of 1965. Civil rights legislation, in declaring racial neutrality as its goal, could not do the job, given the history of deeply entrenched racial and gender discrimination.

In 1961 President John F. Kennedy issued EO 10925, which outlawed discrimination by federal contractors and mandated: "The contractor shall take affirmative action to ensure that applicants are employed . . . without regard to their race, color, creed, or national origin." EO 10925 is noteworthy in that it defined affirmative action as the obligation of the employer. By the mid-1960s it became increasingly clear that EO 10925 had had little impact on the hiring record of government contractors. In September 1965 President Lyndon B. Johnson issued EO 11246, which added several compliance requirements—including goals and timetables—and enforcement authorities to EO 10925. EO 11246 is generally considered to mark the beginning of what is known as affirmative action. The two Executive Orders mandated affirmative action, but failed to define it. Definition came from the courts, with public-affairs groups—including Jewish communal organizations—weighing in on the issue.

The uncertainty over defining affirmative action led to a zone of ambiguity with respect to stances within the organized Jewish community. The range of positions on affirmative action adopted by the various Jewish communal organizations suggests the nuanced complexity of the issue of goals and timetables. The question is: are goals and timetables the same as quotas, abhorred—with good historical reason—by the Jewish community, or are they legitimate vehicles for addressing entrenched discrimination?

In 1969 the umbrella body for Jewish community relations and public affairs in the United States, NJCRAC, noting the traditional Jewish opposition to quotas, adopted a policy that asserted that "equality of opportunity should be based on individual qualification alone" (NJCRAC 1969). In 1971 the first major national debate among Jewish organizations over affirmative action took place under NJCRAC auspices, and the issue came to a head at the 1972

NJCRAC Plenum. The NJCRAC consensus position, adopted after intense debate, is expressed in "Affirmative Action, Preferential Treatment, and Quotas." "We oppose all quotas," it asserted, but this was immediately followed by "but we do not oppose . . . setting specific target goals and time tables . . . so long as such goals and time tables are used to evaluate good faith efforts and not as rigid requirements" (NJCRAC 1981). This nuanced distinction reverberated in subsequent debates among and within Jewish groups.

The NJCRAC position in fact masked several areas of disagreement—some clear, some murky—that were articulated in the 1970s and 1980s. The three "defense" agencies differed in their approaches. The Anti-Defamation League (ADL), an early critic of many forms of affirmative action, viewed affirmative action as a "gateway" and opposed goals and timetables as tantamount to quotas. The ADL objected to all departures from merit selection. The American Jewish Committee (AJC) also opposed quotas, but supported flexible goals and timetables. The American Jewish Congress (AJCongress) opposed quotas, but supported goals and timetables if ordered by a court or administrative agency following a proof or finding of discrimination. Among the religious bodies, the Union of Orthodox Jewish Congregations of America, representing the mainstream, centrist, traditionally observant religious community, opposed anything that suggested group privileges, including goals and timetables. The Union of American Hebrew Congregations (UAHC, now the Union of Reform Judaism) expressed a blanket support of goals and timetables. Two women's groups with considerable membership—the National Council of Jewish Women (NCJW) and Women's American ORT—likewise expressed support for goals and timetables, the latter even supporting quotas in certain circumstances.

The varied positions were played out in cases that reached the U.S. Supreme Court during the 1980s and 1990s and again in 2003. Early cases had the effect of expanding the rubric of acceptable affirmative action practices. The first Supreme Court test of affirmative action was *DeFunis v. Odegaard* (1974), a law school admissions case. DeFunis, a Jewish applicant, challenged the University of Washington Law School's refusal to admit him, while it accepted less qualified minorities under an affirmative action program. Although the school denied having a quota, it did acknowledge that its goal was to achieve a reasonable representation of minorities. The three Jewish defense agencies—the ADL, AJCongress, and AJC—all filed *amicus curiae* (friend of the court) briefs in favor of the student who claimed that he was victimized by the school's affirmative action program. Two Jewish groups—NCJW and the UAHC—supported the program. The case did not reach a decision, but soon thereafter (1978) an almost identical case, *Bakke v. Regents, University of California,* was decided. In *Bakke,* the University of California (Davis) Medical School had reserved a fixed number of places for specified racial minorities, and a number of minority applicants with lower scores than Bakke were admitted, whereas he was not.

Bakke was the first affirmative action case decided by the Supreme Court, and had ramifications for black–Jewish relations. Jewish organizations were split on the case, with the AJC and the AJCongress, together with several white ethnic groups, filing a brief urging that race not be a factor. The ADL filed its own brief along the same lines. The UAHC and NCJW, unlike in *DeFunis,* sat out the case. The Jewish community generally hailed the decision because, although it did say that race could be taken into account, it outlawed rigid racial quotas.

While *Bakke* acknowledged the validity of some race-conscious programs, it also recognized for the first time the validity of reverse discrimination claims, a precedent that concerned blacks. But the main source of black–Jewish tension grew out of the fact that Jewish groups had actually gone into the case. The Leadership Conference on Civil Rights (LCCR), a coalition begun in 1950 by black and Jewish leaders, ducked any number of affirmative action cases—including *Bakke.* The LCCR realized that, without Jewish support, a consensus was impossible, and this exacerbated black–Jewish tensions as well.

Other Supreme Court cases illustrated both Jewish and intergroup sensitivities toward affirmative action. *United Steelworkers v. Weber* (1979) involved not a university but a blue-collar reverse discrimination situation. Most Jewish groups sat out *Weber* (ADL was an exception, filing in opposition to the program) for varying reasons: Jews did not have as clear a stake in the blue-collar world as they did in the university; there was a history of discrimination that needed to be redressed; and, probably, not supporting *Weber* was at least partly intended to improve black–Jewish relations. Nonetheless, affirmative action remained a subject of sharp dispute between blacks—who viewed quotas as a floor, a vehicle to let people in—and Jews—who viewed quotas as a ceiling, a way of keeping people out.

Also expanding the affirmative action rubric was *Fullilove v. Klutznick,* which approved a set-aside for federal expenditures with minority business interests. Only the ADL filed a brief in *Fullilove,* arguing that the set-aside was counter to the principles of color blindness. Other cases in the 1980s (*Firefighters Local Union #1784 v. Stotts* and *Wygant v. Jackson Board of Education*), testing seniority rights, restricted affirmative action. Affirmative action bounced back in two cases—*Local 28, Sheet Metal Workers v. EEOC* (1986) and *U.S. v. Paradise* (1987)—that tested court-ordered quotas where there were judicial findings of prior discrimination. The court allowed the quotas. These cases were significant in terms of Jewish communal involvement. Four major Jewish groups—AJC, AJCongress, the UAHC, and the Central Conference of American Rabbis (Reform)—now joined with blacks (the NAACP Legal Defense and Education Fund, Inc.) in an "Inc. Fund" brief in support of quotas in those circumstances.

Following *Fullilove,* NJCRAC in 1981 revised its position and equated gender discrimination with racial discrimination. In 1995, in a pointed message to hard-liners in the Jewish community, it claimed that the misuse and abuse of affirmative action had been rare and reaffirmed its policy of support of non-quota-driven programs. In an important modification of its policy, the ADL in 1987 said that race could be considered as the determining factor if a history of "egregious discrimination" existed in an industry or workplace.

After *Paradise,* the affirmative action arena was generally quiet, and national Jewish communal involvement in litigation was almost nonexistent in the 1990s. One exception was *Adarand v. Peña* (1995), which established strict scrutiny for federal programs. Jewish groups, whatever their views on goals and timetables, reaffirmed support for these programs. In *Adarand,* a construction company, bidding for a Small Business Administration contract, was denied the contract, even though it had the lowest bid. The contract went instead to a minority contractor. Adarand claimed that race-based presumptions in the bidding process violated the equal protection component of the Fifth Amendment's due process clause. The Tenth Circuit Court of Appeals affirmed a ruling on behalf of the gov-

ernment not requiring strict scrutiny. The U.S. Supreme Court overruled the Tenth Circuit and said in effect that any governmental action based on race needs to be subjected to detailed judicial inquiry—"strict scrutiny"—to ensure that the personal right to equal protection was not infringed. Strict scrutiny became therefore the proper standard for analysis of race-based programs.

On the legislative front, there was Jewish involvement in the embattled Civil Rights Act of 1991, which achieved passage in the 102nd Congress. The bill became a flashpoint in the relationship between President George H. W. Bush and blacks, as well as within the Jewish community. The Civil Rights Act was Congress's first successful effort to reverse the effects of the Rehnquist Supreme Court, which had itself reversed the tide of previous Court decisions that were favorable to affirmative action. Six cases handed down during the 1988–1989 term (and four other rulings since 1985) had restricted the reach of federal laws involving gender, racial, religious, and ethnic discrimination in hiring, promotion, and termination. Passage of the legislation, which would make it easier for a plaintiff to prove the discriminatory effect of employment practices and require employers to defend the legitimacy of such practices—and not the other way around, as the high court decisions would have it—had been frustrated since first introduced in 1989, during the 101st Congress.

The debate over support of the bill exposed numerous fault lines in the Jewish community, again over the question of quotas. At the end of the day Jewish groups, except for two organizations representing Orthodox Jews, Agudath Israel of America and the Union of Orthodox Jewish Congregations of America (OU), supported the measure, acknowledging a consensus position that the bill was not about quotas.

The calm in litigation was ended in 2003 by two cases, *Grutter v. Bollinger* and *Gratz v. Bollinger,* which tested law school and undergraduate admissions policies at the University of Michigan. The Supreme Court, in a 6-to-3 decision, rejected the undergraduate program, which assigned a specific number of points based on an applicant's race. In a narrow 5-to-4 decision, however, it upheld the law school's program, stating that consideration of race within an individualized assessment of candidates is constitutional. Jewish groups were divided on the Michigan cases. The ADL's position in *Grutter* and *Gratz* was that diversity is a laudable goal and that race could be a factor in a plan; the undergraduate program, therefore, which was purely numbers-driven, was flawed, while the law school's individualized approach merited support. Hadassah, the UAHC, and the NCJW joined an AJC brief supporting both Michigan plans. AJCongress and the OU did not file briefs in the cases. The narrowness of the law school decision suggested that divisions over the case were not limited to the Jewish community. Nonetheless, the Michigan cases represented a sea change in the approach to affirmative action, namely that the rationale and justification for affirmative action had moved from a practical means to redress discrimination in the core institutions of society to a recognition that diversity is a societal good.

Overall, the record on affirmative action over thirty years is mixed—who has benefited and who has not? Some data indicate that the main beneficiaries of affirmative action programs over the years have been white women; that, in the black community, blacks who would have been in the education and employment pool in any case (e.g., affluent and other upper-strata blacks) have benefited from affirmative action, but that the overwhelming majority of blacks remain outside the population that apply for these education and employment programs. Data also suggest that white working-class males have not benefited from affirmative action. However, a number of black and Hispanic immigrants, who themselves did not experience discrimination in the United States, have immediately benefited from affirmative action programs.

Jerome A. Chanes

References and Further Reading

Carnegie Council on Policy Studies in Higher Education. 1975. *Making Affirmative Action Work in Higher Education.* San Francisco: Jossey-Bass.

Chanes, Jerome A. 1997. "Affirmative Action: Jewish Ideals, Jewish Interests." In *Struggles in the Promised Land: Toward a History of Black-Jewish Relations in the United States,* edited by Jack Salzman and Cornel West, 295–321. New York: Oxford University Press.

Hacker, Andrew. 1996. "Goodbye to Affirmative Action." *New York Review of Books* (July 11).

Lynch, Frederick R., ed. 1985. "Affirmative Action: Past, Present, and Future." Special Issue. *American Behavioral Scientist* 28,6 (July–August).

National Jewish Community Relations Advisory Council (NJCRAC). 1969. *Joint Program Plan.* New York: NJCRAC.

National Jewish Community Relations Advisory Council (NJCRAC). 1981. "Position on Affirmative Action." Adopted June 1975, amended January 1981. *Joint Program Plan.* New York: NJCRAC.

Sindler, Allan P. 1978. *Bakke, DeFunis and Minority Admissions.* New York: Longman.

Weiss, Robert J. 1987. "Affirmative Action: A Brief History." *Journal of Intergroup Relations* XV,2 (Summer).

Jewish–Christian Relations in the United States in the Twentieth Century

The development of increasingly close Jewish–Christian relationships has been a striking feature of twentieth-century American history. In important ways, American Jews and Christians forged interreligious bonds more successfully than their coreligionists overseas. Indeed, the strengths of Jewish–Christian relations in the United States contributed greatly to the transformation of Jewish–Christian relations worldwide. Historians disagree on why Jewish–Christian relations have taken more positive forms. Some say the change reflects increasing acceptance by American theologians, and within broad social circles, of ideologies of religious pluralism, reflecting the belief that Americans are united by their multicultural and multidenominational heritage (Feldman 1990). Others claim it was a response to perceived threats to common middle-class interests (Cohen 1990).

This divergence reflects differences about the nature of Jewish–Christian relations. While supporters of dialogue—whether historians or practitioners—focus on the universalist and humanitarian ideals that promote neighborly relations, critics argue the rhetoric of Jewish–Christian reconciliation is often a cover for narrow social and political agendas, or for extending the power of mainline churches over the much smaller Jewish population. Scholars explaining the breakthroughs have often focused on changing Christian outlooks, though other accounts stress the changing attitudes of American Jews. These perspectives are further complicated by different interpretations of American antisemitism: while some have emphasized its importance in shaping Jewish–Christian collaboration, others believe antisemitism has long been a marginal phenomenon in American society.

Late nineteenth-century efforts at Jewish–Christian dialogue generally focused on the promotion of a new liberal religion in which the historic divisions between Jew and Christian would no longer matter. The mainly Protestant participants in such dialogue circles—often Unitarian—were confident that Christianity was the most important bridge toward further progress to a unified, universalistic, rational, and scientific religion. Their Jewish interlocutors were predominantly devotees of Isaac Mayer Wise's Reform Judaism (now known as Classic Reform) and were often privately convinced that Judaism, not Christianity, was the more rational religion that would inspire America's future. At the turn of the twentieth century, dialogue groups organized Unity Thanksgiving Services across the country. The ties built up by Reform Jews in the liberal establishment of the Northeast were not the only spurs to this development: from Fort Worth to Chicago, Jewish communities established close ties with Christian congregations by playing a valued role in the building of frontier societies. While this was a time of renewed political and social antisemitism, communities shared choirs, ministers began to exchange pulpits, and many attended sermons in both church and synagogue.

In addition, leading Conservative Jews and Christians formed small scholarly circles to examine the history of Jewish–Christian relations. Protestant interest in the conversion of the Jews had been widespread in the United States since the eighteenth century, and this led individual missionaries to establish relations with American Jews, particularly once the growth of poor urban East European Jewish communities gave them a focus after 1880. Outrage at the Russian pogroms (1880–1921) also moved American Evangelicals to support Jewish causes, including the nascent Zionist movement. Horrified by the pogroms, 413 leading Protestants, Catholics, and Jews across America signed the first Blackstone Memorial (1891), a letter written to the president by William Blackstone, an Evangelical Fundamentalist, which increased public interest in U.S. support for Jewish emigration to the Holy Land. During World War I, the issue was again pressed on the government.

While Protestant, Catholic, and Jewish communities quietly learned much from each other on a secular level, and Catholics and Jews in particular began to draw closer in cities where they represented significant parts of the working-class community, until 1910 there was little dialogue about what was distinctive in Christian and Jewish theologies. For many leaders of the mainline churches, from Roman Catholic to Baptist, Jews were still largely dis-

tant figures, sometimes romanticized, often subjects of vilification, and damned, according to both Protestants and Catholics, unless they converted to the one true faith.

From 1910, a second round of pogroms in Eastern Europe prompted a more deliberate Jewish engagement with Christian thought on both sides of the Atlantic. For Jews to talk of the positive and negative contributions of Christian faith was controversial, and the discussion drew attacks in both Jewish and Christian circles. In the United States, the Reform Rabbi Stephen S. Wise spearheaded attempts to show that there was little in liberal Protestant Christianity that Jews could not accept. Though little he said about Christianity had not also been asserted by other Reform rabbis, his suggestion that it was Christians, or Christendom, not Christianity itself, that failed to live up to the ideals of the prophets provoked repeated controversies within American Jewry.

At this time, a number of leading liberal Protestants, especially Episcopalians and Unitarians, had made concerted efforts to acknowledge the significance of commonalities between the religion of Christians and that of Reform Jews. Wise's position became a feature of the dialogue movements that developed across America in the years between the World Wars. However, Conservative and Orthodox Jews suggested that Christianity and Christians fell short of Jewish ideals—particularly as they refused to affirm the national basis of Israel's calling—and Wise was charged with promoting religious assimilation to Christianity. While many more traditionalist Jews continued to see Christianity as idolatrous, communal leaders bore in mind that popular Christian accusations of ritual murder abroad (the last in the United States was spurred by a young Polish immigrant in 1942) were paralleled by physical and theological attacks on Jews across the United States into the 1940s. Occasionally immigrant Catholic mobs attacked Jews as Christ-killers, while fundamentalist Protestant groups also believed Jews to be in league with the Devil.

From 1900, the dissemination of a new social gospel, or social theology, inspired cooperation among clergy and lay leaders in cities across the United States. From Atlanta to Denver, Christian–Jewish relationships were central to the creation of social welfare organizations such as the Red Cross. Social concerns remained decisive in the development of the first organized national Jewish–Protestant–Catholic cooperation from 1919, with Stephen Wise leading the call for the coordinated defense of workers' rights. The participating church and synagogue organizations soon turned their attention to education against prejudice, particularly in light of the renewed rise of the Ku Klux Klan and its campaign against the Catholic Democratic presidential candidate, Alfred E. Smith, in 1924.

In 1928, Protestants, Catholics, and Jews across the United States established branches of what became known as the National Conference of Christians and Jews (NCCJ). The NCCJ sponsored thousands of radio dialogues among a rabbi, a minister, and a priest, and established Brotherhood Week (in February of each year) in 1942. The Holocaust and World War II underlined the need for this work, and many scholars see patriotic wartime campaigns against prejudice as the catalyst for the decline of American antisemitism. Christian support for the creation of the State of Israel had, however, to be solicited outside NCCJ forums, which still encompassed many anti-Zionists among both liberal Protestants and leading Reform Jewish participants.

Until 1949, Catholics were faced with Church criticism of the NCCJ as indifferentist—in contravention of the teaching that all religions were not of equal value—and had to belong to the organization as individuals rather than as communal representatives, though the NCCJ did have influential supporters in the episcopacy. In 1949, the NCCJ affirmed that members were free to believe that their own religion was superior and agreed that NCCJ would not engage in pulpit exchanges or joint worship exercises. NCCJ constructed itself as a civic organization, unlike the more theologically inclined councils of Christians and Jews on other continents. Its activities soon focused on intergroup dialogue, leaving church and synagogue bodies to create their own programs focused on theological understanding. In the 1950s, leading Conservative Jewish critics argued that this approach did not respect the positive role that religion had to play in public life and, more important, that an alliance of liberal Protestants and Jews in NCCJ meant religious Judaism and Jewish peoplehood were not respected as a separate tradition from the teachings of Jesus and of liberal Protestantism.

With the introduction of a "Jewish document" at the Catholic Church's Second Vatican Council in 1962, thanks to American Jewish and Catholic pressure, representatives of all American Jewish branches urged that the integrity of Judaism be respected. While the document was being drafted, the three main rabbinical movements criticized a proposed reference to the Church's hope for eventual unity (implicitly through acknowledging Christ). None put this more forcefully than the Conservative thinker Abraham Joshua Heschel, widely known among Christians for his *No Religion Is an Island* and *The Sabbath*. However, Modern Orthodox leader Joseph Soloveitchik became more identified with this critique, blaming progressive and secular Jewish leaders for welcoming the Catholic Church's move too eagerly, and warning Jews to focus on common secular interests rather than on theological doctrine. The reference was removed, but Jewish leaders remained unhappy with the resulting declaration, *Nostra Aetate* (1965), until Catholic leaders clarified its implied respect for Jewish peoplehood and theology in 1974 and 1985. Soloveitchik's reported support for a respectful theological dialogue of equals has still to be clarified to the satisfaction of the Modern Orthodox community, many of whom treated his critique as an effective ban on all dialogue.

Nostra Aetate has also been heralded as the beginning of a revolution in Jewish–Christian relations. The document clarified that the Church did not hold subsequent generations of Jews responsible for Christ's crucifixion, or indeed all Jews at the time, and deplored the existence of racist antisemitism. From this time, regular official dialogues among Catholic, Protestant, and Reform, Conservative, and Modern Orthodox Jewish organizations have been accompanied by programs designed to educate Christians about the links between Christian anti-Judaism and antisemitism. American Jews of all stripes greeted Pope John Paul II's consistent enthusiasm for reconciliation as confirmation of the change in Catholic attitudes, though Catholic attempts finally to face the Holocaust gave Jewish leaders repeated cause for concern.

Despite the expectations of many Jews, the 1998 document *We Remember* fell short of the acknowledgment that the Church bore partial responsibility for the Holocaust. The legacy of the wartime pope, Pius XII, continued to provoke vociferous disagreements: *We Remember* provided a brief defense of his responses to the Holocaust, and leading figures in the Vatican and in the American Church regretted that the Jewish community's distress was used by critics who sought to prevent his canonization. A similar tension developed over steps to canonize Pius IX, a pope whose anti-Jewish attitudes marked Catholic–Jewish relations in the middle of the nineteenth century. From the

1980s, cooperation over social concerns returned to the fore of Jewish–Christian dialogue, though divergence between liberal and conservative positions on birth control and homosexuality, for instance, have made for very public differences.

Repeated tensions over the State of Israel have arisen between the churches and American Jewish organizations, which became increasingly concerned with the relationship between anti-Israeli sentiment and antisemitic bias. The sweeping nature of the Presbyterian Church's 2004 endorsement of divestment from Israel, for instance, has been interpreted in this light, and observers believe other churches may follow its example. While some Jewish leaders claimed the Vatican was theologically unable to formally recognize the State of Israel, it finally did, in 1994, when the pace of the Middle East peace process caused it to fear that not to do so risked a loss of influence in the region.

The missionary dimension of church life has also been the subject of ongoing tensions. Fundamentalist Christian missions targeting Jews increased in magnitude following the Holocaust, and a new wave was prompted by the born again movement of the 1960s and 1970s, from which the "Jews for Jesus" movement emerged. Mainline churches began to disown or disarm missionary bodies targeted at Jews, though the extent to which churches have been able to address the effects of triumphalist anti-Jewish theologies (notably supersessionism) remains under debate. From the 1970s, some leading evangelists, including Billy Graham, have welcomed the notion that a partnership with Jews could replace the old missionizing approach, though even Graham appeared privately to share President Richard M. Nixon's hostility to what they believed to be the influence of American Jewish liberals, particularly through the media. The Southern Baptist Church, by contrast, influenced by a growing apocalyptic premillenialism, has recently embraced the conversion of Jews as a central mission, which virtually all Jews view as a spiritual attack. Periodically, fundamentalist Evangelicals and Pentecostal leaders have cast Jews publicly as beyond God's salvific grace, or as agents of the Devil, incurring condemnation from more moderate Evangelicals, particularly Baptists, who remain a significant body in the American Christian community.

American scholarship, religious and secular, has provided a level of guidance to churches not available anywhere else, and this has allowed Americans to give constant impetus to the renewal of Jewish–Christian relations around the world. High-level conferences on the role of churches in the Holocaust and on Jewish–Christian dialogue that were established in the 1960s and 1970s, as well as the new Jewish–Christian dialogue of the 1980s on the relationship between Jesus and the plural Judaisms of his day, remain major influences on international opinion. The welcome given to new Church attitudes by U.S. Jewish theologians in 2000, *Dabru Emet,* was similarly greeted around the world as a long-awaited validation of the steps made by the churches, though it also underlined where divisions within American Jewry now lay. Dominated by Reform Jews, the document's sponsors were criticized by many Conservatives, not for stating what was theologically valid in contemporary Christianity, but for doing it in a form that undervalued what is distinctive in both traditions and what remains difficult in the history of Jewish–Christian relations.

George R. Wilkes

References and Further Reading
Bemporad, Jack, and Michael Shevack, 1996. *Our Age.* Hyde Park, NY: New City Press.
Cohen, Naomi W. 1990. *Essential Papers on Jewish–Christian Relations in the United States: Imagery and Reality.* New York: New York University Press.
Cohen, Naomi W. 1992. *Jews in Christian America: The Pursuit of Religious Equality.* New York and Oxford, UK: Oxford University Press.
Feldman, Egal. 1990. *Dual Destinies: the Jewish Encounter with Protestant America.* Champaign: University of Illinois Press.
Feldman, Egal. 2002. *Catholics and Jews in Twentieth-Century America.* Champaign: University of Illinois Press.
Fisher, Eugene, and Leon Klenicki, eds. 1990. *In Our Time: The Flowering of Jewish–Catholic Dialogue.* New York: Paulist Press.

Joseph Dov Soloveitchik (1903–1993)

Major Shaper of Modern Orthodox Judaism

Joseph Dov Soloveitchik (also known as Joseph Baer) was a pivotal figure in the development of American Modern

Orthodox Judaism. Respected as a challenging thinker even within non-Orthodox and Christian intellectual circles in America and overseas, his influence in the Orthodox world was multiplied through the 2,000 Modern Orthodox rabbis who trained and were ordained during his forty years as head of the rabbinical school at Yeshiva University (YU) in New York. As chair of the Halakhah Committee of the Rabbinical Council of America (RCA) in the 1950s, Soloveitchik also promoted a series of decisions on divorce law and mixed seating in synagogues, rulings that underlined the distinctive nature of Orthodox marriage and synagogue practices, and thereby gave renewed confidence to Modern Orthodox Jews, while ultimately widening the divide between the Modern Orthodox and Conservative movements. His halakhic (Jewish legal) rulings retain unquestioned authority across the Modern Orthodox community in America, and his philosophical output has spread to new audiences following his death.

Born in Pruzhan, Poland, Soloveitchik was tutored at home in Warsaw by his father, Moshe, whose own father and grandfather, as successive heads of the Volozhin Yeshiva (then in Russia, now Belarus), had inspired previous generations of Orthodox scholars to take on new rigorous scholarly approaches to talmudic study. Joseph's mother came from a Hasidic background and opened him up to traditions that construed biblical and talmudic texts as sources of inspiration for a creative approach to religious experience. Soloveitchik's teaching and publications continued to engage with these distinct traditions throughout his life. Traditionalists maintain that his thought was a straightforward, faithful translation of these East European spiritual resources into contemporary language. Soloveitchik's engagement with modernist thought was nevertheless extensive.

Following World War I, Soloveitchik spent a decade studying religious philosophy at the University of Berlin, completing a doctorate on the philosophy of the Jewish neo-Kantian Hermann Cohen. Soloveitchik's first published work, *Halakhic Man* (1944), clarified the relationship between Jewish tradition and ideas of religious experience and knowledge taught in Berlin by contemporaries such as Wilhelm Dilthey. At the same time, Soloveitchik continued his talmudic studies at Berlin's renowned Rabbinic Seminary of Orthodox Judaism. It was here that Soloveitchik first engaged with an Orthodoxy that was deliberately Modern in its marriage of religious

and secular studies and resources. Modern Orthodoxy was not a narrow or settled ideology, and did not become so in the United States, where many liberal Orthodox Jews whose views dovetailed with Soloveitchik's have preferred to call themselves Centrist. In Israel, their counterparts identified themselves as National Religious (*dati leumi*), and a positive engagement with Zionism has become a marker of Modern Orthodoxy outside Israel as well.

In the early 1930s, Soloveitchik joined his father in the United States and, in 1936, founded one of the first Orthodox day schools, teaching both secular and religious subjects: the Maimonides School in Boston. In 1941, he took over his father's position as *rosh yeshiva* of the Rabbi Isaac Elchanan Theological Seminary of YU, an institution that he headed until 1984. As Leib Merkin Professor of Talmud, Soloveitchik inspired YU students with a highly personal and philosophical version of the Volozhin method of talmudic exegesis, already renowned as one of the most analytical approaches to talmudic argument in Europe. In the 1940s, 1950s, and 1960s, the Seminary produced a new generation of Modern Orthodox rabbis, committed to Soloveitchik's engagement with American society, contributing to the revival and dissemination of Orthodoxy across the country.

The Holocaust underlined for Soloveitchik the virtues of life in America, a commitment he honored in urging that American Orthodox Jews celebrate Thanksgiving as a secular holiday. The destruction of Jewish life in Europe also persuaded him to break with the Soloveitchik family's affiliation with the non-Zionist Agudath Israel—the main Orthodox political party in Eastern Europe—in favor of the Religious Zionist Mizrahi Party, a shift he made in the 1940s while membership in the Mizrahi was equated by the Orthodox mainstream with heresy. Soloveitchik saw that their unique sense of religious ethics separated Orthodox Jews from their Christian and non-Orthodox compatriots in America and Israel. In a series of essays, he described religious Jews as sojourning, like Abraham, among the peoples with whom they are connected by fate, by desire for fellowship, and by common beliefs or identity ("*Kol Dodi Dofek*," 1956; "Confrontation," 1964; "Lonely Man of Faith," 1965). To the dismay of some of his closest disciples, interpreters of Soloveitchik's thought have often ignored the tensions between these elements, stressing instead the barriers between the Modern Orthodox and other Jews.

A key factor shaping the reception of Soloveitchik's legacy was the great caution he exercised in promulgating legal judgments. Where professional expertise was needed, he argued against rabbinic interference altogether; he refused to rule against ceding Israeli territory in exchange for peace because the question involved a military competence rabbis did not have. Moreover, his sense of the existential divide between Orthodox Jews, the non-Orthodox, and their Christian neighbors was translated into halakhic rulings only after sustained attempts to reach understanding across communities. In the 1950s, controversies over divorce law and over mixed seating in Orthodox and Conservative synagogues led to a series of ultimately unsuccessful discussions with leading Conservative rabbis, before Soloveitchik was convinced the RCA Halakhah Committee had to issue restrictive rulings. The Modern Orthodox rabbinate's refusal to accept Conservative marriage licenses and divorces signaled a major breach between the movements. This was minor in comparison with the declaration that Orthodox Jews were absolutely forbidden to attend synagogues that sat men and women together, a practice increasingly followed in synagogues affiliated with the Conservative movement, and even found in some American Orthodox synagogues at the time. Soloveitchik insisted that it was better not to go to synagogue at all, even during the holiest festivals, than to attend a service in such a synagogue.

While colleagues in American yeshivot sought then to ban their alumni from joining professional organizations that included the non-Orthodox, Soloveitchik insisted (as leading Modern Orthodox rabbis had since early in the twentieth century) that cooperation with other Jews was needed in the face of secular threats and interests. In 1960, he sought to respond positively, in close coordination with Reform and Conservative rabbis, to the prospect of a document on Jewish–Catholic relations being promulgated at the Second Vatican Council. Disillusioned by 1963 with the direction the Council seemed to be taking, particularly its expression of evangelical hope, he rounded on those Christians and Jews he deemed too impatient to await the conditions for a more equal dialogue between Jews and Christians. The result is reflected in his article "Confrontation," often read as a ban on theological dialogue, though colleagues have long insisted it was a plea for more serious, careful dialogue, not a halakhic ruling. After the document had finally been promulgated as *Nostra Aetate* (1965),

Soloveitchik encouraged Modern Orthodox representatives to join the Liaison Committee established by Vatican and Jewish representatives and gave guidance on Orthodox contributions to this official dialogue for the decade that followed.

George R. Wilkes

References and Further Reading
Besdin, A. 1979, 1989. *Reflections of the Rav.* Vol. 1, Jerusalem: Department of Torah Education and Culture in the Diaspora of the World Zionist Organization; vol. 2: Hoboken, NJ: Ktav Publishing House.
Hartman, David. 2001. *Love and Terror in the God Encounter: The Theological Legacy of Rabbi Joseph B. Soloveitchik.* Vol. I. Woodstock, VT: Jewish Lights Publishing.
Rakeffet-Rothkoff, Aaron, and Joseph Epstein, eds. 1999. *The Rav: The World of Rabbi Joseph B. Soloveitchik.* 2 Vols. Hoboken, NJ: Ktav Publishing House.

Leon Kronish (1917–1996)

Zionist Leader

Leon Kronish, Reform rabbi, Zionist leader, and American Jewish institution builder, was the voice of Jewish Miami Beach during the second half of the twentieth century. Born in New York to East European immigrant parents (Max and Lena Seligman) the same year as the Balfour Declaration, Leon (Asher) never strayed far from its message. Mentored by the great luminaries of the first half of the twentieth century, Rabbis Mordecai Kaplan and Stephen S. Wise, Kronish internalized the principles of Liberal Judaism, cultural pluralism, and Zionism. Migrating to Miami Beach in 1944, he founded Temple Beth Sholom. Under his leadership the congregation became the premier Reform synagogue in South Florida. During his four-decade tenure, Rabbi Kronish played a critical role in bringing an Israeli presence to South Florida and changing the direction of Reform Judaism and Diaspora Jewry.

Brought up in an Orthodox home with parents who spoke Yiddish, Leon attended public school and an after-school Talmud Torah, and he participated in a socialist Zionist youth movement, *Hashomer Hatzair*. Graduating from Brooklyn College in 1936, he attended the Jewish

Theological Seminary, where one of his teachers was Mordecai Kaplan (1937–1938), the founder of Reconstructionism. Kronish received his ordination in 1942 from the Jewish Institute of Religion (JIR) under the mentorship of the Institute's founder, Stephen Wise. Before moving to Florida, Rabbi Kronish married Lillian Austin (1940) and served at the Huntington Center in Long Beach, New York (1941–1944).

Arriving in Miami Beach (1944), a segregated and antisemitic island, Rabbi Kronish viewed his mission as bringing a Zionist and Jewish presence to "the American Negev." The storefront Conservative congregation, the Beth Sholom Center, catered to forty members and World War II servicemen.

Understanding the tensions between cultural pluralism and religio-ethnic parochialism, Zionism and American patriotism, Kronish realigned the congregation with Reform Judaism and renamed it Temple Beth Sholom (1945). He instituted the principles of Liberal Judaism (social justice, cultural Zionism, and religious traditions such as wearing a tallit and kippa) and wrote liturgical innovations for the Jewish holidays. By the mid-1960s, membership exceeded 1,200 households. Kronish's direction for the temple complemented the values of hundreds of thousands of Jews migrating to South Florida and seeking a prophetic guide.

In the 1950s, Kronish joined with members of his congregation to weaken discriminatory practices and change laws throughout South Florida that were antisemitic. He campaigned for nuclear disarmament and for the removal of religion from Miami's public schools. In the 1960s, he challenged Miami Beach residents, nearly three-quarters Jewish, to adopt the policy of one-way busing, that is, busing children from black neighborhoods to their own Miami Beach schools. In addition, he encouraged Judy Drucker, a member, to develop a musical arts program at the temple. The program blossomed and became the foremost musical arts program in South Florida, seeding Miami's musical renaissance.

The Six Day War in 1967 was a watershed for Rabbi Kronish, as it was for Diaspora Jewry. The mission of Liberal Judaism receded, and Israel became his primary focus. Working closely with the leadership of Reform Judaism and American Jewry, in the following years Kronish helped reshape the Israel–Jewish landscape in South Florida, North America, and Israel.

Rabbi Kronish expounded on his ideas in two articles: "*Yisrael Goralenu*" ("Israel Is Our Destiny") in 1968 and "The Zionist *Mitzvot*" ("Zionist Commandments") in 1977. He called on Jews to visit Israel and on youth to immigrate (*aliya*); he called for Jews to absorb Israeli culture and study modern Hebrew, to link with Israeli families and respond politically when Israel is in need. Congregations needed to establish Israel committees and uphold the moral right of Israel's rebirth. His motto was "Bring Israel to America and America to Israel."

Within Reform Judaism, Kronish was instrumental in creating permanent committees on Israel for the Central Conference of American Rabbis (CCAR) and for the Union of American Hebrew Congregations (UAHC), in endorsing a policy that required entering rabbinical students to spend their first year in Israel, and in approving a resolution that the CCAR would host conventions in Israel, the first in 1970. Kronish was a founding member of the Association of Reform Zionists of America (ARZA), Reform Judaism's response to the growing political power of Orthodoxy in Israel, and supported the launching of Reform kibbutzim.

In South Florida, Kronish led the effort for El Al to fly to Miami and for the Israeli government to open an Israeli Consulate. He helped to establish the Miami–Israel Chamber of Commerce and initiated the Alexander Muss High School in Israel Program, first in Miami and then nationally, for students to study in Israel for a semester and receive American credits.

Nationally, Rabbi Kronish worked closely with Labor Zionists, assisting in the founding of the Histadrut Foundation, an American support group for the Labor Federation in Israel (1965). An avid advocate for Israel Bonds since their introduction in 1951, he served as the national chairman in the early 1980s. Golda Meir, Abba Eban, and Yitzhak Rabin were among his many Israeli friends.

Although Kronish believed firmly in linking American Jewry to Israelis and establishing a foothold for Reform Judaism (Progressive Judaism) in Israel, he never strayed from his principles of Liberal Judaism and prophetic mission. Female rabbis were acceptable; patrilineal descent was not. Kronish's commitment was to "Israelization," the transformation of Zionism into a more effective process for American Jewry to bond with Israelis as part of *Klal Yisrael* (Jewish community). Today, programs such as The March of the Living and Birthright are outgrowths of this

Israelization dimension. Kronish Plaza in Miami Beach and the Leon Kronish Memorial Lecture hosted by HUC-JIR in Jerusalem honor his contributions.

Henry A. Green

References and Further Reading
Green, Henry A. 1995. *Gesher Vakesher, Bridges and Bonds: The Life of Leon Kronish*. Atlanta, GA: Scholars Press.

Green, Henry A. 2005. "Leon Kronish: Miami Beach's Twentieth-Century Prophet." In *Jews of South Florida*, edited by Andrea Greenbaum, 162–178. Waltham, MA: Brandeis University Press.

Kronish, Ronald, ed. 1988. *Towards the Twenty-First Century: Judaism and the Jewish People in Israel and America. Essays in Honor of Rabbi Leon Kronish on the Occasion of His Seventieth Birthday*. Hoboken, NJ: Ktav Publishing House.

Jewish–Muslim Relations

The effort to establish a relationship between the representatives of the Jewish and Muslim communities in the United States only started in the early 1990s. These contacts began as part of the Jewish community's long-term policy of building alliances with other ethnic and religious minorities. Traditionally, these alliances have been based on common interests in civil rights, religious freedom, and the separation of church and state. The Jewish community's attempt to reach out to Muslims also derived, however, from an empathy that recalls the early struggles of Jews to acclimate themselves to the American way of life while preserving their traditions. American Jews recognized some parallels between the efforts of Muslims to make their way in American society and those of their own immigrant ancestors. Jews had, however, generally fled from hostile societies, and most came before the State of Israel was founded, while Muslims have emigrated voluntarily, often from Muslim countries or societies with Muslim majorities. The Israeli–Palestinian peace process of the early 1990s and the growth of the Muslim population in the United States provided an additional impetus for these contacts.

The reform in U.S. immigration laws between 1965 and 1996 resulted in an influx of Muslim immigrants. According to the 2000 U.S. Census, the majority of them arrived after 1990. Approximately one-third of the Muslim American population was born in the United States. The largest group of Muslim Americans is of South Asian origin (Bangladesh, Pakistan, India). Others are from Arab lands, Turkey, Iran, the Balkans, West Africa, Indonesia, and other parts of Southeast Asia.

African Americans became interested in Islam during the 1960s and 1970s, and an estimated 700,000 converted to mainstream Islam. Some became followers of Warith Deen Muhammad; others frequented immigrant mosques or smaller African American ones. A minority became supporters of the pseudo-Islamic antisemitic Nation of Islam (NOI)—followers of a demonology based on a grossly distorted version of Islam—and others became adherents of Middle Eastern Islamic extremist movements.

The American Jewish community's perception of Muslims has been strongly influenced by Muslim attitudes toward Jews and Israel. Both before and after the State of Israel was established in 1948, the majority of Arab and Muslim leaders worldwide rejected the Jewish state.

Underlying this rejection of Israel is an intense and pervasive, popular and official, Arab and Muslim antisemitism. As the historian Robert Wistrich observed, "Behind this Arab rejection lies a barrage of derogatory and repulsive images of Jews and Judaism to be found both in the government-backed and opposition media, in popular and academic publications, in television images, caricatures, and in the cassette recordings of clerics who long ago blurred any remaining boundary between anti-Zionism and antisemitism. The stream of vitriolic visual and verbal imagery extends from Morocco to the Gulf States and Iran; it is as strong in supposedly 'moderate' Egypt as it is in openly hostile Arab nations such as Iraq, Libya, and Syria" (Wistrich 2002).

Similarly, radical African American converts to Islam expressed virulent hatred of Jews during the 1977 terror attack and siege of the B'nai Brith building in Washington, D.C., by extremist Hanafi Muslims. Armed with guns, swords, and knives, the terrorists took over the building and held the organization's employees hostage for thirty-nine hours. Throughout the siege, the terrorists' leader, Hamaas Abdul Khaalis, a former Nation of Islam leader, threatened to "blow the heads off" the Jewish hostages and referred to them derogatorily in Arabic as *yahudi*. The siege, which led many Jews to conflate Muslim and Arab attitudes toward Jews, had a chilling effect on the potential for dialogue between American Muslims and Jews.

Muslim extremist expressions of antisemitism from the Middle East have circulated in the Muslim American community for many years. A report by the Center for Religious Freedom states: "The Saudi textbooks and documents spread throughout American mosques preach a Nazi-like hatred for Jews, treat the forged *Protocols of the Elders of Zion* as historical fact, and avow that the Muslim's duty is to eliminate the state of Israel" (Freedom House 2005).

Press reports have revealed that some Muslim schools in the United States have been using textbooks that promote antisemitism, and Saudi-sponsored schools, such as the Islamic Saudi Academy in Virginia, have been teaching antisemitism to their students. Another school in the Washington, D.C., area, the Islamic Educational Center, was reported to be teaching the ideology of Iranian ayatollah Khomeini along with antisemitism. In recent years, Muslim students on American college campuses have also employed antisemitic language and images and disseminated discredited information in their campaigns against Israel.

The growth of the Muslim population in the United States during the 1990s led American Jews to explore the possibility of political coalitions with Muslims. However, prominent Muslim American organizations not only opposed American Jewish support for Israel, but promoted antisemitic characterizations of Jews drawn from the ideology of Middle Eastern terror organizations. The radical agenda of the majority of Muslim organizations made the creation of such coalitions short-lived. As the historian Daniel Pipes observed, "Since leading Islamic groups in the United States are in regular touch with Middle Eastern organizations such as Hamas, Islamic Jihad and Hizballah, it may not be surprising that the rhetoric of the latter, infused with talk of killing Jews and celebrating acts of violence, should have found a home here as well" (Pipes 1999).

The Jewish community remains greatly concerned about the efforts of a significant number of Muslim American advocacy organizations to compete with it for political influence. These organizations promote themselves as the fastest growing non-Christian community in the United States and assert that Muslims already outnumber Jews. Their declared political goal is to neutralize the political power of the American Jewish community and its support for Israel.

Muslim Population

Reports of the numbers of Muslims in the United States vary greatly. Precise data are lacking because the law bars the U.S. Census Bureau from collecting information on religion. The Bureau does, however, collect information on ethnic identification. The first time it collected information on Americans of Arab ancestry was in 1980. It reported 610,000 Americans of Arab ancestry. In 1990, that number grew to 860,000, an increase of over 40 percent. The 2000 Census indicated that there are 1.2 million Arab Americans, an increase of another 40 percent. The Arab American Institute, an Arab advocacy organization, claimed the census underreported their numbers, asserting that there are 3 million Arab Americans.

A 2000 Zogby International survey indicated that, of the 1.2 million Arab Americans counted by the census, the majority is Christian: 42 percent are Catholic, 23 percent are Orthodox Christian, and 12 percent are Protestant, with the remaining 23 percent Muslim. This translates into 276,000 Arab Muslims. This number does not include non-Arab Muslims, such as Iranians, Pakistanis, Bangladeshis, Indians, and Central Asians. The 2000 Census reported 209,273 Pakistanis and 283,225 Iranians.

According to *We the People of Arab Ancestry* (2005), a U.S. Census Bureau report based on the 2000 Census, the largest segment of the Arab American population in the United States has Lebanese ancestry. The report also noted that 46 percent of the foreign-born Arab population arrived between 1990 and 2000, and only 9.6 percent prior to 1970.

Initially, studies of the Muslim population in the United States were carried out by Muslim advocacy organizations and only later by independent demographers. A study by Fareed Nu'man of the American Muslim Council (AMC) in 1992 estimated the population at 5 to 8 million American Muslims. In 2000, Nu'man retracted that figure, revealing that the leadership of the AMC pressured him to arrive at a figure of 6 million to demonstrate parity with the Jewish community. He later told the *Los Angeles Times* that his research pointed to a figure of 3 million.

Nine years later, the Islamic advocacy group, the Council on American Islamic Relations (CAIR), presented a new study that reported between 6 and 7 million Muslim Americans. CAIR's *Mosque Study Project* of 2001 (MSP) was sponsored by four Muslim advocacy organizations: CAIR, the Islamic Society of North America (ISNA), the

Islamic Circle of North America (ICNA), and the Ministry of Imam Warith Deen Mohammed, the Muslim American Society.

Demographers took issue with the methodology of these studies and the data they produced. Statistical Assessment Services (STATS) was highly critical of the MSP as suffering from "serious methodological problems." STATS concluded, based on two studies done by the National Opinion Research Center (NORC) and the American Religious Identification Survey, that the Muslim American population is 2 million, "give or take a few hundred thousand." In a study commissioned by the American Jewish Committee, Tom Smith of NORC reported a possibly slightly higher figure—1.9 to 2.8 million Muslim Americans (Smith 2001).

Motivation for Dialogue

Two overarching developments provide the historical backdrop to the Jewish community's efforts to initiate dialogue with Muslims in the United States. Reports of mass murders of the Muslim population by Serbs and Croats in Bosnia in 1992–1995 led to the creation, for the first time, of a Jewish, Christian, and Muslim interfaith coalition. At the same time, the Oslo Accords (1993), which many at the time assumed would begin the Israeli–Palestinian peace process, served as a major impetus to fostering interfaith dialogues. Still, many in the Jewish community, concerned that some Muslims espouse radical ideologies and support terrorism, remained ambivalent about forming relationships with Muslims.

Since 1992 the debate in the Jewish community over the Jewish–Muslim dialogue has focused on setting aside the difficult issue of Israel and concentrating on local communal issues unrelated to the Middle East conflict. In doing this, the Jewish community faces the painful choice of engaging in dialogue with, and thereby legitimizing, Muslim organizations that may support extremist causes, including terrorism against Israel.

The organized community divided on the terms of the dialogue. The policy of three of the national organizations—the American Jewish Committee (AJC), the American Jewish Congress (AJCongress), and the Anti-Defamation League (ADL)—is to oppose legitimizing Muslim organizations and individuals that support terrorism against Israel, even though the organizations may

condemn terrorist acts against the United States. Other organizations, such as the Jewish Council for Public Affairs and regional Jewish Community Relations Councils, approach the matter from a local perspective and seek dialogue with Muslims to improve communal relations, focusing on individual religious rights and church–state issues.

Muslim American organizations—such as ISNA, ICNA, CAIR, the now defunct American Muslim Council, and the Muslim Public Affairs Council (MPAC)—follow the lead of Sheikh Yusuf Al-Qaradhawi, the Muslim Brotherhood ideologue who condemned the 9/11 terror attacks against the United States but would not condemn suicide bombings against Israel. In 1998 Al-Qaradhawi issued a *fatwa*—an Islamic legal ruling—that maintained that such attacks against Israel are legitimate and should be considered acts of "martyrdom." The *fatwa* had the effect of encouraging and legitimizing suicide bombings against Israel throughout the Muslim world, including among Muslims in the United States. In many instances Muslim organizations' motivation for dialogue is simply to promote their position on Israel as mainstream.

Relations with African American Muslims

The result of Jews' dialogues with African American Muslims has been mixed. The pseudo-Islamic NOI, founded by W. D. Fard in the 1930s, is the oldest African American Muslim organization. After Fard disappeared, Elijah Muhammad became its head. Since its establishment, the NOI has promoted antisemitism along with a black supremacist ideology.

In 1975, Imam Warith Deen Muhammad, the son of Elijah Muhammad, succeeded him as the leader of the NOI. He rejected his father's ideology, began to adopt mainstream Sunni Muslim practices, and renamed the organization the American Muslim Mission. He changed the name of the organization several times—in 2002 from the Muslim American Society (MAS) to the American Society of Muslims (ASM). It is estimated to have 200,000 members and a larger number of followers.

In reaction to Muhammad's theological changes, Minister Louis Farrakhan led a breakaway faction of the group, reestablishing the pseudo-Islamic NOI with himself as its leader. In 2005 the NOI has an estimated 50,000 to 100,000 members with a larger number of followers. As a result of its continued promotion of antisemitic views, the organized Jewish community has not formed a relationship with the NOI.

In the 1990s Jewish communal leaders in major cities throughout the United States established and maintained ties to local leaders of the MAS. The violence in the Middle East has, however, affected relations between the Jewish community and Muhammad's organization. In 1999, for example, Muhammad's MAS, together with extremist Muslim American groups, sponsored the formation of American Muslims for Jerusalem, an anti-Israel organization that promotes what it defines as Muslim rights to the city of Jerusalem.

In February 2000, Imam Muhammad publicly embraced Minister Farrakhan in a symbolic reunification of their movements. At the reconciliation ceremony, Farrakhan pledged to reconcile his extremist theology with mainstream Islam. Nevertheless, he and his followers have continued to promote antisemitic stereotypes of Jews.

Dialogue Efforts

The first efforts to engage in Jewish–Muslim dialogue were initiated in the early 1990s by Rabbi James Rudin, director of the AJC's Department of Interreligious Affairs. In 1992, this outreach resulted in the formation of a coalition with American Muslim organizations to lobby the U.S. government on behalf of Muslims who were being subjected to mass murder in Bosnia. From 1992 to 1995, American Jewish organizations, working with the American Task Force on Bosnia, established in 1992, urged NATO intervention to end the mass killing of Bosnian Muslims. In 1993, the AJC initiated a dialogue with MPAC, one of the American Muslim organizations that had been involved with the Bosnia effort, as well as with Muhammad's MAS.

As a result of those contacts, the first national Jewish–Muslim interreligious conferences were held in the United States. The first conference, "Muslims and Jews in North America: Past, Present and Future," held October 24–26, 1993, was cosponsored by the AJC and the Institute for Islamic and Judaic Studies at the Center for Judaic Studies at the University of Denver. In September 1993, the Union for Reform Judaism published its first guidebook for interfaith dialogue with Muslims, *Shalom/Salaam: A Resource for Jewish Muslim Dialogue.*

The second national conference organized by the AJC and the University of Denver, "Women, Families and Children in Islamic and Judaic Tradition: History and Contemporary Concerns," met on October 23–25, 1994. The AJC and MPAC were scheduled to hold a third national conference in Los Angeles in 1995, but it was canceled after the emergence of irreconcilable differences between the Muslim and Jewish organizers over the suicide bombing attacks initiated by Hamas and Islamic Jihad against Israeli civilians in 1994. Muslim organizations' stance on suicide bombings has remained a central issue of Jewish–Muslim relations ever since.

In August 1999, a group of local rabbis, including representatives of the Reform and Conservative movements, and Jewish representatives in Los Angeles established a new dialogue group with Salam Al-Marayati, the director of MPAC, and Maher Hathout of the Islamic Center of Southern California (ICSC). On December 6, they released their jointly produced "Code of Ethics in Muslim-Jewish Dialogue," and twenty Jewish and Muslim representatives signed the document at City Hall.

Rabbi Gary Greenebaum, Los Angeles regional director of the AJC, criticized the signing. He stated, "I have worked to bring about the day when documents of this sort could be signed in good faith, and I am disappointed that it's being signed as it is today, by co-signers who have not lived up to the statement as it exists." In a separate statement, he elaborated, "They have not proven trustworthy. Time and again they have stepped away from categorically condemning terrorism. They keep rationalizing terrorism and I have a problem with that, as should all Jews." Other critics included Abraham Foxman, national director of the ADL, who noted that Israel and the Palestinians "have moved a lot farther" toward understanding than the Arab community in the United States. "I am not convinced that they are willing to be real partners, and we shouldn't give them a status they haven't earned" (*Los Angeles Times,* December 6, 1999; Jewish Telegraphic Agency, December 10, 1999).

In July 1999, Representative Richard A. Gephardt, the House minority leader, nominated MPAC's Al-Marayati to serve as the Muslim community's representative on the National Commission on Terrorism. After his office received letters of protest from the Conference of Presidents of Major American Jewish Organizations (CPMAJO), the AJC, the AJCongress, the ADL, and the

Zionist Organization of America indicating that Al-Marayati had made statements condoning terrorism, Representative Gephardt withdrew the nomination. The withdrawal caused a national controversy as well as criticism of the Jewish organizations from within the Jewish community.

Nine Muslim organizations, including Al-Marayati's MPAC, released a statement accusing the American Jewish organizations of engaging in "a campaign to silence Americans critical of Israel and to exclude Muslim voices from the public arena. The American Muslim Council, which welcomed the initial nomination of Mr. Al-Marayati, is shocked that Rep. Gephardt (D–MO) bowed to McCarthyist pressure of this sort" (AMC, July 12, 1999).

In 1999, the AJC began a relationship with the Islamic Supreme Council of America (ISCA), a moderate American Muslim organization led by Sheikh Muhammad Hisham Kabbani. ISCA was the first American Muslim organization to condemn publicly and unequivocally Al-Qa'ida's 1998 bombings of the U.S. embassies in Kenya and Tanzania. The relationship is still maintained, as well as with a newer organization, the Center for Islamic Pluralism.

Two years later, the AJC initiated a project designed to advance understanding between Muslims and Jews by publishing two books by scholars of Islam: *Children of Abraham: An Introduction to Judaism for Muslims* by Professor Reuven Firestone of Hebrew Union College–Los Angeles and *Children of Abraham: An Introduction to Islam for Jews* by Professor Khalid Duran. One month prior to the books' publication, CAIR, an extremist organization, denounced the book on Islam as an attack on Islam and launched a campaign of vilification against Duran. The campaign led Abd Al-Munim Abu Zant, the leader of the radical Islamic Action Front in Jordan, to declare Duran an apostate and to issue a call for Muslims throughout the world to kill him. Both books were nevertheless released at the AJC's national convention in May 2001.

Post–September 11 Atmosphere

Immediately following the September 11, 2001, Al-Qa'ida attacks against the United States, Jews made common cause with Muslims on the issue of civil liberties, especially after some Muslims became targets of acts of discrimination and violence. In a case that followed the passage of the 2001 counterterrorism measures enacted by the USA Patriot Act, a Jewish attorney in a Muslim–Jewish dialogue group in Portland, Oregon, assisted in providing twenty-five Jewish lawyers to do pro bono work for Muslims being questioned by the FBI in terrorism investigations.

This sense of commonality lasted only a short time, however. As a result of the position that the Muslim organizations participating in the dialogue groups adopted, justifying suicide bombings against Israel while condemning terrorist attacks against the United States, many rabbis and Jewish communal leaders halted their participation in the dialogue groups. Malcolm Hoenlein, executive vice chairman of the CPMAJO, stated: "We are starting to see many organizations that purport to be in a leadership position in the Muslim community that are associated with supporting terrorist organizations, or that refuse to denounce the suicide bombings, and even now hedge their words carefully in that regard" (*New York Times*, October 22, 2001).

On September 11, 2001, MPAC's Al-Marayati told KCRW radio that Israel should be considered a suspect in the attacks. According to the program transcript, Al-Marayati stated, "If we're going to look at suspects, we should look to the groups that benefit the most from these kinds of incidents, and I think we should put the State of Israel on the suspect list because I think this diverts attention from what's happening in the Palestinian territories so that they can go on with their aggression and occupation and apartheid policies" (*Los Angeles Times*, September 22, 2001).

The statement caused great disillusionment among the Jewish members of the Muslim–Jewish dialogue, and their participation dwindled. Rabbi John Rosove told the *New York Times*, "That was the last straw. I can't sit with a man like this. I'm a moderate liberal, and I assumed that they were, too. But now I'm convinced that the Muslims in our dialogue are very much anti-Israel, and were just using our dialogue to make themselves appear more moderate" (*New York Times*, October 22, 2001).

Although Jewish–Muslim dialogues still take place, considerable ambivalence toward the effort remains in both the Jewish and Muslim communities. As a result of some Muslim organizations' stance on terrorism, many Jewish organizations on the national and local levels have avoided efforts to cooperate and legitimize them as dialogue partners. From the perspective of Islamic extremists in the Muslim world and the United States, the U.S. wars in Iraq and Afghanistan demonstrate only that Americans and Jews are their adversaries. Dialogue with Muslim groups that hold such a view remains tenuous.

Yehudit Barsky

References and Further Reading

Duran, Khalid. 1997. "Muslims and the U.S. Election of '96." *Middle East Quarterly* (June).

Freedom House. 2005. Available at: www.freedomhouse.org/religion/pdfdocs/FINAL%20FINAL.pdf. Accessed March 11, 2007.

Pipes, Daniel. 1999. "American Muslims vs. American Jews." *Commentary* (May).

Smith, Tom W. 2001. *Estimating the Muslim Population in the United States.* New York: American Jewish Committee.

U.S. Census Bureau. 2005. *We the People of Arab Ancestry in the United States: Census 2000 Special Reports.* (March).

Wistrich, Robert. 2002. *Muslim Anti-Semitism: A Clear and Present Danger.* New York: American Jewish Committee.

American Jews in Entertainment and Popular Culture

Yiddish Theater in America

The theater played a vital role in the rich Yiddish subculture generated by the East European immigrant Jewish community in America. A much beloved institution, it catered to and influenced the aesthetic and moral values of its mostly working-class patrons who, while rapidly adjusting to their new homeland, yearned for the home and kin they had left behind. They frequented the Yiddish playhouses to bask in their own language and culture, to watch their American experience reflected and negotiated through a decidedly Jewish lens, and to savor the theatrical representation of familiar types, sentiments, concerns, and dilemmas. In the playhouses they learned a smattering of Jewish history and grappled with Jewish nationalism, labor relations, women's rights, religious observance, acculturation, and Americanization. Nobel laureate Isaac Bashevis Singer noted that the Yiddish theater provided "a remarkable mixture of university and place of amusement" (Singer 1966).

The balance was a delicate one, for though the stage served as an important forum, it never sacrificed pleasure to didacticism. It was mostly a commercial enterprise that tailored its offerings to the tastes of its patrons. These ran the gamut from tear-jerking melodramas, historical plays, and lavish musicals, to sophisticated productions in line with the best of European and American theater. The

boundaries between genres were often lax, with productions offering a mélange of tragedy, domestic melodrama, and low comedy, peppered with music and dance numbers, folkloristic embellishments, and ever-popular replications of religious rituals and prayer. Critic Irving Howe likened the Yiddish theater to Italian opera for its predictability of plots and penchant for spectacle, declamation, and high gesture; its intensely emotional acting style; and its fondness for bravura performance. Enormously popular with all sectors of the community, the Yiddish theater served also as an important locus for social communion where people went to see and to be seen, to meet and socialize with friends and neighbors.

The first Yiddish theatrical production in America took place in New York City in 1882, shortly after mass immigration had begun. Six years earlier the modern Yiddish theater had come into being in Jassy, Romania, when writer Abraham Goldfaden (1840–1908) joined forces with two folk singers, then performing at a local tavern, and provided a skimpy story line that offered narrative continuity to their musical numbers. The public was thrilled, and soon the multitalented Goldfaden was heading his own traveling theatrical company, where he functioned as producer, playwright, director, composer, and librettist. His early offerings resembled *commedia dell'arte* in their combination of a simple, fixed scenario with improvised dialogue and stage business, but soon grew into lavish operettas, some of which—*The Witch* (1879), *The Two Kuni-Lemls* (1880), and *Shulamith* (1880)—became beloved classics of the Jewish stage.

The tales were simple, adopted from a variety of Jewish and European sources, with a musical hodgepodge of Goldfaden originals, cantorial tunes, German and French marches and waltzes, East European folk songs, and melodies lifted from Mozart, Bizet, Handel, Wagner, Meyerbeer, and Verdi. Yet there was genius in the fresh and often fantastic concoctions of the Yiddish bard. The folk loved his tales and hummed his songs, and the names of some of his characters—Schmendrik, Bobbe Yachne, and Kuni Leml—were integrated into the Yiddish thesaurus. Goldfaden's success encouraged the formation of competing itinerant troupes, and in a world with little regard for copyright, his work was soon copied and plagiarized throughout the Yiddish-speaking world.

In August 1882, a minor troupe, headed by brothers Leon and Myron Golubok, introduced Yiddish theater to America. They had been stranded in London when another brother, Abe, working in a New York cigar factory, convinced Frank Wolf, the proprietor of a local saloon, to finance a journey to New York and invest in the production of a Yiddish show. When the troupe, six men and two women, arrived in the city, its ranks were augmented by local talent, including Israel Barsky, a tailor with theatrical aspirations, and the boy soprano Boris Tomashefsky (1866/8?–1939), who became the matinee idol of the Yiddish stage. The company opened in August 1882 at Turn Hall, on East Fourth Street in the Bowery, an area soon to become New York's first Yiddish theater district. The initial offering was Goldfaden's *The Witch*. Although its success was modest at best, the endeavor was timely, as the influx of Jewish immigrants was increasing steadily, and many of the newcomers were young, single, and eager to spend their little extra cash on entertainment.

By year's end the company expanded and moved to the Bowery Garden, a narrow beer hall, though with a proper stage, where it performed Goldfaden operettas and musical melodramas: Barsky's *The Madwoman, Yankele, Young Scamp,* Paysach Tomashefsky's *Rothschild's Biography,* and his son Boris's *The Pogrom in Russia.* In 1883, plagued by financial and personal feuds, the company split in two. Neither troupe fared well, and the 1883 arrival of a more professional troupe from Europe, headed by Maurice Heine, propelled the Goluboks to settle in Chicago and the

Tomashefskys to spend the next three years in Philadelphia. The newcomers, calling themselves the Russian Yiddish Opera Company, leased the Oriental Theater (formerly the Bowery Garden). Their principal playwright was Joseph Lateiner, their resident prompter. At first they produced plays on biblical themes, such as *Esther and Haman* and *Joseph and His Brothers,* then more current titles, such as the highly successful *Immigration to America.*

The rapid rise in Jewish immigration, combined with the 1883 czarist ban on Yiddish-language performances, increased the number of Jewish thespians in New York. The summer of 1886 marked the arrival of a seasoned troupe that included the enormously gifted singer/comedian Sigmund Mogulesco (1858–1914) and dramatic actor David Kessler (1860–1920). Though originally contracted to work in Chicago, they settled in New York, where they rented the National Theater, another Bowery house, renamed it the Roumanian Opera House, and soon enjoyed a major success with Moshe Horowitz's *Tisza Eszlar,* based on the notorious blood libel. A fierce competition developed between the two companies; each used the stage and printed pamphlets to denigrate the other, and each enticed actors from the rival management. At times their plays bore nearly identical titles: when the Roumanian Opera House produced Horowitz's opera *King Solomon,* the Oriental immediately responded with Lateiner's *Solomon's Trial.*

Actors Jacob P. Adler (1855–1926) and Keni Liptzin (1856–1918) came to New York in 1887, as did Abraham Goldfaden, all hoping to partake of the burgeoning theatrical scene. Adler and Goldfaden were not successful and sailed back to Europe. Adler returned in 1890 to become the most revered actor of the Yiddish stage. Goldfaden returned in 1892 but remained a marginalized founding father, often dependent on Adler and Tomashefsky for financial support. He was vindicated shortly before his death when his play *Ben-Ami* proved a major success. His unique role was acknowledged at his funeral, where 75,000 people took part in the procession, the largest such event to date on the Lower East Side.

At first, Yiddish performances were given only on weekends and Jewish holidays. There was no objection to the timing, but the stage respectfully reflected the audience's religious sensibilities. On Friday night and Saturday matinees there was no representation of activities prohibited on the Sabbath. Lights were turned on in advance, matches and cigarettes were not lit, and letters arrived conveniently unsealed. As the theaters assumed a full-week schedule, the company's newest production was usually reserved for the weekend, with Friday considered the gala occasion of the week. During the week, seats were filled through a benefit system whereby social and labor organizations bought out a performance for fund-raising purposes, paying the theater a reduced rate, then selling tickets to their members at full price. Plays for benefit performances were drawn from the company's older repertoire.

At the turn of the century the three major Yiddish theaters, all in the Bowery, were the People's, the Thalia, and the Windsor, houses with seating capacities between 2,500 and 3,500. It was estimated that they were offering more than a thousand performances annually to about 2 million patrons, although the Jewish population in New York in 1900 totaled 580,000. A folksy ambience typified the Yiddish auditorium. Families brought young children, emotional responses to the events on stage filled the air, as did the smell of food. Merchandise was advertised on the stage curtain during intermission, vendors sold sweets and drinks between acts, and the merits of the production were unabashedly discussed in the lobby. Some social critics censured this homeyness as uncouth, suitable to a circus, not a temple of culture. Accordingly, the People's Theater prided itself on not permitting children in the auditorium.

Playscripts were not regarded as literary texts, and actors improvised lines and interjected songs or vaudeville *shticks* that had no bearing on the story line. Boris Tomashefsky brought the house down by inserting his popular song "A Letter to Mother" whenever the pace of the performance slackened. To some extent, ad-libbing resulted from the demands of show business. Appearing in different plays during the week, Yiddish actors often worked with unfinished scripts and had to learn a new role every couple of weeks. Consequently, they improvised, slipped in lines from other plays, and relied heavily on the prompter, a permanent fixture in the Yiddish theater. Moreover, most of the first generation of actors who had begun their careers in the 1880s were reared in the culture of popular entertainment, where scripts served largely as vehicles for the display of performative skills. At the heart of their world stood the actor, not the playwright, and acting was considered most commendable when it raised primal emotions to fever pitch. The emotional atmosphere

was enhanced by the strong bond between audiences and actors, a special feature of the Yiddish theater. Stars were beloved as both family and royalty, with their love lives, personal disputes, weddings, and funerals followed by loyal and at times near fanatical fans.

The theater's popularity and the dearth of a Jewish dramatic corpus created an insatiable demand for new scripts. The best-known and most prolific of the early Yiddish playwrights were "professor" Moshe Horowitz (1864–1910) and Joseph Lateiner (1853–1937). They had arrived in New York in 1882 and 1884 respectively, and between them generated some three hundred playscripts, the vast majority translations and adaptations. Horowitz, it was said, could complete a play in two days, and on occasion he handed in two acts, finishing the final act backstage. Lateiner and Horowitz specialized in quasi-historical extravaganzas, heart-wrenching melodramas, and *tsaybilder*—sentimentalized docudramas depicting recent disasters and sensational events. Though most of these plays were crude, filled with plagiarized scenes and historical inaccuracies, they transported unsophisticated spectators from the dreariness of the tenements and sweatshops to a fantasy world of glamour and amplified emotion.

Young intellectuals were contemptuous of this theatrical fare, labeling it *shund* (trash). Their dream of a Yiddish Ibsen was realized in Jacob Gordin (1853–1909), who introduced literary melodramas into the Yiddish repertoire. A respected writer in Russian, he came to America in 1891 with the utopian *Am Olam* movement. Though he had no theatrical experience, Jacob Adler, who was impressed by his intellect and command of Russian culture, commissioned him to write a play. The play was *Siberia* (1892), followed by the enormously successful *The Jewish King Lear* (1892), both starring Adler. Gordin went on to write more than thirty original dramas, mostly domestic "problem plays," written in the realistic mode. The best known are *God, Man, and the Devil*, with a Faustian theme; *Mirele Efros*, an intergenerational melodrama; *The Wild Man*, the tragic story of an older man married to a young woman; *Dementia Americana*, a satire of Jewish real estate mania; *Homelessness*, which tackled social conditions in a large city; *The Kreutzer Sonata*, on the "New Woman"; and *The Truth*, on mixed marriage. Gordin also translated and adapted more than forty plays, introducing Jewish audiences to the work of Ibsen, Sudermann, Hauptmann, Tolstoy, and Gorky.

Before literary and cultural reformers began to change Yiddish theatrical culture, actors generally delivered their lines in *Daytshmerish,* an artificially Germanized Yiddish deemed more appropriate for higher-class characters. Gordin was important in instituting a more natural stage language. He demanded a faithful rendition of the author's text and terminated ad-libbing and interpolation of unrelated musical and comic numbers. Writing on commission, Gordin provided actors with strong parts, and the reputation of actors associated with his work—Jacob Adler and his wife Sarah, David Kessler, Sigmund Mogulesco, Keni Lipzin, and Bertha Kalich—rested largely on their reputation as the originators and interpreters of specific Gordin roles.

Gordin's success encouraged more Yiddish writers to contribute to the stage. Leon Kobrin (1872–1946) offered realistic portrayals of Jewish life in America, and David Pinski's *The Treasure* and *The Final Balance* were translated into English and produced respectively by the Theater Guild in 1920 and by the Provincetown Players in 1928. In later years the list of dramatists included major writers: Sholem Asch, H. Leivick, Peretz Hirschbein, and Osip Dymov. Yet even culturally oriented managers could not afford to devote themselves entirely to literary plays. The masses who supported the Yiddish stage demanded escapist entertainment. Thus, the biggest hit of the pre–World War I era was the 1909 musical *Dos Pintele Yid* (*The Quintessential Jew*), produced, directed, coauthored, and starring the sweet-voiced Boris Tomashefsky, which packed the People's Theater for the entire thirty-eight-week season.

The prosperity of the Yiddish theater and the belief in its longevity were manifested in the dedication of the Grand Theater (1903), the first house built specifically for Yiddish shows. Located in the Bowery, it opened to much fanfare, with local politicians in attendance. The English-language press noted that it was the first theater in the city's history to be constructed for non-English performances. The Grand, seating 1,700, reflected the social mobility and aesthetic aspirations of its patrons. Its elegant interior, done in red and gold, included an orchestra floor and three balconies, each with its own lobby, cloakroom, and smoking room. Its inaugural performance was *Zion, or On the Rivers of Babylon* by Lateiner, a historical melodrama that alternated between dark moments and burlesque, framed by the destruction of the first Temple in

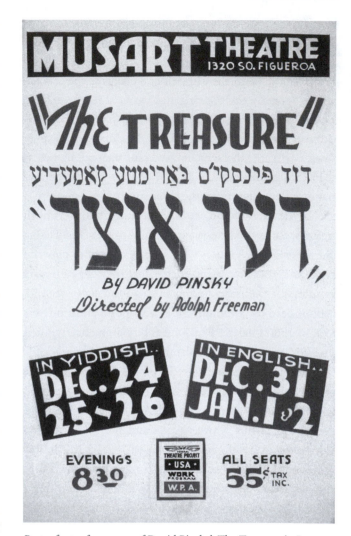

Poster for performances of David Pinsky's The Treasure *in Los Angeles. (Library of Congress)*

Jerusalem and the Jews' return to their homeland by permission of King Cyrus.

Originally, Yiddish theaters were run as stock companies, where the actors shared the profits in accordance with their position, that is, hero, juvenile, comedian. This arrangement was soon replaced by one with the star-manager in charge of a salaried company, a system that was already obsolete in the American theater. The division into management and labor resulted in early unionization efforts. The Hebrew Actors Union, established in December 1900, twenty years before Actors' Equity, held a tight reign on every Yiddish production for years to come. It enforced a salary scale and often required managers to engage actors regardless of ability or choice. It was also reluctant to admit new members. Indeed, until the 1950s, gaining membership was a humbling experience, with applicants forced to audition before the union rank and file. Some accomplished actors, including Stella Adler and Maurice Schwartz, failed their first auditions.

In addition to the actors' union, there were separate unions representing costumers, prompters, chorus people, ushers, stage carpenters, scene shifters, and musicians. Though some of them were tiny—the prompters' union peaked at a membership of twelve—their strength lay in their affiliation with the United Hebrew Trades. If one union had a grievance against a manager, the whole Yiddish theatrical situation was affected. In the ongoing struggle between managers and unions, the latter usually held the upper hand.

Though union wages were fixed, major stars commanded skyrocketing amounts. In 1912 Rudolph Schildkraut, a leading actor in the German theater who came to New York with Max Reinhardt's company, received less than $300 a week on the English-language stage. He was engaged at the People's Theater, where he acted as his own manager, and his weekly income, including his share of the profits, averaged $2,000 a week. Such sums reflect the enormous drawing power of stars on the Yiddish stage.

The prosperity enjoyed during World War I, combined with the decline of the Bowery district and the migration of Jews to Brooklyn and the Bronx, prompted the construction of new theaters. A new Yiddish theater district was established on Second Avenue in Manhattan. This address became synonymous with flagship Yiddish theaters and related businesses, including cafes and restaurants. The most famous was the Cafe Royal, on Twelfth Street and Second Avenue, *the* meeting place of the theatrical crowd, immortalized in Hy Craft's popular Broadway play, *Cafe Crown* (1942). The first theaters to open on this new rialto were the Second Avenue Theater (1911), a 2,000-seat house built for actor–manager David Kessler, and the National, built for Boris Tomashefsky and Jacob Adler, which boasted a covered roof garden and a seating capacity of 1,600. Each house cost about a million dollars. The last two Yiddish theaters on the avenue, opening in 1926, were Maurice Schwartz's Yiddish Art Theater, seating over 1,200, and the Public, with over 1,700 seats.

A new cadre of stars became associated with these theaters during the 1920s and 1930s. The greatest musical comedy star was American-born Molly Picon, the gamine darling of Second Avenue. Other stars included Menasha Skulnik, Herman Yablokoff, Aaron Lebedeff, Ludwig Satz, Mikhel Mikhalesco, Jennie Goldstein, and Zvi Scooler.

However, the interwar era was primarily associated with the art theater movement. Its roots lay with post-1905 immigrants, who generally had a higher level of education than their predecessors, were more politically involved, and had a deep appreciation for literature and drama. Many had become familiar in their native Russia with amateur theatrical clubs that sought to create a Yiddish theater of high artistic merit. In America, quite a few of these young workers joined the newly formed dramatic clubs. One club was the New York–based Hebrew Dramatic League. In 1915 it was adopted as the drama section of the Workmen's Circle, a left-wing fraternal organization. It assumed the name *Fraye Idishe Folksbiene* (The Free Yiddish People's Stage), retaining its amateur status.

The Folksbiene's first production, Henrik Ibsen's *The Enemy of the People,* reflected its highbrow artistic mission. In 1918 they presented *Green Fields,* a low-key tale of Jewish rural life written by Peretz Hirshbein, an early proponent of a Yiddish art theater. The overwhelming reception of this modest literary play, the antithesis of Yiddish theater's traditional glitz, marked the beginning of a more refined Yiddish theater. It also convinced actor–manager Maurice Schwartz of the existence of a younger, intellectually inclined audience. Shortly thereafter Schwartz showcased Hirshbein's *The Forsaken Nook,* a modest production that was enthusiastically embraced by the younger, more sophisticated crowd, launching a golden epoch of meritorious Yiddish drama in America.

Maurice Schwartz (1890–1960), a man of extraordinary talent and energy, founded the Yiddish Art Theater and managed it until its demise in 1950. More than any other individual, Schwartz charted the course of the high-end Yiddish stage. He was an excellent character actor, an occasional playwright, a bold director, a resourceful stage designer, and an astute manager who created a repertory theater with an ensemble of some of the best actors of the time. They included Jacob Ben-Ami, Ludwig Satz, Celia Adler, Bina Abramowitz, Anna Appel, Hyman Mysell, Joseph Sheingold, Joseph Buloff, and Muni Weisenfreund, later known as Paul Muni. Schwartz's taste reflected that of educated Jewish audiences, and in the 1920s he experimented with various theatrical forms, including a constructivist rendition of Goldfaden's *The Tenth Commandment* (1926), designed by Boris Aronson.

Schwartz's most successful productions were *The Brothers Ashkenazi* (1937) and *Yoshe Kalb* (1932) by I. J. Singer. However, Schwartz's extended national and international tours resulted in long absences from New York, which adversely affected the continuity of his Yiddish Art Theater.

The only art theater to sustain activity through the 1930s was the Communist-affiliated Artef Theater, which began as an amateur dramatic studio in 1927 and gradually shifted to professional status in the mid-1930s. Directed by former Habima member Benno Schneider, the Artef was greatly influenced by the Russian avant-garde. Though committed to represent the lives of American Jewish workers, its repertoire consisted mainly of Russian Jewish materials and modern adaptations of folk dramas, notably *Recruits* (1934), *200,000* (1936), and *The Outlaw* (1937). The fortunes of the Artef reflected the position of Jewish communism in America. The company disbanded in the aftermath of the shock waves of the Hitler–Stalin nonaggression pact of 1939.

It was a great tragedy that, while reaching its artistic pinnacle and engaging some of the community's finest artists and writers, the Yiddish theater was losing its audiences. As immigration came to a virtual halt in the mid-1920s, Yiddish culture was swiftly eroded. In 1925 the future still seemed bright—the number of theaters serving the outer boroughs was increasing to four in Brooklyn and four in upper Manhattan and the Bronx, with plans for three additional houses in new Jewish neighborhoods, which would have brought the total of New York Yiddish theaters to twenty. Theater managers regarded the Yiddish stage as a stable American institution, claiming that it attracted some 300,000 New York area families to Yiddish shows. In 1930, the scene had changed. The theatrical season, which traditionally ended by Passover, was brought to a halt in early spring. It was only partly the result of the national financial crisis, of personnel costs proportionately higher than on Broadway, and of the inroads of the talkies. The primary reason was the cessation of immigration and the decline in the number of native Yiddish speakers. Always reflecting the element of the population on whose patronage it depended, the Yiddish theater tried to appeal to the younger, native-born generation by peppering plays with English, with the popular Jennie Goldstein singing, for example, "When I pretend I'm gay, *Es iz mir och un vey.*" However, bilingualism hardly proved to be a panacea.

The dwindling of the Yiddish rialto was a gradual process. In 1927 there were still twenty-five theaters that offered Yiddish productions across America: eleven in New York, four in Chicago, three in Philadelphia, and one each in Baltimore, Boston, Cleveland, Detroit, Los Angeles, Newark, and St. Louis. In 1936, seven Yiddish theaters opened their seasons in New York; in 1945 the number shrank to four, three opening their season with musicals entitled "They All Want to Get Married," "Good News," and "Pleasure Girls." Though efforts to sustain quality Yiddish productions did not cease, they were modest and short-lived.

In the 1950s and 1960s the great names of the golden era were disappearing: actress Sarah Adler, widow of the great Jacob Adler and mother of five performers, of which the best known was actor and coach Stella Adler, died in 1953 at age ninety-five; Joseph Rumshinsky, for fifty years the Yiddish stage's primary musician and the composer of more than a hundred operettas, died in 1956; the queen of tears, Jennie Goldstein, who had made her stage debut at age six, died in 1960. Perhaps most symbolic was the passing of Maurice Schwartz that same year. He was sixty-nine and died in Israel, where he was working on a Yiddish production of Sholem Asch's *Kiddush Hashem.*

By the end of the twentieth century the baton of Yiddish literary drama passed to the Folksbiene, whose enthusiastic members, all amateurs, persist in producing one Yiddish play a year, recently with English over-titles. While the era of Yiddish theater has ended, some of its tales and traditions can be gleaned from the Yiddish talkies of the 1930s and 1940s. Its story continues to excite the imagination of theater and film professionals who produce modern versions of the old plays and documentaries based on its stories, such as playwright Donald Margulies's adaptation of Sholem Asch's *God of Vengeance* and Arnon Goldfinger's film *The Komediant* (1999), an exuberant chronicle of the life and career of actors Pesach Burstein and Lilian Lux and their theatrical family.

Edna Nahshon

References and Further Reading

Berkowitz, Joel. 2002. *Shakespeare on the American Yiddish Stage.* Iowa City: University of Iowa Press.

Burstein, Pesach'ke, with Lillian Lux Burstein. 2003. *What a Life! The Autobiography of Pesach'ke Burstein, Yiddish Matinee Idol,* edited by Gershon Freidlin. Syracuse, NY: Syracuse University Press.

Hapgood, Hutchins. 1967 (1902). *The Spirit of the Ghetto.* Cambridge, MA: Harvard University Press.

Hoberman, J. 1991. *Bridge of Light: Yiddish Films between Two Worlds.* New York: Museum of Modern Art and Schocken Books.

Howe, Irving. 1976. *World of Our Fathers.* New York: Simon & Schuster.

Kadison, Luba, and Joseph Buloff, with Irving Genn. 1992. *On Stage, Off Stage: Memories of a Lifetime in the Yiddish Theatre.* Cambridge, MA: Harvard University Library.

Lifson, David S. 1961. *The Yiddish Theatre in America.* New York: Thomas Yoseloff.

Lipsky, Louis. 1962. *Tales of the Yiddish Rialto.* Cranbury, NJ: A. S. Barnes.

Nahshon, Edna. 1998. *Yiddish Proletarian Theatre: The Art and Politics of the Artef, 1925–1940.* Westport, CT: Greenwood Press.

Rosenfeld, Lulla. 1977. *Bright Star of Exile: Jacob Adler and the Yiddish Theatre.* New York: Crowell.

Sandrow, Nahma. 1977. *Vagabond Stars: A World History of Yiddish Theater.* New York: Harper & Row.

Singer, Isaac Bashevis. 1966. "Once on Second Avenue There Lived a Yiddish Theater." *New York Times* (April 17).

Jews and Broadway

For most of the twentieth century, American Jews selected Broadway as the epicenter of their subculture. Not only a street, Broadway—the New York stage—has been the ebullient showcase for the talents of Fanny Brice, Al Jolson, Eddie Cantor, Bert Lahr, and Barbra Streisand. For over half a century, such performers electrified audiences (and more easily exulted in their ethnicity than they could on screen). Broadway also spawned some of Hollywood's stars, rivaled it in glamour, and incubated the Tin Pan Alley tunes that a nation sang in unison for at least the first half of the twentieth century. The pulse of a common culture could be taken on Broadway.

But the emergence of both rock 'n' roll and television in the 1950s had the effect of weakening the American musical. The center could not hold (or simply shifted to the small screen), which, in retrospect, made the Broadway genre look classier and more estimable. The Broadway musical deserves to be appreciated for having found a European-derived operetta and created an indigenous art form. In particular it flourished from the 1920s, when *Show Boat* (1927) established the groove, until the 1960s, when the social tensions generated by the Vietnam War shattered the consensus that had crystallized around the nation's culture. The vitality of the Broadway musical was evident, however, before and after those dates as well, as the box-office power of *A Chorus Line* (1975) and *The Producers* (2001) suggests. The city that harbored the largest Jewish population in the history of the Diaspora inflected the musical as completely as Vienna marked the waltz and Paris the cancan. Yet this form managed to project a national style as well. Its elements included a compulsive optimism, an electrifying energy, and an immunity to tragedy.

Broadway represented showmanship at its most flamboyant because the goal was to sell tickets. This demotic spectacle was driven by commercialism, not a bid for artistic immortality. Or as lyricist E. Y. (Yip) Harburg wrote: "Mozart died a pauper,/ Heine lived in dread,/ Foster died in Bellevue,/ Homer begged for bread./ Genius pays off handsomely—/ After you are dead" (Lahr 1996). A cantor's son from Dessau, Germany, composer Kurt Weill absorbed the atmosphere upon immigration. Aching badly for success on Broadway, Weill told an interviewer that he was writing "for today" and claimed not to "give a damn about writing for posterity" (Block 1997). Broadway typified the yearning to transform citizens into customers, and yet managed to convert commercial instincts into an art form that has proven itself indelibly enchanting.

Virtually all of the composers and lyricists who heard America singing the songs emanating from Broadway were Jews, and most of them were New Yorkers. Without them it is hard to imagine the history of musical comedy in the United States. There certainly would have been theater, and music, and comedy. But the combination was virtually a franchise enjoyed by one minority group. Two features of the history of Broadway justify its claim to be considered the epicenter of American Jewish culture.

One index is the audience. In 1968 the scenarist and novelist William Goldman speculated that Jews filled half the seats in Broadway theaters, and no scholar has disputed his conjecture. These theaters benefited financially from the parties that stemmed from a tradition of the Yiddish stage. In Abraham Cahan's canonical *Rise of David Levinsky* (1917), the immigrant protagonist recalls his own "considerable passion for the Jewish theater" (Cahan 1960) and participates in the fund-raising activity in which blocks of seats—and sometimes even entire houses—are sold by charitable or fraternal groups. The Broadway audience was more geographically limited—and therefore

Mel Brooks poses before the set of his Broadway show The Producers *in 2001. (AP/Wide World Photos)*

more Jewish—than, for example, the crowds who watched movies. The cinema was obviously far more of a mass art form than Broadway ever aspired to be and had a national (and indeed international) audience that the Broadway stage lacked.

The second factor is talent. When Oscar Hammerstein II was working with composer Jerome Kern on adapting Donn Byrne's biography of Marco Polo, the lyricist inquired: "Here is a story laid in China about an Italian and told by an Irishman. What kind of music are you going to write?" Kern's answer was reassuring: "It'll be good Jewish music" (Fordin 1977). That was the lullaby of Broadway, so that even those who did not satisfy *halachic* (Jewish legal) standards adapted to the prevailing ethnic sensibility.

That was true of Hammerstein himself, whose mother, a Presbyterian, had him baptized as an even more upscale Episcopalian. When he became an adult, however,

Hammerstein practiced no religion (except perhaps for the faith that his next show had to be a hit). But his social and professional circle was so inescapably Jewish that, if any American can be said to have shaped the Broadway musical without actually being Jewish, Hammerstein is the obvious candidate. His first marriage was to Myra Finn, a cousin of his second famous collaborator, Richard Rodgers (who considered himself a Jew on ethnic rather than religious grounds). Hammerstein's career was not unique in demonstrating the liaison's entwining talents. Lyricist Ira Gershwin was a high school classmate of E. Y. Harburg (who wrote the lyrics for the 1939 Hollywood musical *The Wizard of Oz*) and would soon introduce him to composer Burton Lane (*Finian's Rainbow* [1947]), who wrote his first show at the age of fifteen and served as a rehearsal pianist for Ira's younger brother George. Rodgers had served as Kern's rehearsal pianist and was sixteen when he met the twenty-three-year-old Lorenz Hart, who played songs for him that afternoon on his Victrola. Hart had attended the same Catskills summer camp for the German Jewish upper crust as had Rodgers. A fellow camper was Herbert Sondheim, whose son Stephen would meet Hammerstein during the launching of *Oklahoma!* (1943). Sondheim would repay his debts to the lyricist and librettist for his mentoring by dedicating the score for *A Funny Thing Happened on the Way to the Forum* (1962) to Hammerstein, and would also amplify and enhance (as well as upend) the whole musical tradition that Hammerstein and Kern had invented with *Show Boat*. Indeed Hammerstein's death forced Rodgers to work with other lyricists, including Sondheim—so that the intricate mesh of collaborations and personal relationships (and rivalries) stretches from the Americanization of the operetta all the way down to the lingering postmodern death of the Broadway musical.

Because lines of apprenticeship and collegiality were so taut, outsiders had to learn what the indigenes were apparently doing naturally. The most celebrated mimic was a Yale-educated Episcopalian from Indiana, Cole Porter, who allegedly asked George Gershwin for the secret of Broadway success and was told, "Write Jewish." Such a mandate Porter interpreted as a synonym for writing "Middle Eastern." The result was "Just One of Those Things" and "I've Got You Under My Skin"—songs that were noteworthy for their tropical rhythms, their extended melody lines, their moody and exotic aura of romance. Rodgers recalled Porter telling him that Broadway required a talent for writing "Jewish tunes," a claim that Rodgers decoded as the use of strongly chromatic, sensuous "minor-key melodies" that would sound "unmistakably eastern Mediterranean." With "Night and Day" and "Begin the Beguine," Rodgers saw what Porter meant. What Porter thereafter called his "magic formula" was evidenced in "I Love Paris," which one music historian quipped should have been entitled "I Love Russia" (Wilder 1972). In fact most of the Jews who had emigrated from Russia *hated* it. Porter's good friend, Irving Berlin, claimed that his earliest childhood memory of Russia was of a pogrom.

Perhaps some "Jewish tunes" could be traced, in a vague way, to the synagogue. Berlin's father had been a part-time cantor, a job at which the father of composer Harold Arlen had worked full-time. Perhaps there is a resemblance between, say, the folk tune "Havenu Shalom

Aleichem" and the spiritual "It Take a Long Pull to Get There" from *Porgy and Bess* (1935). But in general the direct musical influences on the plangent notes projected from the orchestra pit were unlikely to be liturgical; the Jewish accent on Broadway was not obvious. Nor is there much direct evidence of the impact of the Yiddish theater, which broke attendance records in 1927, the year that *Show Boat* opened. Harburg regularly attended with his father after synagogue on Saturdays. But this lyricist's explicit indebtedness to the Yiddish theater was exceptional. For others, ethnicity was an accident of birth, not a heritage to be cultivated.

Because their shows were often set in New York, its lingo could sometimes be injected into the lyrics. Consider the cinematic (and hence more "universalistic") *West Side Story* (1961), in which the leader of the Jets addresses, "Dear kindly social worker,/ They tell me: get a job,/ Like be a soda jerker,/ Which means like be a slob." But expected to work at a soda fountain as a way to "earn a buck," Riff sneers in the less sanitized version on Broadway—"which means like be a *shmuck*." Or take *Guys and Dolls* (1950), songs by Frank Loesser, who has Nathan Detroit declare his love to Adelaide in a daisy-chain of internal rhymes: "All right already, I'm just a no-goodnik./ All right already, it's true. So *nu*?/ So sue me, sue me, what can you do me?/ I love you." Such sassy, brassy lyrics propelled the momentum of musical comedy far from the ambience of, say, *The Merry Widow* and into the mainstream of American vernacular music.

Though Broadway was popular, its matrix was not populist. Hart had attended Columbia, as had Rodgers and Hammerstein. The latter had also earned a law degree from Columbia; the former was the son of a highly successful physician who took his family to operas as well as to musicals. Kern studied music at the University of Heidelberg. The father of Alan Jay Lerner (*My Fair Lady* [1956]) had founded Lerner Shops and sent his son to Harvard, where a classmate was Leonard Bernstein (*West Side Story*). Sondheim studied advanced composition at Princeton after graduating from Williams College. Of course, not everyone who succeeded on Broadway could brandish such pedigrees. Berlin quit school at the age of fourteen, George Gershwin at sixteen. Frank Loesser's father was a piano teacher and his mother a translator and a lecturer on modern literature. But the future songwriter somehow contrived to get expelled from both high school and college.

That several of Broadway's most prominent creative figures were nevertheless born into comfort may have reinforced a national and generic addiction (to quote from *South Pacific*) to "happy talk." The most glowing dream of the Great White Way was to see your name in lights (even if that name happened to have been anglicized), and thus success was both celebrated and certified. Unlike European operas, musicals encouraged the pursuit of happiness and promised that the goal was within reach. Broadway reinforced the national faith in good fortune; such an ethos could not flourish in the gloom. Thus the operative word is *electricity*, because the dazzling technology of neon lighting reached Broadway in 1924—exactly when the Gershwin brothers did. The raucous exuberance of such musicals, with their jaunty lyrics and their rousing scores, reflected an insouciant spirit that began to vanish only in the era of the Vietnam War.

Broadway itself was a symbol of hope, promising liberation from the shadows of the past. When a cowboy named Curly first strutted onto a stage to exult "what a beautiful mornin'" was glorifying the new state of Oklahoma and to predict that "ever'thin's goin' my way," the contrast with Europe could not have been sharper. The genocidal machinery of the Nazi death camps was operating around the clock; the battle of Stalingrad had ended only a month earlier; and the following month, at Mila 18 in the Warsaw ghetto, a suicidal revolt would erupt. It would end only with the utter destruction of what had once been the largest Jewish community outside of New York City itself. Only in America could Curly's optimism have seemed remotely credible. Musicals committed all sorts of crimes against complexity, which is why it is easy to condescend to the reductiveness that the genre has exhibited. But a cockeyed, optimistic innocence is more deeply implanted in the national sensibility than can be blamed on Broadway alone.

But unlike rock 'n' roll, Broadway was not pitched primarily at adolescents, and its lyricists and composers could therefore prize irony and sophistication. Lorenz Hart had grown up in a German-speaking home and remained fluent in the language, which may account for his absorption in the sheer quiddity of words; he could look at English from the outside. Other Broadway lyricists also reached heights of literacy that were unequalled before or after. They belonged, however indifferently, to a people who entangled piety fully in the interpretation of texts. Who else

could put so polished a spin on language itself, as Hart did in "Bewitched": "I'm wild again, beguiled again, a simpering, whimpering child again"? Who, after the rise of rock 'n' roll, writes that way anymore? Only Stephen Sondheim, who claims to have learned that Broadway is about mind as well as heart while studying mathematics at Williams College, where a music professor robbed art of its romanticism. Music, Sondheim recalled learning, was "a matter of craft and technique. . . . Art is work and not inspiration" (Secrest 1998).

Broadway was not expected to convey verisimilitude, since not even lovers or actors off-stage normally burst into song to communicate their feelings. The aim instead is to provide aesthetic delight—and to impose the bliss of order amid chaos. That task required painstaking creative effort, and to do so with flair entailed genius. The pointless agony of false starts and the desolation of utter failure afflicted even the most gifted. Rodgers and Hammerstein had tried for over a year to solve the problems of adapting George Bernard Shaw's *Pygmalion* and gave up. Refusing to heed Hammerstein's warning that such an adaptation was impossible, Lerner thereupon did it. Indeed *My Fair Lady* proved so triumphant that Nobel laureate T. S. Eliot told Rex Harrison, who starred as Henry Higgins, that the work of another Nobel laureate, "Shaw[,] is greatly improved by music" (Lees 1990). The ordeal of writing musicals nevertheless made Lerner himself a wreck, a chain-smoker who became dependent on amphetamines, a compulsive nail-biter who had to wear gloves to save his cuticles. The result was that he fitted his lyrics and book for *My Fair Lady* so seamlessly to Frederick Loewe's score that it was hard to imagine such sublimity as *constructed*. Shortly before dying, in and out of consciousness, Lerner revealed to a night-shift nurse that he had written *My Fair Lady*. No wonder she thought her patient was delirious.

Broadway offered lyricists a chance to become poets, to show off their virtuosity and wit, and even on occasion to suggest a wider world of literacy and learning. Even to achieve simplicity, arduous work was entailed—at least for Hammerstein, who sometimes needed weeks to lock a particular lyric in place. The work habits of Rodgers, by contrast, gave the impression of inspiration rather than perspiration, of an awesome fluency. Rodgers managed to match melodies to Hammerstein's words while the dinner guests were still sipping their coffee. Preparing for *South Pacific* (1949), Hammerstein gave his collaborator the typed lyric for "Bali Ha'i." Rodgers briefly examined the page before turning it over, went into another room, and five minutes later returned with the finished melody—surely among the most haunting of the thousand songs that he composed in his lifetime.

Such musicals defied snobbery—in the name of gusto, brio, force, robustness. To stir the crowd, those responsible for such shows needed dynamism, and even something daemonic and lunatic, a wild excess of energy, an anarchic superhuman force. The best performers had to project a vividness of personality that could sweep across the footlights and up into the balcony. The stars of these shows did not so much sing as roar, and were not satisfied with wooing the audience; they wanted to knock it out. From such base metals, the golden age of an art form was created, and a little vulgarity proved to be the correct aesthetic choice. The Pulitzer Prize committees formed to honor American drama didn't quite know what to do with Broadway. In 1931, when *Of Thee I Sing* became the first musical comedy awarded the prize, the winners were librettists George S. Kaufman and Morrie Ryskind and lyricist Ira Gershwin, whose brother's score was mysteriously ignored. But George Gershwin enhanced a heritage that is both accessible and blissful, and what endures of it is good music.

But is it, as Kern assured Hammerstein, good Jewish music? A popular answer in the affirmative came only in 1964, when *Fiddler on the Roof* opened. It won nine Tony Awards and ran for 3,242 performances; by 1972, when it closed, *Fiddler* set the record as the longest running musical in the history of Broadway. (That record has since been surpassed.) The musical that Jerome Robbins directed and choreographed even topped the longest run of a non-musical ever produced on Broadway, *Life with Father* (1939)—which would have been an apt title for the adaptation of the Sholem Aleichem tales as well. Any theatrical troupe in the United States that wishes to stage *Fiddler on the Roof* must be licensed to do so—and Music Theatre International has reported that over five hundred different productions are presented annually, elevating this musical consistently into the ranks of the top five nationally.

One New York producer had spurned the chance to mount *Fiddler on the Roof* because he could not envision an audience larger than the constituency for Hadassah benefits. But a musical that exposes the pressures of modernization on a Jewish family in czarist Russia nevertheless became a national and international smash hit as

well. In virtually every country where the show was scheduled to open, backers expressed the fear of a flop. But success was recorded in every country—for example, in Holland, France, Austria, Switzerland, Czechoslovakia, Rhodesia, South Africa, Greece, Turkey, Mexico, Argentina, Brazil, Sweden, Denmark, Finland, Australia. In London, the show ran four and a half years. In the first three decades after *Fiddler* had first opened on Broadway, about a hundred different productions were mounted in West Germany, and within five years after the collapse of the Berlin Wall, twenty-three versions were staged in the former German Democratic Republic. Audiences in Tel Aviv loved the show so much that eventually three Tevyes were needed. (One of them was Chaim Topol, who played the lead in the 1971 Hollywood adaptation.) Even a Yiddish version was introduced in Israel. *Fiddler on the Roof* became the longest running musical in the history of Japan. In Tokyo its producer was introduced to Joseph Stein, the librettist who had brought Sholem Aleichem to Broadway, and asked him: "Tell me, do they understand this show in America?" Stein answered in a characteristically Jewish way—with another question: "What do you mean?" The producer replied, "It's so Japanese!" (Whitfield 2003).

The impact of *Fiddler on the Roof* not only vindicated faith in the extraordinary mass appeal of the American musical, but, paradoxically, Broadway became even more Jewish—even more the cultural expression of one minority—as a result. That particular success reinforces the need to treat Broadway with the seriousness of study that is lavished on other forms and genres stemming from a Jewish sensibility. If the fiction of Franz Kafka can be designated Jewish, or if psychoanalysis can be better fathomed by examining rather than ignoring its Jewish origins, or if the sciences (or professions like law and medicine) can also be considered in the light of Jewish attraction to such fields, why not the musical theater? To neglect it would leave too many works unrecognized and unappreciated. Kern's guarantee to Hammerstein not only promised special pleasures to their audience, but enlarged the boundaries of an American Jewish culture as well.

Stephen J. Whitfield

References and Further Reading

Bergreen, Laurence. 1990. *As Thousands Cheer: The Life of Irving Berlin*. New York: Viking.

Block, Geoffrey. 1997. *Enchanted Evenings: The Broadway Musical from* Show Boat *to* Sondheim. New York: Oxford University Press.

Cahan, Abraham. 1960. *The Rise of David Levinsky.* New York: Harper & Row.

Fordin, Hugh. 1977. *Getting to Know Him: A Biography of Oscar Hammerstein.* New York: Random House.

Furia, Philip. 1992. *The Poets of Tin Pan Alley: A History of America's Great Lyricists.* New York: Oxford University Press.

Gottfried, Martin. 1984. *Broadway Musicals.* New York: Harry N. Abrams.

Gottlieb, Robert, and Robert Kimball, eds. 2000. *Reading Lyrics.* New York: Pantheon.

Henderson, Amy, and Dwight Blocker Bowers. 1996. *Red, Hot and Blue: A Smithsonian Salute to the American Musical.* Washington, DC: Smithsonian Institution.

Jones, John Bush. 2003. *Our Musicals, Ourselves: A Social History of the American Musical Theatre.* Hanover, NH: Brandeis University Press.

Lahr, John. 1996. "The Lemon-Drop Kid." *New Yorker* 72 (September 30): 68–74.

Lees, Gene. 1990. *Inventing Champagne: The Worlds of Lerner and Loewe.* New York: St. Martin's Press.

Most, Andrea. 2004. *Making Americans: Jews and the Broadway Musical.* Cambridge, MA: Harvard University Press.

Sanders, Ronald. 1976. "The American Popular Song." In *Next Year in Jerusalem: Portraits of the Jew in the Twentieth Century,* edited by Douglas Villiers, 197–219. New York: Viking.

Secrest, Meryle. 1998. *Stephen Sondheim: A Life.* New York: Alfred A. Knopf.

Whitfield, Stephen J. 2003. "Fiddling with Sholem Aleichem: A History of *Fiddler on the Roof.*" In *Key Texts in American Jewish Culture,* edited by Jack Kugelmass, 105–125. New Brunswick, NJ: Rutgers University Press.

Wilder, Alec. 1972. *American Popular Song: The Great Innovators, 1900–1950.* New York: Oxford University Press.

Jews and Hollywood

In the rise of the American motion picture industry from modest beginnings around 1900 to become, a century later, a global multimedia entertainment enterprise, Jews played a predominant role as owners and managers of movie companies, and contributed significantly as creative artists. Although Jews had previously been active in arts and communication media such as music, theater, and the press, the emergence of a new, popular medium with unprecedented national influence, apparently dominated by recent Jewish immigrants, fostered opposition and frequent demands for political and cultural control. In the wake of continuing controversies over the consequences of Jewish leadership, scholars have debated the impact of Jewish experience and values on the movies, and the transformations of American Jewish culture and the broader American society that the medium may have wrought.

The first historical question concerns what led Jewish businessmen to recognize the potential in a medium that began as silent, flickering, black-and-white images, telling brief stories or showing newsreel-style actual events, projected as part of vaudeville programs or viewed in penny arcade peep-show machines. The answer generally agreed on is that these men, immigrants from Eastern Europe who had started from the ground up in the clothing trade or in luxury goods such as furs and jewelry, were accustomed to dealing with the public and had a sense of changing tastes. They were familiar with both the working-class and immigrant ghettoes rapidly expanding in large Eastern cities, as well as the consumption desires of the native-born middle class. They began in movies primarily as exhibitors, as investors or operators in vaudeville, penny arcades, or the new storefront nickelodeon theaters that began to proliferate around 1905, at a time when most film producers came from Anglo-Saxon backgrounds and were largely technicians.

A decisive moment of change came several years later when the inventor Thomas A. Edison created a consortium of film companies with the intention of consolidating patents, controlling production, and limiting entry into the motion picture business. Although several Jewish manufacturers and importers, such as Sigmund Lubin of Philadelphia, were included in this group, informally known as the patents trust, the new Jewish entrepreneurs, some of whom had moved into film distribution, were shut out. These excluded figures fought back, expanded their operations as "independents" to include production as well as distribution and exhibition, and outclassed the conservative trust group by developing the feature-length film and promoting individual performers as popular stars. By 1915, when a federal court ruled that the patents trust was an illegal conspiracy to restrain trade, the independents had swept the field and had relocated much of their operations to the Los Angeles suburb of Hollywood, which was soon to become the motion picture "colony" famous throughout the world.

Perhaps the most remarkable aspects of the careers of these Jewish independents are their longevity and the long-term success of the companies they founded in the first quarter of the twentieth century. Paramount, Universal, Twentieth Century Fox, Metro-Goldwyn-Mayer, Columbia, and Warner Bros.: all these familiar names of Hollywood studios stem from their endeavors (even though many of these are now subsidiaries of even larger media conglomerates). Adolph Zukor's Famous Players Film Company (1912) evolved into Paramount. Carl Laemmle, who gave the independents their name with his Independent Motion Picture Corp. in 1909, formed Universal in 1912. William Fox, a distributor since 1904, began the Fox Film Corp. in 1915. Metro-Goldwyn-Mayer developed as a subsidiary of Loew's Inc., a theater circuit started by Marcus Loew in 1919. It combined production companies previously headed by Louis B. Mayer and Samuel Goldwyn; Mayer presided over M-G-M, reporting to Nicholas Schenck at Loew's, while Goldwyn continued as an independent producer. Harry and Jack Cohn, along with Jack Brandt, started a company in 1922 and two years later retitled it Columbia. The four Warner brothers, in the film business since 1907, named their firm after themselves in 1923. All of these men continued for at least several decades as company heads, and several stayed on top into the 1950s or beyond.

Who were they? Zukor (1873–1976), born in Risce, Hungary, had been a furrier. Laemmle (1867–1939), from Laupheim, Germany, ran a clothing business in Wisconsin and Chicago. Fox (1879–1952), born in Tulchva, Hungary, built up a garment industry firm. Loew (1870–1927), born on New York's Lower East Side, was also a furrier. Mayer (1885–1957), from Russia, was in the junk business. Goldwyn (1882–1974), born in Warsaw, was in the glove trade. Schenck (1881–1969), from Russia, operated pharmacies. Harry Warner (1881–1958), the eldest of four brothers, was the only one born overseas, in Kraznashiltz, Poland; they held odd jobs before becoming film exhibitors. Harry Cohn (1891–1958), like Loew from the Lower East Side, was a vaudeville performer before getting an office job at Universal. To this group could be added several additional names, such as Jesse L. Lasky (1880–1958), born in San Francisco, whose pioneering production company merged with Zukor's Famous Players, and Joseph Schenck (1877–1971), older brother of Nicholas, associated with the United Artists company and later a cofounder of Twentieth Century, which took over the Fox studio.

However uncouth and unlettered, as they were sometimes caricatured, these figures clearly comprised a remarkable generation of entrepreneurs. Secular, ambitious, eager to throw off what some saw as the hobbles of Old World Jewish life—scholars have noted how many of these men regarded their fathers as weak and unsuccessful—they were part of an immigrant vanguard who sought to enter, and in the process transformed, mainstream American culture. Working with new technologies and creating novel products, they faced fewer barriers than similar strivers in more traditional fields, and their own enterprises thrived on hyperbole and fantasy, as did few others. As early as 1915 the term *movie mogul* came into use to describe them, and it was not entirely complimentary. Deriving from the name of a sixteenth-century Mongol conqueror, it acknowledged their importance and power, but just as plainly suggested the notion of foreign barbarian invaders. Then, and later, commentators have exclaimed about how they built an empire in Hollywood, one predicated on, and demonstrating, emerging twentieth-century American values of consumption, leisure, and entertainment. But to many influential Americans, this empire was as threatening as it was wondrous.

Any reckoning of the achievements and failures of these business leaders must take into account the impact of antisemitism on their tactics and behavior. It's true that, in the very first years of the movies, before Jews became prominent, many elements in American society saw the new medium as a social danger that needed to be curtailed and controlled. The industry's struggles during later decades over such issues as censorship, monopoly power, and political propaganda might have occurred had no Jews been involved at all, but it was certainly the case that, in critical moments of controversy up through and even after World War II, antisemitism publicly or covertly was brought into play.

Given the political and cultural pressures that the industry steadily faced, for many years no one other than its enemies could afford to discuss what otherwise might seem obvious and intriguing questions: How Jewish were the movies? How were the movies Jewish? In response to facile and ominous answers, it was always intellectually respectable, and factually reasonable, for Hollywood's defenders to say that the industry attracted about as heterogeneous and polyglot a workforce as any community or business in the United States. And that it took its stories from every type of source, perhaps most especially from conservative mainstream periodicals like *The Saturday Evening Post*. And that its popular genres, such as Westerns, melodramas, horror films, crime stories and many others, had their roots in a previous era's dime novels, stage plays, and popular fiction. If Hollywood's fundamental theme was the American Dream, as some commentators have argued, then that cultural construct clearly predated the movies, in the very conception of a nation of immigrants, in the westward movement of the nineteenth century, in the tales of Horatio Alger, and in innumerable rags-to-riches stories. In this perspective, not only were Hollywood's Jewish entrepreneurs assimilatory to the core, so too did their products absorb and recycle the basic narratives that had formed and sustained the national culture.

Still, the questions remained, and long after the pioneers had passed from the scene, along with the traditional forms of antisemitism that had previously pervaded American social and business life, scholars began to feel comfortable in exploring them. The premise stemmed from the incontrovertible facts that these men were the bosses who had the power to tell production supervisors, writers, directors, and actors what to do; that they were Jews; and that most of them were immigrants. Under the circumstances, how could their Jewish experience not find its way onto the nation's movie screens? Nevertheless, the viewpoints that have been put forward so far appear to be conjectural. The most extravagant assertions have come not in scholarly studies but in a documentary film, *Hollywoodism: Jews, Movies, and the American Dream*, which is based on the book *An Empire of Their Own: How the Jews Invented Hollywood*, by Neal Gabler, but which ranges in speculation far beyond it. The film argues that the "nightmare" of nineteenth-century Jewish life in Eastern Europe is reflected in American movies and also gave rise to a counter-fantasy, a "mythical America . . . of boundless optimism, happy endings, and homespun truths." The Hollywood studios, it asserts, became "golden shtetls."

There was more to Old World Jewish life than the shtetl, to be sure, and perhaps one should take into account that, of the Jewish entrepreneurs who built the movie industry, only one, Adolph Zukor, can be said to have had actual experience of shtetl living. A more productive way to understand the role and influence of Jews in the making of

Hollywood and its movies would be to link them much more broadly to transformations in Jewish culture, both in Europe and the United States. Eastern European sites to investigate would be, not only agricultural villages, but cosmopolitan cities like Budapest, Prague, Vienna, and Berlin, where Jews played a role in theater, publishing, music, and, indeed, cinema, simultaneously with the growth of Hollywood. This expansion of Jewish intellectual and artistic endeavors spread to Paris, London, and New York, among other places, en route to Hollywood. On both continents, such steps into the mainstream inevitably involved collaborations that crossed ethnic and religious lines. The assimilatory impulse in such cases concerned more than flight or masquerade; it was an aesthetic necessity. More to the point than trying to find a direct cause-and-effect between Old World trauma and New World fantasy would be an effort to make clear the Jewish traces in hybrid modern popular culture.

The process of Jewish integration relates to larger cultural convergence and conflict in the twentieth century's first half, but is itself illuminated by specific examples. Here are two. Emanuel Goldenberg, born in Bucharest, Romania, emigrated with his family to the Lower East Side at the age of nine, attended public schools and the City College of New York, and, with theatrical ambitions, was admitted to the American Academy of Dramatic Arts. There they told him that he would never succeed with such a name, so he became Edward G. Robinson (1893–1973). After years of working in Yiddish theater and on Broadway, he went to Hollywood with the advent of talking pictures and became a star playing an Italian gangster in *Little Caesar* (1930). Julius Henry Marx (1890–1977), born uptown on New York's East Side, formed a vaudeville troupe with his brothers Leonard, Adolph, and Milton, and soon they became Groucho, Chico, Harpo, and Gummo; Groucho later remarked that the public thought they were Italian. For years they toured the country, and everywhere they stopped they honed their jokes, trying out dozens of variations to see which got the biggest laugh. Later, in their Broadway and movie careers, the Marx Brothers became legendary for bringing Jewish wit and repartee into mainstream culture, yet their verbal play had been shaped and tested in a form of dialogue with countless heartland audiences. In the case of both Robinson and the Marxes, it should be noted, their names, personas, and performance styles had been developed before they set foot on a movie soundstage.

Like the United States, Hollywood was a great absorbent. The American film industry's rise to world dominance was aided by the suspension or curtailment of film production in European countries during World War I, but it was also abetted by the necessity to serve thousands of small-town theaters in the domestic market. The studios became factories of sorts, together producing and distributing well over three hundred films per year between the two world wars. If the upper levels of management tended to be, as far as could be accomplished, closed circles of families and associates, the talent ranks were open and regularly recruited from afar. In comparison to producers, who were by a large majority Jewish in this interwar period, Jews never made up more than a significant minority among directors and writers, and a much smaller percentage among performers (even taking into account masking name changes).

Jewish directors who rose up out of the pool of extras, assistants, and technicians sometimes put on airs, like adding an aristocratic German "von" to their names, as did the major figures Erich von Stroheim (1885–1957), born in Gleiwitz, Silesia, and Josef von Sternberg (1894–1969), born in Vienna. (Stroheim maintained the fiction that he came from a Prussian military heritage, which served him well in his acting roles.) In the 1920s directors who had already built significant careers in European cinemas were lured to Hollywood, such as Ernst Lubitsch (1892–1947) from Berlin and Michael Curtiz (Miháli Kertész, 1888–1962) from Budapest, via Vienna. The coming of sound in the late 1920s led the studios to turn to the New York stage primarily for actors and writers, and also brought Broadway directors such as George Cukor (1899–1983). After Hitler's seizure of power in 1933, Jewish emigrés who managed to become Hollywood directors included Anatole Litvak (1902–1974), Robert Siodmak (1900–1973), and Billy Wilder (1906–2002).

The roster of writers is a long one. A striking number were born on the Lower East Side and had worked as journalists, playwrights, and novelists before becoming screenwriters. A poll of writers in the late 1930s, asking them to list colleagues they most admired, listed among the top ten Robert Riskin (1897–1955), Ben Hecht (1894–1964), Lillian Hellman (1905–1984), and Jo Swerling (1893–1964). The latter, perhaps the least widely known among this quartet, was the only one born overseas, in Bardichov, Russia. Among many others from this interwar period might

also be mentioned Sonya Levien (1888–1960), Samson Raphaelson (1896–1983), Morrie Ryskind (1895–1985), and the twin Epstein brothers, Julius J. (1909–2000) and Philip G. (1909–1952). Sound films also attracted composers, lyricists, and singer-performers from the world of Broadway musicals and variety reviews, including Irving Berlin (1888–1989) and the Gershwin brothers, George (1898–1937) and Ira (1896–1983), among the former and Eddie Cantor (Edward Israel Iskowitz, 1892–1964) and Al Jolson (Asa Yoelson, 1886–1950) among the latter. These names are only a sampling, but they may make a case that Hollywood, along with its business leadership, was also a center for Jewish creative artists rivaling New York and the European capitals before, of course, becoming for some a refuge from the latter.

The arrival of new creative workers from the late 1920s onward coincided with the world crises engendered by the Great Depression and the rise of Nazism, and Jewish figures among them played a central role as Hollywood became increasingly politicized during the 1930s decade. Three issues in particular occupied the film community. In the chronological order of their development, first came the effort to organize talent guilds among, respectively, writers, actors, and directors, with the formation of the Screen Writers Guild (later known as Writers Guild of America) in the forefront. In part out of the writers' struggle, the Communist Party began to recruit members for purposes of fundraising and, perhaps, influencing the ideologies and values that went into motion picture stories. A leader in the movement for a writers' guild was the playwright and screenwriter John Howard Lawson (1894–1977; his family had previously changed its name from Levy), who was unanimously elected the Guild's first president. Considered a moderate at that time, Lawson joined the Communist Party in 1936 and also took a prominent role there, becoming known as the Commissar of Hollywood communists. Later in the decade, prominent figures in the formerly isolated movie colony established the Hollywood Anti-Nazi League to agitate against the German fascist regime. Although many of its members were Jews, and stars like Eddie Cantor performed at its fund-raising events, the League's founders were not Jewish, and they aimed at developing a Popular Front–style group, in which even some studio executives and producers participated.

The historical judgment on the Jewish movie moguls is that they failed to respond to the danger that Nazism posed for German and European Jews. As a group generally, so it has been argued, they were politically conservative, had attenuated their ties to Judaism, and valued their German revenues. To these considerations must be added the political constraints they were under from hostile legislators, which culminated in 1941 with U.S. Senate hearings on "Propaganda in Motion Pictures," in which isolationist senators attacked the Jewish studio heads as foreigners who put their religious and business interests above those of the United States. They cited more than two dozen Hollywood films, among them several tentative screen efforts to deal with Nazism and the persecution of Jews, including *Escape* and *The Man I Married* (both 1940). In addition, as with Jewish leaders in other walks of life, they were given the "friendly" advice by others that to speak out would adversely affect the situation of Jews in America. Nevertheless, at least one industry leader, Harry Warner, has been credited as an unremitting opponent of Nazism, and Warner Bros. produced Hollywood's first anti-Nazi film, *Confessions of a Nazi Spy* (1939).

Even during World War II, when Hollywood's values and goals meshed as never before with those of the U.S. government, the old hostility was never more than in abeyance. In 1943 a senator was critical of allowing "recent citizens" to make U.S. Army information films; in question, among others, was director Anatole Litvak, who worked in the Signal Corps unit making the *Why We Fight* series. As the war came to an end, conservative groups both within and outside the film industry began lobbying for a purge of Hollywood Communists. The U.S. House Committee on Un-American Activities (HUAC) took up the call, although the vocal antisemitism of one of its members, a congressman from Mississippi, proved more embarrassing than effective: the committee wanted the support of Jewish moguls against their left-wing Jewish employees. HUAC got the studio heads to testify at its Hearings Regarding the Communist Infiltration of the Motion Picture Industry and then called the so-called unfriendly witnesses. Ten men were citied for contempt of Congress for refusing to answer whether they were members of the Screen Writers Guild or the Communist Party, and they went to prison when their First Amendment defense was denied. Of the Hollywood Ten, six were Jews, including Lawson, Albert Maltz (1908–1985), Alvah Bessie (1904–1985), Samuel Ornitz (1890–1957), Herbert Biberman (1900–1971), and Lester Cole (1904–1985). Shortly after the hearings, the motion picture industry enacted a "blacklist" against the Ten and all other "alleged subversives." Over the next decade, as HUAC continued its hearings, several hundred studio creative workers were blacklisted, a substantial number of whom were Jews.

The motion picture industry changed fundamentally after World War II with the blacklist; with a Supreme Court decision breaking up the studio system's vertically integrated structure that had controlled production, distribution, and exhibition; and with a rapid defection of the audience to television. After a difficult transition lasting several decades, however, the industry stabilized during the 1970s with new marketing strategies for theatrical movies and greater emphasis on producing shows for television; in subsequent years it thrived with additional revenues from video and DVD sales and film rentals. Throughout this period and beyond, with the gradual postwar decline of overt antisemitism, the prominent role of Jews in all facets of the movies and the wider entertainment industry generally became a taken-for-granted aspect of American cultural life, even though periodic attacks on Hollywood for its alleged excesses and deleterious effects on values and behavior have never entirely gone away.

In the second half of the twentieth century and beyond, the focus of inquiry might shift to another historical question, one concerning the representation of Jews on screen. In the short silent films of the earliest period, before the Jewish moguls gained control of the industry, antisemitic images were not uncommon, along with prejudiced stereotypes of many other nationalities and peoples. Such images did not entirely abate when Jews took responsibility for screen stories depicting Jewish experience: stereotypes have always been a staple of popular entertainment, and they continued to appear in films produced during the 1910s and 1920s about immigrants and life in urban ghettoes. Perhaps the most pertinent generalization is that a substantial number of films dealt with assimilation and intermarriage, such as the popular works *Abie's Irish Rose* (1929) and a multifilm series that was launched in 1926 with *The Cohens and the Kellys*. Before ascribing this emphasis to the moguls' own desire for assimilation and intermarriage, however, it should be pointed out that these films began as Broadway plays, as did the most famous Jewish-themed film of the era, the pioneering part-talkie, *The Jazz Singer* (1927).

Jewish images on screen declined during the 1930s, in part, of course, because of trepidation on the part of producers, but also because of the industry's more general self-imposed limitations on depicting nationalities and types in ways that might cause offense. (Such limitations were not applied to African Americans, however, and some later writers have utilized Hollywood's demeaning portrait of blacks to place responsibility on the Jewish moguls for provoking racial prejudice.) Mention should also be made of Yiddish-language films made outside Hollywood, on the East Coast, including five between 1937 and 1940 from Vienna-born Edgar G. Ulmer (1904–1972), formerly and later a Hollywood director. During World War II the most ubiquitous Jewish character in Hollywood films was a GI from Brooklyn who was part of an inevitably multiethnic Army platoon. As news of Nazi concentration camps emerged after the war ended, the studios produced several lauded movies with antisemitism as a theme, including the Academy Award best picture *Gentleman's Agreement* and another Oscar nominee, *Crossfire* (both 1947); neither film, it might be noted, had a Jewish director.

After a period of caution brought on by the blacklist and Cold War anti-communism, interest in Jewish subjects reawakened in the late 1950s, often impelled by successful novels and stage plays dealing with such themes as the expansion of a Jewish American middle class, the tragedy of the Holocaust, and the establishment of Israel—reflected, respectively, in works like *Marjorie Morningstar* (1958), *The Diary of Anne Frank* (1959), and *Exodus* (1960). At the same time a new generation of writers and directors entered the field, children or grandchildren of immigrants, who were unafraid of previous taboos and, as artists, often viewed Jewish lifestyles (frequently personified in the screen characters they played) with an irreverent, comic approach. This group included versatile writer-performer-directors such as Carl Reiner (b. 1922), Mel Brooks (b. 1926), and Woody Allen (b. 1935), whose *Annie Hall* (1977) won him Academy Awards for best picture, direction, and original screenplay (with Marshall Brickman), as well as a nomination for best actor. Filmmakers Sidney Lumet (b. 1924), who had performed on Yiddish-language stage and radio as a child actor, and Paul Mazursky (b. 1930) were prominent among others who consistently treated Jewish themes. Lumet's works included *The Pawn-broker* (1965) and *Bye Bye Braverman* (1968), based, respectively, on novels by Edward Lewis Wallant and Wallace Markfield. Mazursky's titles included *Blume in Love* (1973) and *Next Stop, Greenwich Village* (1976).

In an era when American cultural interest in ethnicity was beginning to revive, after decades in which assimilation had been the standard, Jewish performers found that "ethnic" appearance and speech patterns could enhance their careers rather than requiring cosmetic alteration or vocal training. (Most name changes had been taken care of by earlier generations.) Singer Barbra Streisand (b. 1942), whose unreconstructed "Jewish" features often drew critics' comments, led the way, bringing her stage role as Fanny Brice (1891–1951), a Jewish stage star of the 1920s, to the screen in *Funny Girl* (1968). Other Jewish women screen notables included Bette Midler (b. 1945), Goldie Hawn (b. 1945), and Gilda Radner (1946–1989). Among emerging male stars of the same period were Dustin Hoffman (b. 1937), Elliott Gould (Goldstein, b. 1938), Richard Benjamin (b. 1938), George Segal (b. 1934), Gene Wilder (Jerome Silberman, b. 1933), and Richard Dreyfuss (b. 1947).

Transformations in American culture and in the film industry after the 1960s were of particular significance to Jewish women creative workers in film. Opportunities for women to direct films in Hollywood had been virtually nonexistent, but, along with the rise of a new feminist movement, the industry's boundaries were becoming more porous, and novel approaches to filmmaking developed among independents outside the old studio system. Elaine May (birth name Berlin, b. 1932), also a performer, directed three films in the 1970s distributed by major companies—*A New Leaf* (1971), *The Heartbreak Kid* (1972), and *Mikey and Nicky* (1976)—with some reference to Jewish themes. Claudia Weill (b. 1947) emerged from the independent documentary movement to direct *Girlfriends* (1978) and *It's My Turn* (1980), both also major studio releases. Joan Micklin Silver (b. 1935) independently directed and produced *Hester Street* (1975), based on an 1896 novel by Abraham Cahan, and went on to make a popular romantic comedy for major studio distribution, *Crossing Delancey* (1988), which linked contemporary Jewish life with old-fashioned Lower East Side traditions. Streisand turned to directing in 1983 with *Yentl*, adapted from an Isaac Bashevis Singer story, which she produced and cowrote, in addition to taking on the title role.

The Jewish filmmaker who has made more top box-office hits than any other in Hollywood history is Steven Spielberg (b. 1947). Even though his career began in the 1970s, amid the upsurge in films featuring Jewish characters and themes, his popular blockbusters over several decades

Director Steven Spielberg and actor Liam Neeson on the set of Schindler's List. *(Universal/The Kobal Collection)*

rarely displayed direct concern with Jewish subjects. This situation changed, however, with *Schindler's List* (1993), hailed on its release as Hollywood's most important film concerning the Holocaust, winning an Academy Award for best picture, and earning for Spielberg his first Oscar as best director. Based on actual events and on a fictional version by Thomas Keneally, the film recounted the successful efforts of a German businessman, Oskar Schindler, to rescue over 1,100 Jews from the Nazi death camps in Poland and Czechoslovakia during World War II. In debates about the film, some critics argued that it drew attention away from the Holocaust as a Jewish calamity—the death of six million—in favor of the uncanny efforts of a gentile father figure.

Following *Schindler's List,* Spielberg took part in founding the Survivors of the Shoah Visual History Foundation, an organization dedicated to creating a visual record of Holocaust survivors and disseminating their accounts through film and television documentaries. *The Last Days* (1998), presenting first-person interviews with Hungarian Jewish survivors, was distributed widely in the-

aters, and *Voices from the List* (2004) appeared as a documentary on the DVD release of *Schindler's List.* In addition to Spielberg's efforts, other Hollywood-based and independent filmmakers were actively engaged in producing nonfiction films concerning the Holocaust and the testimonies of those who came through it. *Into the Arms of Strangers: Stories of the Kindertransport* (2000), a documentary recounting efforts to bring Jewish children from Germany and elsewhere in Europe to Britain before the outbreak of World War II, received a major studio release. At the beginning of a new century, fewer fiction films concerning Jewish life were being made in Hollywood, but interest in building a factual record on film of Jewish tragedy and survival remained strong.

Robert Sklar

References and Further Reading

Avisar, Ilan. 1988. *Screening the Holocaust: Cinema's Images of the Unimaginable.* Bloomington: Indiana University Press.

Birdwell, Michael E. 1999. *Celluloid Soldiers: The Warner Bros. Campaign against Nazism.* New York: New York University Press.

Carr, Steven Alan. 2001. *Hollywood and Anti-Semitism: A Cultural History up to World War II.* Cambridge, UK: Cambridge University Press.

Cohen, Sarah Blacher, ed. 1983. *From Hester Street to Hollywood: The Jewish-American Stage and Screen.* Bloomington: Indiana University Press.

Desser, David, and Lester D. Friedman. 1993, 2004. *American-Jewish Filmmakers: Traditions and Trends.* Urbana: University of Illinois Press/2nd edition (2004).

Doneson, Judith E. 1987, 2002. *The Holocaust in American Film.* Syracuse, NY: Syracuse University Press/2nd edition (2002).

Erens, Patricia. 1984. *The Jew in American Cinema.* Bloomington: Indiana University Press.

French, Philip. 1969. *The Movie Moguls.* London: Weidenfeld and Nicholson.

Friedman, Lester D. 1982. *Hollywood's Image of the Jew.* New York: Ungar.

Friedman, Lester D. 1987. *The Jewish Image in American Film.* Secaucus, NJ: Citadel.

Gabler, Neal. 1988. *An Empire of Their Own: How the Jews Invented Hollywood.* New York: Crown.

Hoberman, J. 1991. *Bridge of Light: Yiddish Film between Two Worlds.* New York: Museum of Modern Art and Schocken Books.

Hoberman, J., and Jeffrey Shandler. 2003. *Entertaining America: Jews, Movies, and Broadcasting.* New York and Princeton, NJ: Jewish Museum and Princeton University Press.

Insdorf, Annette. 1983, 1989, 2003. *Indelible Shadows: Film and the Holocaust.* Cambridge, UK: Cambridge University Press/2nd edition (1989); 3rd edition (2003).

Jacobovici, Simcha [writer and director]. 1997. *Hollywoodism: Jews, Movies, and the American Dream,* codirected by Stuart Samuels. Associated Producers.

Rogin, Michael. 1996. *Blackface, White Noise: Jewish Immigrants in the Hollywood Melting Pot.* Berkeley: University of California Press.

Short, K. R. M. 1981. "Hollywood Fights Anti-Semitism, 1945–1947." In *Feature Films as History,* edited by K. R. M. Short, 157–189. Knoxville: University of Tennessee Press.

Sklar, Robert. 1975, 1994. *Movie-Made America: A Cultural History of American Movies.* New York: Random House/revised and updated (1994).

Zierold, Norman. 1969. *The Moguls.* New York: Coward-McCann.

American Jews and the Catskills

The Catskill Mountains, around a hundred miles from New York City, were a major component of Jewish culture in the twentieth century, providing the first major resort experience for most Jews. Starting with farms in the last years of the nineteenth century, boardinghouses, bungalow colonies, and hotels spread rapidly, and by the 1950s Jewish-owned resorts offered hundreds of thousands each year the opportunity to work and vacation in a safe milieu of Jewish culture, food, communal living, and entertainment.

Ulster, Sullivan, southern Greene, and a small part of southeastern Delaware counties were the location for this resort culture from the turn of the twentieth century up to its current remnants. Its history largely started on the farms. Along with synagogues and social/cultural institutions such as the Jewish Agricultural Society and the Workmen's Circle, the farms provided the base for a year-round Jewish population. The farms were primarily dairy and chicken farms because not much else grew well. But farms were not a profitable proposition for most, so the farmers took in boarders, and many made that their main business. Some boardinghouses became *kuchalayns* ("cook for yourself" in Yiddish), where people rented a room and shared cooking and eating privileges in the kitchen and dining room; these facilities accommodated from ten to forty guests. Kuchalayns frequently developed into bungalow colonies, where people rented a small building, typically two rooms. These colonies consisted of 5 to 120 bungalows, each housing four or five people, and they were often built in a large circle or oval around a central area with a swimming pool, handball court, and other facilities. Some kuchalayns later turned into hotels. For other farmers, the expansion of the boardinghouse led directly to hotels. And many hotels were started from scratch, often built with lumber cut and milled on the premises.

These origins made the Catskills experience a very familial one. In kuchalayns and bungalow colonies, people were together the entire summer, forming very close connections in a mini-society. By the 1950s few kuchalayns remained. But the small (50–250 guests) and medium-sized (250–500 guests) hotels retained the intimacy. The owners, often in-laws, were very hands-on, working in various capacities. They mingled with guests, many of whom were relatives and friends. Even in the large hotels, with 500 to 900 guests, the owners, guests, and staff often knew each other, especially after years of returning to vacation and work in the same resorts.

Over the course of the twentieth century, there were 703 bungalow colonies and 1,133 hotels. At any given time in the 1950s and 1960s, about 500 of the colonies and 550 hotels were operating.

The Catskills had a very strong community orientation. Smaller hotels frequently employed "solicitors" to recruit guests from their neighborhoods. Guests returned year after year, often from generation to generation: a child in the day camp might later be a junior counselor, later still a busboy or waiter in the dining room, and then a guest with a spouse and children. Hotel workers developed close ties with each other, with the owners, and with long-standing guests. Staff–guest romances also contributed to the continuing connections.

People experienced the larger community through frequent visits to delis and shops in nearby towns, in the routine walks past other resorts that were so closely bunched, and in visiting friends and relatives in other hotels and bungalow colonies. Bungalow dwellers were always sneaking into the hotel casinos (night clubs, not gambling casinos) for the shows, guests at the small hotels were doing the same in the larger hotels, and staff visited other hotels for romance.

Catskills hotel owners developed the all-inclusive vacation, with three meals plus a nighttime tearoom, nightly entertainment, many sports and activities, and eventually day camps for children. Nighttime shows included comics and singers on weekend nights, a champagne night (with a guest dancing contest plus dance team exhibitions), a movie night, a bingo night, and a talent show. Sports were common, especially handball, softball, basketball, and tennis; some grander places featured

Entertainment at Grossinger's in the Catskills, 1960. The resort was run by Jennie Grossinger until her death in 1972. (Bettmann/Corbis)

horseback riding and indoor ice skating rinks. Medium-sized and large hotels offered lectures, dance lessons, portrait artists, and other activities. After World War II, the large hotels, operating year-round, added winter sports. A few large hotels had their own golf courses, but most shared the expenses of two municipal courses. During the many decades when gentile hotels kept Jews out, Jews could have a vacation with kosher food, engage in Yiddish conversation, and be entertained by Jewish comedy and song. In the Catskills they could become Americanized while preserving much of their Jewishness. American Jewish humor grew up in the Catskills, where any Jewish comedian worth his laughs got his or her start. The term *Catskills comic* is still widely used.

The range of costs among the resorts led to class stratification, but Jews of all classes came to the resorts. Even the more expensive places were accessible to those with lower incomes, if only for a weekend. People in their teens and twenties worked their way through college and professional or graduate school at these hotels, making the Catskills an important feature of Jewish upward mobility.

Today, the Catskills appear quite different from even two or three decades ago. Hundreds of hotels have ceased to exist since the 1960s, and only a handful remain. Many bungalow colonies remain, most of them Orthodox and Hasidic, though some are secular. Yoga ashrams, Zen meditation centers, drug rehab programs, and mental health and developmental disabilities facilities have taken over many of the old hotels. The town streets, once crowded with guests, workers, and locals who serviced the resorts, are much quieter, and there are many vacant storefronts and high unemployment.

There will not likely be a resurgence of resort building, but the Catskills remain a powerful memory and a draw for people. Many have bought summer homes, including condos developed out of old bungalow colonies and even some hotels. Orthodox Jews of many types continue to make the Catskills a distinctively Jewish location through their widespread network of bungalow colonies, camps, and yeshivas.

Phil Brown

References and Further Reading

Brown, Phil. 1998. *Catskill Culture: A Mountain Rat's Memories of the Great Jewish Resort Area.* Philadelphia: Temple University Press.

Brown, Phil, ed. 2002. *In the Catskills: A Century of the Jewish Experience in "The Mountains."* New York: Columbia University Press.

Lavender, Abraham, and Clarence Steinberg. 1995. *Jewish Farmers of the Catskills.* Gainesville: University Press of Florida.

Richman, Irwin. 1998. *Borscht Belt Bungalows: Memories of Catskill Summers.* Philadelphia: Temple University Press.

American Jews and the Comics

Jewish artists, writers, and publishers have played as important a role in the development of the American comics, as Jews have in Hollywood, in popular and classical music, and in musical theater from the beginning of the twentieth century to the present day. Jews have been involved with the American comics from their very beginning as a mass medium in the 1890s in New York City. Joseph Pulitzer (who was Jewish) and William Randolph Hearst were engaged in a competition to win readers, many of them immigrants who could not read English well, for their newspapers. In the 1890s, Pulitzer began running R. F. Outcault's *Hogan's Alley* and *The Yellow Kid* in *The New York World*. Outcault himself was not Jewish, but he appealed to immigrants, many of them Jews, with these comic strips about life in the tenements. Hearst, understanding that the combined visual and verbal appeal of the comics was especially suited to new speakers of English, soon began a bidding war for Outcault's services, and the race to develop more and more comics was on.

Because, like film, the comic strip was a new and rapidly expanding art form, any talented artist or writer could get into the field at the beginning of the twentieth century. There was no need for an academic education or a pedigree, and an artist did not have to know an exclusively American tradition or style to succeed, since there was none at the time. Moreover, the Jews, like other immigrants from Europe, had the advantage of having seen some of the European comics by the eighteenth-century Swiss Rudolph Topfer (widely credited with creating modern comics) and the nineteenth-century German Wilhelm Busch that had preceded American comics. In addition, Yiddish culture brought its own potential contributions to the comics' affinity for fantasy: the Golem and other Jewish legends.

The story of the Jewish contribution to the comics parallels the larger story of Jews moving from Yiddish and the Lower East Side to English and the mainstream of society. Three main periods in this parallel movement can be discerned. First, from approximately 1900 to 1930, Jews writing comics either avoided their ethnicity by never mentioning it or explored, via ethnic humor, their place as recent immigrants in American society. During the second period, approximately from 1930 to 1960, some Jews produced comics in what might be called a masked style, in which their ethnicity was present, but not obvious. Finally, in the period from 1960 to the present, Jews openly wrote and illustrated comics as Jews about Jewish issues.

In the first period, 1900 to 1930, the dynamic is between the poles of assimilation and ethnic humor, both of which can be seen as attempted Jewish adaptations to America. Rube Goldberg, the first nationally successful Jewish comics artist, never discussed any aspect of Jewish identification in his works. As Martin Sheridan notes, Goldberg's father was a staunch Republican, a land speculator, and at one point the police chief of San Francisco. He wanted his son to take a degree in engineering, which, as a dutiful son, Rube did, while drawing cartoons for the University of California–Berkeley newspaper. But Rube never worked as an engineer. His comics career lasted from the moment he graduated until around the time he was awarded the Pulitzer Prize in 1948, after which he became a sculptor. Goldberg was one of the most successful cartoonists of his time. He made good use of his engineering knowledge in his famous renditions of complicated, nonsensical machines. But there was no Jewish element whatsoever in his work—as in the case of poet Gertrude Stein, who came from the same assimilatory, postimmigrant generation in California.

During this early period, another form of assimilation came in the form of socialism, which replaced Judaism for many Jews. There were political cartoons in the Yiddish press. In 1909, Russian immigrant poet Jacob Marinov started the *Groysser Kibitzer* (Big Joker), which was renamed the *Groysser Kundes* (Big Stick), after Teddy Roosevelt's aphorism—speak softly and carry a big stick (Buhle 1992). This magazine was based on the British journal *Punch* and the German *Simplissimus* and featured the best Yiddish cartoon artists and storytellers, most of whom were committed to socialist themes and a mockery of the rich and the Republicans. In a typical political cartoon, the Jewish American working class was shown toiling in Pharoah's land, from which they would supposedly be led out by Karl Marx, who looked like and replaced Moses. This magazine, which lasted until 1927, was in Yiddish, but it had little traditionally Jewish content.

Other Jews, like members of many minority groups, used ethnic humor to comment on their status as immigrants in America. Like assimilation and socialist universalism, this too was an attempt to adapt to America, in this case by mocking, albeit gently, pronounced Jewish ethnicity. In 1914, Harry Hershfield, who was born in Cedar Rapids, Iowa, and studied in Chicago, began *Abie the Agent.* This was the first comic strip for adults, featuring a lovably stereotypical Jewish salesman, Abie, a companion for other ethnic comics characters like the Irishmen Mutt and Jeff or George Herriman's half-white, half-black Krazy Kat. The other characters in *Abie the Agent* were named Reba, Little Sidney, Minsk, and Sparkbaum. Abie faces many problems, but usually manages to find some solace in his situation. Hershfield became the star of radio shows, including one entitled *Meyer the Buyer,* and was in great demand as a comedian. He published a book with 500 of the best jokes he had heard. As Martin Sheridan notes, *Abie the Agent* was one of the longest running comics strips in history, and at its height brought Hershfield about $125,000 a year, a fabulous sum for the 1920s and 1930s.

Another Jewish cartoonist of the 1920s and 1930s who managed to get into the mainstream by working the vein of ethnic humor was Milt Gross. His comic strip for the *New York World,* wittily entitled *Gross Exaggerations* and republished under the title *Nize Baby,* featured English-Yiddish dialect, as did his other strips, *Dave's Delicatessen* and *That's My Pop.* His *Hiawatta* brilliantly and hilariously renders Longfellow's poem in Yiddish dialect. When reading Gross, we are always in the wisecracking, street-smart New York Jewish immigrant world, and his is an entirely authentic rendering of the linguistic patterns of that rough-and-tumble world. As Martin Sheridan points out, gangster Dutch Schultz was one of Gross's classmates in school in New York, and Gross, a "natural" who never attended art school, perfected his drawing technique with pool chalk between shots. At the age of twelve he went to work in the art department of the *New York Journal,* and, even at that early age, he would ghost work for artists who were late with their drawings. Both Oliver Wendell Holmes and President Calvin Coolidge declared Gross their favor-

Abie the Agent, 1930 (Library of Congress)

ite cartoonist. The very versatile Gross was also a movie writer, talented enough to be chosen to work with Charlie Chaplin on *The Circus.* He was capable of juggling three movie scripts and a bunch of cartoons at the same time. Among his other achievements is a full-length novel without words, perhaps the first American graphic novel—it had thousands of pictures—and was entitled *She Done Him Wrong.*

In the midcentury period, from approximately 1930 to 1960, Jews moved into the mainstream of the comics by expressing their ethnicity in a masked way, somewhat akin to Franz Kafka's masked obsession with antisemitic themes, such as the absurd but deadly ritual murder accusation that is never mentioned but ever-present in his novel *The Trial.* Using stereotypes, if benign ones, Gross and Hershfield had depicted Jews as immigrants undergoing Americanization and had made a commercial success of it. Rube Goldberg became a phenomenally successful cartoonist without mentioning his Jewish identity. But, as successful as these artists were in terms of sales, Jewish creators had not yet produced a mainstream American mythological character. This was soon to happen, in the form of a masked hero.

Superman was created in the 1930s by two young Jewish men from Cleveland, Joe Shuster and Jerry Siegel. The character Superman has been interpreted as the wish fulfillment of two intellectual high school students who, in the transformation from bespectacled Clark Kent to Superman, may have seen themselves imaginatively transformed into athletic musclemen. This transformation might have been particularly appealing to Jewish student intellectuals wishing to fit in with their surroundings during the antisemitic thirties. It is also clearly a Jewish wish-fulfilling response to Hitler, in that only a Superman perhaps could have succeeded in turning back Hitler and restoring Jewish honor.

If we look at the clues in the comic strip itself, Superman's Jewish identity becomes haunting. He has no home planet; it was destroyed—as Judaea was by the Romans. He is an alien in his society, however well he seems to blend into it and share its values as Clark Kent—a typical, if intellectual, American. His father's name was Jor-El, and *El* means God in Hebrew. Superman's own name is Kal-El, or God "lite," because in Hebrew *kal* means lightweight or simple. Superman is in love with Lois Lane, an all-American, obviously Christian girl, but he cannot reveal his true identity to her or to anyone else. And he could have been circumcised with kryptonite. (Al Weisner's "Shaloman," 1997, an Orthodox imitation of a Superman who has come out of the closet as it were, wears a kippa, sports a Hebrew letter *Shin* on his chest, and fights the villains Dr. Traif and H. Porkney Chops.)

Jews seem to have had a special affinity for masked or disguised characters. Bob Kane (Bob Kahn) and Bill Finger, the primary creators of *Batman,* were Jewish, as were Stan Lee (Stanley Martin Lieber), the creator of *Spider-Man,* and Jack Kirby (Jack Kurtzberg), creator of the Fourth World sci-fi series. Arie Kaplan has pointed to many Jewish ideas embedded in their works. Will Eisner created the masked Spirit detective character, while publishers Harry Donenfeld, Jack Liebowitz, and Max Gaines created All-American Comics, featuring many masked characters.

Max Gaines (born Max Ginzberg) was the father of the modern comic book and much more. A salesman, he was out of work and living with his family in his mother-in-law's house when in 1933 he began looking at some Sunday newspaper supplements in her attic. He decided that they could be produced in book form and developed the idea with his friend Harry L. Wildenberg, who worked at a printing plant. In 1934 the first issue of *Famous Funnies* appeared and became a great success. It was Gaines who, now working for the McClure newspaper syndicate, listened when his assistant Sheldon Mayer told him about *Superman,* which had not found a publisher for five years after having been created by Siegel and Shuster. Soon Gaines had turned the strip into a comic book that would be published by the new firm DC Comics, run by Donenfeld and Leibowitz. Within two years of *Superman*'s first publication in 1938, it was appearing in 300 newspapers around the world, and the Superman fan club had 200,000 members. Gaines also founded EC Comics, which meant Educational Comics, and published moralistic children's titles, the Bible, and self-help works, including *Psychoanalysis Comics,* in comic book form.

His son William went on to change EC Comics, whose didacticism was selling poorly, into Entertaining Comics, which published *Tales from the Crypt, The Vault of Horror,* and *Two-Fisted Tales,* among other very popular series. These were the brainchildren of Gaines and his most gifted editors, Harvey Kurtzman and Al Feldstein, all three of whom are legendary in comics. Always a comics devotee, Kurtzman attended the Manhattan High School of Music and Art and started work with Stan Lee of Marvel comics. Feldstein, also a product of the High School of Music and Art, began as a painter, but was soon drawn to the comics.

Unable to sleep because of diet pills prescribed by his doctor, Gaines would think up horror tale "springboards," or basic conceptions, that he would bring in for Kurtzman or Feldstein to elaborate on. Feldstein and Kurtzman, along with Gaines, created the horror, war, and "weird science" series that were secretly read in the 1950s against all parental advice; Feldstein would later say that he felt the success of these series was due to the fact that the EC creators were "writing up" to their youthful readers. Kurtzman was the son of an International Workers Order family, and Gaines and Feldstein, like many other Jews growing up in the thirties and forties, were as left wing as Kurtzman. It is not surprising, therefore, to see in the EC horror comics a leftist tilt, according to which rich, extortionate people always seem to get their comeuppance in a witty but grisly way. A greedy director of a disabled people's home, who has shortchanged the residents' food, is forced to run from a starving dog through dark corridors lined with razor blades. In a story entitled "Dying to Lose Weight," an un-

scrupulous diet doctor named Perdo (from the French *perdu* for "lost") prescribes weight-loss pills containing tapeworms to rich, fat patients, and is himself consumed by a giant tapeworm issuing from the coffin of one of his patient/victims. No less than the future *Mad* magazine, which EC would produce, these stories satirize American society from a "progressive" perspective.

In 1954, psychiatrist Fredric Wertham published *The Seduction of the Innocent,* which called for comic book censorship. After the resulting congressional hearings, the comic book industry imposed a censorship code on itself, and the EC titles were forced out of business. But Gaines placed his hope in a Kurtzman brainchild: *Mad Magazine.* Because it was a magazine rather than a comic book, and therefore presumably for adults, it was not subject to the censorship applied to children's comic books. As Maria Reidelbach notes, this wacky publication, much like the EC comics, employed many Jews, including political refugees and Holocaust survivors. One was Max Brandel, who had escaped death in concentration camps by amusing the Kapos and Gestapo with his caricatures of them. The cover of the very first issue prominently features the Yiddish word *Ganefs* or thieves, and many subsequent issues included Yiddishisms. The favorite *Mad* word *furshluginner* is, according to Philologos, the Yiddish linguist of the New York *Forward,* a concentration camp word composed of Yiddish and German, meaning "stinking." *Mad*'s mascot, a schlemiel named Alfred E. Neuman, has a likeness that has been traced as far back as 1895 by Maria Reidelbach, but whose name is now Jewish. From a left-wing viewpoint akin to that driving the old EC horror titles, *Mad* satirized greed, advertising hype, Senator Joseph McCarthy, and the monolithic Disney organization for imposing white gloves on its characters. With its use of Yiddishisms and other expressions of ethnic identity, *Mad* helped bring about the third period of the comics: the time from the 1960s on, when Jews began to discuss Jewish issues as Jews, openly and confidently, partly no doubt as a result of America's emphasis on identity politics during these years.

Bill Gaines' stand against censorship and *Mad*'s freewheeling social criticism served as the inspiration for the underground comics of the 1960s, which deliberately broke all sexual and other taboos. One of those broken taboos was the masked, hidden tradition of ethnic expression. Now expressions of ethnicity could be open. After he left *Mad,* Kurtzman ran a similar magazine called *Help!*

(1960–1965). *Help!* published many of those who would later become the most famous underground comics creators, including Robert Crumb, who was not Jewish, but was married to a Jewish comics artist. Both of them were attracted to Jewish themes. One of Crumb's most notorious works, published long after he left Kurtzman, "What if the Jews Took Over America," is a fantasy revealing what antisemites think about Jews: wealthy Jews enjoy the fat of the land while non-Jews go begging. Crumb, as the illustrator of David Mairowitz's *Introducing Kafka,* has also produced an empathetic vision of Kafka as a Jewish writer in antisemitic Prague. Gloria Steinem, the feminist writer, also got her start at *Help!* Other women creators of the underground period include Robert Crumb's wife, Aline Kominsky-Crumb, who treats many Jewish themes in the couple's *Self-Loathing Comics,* often from a self-critical perspective, and Sharon Rudahl, whose autobiographical works include scenes of pogroms and other episodes of Jewish history. As Arie Kaplan points out, Trina Robbins, the feminist daughter of a Yiddish journalist, has created a comic book memorial to the Triangle Shirtwaist Factory fire. More traditional artists also began using the comics format to explore Jewish themes. For instance, Morris Epstein in 1963 produced *A Picture Parade of Jewish History,* which used the comics to depict the biographies of great Jewish figures.

The satirical tradition of *Mad* and the underground comics' treatment of serious subjects finally fused with the artistry of Will Eisner to create the graphic or comic book novel, which is the serious and adult form of the comics, freed from all restraints and able to tackle important and complex issues. In 1940, while still in his twenties and drawing and writing the newspaper comic strip *The Spirit,* Eisner prophesied that the comics would one day become a serious art form. He realized this prediction only in 1978, by publishing *A Contract with God,* widely acknowledged as the first American graphic novel (a term that he invented). Set in a 1930s tenement, with a Jewish protagonist, this work has a melodramatic sense of plot, design, and characterization obviously influenced by Eisner's father's work as a set painter in the Yiddish theater. Similarly, Eisner's *A Life Force* (1983) is set in the Depression-era Bronx. Jacob Shtarkah, a carpenter who has built the study hall for a synagogue, has finished his job and is being let go. The novel describes the difficulty of survival among Jewish and Italian immigrants and déclassé native-born

Americans during the Depression. Besides being a pioneer of the graphic novel, Eisner is one of the finest teachers of comic art, as he demonstrates in his textbook, *Comics and Sequential Art.*

The most important Jewish writer/artist working in the new art form that Eisner developed is Art Spiegelman, who has said that he was influenced by the holy Jewish writings of Franz Kafka and Harvey Kurtzman. Spiegelman was the creator of the Topps Garbage Pail kids and, with his wife Françoise, of the avant-garde comics journal *Raw.* He also did the unforgettable 9/11 *New Yorker* cover showing the Twin Towers in a black ink that makes them disappear as the cover is shifted in the light. But his most famous work is the brilliant autobiographical graphic novel *Maus,* which tells the story of his parents' survival during the Holocaust and of his own problems as the son of survivors growing up in Rego Park, Queens. This work, which won the Pulitzer Prize in 1992 in a unique category, and which is comparable in depth and power to some of the creations of Kafka and Dante, is the only work of genius to date in the new genre.

Using mice for Jews, cats for Nazis, and dogs for Americans, *Maus* brings new understanding to the Holocaust and its human costs. On one hand, the animals mask the full horror of what transpired, but on the other, they illustrate the fact that under the Nazis people became animals. As Joseph Witek notes, Spiegelman's most important technique in this work is his juxtaposition of past and present. He shows how the present is always under the shadow of the past, be it in the form of the concentration camp watchtower glimpsed from his studio window, the photos of dead family members that cover up the living, girls seemingly hanging in a forest in the Catskills as his father recounts the outcome of a concentration camp rebellion, or the UPC bar code juxtaposed on the bars of Spiegelman's father's concentration camp uniform on the back cover of volume 2. The word *Catskill* itself becomes a pun on the animals (cats-kill), and Liberty, New York, represents exactly what it says: liberty for Spiegelman's parents. The most harrowing part of this moving autobiographical work, however, occurs when he takes his mouse mask off and speaks as a person about his mother's suicide. This episode, entitled "Prisoner on the Hell Planet," reveals his feelings with brutal honesty, rendered in a surrealistic and dark woodcut style. Yet *Maus* offers hope, too, in the form of several supernatural incidents that offered his parents hope during their struggle, and that seem to indicate divine intervention in human affairs.

Another important and overtly Jewish comics artist of today is Harvey Pekar. His works bring us back to the origin of American Jewish comics in the Socialist tradition. *American Splendor* is realistically set in a Cleveland of telephone poles, garbage cans, and the VA hospital in which he works as a file clerk. He specializes in slices of life that, as Robert Crumb has remarked, are so mundane that they become unusual. A "Big Divorce Issue" and *Our Cancer Year* by him and his wife, artist Joyce Brabner, address the tragedies of everyday life. Pekar's sympathy for the average worker and acknowledgment of his own roots can be seen, for instance, in his nostalgic memorialization of the Jewish ragpickers of an earlier generation in Cleveland. This is proletarian realism with a modern face.

Many other names would have to be added to make this list complete and completely up-to-date. Helena Schlam enumerates and describes the work of dozens of Jewish comics creators at work today. Among contemporary creators, Leah Finkelshteyn especially points to Archie Rand, with his *Amidah* series; Jordan Gorfinkel and his *Promised Land* comic strip; Ben Katchor with *The Jew of New York* and *Julius Knipl, Real Estate Photographer;* and James Strum, creator of *The Golem's Mighty Swing,* the story of a Jewish baseball team. The combination of Jews and the comics is—and will continue to be—as American as apple pie.

Stephen E. Tabachnick

References and Further Reading
Buhle, Paul. 1992. "Of Mice and Menschen: Jewish Comics Come of Age." *Tikkun* 7,2 (March–April): 9–16.
Buhle, Paul. 2003. "The New Scholarship of the Comics." *The Chronicle Review* (May 16): B7–B9.
Finkelshteyn, Leah. 2003. "Thwak! To Our Enemies." *Hadassah Magazine* (June–July): 44–49.
Goodwin, George. 2001. "More Than a Laughing Matter: Cartoons and Jews." *Modern Judaism* 21,2: 146–174.
Kaplan, Arie. 2003. "Kings of Comics." *Reform Judaism* 32,1 (Fall): 14–22, 97; 32,2 (Winter): 10–14, 60–62.
Kaplan, Arie. 2004. "Kings of Comics." *Reform Judaism* 32,3 (Spring): 12–16, 44, 94–95.
Mann, Ron, director. 1988. *Comic Book Confidential.* Sphinx Productions.
Reidelbach, Maria. 1991. *Completely Mad: A History of the Comic Book and Magazine.* Boston: Little, Brown.
Schlam, Helena Frenkil. 2001. "Contemporary Scribes: Jewish American Cartoonists." *Shofar* 20,1: 94–112.
Sheridan, Martin. 1977. *Comics and Their Creators: Life Stories of American Cartoonists.* Westport, CT: Hyperion.
Tabachnick, Stephen E. 1993. "Of *Maus* and Memory: The Structure of Art Spiegelman's Graphic Novel of the Holocaust." *Word & Image* 9,2 (April–June): 154–162.
Tabachnick, Stephen E. 2004. "The Religious Meaning of Art Spiegelman's *Maus.*" *Shofar* 22,4 (Summer): 1–13.
Witek, Joseph. 1989. *Comic Books as History: The Narrative Art of Jack Jackson, Art Spiegelman, and Harvey Pekar.* Jackson: University Press of Mississippi.

American Jews and Television

Jews invented the American television business to an even greater extent than Neal Gabler claims they invented the Hollywood film industry. The movies had been around for twenty years before Jewish moguls took over the major West Coast studios in the mid-1910s. With TV, Jewish owners, executives, and creative personnel dominated the medium from its inception in the late 1940s. Commercial television in the United States evolved from radio. The major radio networks—NBC, CBS, and ABC—became the major TV networks, and they were all run by Jews: David Sarnoff at NBC, William Paley at CBS, and, by the early 1950s, Leonard Goldenson at ABC. (Allen DuMont of the short-lived DuMont network was the sole non-Jewish exception.)

As with motion pictures, however, what could be perceived (and was perceived by antisemites) as Jewish "overrepresentation" *behind* the scenes translated, for the most part, into just the opposite *on* the screen—until quite recently. Since the late 1980s, an unprecedented surge in episodic series, mainly comedies, featuring Jewish main characters has taken place. Around forty such shows have aired in the past fifteen years, compared with no more than seven in the previous forty years (Brook 2003, 2006). Why has this "Jewish" TV trend occurred at this historical moment? And what does the trend say about Jewish identity in postmodern American culture?

The Early Years: We've Come a Long Way . . . Except on TV

Early television was not a wasteland for Jewish images. Indeed, the first successful sitcom was a Jewish show, *The*

Getrude Berg, as Molly Goldberg in The Goldbergs.
(Bettmann/Corbis)

Goldbergs. An adaptation of a long-running hit radio show, *The Goldbergs* (1949–1956) was created and written by Gertrude Berg, who also starred as Molly Goldberg, the cuddly, Yiddish-accented matriarch of an upwardly striving Jewish family living in a tenement apartment in the Bronx. When Molly and family moved in 1955 to a spacious house in the fictive suburb of Haverville, the show's narrative premise seemed to have been fulfilled. This apparent nod to the Goldbergs' good fortunes, however, was largely a reaction to the show's sagging ratings and the changing TV times (e.g., lowest common denominator programming and the shift to the white, middle-class, suburban sitcom), factors that would lead to the show's cancellation a year later.

An additional, ethnically specific ground for the show's demise was the Jewish-dominated entertainment business's time-honored aversion to being "too Jewish." According to *Goldbergs* co-producer Cherney Berg, son of Gertrude, it was network executives, not his mother, who dictated the show's suburban diaspora. Ashamed of their own Jewishness, these men, Berg averred, "had a fit about

the show being Jewish. They wanted the Goldbergs to be the O'Malleys and it just couldn't be done" (Brook 2003). Indeed, Molly's Yiddishisms, neighborly chats, and gefilte fish seemed out of place in the WASPish enclave, and, with a family who now flocked *Father Knows Best*–style around Papa Jake on his return home from work, the thoroughly domesticated Molly was no longer even the center of the Goldberg universe.

No sitcom or other episodic series with explicitly identified Jewish protagonists aired on any of the major networks from the end of *The Goldbergs* until the early 1970s. The implicitly Jewish comedy series *The Jack Benny Program* (1950–1965) made it into the 1960s, but Benny's Jewishness, like George Burns's of *The Burns and Allen Show* (1950–1958), remained closeted and undisclosed. Gone also by the late 1950s were the Jewish-hosted, Yiddish-spiced variety shows that, together with live anthology dramas, had dominated early TV, most notably Milton Berle's *Texaco Star Theater* (1949–1953) and Sid Caesar's *Your Show of Shows* (1950–1954, reprised until 1958). Berle's vaudeville format and Borscht Belt shtick went over particularly well with the East Coast urban audience who made up the bulk of early TV viewership, turning the show into the highest-rated prime-time series and its star into Mr. Television. Caesar's show is Exhibit A for Jewish influence on the creative side of the business. Quantitative studies have confirmed the disproportionate number of Jewish writers and producers, especially in comedy, throughout TV history. The Jewish writers on *Your Show of Shows* are a Who's Who of the genre: Carl Reiner, Woody Allen, Mel Brooks, Larry Gelbart, Mel Tolkin, Neil and Danny Simon. *The Dick Van Dyke Show* (1961–1965), about the behind-the-scenes shenanigans of a TV comedy show, was created by Reiner as a self-reflexive homage to *Your Show of Shows*. The show had to be heavily de-Judaized to get the network's green light (Van Dyke's writer character was "converted" to Christianity, as was Reiner's own show-within-the-show star), a fact that epitomizes TV's wholesale retreat from Jewish imagery in the post-*Goldbergs*/pre-*Bridget Loves Bernie* era.

The latter show, an intermarriage sitcom about a Jewish young man and an Irish Catholic young woman, was a curious way to attempt a re-Judaization of prime time. The theme was neither unfamiliar, nor historically unpopular, to Jewish and non-Jewish audiences. *Bridget Loves Bernie* (1972–1973) was essentially an updating of the 1924 Anne Nichols play *Abie's Irish Rose,* which had spawned a host of imitators and had been adapted for the big screen in 1928 and again in 1946. TV itself had dealt with Jewish outmarriage as early as 1948, the first year of network television, and on occasional episodes and anthology dramas thereafter. *Bridget Loves Bernie* came on the heels of a major survivalist crisis, however, triggered by population surveys showing unprecedentedly high intermarriage rates. In this context, it is not surprising that the reaction to the show, from virtually the entire spectrum of American religious Judaism, was instant and virulently negative. Due to the controversy and despite high ratings, the show was cancelled after one season.

Just as the attempt at a Jewish sitcom revival was part of the overall TV industrial turn in the 1970s to more "relevant" and ethnically specific programming (*Sanford and Son, All in the Family, Good Times, Chico and the Man*), the reaction of Jewish advocacy groups to *Bridget Loves Bernie* was part of a larger trend related to the civil rights and identity politics movements of the 1960s and 1970s. The rise of image monitoring in general, and the harsh reaction to *Bridget Loves Bernie* in particular, makes *Rhoda*'s prime-time existence, much less its survival for five comparatively controversy-free years (1974–1979), all the more perplexing. Spun off from the hugely popular *Mary Tyler Moore Show, Rhoda* starred Valerie Harper (a non-Jew, as was Bernie portrayer David Birney) as a dark-complexioned, nasal-inflected Jewish Woman in Search of Marriage. This was the stereotypical role she had played for four years on *Mary Tyler Moore*: the New York Jewish "wry" to her best buddy Mary Richards's white bread Minnesota WASP. Just two months into her own series, however, Rhoda Morgenstern of the Bronx was exchanging vows with an Italian Catholic construction company owner, Joe Girard (played by the Jewish David Groh).

A common explanation for why Jewish media monitors let the intermarriage issue slide on *Rhoda* but not on *Bridget Loves Bernie* is that, while the latter show was *premised* on intermarriage, the former show was not: Rhoda herself—a much beloved character from her *Mary Tyler Moore* days—was the crux of her sitcom. *Rhoda*'s writers did strive for a certain Jewish "sensibility"—a strong sense of family, Rhoda's self-deprecating humor, her warmth and sensuality—but the show's overall Jewishness, as Executive Producer Charlotte Brown related, "was just 'set dressing'—[mother] Ida's brisket, her plastic on the furniture" (Brook 2003).

Another explanation for the disparate reactions to Rhoda's and Bernie's intermarriage has precisely to do with Jewishness, combined with gender. According to the Jewish tradition of matrilineal descent—since revised by the Reform movement but the normative position of organized Jewry in the 1970s—the children of an intermarried Jewish woman are considered Jewish, while those of an intermarried Jewish man are not. The Jewish Population Survey of 1970 further suggested that an intermarried Jewish mother, rather than a Jewish father, was a greater guarantor of Jewish continuity because she was more likely to raise her offspring Jewish. Narratively speaking, therefore, whatever remained of Rhoda's Jewishness had a much better chance of being passed on than Bernie's, making her, if not exactly a positive role model for Jewish survivalism, at least less of a threat. Nonetheless, the critical assessment of *Rhoda*'s media effect on and for Jewish women, and Jews as a whole, was and remains decidedly mixed, with negative stereotyping and assimilation as the main bugaboos. Rhoda's mother Ida (also played by a non-Jew, Nancy Walker) exemplifies the post-*Goldbergs* downshift from the nurturing *Yiddishe Momme* to the overbearing Jewish Mother, while Rhoda herself is, for many, the very embodiment of assimilation.

Jewish representation on television in the 1970s was also affected by what Howard Suber (1975) terms the platoon trend. Likening TV's then current "obsession with minorities" to Hollywood's rash of pluralist platoon-combat movies during World War II, Suber found "that it didn't really matter which ethnic groups were represented. . . . Characters 'happened' to be Jewish, or 'happened' to be Polish, or 'happened' to be black . . . as if by accident." *Barney Miller* (1975–1982), *Welcome Back, Kotter* (1975–1979), and *Taxi* (1978–1983) offer classic examples of the platoon-type show with a nominally Jewish lead (Hal Linden's Barney Miller, Gabriel Kaplan's Gabe Kotter, and Judd Hirsch's Alex Rieger, respectively). All in all, by the end of the 1970s, one could usefully reverse Edith Bunker's famous quip in an episode of *All in the Family* about the social progress of African Americans—"They've come a long way . . . on TV!"—and conclude about America's Jews: "They've come a long way . . . except on TV!"

1980s Onward: Here Comes the Trend

The situation changed dramatically—literally and figuratively—in the 1980s, largely due to the smash hit 1978 miniseries *Holocaust*. Piggybacking on the phenomenally successful 1977 African American saga *Roots*, *Holocaust*, despite ethical and aesthetic qualms, has been hailed as an epochal event from a Jewish representational standpoint. An onslaught of Jewish-themed made-for-TV movies and miniseries followed, with one or more per year airing throughout the 1980s. Yet this indisputable trend in Jewish TV movies must be contrasted, and reconciled, with a comparative dearth of—indeed a decline in—Jewish episodic programming over the same period, certainly with regard to the situation comedy.

As for dramatic series, the number of recurring Jewish characters increased slightly, if significantly: Mick Belker and Henry Goldblume on *Hill Street Blues* (1981–1987); Stuart Markowitz and Dr. Rebecca Meyer on *L.A. Law* (1986–1994) and *Buck James* (1987–1988), respectively; Joe Kaplan on *Our House* (1986–1988); and Paul Pfeiffer on *The Wonder Years* (1988–1993). Drs. Daniel Auschlanger and Wayne Fiscus were arguably the first Jewish protagonists (albeit in a large ensemble cast) in a dramatic series, on *St. Elsewhere* (1982–1988), and they were followed by the yuppie adman Michael Steadman (and his insecure sister Melanie) on *thirtysomething* (1987–1991). But between the 1979 finale of *Rhoda* and the debut in July 1989 of *The Seinfeld Chronicles* (later *Seinfeld*), Jewish sitcoms consisted only of the quasi-Jewish *Taxi* (1978–1983) and the extremely short-lived *Harry* (March 4–25, 1987), starring Alan Arkin as the Jewish purchasing agent at a New York City hospital. For the generic bulwark of Jewish representation on U.S. television, at least, it appeared that the more things changed, the more they stayed the same.

As did the reasons for the representational stasis: Jews' numerical dominance of the management and creative end of the business, along with anxiety over antisemitic reaction to this perceived imbalance. The long-standing aversion among Jewish executives to drawing attention to themselves had been exacerbated by the *Bridget Loves Bernie* affair. "They don't want to be bothered," opined Eric Goldman, director of the Jewish Media Office, by the sort of controversy that befell the ill-starred intermarriage-comedy. As for the paradoxical rise in Jewish-themed TV movies, Goldman suggested that the occasional rather than regular treatment of Jewish characters and issues was permissible for Jewish executives, because it allowed for a "uniqueness" of presentation but was comparatively "safe" (Elkin 1985).

Even *Seinfeld*, the show that would help launch the Jewish sitcom trend, was initially rejected by (Jewish) NBC head Brandon Tartikoff for its alleged "too Jewishness": the eponymous star's Jewish name and features, his stand-up comic occupation, and the show's "Jew York City" location amounted to ethnic overkill for the network brass. *Seinfeld*, of course, not only survived NBC's self-imposed antisemitism but would go on to become one of the supernovas of the 1990s and arguably the decade's defining series. Moreover, *Seinfeld* was far from a one-hit Jewish wonder. The period from 1989 through the mid-2000s has seen an explosion of sitcoms, and even a few dramatic series, featuring explicitly Jewish protagonists, many of them major critical and/or ratings triumphs: for example, *Brooklyn Bridge* (1991–1993), *Mad About You* (1992–1999), *The Larry Sanders Show* (1992–1998), *The Nanny* (1993–1999), *Friends* (1994–2003), *Dharma and Greg* (1997–2002), *Will and Grace* (1998–2006), *Curb Your Enthusiasm* (2000–2005), *Arrested Development* (2003–2005), and *The O.C.* (2003–).

Several reasons can be offered for this Jewish image efflorescence: a more self-confident generation of Jewish television personnel; the go-ahead from Jewish advocacy groups; narrowcasting and niche programming strategies spurred by the cable/satellite/VCR revolution; the *Cosby Show*'s encouragement of ethnically oriented fare in general; the comparative popularity of the Jewish shows. Another key factor, which contributed to the trend but also problematizes it, is the heightened conflict experienced during this period by Jews, individually and collectively, between assimilation and multiculturalism.

Jews' widespread acceptance in mainstream white America in the 1980s and 1990s came at a moment when a revitalized identity politics was putting a heightened premium on difference. These opposing integrationist and separationist tendencies not only reinforced but also threatened Jews' historically unique insider/outsider status in American society. The commercial and cultural constraints of American television necessarily muted the particularist aspects of the Jewish TV revival, but it is this very muteness that reveals the contradictions inherent in Jews' double investment in assimilation and multiculturalism. For, ultimately, Jews' socioeconomic and cultural success was achieved not through the flaunting but rather the shedding of cultural specificity, a process that not only contradicts identity politics but is also, perhaps,

Cast of the popular television show, Seinfeld. *(Corbis)*

irreversible. The de-Judaized Jews of early television—George Burns, Jack Benny, Carl Reiner—though they may have rejected religious Judaism and the immigrant experience, bore its distinctive traces nonetheless—the inflections, the Yiddishisms, the bodily mannerisms and manifestations. By contrast, the open, even proud Jews of the Jewish sitcom trend, though they may have had less to hide—on TV as in U.S. society—also have had less to show.

One of the few overtly and sympathetically Jewish of the trend shows is, not coincidentally, the one situated in the past, *Brooklyn Bridge.* Betraying its generic roots in the seminal *Goldbergs, Brooklyn Bridge* was creator Gary David Goldberg's serio-comic homage to his mid-1950s New York childhood. While set among an extended Jewish family living in a heavily Jewish neighborhood, the show refrains from ghettoizing the environment as exclusively Jewish. Irish, Italian, and other ethnic families are not only prominently displayed, but a kind of *Bridget Loves Bernie* romance between the teenaged Jewish protagonist, Alan

Silver (Danny Girard), and his Irish Catholic neighbor and sweetheart, Katie Monahan (Jenny Lewis), forms the throughline of the series. *Brooklyn Bridge* is set in the same years (1955/1956) that *The Goldbergs* was leaving the air. Thus an intertextual throughline of assimilation is also established, with *Brooklyn Bridge* extending the Americanizing notion developed in *The Goldbergs* by reflecting it back onto the inner-city environment from which the suburban-bound Goldberg family was ostensibly "movin' on up." By "bringing it all back home," *Brooklyn Bridge* thus functions as a nostalgic bridge between assimilationist and multiculturalist agendas. Assimilation need not mean homogenization, *Brooklyn Bridge* proclaims; through ritualistic remembrance, ethnic identity can be maintained.

A less sanguine assimilationist/multiculturalist inflection informs the 1990s-defining *Seinfeld.* In this series, the "particularist" Jewishness, mocked at a distance in interfaith romance shows like the contemporaneous *Anything But Love* (1991–1993), is transformed into a "universalist" Jewishness that can be derided more openly, not because

Jewishness has been absorbed into the mainstream but because the mainstream has become Jewish. As Carla Johnson (1994) observes in regard to *Seinfeld*'s quartet of *schlemiel-schlimazls* (Jerry, George, Elaine, and Kramer), the same ethno-racial sensitivity that has allowed Jews to withstand adverse social conditions over the millennia has turned them into a sociocultural barometer of these conditions. *Seinfeld*'s ascension in the ratings coincided with a steep downturn in the U.S. business cycle, culminating in the recession of 1992. As for the much touted economic boom beginning in 1993 and lasting through the 1990s, this financial upswing primarily benefited the already wealthy while leaving the average American ever further behind. In other words, the country's reduced expectations and socioeconomic "malaise," proclaimed and disavowed since the 1970s, came home to roost in the show "about nothing." On the TV-industrial front, the multicultural incursions into Seinfeld and company's once privileged white middle-class space are also uncannily reflective of the networks' shrinking audience share in the face of the cable, satellite, and videocassette revolutions. The show's ethno-spatial implosion can thus be taken as a metaphor not only for the overall middle-class economic contraction but for the breakdown of the network hegemony as well.

Besides its commercial encouragement to pursue explicitly Jewish projects, *Seinfeld* offered itself in other ways as a model for emulation—or rejection. The darkly satirical sitcom had broken a cardinal rule of the business, what Jane Feuer (1984) calls the "likeability factor": not only *Seinfeld*'s eponymous protagonist but all four of the show's main characters are insults to humankind. But Seinfeld's breach of characterological etiquette is precisely where the two shows regarded as *Seinfeld* clones—*Mad About You* and *Friends*—diverge most strikingly from their alleged model. While the main characters of *Mad About You* and *Friends* may collectively share some of *Seinfeld*'s hedonism and social irresponsibility, they differ in their pointed rejection of the latter's "no hugging, no learning" premise. *Mad About You*'s lovers and *Friends*' friends are precisely that, indeed both of these things, to one another—just the opposite of *Seinfeld*'s foursome, for whom sex and friendship are mutually exclusive and love a four-letter word. Yet while *Mad About You* and *Friends*' multiple protagonists certainly trump *Seinfeld*'s in regard to "likeability," how they compare in terms of Jewishness is another matter.

Mad About You's discursive claims to Jewishness rest mainly on the presumed Jewishness of Paul Buchman, whose character is patterned after his portrayer, the show's co-creator, Paul Reiser—"he of the way overdone Jewish accent and mannerisms" (Kaplan 1996). Joyce Antler (1998) finds a rare "positive image" of Jewishness in Paul's sister Debbie (Robin Bartlett), although "her proud lesbianism is more openly flaunted than her Jewishness." The tendency to erase female, as opposed to male, markers of Jewishness is also at work in *Friends*' high school chums, Monica Geller and Rachel Green (the non-Jewish Courteney Cox and Jennifer Aniston). What ultimately renders Monica and Rachel most Jewish (or half-Jewish, on their fathers' side) is an emergent form of Jewish representation termed "conceptual Jewishness" (Brook 2003). Partly an extension of Herbert Gans's (1956) notion of "symbolic Judaism," "conceptual Jewishness" refers sociologically to recent Jews' ever more abstract and attenuated links to identifiable ethnic and cultural, never mind religious, expression. Televisually, the term derives from the fact that in shows like *Friends*, "Jewish" characters are literally *conceived* (by their sitcom creators), more than they are *represented* (in the narrative), as Jews.

While conceptual Jewishness may be *Friends*' unique contribution—for better or worse—to Jewish representation, the show's propensity for "perceptual Jewishness" (Brook 2003) clearly relates, once again, to *Seinfeld*. Perceptual Jewishness occurs when characters are perceived as Jewish—by Jews or non-Jews—despite their *not* having been conceived as such by the show's creators. George Costanza's (Jason Alexander) pansemitic *schlemiel* provides the prima facie case in this regard. Is George now or has he ever been Jewish? Textually and extratextually, nobody knows for sure. Jerry Stiller, portrayer of papa Costanza, perfectly captured the paradox of the Jewish Question in regard to George when he joked in an interview, "I think we're a Jewish family living under the Witness Protection Program under the name Costanza" (Fretts 1988).

The Jewish sitcom protagonist most conspicuously conceived, perceived, and *performed* as Jewish is *The Nanny*'s Fran Fine—with surprisingly successful results. Despite what was for many a demeaning portrait of a Jewish American princess by the show's co-creator and star Fran Drescher, *The Nanny* also proved a major breakthrough in female Jewish representation. Notwithstanding the nanny's loud dress, gold-digging aim, and "accent that could etch glass" (Jarvis 1993)—not to mention her even more outrageous and opportunistic mother (played by Renee Taylor)—*The Nanny* not only proved popular with many Jews, including Jewish critics, but it sailed through the media-monitoring shoals largely unscathed. The key to the paradox, as with *Rhoda*, relates to gender. Where Drescher's nanny crucially parts company from the stereotypical Jewess is in regard to sexuality. Hyper- rather than de-sexualized, Drescher's character constructs a variation on the Jewish American Princess whose body is possessed of more than oral appetites and whose persona is—nasal whine and all—romantically desirable. By no means ideal as a revisionist Jewish-feminist text, *The Nanny* nonetheless must be credited with challenging the postwar myth of Jewish female passivity and frigidity embodied in the Jewish princess stereotype.

Although the (non-Jewish) sitcom *Ellen* (1994–1998) was the first regular prime-time series to openly disclose its protagonist's (and actor Ellen DeGeneres's) gayness, this epochal outing occurred near the end of the series' original run. The Jewish sitcom *Will and Grace* (1998–2006) was the first network series to *originate* with an openly gay protagonist, the gentile Will Truman (played by Eric McCormick). Through its leading lady Grace Adler (Debra Messing), the show introduced another unique sitcom character: the Jewish fag-hag. Unlike the tendency of some real-life female homophiles, however, Grace's affinity for gays and queer culture does not come at the expense of or as partial compensation for Jewish particularism. Her Jewishness is more than parenthetical, and the Jewish–gay connection is to a considerable extent reciprocal. Overt references to Grace's ethnicity outnumber those of all Jewish-trend protagonists with the possible exception of *The Nanny*'s Fran Fine. As for reciprocity, Will is in many ways as romantically, and carnally, obsessed with Grace as she with him. Jewish–gay bonding is, from a historical and institutional standpoint at least, a "natural" fit. That the Jewish male already "resembles the homosexual" through physical imputations of effeminacy is well documented (Seidman 1998). Just as evident, and increasingly acknowledged, are the historical "affinity with the closet" that the Jewish and gay (sub)cultures have shared and the degree to which Jews and gays, often in the same person, have dominated the entertainment industry (Seidman 1998).

Four of the eight Jewish sitcoms that premiered in the late 1990s—*Dharma and Greg* (1997–2003), *Alright Already* (1997–1998), *Rude Awakening* (1998–2001), and *Will and Grace* (1998–2006)—featured Jewish female protagonists. Given that all four women—Dharma Finkelstein (Jenna Elfman), Carol Lerner (Carol Leifer), Billie Frank (Sherilyn Fenn), and Grace Adler (Debra Messing)—were attractive and sexually confident indicates that post–*Seinfeld* era Jewish sitcoms were, at least initially, taking their ethnocultural cues less from the decade-defining show than from *The Nanny*. *Seinfeld*'s influence was far from spent, however. Besides its own perpetuation in endless re-runs and its imprint on gentler, kinder "clones" like *Mad About You* and *Friends*, *Seinfeld*'s unlikeability factor has been resurrected, and then some, in two of the most recent Jewishcoms, *Curb Your Enthusiasm* (2000–2005) and *Arrested Development* (2003–2005)—shows that carry individual and family dysfunctionality to comedic extremes.

Created and starring *Seinfeld* co-creator Larry David, *Curb Your Enthusiasm* confirms whence the earlier show's darkly absurdist thrust derived. Working without observational comic Jerry Seinfeld's ameliorative influence and with the greater creative license cable affords (the show aired on HBO), David has given his Kafkaesque proclivities full rein and allowed a postmodern fudging of fact and fiction—he plays himself as the famous and wealthy producer of the earlier show—to predominate. The result is one of the gems of television comedy—Jewish or otherwise—in which an accretion of existential calamities comment simultaneously on the perils of *schlemiel*dom, the contradictions of U.S. society, and the absurdities of the human condition. *Arrested Development*'s ambitions may approach *Curb*'s, but its attainments—critical encomiums notwithstanding—are more measured. A meaner, nastier, upscale *Married with Children* (1987–1997), *Arrested* is noteworthy not as a barometer of social or human conditions but rather of how far Jews have—or have not—come in twenty-first-century America. If they can present themselves in as scathing a fashion as the filthy rich and just plain filthy Bluth family are on *Arrested*, and if they can not only get away with it but be universally lauded—the show even received a Jewish Image award!—then U.S. Jews, as a people, have surely "arrived."

Vincent Brook

References and Further Reading

Antler, Joyce. 1998. "Epilogue: Jewish Women on Television: Too Jewish or Not Enough." In *Talking Back: Images of*

Jewish Women in American Popular Culture, edited by Joyce Antler, 242–252. Hanover, NH: Brandeis University Press.

Auster, Albert. 1993. "'Funny, You Don't Look Jewish': The Image of the Jews on Contemporary Television." *Television Quarterly* 36,3 (October): 65–74.

Brook, Vincent. 2003. *Something Ain't Kosher Here: The Rise of the "Jewish" Sitcom.* New Brunswick, NJ: Rutgers University Press.

Brook, Vincent, ed. 2006. *You Should See Yourself: Jewish Identity in Postmodern American Culture.* New Brunswick, NJ: Rutgers University Press.

Elkin, Michael. 1985. "Jews on TV: From 'The Goldbergs' to 'Hill Street's' Cops." *Jewish Exponent* (June 28): 25–27.

Feuer, Jane. 1984. "The MTM Style." In *MTM: "Quality Television,"* edited by Jane Feuer, Paul Kerr, and Tise Vahimagi, 32–60. London: British Film Institute (BFI).

Fretts, Bruce. 1988. "Cruelly, Madly, Cheaply." *Entertainment Weekly* (May 4): 44–45.

Gabler, Neal. 1989. *An Empire of Their Own: How the Jews Invented Hollywood.* New York: Anchor Books.

Gans, Herbert J. 1956. "American Jewry: Past and Future." *Commentary* (May): 244–249.

Gilman, Sander. 1991. *The Jew's Body.* New York and London: Routledge.

Jarvis, Jeff. 1993. "The Nanny." *TV Guide* (December 18): 8–9.

Johnson, Carla. 1994. "Luckless in New York: The Schlemiel and the Schlimazl in *Seinfeld*." *Journal of Popular Film and Television* (Fall): 116–124.

Kaplan, Susan. 1996. "From *Seinfeld* to *Chicago Hope*: Jewish Men Are Everywhere, but the Few Jewish Women Perpetuate Negative Stereotypes." *Forward* (November): 16–18.

Pearl, Jonathan, and Judith Pearl. 1999. *The Chosen Image: Television's Portrayal of Jewish Themes and Characters.* Jefferson, NC: McFarland.

Prell, Riv-Ellen. 1995. "Why Jewish Princesses Don't Sweat: Desire and Consumption in Postwar American Jewish Culture." In *Too Jewish? Challenging Traditional Identities*, edited by Norman Kleeblatt, 74–92. New Brunswick, NJ: Rutgers University Press.

Seidman, Naomi. 1998. "Fag Hags and Bu-Jews: Toward a (Jewish) Politics of Vicarious Identity." In *Insider/Outsider: American Jews and Multiculturalism*, edited by David Biale, Michael Galchinsky, and Susannah Heschel, 254–268. Berkeley: University of California Press.

Suber, Howard. 1975. "Television's Interchangeable Ethnics: 'Funny, They Don't Look Jewish.'" *Television Quarterly* (Winter): 53–58.

The Marx Brothers

Born on the Lower East Side to immigrant Jewish parents from Alsace and Germany, the five Marx Brothers—Leonard

The Marx Brothers. Pictured from top to bottom: Chico, Harpo, Groucho, and Zeppo. (Library of Congress)

("Chico"), Adolf (later Arthur, "Harpo"), Julius ("Groucho"), Milton ("Gummo"), and Herbert ("Zeppo")—carried their legendary zany comedic antics from vaudeville to stage to screen, and in Groucho's case to radio and television. Though they never played stock Jewish characters during their mature careers, the Marx brothers' comedy had roots in the irreverent medieval Jewish tradition of the Purim *shpil*, and captured both the assimilation-minded exuberance and the alienated impatience of Jewish (and other) immigrants and their children. They were also fierce opponents of antisemitism.

Simon Marrix (changed to Marx), an Alsatian Jew who spoke *Plattdeutsch* (low-country German) and French and learned the tailor's trade, was married in 1884 on the Lower East Side to Minna (later Minnie) Schoenberg, born near Hanover, Germany, the daughter of a traveling magician. They had six sons; the eldest, Manfred, died in infancy. The other five—Chico (1887–1961), Harpo (1888–1964), Groucho (1890–1977), Gummo (1897–1977), and Zeppo (1901–1979)—grew up to become a collective icon of twentieth-century American popular culture.

The Jewishness of the Marx brothers' origins is incontestable, but not so the extent of their Jewish identification and the Jewish character of their comedy. Groucho himself summed up the poles of the debate when he reacted to one reviewer's praise of the act as "the symbolic embodiment of all persecuted Jews for 2,000 years" with, "What sort of goddamned review is that?" (Erens 1984). When the musical biography, *Minnie's Boys* (1970), was in preparation, Groucho angrily vetoed "that Jew broad" Totie Fields from playing his curvaceous, blonde mother Minnie. When asked, "Wasn't your mother Jewish?" he replied, "But the world thinks we're Italian" (Kanfer 2000). (Jewish and plump but blonde Shelley Winters got the role.)

The ambiguous facts are these. The family lived in Yorkville, still a German (and German Jewish) bastion on New York's East Side in the late nineteenth century. They did not so much resist as ignore the *Yiddishkeit,* cultural and political, that the *Ostjuden* brought with them as proud baggage. The attempt to maintain traditional observance died with the children's maternal grandmother. Her widower, the boys' maternal grandfather, was able to maintain only a semblance of it, seeing to it that the boys attended synagogue occasionally and received bar mitzvah preparation, which was even more perfunctory than their regular schooling (only Chico finished high school).

The mind of Minnie, the family's dynamo, was on other things. Credited in Alexander Woolcott's obituary of her in the *New Yorker* with "inventing" the Marx brothers, she was the archetypal stage mother who formed the boys as a singing act (Groucho was the falsetto crooner), the Nightingales, which was their launching pad into vaudeville. Though Gummo at one point was billed as "a Hebrew Boy," none of the mature Marx brothers played explicitly Jewish characters either on the stage or screen. Modeling himself on his maternal uncle, Al Shean (later of the Gallagher and Shean vaudeville team), Groucho played a German or "Dutch comic" until the anti-German backlash in the wake of the *Lusitania* debacle in 1915 sunk that role. This was when Harpo also changed his name from Adolf to Arthur. Chico won his enduring fame by assuming an Italian immigrant persona. Blackface was never the Marx brothers' forte, though they do blacken up in one scene in *A Day at the Races* to escape the sheriff.

In his autobiography, Harpo remarks that the boys, when appearing with Jewish boxer Benny Leonard on the Iowa vaudeville circuit during World War I, were criticized

for a parody of "The Spirit of '76." He added that, to avoid any more criticism, they "never worked dirty" (used off-color language) or "used any Jewish expressions on stage" (Marx 1961). In the stage version of *The Cocoanuts,* Groucho introduced Spanish dancers as "Span yids." This and similar allusions were dropped from the movie version, though Groucho, playing African explorer Captain Spaulding in *Animal Crackers,* does ask, "Did someone call me *schnorrer?*"

When the brothers returned to New York in the 1920s, two events symbolized their ambivalent relation with their Jewish roots: Groucho took the first of his three gentile wives (a small-town midwestern girl) at a ceremony where no rabbi or minister was willing to preside. (A Jewish justice of the peace who was a retired vaudevillian did the honors.) And when the brothers' act opened before a predominantly Jewish audience at the Royal Theater, preparatory to playing the Palace Theater, the audience sat on its hands because it did not hear the comic Yiddishisms it expected.

Groucho never abandoned his disdain for ethnic comedians who played what he called "the professional Jew." It should also be remembered that Groucho's most famous quip—"I wouldn't want to be a member of any club that would have me"—was a slap at the *Jewish* Hillcrest Country Club in Los Angeles (Kanfer 2000).

On the other hand, the Marx Brothers were Jewish—and proud of it—if the measure was sensitivity to, and defiance of, the scourge of antisemitism. All the brothers sharply responded to "No Jews need apply" discrimination in hotel accommodations. When his son, Arthur, was denied swimming privileges at a country club, Groucho countered with a telegram asking, "Since my son is only half-Jewish, would it be all right if he goes in up to his waist?"

On the way to touring Russia in 1933, Harpo stopped over in Hitler's new Reich. He remarked, "I hadn't been so wholly conscious of being a Jew since my Bar Mitzvah. It was the first time since I had the measles that I was too sick to eat. I got across Germany as fast as I could" (Marx 1961). In Moscow, where he was feted and shepherded by the fellow-traveling *New York Times* reporter Walter Duranty, Harpo's eyes were drawn to an old stage hand in a yarmulke whom he asked if it were true that there were "no shuls in Moscow." The stage hand's reply: "No shuls—but there are no pogroms, either."

A notorious agnostic, Groucho humored his first wife's family by allowing his son, Arthur, to attend Christian Sunday school. Yet when the boy returned home, his father would grill him in order to debunk Christological teachings. The octogenarian Groucho sometimes attended synagogue, perhaps at the insistence of Erin Fleming, his final companion and keeper, who converted to Judaism.

A disappointed romantic in matters of the heart, Groucho was never a patsy politically. He liked Winston Churchill's history of World War II, but had doubts about his Cold War politics as a prescription for the United States. His views were progressive enough in the Hollywood of the 1940s to win the McCarthyite designation "poolside pinko," but he never trusted Stalin and had no use for the American Communist Party, as he told his daughter Miriam after she resigned membership.

Marx's refusal to be pigeonholed continued in later years when, in 1964, he followed a visit to Israel with a London stopover to meet "his celebrated pen pal" anti-semite T. S. Eliot, who (rather unconvincingly) also expressed admiration for the Jewish state (Kanfer 2000). Groucho lived long enough to become the sort of honorary cranky grandpa of the New Left, whose hearts he won by blurting out to a *Berkeley Barb* reporter in 1972 that it might not be a bad idea if President Richard Nixon were assassinated. It was no coincidence that French radical Daniel Cohn-Bendit called himself a "Marxist à la Groucho."

Yet Groucho never shared the post–1967 War anti-Israel stirrings on the left and was so upset by the murder of the eleven Israeli athletes at the 1972 Munich Olympics that the news may have precipitated a stroke, which delayed his opening in a Los Angeles theatrical revue. Harpo symbolically bequeathed his harp to Israel. Ambivalent to the end, Groucho in his will coupled instructions that he be buried in a nonsectarian cemetery with a large bequest to the Jewish Federation of Los Angeles.

To return to the question of the Jewishness of the Marx brothers' inspired screen anarchy: with roots in the irreverent medieval Jewish tradition of the Purim *shpil* of annually authorized irreverence, it captured both the assimilation-minded exuberance and the alienated impatience of Jewish immigrants (and not only Jewish immigrants) and their children. When Groucho mocked Margaret Dumont—his perfect foil in *The Cocoanuts, Ani-*

mal Crackers, Duck Soup, A Night at the Opera, and *A Day at the Races,* who was the personification of inanely respectable WASPishness—the urban ethnic audience howled with laughter at a common enemy. This was "coalition building" between Jews and other American newcomers at a deeper level than mere politics.

Harold Brackman

References and Further Reading

Allen, Miriam Marx. 2002. *Love, Groucho: Letters from Groucho Marx to His Daughter Miriam.* New York: Da Capo Press.

Erens, Patricia. 1984. *The Jew in American Cinema.* Bloomington: Indiana University Press.

Kanfer, Stefan. 2000. *Groucho: The Life and Times of Julius Henry Marx.* New York: Alfred A. Knopf.

Marx, Groucho. 1959. *Groucho and Me.* New York: Bernard Geis.

Marx, Harpo, with Rowland Barber. 1961. *Harpo Speaks!* New York: Limelight Editions.

Mitchell, Glenn. 2003. *The Marx Brothers Encyclopedia.* London: Reynolds and Hearn.

Reference.com. 1968. Available at: www.reference.com/browse/wiki/May_1968. Accessed March 11, 2007.

American Jewish Comedians

For most of the twentieth century, Americans identified comedy with Jewish performers. Indeed, in 1979 *Time* magazine observed that, while Jews made up about 3 percent of the population, they accounted for 80 percent of working comedians. From vaudeville through radio, nightclubs, motion pictures, and television, Jewish comedians have been major comedic entertainers. A list of just a few of them reveals their centrality to American culture: George Burns, Fanny Brice, Jack Benny, Milton Berle, Gertrude Berg, the Marx Brothers, Sid Caesar, Woody Allen, Mel Brooks, Joan Rivers, Lenny Bruce, Don Rickles, Jerry Lewis, Rodney Dangerfield, the Three Stooges, Jerry Seinfeld, among hundreds of others.

Although Jewish comedians varied widely, some generalizations can be made. Almost all drew their sensibilities from a particular East European Jewish culture. Most of the Jewish immigrants who came to America after 1881 had lived in a small town (*shtetl*) or city in Poland or Russia. Shunned by their gentile neighbors, they had developed tightly knit communities and a clear cultural identity.

Jewish life in Eastern Europe was characterized by intermittent persecution and economic deprivation. These conditions led to feelings of both depression and fear. Jews were outsiders, marginalized from mainstream society. The insecurity of being a despised minority group profoundly shaped Jews' psychological outlook. Faced with overwhelming power, Jews were generally unable to defend themselves forcefully.

These conditions produced a deep need to escape. Physically, they fled to America where, far from Cossacks and czars, they would more openly express their anxieties and beliefs. The anxieties often surfaced as humor. The humor that emerged on American shores was also a nervous reaction to having survived and escaped the constraints and terrors of Jewish life in Eastern Europe. Indeed, humor provided Jews with their means of coping with unfairness and cruelty, of handling the tensions between what Jews thought life should offer and what it actually allowed. Throughout the twentieth century, the smile from Jewish humor remained haunted by an awareness that the humor served as a vital escape from horror.

Jews had responded to the rigors of their lives in part by developing strong family bonds, which not only continued to sustain them in America, but also provided a trove of material for Jewish comedians. The Jewish immigrants also brought with them a deep distrust of external authority, which in America led them to question arrangements that old-stock Americans often could not recognize, or were reluctant to challenge. Moreover, although many Jews remained skeptical that they would really be accepted in America, they soon became both outsiders and insiders, providing a crucial vantage point they had not known before. Had they just been insiders, they would not have had the perspective necessary to see the humor in American life, and had they just been outsiders, American audiences may not have listened to them.

Another attribute that Jews had developed in response to extreme adversity was to use language as a substitute for weapons—now transformed into an important comedic skill. Armed with selected, pungent Yiddish words and phrases, which frequently combined humorous sounds and deeper emotional expressiveness than their English counterparts, the emerging Jewish comedians had a resource not immediately available to other performers. Yiddish offered acute observations of human foibles and characteristics. And to the ear attuned to English, some of

the words sounded funny. Comedians seized on those words, which eventually became part of the common American vernacular. Indeed, these words allowed Jewish comedians to create characters. A *schlemiel* is a pitiful, unlucky, maladjusted loser. Jerry Lewis forged his character largely from the *schlemiel*. Yiddish was filled with acute, tiny observations of the sort that Jerry Seinfeld later made famous.

Upon arriving in America, a number of Jews were attracted by the opportunities afforded by the dynamic, new urban entertainment form of vaudeville. And because vaudeville was still marginal and opposed by the Victorian elites, there were no entrenched interests barring their entry. However, the Jewish children who entered vaudeville—and they did enter as children—violated every Jewish stereotype. Although Jews had long had a powerful commitment to education, these children hated school. Buddy Hackett used to say, "Ah, school. What fun I had that day." George Burns lost the battle with mathematics and quit early. Harpo Marx was tossed out of school in the second grade—not by the authorities, but by rough classmates. Harpo went back, was thrown out the window again, and decided that school was not for him. Instead of learning, these young children of Jewish immigrants wanted money and fame. They were also young thieves. Phil Silvers stole from pushcarts. Fanny Brice shoplifted. When Eddie Cantor was thirteen, he stole a purse. Bert Lahr stole a pumpkin—from a police officer. They turned out to be better comedians than thieves. As youths, they had rejected education and small business, the means by which most Jews advanced. Instead, as the leisure industry began to take shape, they became its pioneers, achieving success by using their wits to entertain the new urban masses.

Still, like many other American Jews, they were driven by a deep need to succeed, to take advantage of the new opportunity offered them, and they did whatever they could to get a job. George Burns (born Nathan Birnbaum) kept changing his stage name when he found that managers would not hire him. He called them and claimed to have every expertise they wanted. He worked with a trained seal. He tried, with minimal success, to tell jokes. Only when he met Gracie Allen did he succeed. Burns changed the traditional Dumb Dora acts of vaudeville, making the woman partner not stupid, but sympathetic, having what he called an "illogical logic":

George: Gracie, let me ask you something. Did the nurse ever happen to drop you on your head when you were a baby?

Gracie: Oh, no. We couldn't afford a nurse. My mother had to do it.

George: You had a smart mother.

Gracie: Smartness runs in my family. When I went to school, I was so smart my teacher was in my class for five years.

George: Gracie, what school did you go to?

Gracie: I'm not allowed to tell.

George: Why not?

Gracie: The school pays me twenty-five dollars a month not to tell (Epstein 2001).

Injecting American humor with Jewish soul, Burns also used his strong affection for his mother, as well as the high regard in which Jews held their mothers, to alter American entertainment. Eddie Cantor was so popular with audiences because they loved his energy and sensed that he was one of them. It was not unusual for him to interrupt his act to make an announcement from an anxious parent to have her child, who was in the audience, come home.

Born Benjamin Kubelsky, Jack Benny fashioned a persona far from his real self. "Jack Benny" was cheap. He would not buy his girlfriend flowers, but seeds. Once, Benny was invited to throw out the first pitch at a baseball game. He held the baseball, put it in his pocket, and sat down, delighting the crowd. Although the character drew on antisemitic stereotypes about Jews and money, this did not reinforce the negative image because Benny was not widely recognized as a Jew.

Benny was also famous for being eternally thirty-nine and being a bad violin player. Indeed, during President Lyndon B. Johnson's administration, Benny approached the White House gates. A marine guard stopped him and said, "Excuse me, Mr. Benny, what's in the case?" Benny responded, "It's a machine gun." The guard said, "Okay, then, you can go in. For a minute I thought it was your violin" (Epstein 2001).

Benny achieved enormous popularity with his radio appearances, beginning in 1932. Trying to create laughs after the Great Depression began in 1929, Benny used his cheap persona to give emotional permission to his audiences to be cheap themselves. Often unable to earn an adequate living, guilty that they could not provide for their families, radio listeners found in Benny a character even

Jack Benny. (Library of Congress)

cheaper than they. And if he could laugh about his situation, so could they.

Huge numbers of non-Jewish Americans responded so positively to Burns, Benny, and other Jewish comedians in these years because they recognized a certain shared experience in their humor. The Jews were part of a vast movement of people who had left Eastern and Southern Europe, as well as the farms and small towns across America, to come to the rapidly industrializing cities in search of work. These external and internal immigrants often felt uprooted, alienated, and out of place, anxious about their skills and future. It is therefore not entirely surprising that they turned to comedians emerging from a people who, throughout their history, had frequently been forced to move to a new place and to adapt quickly, and who had found ways to survive with their families and pride intact. That is, the Jewish comedians brought with them a past that resonated with the emotional needs of a wide American audience.

Similarly, during the Depression audiences could learn much from those who had endured centuries of economic adversity, turning to the Jewish comedians for amusing lessons on survival. Whether consciously or not, the comedians drew on a great Jewish tradition of using humor to survive.

Yet for all their success in vaudeville and radio, Jews did not succeed as well in film—before the era of sound. Jewish humor was driven primarily by language, not pantomime or visual antics. Although many audiences incorrectly believed Charlie Chaplin to be Jewish because of his immigrant tramp character, silent film comedies were, in fact, dominated by non-Jews such as Chaplin, Buster Keaton, and Harold Lloyd.

With the arrival of sound in 1927, however, Jewish comedians quickly appeared on the screen. The most prominent were the Marx Brothers. Driven by an indomitable mother, the brothers started in vaudeville, went to Broadway, and achieved lasting fame in a series of brilliant films mocking all forms of authority. The Marx Brothers elaborated a clever comedic technique. In vaudeville, each brother represented a different ethnic type: Chico was the Italian, Harpo originally played an Irish lad, and Groucho was a German until the sinking of the *Lusitania* led him to switch to a Jewish character. In films, they broadened this approach, with each representing a different level of linguistic comedy. Groucho became the wisecracking verbal comic, Harpo the pantomimist, and Chico in-between, able to speak but having to do so in a thick accent. In *Duck Soup*, for example, Groucho's verbal assault on Margaret Dumont exemplifies his approach:

> *Dumont:* I've sponsored your appointment because I feel you are the most able statesman in all Freedonia.
> *Groucho:* Well, that covers a lot of ground. Say, you cover a lot of ground yourself. You'd better beat it. I hear they're going to tear you down and put up an office building where you're standing. You can leave in a taxi. If you can't leave in a taxi you can leave in a huff. If that's too soon, you can leave in a minute and a huff (Epstein 2001).

Although Jews found a greater degree of acceptance in America than in Europe, considerable suspicion and distrust persisted, and Jews were barred from, or their access was severely restricted to, elite colleges, private clubs, hotels, many businesses, and other areas of American life. As a result, many performers found it necessary to hide or disguise their Jewishness. Indeed, when performers like

George Jessel retained a Jewish persona on radio, they were less successful than those like Jack Benny, who did not. Jessel spoke rapidly in a recognizably Jewish accent and talked about urban subjects. Despite his stable marriage to a Jew and his ongoing relationship with the Jewish community, Benny managed to avoid being widely perceived as Jewish by carefully eschewing Jewish accents or jokes and by sticking to wider American subjects.

The 1930s witnessed the spread of Nazism in Europe, and the intensification of antisemitism in America. Fearful of losing European, and particularly German, distribution rights, American film companies chose not to make movies that challenged the rise of Hitler. Indeed, even stereotyped Jewish characters disappeared from film. The Yiddishisms in the Marx Brothers and Eddie Cantor movies vanished.

There were some attempts to pierce the silence about the Nazis. In comedy, the most famous case was that of Charlie Chaplin, who was repeatedly warned not to make *The Great Dictator* (1940). Chaplin was not, however, the first actor to portray Hitler on film. That honor belongs to Moe Howard of the Three Stooges. The three Jewish comedians who made up the Stooges starred in three anti-Nazi films, beginning with *You Nazty Spy* in 1940. The Stooges smuggled Yiddish into their films. They kept the immigrant sensibility of fighting to survive. They borrowed their physical humor from earlier Jewish vaudeville acts, especially Joe Weber and Lew Fields.

Stung by rejection in society and on screen, the Jews developed their own institutions. The most important of these were the private resorts in the Catskill area, northwest of New York City. The resort colonies began a century ago, and by the 1950s some nine hundred hotels brought in more than a million guests a year. The Borscht Belt (also called the Jewish Alps) was the training ground for a generation of Jewish comedians. Starting as teenagers, the young men and women who went to the Catskill resorts became *tummlers,* social directors of entertainment. Their job was to amuse customers constantly, and it became a Catskill tradition to do anything for a laugh. The audiences were tough, and young, would-be comedians—like Sid Caesar, Jackie Mason, Danny Kaye, Joan Rivers, Alan King, Red Buttons, and Jerry Lewis—quickly learned that they needed a ready wit and especially nerves of steel. Joan Rivers, who only landed a job because she could drive male comedians around in her car, once played to an audience

The Three Stooges, Moe Howard (left), Curly Howard (center), and Larry Fine (right), performing a comedy routine. (Library of Congress)

that only understood Yiddish. She quickly found a translator. She would tell a joke in English, and the uncomprehending audience did not laugh. The translator told the joke again, and they still did not laugh. As she later recalled, it was the only time in her life that she bombed twice with every line. Jerry Lewis used his Borscht Belt training to great effect in developing his act with Dean Martin, an act in which the wild Lewis character knew no bounds in seeking laughs.

When television arrived, Jewish comedians were among the first to explore the new art form. Many radio performers did not like or trust television. The new medium ate up material quickly—Ed Wynn called it the glass furnace—and required physical dimensions, which radio depended on a listener's imagination to provide.

Milton Berle was among the first of the Jewish comedians to recognize television's possibilities. Berle had worked in vaudeville but had been less successful on radio. He, unlike some other comedians, was therefore willing to experiment with the new medium. In 1948, Berle received funding for a test show that would determine his career. He bravely hired Pearl Bailey, an African American singer, and Señor Wences, a foreign-sounding ventriloquist, whose father was, in fact, a Sephardic Jew. Berle was an enormous success and is often credited with creating the market for televisions. There were even jokes about it. Joe E. Lewis observed, "Berle is responsible for more television sets being sold than anyone else. I sold mine. My father sold his" (Epstein 2001). But Berle's early success was deceptive. Televisions were originally in more affluent, urban areas that understood Berle's fast talk, city ways, wild costumes, and manic behavior. That is, Berle had not changed his approach for television, keeping his urban, Jewish performance intact. As the show came to be broadcast far beyond the cities, however, audiences did not find Berle as appealing. His original, groundbreaking shows lasted from 1948 until 1956.

Sid Caesar suffered a similar fate. A brilliant mimic who got his start by imitating customers in his father's restaurant, Caesar's major shows were *Your Show of Shows* (1950–1954) and *Caesar's Hour* (1954–1958). The latter was eventually canceled when Lawrence Welk was aired opposite him. Still, Caesar had gathered the most brilliant comedy writers in television history. At various times, Woody Allen, Mel Brooks, Larry Gelbart, Carl Reiner, and Neil Simon wrote for him.

Other Jewish comedians appeared on television as well. Like Berle, Phil Silvers depended on the joke, but, unlike the variety shows Berle and Caesar explored, Silvers focused on a new kind of show, the situation comedy. Here Silvers developed the character of Sergeant Bilko to perfection. Bilko was the fast-talking guy using his wits to struggle against a more powerful institution. He was a perfect metaphor for American Jews. Soupy Sales created what seemed like a show for children, complete with old films, silly puns and gags, and puppets. But Sales was extremely clever and quick, and made the old art of taking a pie in the face fresh again.

Berle and Silvers were joke-a-minute comedians, while Caesar relied less on the joke than on humor emerging from character. Other Jewish comedians expressed a clear nostalgia for a warm, Jewish past. Gertrude Berg was America's Jewish mother, who, on radio and television, used food, common sense, and a lilting accent to solve problems. Sam Levenson and Myron Cohen became storytellers, providing insights into life and the travails of marriage. Cohen told about a time when he was on a plane and saw a woman wearing a beautiful diamond. "Excuse me," he said, "I don't mean to be forward, but that's a beautiful diamond. The woman nodded, "Thank you. It's called the Klopman Diamond. It's like the Hope Diamond. It comes with a curse." "What's the curse?" Cohen asked. "Klopman," she sighed (Epstein 2001). Cohen invited audience members to tell the story substituting a name from their own lives.

Alan King also avoided the rapid-fire joke telling, but his stories, told at first in nightclubs and later on television, were especially well received by a new Jewish generation that had moved to suburbia. King went after the institutions that bothered people. "If banks are so friendly," he would say, "why do they chain down their pens?" Suburban Jews had become American, but they still retained a healthy distrust of the powerful, and of institutions in general. King's anger gave voice not only to Jewish suburbanites, but also to everyone's frustrations with what was supposed to be paradise.

The storyteller's humor was one of reconciliation. These storytellers made the present more palatable, either by recalling a warm past, thereby letting the present slip away for a few minutes, or by expressing anger at institutions, enabling people to handle their anxieties through humor. This strategy explicitly relied on the heritage of Jewish comedy from Eastern Europe, where Jewish audiences, bereft of power, had used humor, along with religion, to learn to accept what they could not change.

Unlike these storytellers, there arose a group of Jewish comedians in the late 1950s and early 1960s who did not want their audiences to reconcile themselves with social or political reality. They were the exemplars of the Jewish tradition of challenging those in power, norms (of language in the case of Lenny Bruce), and even views of what is sane. Mort Sahl wanted audiences to understand the political strings that operated the country. Always sharp and timely, his humor was that of a prophet seeking to alert the masses to a hidden reality, beyond their vision until he reveals it. Sahl's prophecy was not about the sacred, but about secular power. Lenny Bruce, angry about hypocrisy wherever he saw it, used obscenity as a weapon to puncture the illusions audiences held about society. Shelley Berman provided psychological insights about relationships and the fragile relationship of the self confronted with an uncaring society. He was among the first who talked openly about personal psychological issues.

It was also an era of improvisational comedy, a perfect metaphor for a society that felt that the old, pre–World War II rules no longer applied in these years of economic expansion, of supposed suburban paradises, that masked a stifling conformity, and of the threat of nuclear destruction. Certainly, Jews were attracted to the very idea of improvisation, of having to rely on quick mental agility and having to make up their lives as they went along. Such an idea precisely matched the Jewish condition, especially in East Europe for centuries. Improvisational comedy also matched America's uncertainty about where the society was heading, while easing the journey with laughter. Mike Nichols and Elaine May did scathing improvisational bits about family relationships, charting the increasingly complex battle of the sexes and the widening chasm between parents and children. Jerry Stiller and Anne Meara presented a softer version of Nichols and May. They developed characters, based on their real relationship, about a Jewish man and a woman born Irish Catholic.

Audiences were hungry for direct talk, and these new comedians gave it to them. Their comedic heirs continued this tradition. Woody Allen began writing jokes in high school, became a shy stand-up comedian, and eventually found his voice in films that made it unmistakably clear to the audience that he was Jewish. In *Annie Hall,* for example, there is a scene at the Hall family table at which everyone is praising grandma's ham. Woody's character appears in Hasidic garb as he imagines how Annie Hall's gentile family sees the New York *schlemiel* that he plays. Allen was among the first to make sure everyone knew that they were laughing because someone Jewish had made the jokes. Allen did this even though he had a difficult relationship with his own Jewishness.

Mel Brooks was the other great Jewish filmmaker of this era. After leaving Sid Caesar's employ, Brooks teamed up with Carl Reiner to make a series of records about a 2,000-Year-Old Man, who spoke with a Yiddish accent and clearly had Borscht Belt training. Brooks went on to make a series of movies. His first film, *The Producers,* was a wild tale of producers who try their best to create a failure on Broadway by putting on a musical about the Nazis. In a series of later films, he gently mocked various film genres, starting with the Western in *Blazing Saddles.* He was the film insider and Jewish outsider, whose vantage point let him look at the conventions of film—that is, the conventions of American culture—and both see and expose their premises, which were simply accepted by Americans who were only insiders.

There were only a few other Jewish filmmakers. Albert Brooks made movies, but any Jewish themes were hidden under the broader American concerns of his characters.

In the sixties, Jews and Jewish culture became widely accepted by the larger society, and Jewish stand-up comedians became very successful. Shecky Greene had to battle in Las Vegas to talk about being Jewish on stage, but, once he did, audiences loved it. Rodney Dangerfield created a character with bulging eyes, sweat, and endless movements, who "didn't get no respect." Buddy Hackett used his body, face, and voice to perfection. Don Rickles

made insult comedy an art. It was a difficult art that almost no one else managed to get right. Norm Crosby developed a unique comedic style, built on malapropisms: "The Etruscans vanquished the Trojans and pushed them out of Trojia down the Agamemnon Valley which led to the Connecticut Valley" (Epstein 2001).

Almost all Jewish comedians were men. The failure of large numbers of Jewish women to enter the ranks of comedians is not simply an ethnic example of the broader exclusion of women from the field. The situation for Jewish women was particularly difficult because of the nature of the material on which many male Jewish comedians depended for their laughs. The standard material of the successful Jewish comedian Henny Youngman relied on lines like: "I went on a pleasure trip. I took my mother-in-law to the airport." Or, "My wife asked me to take her someplace she'd never been before, so I took her to the kitchen." Or his signature line, "Take my wife, please." The humor was based on a particular view of Jewish women. Had Jewish women become successful comedians in the 1960s and 1970s and talked humorously about Jewish women, they would have seriously undermined the images of them that were central to many Jewish male comedians' routines. Thus Jewish male comedians opposed the hiring of Jewish women comedians, not only because of the unwanted competition, but also because their material would have rapidly become dated.

Some Jewish women, however, entered comedy in the 1950s and 1960s. Some, like Rusty Warren and Pearl Williams, chose to create sexually suggestive material, performing in clubs and on "party" records. Gertrude Berg was still around, although the ratings for her television show steadily declined, the victim of the iconoclasm of the new era. Some Jewish women tried to enter mainstream comedy. Totie Fields had to rely on self-mockery, making fun of her own weight, and when she lost a leg, even about her disability.

It was Joan Rivers who made the breakthrough for Jewish women comedians. At first, in the early 1960s, she used the self-mocking humor that women were forced to employ. She was not so influenced by feminism as she was by other comedians, especially Woody Allen and Lenny Bruce. Bruce's honesty and directness on stage deeply affected her, so that by the late 1960s she began to develop lines that mocked men's traditional views of women. In the 1970s and later, she made fun of the women whom men considered beautiful, such as Elizabeth Taylor or Bo Derek. Rivers thereby undermined the very image of women that men brought with them to a comedy act. She paved the way for women to explore new subjects and to do so from a position of authority. Her comedic heirs, such as Gilda Radner, Elayne Boosler, Roseanne, Fran Dresher, and Rita Rudner, thus had the freedom to develop fuller characters.

Several members of the next generation of male Jewish comedians became major stars. Billy Crystal went from television to movie stardom, appearing in one of the most insightful films about performers, *Mr. Saturday Night* (1992). Andy Kaufman was less a comedian than a performance artist, someone who deliberately annoyed or confused audiences to force them to see entertainment or comedy through new eyes. He did not tell jokes. He simply acted strange. From his signature role on the television show *Taxi* to his odd experiments with wrestling, Kaufman pushed the borders of what was comedic. Not all audiences wanted to escape the traditional way of experiencing comedy—by laughing at one joke and then another. He wanted them to see the absurdities of life and learn to laugh at them. Other comedians loved him.

Jerry Seinfeld became one of the most popular entertainers in American history. The last episode of *Seinfeld* in 1998 attracted 76 million viewers. Seinfeld's early efforts, however, were not auspicious. On the day he graduated from college, he appeared in a comedy club and froze. Instead of telling jokes, he recited the subjects of the jokes. Unwilling to quit, Seinfeld began to make observations about the minutia of daily life, providing characters with whom his audiences readily identified and situations that made them laugh. "I grew up in Massapequa," he might say. "It's an old Indian word meaning 'by the mall.'"

Other Jewish comedians also explored the smaller, more personal universe that became important to the inward-turning American audiences after the 1970s. Richard Lewis perfected the manic comic, always moving, always neurotic. Garry Shandling created the brilliant *The Larry Sanders Show* about a late-night comedy program. *Sanders* was a dead-on satire about late-night television, comedians, and the entertainment industry. Shandling was unafraid to make himself look manipulative and less than perfect.

More Jewish comedians achieved renown in the 1990s and the beginning of the twenty-first century. Jerry Stiller's

son, Ben, became a major movie star. So did Adam Sandler, who first worked on *Saturday Night Live.* Sandler perfected the loser who uses his anger to achieve success, a character who apparently matched the psychological profile of many in his audience. Jeffrey Ross became famous for his work at the Friars Club. On television, Jon Stewart developed a wide following for his political satire and comedy. Larry David was crucial in creating *Seinfeld.* His sensibility and experiences allowed him to write scripts that deeply probed the American psyche. After leaving *Seinfeld,* he later developed *Curb Your Enthusiasm,* a mostly improvised comedy for HBO about a man who seems to have it all but keeps getting into trouble.

Jewish comedy's past was glorious, the present strong, but its future appears uncertain. Traditional Jewish comedy had mined the inheritance of *shtletl* culture, Yiddish, and the immigrants' feelings of dislocation. As later generations of American Jews acculturated and assimilated into American life, memories of that Eastern European past increasingly dissipated, and may soon be consigned only to the nostalgic. It remains unclear, however, if future generations of American Jews will assimilate so completely that the crucial status of being simultaneously inside and outside the society will disappear. Moreover, the earliest comedians entered the marginal world of vaudeville because many economic routes were closed to Jews. At the beginning of the twenty-first century, by contrast, almost no jobs remain off-limits. As Jews have become more accepted by the larger society, the old hunger for approval, so evident in the first generations of Jewish immigrants, is no longer as strong. Still, remnants of the linguistic constructions, the distrust of authority, the laser-sharp observations, and the ability to create a variety of characters remain strong. Generations of Jewish comedians have left an extraordinary legacy for anyone interested in becoming a comedian.

There is another reason to suspect that Jewish comedy may persist. One definition of comedy is that it is tragedy plus time. After enough time has elapsed since the events of September 11, 2001, Americans may, as they have in the past, turn to Jews and the Jewish experience to understand how a people absorbs and copes with great tragedy. Just as Jewish comedians helped provide emotional resilience for the many Americans dislocated by immigration and later by the Great Depression, young Jewish comedians may once again draw on the Jews' long experience with unbearable tragedy, with countless innocents killed and terrorized, to help cure an ailing America.

In this way, tomorrow's Jewish comedians could carry on a noble tradition that brought Americans endless laughs and, perhaps as importantly, the strength to accept pain and difficulties and to go on, buoyed by humor. Jewish comedians have given America a great gift, and Americans have been grateful.

Lawrence J. Epstein

References and Further Reading

Adamson, Joe. 1973. *Groucho, Harpo, Chico, and Sometimes Zeppo.* New York: Simon & Schuster.

Boskin, Joseph. 1997. *Rebellious Laughter.* Syracuse, NY: Syracuse University Press.

Epstein, Lawrence J. 2001. *The Haunted Smile: The Story of Jewish Comedians in America.* New York: PublicAffairs.

Goldman, Albert. 1971. *Ladies and Gentlemen, Lenny Bruce!* New York: Ballantine Books.

Kanfer, Stefan. 2000. *Groucho: The Life and Times of Julius Henry Marx.* New York: Alfred A. Knopf.

Levy, Shawn. 1996. *King of Comedy: The Life and Art of Jerry Lewis.* New York: St. Martin's Press.

Lyman, Darryl. 1989. *The Jewish Comedy Catalog.* Middle Village, NY: Jonathan David.

Romeyn, Esther, and Jack Kugelmass. 1997. *Let There Be Laughter! Jewish Humor in America.* Chicago: Spertus.

Woody Allen (b. 1935)

Filmmaker

Woody Allen, the Academy Award–winning filmmaker, is in the Jewish comic tradition of the *shlemiel*. The chronic outsider, he has exploited his ambivalence toward both American and Jewish culture to win insider celebrity and mainstream success.

Born Allen Stewart Konigsberg in the Bronx, New York, in 1935, Woody Allen was the son of Martin Konigsberg and Netty Cherrie, the American-born children, respectively, of Austrian Jewish and Russian Jewish immigrants. His Orthodox family spoke German as well as Yiddish at home, and while growing up in Brooklyn he lived at times with relatives who were refugees from Hitler's Germany. Allen prayed each morning with phylacteries, attended synagogue every Saturday with his paternal grandfather, and went to Hebrew school in the afternoons for eight years until his bar mitzvah, at which he showed his true vocation by appearing in a blackface imitation of Al Jolson.

Three-time Academy Award–winner, including as director of best picture *Annie Hall* (1977), Allen started as a teenage joke writer for comedian Sid Caesar and *The Tonight Show,* and evolved into a stand-up comic. He wrote plays as well as movie scripts, shaped from behind the scenes the television success of *Saturday Night Live,* and graduated from slapstick comedy to films that explored the meaning of life. He is celebrated in France as a great *auteur.* What is the relation of Allen's Jewish roots to his serio-comic gift?

According to Michael Abbott, "Allen's didacticism, his tortuous self-questioning, his familiar use of a question in reply to a question, his mosaic storytelling style—all are rooted deeply in Talmudic thought and tradition" (Abbott 1996). Allen views matters differently: "I was unmoved by the synagogue, I was not interested in the *Seder,* I was not interested in the Hebrew school, I was not interested in being Jewish. It just didn't mean a thing to me. I was not ashamed of it nor was I proud of it. It was a nonfactor to me. I didn't care about it. It just wasn't my field of interest. I cared about baseball, I cared about movies. To be a Jew was not something that I felt 'Oh, God, I'm so lucky.' Or 'Gee, I wish I were something else.' I certainly had no interest in being Catholic or in any of the other Gentile religions" (Lax 2000).

Allen also attributed little of value to his secular education. He attended Public School 99—where Irish teachers were reputed to let little Christian pupils out early, while keeping the Jewish kids after class, so they would be late for Hebrew school—and then Midwood High School. He mainly excelled as an amateur magician and dreidel hustler, who spun the little lead top with a Hebrew letter on each of its four sides until the smoothed-down edges ensured that he knew which side would come up more often than not. As a college student, he dropped out of New York University before briefly attending the City College of New York. He explains the reasons for his college failures, alternatively, as being caught cheating in "a delicate situation with the Dean's wife" or misbehavior during a metaphysics final ("I looked into the soul of the boy sitting next to me"). Despite his love affair with New York, he also did not absorb much of the city's high culture: "I didn't go to a play until I was about eighteen years old, almost never went to a museum, and never read at all" (Whitfield 1986).

Yet despite, or because of, the limitations of his education, Allen developed a persona very much in the tradition of Jewish humor. First, in his comedy monologues and early films like *Take the Money and Run* (1969), he was the *nebbish*—a comic nonentity. But then he graduated to the role of shlemiel—the failure with a brain and a sense of humor—playing an Americanized version of Menashe Skulnik of the Yiddish theater. His great achievement, in the words of Andrew Heinze, "was to take the heroic little man of American comedy (Buster Keaton, Charlie Chaplin) and make him a verbally heroic little man, unafraid of publicizing the angst within" (Heinz 2004).

Allen's breakthrough film, *Annie Hall,* infused Jewish content into the very non-Jewish tradition of great film romantic comedies going back to the 1930s. Perhaps for the first time in American popular culture, Allen's alter ego, Alvy Singer, broke with the history of Jewish comedians, who never played Jews, in order to recast the traditionally suspect male Jewish fascination with the *shiksa,* or blonde goddess, into an eccentric yet popular love story. Through Allen, Philip Roth's Portnoy thereby entered the American mainstream as a romantic hero rather than just a comic foil—with his love interest, a proper midwestern middle-class WASP, replacing Portnoy's nymphomaniac "monkey." Alvy gives his rueful experience a Jewish frame of reference from the first—when he invokes Sigmund Freud and Groucho Marx (applying Groucho's crack that "I wouldn't want to be a member of any club that would have me" to his own "relationships with women")—to the last, when he ends the film with another Jewish joke (Whitfield 1999). In a flashback, Alvy rejects the plea of his first wife, Allison Portchnik, to come to bed because he prefers to read the Warren Commission Report on the assassination of President John F. Kennedy. When she protests that he is rejecting her, Alvy responds: "She's right! . . . She was beautiful. . . . She was real intelligent." Alvy is once again spurning in the person of the Jewish feminine "any club" that would want him as a member.

The film's dramatic centerpiece is the contrast of Thanksgivings at the two homes: the WASPiness of Annie's ham-consuming family, including Grammy Hall's hostile gaze at the visiting "real Jew" Alvy, who for a moment is transformed into a Hasidic rabbi, in contrast to the Singers' frenetic, noisy digestion of the family brisket. Yet underlying the Halls' blandness is the craziness of Annie's clean-cut brother Duane, who brags over dinner of 4H-Club activities, yet later tells Alvy that he contemplates suicide by car crash. The Singers, on the other hand, are redeemed by their honesty and vitality. Annie's triumph is that—mentored by Alvy—she proves capable of outgrowing her own background, symbolized by her going on her own to see the film *The Sorrow and the Pity.* Alvy's tragedy is that—the victim of his insecurity and inability to combine sex with love in the same object—he is not capable of outgrowing his. His is a twinned Freudian and Jewish-American tragicomedy.

Allen began exploring the love-and-death theme with his film *Love and Death* (1975), his comic take on a Jewish peasant in czarist Russia. In the 1980s, he continued the exploration in the melodramatic mode with *Hannah and Her Sisters* (1986) and *Crimes and Misdemeanors* (1989). In *Hannah,* Allen plays a secondary character, Mickey Sachs, who shocks his parents by converting to Catholicism—buying a crucifix, icons, white bread, and mayonnaise—yet ultimately rejects it as a "die now, pay later" religion. In *Crimes,* the centerpiece is a flashback to a *seder* meal at which the characters passionately debate what is evil and whether God punishes it.

Crimes and Misdemeanors tells the parallel stories of Judah Rosenthal, a successful ophthalmologist who pays to have his mistress killed to prevent her from revealing their affair, and Cliff Stern, a filmmaker who ultimately refuses to complete a documentary film glorifying the egomaniacal television personality Lester. Cliff along the way falls in love with the film's producer, Halley, who rejects him because he is married. When Cliff divorces, Halley again rejects him and marries Lester. Cliff's hero and mentor is the philosophy professor Louis Levy, who lost his whole family in the Holocaust, yet who still believes that "it is only we with our capacity to love that give meaning to the indifferent universe." In the film's finale at a Jewish wedding, Cliff meets Judah, who relates the plot of a film script in which an adulterer kills his mistress and gets away with it. Judah, at least in his own mind, had eluded God's judgment without suffering the ravages of guilt. Cliff, on the other hand, refuses to abandon his Jewish ethical moorings.

Woody Allen's paradox is that he is the chronic "outsider"—and critic of both American and Jewish culture—who yet has found ways to win "insider" celebrity and acclaim despite his complaints that he has never been adequately appreciated by greedy Hollywood studios and banal American audiences. Has Allen mellowed over the years, particularly in relation to his own American and Jewish roots? For the first time, he appeared in 2002, in the wake of 9/11, at the Academy Awards ceremony, urging that films be made in New York City. Yet his expatriate alienation seems to have reasserted itself, to judge from his observation in 2005 to *Der Spiegel:* "The history of the world is like, he kills me, I kill him—only with different cosmetics and different castings: so in 2001 some fanatics killed some Americans, and now some Americans are killing some Iraqis. And in my childhood, some Nazis killed Jews. And now, some Jewish people and some Palestinians are killing each other" (*Der Spiegel,* June 20, 2005).

Specifically regarding his Jewish roots, Allen initially made a living from jokes negatively stereotyping Jews, explaining how his parents, when he was kidnapped, "rented out my room," and how "my grandfather, on his death bed, sold me his watch" (Telushkin 1992). In *Deconstructing Harry* (1997), he juxtaposed a tale of a Jewish retiree to Florida who admits that he literally cannibalized his first family with an encounter between Harry and his Zionist brother-in-law, in which Harry accepts the fact that Hitler killed six million Jews because he knows that "records are made to be broken." Yet more recently, Allen waxed more philosophical about his own Jewishness: "I'm not a religious person, but in the Jewish families that I've known and grew up in there were certain social values that were common to them—appreciation of theater, of classical music, of education, certain professions like medicine, law. When that appears in your comedy, it has the patina of Jewish humor" (Fox 2001).

Yet here also he regressed from mellow to mawkish in his rationalization—regarding the scandal over his romance with the teenage adopted daughter of his longtime companion Mia Farrow—that he learned from "all the reading I'd done through my life on the Holocaust. . . . Those who focused on what was actually happening to them—the daily horror . . . the reality of it—they survived" (Atzmon and Greenstein 2005). Then he mused to a *Washington Post* reporter, comparing his own declining virility and prospective mortality to the experience of the Holocaust: "You do the best you can within the concentra-

tion camp. If you face reality too much, it kills you. . . . It's just an awful thing, and in that context you've got to find an answer to the question: why go on?" Leon Wieseltier offered this diagnosis: "So that's it: nobody is coming upstairs to see his kvetchings. He isn't getting laid and it's Auschwitz. This is not what Primo Levi had in mind" (Wieseltier 2006).

Like the antihero of his pseudo-documentary *Zelig* (1983)—about the son of a Jewish actor who becomes a shape-changing chameleon, turning himself into a Hasid, a Christian, a black, and even a Nazi—Allen can neither reconcile himself to his Jewishness nor completely reject it, as he reverts to ambivalent form. Allen's shape-shifting Jewish antihero personifies the Jews' "long historical apprenticeship in cultural mimicry" (Stam and Showat 1985). *Zelig* in Yiddish means "blessed"—an ironic name in this context and a condition that Allen, to his credit, is honest enough not to claim for himself: "I've often said that the only thing standing between me and greatness is me" (Agence France Press 2005).

Harold Brackman

References and Further Reading

Abbott, Michael. 1996. "Talmudic Tradition in the Films of Woody Allen." Paper presented at Society for Cinema Studies Conference, Dallas, Texas.

Agence France Press. 2005. "Woody Allen Is Mediocre and Makes Miserable Films: Woody Allen." (December 18).

Atzmon, Gilad, and Tony Greenstein. 2005. "Debate." *Peacepalestine.* Available at: http://peacepalestine.blogspot.com/2005/06/gilad-atzmon-tony-greenstein-debate.html. Accessed March 7, 2007.

Fox, Michael. 2001. "Deconstructing Woody." *Los Angeles Jewish Journal* (August 24).

Heinze, Andrew W. 2004. *Jews and the American Soul: Human Nature in the Twentieth Century.* Princeton, NJ: Princeton University Press.

Lax, Eric. 2000. *Woody Allen: A Biography,* 2nd rev. ed. Cambridge, MA: Da Capo Press.

Stam, Robert, and Ella Showat. 1985. "Zelig and Contemporary Theory: Meditation on the Chameleon Text." *Enclitic* 9: 176–193.

Telushkin, Joseph. 1992. *Jewish Humor: What the Best Jewish Jokes Say about the Jews.* New York: William Morrow.

Whitfield, Stephen J. 1986. "The Distinctiveness of American Jewish Humor." *Modern Judaism* 6,3: 245–260.

Whitfield, Stephen J. 1999. *In Search of American Jewish Culture.* Hanover, NH: Brandeis University Press.

Wieseltier, Leon. 2006. "Reinie and Woody." *New Republic* (September 11–18).

American Jewish Women Entertainers

Twentieth-century America offered women, including Jewish women, opportunities to perform in a public venue. The commercialization of entertainment, which turned home- and church-based music and theatrical productions into a for-profit business in the new cities, enabled women to sing, dance, and act for diverse audiences. Talented Jewish women displayed their skills on the Yiddish stage, many coming to New York's Lower East Side from Eastern Europe. Some had been veteran actresses in Warsaw, Lublin, or the many other cities with large Jewish populations. Stars such as Bertha Kalich and Bessie Thomashefsky performed throughout Eastern Europe and came to New York as established stars. Others, such as Molly Picon, born on the Lower East Side, won acclaim in the Yiddish theater in America. For many actresses, the Yiddish stage was their only outlet, and they worked happily on it for decades. Others were lured to the English-speaking entertainment world, and they measured their success by the acceptance they received from American audiences, of Jews and non-Jews alike.

Jewish entertainers in early twentieth-century America were also attracted to vaudeville and burlesque houses, the epitomes of secular mass culture, which arose just when the Jewish migration was in full swing. Like their Christian counterparts, Jewish women played stereotypical roles in the variety shows, serving as the butt of humor in comedy duos, as well as the singers and dancers in musical numbers. For comic purposes, all women were treated as simpleminded, guilty of malapropisms, naïve comments, and general silliness. As females and members of a minority group, Jewish women entertainers were doubly handicapped. But in private enterprise a Jewish woman with a large and loyal following was as valuable a commodity as a popular WASP entertainer. Generally, it was the daughters and granddaughters of the immigrants who played in vaudeville. As women, they had to subscribe to the gender role expectations of American culture: their physical appearance determined the role they played. Those with delicate features and slim bodies were favored as dancers and heroines. When amply built Sophie Tucker appeared on stage in her early years of performing, she had to don blackface to be seen comically, the only role open to a large woman. Her girth prevented her from being the appealing

American Jewish entertainer Bertha Kalich performed in German, Yiddish, Romanian, and English. (Library of Congress)

ingénue. Immigrant Jewish women with thick accents were rarely allowed on the American stage. When Bertha Kalich, an exception, made the transition to English in New York, critics noted that her accent was slight and therefore acceptable to American audiences.

Jewish women who ventured onto the vaudeville or musical theater stage had already left their traditional religious Jewish culture. They had moved into the larger world of New York City or Chicago or Philadelphia, shedding their Jewish identities, and sometimes changing their names to become acceptable to Gentile audiences. The closer they were to their immigrant past, the greater was the likelihood that they masked their origins. By the third generation, that is, by the post–World War II period, ethnicity was no longer a major stumbling block—as long as it was not highlighted. Still, there were some important exceptions. Sophie Tucker sang some Yiddish songs (usually off-color ones) before her largely Jewish audience in the intimate setting of the new nightclubs in 1910s and 1920s New York and Chicago. Fanny Brice, who did not know Yiddish, learned to sing a song with a Yiddish accent, even performing it successfully in the Ziegfeld Follies, a very American, but Jewish-owned, venue. Ethnic humor, a regular feature of Fanny Brice's repertory, was acceptable to diverse audiences in the early decades of the twentieth century, when they consisted of people who were themselves within a generation of their European pasts.

Many considered appearing in public before mixed audiences, sometimes wearing flimsy costumes, inappropriate behavior for modest, observant Jewish women. Indeed, respectable society in the early twentieth century looked down upon women entertainers of all religions as having questionable morals. Performing removed women from the home, their traditional domain, and exposed them to the corrupt world. Like all entertainers, Jewish women entertainers strove for public recognition and success. Even those who spent their entire career in Yiddish theater sought fame and fortune, albeit in an environment that preserved their connection to secular Jewish culture. All women entertainers were pioneers, creating distinct, individual identities in an era when women had few public roles. The Jewish community, like most other ethnic communities, took pride in the successes of their talented singers and actors, though rabbis lamented the fact that more of their congregants went to the theater on Friday night than to the synagogue.

As the years passed, the Jewishness of Jewish American women entertainers became less and less evident—and less and less relevant to their work. While the Jewish press kept close watch on their favorite Jewish stars, the stars no longer played identifiably Jewish roles or starred in dramas about antisemitism or events in Jewish history. Many of the Jewish stars married Christian men and did not practice Judaism. Their connections to Judaism were tenuous at best. Thus this essay will focus on those who retained their identification with Judaism and/or Jewish American culture in their careers.

Bertha Kalich (1874–1939), born in Lemberg, Poland (then part of Austria-Hungary), displayed musical and dramatic talent at an early age. Encouraged by her mother, an ardent opera fan, she studied privately and at thirteen joined the chorus of the local Polish theater. Adept at languages, she eventually performed in German, Yiddish, Ro-

manian, and English. In 1890, she married Leopold Spachner, with whom she had two children. Four years later, they came to New York, where she performed at the Thalia Theater in a number of Yiddish plays. Beautiful and stately, she quickly developed a following, with women imitating her dignified mannerisms and elegant dress. Her growing fame attracted the attention of English producers, and in 1905 she appeared at the Manhattan Theater and other venues in English dramas. Her facility with languages probably enabled her to erase her accent easily. Ten years later, she returned to the Yiddish stage, where she continued to appear until the late 1920s, when poor health forced her to retire. While the actors in Yiddish theater were known for exaggerated gestures and over-the-top acting styles, Kalich was restrained and understated.

The dramas of the Yiddish theater were usually sentimental, romantic pieces, not known for their high art. The women were generally long-suffering and the men absent-minded or ineffectual. Indeed, Yiddish playwrights shared the same cultural role definitions as their Christian counterparts; men were patriarchs, and women were expected to be subservient and obedient. Comedy and musicals were more often found in Yiddish vaudeville houses, where a variety of acts closely resembled those in the English-language vaudeville shows. Molly Picon (1898–1992) won an amateur acting contest at age five and went on from there. Her natural athleticism and small stature contributed to her ease on the stage as a dancer, singer, and actress. Her sunny personality made her a favorite with audiences for many years. In the 1920s, she played at the Second Avenue Theater in New York, the most famous venue of all. With her husband Jacob Kalich, who wrote and directed many plays, over the years she developed a huge repertory of material that she performed repeatedly. In 1938, she starred in the last Yiddish movie made in Poland—*Mamele*—in which she played a twelve-year-old. She remained active, playing in a one-woman show, until just a few years before her death at ninety-four.

Sophie Tucker (1884–1966) was born in Russia but came to America when only three months old. Her family settled in Hartford, Connecticut, where they ran a kosher diner and rooming house. From an early age, despite her mother's disapproval, Sophie sang for the customers. Though she married at nineteen and had a son three years later, she yearned for the lights of New York and a career in show business. She fulfilled her dream by divorcing her husband Louis Tuck and leaving her son with her mother. With neither conventional beauty nor a lovely voice, Tucker (she added the "er" to her married name), a large woman with a gravelly voice, used her considerable personality to deliver a song, often a bawdy one, to the delight of audiences in supper clubs, like Reisenweber's in New York City. "A Good Man Is Hard to Find" and "I'm the Last of the Red-Hot Mammas" became staples in her repertory. Modeling herself after the popular African American blues singers, whose material was usually off-color, and capitalizing on audiences' (including Jewish audiences') love of the naughty, Tucker became a successful performer for decades. In 1925, Jack Yellen wrote "My Yiddishe Mamma" for her, a song that became part of all her performances. Tucker continued to perform in big city nightclubs until she died in 1966 at the age of eighty-two.

The new popular cultural media of the twentieth century offered opportunities for actresses to reach larger audiences. But the silent, and then sound, movies, as well as the radio, had new requirements that often led women to hide or erase their ethnicity. Being a Jewish woman was not a helpful or even a relevant attribute, except in some situations. *The Jazz Singer* (1927), for example, featured a Jewish family, who could be played by Jewish actors, although this was not essential. Indeed, directors wanted actors who could play any role. The performer's ethnicity was not an asset in popular culture. Moreover, antisemitism remained widespread in 1920s and 1930s America, and the movie moguls, most of whom were assimilated Jews, were not interested in promoting their kinswomen. They counseled discretion and name changes. Accordingly, Theodosia Goodman, a nice Jewish girl from Philadelphia, became Theda Bara in silent film. Depicting her as exotic, Hollywood presented her in ornate costumes and striking makeup.

One of the most successful woman entertainers whose Jewish persona was at the core of her success was Gertrude Berg (1899–1966). Born in New York City, she was an only child, whose family ran a resort hotel in the Catskill Mountains. Gertrude spent every summer there and at an early age began to write and produce skits for the amusement of the guests. After graduating from high school, she took playwrighting courses at Columbia University. In 1919, she married Lewis Berg, with whom she had a son and a daughter. By the late 1920s, she was trying to get her story ideas accepted by radio executives. Finally, in 1929, she

convinced the NBC Blue Network to air the first Goldberg family show. Berg starred in "The Rise of the Goldbergs," which remained on the air for five years. In 1934, she went on tour with the show, and in 1938 persuaded CBS to broadcast it. The program lasted seven years. With television making its debut after the war, Berg sought to move her well-known show to the new medium. In 1949, it became one of the first radio comedies to make a successful transition to television, where it lasted for five seasons.

The character Gertrude Berg created, Molly Goldberg, was a warm, maternal figure who used common sense and chicken soup to solve the various domestic crises that arose in a normal family. With her husband Jake, children Rosalie and Sammy, and boarder Uncle David, she negotiated the everyday struggles of an urban family who only happened to be Jewish. Although she cultivated a Yiddish accent, using Yiddish-inflected rhythms and expressions such as "oy" and "nu," Molly's basic approach was pragmatic American. References were made to Jewish holidays, and her Jewish neighbors in the Bronx apartment building where the family lived listened when she called "Yoo-hoo, Mrs. Bloom," but her Jewishness served mainly as comic relief. Berg's long popularity, however, testified to the public's willingness to watch a second-generation Jewish American family adjusting to American life, confronting problems common to all Americans.

Fanny Brice (1891–1951) had a successful career on the musical stage as well as on the radio. Doing ethnic skits in the Ziegfeld Follies such as "I'm An Indian" endeared her to large audiences. Born in New York City to the Borach family, she changed her name to Brice to avoid the ethnic label. Her smooth, silky voice quickly brought her success, first in amateur contests as a child, then in musicals as a teenager, and eventually in the Ziegfeld Follies, where she was the headliner throughout the 1910s and 1920s. She learned an Irving Berlin song satirizing Salome of the many veils, and Berlin taught her to sing it with a Yiddish accent. It was a big hit, and as a result Brice developed many musical numbers and comic skits based on Jewish family culture. "Mrs. Cohen at the Beach" featured an anxious and possessive Jewish mother. In the "I'm An Indian" number, she is Rosie Rosenstein, a nice Jewish girl who had been captured by the Indians. In the 1930s, she developed the radio persona of a mischievous child, Baby Snooks, a character she had created many years earlier. In this guise, she remained a beloved figure until her death in 1951.

Perhaps the most spectacularly successful Jewish woman entertainer of the twentieth century is Barbra Streisand (b. 1942). A singer and actress who also became a film director, she has won awards for her performances on stage, for her recordings, and her roles in film. Beginning on Broadway as Miss Marmelstein in *I Can Get It for You Wholesale* in 1961, Streisand's extraordinary voice, her fine articulation, and her comic talents distinguished her from other aspiring performers. Her portrayal of Fanny Brice in the stage version of *Funny Girl* two years later enlarged her audience; five years later the film version won her an Oscar. Playing a Jewish singing star was the first of her many filmic portrayals of Jewish American women. Though Streisand did not only play Jewish heroines, she was one in her most memorable films, such as *The Way We Were* (1973), where she is a radical student activist in the 1930s and an advocate of social justice in the 1940s and 1950s; in *Yentl* (1983), where she plays a Jewish girl in Poland who masquerades as a boy so she can study Torah; in *The Prince of Tides* (1991), where she is a Jewish psychiatrist (who falls for a Gentile man and laments the fact); and in the 1996 *The Mirror Has Two Faces*, in which she is a college professor.

Jewishness is a factor in all of these movies, not merely an accident of birth and upbringing. The Streisand character in *The Way We Were* falls in love with the symbol of WASP power and beauty (played by Robert Redford), and the clash of cultures is a major cause of their ultimate divorce. In *The Prince of Tides*, the Nick Nolte character is the object of her affection, and she asks herself why she falls in love with inappropriate Gentile fellows. *Yentl* focuses on the clash within Judaism between the male-dominated Orthodox system of gender roles and the modern one. Thus, while Streisand's music does not deal with her Jewish American identity, many of her cinematic roles do. Streisand always insisted that her prominent nose, a stereotypical Jewish feature, was a part of her and not to be changed. Identified openly as a liberal Democrat, who has become more and more of a political activist, recently Streisand has studied the mystical tradition in Judaism.

Bette Midler (b. 1945) is another very popular concert singer and film star who has identified as a Jew in many of her public pronouncements, as well as in her use of old Sophie Tucker songs. It is primarily on talk shows and in concerts that she refers to herself as Jewish. Midler has written in her comic autobiography *A View from a Broad* (1980) that being white and Jewish in Hawaii, where she grew up, was anomalous, and, she quipped, no one knew what it meant except that it had to do with liking boys. Beginning her career in 1965 by playing a small part in the stage production of *Fiddler on the Roof,* and then playing Tsaytl, Tevye's oldest daughter, on Broadway for several years, Midler went on to play at gay nightclubs, such as the Continental Baths in New York City, in the late sixties and early seventies. She developed her Divine Miss M persona, which included bawdy Tucker songs. In the 1980s, she made successful comedies, such as *Ruthless People* and *Down and Out in Beverly Hills.* In the 1990s she returned to the concert stage and toured the country with an updated version of her 1970s show. Her movie career ran into obstacles when she tried to star in melodramas, and her brief effort at television was unsuccessful. In the twenty-first century Midler has returned to the concert stage, leaving her movie career behind.

Although there have been other Jewish female characters on television, none has enjoyed the enduring popularity of Molly Goldberg. Valerie Harper as Rhoda Morgenstern was a Jewish woman yearning for marriage on "The Mary Tyler Moore Show," but there has not been a family comedy or melodrama openly featuring Jewish Americans since the Goldbergs. Perhaps that show represented the last time Jewish Americans qualified as an ethnic group on television. Since the 1970s, they have been displaced by African American families in situation comedies. Jewish Americans have been largely absorbed, for good or ill, into the American mainstream, and are no longer represented in popular culture as a distinct ethnic group. Consequently, Jewish American entertainers make little or no note of their religious or cultural background in presenting themselves to the American public.

June Sochen

References and Further Reading
Antler, Joyce. 1997. *The Journey Home: Jewish Women and the American Century.* New York: Free Press.
Berg, Gertrude, and Charney Berg. 1961. *Molly and Me.* New York: McGraw-Hill.
Grossman, Barbara W. 1991. *Funny Woman: The Life and Times of Fanny Brice.* Bloomington: Indiana University Press.
Katkov, Norman. 1953. *The Fabulous Fanny: The Story of Fanny Brice.* New York: Alfred A. Knopf.
Lifson, David S. 1965. *The Yiddish Theater in America.* New York: Thomas Yoseloff.

Sochen, June. 1981. *Consecrate Every Day: The Public Lives of Jewish American Women, 1880–1980.* Albany: State University of New York Press.

Spada, James. 1996. *Streisand: The Intimate Biography.* New York: Time Warner Paperbacks.

Tucker, Sophie. 1945. *Some of These Days: The Autobiography of Sophie Tucker.* New York: Garden City Publishing Co.

Harry Houdini (1874–1926)

Magician

Born Ehrich Weiss in Budapest, Hungary, Harry Houdini came to America when he was four. His father led a Reform Jewish congregation in Appleton, Wisconsin. But the Weisses were not spared the immigrant experience, moving to Milwaukee's slums when the rabbi lost his job, and on to New York tenements, where he resorted to selling his books to feed his six children. At eight Houdini was peddling newspapers and shining shoes; at twelve, he hopped a freight car, hoping to send money home. From then on he worked to support the family.

At his father's death in 1892, Houdini quit his job and set out to make his name. It was a bad time for breaking into show business—civic unrest, economic depression—but Houdini had an instinct for right choices. One was his marriage at twenty to Wilhelmina "Bess" Rahner (over her Catholic mother's strenuous objections). As a duo they performed magic tricks, mind-reading acts, song and dance and comedy routines wherever they could: beer gardens, dime museums, medicine shows, variety troupes, traveling circuses, carnival midways. It was a long and thorough apprenticeship; with the Escape Act Houdini discovered his calling. Beginning with handcuff releases, adding padlocks, leg irons, and chains (photographs show him trussed up with such devices like ornaments on a Christmas tree), he hit upon the Challenge Act: daring audiences to challenge *him.* He'd found his key—himself. Short, muscle-bound, with stubborn stocky bowlegs and kinky high-voltage hair, Houdini was compacted of energy, fueled by a fierce sense of competition and conquest. The stage was his arena and all else his adversary. When he combined locks with boxes, the Escape became a minimelodrama and the Magician a Hero: "Nothing Can Hold Houdini."

Magician Harry Houdini. (Library of Congress)

Rising to top billing as a variety act on the vaudeville circuit, Houdini set his sights higher. At the turn of the century he sailed for England and the Continent, accepting his own dare. The bet paid off. His Escape was an act of self-expression and an expression of his times. He was "The American self-liberator," the Little Guy, the Challenger, the personification for the Old World of the chutzpah of the New. Who better than an immigrant—and a Jew—to advertise the label, "Made in America"? The tour would last five years.

Houdini returned home a celebrity in the age of celebrity. From 1906 to 1914 he toured his two worlds, escaping from contraptions ever-more elaborate (and bizarre)—submerged in coffins underwater; stuffed and sewn inside the carcass of a smelly "sea monster" or a giant football strung with padlocks; immersed in vessels filled to overflowing—and performing publicity stunts ever-more daring—wriggling out of straitjackets suspended upside down from the tops of skyscrapers; leaping in anchors and manacles into cold murky rivers. Upping the ante is the imperative of show business. Houdini was returning to his circus roots: strong man, contortionist, acrobat, high-wire act, and all-around daredevil. "It was the easiest way to draw a crowd," he wrote (Silverman 1996). The risk was the act.

World War I cut him off from half his audience. But it offered a respite from the Escape—for all the tricks and gimmicks, the secret compartments and trapdoors, it was physically grueling for a man now in his forties. Ascetic, abstemious, constantly in training, wasting little time in sleep, Houdini concentrated his relentless energies on the war effort: entertaining the troops with patriotic extravaganzas, raising money—more than a million—at Liberty Bond rallies; founding new fraternal and philanthropic organizations; funding Jewish causes; and helping down-and-out magicians. He was depleting his own funds. A novelty act himself, Houdini was fascinated by the new, whether adventure or invention (he holds the record for the first solo plane flight in Australia), and Hollywood had made the fortune of many a rabbi's son. Starting out in serials, Houdini was soon producing, writing, and acting in his own feature films while keeping a cottage industry of ghostwriters going with his ideas for film scripts, magazine articles, short stories, and books: *The Right Way to Do Wrong, The Unmasking of Robert-Houdin, A Magician among the Spirits*. But the enterprise was his only failure; the movies competed with the magic.

Houdini was still "the greatest showman of them all," the highest-paid performer in vaudeville, a household word. With an immigrant's desire for legitimation and a serious interest in the history of magic, he amassed a vast collection of artifacts and memorabilia, now in museums and the hands of hosts of Houdini buffs. And, as often as he could, he bought back the books in his father's library.

Times were changing. Audiences were changing. Vaudeville's days were numbered. The Great War and the 1918 flu pandemic had left political turmoil, disillusion, and loss. Grief was a lucrative business for psychic mediums purporting to call up the spirits of the dead. Houdini's lengthy campaign exposing the fraud was motivated in part by his sense of competition—he had never pretended to be more than "an actor playing the role of magician"—and in part by his own inconsolable grief for his mother. But he was also battling the isolationism, nativism, and superstition of a reactionary postwar America. Astonished at the antisemitism of the Old World, he was encountering it in the New: death threats, hate mail, attacks as a Communist, an agent of the pope, a "Judas," a Jew (Silverman 1996).

He died at fifty-two, on Halloween, after giving a final performance in a high fever, with a broken ankle and a burst appendix. The crowds that had mobbed the streets to watch his escapes thronged to their hero's funeral. Houdini had aspired to nothing less than legend. His secret was not what he did but what he was—the force of his personality. Not captured on film, never more to be recorded, it must have been magic. To this day his name still stands for the thing.

Bette Howland

References and Further Reading
Brandon, Ruth. 1993. *The Life and Many Deaths of Harry Houdini*. New York: Random House.
Silverman, Kenneth. 1996. *Houdini! The Career of Ehrich Weiss*. New York: HarperCollins.

Al Jolson (1886–1950)

Performer

In the 1910s and 1920s, Al Jolson was one of the most popular performers of the American stage. His minstrel character was as recognizable to audiences as Charlie Chaplin's Little Tramp. Scholars consider his debut film, *The Jazz Singer* (1927), to be the birth of the talking motion picture. Jolson's career bridged nineteenth-century minstrelsy and vaudeville and the twentieth-century media of sound and screen, and his career signals the advent of Jews as major participants in the American entertainment industry.

In 1886, Asa Yoelson was born to Rabbi Moshe Reuben and Naomi Yoelson in Seredzius, Lithuania. In 1890, in the wake of a plummeting East European economy and increased antisemitism, Rabbi Yoelson came to the United States in search of work. Four years later he sent for the rest of his family to join him in Washington D.C., where he had found a position as the rabbi of the Orthodox Talmud Torah Congregation. Even after Rabbi Yoelson

Al Jolson entertains U.S. troops at Pusan Stadium, Korea in 1950. (National Archives)

found a congregation, he had to supplement his income with rabbinical odd jobs. Shortly after her migration to America, Naomi died.

In 1899, Asa performed for the first time as a street urchin in the stage production of Israel Zangwill's *The Children of the Ghetto*. He earned 25 cents per show for three shows before Rabbi Yoelson discovered his son's clandestine stage career and stopped it. Perhaps Asa's older brother, Hirsh, who had recently run away to New York to try his luck in the theater, had turned the rabbi against show business. But nothing could keep Asa from performing. He and Hirsh began to serenade the customers of the Hotel Raleigh with the latest popular tunes. "We knew all the popular songs," Hirsh remembered thirty years later: "Sweet Marie, The Sidewalks of New York, Maggie Murphy's Home, Daisy Bell, Say Au Revoir but Not Good-By—

but we found that some of the songs which the gray-haired statesmen and jurists liked best were old ones that carried them dreaming back into the past—Suwanee River, Old Kentucky Home, and When You and I Were Young, Maggie" (Alexander 2001). At age eleven, Asa ran away from home with a tiny carnival called Rich & Hoppe's Big Company of Fun Makers.

Asa moved from carnival show to burlesque house to dime museum, up and down the Eastern seaboard. Usually his job was to "plug" songs from the audience to induce a sing-along for established acts. Occasionally he took the stage himself. At fourteen he was established enough in show business for his face to grace the cover of a piece of sheet music, and he was billed as Al Joelson. Still, Al often turned up at his father's home penniless and unwashed.

In the fall of 1904, Asa settled into the medium of minstrelsy. While still billing themselves as Joelson & Joelson, Al and his brother appeared in a skit, "A Little of Everything," which included the part of a hospital orderly. The part was probably written specifically for blackface, since service positions were typical minstrel roles. Al found himself particularly adept at playing in blackface. It was for this act that Joelson changed his stage name to Jolson (Goldman 1988).

Jolson worked exclusively in blackface for the next five years. He traveled from carnival gig to burlesque house, sometimes with his older brother Harry, sometimes without, while he developed his minstrel performance and honed his comic timing. In 1908 Jolson played Portland, Oregon, where Lew Dockstader and his Minstrels were also playing. Upon seeing Jolson perform, Dockstader offered Jolson a position in his troupe. Lew Dockstader's Minstrel show of 1908–1909, in which Jolson participated, parodied the current fad of the rich to make expeditions to the North Pole. Its second act began in "Boo Hoo Land," a black jungle paradise into which stumbled the provincial explorers Professor Hightower (Lew Dockstader) and his scrawny assistant Acie (Al Jolson). These explorers—inexplicably both in blackface—soon find themselves in the tribal soup pot. By February 1909, after Dockstader's Minstrels played a week at Springer's Grand Opera House in New York, Jolson was blessed by *Variety,* already the premier magazine of the theater: "As it stands now, Jolson's offering is capable of holding down a place in any vaudeville show" (Goldman 1988).

Critics and fans soon learned Jolson's name. When Dockstader's show closed in 1909 for the summer, Jolson began to tour on the vaudeville circuit. The step from minstrel troupe to vaudeville was immense, for even vaudeville was considered highbrow compared to troupe minstrelsy. Jolson's crowning vaudeville appearance took place at Hammerstein's Victoria for a Monday matinee on December 27, 1909. Long famous as the premier vaudeville theater, the Victoria on Monday afternoons housed mainly a show business audience. Fellow performers, producers, and managers went there to scout the best vaudeville talent. To have arrived on Oscar Hammerstein's stage for a Monday show after only a few months on the vaudeville circuit was a testament to both Jolson's comic gift and his ambition.

The producers Jake and Lee Shubert eventually gave Jolson his breakthrough Broadway role in their musical comedy *La Belle Paree.* Jolson took the stage as Erastus Sparkler, described as "a colored aristocrat from San Juan Hill, cutting a wide swath in Paris." This made Jolson the first to perform minstrel comedy in what was then called the legitimate theater. The show was written by Frank Tours and Jerome Kern (the latter would go on to write *Showboat,* the groundbreaking musical about miscegenation), and starred such top talent as Melville Ellis and Stella Mayhew as the mulatto maid, who performed a duet with Jolson:

> *Jolson:* Never going back again to Yankee land.
> *Mayhew:* Got a lot of customs there that I can't stand.
> *Jolson:* Like hanging a coon.
> *Mayhew:* Working in June.
> *Both:* Hunting chicken thieves night and noon.
> *Jolson:* Don't know how to treat us colored gentlemen.
> *Mayhew:* Call us colored ladies "wenches" now and then.
> *Both:* There's one place for the race.

This song, "Paris Is a Paradise for Coons," announced Jolson's presence on Broadway, although the New York *World* introduced him erroneously as Al Johnson (Goldman 1988).

Though the Mayhew-Jolson duet received praise from critics, the show was generally panned. It was four hours long, and its plot was loose even by vaudeville standards, let alone for fancy Broadway. Audiences expected more from a Shubert production. Even with extensive revisions, the second night was no better. On the third night Jolson took extraordinary measures. He addressed the audience directly and without a script, in vaudeville fashion:

> Lot of brave folks out there. Either that, or you can't read. Come to think of it, after the reviews we got, there's a lot of brave folks up here on the stage. Hey, I know you. You was in the audience the last time I played Brighton Beach. You used to like my act. What's the matter, you come into this classy joint you think you shouldn't have a good time? C'mon, this place ain't so much. I remember when it was the Horse Exchange. That's better—now I got a few songs to sing, if you'll listen (Sieben 1962).

According to all reports and biographies, the third night made Jolson's career. He went on to two full decades in theater without a single flop. According to Jolson's best biographer, Herbert G. Goldman, in the next decade Jolson would perfect his stage character Gus in various Broadway roles, including "a gondolier, Robinson Crusoe's Man Friday, Inbad the Porter in the age of Sinbad, and Bombo, Christopher Columbus' black navigator" (Goldman 1988).

Jolson became so successful that, at the height of his stage career, he took out an ad in the 1919 New Year's issue of *Variety:* "Everybody likes me. Those who don't are jealous! Anyhow, here's wishing those that do and those that don't a Merry Christmas and a Happy New Year—Al Jolson" (Sieben 1962). Detractors often cite such conduct as evidence of Jolson's egomania. In fact, no mania is evident. In the same year that Jolson took out his ad there were two big musical comedy productions in America, Ziegfeld's *Follies* and the Shuberts' *Sinbad.* For the *Follies* of 1919, its classic year, Florenz Ziegfeld had enlisted a legion of talent including Eddie Cantor, Will Rogers, Bert Williams, Fanny Brice, Van and Schenck, Marilyn Miller, Anne Pennington, and the mordantly brilliant W. C. Fields. The Shuberts had only one star—Al Jolson. Alone, Jolson stood fast and favorably against the entire cast of the *Follies,* as he had for each year in the preceding decade in every musical comedy in which he appeared. Much of Jolson's appeal can be traced to his stage presence and comic timing, which by all accounts were flawless. Yet it was also Jolson's ability to deliver a song that made him a star. Among the numbers Jolson introduced in *Sinbad* were "Swanee," "Rock-a-Bye Your Baby with a Dixie Melody," and the melody by which he has been known since, "My Mammy."

Samson Raphaelson, an undergraduate at the University of Illinois, went to see Al Jolson star in "Robinson Crusoe, Jr." Sometime in the course of the show, Raphaelson claimed he had an epiphany: "My God, this isn't a jazz singer," he realized. "This is a cantor!" (Alexander 2001). The image of the blackfaced cantor remained in Raphaelson's mind until he wrote a short story, "The Day of Atonement," a fictionalized account of Al Jolson's life. Shortly after its publication, Jolson read the short story and decided that a comedic version of it, starring himself, would look good on the screen. D. W. Griffith, director of *Birth of a Nation,* agreed that the stage's most celebrated talent should work in film, and Griffith considered directing the picture himself. Ultimately he dropped that idea because even he considered the story "too racial," by which he meant its subject was too Jewish. As Jolson looked for a studio and director to film his biography, he found that most of Hollywood agreed with Griffith. For modern

movie audiences "The Day of Atonement" was too Jewish. Raphaelson turned his short story into a dramatic play, which he called *The Jazz Singer,* and brought it to Broadway on September 15, 1925. For the next two years it performed successfully to mostly Jewish audiences.

Meanwhile, four Jewish brothers, Sam, Harry, Albert, and Jack Warner, had successfully premiered Vitaphone technology to an audience of industry elites in 1926 with a film short, *Don Juan.* But the new technology was not yet proven before paying audiences. Because the Warners made two Vitaphone feature films that flopped after the premier of *Don Juan,* they knew that the new and expensive technology required a perfect vehicle. Yet, for many reasons, *The Jazz Singer* was not a sure hit. For one, Warner Brothers originally signed George Jessel, the virtually unknown lead of the Broadway production, to star. Even Sam Warner's later hiring of Jolson did not assure the film's success. Jolson's experience was entirely in stage comedy, and *The Jazz Singer* was a drama. Jolson's name had never sold a single movie ticket.

Moreover, D. W. Griffith was right. The subject matter of *The Jazz Singer* was indeed "racial." Some film companies enjoyed moderate success with ethnic themes targeted at ethnic audiences, although this practice was less popular in the 1920s than it had been earlier. Warner Brothers, however, achieved most of its previous successes by producing movies with universal appeal; *Rin Tin Tin* was by far its largest grossing picture before 1927. The explicit theme of the film is the conflict of competing ethnic musics. Specifically, *The Jazz Singer* compares the liturgical music of Jews and the imagined music of African Americans. Prayer and jazz become metaphors for Jews and blacks.

The movie was an enormous success with gentile and Jewish audiences alike. In its review of *The Jazz Singer,* the *Morgen Zhurnal* (*Morning Journal*) spoke characteristically for all the Jewish papers. "Is there any incongruity in this Jewish boy with his face painted like a Southern Negro singing in the Negro dialect?" a critic asked. "No, there is not. Indeed, I detected again and again the minor key of Jewish music, the wail of the Chazan, the cry of anguish of a people who had suffered. The son of a line of rabbis well knows how to sing the songs of the most cruelly wronged people in the world's history" (Diner 1977). African American music, according to another article, "was born on the plantations of the South and in [it] one can hear the cracks of slave-drivers' whips and the clanging of chains and the pain of expression" (Diner 1977).

East European Jews, many of whom had come from the bleak Russian Pale, believed they were uniquely qualified to interpret that music. Al Jolson himself made the comparison of Jewish and African American exiles in his film *Big Boy.* On the lawn of a plantation, in overalls, burnt cork, a wig of wool, and a broken hat of straw, Jolson leads a group of recently freed slaves, played by African American actors, through verses of the classic slave spiritual "Go Down Moses." Exile was the shared sacred history to which the *Kalifornia Yidishe Shtime* (*California Jewish Voice*) referred in its praise of Jolson's blackface performance: "In every fluctuation of Jolson's voice, and in the smallest movement of his body, there is such religious tragedy that a shiver courses through the bones" (Alexander 2001).

That same newspaper posited a larger meaning to Jolson's minstrelsy: "When one hears Jolson's jazz songs, one realizes that jazz is the new prayer of the American masses, and Al Jolson is their cantor. The Negro makeup in which he expresses his misery is the appropriate *talis* for such a communal leader" (Alexander 2001).

The Jazz Singer made film a legitimate subject for review to some Jewish papers. Many motion pictures and reviews followed. Jolson did well in some, not so well in others. His last starring role was in *The Singing Kid* (1936); American perceptions of minstrelsy had changed during the Depression and thus ended Jolson's career.

Jolson sang for troops in World War II, and, due to his resurging popularity, a movie was made about his life, *The Jolson Story* (1946), in which Jolson himself dubbed the songs for star Larry Parks. The film's success resulted in a sequel, *Jolson Sings Again* (1949). Jolson also entertained troops in Korea, after which he died of a heart attack in San Francisco, on October 23, 1950.

Michael Alexander

References and Further Reading
Alexander, Michael. 2001. *Jazz Age Jews.* Princeton, NJ: Princeton University Press.
Diner, Hasia R. 1977. *In the Almost Promised Land: American Jews and Blacks, 1915–1935.* Westport, CT: Greenwood Press.
Goldman, Herbert G. 1988. *Jolson: The Legend Comes to Life.* New York: Oxford University Press.
Sieben, Pearl. 1962. *Immortal Jolson: His Life and Times.* New York: Frederick Fell.

Samuel "Roxy" Rothafel (1882–1936)

Co-creator of the Movie Palace Experience

Radio broadcasting pioneer, showman, filmmaker, author, and co-creator of the movie palace experience, Roxy Rothafel transformed moviegoing into grand entertainment. Theaters around the world are named for him.

Samuel Lionel "Roxy" Rothafel was born in Germany in 1882 and immigrated to the United States in 1886. He grew up in the lumber town of Stillwater, Minnesota, the son of a poor Jewish cobbler. By the turn of the century, Roxy had joined the hordes of immigrants in New York City searching for something that a man with dreams, but little education or training, could accomplish. He enlisted in the Marines (1901–1905), where he found the discipline and skills he would use to build his empire.

After his service ended, he became a traveling bookseller and a semipro baseball player in northeastern Pennsylvania. It was on the baseball diamond that his famous nickname was coined.

He opened his first movie house, the Family Theatre, in 1908 in a large room behind a Forest City, Pennsylvania, tavern. Although his clientele were mostly coal miners and their families, Roxy insisted on bringing high-class films, vaudeville, and musical acts to the Family Theatre that were often in stark contrast to the offerings at many contemporary nickelodeons.

By 1910, Benjamin F. Keith hired Roxy to add motion pictures to his vaudeville theaters and to enhance their presentation, from interior decoration to the ushers' appearance. The following year, he converted the 3,000-seat Alhambra Theatre in Milwaukee, formerly used for "legitimate" productions, into the largest venue in the country dedicated solely to motion pictures. Roxy next made over the 1,700-seat Lyric Theatre in Minneapolis, thereby attracting the middle class to both theaters. By the time he left the Lyric in mid-1913, patrons included prominent members of the city's academic, legislative, business, religious, and cultural elite (including the state's governor), all now supporters of this once shunned medium.

Roxy left each theater more elegant and yet more accessible to the lower and middle classes than it had been. A Roxy theater offered carefully selected motion pictures with classical musical accompaniment, professionally

Samuel "Roxy" Rothafel, a creator of the modern movie palace, seated in Capitol Theater in New York, ca. 1923. (Library of Congress)

managed and dressed ushers, a meticulous staff, and magnificent theater—all with the goal of providing as fine a performance as at the symphony, at a price everyone could afford.

His marriage of fine music, better films, and a staff that treated even its poorest patron the same way it did the governor sitting only a few rows away enabled Roxy to democratize culture, wresting it from the hands of the elite and making it available to all. Roxy, and the contemporaries he influenced like Marcus Loew, William Fox, and Balaban & Katz, spent the next two decades hiring conductors, musicians, opera singers, dancers, and choreographers who were every bit as talented, if not more so, than those who worked in posh society venues.

He was not the only showman working to elevate motion pictures and motion picture theaters, but by 1913 he

was certainly the best known within the industry. He moved to New York City's Regent Theatre in November 1913, to the city's Strand in 1914, to the Knickerbocker in 1915, to the Rialto in 1916, and managed both the Rivoli and Rialto from 1917 to 1919, always guided by an unrelenting desire to elevate the lives and cultural education of people with backgrounds similar to his own. "I have little interest in the exclusive few," he told the journal *Etude*, in 1927. "My work must reach all or none."

Roxy increased the size of his orchestra at each successive venue he managed, and soon pioneered, along with his West Coast counterpart, Sidney Patrick Grauman, the prologue, a short stage performance, usually with a thematic and/or stylistic connection to the feature film presented. Prologues later grew in size and scale to become full-blown stage shows, a cornerstone of the movie palace experience.

The Hollywood Reporter's W. R. Wilkerson noted in 1936, "He created the presentation house, the picture stage show; he brought into movie theaters the big concert orchestras, the ballets, the concert and opera singers. Every important feature of motion picture presentation in the theater today was the inspiration of Roxy."

With America's entry into World War I, Roxy devoted much of his time to encouraging enlistment and patriotic vigor, stationing Marines at the entrances of his theaters and even incorporating them into his stage shows. He reenlisted in the Marine Corps Reserves and directed and/or edited several war films for the Committee on Public Information.

After leaving the Rialto and Rivoli in January 1919 for an ill-fated attempt at producing motion pictures, Roxy returned to exhibition, managing the Park Theatre in Manhattan and, for Samuel Goldwyn, the California Theatre in Los Angeles. By June 1920, Roxy was back in Manhattan to revive the 5,300-seat Capitol Theatre where, to boost its sagging box office, he lowered the theater's ticket prices, expanded its orchestra and stage shows, and added foreign films and documentaries to its repertoire, making it the country's highest-grossing movie theater.

During specific holidays Roxy would incorporate religious hymns, like "Kol Nidre," into the Capitol's live entertainment. Jewishness, however, remained a secular component of his life, and he viewed religious services and songs as just another element of entertainment. Roxy, like Fox, Loew, and other Jewish moguls, would become increasingly active in Jewish charities and organizations.

His position as the industry's most prolific motion picture exhibitor was further solidified when he began broadcasting the Capitol's live performances over radio station WEAF in November 1922. In February 1923, he constructed a special recording studio inside the theater for his cadre of performers, now known as *Roxy and His Gang* (one of the first variety shows on radio), which was soon picked up by stations across North America. Thanks in part to "Roxy and His Gang"'s instant popularity, the variety show format became a mainstay on radio for decades, and later on television. With millions of adoring fans from Cuba to Canada, "Roxy and His Gang" frequently toured North America to raise money for charity and were greeted by parades and an invitation to the White House.

Roxy co-wrote *Broadcasting: Its New Day,* began a nationally syndicated newspaper column, and was named president of the Radio Announcers of America—all in 1925. He soon became a pitchman as well, appearing in ads for grape juice, cigarettes, radios, and other products.

Given his influence and fame (his broadcasts reached an estimated 10 million listeners at their peak), he was offered the management of a new movie palace that was to be named for him, the 5,920-seat Roxy Theatre, whose opening on March 11, 1927, marked the pinnacle of the movie palace era. With its cavernous auditorium and rotunda, its battalion of well-drilled ushers, its ever-expanding stage shows, and its 110-piece orchestra and 110-member chorus, the Roxy Theatre exemplified the excess emblematic of the era. Less than two weeks after its debut, the theater was purchased by William Fox for $15 million.

Roxy was lured away in 1931 to manage two new theaters at Rockefeller Center: the 5,960-seat vaudeville-only Radio City Music Hall and a 3,500-seat movie house, the RKO Roxy Theatre. A new troupe of Roxyettes was commissioned for the Music Hall by the group's founder, Russell Markert, who had initially brought them to the original Roxy Theatre. (These precision dancers live on as the Rockettes.)

Radio City's opening night on December 27, 1932, was a critical disaster, and Roxy, gravely ill at the time, left the theater on a stretcher. He returned two days later to oversee the opening of the RKO Roxy Theatre before reentering the hospital for surgery. He rejoined Radio City in April 1933, but with his responsibilities and salary cut in half, he resigned in January 1934.

A subsequent unprofitable tour of "Roxy and His Gang" at Paramount's deluxe movie houses was followed by yet another failure when he reopened the 4,300-seat Mastbaum Theatre in Philadelphia that December, only to have it close ten weeks later. Sound motion pictures, coupled with the Depression, had made Roxy's brand of stage show and orchestral extravagance passé and often fiscally untenable. (Roxy blamed the failure on a local cardinal who forbade parishioners to attend any movie theater in Philadelphia.)

His radio efforts were now the lone bright spot in his life, with "Roxy and His Gang" appearing on the CBS radio network for a one-year engagement that began in September 1934, each week adding to the seven million fan letters he had collected during his thirteen years on the radio.

In January 1936, NBC and CBS began vying to bring Roxy back on the air for a new radio show, while Paramount was negotiating to reinstall him as managing director of the original Roxy Theatre. Days away from returning to the institutions he loved most, he fell asleep on January 12 and never awoke. He was fifty-three.

Today, his famous nickname still adorns the marquees of hundreds of unaffiliated theaters and nightclubs throughout the world, extending the brand name that has come to embody the very word *entertainment*.

Ross Melnick

References and Further Reading

Hall, Ben M. 1961. *The Best Remaining Seats.* New York: C. N. Potter.

Melnick, Ross. 2003. "Rethinking Rothafel: Roxy's Forgotten Legacy." *The Moving Image* (Fall): 62–95.

Melnick, Ross, and Andreas Fuchs. 2004. *Cinema Treasures.* St. Paul, MN: MBI Publishing Company.

Sammy Davis Jr. (1925–1990)

Singer, Dancer, Entertainer

Sammy Davis Jr. was one of America's most beloved entertainers in the second half of the twentieth century. He was a singer, dancer, and comedian, a star of vaudeville, Las Vegas nightclubs, Broadway, and Hollywood. His conversion to Judaism, his many relationships with white women, and his strained rapport with the American black community made him controversial in his time.

Sammy Davis Jr. was born into an entertainment family in Harlem, New York. His parents soon separated, and at age eleven Davis joined his father and Will Mastin to form the Will Mastin Trio, the vaudeville team with which Davis worked for the next quarter of a century. All three performers played in blackface occasionally, which was normal for black performers of the time, but Davis was particularly adept at the practice since he enjoyed mimicking the act of Al Jolson, one of his heroes.

As a teenager, Davis became an expert dancer and comedian. By all accounts he had tremendous energy and did not want to leave the stage at evening's end. His shows were characterized by manic and impromptu dance numbers interspersed with songs and comic impressions of Hollywood actors. These became the mainstay of his long career.

After service in the U.S. Army during World War II, Davis returned to the Will Mastin Trio and became its lead. Davis found his first national recognition as the opening act for a tour by Mickey Rooney. In 1952, the Will Mastin Trio became regulars on television's *The Colgate Comedy Hour,* hosted by Eddie Cantor. During this time Davis became lifelong friends with many Jewish performers, including Jerry Lewis and Tony Curtis.

The reasons for Davis's conversion to Judaism in 1954 remain obscure. During the summer of that year, Davis read a history of the Jews and found himself moved by their story. Soon after, in a car accident near San Bernardino, California, Davis badly damaged his eye. According to Davis's account of his conversion experience, after the accident he realized that he had not been carrying a mezuzah given to him by Eddie Cantor. Then, just before surgery to remove his eye, actress Janet Leigh pressed a Star of David into his hand. All of this prompted Davis to seek out Rabbi Max Nussbaum of Temple Israel, Los Angeles, for conversion procedures. For the next several years he was often seen around Los Angeles reading *Everyman's Talmud.* Jewish friends did not encourage the conversion or believe its sincerity. Tony Curtis thought the conversion "a bit gratuitous," while Jerry Lewis commented, "You don't have enough problems already?" (Haygood 2003). Nevertheless, Davis became a lifelong observer of the High Holidays and other Jewish practices. Indeed, it was as a Jew that Davis reproved a friend who had read a history of the Jews but remained unimpressed:

> Baby, you'd better read it again. These are a swinging bunch of people. I mean I've heard of persecution, but what they went through is ridiculous. . . . They'd get kicked out of one place, so they'd just go on to the next one and keep swinging . . . , believing in themselves and in their rights to have rights, asking nothing but for people to leave 'em alone and get off their backs, and having the guts to fight to get themselves a little peace (Haygood 2003).

In 1960 Davis married Swedish actress May Britt in a home ceremony performed by Reform Rabbi William M. Kramer of Temple Israel, Hollywood. Britt had converted to Judaism several months before. This was only the latest relationship between Davis and a white woman in a series that had also included actress Kim Novak. Racists protested the marriage, while American Nazis picketed

Davis's shows with placards reading "Sammy Davis Jewnior." In celebration of Lincoln's birthday the following year, Davis and his wife, along with other prominent blacks, were officially invited to a White House event. However, when President John F. Kennedy realized at the last minute that the mixed race couple had been invited, he refused to see them and had them escorted from the room before photographers arrived. Davis never forgot the slight and eventually cultivated a relationship with Richard M. Nixon, which further estranged Davis from the black community (Haygood 2003).

On Broadway, Davis is known principally for two shows. In *Mr. Wonderful* he played a nightclub entertainer. The play climaxed with Davis impersonating Al Jolson in blackface, which critics considered the show's highlight (Haygood 2003). *Golden Boy* also achieved longevity and much acclaim. In film he is best remembered for his portrayal of Sportin' Life in *Porgy and Bess,* and for his appearance with Frank Sinatra, Dean Martin, Peter Lawford, and Joey Bishop in *Ocean's 11.* In song Davis was known for his renditions of "I've Gotta Be Me," "The Birth of the Blues," and "Mr. Bojangles," the latter about the minstrel life. He considered "Mr. Bojangles" somewhat autobiographical and pursued the rights to record it for some time before he was finally permitted to do so.

Davis published two autobiographies and one essay about Hollywood. He died of throat cancer in Los Angeles. He received a Jewish funeral from Rabbi Allen Freehling.

Michael Alexander

References and Further Reading
Davis, Sammy, Jr., Jane Boyar, and Burt Boyar. 1989. *Why Me? The Sammy Davis Jr. Story.* New York: Farrar, Straus and Giroux.
Fishgall, Gary. 2003. *Gonna Do Great Things: The Life of Sammy Davis, Jr.* New York: Scribner's.
Haygood, Wil. 2003. *In Black and White: The Life of Sammy Davis, Jr.* New York: Alfred A. Knopf.

American Jews and Science Fiction

Jewish science fiction is a subcategory of the science fiction genre that explores the universe and humanity's place in it by using Jewish concepts, beliefs, and traditions. Although science fiction is commonly seen as a literature of the future, it is in fact a literature of ideas and thus lends itself to the intellectual and inquiring tradition of Judaism.

Science fiction as a distinct literary genre can be dated to the creation by Hugo Gernsback of the magazine *Amazing* in 1928, although stories recognizable as science fiction predate Gernsback's magazine. Jewish characters and ideas have appeared in that literature since before Gernsback, although many of the stories contained little, if any, Jewish content beyond the inclusion of Jewish characters or artifacts drawn from Jewish folklore.

From the earliest days of science fiction as a defined literary genre, authors tackled Jewish themes and included Jewish characters in their works, although it would still be many years before those themes, whether based on *halacha* (Jewish law) or Jewish history, became integral to the story rather than added on for flavor. Similarly, Jews have written science fiction from the very beginning, although there was a large influx of contributors in the late 1930s and 1940s with the publication of works by Isaac Asimov, Lester del Rey, H. L. Gold, C. M. Kornbluth, Judith Merril, and Sam Moskowitz, among others.

For many people, Jack Dann's 1974 anthology *Wandering Stars* is the *aleph* and *tauf* of Jewish science fiction. However, science fiction acknowledged Jews and Jewish themes long before this.

Given the number of practitioners of science fiction who can be considered Jewish, from the nonpracticing Isaac Asimov to the orthodox Avram Davidson, it is not surprising that Jewish themes and Jewish humor have long pervaded the genre. Asimov, Judith Merril, and Harlan Ellison are among the more famous Jewish practitioners of science fiction, but a complete list of Jewish writers in the field would go on for pages. However, that a science fiction story is written by a Jew does not automatically make it Jewish, and a story written by a non-Jew may contain Jewish themes.

Jewish science fiction can be separated into four categories. The first, science fiction and fantasy that use Jewish characters or situations, is Jewish in name alone. The second, like the fiction and fantasy of the Borscht Belt, uses Jewish themes, characters, and tropes to create humor. The third category is that of wish fulfillment, wherein Jews, after centuries of oppression, have gained the ability to strike back. Finally, there is the serious Jewish science fiction and fantasy that use the tropes of the genre to study questions of importance to Jews and possibly to other ethnic groups. Several works fall into more than one category.

Type I: In Name Only

A story that includes nominally Jewish characters is not necessarily a Jewish story, just as the appearance of Jewish characters in television sitcoms does not mean the characters have a Jewish outlook on life (and frequently only appear Jewish when necessary). The early science fiction stories that added a Jewish character or artifact did not explore how its Jewishness affected the story. A cinematic example is *Raiders of the Lost Ark*. While the Ark is Jewish, nothing else about the film draws on Jewish tradition.

In his "Guardians of the Flame" novels, particularly the early ones, Joel Rosenberg introduces a Jewish character, Doria Perlstein. Although there are some vague references to her upbringing, the religious and cultural identity of the character is intrinsic neither to Doria's actions nor to the plot. In his later works, such as the "Metzada" sequence or "The Keepers of the Hidden Way" series, the characters' Jewishness becomes more important.

This type of Jewish presence occurs frequently in science fiction that is set in a historical period. Jews are added for a feeling of authenticity, but their religion and their associated outlook on life do not add anything to the story. As far as the story is concerned, these Jews could just as easily be Christians, Hindus, or aliens, depending on the scenario. In Orson Scott Card's *Enchantment* (1999), a retelling of the story of Sleeping Beauty, the protagonist is a Jewish boy from New York who gets involved in an ancient curse. While his Jewishness adds an extra layer of intrigue, it is not essential to the plot or character. Jane Yolen's retelling of the same fairy tale in *Briar Rose* (1992), on the other hand, uses Jewish themes in a much more integral manner, as her characters must contemplate how their Judaism defines them in the aftermath of the Holocaust.

Type II: For Comic Effect

Often the Jewish content of a story is no more than a hook on which to hang Borscht Belt–style humor, as in Harry Turtledove's "A Different Vein" (2000) or Adam-Troy Castro's "The Curse of the Phlegmpire" (1996). Harlan Ellison's "I'm Looking for Kadak" (1974) is based on *gilgul*

(reincarnation), but it is most notable for its inclusion of numerous Yiddish terms (and a glossary) used for comedic effect. Other Ellison stories, including "Mom" (1981) and "Go Towards the Light" (1997), also rely heavily on humor.

The story can be considered Jewish in the same way a Jackie Mason or Henny Youngman joke is labeled Jewish. It has grown out of the Jewish tradition, which can be traced back to the tales of Sholom Aleichem and Jewish oral usage. It is a style of telling a story that goes deeper than just the speech patterns associated with Brooklyn or Eastern European Jews. An instance of this is Avram Davidson's "The Golem" (1955), which refers to Jewish folklore, but could just as easily refer to Frankenstein's monster. Still, the speech patterns and the world-weary attitude of the Gumbeiners clearly indicate the culture from which they came, as does their low-key method of dealing with the animated menace that appears before them.

Because of the obvious link of the golem to the Frankenstein story (although the moral of Rabbi Lowe's tale is different from Shelley's), it is not surprising that the golem recurs throughout science fiction and fantasy. Harry Turtledove's "In This Season" (1992) tells the story of a Jewish family rescued by a golem during the Holocaust. In both the Davidson and Turtledove tales, the Jews are able to succeed because of their knowledge of Jewish folklore, whether in destroying or creating the clay guardian.

Another practitioner of the Jewish comedic tale is Mike Resnick. While his novel *The Branch* (1984) is a more serious book about the Jewish messiah, his short stories rely on Jewish humor to make their point. "The Kemosabee" (1994) mixes Jewish culture, American folk heroes, and the legend that the Native American tribes are descended from the lost tribes of Israel to deliver a punchline. "Mrs. Hood Unloads" (1991) uses the stereotypical Jewish mother of comedy routines to provide a humorous take on the Robin Hood story.

Woody Allen's "The Scrolls" (1974), reprinted in *More Wandering Stars* (1981), relies on a rudimentary knowledge of the Bible and Jewish history, as well as recent archaeology, to parody the traditional interpretations of Biblical stories. Christopher Moore uses a similar technique in the novel *Lamb* (2002). Although *Lamb* focuses on the life of Jesus, it places the character (and his companion) in a well-researched Jewish milieu and shows their Jewish perceptions in just about everything they do.

Type III: Wish Fulfillment

The greatest wish fulfillment stories are Joel Rosenberg's two-volume "Metzada" sequence, *Not For Glory* (1988) and *Hero* (1990). In these novels, Jewish mercenaries, who have long since left Israel, have developed a military culture that places them in high demand across the galaxy. They need never fear a reprise of the Holocaust, not only because they can defend themselves, but, for the right price or cause, they can go on the offensive. Just as science fiction in general is an extrapolation from modern theories, the Jews in these books are an extrapolation from the feats of the Mossad and the Israeli army in the sixties and seventies against overwhelming odds.

Susan Shwartz and S. M. Stirling both used Judaism as the basis for their stories in Jerry Pournelle's "War World" series. Like Rosenberg's volumes, these stories are set in a far future among Jews of an interstellar Diaspora. While they face overwhelming forces, in a race of genetically modified supermen, their HaBandari are pastoral peoples who prove themselves capable warriors when the need arises.

In contrast to Rosenberg's tales is Turtledove's "Next Year in Jerusalem" (2003), which posits a world in which the Jews have been driven from Israel and an Arab state has displaced the Jewish state. In this unsettling story, Jewish fighters return to the Holy Land in an attempt to reclaim it. While their ability may fall into the wish-fulfillment mode, most Jews, and certainly those who support Israel, will find the portrayal of the Jewish invaders appalling.

More than anything else, the Holocaust is the defining event of modern Jewish history. Without the Holocaust, it is quite possible that the quest for a Jewish state would be no further along than it was when Theodor Herzl espoused the idea in the late nineteenth century. Many of the science fiction and fantasy stories that focus on Jews do so in the context of alternative histories in which the Nazis won. This is the case in Martin Gidron's *The Severed Wing* (2000) and in time travel stories, such as J. R. Dunn's *Days of Cain* (1997) and Stephen Fry's *Making History* (1996), in which an attempt is made (with varying results) to change Hitler's success.

Rather than realizing desires for the Holocaust never to happen again, these tales are a wish fulfillment that the Holocaust had never occurred or that it could have been made less horrific. P. D. Cacek's short story "A Book by Its Cover" (2002) presents a method of ameliorating the effects of the Holocaust by enabling the salvation of individual Jews through fantastic means, while hewing closely to the view of Judaism as a religion of the Book.

Type IV: Serious Issues

The science fiction stories that most strongly emphasize Jewishness are those examining what it means to be Jewish. Jack Dann's "Jumping the Road" (1992) explores a race of Jews on a distant planet removed from the rest of their coreligionists, calling to mind the Jews of Ethiopia or India. Similarly, "Kaddish for the Last Survivor" (2000), Michael Burstein's tale of a Holocaust survivor's granddaughter who is struggling with issues of assimilation, reflects on what it means to be Jewish, perhaps as no other story since William Tenn's "On Venus, Have We Got a Rabbi" (1974).

While the Holocaust is often at the core of stories of wish fulfillment, it has also been used to highlight questions of Jewish identity. Burstein's "Kaddish for the Last Survivor" indicates that the Holocaust has created a new urgency in the maintenance of a Jewish identity, for, if Jews forget who they are, the Nazis will have won. Philip Roth's *The Plot against America* (2004) places an antisemitic president in the White House during the rise of the Nazis; it considers what it means to be Jewish and what it means to be American, and which takes precedence in an increasingly hostile environment.

Burstein's "Kaddish for the Last Survivor" and Carol Carr's "Look, You Think You've Got Troubles" (1974) both take a serious look at intermarriage, one of the major issues of American Jewish identity. Both address the issue of a Jewish woman marrying a non-Jewish man, and, although they come to very different conclusions, both reaffirm a sense of Jewish identity.

Judaism, which existed long before Christianity, is much more than a rejection of Jesus. As Mike Resnick has frequently said, his novel *The Branch* was an attempt to show what a messiah based on the Old Testament would be like. By returning to the G–d of the Old Testament, and exploring how Judaism differs from Christianity, Resnick presents a messiah who is anything but the Christian prince of love.

Some authors explore serious issues other than identity and religion. In Israel several authors, who may be responding to recent events there and the radicalization of

Islam, warn of a takeover of Judaism and the country by the religious right. Such works include Yitzhak ben Ner's *HaMalachim Baim* (1987) and Amos Kenan's *HaDerech L'Ein Harod* (1984), dystopian novels similar to George Orwell's *1984* or Anthony Burgess's *A Clockwork Orange,* that sound the alarm of the consequences if events continue along their current path.

Non-Jewish authors Barry B. Longyear and Robert Zubrin have also looked at the Arab–Israeli conflict and have offered their own solutions in a science fiction setting. Longyear's *The Last Enemy* (1998), a sequel to his "Enemy Mine," presents two races, humans and Drac, exploring how they resolve their differences. Longyear's novel provides an analog for the Jewish Bible and Talmud. Zubrin's more political satire addresses not only the conflict in Israel, but also the perceptions of Israeli actions.

W. R. Yates's novel *Diasporah* (1985) looks at the Jewish community after Israel has been destroyed. While Turtledove postulated an attempt to reclaim Israel in "Next Year in Jerusalem," Yates sees a future in which even after the destruction of the Jewish state, the Jewish people are still being attacked, not just by Arabs, but by governments elsewhere in the world. The response is to turn to an Orthodox form of Judaism as they attempt to leave the solar system.

Other stories that focus on Jewish themes do so in a more lighthearted manner, partly because they are retellings of Jewish legends. Although these stories often feature golems, Jewish folklore is not only the province of golems, as seen in Lisa Goldstein's novel *Red Magician* (1993) or in the series of short stories by James Morrow, a non-Jew, "Bible Stories for Adults."

Steven H. Silver

References and Further Reading

Berkwits, Jeff. 2004. "Stars of David." *San Diego Jewish Journal* (October): 31–36.

Dann, Jack. 1974. *Wandering Stars.* New York: Harper & Row.

Dann, Jack. 1981. *More Wandering Stars.* New York: Doubleday.

Dern, Daniel P. "Jews in/and Science Fiction." Available at: http://www.dern.com/Dern_Jews_in_Science_Fiction_Shavout_2002.txt. Accessed March 6, 2005.

Meth, Clifford, and Ricia Meinhardt. 1996. *Strange Kaddish.* Morristown, NJ: Aardwolf Press.

Oppenheimer, Daniel. "Space Odyssey." Available at: http://www.nextbook.org/cultural/feature.html?id=68. Accessed November 19, 2004.

Peterseil, Yaacov. 1999. *Jewish Sci-Fi Stories for Kids.* New York: Pitspopany Press.

Reeber, Jim, and Clifford Meth. 1997. *Stranger Kaddish.* Morristown, NJ: Aardwolf Press.

Schneider, Ilene. "Jewish Science Fiction." Available at: http://www.totse.com/en/ego/science_fiction/jewscifi.html. Accessed March 6, 2005.

Silver, Steven. "Jewish Science Fiction and Fantasy." Available at: http://www.sfsite.com/~silverag/jewishsf.html. Accessed February 23, 2005.

Isaac Asimov (1920–1992)

Science Fiction Writer

The author, editor, or co-editor of nearly five hundred volumes of science fiction (SF) and popular science, Isaac Asimov also published books on literature, the Bible, history, and other topics. He was one of the three most influential science fiction writers in the world between 1940 and 1980 (the others were Robert A. Heinlein and Arthur C. Clarke). In 1977, his enormous popularity led to his name being used in the title of the new *Isaac Asimov's Science Fiction Magazine,* which quickly became the field's leading market for short stories. Though his influence on other writers waned in his final years, several of Asimov's late novels achieved best-seller status.

Asimov was born in Russia, in the *shtetl* of Petrovichi, probably on January 2, 1920. His father was a relatively successful merchant who had a traditional Jewish education. The family immigrated to the United States in 1923, eventually settling into the American middle class. Asimov's father bought a candy store, and it was in the store's magazine racks that the writer-to-be discovered science fiction for the first time. Even though he had been bar mitzvahed, Asimov's father was not particularly religious, and the family did not keep kosher once they came to the United States. Asimov received little if any religious education and has variously described himself as a "freethinker" and a "second-generation atheist."

Although he wrote many memorable short stories early in his career, including "Nightfall" (1941), "The Martian Way" (1952), and "The Ugly Little Boy" (1958), Asimov is best remembered for two series: his Foundation trilogy and its later sequels, and his many robot stories.

Foundation, Foundation and Empire, and *Second Foundation* first appeared between 1942 and 1953 as a series of magazine stories and truncated paperback volumes before being restructured in 1963 into a trilogy, as they are known today. They tell the story, heavily influenced by Gibbon's *Decline and Fall of the Roman Empire,* of the latter years of a far-future galactic empire and of Hari Seldon, creator of the science of psychohistory, which can predict large-scale historical trends. Seldon envisions a plan, not to save the empire, but to limit the dark age that will follow its fall, and he sets up two organizations, the public Foundation and a secret Second Foundation, to carry out his work long after he is gone. Although static and talky by modern standards, the books addressed a variety of serious political, philosophical, and sociological issues on a level rarely seen in the genre at the time. They have never been out of print and in 1965 earned a Hugo Award, voted by hard-core science fiction fans as the best SF series of all time.

The robot series began with "Robbie" (1940). Then, in "Reason" (1941) and "Liar!" (1941), Asimov introduced one of the most influential concepts in the history of science fiction, the Three Laws of Robotics: (1) a robot may not injure a human being or, through inaction, allow a human being to come to harm; (2) a robot must obey the orders given by human beings, except when such orders conflict with the First Law; (3) a robot must protect its own existence as long as such protection does not conflict with the First or Second Law. These stories and others were reprinted in book form in *I, Robot* (1950) and in later collections, and there were also two early robot novels, both featuring a robot detective, R. Daneel Olivaw: *The Caves of Steel* (1954) and *The Naked Sun* (1957).

In both the Foundation and the robot stories Asimov explored the theme of reason versus irrationality, always coming down firmly on the side of the former. Politically, he was essentially a liberal technocrat. His fiction rarely, if ever, contained explicitly religious material, beyond the occasional use of a biblical quote for a title, as in "That Thou Art Mindful of Him" (1974), but the robot stories frequently served as vehicles for the implicit exploration and condemnation of both racial and religious prejudice. "The Bicentennial Man" (1976), in which a robot tries to overcome society's and its owners' irrational refusal to recognize it as a full-fledged person, develops this theme particularly well. Over a period of many years, as the technology becomes available, the story's robot protagonist literally has its machine parts replaced by organic ones, finally sacrificing its "positronic" computer brain for human gray matter, in effect giving up virtual immortality to gain full equality.

During the years between 1960 and 1980, Asimov published very little science fiction, concentrating almost exclusively on nonfiction. His one novel from this period, however, *The Gods Themselves* (1972), is widely recognized as the author's finest full-length work. Winner of both the Hugo and the Nebula Awards (the latter given by fellow SF writers), it focuses on a misguided, near-future attempt to end the energy crisis by pulling energy out of a parallel universe, in the process nearly destroying the fascinating alien species that lives there and humanity itself. The well-developed aliens are especially noteworthy because the author had previously studiously avoided writing about such beings in either of his major series.

In the 1980s Asimov returned to science fiction, writing such best-selling novels as *Foundation's Edge* (1982), *The Robots of Dawn* (1983), *Robots and Empire* (1985), and *Prelude to Foundation* (1988), in which he extended his two major series and tried, with mixed success, to tie them together. Although *Foundation's Edge* received another Hugo Award, the later novels are generally considered inferior to their predecessors. Asimov's prodigious output of fiction also included mysteries and children's novels, collaborating on many of the latter with his second wife, Janet. *The Complete Stories,* published in two volumes (1990–1992), is his definitive short story collection. He also edited or co-edited many dozens of short story anthologies, although in later years his less well-known collaborators, most notably Martin H. Greenberg, tended to do most of the work.

Although Asimov is best remembered as a science fiction writer, it is estimated that less than 15 percent of his published work was actually SF. An incredible polymath with a doctorate in chemistry who taught for a number of years at the Boston University School of Medicine, Asimov took the entire universe as his subject matter. His major publications include his first nonfiction book, *Biochemistry and Human Metabolism* (1952), co-authored with Burnham Walker and William C. Boyd. *Fact and Fancy* (1962) was the first of many volumes collecting the popular science essays he published in *The Magazine of Fantasy and Science Fiction.* Among his other notable science books are *Inside the Atom* (1956); *The Intelligent Man's Guide to*

Science (1960), with several revised editions; *Asimov's Biographical Encyclopedia of Science and Technology* (1964); *The Collapsing Universe: The Story of Black Holes* (1977); and *In the Beginning: Science Faces God in the Book of Genesis* (1981), which presents his take on Creationism.

Although he was not religious, Asimov published a number of works on the Bible, including the two-volume *Asimov's Guide to the Bible* (1968–1969), a respectful, but resolutely secular, attempt to explicate virtually every potentially obscure bit of historical, theological, liturgical, scientific, or geographical information in the Old and the New Testaments. His forays into literature produced, among other books, *Asimov's Guide to Shakespeare* (1970), also in two volumes.

Michael Levy

References and Further Reading

Asimov, Isaac. 1979. *In Memory Yet Green: The Autobiography of Isaac Asimov, 1920–1954.* Garden City, NY: Doubleday.

Asimov, Isaac. 1980. *In Joy Still Felt: The Autobiography of Isaac Asimov, 1954–1978.* Garden City, NY: Doubleday.

Asimov, Isaac. 1994. *I, Asimov, A Memoir.* Garden City, NY: Doubleday.

Gunn, James. 1996. *Isaac Asimov: The Foundations of Science Fiction,* rev. ed. Lanham, MD: Scarecrow Press.

American Jews in Sports

American Jewish Men in Sports

Although for centuries gentiles derided Jews as weak and craven, lacking the masculine attributes necessary for athletic success, Jewish men in the United States became prominent in several sports during the early twentieth century and were overrepresented in boxing and basketball, as well as in sportswriting. Sports helped American Jewish men forge a tougher, more combative image, undermining pernicious stereotypes in a period of dramatically intensifying antisemitism in both Europe and America. After World War II, Jewish men's participation in top-level sports competition declined. The weakening of barriers against Jews in employment and education significantly expanded their opportunities, reducing the importance of sports as a means of achieving upward mobility for the third generation. Postwar suburbanization removed many Jews from dangerous urban neighborhoods, where the development of athletic skills had afforded protection against antisemitic assault. The establishment of Israel, with its proficient armed forces, surrounded by enemies that threatened its destruction, provided a new model of Jewish strength and determination to withstand attack.

Jewish underrepresentation in athletics prior to the twentieth century is attributable in part to gentiles' determination to exclude Jews from competition, but also to manliness not being as problematic for Jews as for Chris-

tians. For centuries, Christian males appear to have been more insecure in their manhood than Jewish men. Jews traditionally defined manliness very differently from Christians, not conflating it with physicality. In the United States, Jewish boys were less likely to grow up in a father-absent household than boys of most other ethnic groups, because Jews tended to emigrate as intact families, and fewer fathers deserted. Jewish boys also interacted with other adult males as they prepared for their *bar mitzvah*. A Jewish wife often ran a small business, enabling her husband to study, and he did not believe that his wife's working undermined his manhood. Men dominated the *shul*, which was not the case in many American churches since the nineteenth century. In prayer, the Jewish male assumed a more manly posture than the Christian, standing rather than kneeling. Unlike the Catholic priest, the rabbi married, and his beard accentuated his masculinity. Insecurity about manliness among Protestants during the late nineteenth and early twentieth centuries resulted in a Muscular Christianity movement designed to overturn the feminine orientation of churches, which had no counterpart in Judaism (Norwood 1993).

Influenced by the need for self-defense against antisemitic assault, a significant danger in many American neighborhoods at least through World War II, Jewish men became a major presence in boxing from 1900 to 1940. Surrounded for centuries by a large, hostile, and much better armed gentile population, Jews had generally refrained from violent response to antisemitic provocations because they understood it to be counterproductive. However, the waves of pogroms in Eastern Europe, beginning in 1881–1882, had made Jews more receptive to using physical force to protect themselves. Many of those who emigrated to the United States had participated in defense units organized by Zionist and Bundist groups. The attack by Christian pogromists on the Jews of Gomel in Russia, which followed the slaughter at Kishinev in 1903, resembled a battle because of the Jewish defense units' fierce combativeness. Many second-generation Jewish men in America were inspired to defend themselves with their fists against antisemitic violence by what Jewish immigrants had taught them about their struggle against pogromists in Eastern Europe. By 1928 Jews had more contenders in the various weight divisions than any other ethnic group. Moreover, many Jewish prizefighters placed the Star of David on their trunks to express pride in their Jewishness and, during the 1930s, their opposition to Nazism.

The first prominent American Jewish boxer was Joe Choynski (1868–1943) of San Francisco, who as a schoolboy had been frequently harassed as a Jew. Although only about 165 pounds, Choynski fought most of the top heavyweights of his time. In 1897 he battled future heavyweight champion Jim Jeffries, who outweighed him by sixty pounds, to a twenty-round draw. In 1901, Choynski knocked out Jack Johnson, an African American who became one of the greatest heavyweight champions ever, in three rounds in Galveston. For violating an anti-prizefighting law, Choynski and Johnson were jailed for nearly a month. During their imprisonment, Choynski helped Johnson improve his boxing technique, preparing him to become a heavyweight contender.

During the first quarter of the twentieth century, American Jews won two world boxing titles: Abe "The Little Hebrew" Attell was featherweight champion from 1901 to 1912, and Benny "The Ghetto Wizard" Leonard (born Benjamin Leiner) was lightweight champion from 1917 until he retired undefeated in 1925, arguably the best ever in his division. Growing up in an Irish American neighborhood in San Francisco, Attell learned to fight to protect himself. Leonard (1896–1947), the son of Russian Jewish immigrants, was raised on New York's Lower East Side. Considered the most skilled of all American Jewish boxers,

Leonard would not fight on Jewish holidays. His model was the great Jewish lightweight Leach Cross (1886–1957) (born Louis Wallach), a dentist "who repaired teeth in the daytime and knocked them out at night" (Blady 1988). Cross, who also grew up on the Lower East Side, the son of Austrian Jewish immigrants, was the first boxer to become wildly popular among New York's Jewish population.

In 1935 Max Baer (1909–1959), who strongly identified as Jewish and anti-Nazi, won the world heavyweight title, greatly prized in America as a symbol of both manliness and national prestige. Baer's father, an Omaha cattle dealer, was Jewish, but his mother was not. Baer referred to himself as the first Jewish heavyweight champion and noted that the Nazis considered him a Jew. Physically, Baer defied press stereotypes of the Jew, but not temperamentally. Sportswriters described him as a powerfully built Adonis, very attractive to women, but also as somewhat of a buffoon. The press tended to assume that Jewish fighters, like African Americans, were handicapped by a lack of self-discipline and an inability to concentrate. In the 1930s, reporters referred to Baer, to Jewish light heavyweight champion "Slapsie Maxie" Rosenbloom, and to Jewish heavyweight contender Kingfish Levinsky (born Hershel Krakow) as clowns.

In June 1933, shortly after the Nazis came to power in Germany, Max Baer faced German heavyweight Max Schmeling, former world champion, whom ring announcers now introduced as the Fighting Son of the Fatherland, emphasizing that he represented the Third Reich. Schmeling proclaimed before the bout that he had never seen Germany more peaceful than under Nazi rule. Openly proclaiming his hatred of Nazism, Baer wore the Star of David on his trunks for the first time in his career. Between rounds he deliberately grabbed the embroidered Star of David and displayed it to Schmeling. Baer scored a stunning upset victory over the German, knocking him out with pile-driving right hand blows in the tenth round. To soften the humiliation of Schmeling's loss to a Jew, the Nazi press referred to Baer only as a German American. But in March 1935, the Nazi propaganda ministry banned the film "The Prizefighter and the Lady," in which Baer starred, because he was Jewish.

Baer's victory positioned him for a shot at the heavyweight title, which he won a year later from Primo Carnera. Expressing outrage at Nazism, Baer clamored for another fight against Schmeling, even offering to fight him

Max Baer placed a large Star of David on his trunks for his bout against German heavyweight Max Schmeling in 1933 as an anti-Nazi statement and always wore it in the ring after that. Although his mother was not a Jew, fight fans considered Baer, world heavyweight champion (1934-1935), to be Jewish. American Jews were proud that Baer forcefully denounced Adolf Hitler. The Nazis banned from Germany the film The Prizefighter and the Lady, *in which Baer starred, because they considered him Jewish. (Library of Congress)*

in Germany. Moreover, he publicly wished that he could work Hitler over with his fists. But Hitler would never again permit Schmeling to face a Jew in the ring. Baer held the heavyweight title for a year, before losing it to Jimmy Braddock.

The last American Jewish boxing great, Barney Ross (born Barnet [Beryl] Rosofsky), who held the lightweight and welterweight titles during the 1930s, was also an important symbol of Jewish pride. Ross (1909–1967) was born on New York's Lower East Side, but his father, a Talmudic scholar, moved the family to a rough neighborhood on Chicago's West Side, where he ran a small grocery store. After his father was killed in a holdup, Barney became a boxer to enable his family to survive. During a nine-year professional career, Ross was never knocked down. After the Nazis assumed power in Germany, he

knew that his rabbi was counting on him to challenge in the ring "the horrible lies Hitler is telling" (Levine 1992). When the Japanese bombed Pearl Harbor, Ross enlisted in the Marine Corps, determined to fight the Axis. He was decorated for heroism in combat on Guadalcanal, where he was wounded. A passionate Zionist, Ross ran guns to Israel in 1948.

Jews were also prominent in boxing as promoters and trainers. "Uncle Mike" Jacobs was the world's leading boxing promoter from 1937 to 1946, staging Joe Louis's title defenses and three-million-dollar gates. He offered to donate 10 percent of the profits from the 1938 Louis–Schmeling bout to assist refugees from Nazi Germany. Ray Arcel (1899–1994) and Charley Goldman (1888–1968) were among the leading trainers in twentieth-century boxing. Arcel recalled that, as a Jew growing up in overwhelmingly non-Jewish East Harlem, he had to fight to protect himself every day. He trained and worked the corner for over twenty champions. His favorite was Benny Leonard, whom he preferred because of his great ring savvy. Goldman, born in Warsaw, Poland, and once a bantamweight contender, was credited with developing Rocky Marciano into one of the greatest heavyweights of all time. He also trained four other champions. The leading boxing gym, Stillman's in New York, and the leading manufacturer of boxing gloves and equipment, Everlast, were run by Jews.

Jews became heavily involved in the new sport of basketball in the early twentieth century and assumed a dominant role during the 1930s. The sport was particularly accessible to Jews because of its relatively low prestige, marginality on most college campuses, and recent origin, having been invented only in 1891. Poor earning potential in professional basketball, resulting from a small fan base, rendered basketball unattractive to mainstream athletes. The sport was concentrated in northeastern cities, where most of the Jewish population resided. Moreover, basketball required little space or equipment, making it easy for urban institutions that sponsored leisure activities in Jewish neighborhoods, like settlement houses and Young Men's Hebrew Association chapters, to sponsor teams.

By the 1920s, Jewish players had achieved great prominence in professional basketball. Barney Sedran, raised on New York's Lower East Side, although only 5 feet 4 inches tall, became one of basketball's earliest professional stars, a standout on both offense and defense. Nat Holman (1896–1995), also from the Lower East Side, won fame with the barnstorming Original Celtics, the decade's dominant team, with whom he played from 1921 to 1927. The Celtics touted Holman as the greatest basketball player in the world. He significantly influenced basketball as a highly successful coach at City College of New York (CCNY) for almost forty years until he retired in 1960, and as the author of several manuals on how to play basketball. Holman, whom sportswriters nicknamed Mr. Basketball, helped shape the game by promoting the Northeast style of play that kept the offense in motion and emphasized ball control and patient teamwork, carefully setting up shots near the basket.

Several identifiably Jewish professional teams in eastern cities established reputations as basketball powerhouses during the 1920s. The SPHAs in Philadelphia, named after the South Philadelphia Hebrew Association, sported the Star of David on their jerseys and played successively in the Philadelphia, Eastern, and American (ABL) Basketball Leagues. Team founder Eddie Gottlieb, who had emigrated as a child from the Ukraine, later became one of the nation's leading sports promoters, as well as owner of the National Basketball Association's (NBA) Philadelphia Warriors.

During the 1930s, the SPHAs and the Brooklyn Jewels, another largely Jewish outfit, whose coach was Barney Sedran, were the premier teams in the ABL, the East's leading professional basketball circuit. Nearly half the ABL's players during the 1937–1938 season were Jews, as were the eight leading scorers in 1940–1941 (Levine 1992).

The significant Jewish presence in basketball was reflected in the NBA's having a Jewish commissioner, Maurice Podoloff, when it was established in 1949, as well as a Jewish public relations man, Haskell Cohen, along with prominent Jewish players. Podoloff, who served as commissioner until 1963, and Cohen, also a sportswriter for Jewish newspapers, were elected to the Basketball Hall of Fame. The two men had together constituted the NBA's original front office. Several Jews starred in the NBA during the 1950s, although the number playing in the league dropped off markedly. Dolph Schayes of the Syracuse Nationals, son of Rumanian Jewish immigrants who settled in the Bronx, was the NBA's leading scorer when he retired in 1964. Max Zaslofsky, raised in an Orthodox Jewish household in Brooklyn's Brownsville section by Russian Jewish immigrant parents, was the NBA's third-highest scorer ever when he stopped playing in 1956. Red Auerbach, whose father was a Russian Jewish immigrant, coached the Boston Celtics to nine NBA championships in the decade 1956–1966 and later assumed the general managership and presidency of the club. As general manager, he appointed the NBA's first African American head coach, Bill Russell. In 1984 David Stern, son of New York delicatessen owners, became the NBA's fourth commissioner and the second Jew to assume that post.

Jews excelled in college basketball as well from the 1920s through the 1940s, often constituting a majority of starters on the best eastern college basketball teams, such as Nat Holman's CCNY, New York University (NYU), Long Island University (LIU), and even from 1928 to 1931, St. John's University. Jewish collegians' strong interest in the sport was apparent as early as 1923, when the Syracuse University student government denounced Jewish undergraduates for their alleged lack of involvement in campus athletics, except for basketball. In 1950 Holman's CCNY squad, with three Jewish starters, became the first team to win both major college basketball titles, the National Invitation Tournament and the National Collegiate Athletic Association, achieving a Grand Slam, never again duplicated.

Jewish players often encountered antisemitic harassment from opposing college fans during this period. Students at Manhattan College, a Catholic school, taunted NYU's players by yelling "NY Jew," and in 1936 the student newspaper of NYU's downtown campus demanded that the school break athletic relations with Georgetown. An editorial declared that Georgetown students had threatened to physically harm NYU's Jewish players and had constantly yelled antisemitic epithets.

Nat Holman's reputation was tarnished and the basketball programs at the New York–area college powerhouses were damaged by the 1951 point-shaving disclosures, among the most serious sports gambling scandals in history. Thirty-two players—about a quarter of them Jewish—at seven colleges and universities, including CCNY, LIU, and NYU, were charged with taking bribes from gamblers to shave points in games, and several received prison sentences. But in part because large numbers of non-Jewish players at midwestern and southern universities also accepted bribes and shaved points, the resulting public outcry was not tinged with any significant degree of antisemitism. The New York Board of Education suspended Nat Holman from coaching despite his insistence that he was unaware of his players' contacts with gamblers, but he was reinstated in 1953.

The founder and owner of the most successful and long-lasting barnstorming basketball team, and probably the most well-known sports franchise in the world, the Harlem Globetrotters, was a Jew, Abe Saperstein. Saperstein organized the team, always composed of African American players, in 1927. During the 1930s, the Globetrotters began to mix comedy routines with a flashy but highly skillful style of play, featuring dazzling displays of dribbling and ball handling. Saperstein explained that, although he had formed the team in Chicago, he named it for Harlem because that district meant to African Americans what Jerusalem did to Jews. Saperstein experienced serious financial difficulties in the team's early years, often personally chauffeuring his squad in rundown cars from one small-town arena to another and sometimes even serving as a substitute player. By the 1950s, however, the franchise had become very profitable. The Globetrotters have been accused of perpetuating racist stereotypes through clowning on the court, but they also typified athletic excellence and often made their white opponents, whom they invariably defeated, appear laughingly inept. Saperstein also established the American Basketball League as a rival to the NBA in 1961 and served as commissioner, but it folded after a year and a half.

Unlike basketball, Jews have always been underrepresented in baseball, although one of the game's greatest all-time pitchers, Sandy Koufax, and a leading long-ball hitter, Hank Greenberg, were Jewish. Lipman "Lip" Pike, a left-handed infielder, played for several of the nation's premier professional teams, including the Brooklyn Atlantics beginning in 1869, but there were very few Jews in the major leagues prior to the 1930s. Baseball's prestige as the national pastime, which was far greater than basketball's, along with its existence for decades before many Jews arrived in the United States, made it difficult for Jews to gain acceptance as participants. It also required more space to play than basketball, and space was not available to first- and second-generation Jews in congested urban neighborhoods. Jewish youth resorted instead to stickball and stoop ball, games partially resembling baseball but designed to be played in cramped city streets. Many Jewish parents accepted boxing as practical training in self-defense, necessary if their sons were to survive in an antisemitic environment. Basketball at least brought their sons into contact with other Jews. Because Jewish boys were disproportionately raised in two-parent households, and thus less influenced by their peers, they were more easily discouraged from engaging in activity their fathers and mothers considered frivolous.

The first Jewish baseball player to attract significant attention was New York Giants second baseman Andy Cohen, whom manager John J. McGraw recruited in 1928 in an effort to draw Jewish fans to the Polo Grounds. Some "greenhorns," lacking familiarity with baseball but thrilled that the Giants had acquired a Jewish player and anxious to see him, asked at the stadium ticket window for seats right behind second base. McGraw released Cohen after he hit .294 in 1929, suggesting that Jewish players probably had to perform above the average to survive in the big leagues.

During the 1930s and 1940s, Jewish players compiled solid records in the major leagues, including Buddy Myer (whose father was Jewish), a lifetime .303 hitter who won the American League batting title in 1935; New York Giants all-star catcher Harry Danning, a lifetime .285 hitter; and outfielders Goody Rosen and Morrie Arnovich. The Jewish press praised Phil Weintraub of the Philadelphia Phillies for eating only kosher meals. Moe Berg, a catcher who played in the majors for fifteen years, was considered one of the most intelligent men in baseball, but a weak hitter: it was said that he spoke ten languages but couldn't hit in any of them.

Besides Koufax and Greenberg, a few Jews made their mark in the majors after World War II, including relief pitcher Larry Sherry, slugging first baseman Mike Epstein, all-star pitchers Ken Holtzman and Steve Stone, and most recently outfielder Shawn Green. Sherry dramatized the importance of relief pitching when he won or saved each of the Los Angeles Dodgers victories in their 1959 World Series triumph. His brother Norm, a catcher, helped Sandy Koufax conquer his early wildness, enabling him to become one of the greatest pitchers of all time. Today there are about a dozen Jews playing in the major leagues.

Players and fans routinely subjected Jewish major leaguers to antisemitic insults through the 1950s. Hank Greenberg was constantly taunted during his career, which extended from 1933 to 1947: "Every day . . . some son of a bitch call[ed] you a Jew bastard and a kike and a sheenie. . . . If the ballplayers weren't doing it, the fans were" (Greenberg 1989). During the 1934 World Series, the St. Louis Cardinals subjected Greenberg, the Detroit Tigers first baseman, to a barrage of antisemitic epithets. The Chicago Cubs did the same in the Fall Classic the next year, voicing antisemitic insults so frequently that the umpire ordered them to stop. But because the umpire used profanity in doing so, baseball commissioner Judge Kenesaw Mountain Landis fined him. In 1949, National League bench jockeys' relentless harassment of Giants outfielder Sid Gordon caused the Anti-Defamation League to contact every major league club to determine whether there were regulations prohibiting such conduct. During the 1950s, Cleveland Indians slugger Al Rosen, who as a youth in Miami had taken boxing lessons to protect himself against antisemitic assault, on several occasions physically confronted opponents on the diamond who taunted him for being Jewish, much like Hank Greenberg had done earlier.

Such antisemitic harassment in baseball persisted even into the 1970s. African American slugger Reggie Jackson recalled his disgust when, shortly after he joined the New York Yankees, he witnessed his manager Billy Martin and several Yankees, including stars Thurman Munson, Graig Nettles, and Sparky Lyle, hurling vicious antisemitic insults at Jewish teammate Ken Holtzman. Antisemitism may have been a factor in Martin's unwillingness to use Holtzman, a former all-star who had hurled two no-hit games, after the Yankees acquired him in 1976.

Antisemitism was also expressed in more subtle ways. The African American players on the Los Angeles Dodgers in the 1960s were disturbed that club management gave blond, blue-eyed gentile pitcher Don Drysdale a higher profile in its press guides and yearbooks than the Jewish Sandy Koufax, although the latter was then unquestionably the best pitcher in baseball.

The first Jewish umpire, Albert "Dolly" Stark, was hired by the National League in 1928. In a period when most umpires remained fairly stationary, Stark introduced a more mobile approach, moving rapidly around the infield and down the foul lines, as a result missing far fewer calls. League officials considered Stark highly proficient, but players were often abusive because he was a Jew, and he retired without explanation in 1940. Stark gave young Tigers first baseman Hank Greenberg important emotional support during the 1934 World Series when the Cardinals repeatedly shouted antisemitic insults at him. During the World Series the next year, the Cubs taunted both men as "Christ Killers."

Until recently, Jews were greatly underrepresented as club owners in baseball as well. During the early twentieth century, Andrew Freedman had owned the New York Giants, Barney Dreyfuss the Pittsburgh Pirates, and Judge Emil Fuchs, who was exposed to baseball as a youth at the University Settlement on New York's Lower East Side, the Boston Braves. Nate Dolin, part of a Jewish group that purchased the Cleveland Indians in 1949, recalled that the other owners isolated him and his colleagues, barring them from their private clubs where important business was transacted. In 1998, however, Bud Selig, Jewish owner of the Milwaukee Brewers, became commissioner of major league baseball, after having served as acting commissioner since 1992.

Jews were even less represented in football than in baseball. Nevertheless, Jews contributed some of the sport's greatest performers, like Hall of Fame quarterbacks Benny Friedman and Sid Luckman, each of whom profoundly transformed offensive play, and Hall of Fame offensive tackle Ron Mix. Jews' relatively low rate of participation was partly due to the absence of a significant presence at the colleges that developed major football programs. Quotas sharply restricted Jewish admission to the elite northeastern colleges where football first emerged and later at many of the large state universities that emphasized football, which were also geographically distant from the principal areas of Jewish settlement. The metropolitan commuter colleges that Jews disproportionately attended in the pre–World War II era generally lacked the space and facilities for football, and they sponsored basketball instead. Professional football originated in mining and steel mill towns, where few Jews resided, and until the 1950s had a relatively small fan base.

Phil King (1872–1938) of Princeton, acclaimed as the best all-around player in the country, was the first Jew to gain prominence in football. Walter Camp, who elaborated the rules that made football a distinct sport in the early 1880s, selected King, a quarterback and halfback, to his all-American team all four years that he attended Princeton, from 1890 to 1893. Like Paul Robeson, King combined gridiron prowess with excellent academic performance, graduating as class salutatorian. He was the first Princetonian elected captain of both the football and the baseball teams. Woodrow Wilson, a football enthusiast, as well as student, professor, and president at Princeton, rated King the best player he had ever watched.

A Jewish tailback and Jewish quarterback played central roles in developing football's modern pass offense. Benny Friedman (1905–1982), son of Russian Jewish immigrants to Cleveland, starred at both the University of Michigan, where he won All-American honors, and in the National Football League (NFL) from 1927 to 1934. He belonged to a Jewish fraternity at Michigan. The New York Giants acquired Friedman from the Detroit Wolverines in 1929, in part to attract Jewish fans. That year, as a single wing tailback, he set a new NFL record for most touchdown passes in a season, more than triple the previous total. Friedman's aerial exploits influenced NFL authorities to alter the shape of the football so that it was easier for passers to grip. Red Grange, one of football's all-time greats, pointed to the Jewish phenom as the embodiment of masculinity: "Benny Friedman can, and does, take a terrific pounding without crying about it. That . . . is my conception of a man!" (Grange 1932). After retiring, Friedman coached football at the overwhelmingly Jewish CCNY and at Jewish-founded Brandeis University, where he was also athletic director.

Sid Luckman (b. 1916), who was with the Chicago Bears from 1939 to 1950, was the first in the NFL to play quarterback in the modern T-formation, a new alignment that opened up the offense and resulted in a significant increase in passing. Luckman grew up in Brooklyn and played football at Columbia University, which he selected for its academic program. Like Friedman, adept at deciphering defenses, Luckman won coaches' praise for mental acuity. He led the Bears to four NFL championships, including a 73-0 win over the Washington Redskins in 1940. In 1943, he set an NFL record that has never been surpassed, hurling seven touchdown passes in a game. Both Luckman and Friedman were inducted into the Pro Football Hall of Fame.

Two other Jews, Harry Newman and Marshall Goldberg, achieved prominence in college and pro football prior to World War II. Starring at Michigan from 1930 to 1932, Newman succeeded Benny Friedman as the NFL's best passer, playing with the New York Giants from 1933 to 1935, and then in the rival American Football League in 1936 and 1937. Head counselor Friedman took Newman under his wing at a summer camp he attended after finishing high school and taught him to pass. Goldberg, originally from West Virginia and therefore nicknamed the Hebrew Hillbilly, excelled as a running back at the University of Pittsburgh from 1936 to 1938, helping the Panthers win the 1937 Rose Bowl, and then for several years in the NFL with the Chicago Cardinals.

Several Jews had highly successful careers as head coaches in pro football, the most complex of all sports, where formulating strategy and mental insight are especially important. Sid Gillman, a coach inducted into both the Professional and College Football Halls of Fame, directed the Los Angeles Rams from 1955 to 1959 and then the San Diego Chargers from 1960 to 1969 and 1971, where he was credited with developing the team's renowned wide-open pass offense. He won an American Football League (AFL) championship with the Chargers in 1963. Marv Levy coached the NFL's Buffalo Bills to four consecutive Super Bowls, 1991–1994. Allie Sherman, who had played quarterback with the Philadelphia Eagles, was the New York Giants head coach from 1961 until 1969, winning division championships his first three seasons.

That NFL and college football teams today often gather together for Christian prayer prior to games suggests that Jews have little presence in the sport. Ron Mix was the best of a small handful of Jewish players in the NFL and AFL of the post-1960 era. Considered the AFL's best offensive tackle of the 1960s, referees flagged him for holding only twice in his ten years with the San Diego Chargers, an incredible feat that helped earn him the nickname the Intellectual Assassin. In 2000, Jay Fiedler, a Dartmouth graduate, became the NFL's first Jewish starting quarterback since Sid Luckman.

Jewish athletes and coaches engaged in a movement to boycott the 1936 Olympic games in Berlin to protest Nazi government antisemitism and repression. Although the boycott movement ultimately failed, CCNY basketball coach Nat Holman publicly spoke out for the boycott, as did Jewish sportswriter Shirley Povich (1905–1998) in his *Washington Post* column. The players on the predominantly Jewish LIU and NYU basketball teams even voted not to play in the elimination tournament to select a squad to represent the United States in Berlin.

An incident at the Olympics involving the U.S. 400-meter relay team precipitated charges of antisemitism on the part of American athletic authorities. On the morning of the race, American track coach Dean Cromwell replaced the team's two Jews, Marty Glickman and Sam Stoller, with other runners. Glickman, later a prominent sports announcer, and many others believed that

Cromwell had removed the Jewish runners to placate his Nazi hosts. Both Cromwell and Avery Brundage, head of the U.S. Olympic Committee, were purportedly Nazi sympathizers and later members of the America First Committee, a group organized to prevent U.S. assistance to Britain in the European conflict.

Until the post–World War II period, Jews were only marginally involved in golf and tennis. These sports were primarily confined to the affluent, and often played at country clubs and resorts that barred Jews. Few facilities offering golf and tennis were available to the urban, working- and lower-middle classes, in which Jews remained concentrated. Jewish participation increased during the 1950s and 1960s as a result of upward mobility and suburbanization, along with some decline in discrimination. Still, because many facilities continued to exclude Jews, as they became more affluent in the postwar period, Jews established their own country clubs and resorts, which featured golf courses and tennis courts.

By contrast, Jews dominated ping pong during the 1930s, a sport related to tennis, but much less prestigious, popular in cities because it required far less space and was played indoors. The equipment and facilities required for play were much less expensive than those used in tennis or golf. Jews were instrumental in transforming ping pong from a slow parlor game into a highly skilled competition, renamed table tennis and characterized by rapid-fire shots, powerful serves, and dramatic backhands, with players positioned much farther from the table. By 1938 at least eleven Jews had held the U.S. table tennis men's title. These included Abe Berenbaum, Sol Schiff, Marcus Schussheim, and Sidney Heitner.

Before World War II, Jewish men were not very involved in competitive swimming, largely due to the lack of access to facilities. Public swimming pools in urban Jewish neighborhoods and city beaches were usually very crowded and not suitable environments for developing the skills necessary to attain the highest level of proficiency. After 1945, upward mobility and suburbanization exposed Jews to better facilities, promoting greater interest in swimming. The first Jewish man to become a prominent competitive swimmer was Mark Spitz (b. 1950) of Indiana University, who grew up in California and Hawaii. Spitz accomplished the most spectacular feat in the sport's history by winning seven gold medals in the 1972 Olympic games in Munich, a record no other swimmer has equaled.

Spitz experienced a significant amount of antisemitic harassment from other American swimmers at the Olympic trials. After Palestinian terrorists murdered eleven Israeli athletes at the Munich Olympics, security officials had Spitz leave Germany immediately under heavy guard. In 1985, Spitz paid tribute to the slain Israeli athletes by lighting the torch to begin Israel's Maccabiah games, in which he had participated in 1965 and 1969. The daughters of three of the murdered Israeli athletes escorted him into the stadium with the torch.

By the middle of the twentieth century, Jews were extensively involved in sportswriting, a field they transformed. Journalists had consigned sportswriting to a low status, thereby facilitating Jewish entry. Nonetheless, some Jewish sportswriters found it necessary to anglicize their names to obtain employment or to win acceptance from editors. The *New York Herald* did not permit the first prominent Jewish sportswriter, Dan Margowitz (1890–1981), to use his identifiably Jewish surname, so he introduced the byline Dan Daniel not long after he began writing for the paper in 1909. Dan Daniel worked for several New York dailies and the *Sporting News* and was an associate editor of *Ring* magazine, the leading boxing periodical. In the 1940s, Al Horwits of the Philadelphia *Evening Ledger* became the first Jew elected president of the Baseball Writers Association. Jesse Abramson (1904–1979) of the *New York Herald Tribune* was considered America's leading track and field journalist, nicknamed the Book because of his encyclopedic knowledge of the sport. He also covered boxing and college football. Al Hirshberg covered sports for Boston newspapers from 1930 to 1968 and wrote numerous books about sports. Most notably, he collaborated with Jimmy Piersall on *Fear Strikes Out*, which chronicled the ballplayer's recovery from a serious mental breakdown.

Although most sportswriters were indifferent to, or supportive of, baseball's color bar, many Jews in the profession clamored for an end to it. Jewish sportswriters tended to be more sensitive to the suffering of African American athletes than other white journalists. As Jews, they were sometimes barred from hotels that accommodated their gentile colleagues, an experience shared with African American athletes, although not on as large a scale. Before U.S. entry into World War II, *Washington Post* sports columnist Shirley Povich, raised as an Orthodox Jew, called for baseball to desegregate. In 1953, Povich published a fifteen-part series in the *Post* on desegregation and the

African American contribution to baseball, and he denounced the Washington Redskins' unwillingness to sign black players. Roger Kahn of the *New York Herald Tribune* repeatedly denounced baseball's rampant racism and gave significant attention to how Jackie Robinson was mistreated during his career. Kahn's editor refused to publish Kahn's denunciation of major league baseball's lodging their white players at a St. Louis hotel that excluded blacks. Kahn became a close friend of Jackie Robinson and joined with him in criticizing the major leagues during the 1950s for their lackluster effort to desegregate. Like Kahn, Milton Gross, who became a frequent columnist for the Jewish-owned *New York Post* in 1949, displayed particular empathy for the plight of African American athletes. Gross too developed a friendship with Jackie Robinson and joined with him in challenging baseball club owners' unwillingness to hire blacks as managers, a barrier that lasted a generation after Robinson made the breakthrough into the majors. Povich, Kahn, and Gross all had long and distinguished careers as sportswriters.

Many African American athletes expressed appreciation to Jewish sportswriters for their support, and several—including Roy Campanella, Floyd Patterson, Satchel Paige, Rod Carew, Willie Mays, and Walt Frazier—collaborated with Jewish sportswriters in preparing books about their experiences. When the Baseball Hall of Fame established a committee to determine which players from the Negro Leagues should be inducted, its chairman Monte Irvin, who had starred in both the Negro and major leagues, selected Jewish sportswriter Dick Young and promoter Eddie Gottlieb to be on it.

A new cohort of sportswriters, nearly all of Jewish background, dramatically transformed the craft during the 1960s, introducing a more iconoclastic approach to sports coverage. Known as the Chipmunks, they examined the impact of larger social and cultural issues on sports, and viewed athletes more critically than their senior colleagues did. Their interviews with players and team officials were often contentious. Chipmunks included Leonard Shecter (1926–1974), Maury Allen, and Larry Merchant, all of the *New York Post,* and Stan Isaacs of *Newsday.* Shecter collaborated with former major league pitcher Jim Bouton on the 1970 best-seller *Ball Four,* whose portrayal of puerile ballplayers acting unkindly to fans, unscrupulous team management, and racism in the majors angered baseball's establishment.

Nat Fleischer (1887–1972), raised on the Lower East Side, and A. J. Liebling (1904–1963), the most important writers on boxing for American periodicals, were of Jewish background. In 1922, Fleischer founded *Ring* magazine, which became the nation's premier boxing publication. Fleischer set up rankings for each weight category and carefully checked fight data, making it difficult for boxers to distort their records, a practice that had long plagued the sport. Fight promoters, managers, and journalists considered his rankings definitive. Fleischer was also committed to documenting the African American contribution to boxing, writing a five-volume history of the subject.

Liebling, son of a New York furrier, was a longtime contributor to the *New Yorker,* which he joined in 1935. Dartmouth College expelled him for refusing to attend chapel. Liebling also served as a war correspondent during World War II, and wrote about politics and gastronomy as well as boxing. He developed keen insight into the sport by talking with veteran cornermen in New York fight gyms. Red Smith, one of the nation's most respected sports columnists, maintained that no one wrote about the "sweet science" as gracefully as Liebling.

In broadcasting, Mel Allen (1913–1996) and Howard Cosell (1918–1995), arguably the most well-known baseball play-by-play announcer and football and boxing commentator respectively, were also Jewish. Both men anglicized their surnames. Allen was born Mel Israel to Orthodox Russian Jewish parents who settled in Alabama. CBS executives prevailed on him to change his name so that it would not be recognizably Jewish. Allen served as head broadcaster for the New York Yankees from 1939 to 1942 and from 1946 to 1964, with time out for World War II military service. Not only New Yorkers but fans across the country who heard him call twenty World Series and twenty-four All-Star games were enchanted by his voluble and excitable style. Allen and Red Barber, who announced Yankees games with him from 1954 to 1964, were the first to enter Baseball's Hall of Fame as broadcasters.

Cosell was best known as the longtime analyst on Monday Night Football from 1970 to 1983, which he helped make enormously popular. Born Howard Cohen, the son of an accountant for a clothing store chain, he changed his name while attending NYU, but never concealed his Jewish identity. Selected as editor of the law review at NYU Law School, Cosell briefly practiced law, an unusual, if not unique background among sports broadcasters. He joined the American Broadcasting Company (ABC) full-time in 1956 and came to national attention as a result of his boxing coverage on that network's televised Wide World of Sports.

Cosell adopted a more critical stance toward athletes and sports than was common in radio and television during the late 1950s and early 1960s, and he displayed concern for the racist harassment and discrimination that African American athletes encountered. As a result, until his retirement he received much racist hate mail, usually antisemitic as well. Cosell conducted numerous interviews with Jackie Robinson and criticized major league baseball for not offering him a managerial position. He also developed a friendly relationship with Muhammad Ali during the 1960s, when Ali was widely disliked, and he backed African American outfielder Curt Flood's court challenge to baseball's reserve clause. Cosell was horrified by the Palestinian terrorists' murder of Israeli athletes at the 1972 Munich Olympics and declared that it had strengthened his Jewish identity.

Marty Glickman became the first to make the transition from athlete to long-term sports broadcaster. He was a highly popular radio announcer for both the New York Knickerbockers basketball and the New York Giants football teams for over twenty years, beginning in 1946 and 1948 respectively, and the New York Jets football team for eleven years. Glickman's excitability entranced even the Beats of the 1950s, who found listening to him provided the intense emotional experience they craved. In *On the Road*, Jack Kerouac has Dean Moriarty ask Sal Paradise: "Man, have you dug that mad Marty Glickman announcing basketball games—up-to-midcourt-bounce-fake-set-shot, swish, two points. Absolutely the greatest announcer I ever heard" (Kerouac 1957).

Stephen H. Norwood

References and Further Reading
Blady, Ken. 1988. *The Jewish Boxers' Hall of Fame*. New York: Shapolsky.
Bodner, Allen. 1997. *When Boxing Was a Jewish Sport*. New York: Praeger.
Cosell, Howard. *Cosell*. 1973. Chicago: Playboy Press.
Glickman, Marty. 1996. *The Fastest Kid on the Block: The Marty Glickman Story*. Syracuse, NY: Syracuse University Press.
Grange, Red. 1932. "The College Game Is *Easier*." *Saturday Evening Post* (November 5).
Greenberg, Hank. 1989. *Hank Greenberg: The Story of My Life*, edited by Ira Berkow. New York: Times Books.
Gurock, Jeffrey S. 2005. *Judaism's Encounter with American Sports*. Bloomington: Indiana University Press.
Halberstam, David. 1994. *October 1964*. New York: Villard Books.
Holtzman, Jerome, ed. 1995. *No Cheering in the Press Box*. New York: Henry Holt.
Kerouac, Jack. 1957. *On the Road*. New York: Penguin.
Leavy, Jane. 2002. *Sandy Koufax: A Lefty's Legacy*. New York: HarperCollins.
Levine, Peter. 1992. *Ellis Island to Ebbets Field: Sport and the American Jewish Experience*. New York: Oxford University Press.
Norwood, Stephen H. 1993. "My Son the Slugger: Sport and the American Jew." *Reviews in American History* 21,3: 465–470.
Norwood, Stephen H., and Harold Brackman. 1999. "Going to Bat for Jackie Robinson: The Jewish Role in Breaking Baseball's Color Line." *Journal of Sport History* 26,1: 118–144.
Norwood, Stephen H. 2007. "American Jewish Muscle: Forging a New Masculinity in the Streets and in the Ring, 1890-1940." *Studies in Contemporary Jewry* 23.
Ribalow, Harold U., and Meir Z. Ribalow. 1985. *The Jew in American Sports*. New York: Hippocrene Books.
Riess, Steven, ed. 1998. *Sports and the American Jew*. Syracuse, NY: Syracuse University Press.
Sammons, Jeffrey. 1988. *Beyond the Ring: The Role of Boxing in American Society*. Urbana: University of Illinois Press.
Simons, Bill. 1990. "Andy Cohen: Second Baseman as Ethnic Hero." *The National Pastime* 10: 83–87.
Voigt, David Q. 1984. "From Chadwick to the Chipmunks." *Journal of American Culture* 7 (Fall): 31–37.
Whittingham, Richard. 1984. *What a Game They Played*. New York: Harper & Row.

American Jewish Women in Sports

American Jewish women have long participated in sport as athletes, administrators, and advocates. They have achieved national or even international success in basketball, swimming, track and field, tennis, and golf. In the late nineteenth and early twentieth centuries, first at Jewish settlement houses and then at Young Men's–Young Women's Hebrew Associations, middle- and upper-class reformers promoted immigrant Jewish women's physical exercise and sport as part of their Americanization process—albeit within Jewish institutions. Although some Jewish women and girls engaged in sport for their physical health, others displayed their athletic skill in competitions with Jews as well as gentiles.

Some of these Jewish women challenged traditional gender and ethnic boundaries to secure sporting opportunities in Jewish institutions and mainstream American sites. Charlotte Epstein in competitive swimming and the Olympic games, Lillian Copeland as an Olympic track and field star, Elaine Rosenthal in competitive golf, and Jewish women basketball players all opened sporting opportunities for other women. Their activities belied the early twentieth-century stereotype of the American Jewish woman as lacking in physical energy and sporting ability. Yet the white Anglo-Saxon Protestant perception that, unlike other immigrants, Jews were "people of the book, rather than men and women of the bat" persisted (Riess 1998). Several American Jewish women demonstrated exceptional leadership abilities, shaping women's sports in their communities, in Jewish organizations, and even in the Olympics.

Jewish immigrant women were first exposed to American sports in settlement houses and immigrant aid associations in the late nineteenth century. German Jews, who by the 1880s had become oriented to American culture and institutions, sought to Americanize the newest Jewish immigrants. They wanted to promote the spiritual and bodily well-being of Jewish females. Sport and physical activities became increasingly important for the East European newcomers, as in the larger American society. The emphasis in the Progressive Era on physical health and on athletics was related to middle-class fears that immigrants were bringing disease to America, to the determination to strengthen the Anglo-Saxon Protestant population, and to the promotion of nationalism through military and athletic events. Reformers stressed the need for women to engage in health-building exercises and athletics to increase their stamina and better fulfill their domestic roles. Jewish women's

U.S. women's 1924 Olympic swimming team as they sail for France. The team included American Jewish athlete Charlotte Epstein, top row, fourth from left. (Underwood & Underwood/Corbis)

physical well-being and participation in sports demonstrated that they could be fit for American life and could be assimilated.

In 1885 Jewish women founded the Young Women's Union in Philadelphia, the oldest Jewish settlement house in the United States. It offered domestic instruction, classes in English and reading, and opportunities for recreation and sports. Jewish women taught calisthenics and gymnastics to Jewish women and girls. Philanthropists who founded the Irene Kaufmann Settlement House in Pittsburgh in 1895 incorporated sport and physical education in their program, offering women volleyball, gymnastics, track, and other sports. New York's Educational Alliance and Hebrew Technical Institute for Girls, Boston's Hebrew Industrial School, Detroit's Hannah Schloss Memorial Building, St. Louis's Jewish Educational Alliance, and other immigrant aid organizations integrated sport into educational programs for Jewish women and girls. Many immigrant Jewish girls first learned about sport at settlements, preparing them for participation in these American activities at the public high schools that offered sports.

At other Jewish institutions that provided athletic facilities for men, females wanted to participate in more vigorous and competitive sporting activities. The Chicago Hebrew Institute (CHI), the forerunner of today's Jewish Community Centers (JCC), was organized in 1903 by a group of young men who sought to promote the moral, physical, religious, and civic welfare of Jewish immigrants and residents. From its earliest years, the Hebrew Institute emphasized the importance of physical fitness for males and females. The opening of a new gymnasium and swimming pool at the CHI in 1915, with separate facilities for men and women, promoted women's athletic participation. Girls now had their own gym in which to develop their basketball ability and competitive spirit. The 1921 team went undefeated in twenty-six games. They played teams from the Hull House settlement, the Illinois Athletic Club, church teams, and working-class girls' teams. The Institute girls won the Central Amateur Athletic Union (AAU) Girls' Basketball Championship against other midwestern teams. In volleyball, too, these Jewish girls earned victories. At the Jewish People's Institute (the CHI changed its name in 1922), girls demonstrated prowess in swimming and won events in Chicago's city-wide competitions.

The New York City Young Women's Hebrew Association (YWHA) served as one of the most important organizations for Jewish women desiring to participate in sports at the turn of the century. The oldest YWHA in the United States, it was founded in 1902 under the leadership of a small group of philanthropic Jewish women. It was developed to strengthen the ethnic and religious identity of young Jewish women and to counter the Young Women's Christian Associations and church-related athletic programs. Unlike the many YWHA ladies auxiliaries that were formed when women could not gain membership in Young Men's Hebrew Associations (YMHA), this YWHA was independent of the YMHA. The number of women using the facilities led to new, larger quarters. In 1914 the new YWHA opened, offering a comprehensive program in sports and physical culture training. It featured a swimming pool, a gymnasium, and a roof garden with tennis courts. Jewish women and girls participated in the Young Women's Hebrew Athletic League and competed against other YWHAs and YWCAs. Schedules had to be carefully arranged because the YWHA often closed on the Sabbath until later in the afternoon, and YWCAs kept their Sabbath as well.

Most YWHAs, however, had neither their own funding nor female staff trained in physical education and sports. During the early twentieth century, most YWHAs were affiliated with YMHAs, and YMHA athletic spaces usually remained male domains. Over time, with the aid of National Jewish Welfare Board (JWB) staff and funding, YMHA-YWHAs in various communities made athletic spaces more available to women. The JWB, organized in 1921, became the national governing body for YMHAs and YWHAs and the National Council of Young Men's Hebrew and Kindred Associations. The JWB promoted the merger of YMHAs and YWHAs and by the mid-twentieth century sought to develop them into JCCs. Today JCCs across the country serve Jews of both sexes.

So many Jewish women and girls engaged in sporting activities that they quickly outgrew YMHA rooms. Although founded in 1915, the Hartford, Connecticut, YWHA needed new quarters by 1919. Hartford YWHA members participated in swimming, tennis, basketball, volleyball, baseball, track and field, and bowling. The American Jewish press, such as the *Connecticut Hebrew Record* and Boston's *Jewish Advocate*, covered these girls' basketball games. The YWHA basketball team played in the Hartford County Basketball Girls League against teams of the Travelers Insurance Company, Aetna Fire, YWCA, and others, but the Jewish girls preferred playing YWHA organizations. A game between Hartford and New Haven YWHAs in 1920 held special significance for charity work undertaken by Jewish women. Proceeds went to the Jewish Home for Orphans and the Home for the Aged. The number of spectators who watched New Haven defeat the Hartford YWHA equaled those at men's basketball games. In 1930 and 1931, the Hartford YWHA team won the Connecticut State Championship, playing against Jewish and non-Jewish teams.

Basketball held wide appeal for women and girls at YWHAs. Women's basketball differed from the men's game to accommodate the concerns of women's physical educators, male athletic directors, and doctors that basketball was too rough on a woman's body. Some medical commentators worried that too much physical exertion harmed women's reproductive ability and that strenuous athletics promoted competition rather than cooperation, which was deemed appropriate for females. Jewish immigrant Senda Berenson became a leading physical educator of women and was known as the Mother of Women's Basketball. After attending the Boston Normal School for Gymnastics, she became interested in women's physical education. In 1892 Berenson was appointed the director of physical training at Smith College, the elite women's school in Northampton, Massachusetts. After observing Dr. James Naismith's new basketball game at Springfield College, Berenson organized the first women's basketball game at Smith College in 1892. She adapted the rules for women, dividing the court into zones, prohibiting snatching the ball from another player, allowing five to ten players on a team, and emphasizing teamwork. Women's basketball gained popularity for Jews and gentiles at colleges and schools, in YWHAs and YWCAs, and in working-class leagues. In honor of her vital role in the sport, Berenson was the first woman inducted into the Basketball Hall of Fame.

American Jewish women—as well as gentiles—wanting to pursue competitive swimming benefited from the leadership of Charlotte Epstein, known as the Mother of Women's Swimming in America. Born in 1884 in New York, Epstein swam in competitions and won some of the diving events. In 1911, she joined the recently formed National Women's Life-Saving League and in 1913 served as chair of its Athletic Branch, responsible for directing all competition. As an athlete, as an administrator promoting

competitive aquatic sports for women in the Women's Swimming Association (WSA), and through her major involvement in the Olympic games, the Maccabiah games (the Jewish Olympics, begun in 1932), and YWHAs, Epstein changed the sporting culture for women. During the early twentieth century, male officials governing amateur athletics prohibited women swimmers from participating in sanctioned swim races, national championships, and the Olympic games. They expressed concern about young women and girls engaging in vigorous competitions and being observed by spectators. Epstein led the way in overcoming gender restrictions for Jewish and non-Jewish swimmers alike. Gertrude Ederle, Olympian, and the first woman to swim the English Channel (1926), learned to swim at Epstein's swimming club and credited "Eppie" and the WSA for launching the careers of many early American champions.

Epstein and fellow lifesaving teammates, several of whom were Jews, campaigned to reform gender constraints in aquatic sports. In January 1915, the *American Hebrew* reported on Epstein's Jewish swimmers: Lucy Freeman (440-yard champion), Rita Greenfield, Sophie Freitag, and Frances Ricker. Epstein's effort to have the AAU recognize women's swimming held promise for women to compete in the Olympics. In October 1917 Epstein founded the renowned New York City WSA, a nonprofit club, to advance the sport of women's swimming. She became team manager of WSA, chairman of the Sports Committee, and, in 1929, president. From these positions, she promoted the national and international success of WSA swimmers, including the Olympians and national champions Aileen Riggin, Helen Meaney, Gertrude Ederle, Alice Lord, and Eleanor Holm.

Epstein battled the U.S. Olympic Committee for the right of American female swimmers and divers to go to the 1920 Olympics in Antwerp, Belgium. Once she succeeded and females competed in the sport in the Olympics for the first time, Epstein provided exemplary leadership as the manager-chaperon of the U.S. Women's Olympic Swimming Team. Under her direction at the WSA and as Olympic manager from 1920 to 1936, WSA members won Olympic championships and set numerous world records. Epstein became the official team manager of the U.S. Women's Swimming Team in the 1920, 1924, and 1932 Olympic games. She served as chair of the Swimming Committee in the 1935 Maccabiah games held in Palestine.

Jewish athletes from thirty countries competed in this second Maccabiah. Eppie's swimmers included Doris Beshunsky and Janice Lifson, a WSA teammate, who triumphed in the Maccabiah games. In 1936, Epstein refused to attend the Berlin Olympic games. As a Jew, she boycotted American participation in the Nazi Olympics and withdrew from the American Olympic Committee (AOC) in protest of Nazi policies. Epstein's swimming career continued until her death in 1938. In 1939, the AOC issued a resolution to honor her. She was inducted into the International Swimming Hall of Fame and the International Jewish Sport Hall of Fame.

American Jewish women also competed at YWHAs and the Olympics in track and field. In the 1920s Lillian Copeland became an outstanding track and field athlete at the University of Southern California. She won nine national titles and set world records in the javelin throw and the discus toss. In the summer 1928 Olympics she earned a silver medal in the discus. At the 1932 Los Angeles Olympic Games, Copeland won the gold medal in the discus throw, setting a world record. Both the *American Hebrew* and the *Los Angeles Times* highlighted her achievement. Sybil "Syd" Koff Cooper of New York was another track and field star in national competitions. At nineteen, she was a star at the first Maccabiah in 1932. She again excelled in the 1935 Maccabiah, winning seven gold medals in these first two Maccabiads. Although qualifying for the American track team, in 1936 both Koff and Copeland boycotted the Nazi Olympics.

Golf drew the interest of middle- and upper-class Jewish women at Jewish country clubs. Elaine Rosenthal Reinhardt became one of the most prominent golfers in the early twentieth century, playing at Ravisloe Country Club, a Jewish Club in Homewood, Illinois, outside Chicago. In 1914, at age eighteen, Rosenthal reached the finals in the U.S. women's national golf championship in New York. In 1917, 1918, and 1925, she won the prestigious Western Women's Golf Championship, becoming the first woman to do it three times. When she won for the third time, both the *American Hebrew* and the *Chicago Tribune* reported on her success. At times antisemitic behavior occurred in the Western Women's Golf Association. In 1923, for example, Jewish women golfers from six Jewish clubs in or near Chicago were barred from competing in the championship. During World War I, golf matches were halted, but Rosenthal was among the elite golfers invited to participate in American Red Cross golf exhibitions, where she raised funds with stars like Bobby Jones.

Champion tennis player Julie Heldman of Houston, Texas, won gold, bronze, and silver medals in singles and doubles events at the 1968 Olympics in Mexico City, where tennis was an exhibition sport. She also excelled in the 1969 Maccabiah games, winning three gold medals. Heldman was ranked as high as Number 2 in the United States in 1968–1969 and Number 5 in the world in 1969. Her mother, Gladys Heldman, born in 1922, had been the top amateur player in Texas and had competed in the U.S. Open and Wimbledon. In 1953 Heldman founded *World Tennis* magazine, selling it in the 1970s. She championed women's tennis and pioneered the formation of women's professional tennis. In 1970 Heldman spearheaded the movement of the best women's players, like Billie Jean King and Rosie Casals, to form their own pro tour to protest sex discrimination and the lack of prize money for women. They, as well as Julie Heldman, played in the first Virginia Slims Circuit tournament, held in Houston in 1970. The Virginia Slims Circuit gained popularity and later merged with the U.S. Tennis Association. In recognition of her achievements, Gladys Heldman, who died in 2003, was inducted into the International Tennis Hall of Fame in 1979 and the International Jewish Sports Hall of Fame in 1989. Julie Heldman was inducted into the latter in 2001.

Contemporary Jewish women honored in 2003 at the Jewish Sports Hall of Fame include professional golf champion Amy Alcott, ESPN sportscaster Linda Cohn, Olympic world record swimmer and Maccabiah champion Marilyn Romanesky, and Olympic gold medal figure skater Sarah Hughes.

Linda J. Borish

References and Further Reading

Borish, Linda J. 1998. "Jewish American Women, Jewish Organizations and Sports, 1880–1940." In *Sports and the American Jew*, edited by Steven A. Riess, 105–131. Syracuse, NY: Syracuse University Press.

Borish, Linda J. 1999a. "'Athletic Activities of Various Kinds': Physical Health and Sport Programs for Jewish American Women." *Journal of Sport History* 26,2 (Summer): 240–270.

Borish, Linda J. 1999b. "'An Interest in Physical Well-Being among the Feminine Membership': Sporting Activities for Women at Young Men's and Young Women's Hebrew Associations." *American Jewish History* 87: 61–93.

Borish, Linda J. 2000. "Senda Berenson Abbott" and "Lillian Copeland." In *Encyclopedia of Ethnicity and Sports in the United States,* edited by George B. Kirsch, Claire E. Nolte, and Othello Harris, 63, 110. Westport, CT: Greenwood Press.

Borish, Linda J. 2002. "Women, Sports, and American Jewish Identity in the Late Nineteenth and Early Twentieth Centuries" In *With God on Their Side: Sport in the Service of Religion,* edited by Tara Magdalinksi and Timothy J. L. Chandler, 71–98. New York: Routledge.

Borish, Linda J. 2004. "'The Cradle of American Champions, Women Champions . . . Swim Champions': Charlotte Epstein, Gender and Jewish Identity, and the Physical Emancipation of Women in Aquatic Sports." *The International Journal of the History of Sport* 21 (March): 197–235.

Senda Berenson (1868–1954)

Creator of Women's Basketball

In March of 1892, Senda Berenson, a diminutive young woman with thickly accented speech, introduced the students of Smith College to her adaptation of James Naismith's new game of basketball. From the Lithuanian village of Butry-Mantsy, Senda Berenson (b. March 17, 1868) had been brought to Boston in 1875 by her mother a year after her father had come to America. A lumber merchant who had been suspiciously burnt out of home and business, he had saved enough money as a peddler to send for his wife and five children. Never advancing beyond this meager financial position, his family remained impoverished until the eldest child, Bernard, began to make his fortune as an art broker for the wealthy. It was under his tutelage that Senda came to aspire to an artistic life. But Senda's development as a pianist, dancer, and painter became seriously limited by worsening physical problems. In the fall of 1890, hoping to strengthen her back before returning to more treasured pursuits, she enrolled in the Boston Normal School for Gymnastics (later absorbed by Wellesley College).

The changing social and cultural climate of these last years of the Gilded Age had encouraged her dreaming. Suffragist activism and women's labor unionism promised a new order for women. Senda, seeking to play a role in the world beyond her impoverished Jewish immigrant North End neighborhood, imagined herself a part of this Boston Bohemia. Through her brother, she had found a place in the avant-garde world of George Santayana and Ralph Adams Cram, into which she hoped permanently to escape.

Each of these elements—a Jewish immigrant beginning, the search for a place in the larger American society, artistic aspirations, and the desire for a changing order—found their voice on a March afternoon in 1892 when Senda stepped beyond her assigned role as a substitute for the college's ailing athletic director and daringly introduced the game of women's basketball. Midway through her course of study at the normal school, she had caught the eye of its director, who had been captivated by Senda's budding zeal for athletics. Still a student, she was only to be a one-semester replacement at Smith. Thus, whatever reluctance the college, an avowedly Christian school, may have had about hiring a Jew as a permanent faculty member, it did not interfere with the appointment. Once Berenson proved so overwhelmingly successful in her work with the students, the college apparently overlooked her religion and ethnicity. (There were a handful of Jewish students on campus, mostly from wealthy families, and in time a second low-profile Jewish faculty member, who became one of Senda's closest friends.)

Not long after arriving on campus, Senda traveled to the YMCA in Springfield, Massachusetts, to see the new game of basket ball, which James Naismith had presented to his reluctant students. She had read about this new team activity in the Y's journal and thought that it might be adaptable for her women. She changed the freewheeling men's game into a more genteel affair, with zones established to restrict movement and passing substituted for dribbling. It was to be a more civilized and ladylike pursuit. Players merely passed the ball forward until it was close enough to be tossed into the closed-bottom basket. A ladder was then brought forth, and the ball was retrieved and brought to center court for another toss-up. Repeatedly modified under Senda's guidance for the next quarter century, beginning in 1899 the Spalding Company published an annual edition of her rulebook. Berenson's insistence on maintaining the more genteel side of the game continued to shape athletic life at Smith College until the early 1970s, when it at last departed from her vision and played its first interscholastic games.

Until Senda's innovations at Smith and their rapid spread nationwide, little in the way of athletics was available to women beyond gymnastics and exercise regimens. The occasional baseball game, played in full dress, represented one of the rare exceptions to this situation. Surrounded by her students, dressed in far briefer garments than they, on that March day in 1892, Senda stood in disbelief before a full house as she tossed up the ball for the first time. She did not at first understand the larger forces at work on that small campus that would carry her game to schools, colleges, and settlement houses across the country within a few years—and in 1967 force the male-dominated Basketball Hall of Fame to admit her as its first female honoree. Women were attempting to break free of the old roles imposed by a patriarchal social order, and basketball was quickly perceived as a means to this end, first by Senda and soon after by many others.

Senda came to recognize that the "remarkable success" of her "dubious experiment" owed to its being introduced at "*the* psychological moment in the development of the American girl," as she later explained (all quotes from Senda Berenson Papers, n.d.). Unlike those "anxious mothers who . . . feared their daughters would become tomboys if they wore loose clothing and played games," she had provided a "natural outlet of the play instinct" through which young women could develop the "endurance and physical courage" needed in their search for equal standing in society. It was the "simultaneous quickness of thought and action," developed through basketball, that would serve this goal of equality, she felt certain.

It was as a social activist that Senda first came to the attention of other progressive American women, Jane Addams and Margaret Sanger among them. As she later recalled, "Something had to be done to counteract all those evils . . . of a civilization which does anything it can to undo what nature strives to do for us—making us crowd into large cities where there is little opportunity for natural exercise—where occupations tend to make us narrow chested [and] stoop shouldered," physically and in spirit.

Nowhere were these conditions more prevalent than among poor women, whose lives were "apt to be so monotonous. They work (and it is something that is generally not stimulating intellectually) all day long," she noted in her effort to bring a sense of liberation to those confined and overworked women, about whom she spoke tirelessly in her many public talks throughout these years. "They come back home where they generally have to help in the housework—where the mother is apt to be sad and tired and often complaining, where often someone is ill. Such a person soon gets into a deadening round of monotonous depression." Unlike most of her students and colleagues at Smith, Senda had known this world intimately in her youth and felt the need to offer a stimulant for change. She claimed, "a person can perhaps be saved more quickly through exercise and games than in any other way." They alone "absorb the whole person, the physical, the mental, and if well-guided, the moral," enabling them to "mix in the affairs of the world."

From the start, Senda had stressed the moral as well as the practical value of basketball. There seemed little point in forming New Women if they could not also transform the world in which they lived. Thus, in an atmosphere where "group games of any kind were unheard of" for college women, "we made a point from the beginning to develop good sportsmanship."

This spirit was missing from the growing world of American athletics, Senda repeatedly observed. The unpleasant consequences of this were already evident. "The great evil in athletics today is that we lose sight of all things except the desire to win—to win by fair means or foul. . . . Hence . . . the joy in the playing—is entirely lost. . . . [W]e spend enormous amounts of money to see a few overtrained men play football or baseball while thousands, who were not prepared to take any exercise themselves, look on and shout themselves into a frenzy." "To win always has a great element of seeing the other person lose—not a noble thing," she complained.

Rather, Berenson urged the young to "study appreciation of the arts, read as much as possible, go abroad the first opportunity you have," and engage with the political and social issues of their time. This was the path she followed in her own life from early adolescence through her days as a student and teacher in America and Europe, where she had gone in 1897 to study at the Royal Central Institute of Gymnastics, and in the following years when she often accompanied her brother through the cultural capitals of the Continent. Even when slowed by deteriorating health in her last years, she locally aided those suffering through the Great Depression and in the 1940s worked with the Red Cross in the war effort.

She retired from Smith College in 1911 upon her marriage to English professor Herbert Abbott. Though Senda had not abandoned Judaism, she was a confirmed atheist, and her famed father-in-law, the Reverend Lyman Abbott, performed the ceremony. In 1917 she resigned from chairing the national Basketball Committee for Women, only to experience the loss of her husband in 1925. For the rest of her life, Berenson remained deeply concerned about the human condition. After World War II, she was especially concerned with what she considered the march toward nuclear madness. She always hoped to set things right by sharing her vision of what life could be. She died in Santa Barbara, California, on February 16, 1954.

Ralph Melnick

References and Further Reading

Melnick, Ralph. 2007. *Senda Berenson: The Unlikely Founder of Women's Basketball.* Amherst: University of Massachusetts Press.

Senda Berenson Papers. No date. Smith College Archives. Northampton, MA.

Hank Greenberg (1911–1986)

Star Baseball Slugger

Henry "Hank" Greenberg, one of baseball's greatest sluggers, provided a much idolized symbol of Jewish prowess in a time of Depression, world war, and intensified antisemitism at home and abroad. As a Jew in the overwhelmingly gentile environment of professional baseball, Greenberg's life exemplified the challenges that would confront the American Jewish community at large in an increasingly assimilated milieu.

Born in Greenwich Village (in New York City) to religiously observant parents who had immigrated from Romania, Greenberg grew up in the Bronx. A star athlete at James Monroe High School, the powerfully built six-foot-three-inch first baseman attracted the interest of the nearby New York Yankees. The Yankees' interest in the box office potential of a homegrown Jewish star was nullified, however, by Greenberg's astute recognition that the formidable Lou Gehrig stood between him and a first base starting slot on the Bronx Bombers. Instead, Greenberg signed a contract with the Detroit Tigers, and, after one semester at New York University, joined the Tiger organization in the spring of 1930.

After several years in the minor leagues, Greenberg became the Tigers' starting first baseman in 1933, hitting .301 in his rookie season. The next season, Greenberg raised his batting average to .339 while leading the American League in doubles and hitting twenty-six home runs, as the Tigers won their first pennant in a quarter century. Late that season, with Tiger games scheduled on the Jewish High Holidays, Greenberg's religious identity became the subject of widespread attention and debate. The year before, Greenberg had sat out those games, without comment being made. In early September 1934, however, the Tigers were battling for the pennant in a tight race with the Yankees. Greenberg, pressured by the press and his teammates and not wanting to let his team down, decided to play on Rosh Hashanah—to his father's chagrin. His two home runs won the game for Detroit. The next week, with the Tigers now holding an all but insurmountable seven-and-a-half game lead (with only eleven games left to play), Greenberg did not play on Yom Kippur. He attended services at a Detroit synagogue, where he was applauded by the congregation and attracted favorable, albeit somewhat condescending, notice in the press for fidelity to his religious beliefs.

The next year, Greenberg led the American League in home runs and runs batted in as the Tigers repeated as American League pennant winners and won their first world championship. Greenberg continued his robust hitting throughout the decade. In 1937 he drove in 183 runs (third-best on the all-time list), and the following year he challenged Babe Ruth's 60-home-run record, falling just short with 58 (still the top single-season American League mark for a right-handed batter). After leading the league in home runs, runs batted in, doubles, and slugging percentage, and after playing in his third World Series in 1940, Greenberg was drafted into the army in the spring of 1941. Discharged in early December, he reenlisted immediately after Pearl Harbor. His wartime service included overseas duty with the Army Air Forces in the China-Burma-India theater and several bombing missions over Japan.

Having lost the equivalent of four full seasons at the peak of his career, Greenberg returned to the Tigers in July 1945. He hit a home run in his first game back and finished his abbreviated season with a batting average of .311, as the Tigers won their fourth league pennant with Greenberg in the lineup and then defeated the Chicago Cubs in the World Series. After a 1946 season in which he again led the American League in home runs and runs

Baseball slugger Hank Greenberg. (National Baseball Hall of Fame Library, Cooperstown, NY)

batted in, the thirty-six-year-old Greenberg was released by the Tigers. In 1947, he concluded his career with the Pittsburgh Pirates, hitting 25 home runs and offering much appreciated encouragement to Jackie Robinson in his difficult rookie season with the Dodgers.

Greenberg compiled a lifetime batting average of .313 with 331 home runs and 1,276 runs. He led the American League four times in both home runs and runs batted in, and his career slugging average and home run percentage still rank among the sport's all-time best. Voted the American League's Most Valuable Player in 1935 and 1940, Greenberg was named to four All-Star teams and appeared in four World Series—a notable feat for a non-Yankee in that era—hitting .318 with five home runs. After his retirement, Greenberg enjoyed a successful career as a baseball executive with pennant-winning teams in Cleveland and Chicago, proving as tough a bargainer from management's side of the negotiating table as he earlier had on his own

behalf as the sport's highest-paid player. He was elected to the Baseball Hall of Fame in 1956.

Playing at a time of widespread discrimination against Jews in business, society, and education, and in the Detroit of Father Coughlin, Greenberg had to contend with antisemitic attitudes and utterances among both fans and players. Greenberg was fully prepared to confront his tormenters, physically if necessary, but was generally uncomfortable in situations that called attention to his religious identity. Early in his career, he was embarrassed when his father signed baseballs in Hebrew for fans outside Yankee Stadium. Greenberg felt himself to be very much the unwilling man-in-the-middle in the controversy over whether he should play on the High Holidays in 1934. Apparently, his discomfort colored his recollection of that event. He later remembered that 1934 was the only time that he faced the issue of playing on Yom Kippur, although Yom Kippur actually conflicted with his team's schedule in several other years, and Greenberg never played on any of those days. The children of his first marriage, to the daughter of department store magnate Bernard Gimbel, were raised without any religious training and minimal Jewish self-awareness. His daughter recalled that he felt that "I had to go through this stuff and I hated it, and I thought I'd spare my kids." One son found himself so bereft of religious identity that he listed himself as a Congregationalist on a college enrollment form. Yet Greenberg's posthumously published autobiography quoted him as saying that "I came to feel that if I, as a Jew, hit a home run, I was hitting one against Hitler," and that "I find myself wanting to be remembered not only as a great ballplayer, but even more as a great *Jewish* ballplayer" (Greenberg 1989).

Henry D. Fetter

References and Further Reading
Greenberg, Hank. 1989. *Hank Greenberg: The Story of My Life,* edited and Introduction by Ira Berkow. New York: Times Books.
Levine, Peter. 1992. *Ellis Island to Ebbets Field: Sport and the American Jewish Experience.* New York: Oxford University Press.

Hall of Fame pitcher Sandy Koufax. (National Baseball Hall of Fame Library, Cooperstown, NY)

Sandy Koufax (b. 1935)

Baseball Pitching Star

Sanford "Sandy" Koufax, generally recognized as baseball's best pitcher in a period of outstanding pitching, is arguably the greatest left-handed pitcher of all time, despite a career cut short by injury in his prime. Like Hank Greenberg in an earlier time, Koufax inspired a generation of Jewish baseball fans by demonstrating that a Jew could star in the national pastime while respecting religious tradition.

Born in Brooklyn, New York, to parents who divorced a few years later, he took the last name of Irving Koufax, whom his mother married when Sandy was nine years old. At Lafayette High School in Brooklyn, his primary sport was basketball, which he played, along with baseball, at the University of Cincinnati when he enrolled in the fall of 1953. In December 1954, he was signed by the Brooklyn Dodgers, for a $14,000 bonus and a first-year salary of $6,000.

For decades, New York baseball owners and managers had dreamed of fielding a star Jewish player, who could attract the city's baseball-mad Jewish fans to the ballpark. This dream was frustrated, however, as Koufax struggled through his first years with the Dodgers, his raw pitching power and enormous potential outweighed by persistent control problems and the difficulty of gaining a regular place in the rotation of the pennant-winning team's well-established pitching staff. More importantly, the Dodgers moved to California after the 1957 season. Koufax would only achieve greatness in Los Angeles, a continent away from his Brooklyn home.

In the spring of 1961, Koufax finally began to heed the advice he had been receiving for years—to concentrate on getting the ball over the plate, not on throwing as hard as he could—after it was proffered by a Jewish teammate, reserve catcher Norm Sherry. It was the turning point in his career. After winning 36 games and losing 40 in his first 6 seasons with the Dodgers, in 1961 Koufax won 18 games and broke the National League season record for strikeouts with 269. His 1962 season was cut short by injury, but everything came together in 1963. With a blazing fastball, sharply breaking curve, and pinpoint control, that year he led the league in wins (25), strikeouts (306), and earned run average (1.88), and won two games in the Dodgers' four-game World Series sweep over the New York Yankees. He was named the National League's Most Valuable Player and won the first of his three Cy Young Awards as the best pitcher in the major leagues. Dodger teammate Don Drysdale, a Hall of Fame pitcher in his own right, commented, with only slight hyperbole, "He's the only pitcher who wouldn't surprise me a bit if he pitched a no-hitter every time he went out there" (*New York Post*, September 30, 1963).

Although Koufax's 1964 season was curtailed by injury, he still won 19 games and again posted the National League's lowest earned run average. In 1965, he won a league-leading 26 games, struck out a record 382 batters, and pitched a perfect game (his fourth no-hitter in as many seasons), as the Dodgers again won the National League pennant.

The first game of that year's World Series, which Koufax was due to start, fell on Yom Kippur. In keeping with his customary practice, he did not pitch that day, a decision that did not arouse the controversy sparked three decades earlier when Hank Greenberg faced a similar situation. This may have reflected a greater tolerance and understanding of Jewish religious observance in the post-Holocaust era. Drysdale took Koufax's place on the mound for the Series opener, was hit hard, and, when taken out of the game, reportedly remarked to the Dodger manager, "Skip, I bet you wish I was Jewish too" (Leavy 2002). Although Koufax lost the Series' second game, he won his next two starts, hurling a three-hit shutout in game seven, as the Dodgers came from behind to win the world championship.

In 1966, Koufax pitched the Dodgers to their third pennant in four years, winning a career-high 27 games, striking out 317 batters, and again compiling the league's lowest earned run average. This would be his last season. Suffering from an arthritic elbow, Koufax announced his retirement after the Dodgers lost that year's World Series to the Baltimore Orioles. He was thirty years old.

In twelve seasons with the Dodgers, Koufax won 165 games and lost 87, a winning percentage of .655. His career earned run average was 2.76, and he struck out 2,396 batters, more than one per inning. Koufax led the National League in games won three times, in strikeouts four times, and in earned run average for five consecutive years. He was elected to the Baseball Hall of Fame in 1972, his first year of eligibility.

Pitching in the pastoral setting of Los Angeles' Chavez Ravine Stadium, Koufax symbolized the demographic shift in American Jewry—in the decades since Hank Greenberg had starred for the Detroit Tigers—away from the industrial inner cities of the Northeast and Midwest, to a suburban environment. Similarly, his two marriages (which each ended in divorce) to non-Jewish women anticipated another trend in American Jewish life. Although he rarely encountered severe antisemitism, stereotypical attitudes surfaced in a gratuitous magazine report that the Dodgers set aside a platter of bagels, lox, and chopped liver for him in the team clubhouse or in the offensive taunt of a Minnesota sportswriter during the 1965 World Series that the "Twins love matzoh balls." A predisposition to resort to ethnic clichés may have motivated the press to portray this well-muscled six-foot-two-inch power pitcher who happened to be Jewish as an aloof highbrow who listened to classical music and read books by Aldous Huxley, did not socialize with his teammates, had become a ballplayer by chance, and did not even like baseball—a characterization that, Koufax repeatedly insisted, was inaccurate.

Once his playing days ended, Koufax's laconic manner and reserve doomed his brief foray at broadcasting. A minor league pitching instructor for the Dodgers in the 1980s, he thereafter made periodic spring training appearances as a coach at Dodgertown, but for the most part Koufax has lived quietly, almost entirely out of the public eye, in the decades since he retired at the peak of his game. The ranks of comparably preeminent Jewish athletes have been thin since Koufax's time; only swimmer Mark Spitz comes to mind. Perhaps increasing affluence has sapped the all-consuming competitive hunger that great athletes must have. And, as ongoing assimilation has vitiated traditional definitions of who is a Jew, the determination of religious identity has become ambiguous in many cases. But if another Jewish "Koufax" has yet to appear, neither has a gentile one.

Henry D. Fetter

References and Further Reading
Koufax, Sandy, with Ed Linn. 1966. *Koufax*. New York: Viking.
Leavy, Jane. 2002. *Sandy Koufax: A Lefty's Legacy*. New York: HarperCollins.

Richler, Mordecai. 1966. "Koufax the Incomparable." *Commentary* (November): 87–89.

Marvin Miller (b. 1917)

Labor Leader

Marvin Miller created the most powerful American professional trade union in the twentieth century, the Major League Baseball Players Association. Starting with his election to head the union in 1966, during his sixteen-year tenure Miller changed the labor landscape of modern professional team sports and, in the process, goaded club and league management into meeting the challenges of the global entertainment market. Reviled by owners and many fans as the epitome of greed, Miller triumphed repeatedly with the backing of a unified union membership.

An economist by training and practice, Miller accepted the challenge of transmuting a fraternity of baseball players ruled by feudal management into a trade union. United, the Players Association effectively secured improved terms and conditions of employment through the use of the strike. When baseball management locked out the ballplayers, no one on the union side broke ranks. As a result, through collective bargaining the Players Association achieved significant improvements in pension rights and benefits, licensing revenues, scheduling, and even padded outfield walls. At the same time, the multibillion-dollar business of baseball enjoyed record attendance and enhanced franchise values.

Miller understood that the integrity of contract promises depended on a readily available means of enforcement. Schooled in traditional labor relations, in 1970 Miller sought and obtained a provision at the bargaining table for labor arbitration of disputed contract issues before an impartial party. In 1975, before noted arbitrator Peter Seitz, who was jointly selected by baseball management and the union, General Counsel Richard Moss presented evidence to support the Players Association's claim that, under the terms of the uniform player contract, a club may only reserve a player's services for a single option year. Seitz ruled in favor of the union. Miller had won a player's right to free agency, ending the century-old baseball practice of the strict lifelong reserve system that bound a player to one

Marvin Miller, executive director of the Major League Baseball Players Association (1966-1982). (Bettman/Corbis)

club for his entire career. After negotiations, the club owners and the union agreed to the current system that allows a player to declare free agency after six years of major league service and market his services to any baseball club.

Miller's greatest talent was his ability to listen to his members and seek their input. He established a representative structure that offered genuine participation for rank-and-file ballplayers in the development of union policies. When asked early on by one of his members whether they were really a union, Miller responded that national law protected the right of any group of people who worked together to advance their collective interests. The Players Association was a genuine union, and Miller would make it a very powerful one.

When Miller took over as executive director, the union owned a file cabinet and had $5,400 in its bank account. He immediately negotiated a deal with Coca-Cola to put players' pictures under bottle caps, raising $66,000, the modest beginning of a licensing program that subsequently produced millions in revenue for all major league baseball players.

Born in 1917 in the Bronx, Marvin Julian Miller was raised in Brooklyn. A Dodgers fan, young Miller would sit in the bleachers and root for his favorite pitcher, Dazzy Vance. Miller knew the statistics, batting stances, and pitching motions of every player. He entered high school just as the Great Depression began, and his parents joined unions to protect their jobs. Miller's father sold women's coats on the Lower East Side of Manhattan, working seven days a week. Miller walked the picket line with his father. His mother was a public school teacher and one of the early organizers of the teachers' union. Miller learned from them the lesson that in the union there is strength.

Miller graduated from New York University in 1938 with a degree in economics. He worked for the War Labor Board during World War II and then joined the staff of the International Association of Machinists. In 1950, Miller became research director and chief economist for the United Steelworkers of America. Working for various union presidents and Steelworkers general counsel Arthur Goldberg, Miller became an expert in collective bargaining. He was considered a quiet and industrious "technician."

George Taylor, the nation's leading academic labor economist, recommended Miller to the baseball players for the position of executive director of their Players Association. A dapper New Yorker with a pencil-thin moustache, Miller was not a natural choice for the job. (In fact, two others had already rejected the position before Taylor suggested Miller.) Miller would have to win the respect of the membership and withstand the onslaught of attacks by the owners who were used to dominating the compliant players. His membership had almost no work experience outside of baseball and knew nothing about unions. He patiently explained to the players their rights under national law as he traveled from city to city, and he encouraged their questions and comments. Miller won the support of his membership, and his organizational skills proved legendary. When management refused to supply salary information in violation of federal law, Miller simply accumulated the data from the players themselves. He would need all his negotiating skills if he were to prevail at the bargaining table.

Miller's greatest challenge was convincing the owners to take a union of pampered professional athletes seriously.

Miller achieved immediate success in negotiations, however, raising the minimum salary from $7,000 to $10,000 and improving pension rights in 1968. Then the owners vowed to stand fast, perhaps in a futile effort to break the union. Miller understood that success at the bargaining table depended on economic strength. Although the Players Association bargained hard as each contract expired, club owners had difficulty believing the players would jeopardize their status by striking or withstanding an owner-directed lockout—an incorrect, but long-lived, assumption that would prove disastrous to baseball management for decades. The sports media were strongly and incessantly anti-union in tone and content. Miller kept his troops together, however, unlike the experience in other professional sports unions, such as the National Football League Players Association. And he, along with his devoted membership, triumphed. During his tenure, the average salary of a major league baseball player increased from $19,000 to $240,000. More importantly, he had established a market-based salary system that would increase the average player salary to over $2 million a year by the turn of the century.

The ultimate challenge to Miller's success came in 1981 when the owners provoked the union to strike to defend the significant gains it had achieved. Claiming that twenty-one of its twenty-six clubs were losing money, the owners sought to limit free agency salaries. Under their plan, a club signing a free agent would have to assign one of its current players to the free agent's former club. This "forced trade," similar to football's Rozelle Rule, would have gutted the union's previous victories and effectively ended free agency. Management had prepared for the battle by taking out strike insurance from Lloyds of London. Miller and his troops stood fast through a fifty-day walkout from June until the end of July. When their insurance ran out, the owners backed down. As was his custom, Miller gave the players full credit for prevailing.

During Miller's tenure as executive director from 1966 to 1982, the owners and the Players Association negotiated five basic collective bargaining agreements that included greater improvements in employee working conditions than in any American industry in a comparable period. They included the introduction of salary arbitration to resolve pay disputes without player holdouts and the introduction of a player's right to veto trades. In that same period, five pension and insurance agreements were negotiated, vastly improving all the benefits and adding many new ones. All of this was accomplished with a minimum of lost work time.

Miller retired in 1982, but he continued to informally advise his successor, Donald Fehr, and to comment publicly on baseball labor relations issues. His 1991 memoir, *A Whole Different Ballgame: The Sports and Business of Baseball*, recounts Miller's version of events on the business side of baseball. He donated his papers to New York University's Tamiment Library for future generations of scholars. His wife of over sixty years, Terry Miller, earned her doctorate in psychology in 1961 and, after working in clinical and experimental psychology, retired as an associate professor at the City University of New York.

Although he never fielded a ground ball or stroked a hanging curve, Miller pounded the opposition with genius and tenacity. Miller was the most effective union leader of his time. Beloved by many of his members and detested by many on management's side and among the public, Marvin Miller lived a Hall of Fame career that should eventually result in his induction into the shrine of the national pastime at Cooperstown, New York.

Roger I. Abrams

References and Further Reading

Abrams, Roger I. 1998. *The Legal Bases: Baseball and the Law*. Philadelphia: Temple University Press.

Korr, Charles P. 2002. *The End of Baseball as We Knew It: The Players Union, 1960–1981*. Urbana: University of Illinois Press.

Miller, Marvin. 1991. *A Whole Different Ball Game: The Sport and Business of Baseball*. New York: Birch Lane Press.

American Jewish Novelists, Essayists, Poets, and Playwrights

Early Jewish Writers in America

The opening chapters of Jewish American literary history span the first two and a half centuries of Jewish settlement in North America, from the mid-seventeenth to the late nineteenth century, when the mass immigration from Eastern Europe significantly altered the dynamic of Jewish life and literature in America. To begin with, these chapters chronicle the imaginative responses expressed in a range of documents, from petitions and letters to sermons and liturgy, of the earliest Sephardic and Ashkenazic immigrants and their descendants to the unprecedented opportunities and challenges of the New World: their protests and prayers, their translations and transformations, their affirmations and renunciations. These chapters narrate as well the earliest attempts of Jewish writers to join in the literary and intellectual life of the United States—the first poems, plays, novels, and criticism they wrote as Americans for American audiences—the development of Jewish intracommunal literary culture, and the gradual emergence of a self-confident, integrated, mainstream mode of Jewish American ethnic expression.

The Seventeenth Century

Although a number of literary figures lived in several of the Dutch Jewish communities in South America and in the Caribbean, none were among the twenty-three Jews who fled Recife, Brazil, after the Portuguese reconquest and landed in New Amsterdam in 1654, and none were among those who followed for the next half century. The literary remains of these earliest Jewish settlers consist mainly of petitions addressed to the Dutch West India Company protesting the exclusionary policies of Governor Peter Stuyvesant and demanding economic and political rights. While hardly literature in the strict sense, these defiant Dutch petitions are the first examples of Jewish self-expression to emerge out of the immediate experience of Jews in North America.

The Eighteenth Century

The resistance of the early Dutch Jewish settlers to anti-Jewish practices, their insistence on participating in the political life of the colony while remaining practicing Jews, stands nobly, if somewhat deceptively, at the threshold of the history of Jewish American letters, for the course of that history takes a different turn when the first Jewish-authored literary texts are published in the eighteenth century. By then, much of the overt bigotry encountered by the early settlers had been rebuffed and reversed, and the vicissitudes of life in the various British colonies exerted their influence on the Jewish imagination in more subtle and complex ways.

A case in point occurred around 1720, when an Italian Jew, probably of Portuguese descent, named Judah Monis (1683–1764) arrived in Puritan Boston. While steeped in Christian anti-Judaism, the Puritan attitude toward Jews, epitomized by Increase Mather's *The Mystery of Israel's Salvation, Explained and Applyed* (1669), proved to be more nuanced than the aggressive antipathy of Stuyvesant. While later claims of "Jewish" influence on Puritan New England and, hence, on American culture in general are grossly overstated, the typological mind-set of the Puritans did keep the Old Testament and the biblical Hebrews in the forefront of their imaginations. Moreover, like other Protestant millenialists, the Puritans believed that the survival of the Jews as a distinct people despite their dispersion among the nations was an indication that the Jews still had a special role to play in Christian history. They looked forward to the conversion of a remnant of the Jews, their redemption from obstinacy and error, as a sign that the end of times was near.

When Monis appeared in Boston, he was welcomed warmly by Mather and his colleagues as a learned scholar and religious figure with an insider's knowledge of Hebrew and the Bible. When he converted to Christianity, his apostasy was seen as an affirmation of the Puritans' conception of sacred history. As a converted Jew, Monis never renounced his Jewish identity—he is said to have continued to observe his Sabbath on Saturdays—but parlayed it into a respected position in Puritan society, becoming instructor of Hebrew at Harvard College and, hence, its first Jewish faculty member. The volume of conversionist discourses that appears under his name (*The Truth, The Whole Truth, and Nothing But the Truth*, published soon after his conversion in 1722) makes him the first Jewish author in America. The volume is remarkable for its coupling of classical Jewish erudition with a direct and frank address to "my Brethren *According to the Flesh*." Monis admits: "I do expect the News of my Embracing the Christian Religion that came to your Ears some time ago, has been somewhat surprizing to you all; and I am afraid you did not think it to be the best you ever have heard." Still, he prayed that God would "in due time take the Vail [sic] from before the eyes of your Understanding, that so you may see the veracity of his Christ."

Not all scholars accept without skepticism Monis's authorship of these discourses, but his place as the first Jewish American author is nevertheless secured by *A Grammar of the Hebrew Tongue*, published in 1735 and used for decades by his students at Harvard. (He also composed a Hebrew lexicon that was never published.) The irony of the apostate's position in Jewish American literary history is compounded by the fact that, while Monis labored to spread the knowledge of Hebrew among the Puritans, American Jews, loyal to Judaism but far from centers of Jewish learning, were evidently losing their facility in the Holy tongue.

More ironic still is the fact that this Jewish linguistic erosion engendered Jewish literary creativity, for the next significant Jewish-authored publications in America were translations. Noting that Hebrew was "imperfectly understood by many, by some, not at all," a New York Jew named Isaac Pinto (1720–1791) took it upon himself "to translate our Prayers, in the Language of the Country wherein it hath pleased the divine Providence to appoint our Lot." His *Prayers for Shabbath, Rosh-Hashanah, and Kippur* appeared in 1766. (An earlier, anonymous volume, *Evening Service of Rosh Hashanah and Kippur*, appeared in 1761 and has also been attributed to Pinto.) While he makes clear in his preface that prayer in Hebrew was greatly preferred, as a sign both of "veneration for the Language . . . in which it pleased Almighty God to reveal himself to our Ancestors" and of the conviction "that it will again be re-established in Israel," Pinto bowed to the exigencies of Jewish life in America, hoping that his reluctant literary effort would "tend to the Improvement of many of my Brethren in their Devotion."

Another sign of the undeveloped literary state of the Jewish community in eighteenth-century America is the fact that the first Jewish sermon printed in the British colonies was composed by a visitor from Hebron, Rabbi Raphael Hayyim Isaac Carigal (1729–1777). Carigal arrived in Newport, Rhode Island, in 1773, just before Purim, and preached a sermon in Ladino in the synagogue there three months later, on the holiday of Shavuoth. (It was soon translated by Abraham Lopez into English and published later that year as *The Salvation of Israel*.) Woven with strands of the Bible, Talmud, and ancient history, the sermon took as its theme the dangers of religious innovation and the arrogance of human reason, warning his audience in those turbulent times that "public commotions & revolutions are effects proceeding from the council of the divine creator, who establishes and destroys kingdoms and empires for reasons reserved only to his infinite wisdom."

By the time Carigal preached in Newport, however, the American-born Gershom Mendes Seixas (1745–1816) had been the *hazzan* (cantor) of Shearith Israel for five years, and, in the decades following the Revolution, Seixas became a significant representative of the fledgling Jewish American community. Shaped by the Revolutionary years, Seixas's homiletics—as seen in his two published sermons, *A Religious Discourse* (1789) and *A Discourse Delivered* (1798)—are characterized by a tension between traditional religio-ethnic conservatism and the headiness of Revolutionary promise, between a Jewish narrative of exile and a new, secular Jewish *American* narrative of liberation. The most well-known version of this new narrative was articulated by the hazzan's brother, Moses Seixas (1744–1809) of Newport, in a letter written in 1790 to newly elected President George Washington: "Deprived as we have hitherto been of the invaluable rights of free citizens, we now . . . behold a government, erected by the majesty of the people, a government which to bigotry gives no sanction, to persecution no assistance, but generously offering to all liberty of conscience and immunities of citizenship, deeming every one, of whatever nation, tongue, or language, equal parts of the great governmental machine." Gershom's congregants had to be reminded that this new American narrative did not supersede the older, Jewish one. Recalling the history of the Jews from God's promise to Abraham to the destruction of the Temple, Seixas concludes in *A Religious Discourse:* "From that period even until now, our predecessors have been, and *we are still at this time* in captivity among the different nations of the earth; and though we are . . . made equal partners of the benefits of government by the constitution of these states . . . still we cannot but view ourselves as captives in comparison to what we were formerly, and what we expect to be hereafter, when the outcasts of Israel shall be gathered together" and "we shall be established under our own king—the Messiah the son of David."

The Early Nineteenth Century

In the early decades of the new republic, patriotic American writers turned their energies to producing what they believed could and should be a distinctly American literature. On this note, American Jews proudly entered into the cultural life of the new nation as well, striving to write as Americans and succeeding, authoring plays, poems, and romances that broadly resembled those of their non-Jewish compatriots.

Among these Jewish American aspirants was New York's Samuel B. H. Judah (1799–1876), who authored a number of melodramas, including *The Mountain Torrent* (1820) and *The Rose of Aragon* (1822), along with a patriotic comedy called *A Tale of Lexington* (1823), a long Romantic dramatic poem *Odofriede, the Outcast* (1822), and a novel *The Buccaneers: A Romance of Our Own Country* (1827). Plainly an ambitious young writer, Judah also produced a scurrilous account of the political and literary life of New York City called *Gotham and the Gothamites* (1823), in which he suggests that his fellow playwright Mordecai Noah was "descended from Mordecai of old, that hanged Haman, for his desires, like that worthy's, are entirely bent toward the gallows." Although published under the pseudonym Terentius Phlogobombus, Judah's authorship was nevertheless revealed and he was jailed for his efforts. (A number of freethinking biblical dramas published in the 1830s have also been ascribed to Judah, but his authorship of these is doubtful.)

More successful in his literary endeavors was Philadelphia-born Jonas B. Phillips (1805–1869). After publishing a collection of gothic stories, *Tales for Leisure Hours* (1827), he authored a number of popular melodramas, including *The Evil Eye* (1833), based on a story by Mary Shelley, and *Jack Sheppard, or The Life of a Robber* (1839), based on a novel by Henry Ainsworth, notable as the first dramatic work to include, albeit briefly and inconsequentially, a Jewish character. Phillips also penned a tragedy, *Camillus; or, The Self-Exiled Patriot* (1833), and a collection of verse, *Zamira: A Dramatic Sketch, and Other Poems* (1835). A number of his lyrics were set to music by popular composer Henry Russell.

Like Judah and Phillips, Isaac Harby of Charleston (1788–1828) enters American literary history through the stage: Harby's early gothic melodrama *The Gordian Knot* (1807, produced in 1810) is credited with being the first Jewish-authored literary work published in the United States, and his later *Alberti* (1819), a play about the Medici, was honored by the presence of President James Monroe at its premiere. (Harby is also said to have authored, at seventeen, a tragedy about Roman emperor Alexander Severus.) A noted newspaper editor, Harby also produced a considerable and respectable body of general political, literary, and dramatic criticism. (*Selections from the Miscellaneous*

Writings of Isaac Harby, containing *Alberti* and a generous sampling of his critical writing, was published posthumously in 1829.) These literary works are for the most part, like the works of Judah and Phillips, indistinguishable in style and theme from those of his non-Jewish American contemporaries.

Yet Harby figures more prominently and significantly in the history of Jewish American letters. What distinguishes him, first and foremost, is his critique of anti-Jewish bigotry, whether in his 1816 letter to President James Monroe protesting the removal of Mordecai Noah as United States consul in Tunis, or, more publicly, in an essay on Shakespeare's *Merchant of Venice.* "When we observe in a drama, an Irishman represented as a *rogue,* an Englishman a *sot,* a Frenchman a *monkey,* and a Jew a *usurer,*" he writes, "we evidently are aware, that the author's sole object is to gratify the malignant passions of mankind," accusing the otherwise irreproachable bard of "bow[ing] his great genius to the prejudices of an ignorant age" (*Miscellaneous Writings*). Still, glimpses of Jewish sentiment are rare indeed in Harby's literary writing, and it is worth noting that his critique of antisemitism draws sustenance from his Jeffersonian liberalism as much as it is fueled by his Jewishness.

More than on his plays or criticism, Harby's Jewish reputation rests on his literary activity within the Jewish community of Charleston. As a founding member of the Reformed Society of Israelites for Promoting True Principles of Judaism According to Its Purity and Spirit, the first proto-Reform congregation in America, Harby contributed to its revisionary prayer book and penned a discourse (1825) that articulated its beliefs and goals. Here Harby speaks unequivocally *as* a Jew—and, more precisely, as an American Jew. Not only did he configure progressive American values as Jewish values, he also envisioned America as the culmination of *Jewish* history. "Thus appreciating, thus enjoying the natural and political blessings of our country," he wrote, "we are willing to repose in the belief that America truly is the land of promise spoken of in our ancient scriptures, that this is the region to which the children of Israel, if they are wise, will hasten to come." Such beliefs would find their full articulation decades later in the writings of German reformers Isaac Mayer Wise and Kaufmann Kohler.

Ridiculed by Judah and defended by Harby, Mordecai Manuel Noah (1785–1851) of New York was unarguably the most prominent Jew in antebellum America, as well as the most flamboyant—and the most maligned. Consul to Tunis, grand sachem of Tammany Hall, and editor of the *National Advocate,* he was also a prolific essayist, publishing two collections of essays: *Essays of Howard on Domestic Economy* (1820) and *Gleanings from a Gathered Harvest* (1845). More important, he was a popular and successful American playwright. His plays include *The Fortress of Sorrento* (1809), *Paul and Alexis* (1812; later known as *The Wandering Boys*), *She Would be a Soldier* (1819), *The Siege of Tripoli* (1820), *Marion; or, The Hero of Lake George* (1822), and *The Grecian Captive* (1822). Some of these plays used American materials, others more elliptically addressed American themes, but all were deliberate attempts to create a national literature. It bears mentioning, though, that Noah's most notable and notorious contribution to the American drama may very well be his unconventional theatrics: an inveterate showman, Noah experimented with the use of live animals on stage, including a camel and an elephant, with embarrassing results.

Still, Noah is remarkable in Jewish American literary history primarily for his willingness, indeed his insistence, on appearing before the public not simply as an American writer but also as a *Jewish* American writer. In his *Travels in England, France, Spain, and the Barbary States* (1819), an account of his diplomatic travels, he presents himself both as an American writer contributing to "the stock of American literature" and, in his fascinating account of the Jews of North Africa, as a Jew "professing the same religion, and representing a Christian nation."

Noah was also a self-appointed, outspoken champion of Jewish causes and wrote frequently on Jewish themes, often marked by his penchant for the unusual and the flamboyant. Noah's most notable and most notorious scheme and his most characteristic bit of Jewish American writing, however, came earlier in his life. In 1820, just as his career as an American dramatist was taking off, Noah petitioned the New York State Assembly for permission to buy Grand Island in the Niagara River, near Buffalo, to build a colony for immigrant Jews—not as a home in their new promised land, as Harby suggested, but as a preparatory stage to their restoration to Palestine. With a self-promoting nod to the biblical Noah, he called it Ararat. On Thursday, September 15, 1825, Noah organized a grandiose, theatrical procession of musicians, soldiers, politicians, clergymen, and masons, with Noah himself, dressed ostentatiously as the Judge of Israel. When the procession ended, he delivered an elaborate address, a pastiche of American and biblical rhetoric, a traditionalist vision of a return to Zion in which America also played a central, catalytic role. It was a plea to help persecuted Jews that combined well with the histrionic American patriotism of his plays and even more so with the millennialist fervor that was over-taking America, in particular upstate New York, in the 1820s. Over the next two decades, Noah would return in more detail to the themes he touched upon in his Ararat address. In 1837 he wrote a quasi-learned discourse reviving the old claim that the American Indians were the de-scendants of the ten lost tribes of Israel. In 1840 he wrote an introduction to and published an English translation of the seventeenth-century pseudo-midrash, *The Book of Jasher*. In 1845 he delivered the proto-Zionist *Discourse on the Restoration of the Jews* and in 1849 an *Address to Aid in the Erection of the Temple at Jerusalem*. Although the Ararat project failed miserably, it did succeed in firing the imagi-nations of a number of Jewish writers since then, including British man of letters Israel Zangwill, American graphic novelist Ben Katchor, and, most recently, Israeli novelist Nava Semel.

Brief mention should be given to two unique figures, who, for very different reasons, remain on the margins of the history of Jewish American literature: Alexander Bryan Johnson (1786–1867) of Utica, New York, and Rebecca Gratz (1781–1869) of Philadelphia. Born to a Jewish family in England, Johnson immigrated to America with his par-ents when he was eighteen. A banker by profession, John-son was also a noted philosopher, whose works enjoyed a brief revival in the 1960s. Among his many writings are *A Treatise on Language* (1836); *The Philosophical Emperor* (1841), a political satire; and *The Meaning of Words* (1854). However, Johnson was raised as an Episcopalian, joining the Presbyterian Church upon marrying a granddaughter of John Adams. And unlike Judah Monis, Johnson did not make anything of his Jewish origins.

Fully integrated into Philadelphia society, acquainted with such distinguished literary figures as Washington Ir-ving and James Kirke Paulding, Rebecca Gratz was proba-bly the most cultured and literate Jew of her time. (Legend has it that she was the original for Walter Scott's Rebecca in *Ivanhoe*.) But she never published a word. Still, she was one of the most significant Jewish American literary figures of her time. Most notably, she was a prolific letter writer,

maintaining correspondences with such figures as Grace Aguilar, Maria Edgeworth, Fanny Kemble, and Catherine Sedgwick, as well as with various members of her family. Collected and published in 1929, her letters show her to be impressively informed on both contemporary Jewish and secular matters: she could reflect as comfortably on Noah's edition of *The Book of Jasher* or a new translation of Mendelsohn's *Jerusalem* as on the latest novel. Johnson and Gratz comprise an invaluable example of the hybrid nature of Jewish cultural identity in early America.

The Later Nineteenth Century

The Jewish literary scene changed substantively with the German migration of the second quarter of the nineteenth century. When Isaac Mayer Wise (1819–1900) arrived in New York from Bohemia in 1846, he later recalled, he was appalled by the low level of Jewish literacy and the paucity of Jewish literary activity. He did acknowledge the accom-plishments of Mordecai Noah and Charleston poet Penina Moise, but seemed to feel that the list began and ended with them. As the new wave of immigration continued, however, the audience for Jewish-themed literature grew, and in the decades that followed, the amount of literature produced and read by American Jews grew considerably, and its character and range changed significantly, in large part due to Wise himself and to others such as Isaac Leeser of Philadelphia (1806–1868) who were pioneers of the Jewish press in America. (Leeser founded *The Occident and American Jewish Advocate* in 1843, and Wise's *American Is-raelite* first appeared in Cincinnati in 1854.) Described on its cover as "devoted to the Diffusion of Knowledge on Jewish Literature and Religion," *The Occident* understood "literature" broadly to include scholarly essays and ser-mons: indeed, no poetry or fiction at all appeared in *The Occident's* first issue. But soon its pages, like those of Wise's *Israelite* and other early Jewish periodicals such as *The As-monean, The Jewish Messenger,* and *The American Hebrew,* became the central venue for Jewish belletristic writing in America.

From the outset, this literature was meant to be intra-communal, to foster religious and communal feelings and allegiances, and to provide a bulwark against Christian missionaries. At the same time, it also served the purposes of acculturation, as it prepared the immigrants and their children to be Americans. Similarly, while the prose and poetry of this period were written by Jews for Jews, they also display a variety of strategies for reaching a broader audience.

In the beginning, to be sure, American-authored works were not easy to come by. Often, the editors turned to English authors such as Grace Aguilar and sisters Celia Moss and Marion Hartog. Sometimes they published translations from the French and German. In his quest for Jewish American literature, however, Wise often turned to his most reliable resource: himself. Along with the news, sermons, and history, Wise also authored a number of fictions in English, published serially in the *Israelite* under the byline, "The American Jewish Novelist." He authored a number of fictions in German as well, published in the *Israelite*'s German supplement, *Die Deborah*.

Two of Wise's novels were later published in book form: *The Combat of the People, or Hillel and Herod* (1859) and *The First of the Maccabees* (1860), both historical romances of the Second Temple period. As in many of his writings, one of Wise's goals in these novels was to recast Jewish history in American terms, blurring the differences between the two. In *Maccabees*, for instance, Wise has Matathia, father of Judah Maccabee, sound much like Thomas Jefferson: "The despotic will of Antiochus will shatter into atoms on the rock of Israel's fortitude. The blood of our saints impregnates the tree of liberty with new strength." (This sort of rhetoric would find its culmination in Kaufmann Kohler's sermon series, *Backwards or Forwards?* [1885].) Among Wise's many other works of history and theology are *The History of the Israelitish Nation from Abraham to the Present Time* (1854), *The Essence of Judaism* (1861), *The Cosmic God* (1876), and *History of the Hebrews' Second Commonwealth* (1880). His *Reminiscences* were translated from the German by David Philipson and published in 1901.

As in so many other areas of Jewish American culture, Wise's influence on the development of Jewish American literature was considerable, though not always as he may have imagined or approved. For instance, the first Hebrew book wholly written and published in America—Elijah M. Holzman's *Emek Refaim* (1865)—was an Orthodox polemic satirizing Wise and other American Reform rabbis.

Wise would have seen his influence more approvingly in the work of several writers who produced serial fiction for *The Israelite*. One such writer, Herman M. Moos

(1836–1894), also served as literary editor for the paper. Moos's gothic romance, *Hannah; or, A Glimpse of Paradise*, was published serially in 1865 and in book form in 1868. The romance follows the trials and tribulations of the Armholds, a German Jewish family who immigrate to Cincinnati, and, in particular, their two sons, Edgar and Reuben, one of whom becomes a novelist, the other a drunk. Moos obviously desired to reach an audience broader than the readers of the *Israelite*, as his stated goal was "to dispel some prejudices that, like an impenetrable mist, have kept Jew and Gentile from understanding one another better" and to raise "the claims of Israel to a partial acknowledgment of its desserts." *Carrie Harrington*, the sequel to *Hannah*, is a tale of seduction and betrayal in which a virtuous but naïve Jewish heroine is abducted by a handsome but callous Christian. The volume is notable for a long and vigorous defense of such novels as those of George Sand, Eugene Sue, and Monk Lewis, delivered by a progressive Jew named Mr. Aaron against the charges of a prissy Christian critic, Mrs. Flintweasel. Moos was also the author of a long narrative poem on the Mortara case of 1858, published along with other verse in *Mortara: or, The Pope and His Inquisitors* (1860).

Another disciple of Wise, businessman Moritz Loth, offered a didactic novel about the dangers of wealth in *Our Prospects: A Tale of Real Life* (1870), though his narrative strategy differed markedly from those of Wise and Moos. Rather than people his novel with virtuous or Americanizing Jewish characters, Loth approached the question of Jewishness indirectly, choosing rather to portray two Christian Cincinnati families, the Huntings and the de la Mottes, while infusing the novel with a morality that is suspiciously similar to that of Reform Judaism, inserting here and there a poem by Wise, and assigning frankly philosemitic attitudes to the most praiseworthy characters. One upstanding young and handsome Christian man, for instance, refuses to go to church, preferring rather to be tutored in Hebrew at home and to read the Bible in the original. Another moral tale, *The Forgiving Kiss: or, Our Destiny*, followed in 1874, and *On a Higher Plane* in 1899. He also published *Pearls from the Bible* in 1894.

Nathan Mayer (1838–1912) has been called the most accomplished of the early Jewish American novelists. A physician by profession who served with distinction with Union forces during the Civil War, he also wrote music and drama criticism (for the *Hartford Times*) and verse, including a poem read at the dedication of a monument to those who fought at Antietam, published as a pamphlet in 1894. Following Wise's lead, he published a number of historical romances in *The Israelite,* including *Plots and Counterplots,* which was published in book form in 1858, and *The Count and the Jewess* (1865). In 1867, however, he published the first fictional account of contemporary Jewish life in America, *Differences,* a novel of the Civil War and its aftermath, whose central character is Louis Welland, a young German Jewish immigrant caught in the web of interfaith and intersectional tensions. As in the other early novels—though uniquely in a realistic, contemporary setting—the Judaism promoted through its virtuous characters is that of Wise and the Reformers. Commenting on intermarriage, for instance, Welland remarks assuredly that many "ancient customs have been disregarded of late, and the heavens have not fallen." The novel interweaves romantic alliances with the North–South conflict, moving resolutely toward a conciliatory ending where the lovers declare themselves "United in love . . . notwithstanding former differences." And, with a nod toward a broader reading public still suffering from the wounds of war, the novel closes with the words, "United forever."

Although the development of Jewish American poetry over the course of the nineteenth century was also significantly facilitated by the Jewish press, the influence of Wise and the Reform movement was far less dominant than it was in fiction. The imaginative range and intellectual sophistication of the poetry is evident in the work of the four most significant poets of the period.

Penina Moise (1797–1880) of Charleston was the first Jewish poet of note in America. A student of Isaac Harby, Moise published widely in the newspapers of her day, both secular and Jewish, and in 1833 she published *Fancy's Sketch Book,* the first book of original poetry published by a Jew in America. Written in neoclassical style, the volume displays the range of interests of a cultured American woman. Poems on Greek myths are followed by others on biblical characters; poems on world politics (Greek independence, Napoleon) are joined by poetic eulogies for Isaac Harby and Felicia Hemans. One patriotic poem, "To Persecuted Foreigners," stands out for its rhetorical address to Jews, encouraging them to immigrate to America: "If thou art one of that oppressed race,/ Whose pilgrimage from Palestine we trace,/ Brave the Atlantic—Hope's broad anchor weigh,/ A Western Sun will

gild your future day." The poem was originally published in *The Southern Patriot.*

Throughout her long and often difficult life, Moise continued to write poetry, including occasional poems on Jewish political themes such as the Damascus blood libel of 1840. Far more popular than her secular poetry, however, was her spiritual verse: *Hymns Written for the Use of Hebrew Congregations* (1856) went through several editions. Her collected poetry was published as *Secular and Religious Works of Penina Moise* in 1911.

Born in Philadelphia to a Jewish father and a Christian mother, Rebecca Gumpert Hyneman (1812–1875) formally converted to Judaism after marrying Benjamin Hyneman in 1845, and soon after her verse began appearing in Leeser's *Occident.* Hyneman also wrote a number of sensationalist fictions after the disappearance and presumed death of her husband in 1850, including *The Fatal Cosmetic* (1853), a gothic tale about a female vampire who preys on young girls in Philadelphia, and *The Doctor* (1860), a dark romance no doubt inspired by the Brontes. But it is with her verse that she makes her mark on Jewish American literary history. In 1853 she published *The Leper and Other Poems,* the first volume of verse on primarily Jewish themes published in America. Quoting from the introduction to *The Scarlet Letter* in her preface to *The Leper,* Hyneman takes on Hawthorne's studied self-effacing persona in presenting her poetry, previously addressed to the narrow circle of Jewish readers, to the wider American public, thus making her volume the first self-consciously Jewish literary work in America since Noah's *Travels.* Particularly noteworthy are her two series of poems on "Women of the Bible." Unlike Moise's verse, Hyneman's poetry is heavily Romantic, her Jewishness colored by the exoticism of the East and a history of suffering and martyrdom. In a poem on the biblical Rebekah, for instance, Hyneman writes: "Deep in each earnest Jewish heart/ Are shrined those memories of the past,/ Memories that time can ne'er efface,/ Nor sorrow's blighting wing o'ercast."

Of all the midcentury "Jewish" poets, Adah Isaacs Menken (1835–1868) was the most well-known in her day, though not for her poetry. A stage actress who played male roles (most famously Mazeppa) and titillated audiences with her risqué costumes and scandalous off-stage behavior, Menken also maintained an active literary life, publishing dozens of poems and essays, and counting among her acquaintants Whitman, Dickens, Swinburne, and Dumas.

Her early life and ethnicity are obscure—it is unlikely that she was born Jewish, as she once claimed, or that she ever formally converted to Judaism—but after she married Alexander Isaac Menken, a musician from an affluent Cincinnati Jewish family, in 1856, she took his name and claimed his religious identification. Part of their married life was spent in Cincinnati, where she published over a dozen poems and essays of palpable Jewish content, mostly in Wise's *Israelite,* including a poem to novelist Nathan Mayer and an essay on Shakespeare's Shylock. The marriage lasted only three years, but she retained Menken's name and a Jewish identity throughout her life and travels—which took her to New York, San Francisco, London, and finally Paris, where she died—and despite subsequent marriages and liaisons. Her later poetry—including a violently dramatic poem on the apocryphal Judith and another, supposedly from the Hebrew, called "Hear, O Israel"—was published posthumously in *Infelicia* (1873), the volume bearing a dedication to Dickens, an epigraph from Swinburne, and the unmistakable prosodic influence of Whitman. The strident, histrionic Jewishness she depicts in these late poems departs markedly from the conventional self-definitions of the era.

Plainly the most talented and literate of all these poets and novelists was Emma Lazarus (1849–1887). She was certainly the most accomplished, the most centrally situated in the literary scene of the period, and the most successful in addressing both Jewish and non-Jewish audiences. In little more than two decades, Lazarus published five volumes of verse while also trying her hand at fiction—publishing a novel, *Alide: An Episode of Goethe's Life* (1874), and a melodramatic short story about an immigrant artist, "The Eleventh Hour" (1878)—and penning numerous, often powerful essays on a variety of literary and political themes, from "American Literature" to "The Jewish Problem." A two-volume collection, *The Poems of Emma Lazarus,* was published by her sisters in 1888, the year following her death.

Born into a wealthy Jewish family that could trace its history in America to the Revolution, Lazarus was raised in the elite cultural circles of New York and given a private, classical education. She began writing poetry seriously as an adolescent, and her first book, *Poems and Translations* (1866), was privately published by her father and sent to Ralph Waldo Emerson, who responded with warm praise. Her second volume of poetry, *Admetus and Other Poems*

(1871), was dedicated to Emerson, and she sent him her next volume of verse in manuscript, a poetic tragedy called *The Spagnoletto,* which was eventually published in 1876. Their mentor–disciple relationship continued for the rest of Emerson's life, surviving Lazarus's severe disappointment at not being included in Emerson's anthology, *Parnasus* (1874). After his death, Lazarus published a eulogistic essay, "Emerson's Personality," in 1882, and a poem, "To R.W.E.," in 1884.

Despite her embeddedness in American literary culture, Lazarus would doubtless have remained little more than a footnote in literary history had she not turned to Jewish themes and concerns in the early 1880s. Although she had written "In the Jewish Synagogue in Newport" (1867) as a more optative response to Longfellow's elegiac "The Jewish Cemetery at Newport," Lazarus did not present herself as a Jewish writer until the first reports of the pogroms in Russia reached America and the first East European immigrants began to arrive at Ward's Island. Then, encouraged by Edmund Clarence Stedman and inspired by George Eliot, she began to publish poetry and prose in the Jewish press, especially in the *American Hebrew,* which also brought out her boldly titled *Songs of a Semite* in 1882 and carried a controversial fifteen-part series of proto-Zionist essays called *An Epistle to the Hebrews* (1882–1883), which she dedicated to George Eliot. (*Epistle* was posthumously published in book form in 1900.) Lazarus carried her cause to the general press as well: spurred by the publication in *The Century* of "Russian Jews and Gentiles," a wildly antisemitic essay by Mme. Z. Ragozin, Lazarus responded by contributing two essays to the journal, "Russian Christianity vs. Modern Judaism" (1882) and "The Jewish Problem" (1883), in which she turns the tables on Ragozin, attacking Christian antisemitism, offering a compassionate view of Jewish history, and promoting the establishment of a Jewish homeland in Palestine.

Lazarus read voraciously, and her literary Jewishness displays something other than the exoticism of Hyneman and the histrionics of Menken: an audacious and intensive intellectual engagement with Jewish texts and history. She did not follow the beaten path, combining the theological progressivism of Wise and his followers with a fervent Jewish nationalism unheard of in Reform circles or among American Jews in general since Mordecai Noah. Nor did her ethnic awakening lead her to give up on America or on Western culture, though she sometimes understood her dual allegiances in oppositional terms. Her model in this was clearly Heinrich Heine. (Her *Poems and Ballads of Heinrich Heine* was published in 1881.) "A fatal and irreconcilable dualism formed the basis of Heine's nature," she wrote in *The Century* in 1884. "He was a Jew, with the mind and eyes of a Greek."

Nowhere is the complexity of Lazarus's cultural allegiances more at play than in her most famous poem, "The New Colossus." Written in 1883 to help raise funds to erect a pedestal for Frédéric-Auguste Bartholdi's "Liberty Enlightening the World," the sculptor's monumental statue of the goddess Libertas modeled on the Colossus of Rhodes, Lazarus's sonnet daringly wrenches the statue from its classical foundations and places it firmly within the context of immigration and myth of American asylum, changing its name to "Mother of Exiles" and placing into its "silent lips" welcoming words that echo the Hebrew prophets: "Send these, the homeless, tempest-tost to me,/ I lift my lamp beside the golden door!" Embossed on a bronze plaque in the base of the Statue of Liberty, looking toward the arrival of the East European immigrants, the sonnet establishes Lazarus as the writer whose work is the culmination of early Jewish American literary history.

Michael P. Kramer

References and Further Reading

Chametzky, Jules, et al. 2000. *Jewish American Literature: A Norton Anthology.* New York: W. W. Norton.

Harap, Louis. 1974. *The Image of the Jew in American Literature: From the Early Republic to Mass Immigration.* Philadelphia: Jewish Publication Society.

Karp, Abraham. 1975. *Beginnings: Early American Judaica.* Philadelphia, PA: Jewish Publication Society.

Karp, Abraham. 2000. "The Hebrew Book in the New World: From Bibliography to History." Available at: http://www2.jewishculture.org/jewish_scholarship/jewish_scholarship_feinstein_karp.html. Accessed March 12, 2007.

Kohut, George Alexander. 1895. "Early Jewish Literature in America." *Publications of the American Jewish Historical Society* 3: 103–147.

Kramer, Michael P. 1992. "New English Typology and the Jewish Question." *Studies in Puritan American Spirituality* 3: 97–124.

Kramer, Michael P. 2001. "The Conversion of the Jews and Other Narratives of Self-Definition: Notes toward the Writing of Jewish American Literary History; or, Adventures in Hebrew School." In *Ideology and Jewish Identity in Israeli and American Literature,* edited by Emily Miller Budick, 177–196. Albany: State University of New York Press.

Kramer, Michael P. 2003. "Beginnings and Ends: The Origins of Jewish American Literary History." In *The Cambridge Companion to Jewish American Literary History,* edited by Michael P. Kramer and Hana Wirth-Nesher, 12–30. Cambridge, UK: Cambridge University Press.

Lichtenstein, Diane. 1992. *Writing Their Nations: The Tradition of Nineteenth-Century American Jewish Women Writers.* Bloomington: Indiana University Press.

Marcus, Jacob Rader. 1989–1993. *United States Jewry, 1776–1985.* Detroit, MI: Wayne State University Press.

Schappes, Morris U., ed. 1952. *Documentary History of the Jews in the United States, 1654–1875,* rev. ed. New York: Citadel Press.

New Jewish Immigrant Writing

According to most critics of Jewish American literature, we are currently in the midst of a surprising literary revival, a creative surge of literary energy expressive of a rising generation of authors, many of whom are not native-born, indeed some writing from positions within religious orthodoxy itself. What is surprising about the current literary scene is its implicit challenge to a famous prediction by the powerful literary critic Irving Howe, who imagined the end of Jewish American literature with the passing of the immigrant-saturated memories of its earlier practitioners. In light of the startling achievement of a host of new immigrant writers, Howe's bleak forecast seems to have been premature.

A year after his elegiac chronicle of the migration of East European Jews to America, *World of Our Fathers* (1976), Irving Howe announced the apparent exhaustion of a once flourishing genre: Jewish American fiction. As a result of the absorptive power of *Americanization*—the term invoked by early twentieth-century critics to describe the eventual embrace of New World ideals by arriving immigrants—Howe argued that later writers were unlikely to bridge the chasm separating their assimilated lives from the shaping crucible of the immigrant generation, the creative source of much Jewish American writing.

For Howe, the emotionally charged landscape of immigrant family life produced a range of complex responses that he associated with growing up Jewish in the New World. "Nostalgia, return, hatred, nausea, affection, guilt— all these are among the familiar, urgent feelings which memories of immigrant streets, tenements and (most of all) families can stir up in the American Jewish writers." In the wake of inevitable memory loss ("America makes one forget everything," cautioned the advice columnist for the Yiddish *Daily Forward* in 1908), will there remain, Howe asked, "a thick enough sediment of felt life to enable a new outburst of writing about American Jews?" (Howe 1977a) as in the 1930s, with Henry Roth's harrowing immigrant novel, *Call It Sleep,* and again in the 1950s, with the arrival of Saul Bellow, Bernard Malamud, and the young Philip Roth.

Howe was not optimistic. In the contemporary literary scene there was relatively little in what he termed the "post-immigrant Jewish experience" for the imagination to draw on. A generation later, however, his prediction—now dubbed the Howe Doctrine by students of Jewish American literature—seems to have been dead wrong. Rather than chanting *kaddish* over the demise of Jewish American fiction, the years at the end of the twentieth century and beginning of the twenty-first have witnessed a Jewish literary revival, a flowering by a rising generation of writers who have made, in Morris Dickstein's description, "their Jewish fantasies, feelings, and experiences absolutely central to their work" (1997).

Dickstein has in mind authors as various as Allegra Goodman, Ehud Havazelet, Steve Stern, Nathan Englander, and Jonathan Safran Foer. In addition, there now exists a serious body of literature (and scholarship) by children of the Holocaust, second-generation "survivors" who continue to grapple with embers of *postmemory,* the term Marianne Hirsch applies to the traumas of family history visited upon the victims' surviving sons and daughters. These writers include Melvin Jules Bukiet, Thane Rosenbaum, Eva Hoffmann, and most brilliantly Art Spiegelman. A thriving creative realm also explores the bounded world of Jewish orthodoxy by writers and filmmakers now estranged, but at one time either inside the fold (like Pearl Abraham and Pearl Gluck), or straddling the margins of that world, curious (from a secular perspective) about the claims of religious faith, fascinated by the clarifying power of undoubting belief. These writers include Areyeh Lev Stollman, Dara Horn, and Tova Mirvis, especially her novel, *The Outside World* (2004).

Unswerving in his convictions about the inevitable trajectory of Jewish assimilation (subsequently borne out, statistically at least, by sociological data on rates of inter-

marriage and religious affiliation and observance), Howe did not anticipate the array of returns to the marrow of Jewishness that have come to mark the beginning of a new century: the return to memory (as in Foer's critically acclaimed 2003 novel *Everything Is Illuminated*); to orthodoxy; to earlier, often comic, traditions of Yiddish writing; above all, to a host of engagements with the labyrinth of Jewish identity itself. "I am in-between and unsettled," remarks Nathan Englander, among the more heralded members of the Revival (Englander 2002). His fluid sense of Jewish identity captures perfectly the exhilarating moment of contemporary self-consciousness.

Howe also assumed, incorrectly, that the historic twentieth-century story of migration was virtually completed, at least in its Jewish incarnation. What Howe could not have predicted (he died in 1992) is a postcolonial world shaped by constant movement and upheaval, of orbiting families (to borrow the title of a Bharati Mukherjee story), unsettling their host nations' fixed identity. Howe was also skeptical about the debates over multiculturalism and identity politics in the academy; above all, he was irritated by the collective "fever" of ethnicity and mania over "roots" in American society, which his own best-selling study of Jewish life on the Lower East Side helped, ironically, to legitimate (Howe 1977b, 1986).

Yet in identifying immigrant experience as *the* energizing source for the literary imagination, the Howe Doctrine appears ironically to have anticipated the emergence of a remarkable cohort of new immigrant writers from the former Soviet Union who are in creative dialogue with the traditions of Jewish immigrant literature. Still in their early thirties, Gary Shteyngart, Lara Vapnyar, and David Bezmozgis transcribe in startling new ways the narrative of immigrant families' ordeal of transition, the familiar struggle to decode an often bewildering, disorienting new world. Confirming the sociological–aesthetic assumptions of the Howe Doctrine, they represent a new chapter in a long tradition of Jewish immigrant writing.

"To rehash the old immigrant narrative," groans Gary Shteyngart, regarding his vexed relation to literary history. "What a job, eh? Who would want it?" (Shteyngart 2003). Rather than feeling weighed down by literary giants like Bellow and Malamud, in his award-winning *The Russian Debutante's Handbook* (2002) Shteyngart mischievously liberates the American immigrant story, *reversing* the canonical narrative's Old-World-to-New-World journey of rebirth and transformation (as in the fiction of Anzia Yezierska or memoirs by Mary Antin). Instead, he sends his alienated alter ego hero, Vladimir Girshkin, back to Eastern Europe, to Prava (Prague), the new playground of a spoiled expatriate generation seeking the pleasures of easy nostalgia and quick fixes, both monetary and sexual. "The whole point of coming to the Old World," explains a would-be poet, who knows no poetry, "is to chuck the baggage of the new."

Vladimir would also like to chuck the cultural burdens packed into *his* New World baggage, would like, above all, to overcome the mythic expectations of American success ("the old immigrant narrative"), but his endlessly ironic sensibility prevents any easy deliverance. In their rebuking example, Girshkin's Russian émigré parents project the boundless energy of the "alpha" immigrant; as explained by Girshkin's weary (alpha-drained) father, "emigrating to this country, leaving one's hut, one's yurt, one's Soviet-era high-rise requires an ambition, a madness, a stubbornness, a stamina." In dissent, Vladimir chooses the role of an inertia-ridden "beta" immigrant son, a *failurchka* (his alpha mother's endearing nickname). Seeking redemption, a new life in the *Old* World, Girshkin arrives in Prava as a self-styled "Vladimir the *Re*patriate, in this case signifying a homecoming, a foreknowledge, a making amends with history. . . . Back to the part of the world where the Girshkins were first called Girshkins!"

In the end Vladimir remains unsettled, like his creator, neither at home in the Old nor at ease in the New. In various interviews Shteyngart speaks of the empowering disjunctions that come with the territory of new-world displacement, his "*Zelig*-like" condition, relishing "a constant state of movement, of migration" (National Public Radio, June 6, 2003). The allusion to Woody Allen's chameleon man of the fluid 1920s seems apt; indeed, reading Shteyngart's work the novelist Chang-rae Lee (whose canonical *Native Speaker* also plays with the traditions and tropes of the immigrant novel) recognized that Shteyngart's antic mode of comedy and wicked satire, channeled through the anti-hero Girshkin, seemed "as if Woody Allen had been an immigrant" (Zalewski 2002).

Yet Shteyngart remains deeply conscious of his multiple positions as "ex-Soviet, Russo-Judeo-American immigrant writer," a situation, he confesses, which "is not all borscht and laughter for me" (Shteyngart 2003). Along with his haunted alter ego, he remains attuned to those "wispy force fields of desire and history that enfold Manhattan, a simple result of the number of foreigners that inhabit the island and cannot express themselves in their true language at any given moment" (Shteyngart 2003). Despite feeling adrift in the new world, Shteyngart ultimately celebrates his marginal relation to the shape-shifting potential of the American landscape. *The Russian Debutante's Handbook* speaks on behalf of those who (like his literary forebear, Bellow's Tommy Wilhelm, schlemiel anti-hero of *Seize the Day*, drowning in the material 1950s) continue to resist the alpha immigrant success narrative; at the same time, its soulful hero imagines becoming the father of a New World son "free of the fear and madness of Vladimir's Eastern lands. . . . An American in America."

In sharp contrast to Shteyngart's extravagant comic imagination, the stories collected in Lara Vapnyar's *There Are Jews in My House* (2003) and David Bezmozgis's *Natasha and Other Stories* (2004) are more subdued, modest in their rich evocation of the emotional strains that afflict immigrant families in the wake of migration. Unlike Shteyngart and Bezmozgis, who emigrated as children, Vapnyar arrived in New York as a young woman in 1994, with virtually no English; she learned to speak and write by watching soap operas and reading Jane Austen. As a result, her stories, told mostly from the perspective of an attentive child, achieve a certain power through intimation, by what remains unspoken. In the process they also convey the excitement of discovery, the enchanting power of linguistic newness. In this respect she could be a sister to the early twentieth-century immigrant writer Anzia Yezierska, marveling at her own New World linguistic condition: "And every new word made me see new American things with American eyes. I felt like a Columbus, finding new worlds through every new word" (Yezierska 1923).

While most of the quiet, delicate stories in *There Are Jews in My House* are set in a drab post-Soviet society haunted by the Chernobyl disaster and feelings of unspeakable loss and uncompleted mourning, one story conveys the palpable excitement of linguistic and, it appears, romantic discovery. In "Mistress," the only story set in America, in the Russian Jewish immigrant enclave of Brooklyn, Vapnyar distills a family drama reminiscent of the "sweatshop romances" of immigrant writers like Abraham Cahan and Yezierska. "Mistress" narrates the poignant relationship between a grandfather and grandson, each strangely speechless in the New World, each yearning to find a New World voice. Back in the old country, Misha communicated instinctually with his beloved grandfather. In their cramped existence in Little Odessa, however, the grandfather remains "immobile." Only after he starts taking English lessons does the grandfather begin to recover his old world energy and his voice. As Misha discovers, indirectly, the agent of his grandfather's newfound loquacity is a woman, a fellow immigrant he has met in English-language school, "with a gray braid and an amber brooch . . . his and the grandfather's secret."

At the end of "Mistress" is a scene of powerful verbal release, a flood of New World emotion no longer under repression. Misha "talked nonstop, breathlessly, sputtering, chuckling in excitement, interrupting one story to tell the next." The grandfather, now "focused on Misha," now alive to the world, keeps repeating "Imagine!" in response to the grandson's chatter. In Vapnyar's adopted lexicon, the word registers as both exclamation and injunction. Old and new generations bond through mutual discovery, sharing the untold revelations available in the new world.

An even more evocative rendering of the closed world of immigrant family life may be found in David Bezmozgis's *Natasha and Other Stories,* a series of linked stories about a fiercely protective and loving Jewish family who fled Latvia for a new life in the émigré Russian Jewish enclaves of Toronto. (Bezmozgis left Riga with his family in 1980 and settled in Canada.) Narrated chronologically by young Mark Berman, the stories capture the intimate accents of immigrant experience voiced from the inside, from within a nation less burdened by the mythic promise of America, in contrast to Shteyngart's playful troping of the cosmic *American* immigrant narrative. The family Berman (would-be "Baltic aristocrats," in their son's knowing eyes) huddles together, in anxiety and hope, desperately grasping at any promise of social-material connection in its dream of moving up in the world, "one respectable block from the Russian swarm."

Like so many immigrant sons, from the very beginning Bezmozgis's Mark is conscious of his default status as the family's cultural translator, the necessary mediator between baffled family and alien linguistic territory. In the daily ritual of going off to first grade ("with our house key hanging from a brown shoelace around my neck") and coming home "bearing the germs of a new vocabulary," Mark feels the weight of family need and expectation. And as he grows older, Mark also gains an intimation of the

menacing totalitarian world the family left behind, in Soviet-controlled Riga, along with an altered sense of his relation to another repressed past, the meaning of Jewish memory and history, now slowly dislodged in the freer atmosphere of Canada.

In apparent dialogue with the traditions of Jewish American literature, Bezmozgis follows Mark's journey into a complicated consciousness of filiality. But unlike Henry Roth's *Call It Sleep* (1934), about a tormented immigrant father bent by paranoia and humiliation, who takes out his rage by savagely beating his son, Bezmozgis's fictional father, Roman Berman, manages to survive his New World indignities through strength of character and unconditional love. In the wrenching story "Roman Berman, Massage Therapist," the father seeks "to improve his chances" by bringing Mark along to meet a local rabbi, hoping that the presence of his bright Canadian son, able to speak rudimentary Hebrew and sing "Jerusalem of Gold," will somehow help the father realize his dreams. "Seated across the table from the rabbi," Mark observes, "my father wrestled language and dignity to express need. . . . I was sufficiently aware of our predicament to feel the various permutations of shame: shame for my father, shame for my shame, and even shame for the rabbi, who seemed to be a decent guy."

Of course, scenes of filial shame may be found throughout immigrant expression, Jewish and non-Jewish. Rather than flight or separation (the memorable response to filial shame in Yezierska, Isaac Rosenfeld, and, in his memoir *A Margin of Hope,* Irving Howe himself), what distinguishes Bezmozgis's Mark is his profound empathy, his desire to see past the father's humiliation. As the comic quest for connections unfolds, the Bermans find themselves hosted by an orthopedist's family, parvenus who have invited the greenhorns in bad faith, in order to hear tear-jerking testimony from (they presume) "refuseniks" about the execrable fate of Jews living in the oppressive Soviet Union. "If it wasn't too personal," Dr. Kornblum "wanted to know how bad it really was." Grasping at any opportunity, "My mother . . . admitted that. . . . She knew some refuseniks, and we were almost refuseniks, but we were not refuseniks."

Such comic moments, born of desperation, fill this story about a family's doomed effort to impress the hypocritical Jewish bourgeoisie, living in "fully detached" material splendor. In the end, the son is witness to another scene of humiliating exposure, another kind of self-indulgent *use* by the shady Kornblums. Caught massaging Mrs. Kornblum's neck in the master bathroom ("She said it was wonderful, my father was a magician, if only she could bottle his hands and sell them"), the father sits helplessly on the bed, beneath "a large family portrait taken for Kornblum's daughter's bat mitzvah," struggling to explain: "He said, Tell me, what am I supposed to do? Then he got up, took my hand, and we went back downstairs."

For Bezmozgis, there are no easy responses to the father's embarrassment. What *are* helpless fathers supposed to do to achieve a life, a livelihood, in an unforgiving new world? In *Natasha,* achieving dignity involves an altered way of perceiving, really of *feeling* the world, of approaching what might be called a secular version of *rachmones,* the Yiddish term for compassion.

Compassion takes many forms in Bezmozgis's stories. The reader glimpses it at the end of the title story, "Natasha," when the older narrator—living out a fantasy of adolescent rebellion in his parents' dark basement, reading Kafka, selling drugs and getting stoned, brooding about his torrid affair and humiliating rejection by his Lolita-like émigré cousin Natasha—begins to see his chaotic world through her eyes: "standing in our backyard, drawn by a strange impulse, I crouched and peered through the window of my basement. I had never seen it from this perspective, the opposite perspective. . . . In the full light of summer, I looked into darkness. It was the end of my subterranean life." And the beginning of Mark's self-dignity.

Above all, the reader is moved, with the narrator, by the application of rachmones in Bezmozgis's powerful final story, "Minyan." If the unsavory Kornblums offer only false compassion, spilling liberal tears over the indignities of Soviet Jews, in "Minyan" an older Mark Berman gains a lesson in Jewish mercy through the example of the older generation, now retired in rent-controlled, high-rise comfort. "Minyan" chronicles the subterranean intrigue involved in maintaining a *minyan* (quorum required for Jewish communal worship) for the building's basement synagogue. Potential renters have to go through the elderly Zalman, who has the ear of the building's manager, and convince him of their spiritual commitment. Charged with gathering ten Jews for services on Friday nights and Saturday mornings, Zalman alone has the power to decide someone's residential fate.

In relating this story, Mark confesses a powerful connection to the world of his widowed grandfather, who already lives in the building: "Most of the old Jews came because they were drawn by the nostalgia for ancient cadences, I came because I was drawn by the nostalgia for old Jews. In each case, the motivation was not tradition but history."

How would Irving Howe have responded to this confession of a grandson's nostalgia for his grandfather's nostalgia? At the height of the ethnic revival in the late 1970s and 1980s, Howe remained "a little irritated [by] the upsurge of nostalgia I detect among a good many young people for the immigrant world to which I was already a latecomer, and of which they barely know" (Howe 1986). Yet in Bezmozgis's imagination the voice of Jewish compassion feels earned, transforming a potentially breezy emotion ("unearned nostalgia" in Howe's dismissive phrase) into an act of generational rededication. What does it mean to be a Jewish son (or grandson) in the fiercely loving world of the Bermans, unsettled in their exile? For Bezmozgis the answer seems to be in performing acts of memory and compassion as a way of salving the pain of new world indignity.

In this respect, Bezmozgis's debut offers a powerful answer to Howe's pointed questions, asked of an emerging cohort of Jewish American writers decades earlier: "Does it [Jewish American experience] form the very marrow of their being? Does it provide images of conflict, memories of exaltation and suffering, such as enable the creating of stories?" (Howe 1977a). To judge from the stunning achievement of the "new" immigrant writers, the answer appears to be a resounding yes. Their unanticipated presence both fulfills *and* confounds the strictures of the Howe Doctrine. If Howe could not see beyond his own biography, he nevertheless understood the profound literary potential of the immigrant experience: upheaval, transition, adjustment, the nostalgic impulse of looking back, the forward dream of imagining a future. In the end, the immigrant narrative may well provide the most enabling, creative source for those writers seeking to engage the new world—any new world.

Donald Weber

References and Further Reading
Bezmozgis, David. 2004. *Natasha and Other Stories.* New York: Farrar, Straus and Giroux.

Dickstein, Morris. 1997. "Ghost Stories." *Tikkun* 12: 34–36.

Englander, Nathan. 2002. "On Coming Home." *Lincoln Center Theater Review* 31: 11.

Howe, Irving, ed. 1977a. *Jewish-American Stories.* New York: New American Library.

Howe, Irving. 1977b. "The Limits of Ethnicity." *The New Republic* 176 (June 25): 17–19.

Howe, Irving. 1986. "Immigrant Chic." *New York Magazine* 19 (May 12): 76.

Shteyngart, Gary. 2002. *The Russian Debutante's Handbook.* New York: Riverhead Books.

Shteyngart, Gary. 2003. "Several Anecdotes about My Wife." In *Lost Tribe: Jewish Fiction from the Edge,* edited by Paul Zakrewski, 22–25. New York: Perennial Books.

Vapnyar, Lara. 2004. *There Are Jews in My House.* New York: Pantheon.

Yezierska, Anzia. 1923. *Children of Loneliness.* New York: Funk & Wagnalls.

Zalewsi, Daniel. 2002. "From Russia with Tsuris." *New York Times Magazine* (June 2).

Jewish American Women Fiction Writers

Although there were Jewish women writers in nineteenth-century America, in the twentieth century their numbers increased significantly, and they found a new voice. The Jewish woman writer became recognized as an important addition to both the Jewish and American literary scenes. Immigrant Jewish women joined the American-born to write imaginative stories about their experiences, doubts, and self-discovery in the new land. The United States offered particularly fertile ground for Jewish women to realize their literary ambitions. Early in the twentieth century, the woman suffrage movement gave young girls ideas about freedom and independence; public education enabled Jewish daughters to study a wide variety of subjects; and the rhetoric of individualism applied to women for the first time, sparking the flame for talented and energetic women to write creatively. As the magazine and book publishing world grew in the 1920s and 1930s, outlets for women's writing also increased, and some of the new Jewish women writers earned a handsome living from their work.

Not all Jewish women who became writers addressed Jewish subjects, but many who did found an audience for their writings. Newcomer Anzia Yezierska (1880–1970) and American-born Fannie Hurst (1889–1968) became successful writers in America during the first third of the century. While the traditional religious culture dominated Yezierska's fiction, Hurst's early stories focused on the immigrant Jewish experience and adjusting to the new world. Hurst became one of America's most popular writers, with many of her stories dramatized in the movies. Sensitive to the struggles of minorities in a majority Protestant culture, she enlarged her subject matter to include sympathetic portrayals of African Americans, as well as the challenges facing women alone. Hurst's later writings contain no specific references to Jewish culture, while Yezierska remained concerned with Jews'—particularly Jewish women's—adjustments to American life. Yezierska's celebrity rose dramatically in the 1920s only to decline rapidly by decade's end.

Raised in St. Louis in a German Jewish family, Hurst moved to New York as an adult and observed the thriving Jewish culture on the Lower East Side much like an anthropologist viewing an exotic culture. "The Gold in Fish," a 1927 story, describes the conflicts between the generations, with Morris announcing to his immigrant parents that he has changed the family name to Fish. "You hear that, papa," says the mother, "the name that was good enough for you to get born into, and for me to marry into, is something to be ashamed of" (Hurst 1927). Hurst sympathizes with the older generation but resignedly documents its failure to prevail against the younger generation and its Americanizing ways. Anzia Yezierska, a fiercely ambitious daughter of an autocratic father, came to the United States from Eastern Europe and wrote frequently about the clashes between a daughter who insisted on carving out her own adult path while rejecting the traditional road prescribed by *shtetl* culture and her parents.

Yezierska, like so many Jewish American women writers of all generations, looked at Jewish life vertically—at the interaction of at least two generations—elaborating on the tensions experienced by the protagonist, usually a member of the younger generation. A family-centered story allows the writer to offer contrasting patterns of behavior—how they change over time, and how tradition and modernity coexist or clash. For Jewish writers whose subject matter remains Jewish, this genre is indispensable. The dynamic of parents and children, of inheritances and rejections, becomes the fabric of the fiction. In *Bread Givers* (1925), one of Yezierska's most popular novels, heroine Sara Smolinsky defied her father, refused to marry as her sisters had done before her, and separated from the family. She studies and becomes a teacher, but in the end reconciles with her father and marries a Hebrew teacher. In this story, Yezierska finds a middle ground between the traditional Jewish and modern American cultures, suggesting that it is possible to retain aspects of religion and Jewish culture while participating in the secular American world. How to negotiate both sides of this duality remains a major theme for the writers, from the first generation to the contemporary one.

The second generation of Jewish American women writers, born 1910–1930 in this country, continued the motifs of the first generation. While comfortable as Americans, some writers consciously chose to define themselves as Jewish, struggling to balance their Jewishness with the larger secular culture. Hortense Calisher (b. 1911), who began writing stories in the 1930s, published her fifteenth novel in 2002, at the age of ninety-one. In *Sunday Jews* (2002), Calisher returned to a subject she had explored early in her career but had left for many years. In a group of early stories about the Elkins, an assimilated German Jewish family (perhaps like her own family), Calisher showed sympathy toward the Jews who acknowledged their religio-cultural identity. In her latest work, she favors the fully assimilated Jews, arguing that they are enriched by the larger culture, even as the Jewish culture has enriched it. Her longevity has enabled her to witness the absorption of Jews into American society, and, in her judgment, the partnership has been fruitful for both sides. In Calisher's world, Jews who remain staunchly observant are parochial and limited.

Two additional writers from the second generation, Tillie Olsen (1913–2007) and Grace Paley (b. 1922), were philosophically left-of-center and tried to free themselves from what they perceived to be the segregated world of religion. They were secular humanists and socialists, two minorities who rejected the capitalist, materialist, and religious cultures surrounding them in America. Olsen's *Tell Me a Riddle* (1976) presents three generations of a family, with the grandmother Eva instructing her children to write on her tombstone: "Race, human; Religion, none" (89). Unlike in most writings by second-generation Jewish women, Eva, the old woman, is the emotional center of the novel, and her frustrations with a life that denied her expressive opportunities demonstrate Olsen's feminist sensibilities. Indeed, in the 1970s the women's movement

rediscovered Olsen, and contemporary critics laud her feminism, not her exploration of Jewish themes. Yet, in this story, her characters are demonstrably Jewish.

Grace Paley, a short story writer, has published many stories about a fictional family called Darwin, the irony probably intended. It is a three-generation family, with the grandparents, cultural Jews, living in the Children of Judea retirement home. The middle generation, Faith, Hope, and Charles, particularly Faith, are wracked with self-doubt and constant anxiety. Faith's husband, Ricardo, abandoned her, and she was left to raise her sons, Anthony and Richard, alone. While Hope's and Charles's voices are heard in some of the stories, Faith is the central character. What she has faith in is unclear. In one story, "Faith in a Tree," she wonders why her mother sent her on an airplane trip alone when she was a child. She speculates that her mother was probably trying to make her independent, "That in a sensible, socialist, Zionist world of the future she wouldn't cry at my wedding? You're an American child. Free. Independent" (Paley 1975). If that was the Mother's intention, she failed. In story after story, Faith never answers her many questions. She does not share her parents' vision of a socialist-Zionist utopia, she has no knowledge of the Jewish religion, and her contemporary American culture only reinforces her doubting nature.

The youngest member of this second generation, Cynthia Ozick (b. 1928) differs considerably from the three older members of her cohort. Her stories, novellas, and novels are all about Jewish subjects. She is also a formidable essayist whose nonfiction focuses on Jewish themes. Indeed, while Judaism is central to all of Ozick's writing, the depictions of characters in her stories range from the realistic to the magical. In *The Pagan Rabbi* (1971), Ozick grapples with a learned Mishnah expert whose intense studies lead him into mysticism and a preoccupation with nature that smacks of paganism. Ozick is intrigued by the creative process and how the writer's work competes with the work of God. Judaism prohibits the worship of idols and the creation of graven images. Ozick wonders in her writings whether Jewish writers are not violating this sacred principle, yet she cannot stop from imagining and creating new stories.

In *The Puttermesser Papers* (1997), a collection of five stories about Ruth Puttermesser, a single civil servant, Ozick continues to grapple with the creation of Jewish fiction. Puttermesser is always searching for truth, understanding, and ultimately paradise (in Hebrew, *gan edyn*, the Garden of Eden), to no avail. Ozick states in her essays that she considers Judaism a lifelong process in which Jews engage and, in the very process, demonstrate their Judaism. Ruth Puttermesser, the first significant female character in Ozick's fiction, participates in this process until she dreams, when she is dying, of Paradise as a place where chocolate can be eaten forever. Though a seemingly trivial ultimate wish, Puttermesser remains Jewish in her constant behavior of questioning, analyzing, and seeking knowledge.

Born in the 1930s and 1940s, the third generation of Jewish women writers was comfortably settled in American culture. As the children or grandchildren of immigrants, they never experienced personal conflicts between leading a religiously oriented life and secular American patterns of living. They grew up as American children, too young to remember the Holocaust. Rona Jaffe (1932–2005) and Gail Parent (b. 1940) shared the family genre with their predecessors, but they viewed the family with derision and sarcasm. Thanks to psychoanalysis and women's liberation, they looked at their family background clinically and critically. Still, though they were assimilated in many ways, they identified themselves and their fiction as Jewish.

Jaffe's *Family Secrets* (1974) presents a three-generation Jewish family, with the patriarch Adam Saffron, a self-made immigrant millionaire, bequeathing to his children and grandchildren a love of materialism, a shallow connection to Jewish ritual, and no moral framework. One grandson, Richie, who was studying to be a rabbi, quits three months before ordination because he is no longer eligible for the draft. Among Saffron's other grandchildren, one becomes a flower child in the sixties, another is devoted to running, and the others become all-American achievers. The Jewish calendar, religious observances, and the Jewish perspective on learning, self-analysis, and social justice are all forgotten. Gail Parent's two comic novels, *Sheila Levine Is Dead and Living in New York* (1972) and *David Meyer Is a Mother* (1977), use humor to dissect the modern Jewish American family. Sheila is an overweight, unmarried woman whose parents worry about her not finding a mate. David is a Jewish "prince," spoiled and unsure of himself. His parents, like Sheila's, think about the most superficial things and never impart a Jewish value system to their offspring. Both books portray unattractive and unsympathetic Jews, whose connection to their religion and their

heritage is tenuous at best. Jewish American adjustment has become maladjustment to Judaism and neurotic adaptation to America.

Fourth-generation Jewish women writers, born in the 1950s and 1960s, offer a lively return to themes of the first generation. Rebecca Goldstein (b. 1950), Pearl Abraham (b. 1960), and Allegra Goodman (b. 1967) all write fresh new treatments of the perennial subject: being a Jew in free America. Many of the youngest generation were raised in Orthodox Jewish families, providing them with the religious education and tradition common to immigrant Jews but rejected by later generations. Raised within a Jewish calendar year, they knew firsthand how tradition can blend, or clash, with the lures of American culture. Though they received above-average secular educations (Goldstein and Goodman both have doctorates), they were also learned in Jewish tradition. Their themes offer a new twist on the first two generations' concerns about assimilation, acculturation, or rejection: their challenge is how to retain their religious Judaic culture in the open environment of America.

For these writers, their immersion in religious Judaism is all encompassing. Getting out while staying in becomes the struggle. In Goldstein's first autobiographical novel, *The Mind-Body Problem* (1983), the protagonist, blonde and beautiful Renee Feuer, was raised in a traditional home. Her father was a cantor. At seventeen, she rebels against Orthodoxy while still attending the Baas Yaakov Girls High School. She goes on to study philosophy at Barnard and to graduate school at Princeton (all of which Goldstein did). Though Renee rejects religious culture for the secular, intellectual world of philosophy, she observes her new world through traditional Jewish eyes. She refers to *treyf* (unkosher) food, describes herself as a lapsed Jew, but still notes the holidays. At the end of the book, it is autumn, the time of Rosh Hoshanah and Yom Kippur, the Day of Atonement, and she remembers her father chanting the somber words as to who shall live and who shall die and the congregation responding: "But repentance, prayer, and charity cancel the stern decree." She comments that, though she doesn't believe those words any longer, she still gets a tingle in her spine and teary eyes " . . . as there is often a lag between one's rationality and emotive responses" (Goldstein 1983).

In *Mazel* (1995), Goldstein's fourth novel, three generations of Jewish women are portrayed. The grandmother Sasha is a famous Yiddish actress, while her daughter

Chloe is a professor of classics at Columbia, and the grand-daughter Phoebe is a physicist and expert on the mathematics of soap bubbles. Though Sasha and Chloe have a hard time communicating with each other, Phoebe brings them together and they live with the tensions. The youngest member of the family has returned to traditional Judaism, and she brings her mother and grandmother, however reluctantly, back into the orbit. In an afterword for the paperback edition, Goldstein asks: "How does one reconcile the pull of one's membership in a particular people's existence with one's pull to partake in the whole wide world?" (Goldstein 2002).

Pearl Abraham grew up in both New York and Israel, learning Yiddish before English in a Hasidic home. For years, she could read English more proficiently than Yiddish though she wrote more comfortably in Yiddish. She has described her first novel, *The Romance Reader* (1995), as an English translation of a Yiddish novel (Abraham 1996). Her protagonist, Rachel, is the oldest daughter of a Hasidic rabbi. She reads forbidden books and yearns for experience and knowledge beyond the limited confines of her strict religious environment. In a conversation about the sixteen girls who graduated with her from high school, and who was getting married when, everyone said: "God willing, she (Rachel) will be next." Rachel thinks: "Should I say, Not ever, God willing? That would cause a scandal, and then it might be never. I don't know what I want" (Abraham 1996). Eventually, she marries and divorces, returns home temporarily, but is uncertain about her future.

In her second novel, *Giving Up America* (1998), Deena, her main character, is raised in the Hasidic tradition and marries a modern Orthodox Jew. What she discovers is that her husband Daniel represents a culture as alien as that of assimilated Jews or even non-Jews. The difficulties that all marriages encounter, including renovating an old house and facing the prospect of an unfaithful husband, force Deena to consider the clash of cultures even within Judaism. Drawing on autobiographical material, Abraham explores topics that have resonance beyond Hasidism. What is the nature of compatibility between two people? How can unique individuals form partnerships with other unique individuals, particularly in a new world where women's wishes are given new respect and consideration? Finally, how can Jewish women preserve their connections to religious observance while expanding their intellectual horizons?

These same questions appear in the fiction of the youngest member of the contemporary generation, Allegra Goodman. Born in Hawaii to Orthodox parents, and with an undergraduate degree from Harvard and a doctorate in literature from Stanford, Goodman has been publishing fiction since she was a freshman at Harvard. Her first short story collection, *Total Immersion,* was published when she was twenty-one years old. *The Family Markowitz* (1996), a series of interrelated stories, features characters whose Jewishness is culturally, not religiously, based. Sara, the subject of one chapter, is a mother, writer, and teacher of creative *midrash* at the Jewish Community Center in Greater Washington. Her problems can be shared with all working women. Goodman's first novel, *Kaaterskill Falls* (1998), focuses on an Orthodox community in a small town in upstate New York where the followers of Rav Elijah Kirshner gather in the summer. The protagonist is a restless young mother of five daughters who wants to run a business, a wish she eventually fulfills.

Paradise Park (2001) takes the prolific Goodman onto new territory: her heroine (or anti-heroine), Sharon Spiegelman, at the beginning of the novel is a twenty-year-old searcher for truth, alone in Hawaii, having been abandoned by her boyfriend. The reader follows Sharon's next twenty years of traveling, wandering, and searching for herself. She tries Christianity, Buddhism, marijuana, whale watching, folk dancing, and eventually Hasidism in Crown Heights, Brooklyn. The novel is both comic and serious in tone, with the reader both sympathetic to, and exasperated with, the self-indulgent Sharon. Her return to tradition after her open-ended search can be viewed as rejecting the secular world and its temptations for the predictable and certain truths of a closed religious community.

Goodman, Goldstein, and Abraham use their own experiences as the basis for their fiction, but, while they have chosen to dwell in the larger American culture, their fictional heroines often return to the religious fold. Their fiction demonstrates the struggles within Orthodoxy by women with feminist sensibilities. Perhaps this cohort may offer us the most vibrant fictional experience of the tensions experienced by modern religious Jewish women and, by extension, all American Jews who try to identify with some aspects of religious and cultural Judaism while living in the secular world of twenty-first-century America.

June Sochen

References and Further Reading

Abraham, Pearl. 1995, 1996. *The Romance Reader*. New York: Riverhead Books.

Goldstein, Rebecca. 1983. *The Mind-Body Problem*. New York: Random House.

Goldstein, Rebecca. 1995, 2002. *Mazel*. New York: Viking/2002. Madison: University of Wisconsin Press.

Goodman, Allegra. 2001. *Paradise Park*. New York: Dell.

Hurst, Fannie. 1927. *Song of Life*. New York: Alfred A. Knopf.

Olsen, Tillie. 1976. *Tell Me a Riddle*. New York: Dell.

Ozick, Cynthia. 1997, 1998. *The Puttermesser Papers*. New York: Vintage Paperback.

Paley, Grace. 1975. *Enormous Changes at the Last Minute*. New York: Dell.

Sochen, June. 1981. *Consecrate Every Day: The Public Lives of Jewish American Women, 1880–1980*. Albany: State University of New York Press.

Yezierska, Anzia. 1925, 1975. *Bread Givers*. New York: George Braziller/Reprinted (1975).

Sholem Asch, novelist and playwright. (American Jewish Archives)

Sholem Asch (1880–1957)

Yiddish Playwright and Novelist

One of the most prominent modern Yiddish playwrights and novelists, Sholem Asch was one of very few writers in that language to succeed widely in English translation and garner attention from broader American, non-Jewish audiences. However, his controversial writings, most notably his trilogy of "Christian" novels written late in his career, alienated some of his most ardent Yiddish supporters while becoming English-language best-sellers.

Asch was born into a large Hasidic family in Kutno, a small Polish market town; his father, Moyshe Gombiner Asch, was a well-off livestock trader. Not particularly learned himself, Moyshe recognized Sholem's intelligence and hoped he would enter the rabbinate. Asch's own interests, however, ran to questioning Jewish orthodoxy, not perpetuating it; while still at religious school, he began reading secular material at a classmate's home, leaving home when discovered.

By the late 1890s, Asch was teaching Hebrew and earning money writing letters for illiterate inhabitants of Włocławek; while there, he also began writing fiction. In the summer of 1899, Asch visited Warsaw and met the noted Yiddish writer I. L. Peretz. Asch began regularly visiting Peretz's literary salon; thanks to Peretz's support, Asch's

Hebrew and Yiddish stories began appearing in Eastern European periodicals. He soon moved to Warsaw and in December 1901 married Madzhe Spiro, the daughter of a well-known Warsaw Jewish educator.

Asch's first book of stories appeared a year later, and his 1904 novella *A shtetl*, with its idyllic portrait of traditional Polish Jewish life, helped to establish the fledgling writer's reputation. But Asch's dramatic work elevated him to international celebrity. His first play, best known as *Mitn Shtrom* (*With the Current*), written as early as 1905, was performed in Krakow's National Theater, and in 1906 Asch met noted actor/director Jacob Adler to discuss producing his play *Meshiekhs tsaytn* (*The Messianic Era*) in New York, where the demand for Yiddish theater was exploding along with the city's immigrant Eastern European Jewish population. But his next play would cause the true explosion.

Got fun nekome (*God of Vengeance*), set in a Jewish brothel, focuses on the traditionally observant brothel owner's attempts to maintain his daughter's purity—and his own conscience—while operating his business. His failure to do so, accompanied by scenes of prostitution, lesbian seduction, and the blasphemous use of a Torah scroll, created a work so controversial it was bound to become famous. Asch first offered the play to Max Reinhardt and Rudolph Schildkraut, the leading director and actor of German Jewish theater; opening at the Deutsches Theater on March 19, 1907, the play ran for six months. It opened at New York's Thalia Theater, with noted Yiddish actor David Kessler in the starring role, on October 13, 1907. Translated and performed in a dozen European languages, it came to Broadway in English in 1923.

Some Yiddish critics claimed Asch was trying to curry favor with non-Jews by presenting Jewish life as immoral; others, including Peretz, felt his crime was misrepresenting details of Jewish life. But the sexual elements remained the most controversial: the 1923 Broadway production led to prosecutions against its star and producer for "obscenity and immorality," with figures no less prominent than Konstantin Stanislavsky and Eugene O'Neill speaking in the play's defense.

In 1909 and 1910, Asch traveled through the United States and Canada. Though worried about America's materialism, his greater concerns about Jews' long-term prospects in Russia would lead to his emigration from Eastern Europe. After spending several years in France, he moved to New York following the outbreak of World War I. After living briefly in Greenwich Village, the Bronx, and Brooklyn, Asch and his family moved to Staten Island in 1920, the year he became a citizen. The war—particularly the savage treatment of Jews by combatants on both sides—pushed the cosmopolitan, pan-European Asch to think more about questions of Jewish national identity and to participate more actively in Jewish public life, particularly on behalf of Jewish war victims; Asch became a founding member of the American Jewish Joint Distribution Committee (1914).

After arriving in America, Asch increasingly earned his living by writing for the *Forverts,* America's largest Yiddish newspaper, edited by one of Asch's strongest supporters, the powerful and opinionated Abraham Cahan. Asch's first novel written in America, *Onkl Mozes* (*Uncle Moses*), was first serialized in the *Forverts* in 1917. *Onkl Mozes,* the story of an immigrant who achieves financial success on others' backs but whose catastrophic marriage to a younger American-born woman proves his undoing, illustrates the fraught nature of the unrestrained pursuit of "the American dream."

The next fifteen years marked the height of Asch's celebrity and success: though another novel on American themes, *Di muter* (*The Mother*), appeared in the *Forverts* in 1923, he returned to Europe that same year, staying mostly in Warsaw for two years before settling in the Bellevue suburb of Paris. Though continuing to write for American and European Yiddish newspapers, Asch spent much of the late twenties and early thirties writing the massive trilogy known as "Three Cities": *Petersburg* (1929), *Warsaw* (1930), and *Moscow* (1931). The trilogy, originally titled *Farn mabl* (*Before the Deluge*), focuses on the Russian revolution's impact on the eponymous cities' Jewish communities. This second European period's apotheosis came in 1930, with months-long international celebrations marking Asch's fiftieth birthday and his thirtieth anniversary as a writer.

Asch spent much of the early thirties in and around Nice, where he wrote his next major novel, *Der tilim-yid* (1934; published in English as *Salvation*), and worriedly watched fascism's rise. In 1933, he was a major speaker at a Nice anti-Nazi rally and in 1934 wrote *The War Goes On,* about the roots of fascism in Weimar Germany. In 1936, Asch visited Palestine; the trip would result not only in *Dos gezang fun tol* (*Song of the Valley*), a picture of the Jewish pioneers working in the Jezreel Valley, but also the beginnings of a novel about the life of Jesus planned since his first 1907 visit to Palestine. Right before World War II began in 1939, Asch returned to America, moving first to Stamford and then to Miami Beach; that same year, his novel *The Nazarene* was published in English. The book received excellent reviews in the English press and became a best-seller (ninth in national sales in 1939 and fifth in 1940).

The novel's catalyst is a contemporary Polish researcher's discovery of a fifth gospel, ostensibly written by Judas Iscariot. The researcher, though an antisemite, seeks a young Jewish scholar's assistance in translating the manuscript; it emerges that the Pole is (or believes himself to be) the reincarnation of a Roman military governor, Pontius Pilate's assistant, and the scholar a "wandering Jew" figure who had actually been a Pharisaic rabbi during Jesus' lifetime. These developments allow Asch the opportunity to write a lively re-creation of Jesus' milieu and his personal history.

Asch's non-Jewish critics praised the prodigious research that went into the book's composition and the rich, detailed portrait of historical Palestine that resulted, a worthy fictional entry in the numerous volumes dedicated to the "quest for the historical Jesus." Asch himself, however, claimed motives beyond the purely historical or simply aesthetic for the novel's composition. Highly mindful of the contemporary situation in Europe, Asch believed anti-semitism resulted from Christian and Jewish misunderstanding of the two religions' common origins and, further, from the religions' subsequent divergence from each other. In *The Nazarene*, Asch's attempt to rectify this situation consisted of portraying Jesus as a Jewish leader, a prophetic or almost Hasidic preacher, reminding readers of deep continuities between the religions even millennia later. Characters in the novel refer to Jesus as divine or the son of God, but the book itself makes no such claims, allowing for liberal constructions of the book's ecumenical intent.

Throughout the 1940s, however, Asch's sympathetic attitude toward Christianity grows significantly: in nonfiction works of philosophy and theology like *What I Believe* (1941) and *One Destiny: An Epistle to the Christians* (1945), and especially in the remaining two volumes of the trilogy, *The Apostle* (1943) and *Mary* (1949), Asch increasingly presents a view of Jesus and the Christian religion at odds with any normative expression of Judaism. Though still claiming his motives were simply those of rapprochement and ecumenical understanding, he referred to Jesus in a 1944 interview as the son of God and the son of Man, claimed him as the continuation of Judaism, and presented Jesus as a divine figure throughout the novel *Mary*. Even other contemporary figures like Marc Chagall, who had used Jesus as a Jewish figure or symbol in their work, never made such sweeping claims.

In the Yiddish-speaking world, however, the controversy over Asch's Christological intentions had begun as early as the 1939 publication of *The Nazarene*. For Asch's Yiddish readers, though, the controversy was necessarily secondhand: Asch's usual publishers, especially his former champion Cahan, refused to serialize or publish the Yiddish version of the novel, arguing that this sympathetic account of Christianity's founder, perhaps offensive to traditional Jewish audiences at any time, was singularly inappropriate at this historical moment, possibly even constituting national betrayal. Cahan also accused Asch of

attempting to gain popularity with non-Jews by actively proselytizing for Christianity. Though Asch attempted to respond to his critics throughout the forties, the opposition to his work remained unchecked, with the result that the Yiddish version of *The Nazarene* (*Der man fun natseres*) would not be published until 1943, and the trilogy's second and third volumes never appeared in Yiddish, though *Mary* would reach third place on the English bestseller lists.

Asch would continue to write and publish prolifically: in October 1943, no longer able to write for the *Forverts,* he joined the Communist paper the *Morgn Frayheyt.* Though the paper boasted of having one of Yiddish literature's most important writers in its pages, Asch himself was no Communist; his essays on current events and his short fiction (including excerpts of *The Apostle* and *Mary*) appeared there solely as a matter of financial necessity. Though his attitude toward the Soviet Union briefly changed during World War II, as the Soviets saved large numbers of Jews from the Nazis, he would eventually break with the Communist Party in the late forties over Stalinist repression of Soviet Yiddish writers and Yiddish literary culture. Despite his generally staunch anti-Communism, his writing and wartime activities would lead to his questioning by the House Un-American Activities Committee in 1952.

Despite his continued literary activity in the forties, he became increasingly alienated from his original readers; mock trials of Asch were staged internationally, and, in April 1944, he was asked to leave when he attended a memorial service in New York for Warsaw Ghetto victims. Many of his later novels—even one of his masterpieces, *East River* (1946), a novel of immigrant Jewish life around World War I—were largely ignored or dismissed in Yiddish circles even as his star continued to rise in the English-speaking world: in 1943, he became the first Yiddish writer nominated for the Nobel Prize. *East River* is itself a testament to Asch's shift in perspective: though set in the heyday of Eastern European Jewish immigration, between 1910 and 1916, the novel takes place not on the Lower East Side, but in the multi-ethnic neighborhood of the East Forties, not only among first-generation immigrants, but their children. The novel soberly discusses acculturation and the loss of identity, and poses the impossible question of the relationship between intermarriage and full participation in the Americanization process. These complexities and Asch's continued growth as a writer, however, went largely unrecognized by an increasingly hostile and uncaring audience.

The animus against Asch reached its height in the early fifties; a 1950 book by *Forverts* staffer Khayim Liberman, *Sholem Asch un kristentum* (*Sholem Asch and Christianity*), was so vitriolic it both provoked some sympathetic backlash and contributed to Asch's decision to leave America for good in 1953. In his remaining years, he divided his time between Europe, especially London, and the Israeli city of Bat Yam, where he had built a house at the request of the city's mayor. Asch had paid his first visit to the State of Israel in 1952; though some there, especially more traditional Jews, were still angry with him, his warm reception from many others, most notably a group of former inhabitants of his birthplace, encouraged Asch to settle there. Asch died on a visit to London on July 10, 1957, and was buried there.

Jeremy Dauber

References and Further Reading
"Asch, Sholem." 1956–1981. In *Leksikon fun der nayer yidisher literatur* (*Lexicon of New Yiddish Literature*), Vol. 1, cols. 183–192. New York: International Yiddish Culture Congress.
Madison, Charles. 1968. *Yiddish Literature: Its Scope and Major Writers.* New York: Frederick Ungar.
Mazower, David. 2004. "Sholem Asch: Images of a Life." In *Sholem Asch Reconsidered,* edited by Nanette Stahl, 3–31. New Haven, CT: Beinecke Rare Book and Manuscript Library.
Niger, Samuel. 1960. *Sholem ash: zayn lebn, zayne verk* (*Sholem Asch: His Life, His Works*). New York: Congress for Jewish Culture.
Siegel, Ben. 1976. *The Controversial Sholem Asch.* Bowling Green, OH: Bowling Green University Popular Press.
Stahl, Nanette, ed. 2004. *Sholem Asch Reconsidered.* New Haven, CT: Beinecke Rare Book and Manuscript Library.

Saul Bellow (1915–2005)

Novelist, Winner of Nobel Prize for Literature

Few novelists dominated American fiction in the second half of the twentieth century as did Saul Bellow. He had perhaps the most distinguished literary career of any contemporary novelist in the United States. His numerous honors and awards included National Book Awards in 1954, 1965, and 1971. In 1968 the Republic of France awarded him the Croix de Chevalier des Arts et Lettres, the highest literary distinction that France awards to non-citizens. In March 1968, he received the B'nai B'rith Jewish Heritage Award for "excellence in Jewish Literature," and in November 1976 the Anti-Defamation League awarded him its America's Democratic Legacy Award—the first time this award had been given to a literary figure. In 1976, Bellow became the seventh American writer to win the Nobel Prize. His fiction was published in *Partisan Review, Playboy, Harper's Bazaar, The New Yorker, Esquire,* and various literary quarterlies. His essays and reviews appeared in *The New York Times Book Review, Horizon, Encounter, The New Republic,* and *The New Leader,* among other publications. During the 1967 Arab–Israeli conflict, he served as a war correspondent for *Newsday.*

Bellow remained a literary force to the end of his life, continuing to produce fiction that commands attention and respect. Even critics not favorably disposed toward his work acknowledge his intellectual brilliance, his eye for detail, his wry humor and comic gifts, and his masterful control of his prose—not to mention his refusal to bend to shifting cultural winds.

For six decades Saul Bellow wrote fiction and nonfiction that rejected the negative intellectual and cultural forces that have shaped the literature of the twentieth—and now the twenty-first—century. He showed little patience for existential nihilism and wasteland pessimism. As an undergraduate at the University of Chicago and then at Northwestern, Bellow was an active Trotskyist. He clung to his leftist views until World War II, when the machinations of Hitler and Stalin opened his eyes to the extremes of both right and left. Some critics today refer to him as a neoconservative, but Bellow preferred to think of himself as a liberal who had been abandoned by a liberalism that shifted decidedly to the left. He can more precisely be described as an old-style humanist whose values, derived primarily from the University of Chicago's Great Books program, coincided closely with traditional Judaic principles. In novel after novel, as well as in stories and essays, he emphasized the basic integrity of the private life, the value of familial ties, and man's inherent awareness of his social contract. He did so while proclaiming the individual's need to adhere to humanity's behavioral principles of order, logic, decency, and self-control.

Portrait of twentieth-century novelist Saul Bellow (UPI-Bettmann/Corbis)

He was born Solomon Bellow, on July 10, 1915, in Lachine, a small suburb of Montreal, in Quebec, Canada. (In Europe, the family name was spelled Belo—from *byelo*, white, in Russian.) His parents, Abraham and Liza (Gordin) Bellow, were deeply religious Jewish immigrants from Russia. Two years earlier they had brought their family to Canada from St. Petersburg, where Abraham had been an importer of Egyptian onions. There were three older children: two sons and a daughter. When Solly—as he was called—was three, his family moved from Lachine to Montreal. The once successful and proud Abraham Bellow now found himself an abject failure. In an early version of *Herzog*, Bellow catalogued his father's failures: "The bakery, the sacks, peddling, jobbing, buying the produce in the country and selling it door to door, the dry goods store was a failure; matchmaking, insurance schemes, selling cemetery lots—all failed." For the next six years the Bellows lived in an old, rundown section of Montreal. It was a mul-

tilingual neighborhood, and Solly absorbed four languages as he grew up—English, French, Yiddish, and Hebrew. This last tongue he used at *cheder* (Hebrew school), where he was taught to read in the Old Testament.

Bellow had occasion to look back at this early awareness of his Jewishness. "We observed Jewish customs, reciting prayers and blessings all day long. Because we read Genesis again and again, my first consciousness was that of a cosmos, and in that cosmos I was a Jew." To deny this past strikes Bellow as treasonous. "It would be a treason to my first consciousness to 'un-Jew' myself" (Bellow 1994). Despite this early sense of communal togetherness, Bellow was not a joiner and never belonged to an orthodox congregation. The last truly orthodox thing he did, he admitted, was to have his bar mitzvah. But if he did not embrace orthodoxy, the adult Bellow was hardly irreligious. "I could never describe myself as an atheist or agnostic. I always thought those were terms for a pathological state and that people who don't believe in God have something wrong with them. Just say I am a religious man in a retarded condition and the only way I can square myself is to write" (Bruckner 1984).

In 1924, when Solly was nine, the family moved to Chicago. There Abraham Bellow, after a series of business failures and dead-end jobs, went into the business of peddling wood chips for bakers' ovens. The demand for these chips was great, and the Bellow family, for the first time in the New World, enjoyed a newfound prosperity. But Solly's initiation into Chicago street life was not easy. The neighborhood kids at first proved hostile. They made him "feel like a foreigner, an outsider," he later recalled, by poking fun at his accent and calling him a Canuck (Weinstein 1985). He remembered vividly his sense of being both a participant in and a marginal observer of the new life. But before long he was at home in both that city's streets and libraries. At Tuley High, he made friends with such other budding writers and intellectuals as Isaac Rosenfeld, Sidney J. Harris, Oscar Tarcov, Sam Freifeld, and Sam Wanamaker—all of whom would figure in both his life and fiction.

In 1933, Bellow entered the University of Chicago, where Robert M. Hutchins had recently introduced his "return to the classics" program. Later claiming to have been oppressed by that campus's "dense atmosphere of learning, of cultural effort," Bellow transferred to Northwestern in 1935 to study sociology and anthropology. A favorite teacher there was the noted anthropologist Melville Her-skovits, whom Bellow mentioned often. Graduating with honors from Northwestern in 1937, Bellow considered doing graduate work in English there, but he was rebuffed by the chairman of that department, who told him that the son of Russian Jewish immigrants could never have a proper feeling for the English language. Angered and frustrated, but armed with a scholarship, Bellow began work on an advanced degree in anthropology at the University of Wisconsin in Madison. But he quickly found himself unsuited for graduate study. "Every time I worked on my thesis, it turned out to be a story," he explained to an interviewer. "I disappeared for the Christmas holidays and I never came back" (Breit 1953). In fact, he had made at that moment two significant changes in his life. One was that on New Year's Eve he married Anita Goshkin, a social worker. The second was that he returned to Chicago, where he had decided to live while devoting himself to writing fiction. He was employed briefly by the Depression-spawned Works Progress Administration (WPA) Writers Project, writing short biographies of midwestern novelists and poets. He then taught for approximately four years at Pestalozzi-Froebel Teachers College in Chicago. He also served briefly in the Merchant Marine during World War II and worked on the editorial staff of the *Encyclopedia Britannica*, helping to assemble the *Synopticon*, or index, to Mortimer Adler's Great Books series.

In 1941 Bellow published his first stories. "Two Morning Monologues" reveal the internal agonizings of an unemployed young man waiting and indeed wishing to be called up for military service, and the inner musings of a compulsive horseplayer driven to assert his freedom and identity through gambling. Bellow developed this initial idea of the waiting draftee into the story "Notes for a Dangling Man" (1943) and then into his first novel, *Dangling Man* (1944). Turning here to the familiar literary form of a journal, Bellow relates the tribulations of a young pacifist awaiting his draft call during World War II. The critics were encouraging. The tough-minded Edmund Wilson described the novel "as one of the most honest pieces of testimony on the psychology of a whole generation who have grown up during the depression and the war" (Wilson 1944). In its differing forms, this short novel introduces some of the key characters and themes to be found in Bellow's later work. His hero Joseph repeatedly asks, "How should a good man live, what ought he to do?" Either re-

phrased or implied, these moral questions echo throughout Bellow's fiction.

Three years later, Bellow finally decided to assert his Jewishness in his fiction. He chose to do so by means of an intellectually challenging, tightly structured, full-length narrative that confronted head-on antisemitism's moral, social, and intellectual complexities. At first glance *The Victim* (1947), Bellow's second novel, suggests merely one more retelling of the story rendered painfully familiar by Jewish novelists in the 1930s and 1940s—that of an innocent Jew beset by a fanatical antisemite. But Bellow alone had the chutzpah to portray the eternal patsy as both victimizer and victim. In somber, slow-paced prose, he delineates the postwar Jew's growing self-awareness of his collective character and place. He does so through the endurance and violence, good intentions and guilty uncertainties of Asa Leventhal, a moderately successful journalist who is confronted by the reappearance of a strange apparition from his troubled past named Kirby Allbee. Only a few discerning critics grasped the depth of Bellow's psychological probings of antisemitism in *The Victim*, and most readers were not overly enthusiastic. Later, critics would come to see in these early works another recurrent motif of Bellow's fiction. For instance, Marcus Klein, in *After Alienation* (1964), his study of midcentury American novelists, pointed to the basic tensions even in Bellow's early fiction between the individual who inevitably desires self-preservation and his society that insists on self-sacrifice.

Throughout his career Bellow would divide his time between writing and teaching, and for a number of years he held a series of short-term university appointments. He taught at the University of Minnesota (1946–1948, 1957–1959); New York University (1950–1951); Princeton University (1952–1953), where he became close friends with the poet John Berryman; and Bard College (1953–1954). Between 1948 and 1950 Bellow lived in Paris and traveled in Europe, and afterward he spent over ten years in New York City and Dutchess County, New York. His first long-term university tenure began in 1963, when he returned to the University of Chicago as a professor in a new department called the Committee on Social Thought. Beginning in 1993 he taught at Boston University.

Like most fiction writers, Bellow draws from his own life for the general outlines of his plots. Although he had until the last years of his life played down the autobiographical elements in his fiction, his novels reveal his keen awareness of his Jewish family background and his cultural roots in both Eastern Europe and North America. Ironically, Bellow, during most of his career, resisted the label of "Jewish writer." Yet it was Bellow, notes Ruth Wisse, "who demonstrated how a Jewish voice could speak for an integrated America. With Bellow, Jewishness moved in from the immigrant margins to become a new form of American regionalism." Wisse perceptively points out that Bellow "did not have to write about Jews in order to write as a Jew." For his "curious mingling of laughter and trembling" is to be found throughout his fiction. This is especially true in a novel like *Henderson the Rain King,* where the narrative "follows an archetypal Protestant American into mythic Africa" (Wisse 2003).

Bellow did not merely influence and prepare the way for other American Jewish writers like Bernard Malamud and Philip Roth, Herbert Gold and Grace Paley and Cynthia Ozick, but, Wisse adds, he also "naturalized the immigrant voice." In his hands, the American novel seemed "freshly authentic when it spoke in the voice of one of its discernible minorities" (Wisse 2003). His every narrative centered on a sensitive, thinking social adventurer keenly aware of the personal cost of modern existence. Other writers (Jewish and non-Jewish) then emerging found in his work a means of confronting the day's social and human dilemmas. No other novelist depicted as effectively the postwar confusions. Bellow transformed America's urban complexities into a sort of principle, "a mixture of health and sickness," that exemplified the modern condition. Here his Jewishness proved significant. "Would it be excessive to say," asked Irving Howe, "that this principle draws some of its energies from the Jewish tradition, the immigrant past?" (Howe 1976).

In 1948 Bellow received a Guggenheim Fellowship and headed for Europe. Dividing his time between cities like Paris and Rome, he wrote a long picaresque novel about Chicago and a young man's determination to live his life on his own terms. Few American novels have evoked as much interest and excitement upon publication as did *The Adventures of Augie March* (1953). It proved Bellow's major breakthrough work and won him his first National Book Award for fiction (1954). In it and later works, Bellow also "brought to completion" what critic Irving Howe would hail as "the first major new style in American prose fiction since those of Hemingway and Faulkner: a mingling of high-flown intellectual bravado with racy-tough street

Jewishness, all in a comic rhetoric that keeps turning its head back toward Yiddish even as it keeps racing away from it" (Howe 1976). The novel represented then a literary as well as a personal leap forward, as in it Bellow fuses a number of literary traditions. A contemporary coming-of-age novel, *Augie March* also embodies elements of the picaresque and comic traditions, as well as of the American, Jewish, and Yiddish ones.

Saul Bellow was now a presence on the American literary scene. He quickly followed up his previous successes with *Seize the Day* (1956), which consisted of a short novella bearing the volume's title, three short stories, and a one-act play. The stories—"A Father-to-Be," "Looking for Mr. Green," and "The Gonzaga Manuscripts"—have been much anthologized. Achieving even stronger recognition has been the novella, *Seize the Day,* which Alfred Kazin declared to be the "most moving single piece of fiction" that Bellow had written to that point (Kazin 1956). Many academic readers have agreed with Kazin, for this short novel has remained a staple on reading lists in American contemporary fiction classes. In it, Bellow focuses on Tommy Wilhelm, an unemployed salesman who insists that his reluctant, tightfisted father be a father to him. Rejected and vulnerable, Tommy is easy prey for Dr. Tamkin, a fast-talking charlatan who separates him from his last few dollars. In effect, Bellow felt he had to come to terms—as a writer and a Jew—with a highly advanced, modern world that had produced the Nazi death camps. But he found he had to do so in American, not European, terms. Three years later Bellow published another major novel, indeed one unusual even for him, *Henderson the Rain King* (1959). Drawing on his middle-aged American's fantastic quest for ultimate truth and his own identity among primitive African tribesman, with wry humor, Bellow makes clear that these so-called primitives at times reveal more insight and integrity than are evident in the supposedly civilized society his hero has left behind.

Five years later Bellow brought out what many critics consider his best and most personal novel, *Herzog* (1964). He is reputed to have written fifteen revisions, but this richly detailed account of the troubled love life of a quirky, distracted Jewish scholar quickly proved an international best-seller and won Bellow, among other awards, a second National Book Award and the $10,000 Prix International de Littérature. Moses Herzog is the quintessential Bellow hero. An urban intellectual, well-meaning but ineffectual,

Jewish professor of history, Herzog, like Bellow, can recall a poverty-stricken boyhood in Montreal. Now he struggles valiantly but comically to relate his humanistic values and traditional Jewish desires for intellectual and spiritual clarity to an increasingly dehumanized and uncaring modern world. A specialist in the Romantic period, he is forced to cope with the painful contradictions between his inner life of romantic aspirations and his external life's harsh realities. Among the most painful of these realities is his discovery of his wife's lengthy affair with his best friend. Shaken to the core, Herzog struggles to regain his emotional stability and shattered self-confidence. His efforts toward self-analysis cause him to write numerous letters, to friends and strangers, to world and mythic figures, both living and dead—none of which he mails. Departing from the always popular mode of the "victim" novel, Bellow ends *Herzog* on an upbeat note. His hero accepts his human condition and rejects any further attempts at self-justification. Nearly every Bellow narrative reveals a strong sense of his own Jewishness, but no story of his, short or long, does so as clearly and poignantly as *Herzog*.

In 1964, *Herzog* became a Literary Guild selection and a best-seller, and Bellow's first produced full-length play, *The Last Analysis,* opened in New York. Bellow had initially titled it *Bummidge,* and he clearly had in mind a different or unconventional play—both a good-natured farce and a spoof of Freudianism. His central figure was Philip Bummidge, an aging Jewish comedian who planned to send the results of his self-analysis electronically to a group of psychiatrists gathered for the purpose. Some critics appreciated Bellow's introduction of ideas to the Broadway stage, but most found the play too "talky" and Bellow more the novelist than playwright. The production closed after twenty-eight performances. (Bellow later rewrote the play, and it had a more successful off-Broadway run in 1971.) Four years after *Herzog,* Bellow published his first short-story collection, *Mosby's Memoirs and Other Stories* (1968). Here he brought together five stories carefully crafted over the preceding decade ("Leaving the Yellow House," "The Old System," "Looking for Mr. Green," "The Gonzaga Manuscripts," "A Father-to-Be," and "Mosby's Memoirs"). Not surprisingly, these stories either prefigure or look back at the thematic concerns of his novels, as his troubled protagonists struggle with their inner uncertainties and outer realities while striving to determine their self-worth and social place.

Bellow topped off the turbulent sixties with *Mr. Sammler's Planet* (1970), a novel many critics have ranked with his finest work, which won him his third National Book Award. He presents the poignant figure of Artur Sammler, an unlikely survivor of the Holocaust, who finds himself in New York in the chaotic 1960s. A lifelong humanist and believer in the societal values of order, discipline, and reason, the elderly Sammler is caught up in what appears to him to be a general breakdown of Western civilization. Neither prude nor Puritan, he recognizes better than most the soul's individuality. What he deplores is not the need to be unique, but the current mass obsession with an originality that rejects tested cultural models for the grotesque and bizarre. For if he is past passion, he is hardly dispassionate as he muses on the connections between human madness and death. The Holocaust and his own escape from the grave are the experiences by which Sammler measures all events. These have strengthened his belief in limits, dignity, tradition. Family members and friends, as well as acquaintances and strangers, force him to be a reluctant witness to their sordid sexual escapades, harebrained money schemes, or public misdeeds. Each seeks not Uncle Sammler's advice but his moral approval. For his part, Sammler, who now considers himself less a survivor than a marginal figure, wants only to spend undisturbed afternoons in the New York Public Library reading Meister Eckhardt and other medieval mystics. But life, he finds, is not yet ready to release him from its grip.

Five years later Bellow published *Humboldt's Gift* (1975), another novel that retraces his ongoing effort to understand his own literary success, as well as the success of other Jewish writers during the two decades following World War II. Through the characters of Charlie Citrine and Von Humboldt Fleisher, Bellow examines the complex relationship of the serious writer to American society in the heady postwar years. Bellow does so by means of the tumultuous emotional bonds he himself shared with the brilliant but self-destructive poet/writer/critic Delmore Schwartz, his New York literary mentor, who died alone and in poverty in 1966. Bellow makes it clear that talent and ambition are too often not enough to sustain success or to ensure a satisfying life.

In addition to talent and ambition, then, what other qualities help explain Bellow's literary success? Certainly he had inherited a relatively brief but rich tradition of Jewish writing in America, one stretching from Abraham

Cahan through Ben Hecht and Ludwig Lewisohn to his own postwar generation. He emerged when Jews were entering America's cultural flow. Single-minded and gifted, Bellow alone so grasped the American imagination that—in fictionalizing this Jewish entrance into American life—he penetrated to the nation's cultural core. He did so without compromising his standards, and while avoiding the tempting but often insipid values of comfortable middle-class life. Bellow's literary themes may have resembled those of middlebrow Jewish novelists like Herman Wouk or Irwin Shaw—in step with whom he established his reputation—but he somehow transformed the most familiar material into art. Other Jewish novelists like Bernard Malamud, Herbert Gold, and Philip Roth were quick to follow his lead.

Bellow was now a well-known novelist receiving invitations from many quarters. In late 1975 he chose to spend several months in Israel, where he had earlier covered the 1967 Six Day War for *Newsday*. This time he went to tour that country's historic sites and current trouble spots, to talk to spokesmen from every political faction, and to familiarize himself with the nation's political, cultural, and social conditions, as well as the people's hopes and anxieties. He wanted to make sense of the many tragic and complex issues facing the embattled nation. Returning home, he published his first nonfiction book, *To Jerusalem and Back: A Personal Account* (1976), which proved to be not only a personal memoir, but also his perceptive ruminations on his stay. Ironically, Bellow had through the years repeatedly rejected the label of "Jewish writer" for himself as too parochial or limiting. But here he defended with passion and eloquence, as an engaged Jew, Israel's right not only to exist but also to take her rightful place among the world's nations. He vents most of his anger against France, accusing its government, newpapers, and intellectuals of moral and political hypocrisy for the positions they have taken against Israel in recent decades. Shortly thereafter, in 1977, Bellow was awarded the Nobel Prize for Literature, only the eighth American—and the first Jewish one—to be so honored.

Seven years after *Humboldt's Gift*, Bellow brought out his next significant novel, *The Dean's December* (1982). Not only a tale of two cities, Chicago and Bucharest, it is also a scathing portrait of the bitter internal battles of university life. Albert Corde, a onetime highly successful journalist, is now dean of students at a Chicago college. But he is spending a cold, bleak month in Rumania with his wife, a noted astronomer, who has returned to her native city to be with her dying mother. There, despotic Communist officials control all lives—and deaths. Trying to help his wife through the mechanics and bureaucratic red tape of a last bedside vigil, cremation, and burial, the dean experiences both the privations and humiliations of life under Communism. These are not his only problems. Before leaving Chicago, Corde had stirred up a commotion by publishing, in *Harper's*, a harsh two-part study of that city's judicial system. To make matters worse, he had also demanded an investigation into the "accidental" death of one of his white students at the hands of a black prostitute and her pimp. Therefore, upon returning home, Corde does not find life much pleasanter in Chicago's harsh streets than it had been in Bucharest's lockstep bureaucracy.

Two years later, in 1984, Bellow published his second short story collection, *Him with His Foot in His Mouth and Other Stories*. Strongly reminiscent of his earlier *Mosby's Memoirs and Other Stories* (1968), these five stories ("Him with His Foot in His Mouth," "What Kind of Day Did You Have?" "Zetland: By a Character Witness," "A Silver Dish," and "Cousins") recall his familiar emotional terrain and traditional humanistic values. With wry, ironic humor, Bellow offers variations on his quintessential antihero. Each central figure is an aging urban intellectual, from an immigrant Jewish family, who still thinks big or transcendent thoughts about man, art, and the soul, yet feels he has outlasted his brief significant moment. None seems able to deal with life as he finds it. Collectively, their quirky personalities render them perpetual outsiders—whether Jews among gentiles, immigrants among "real Americans," or, most painfully, near-strangers in their own families.

Despite his now more than seventy years, Bellow seemed to be working without pause. In 1987, he published *More Die of Heartbreak*, a big novel with a cast of naïve academics, scheming social opportunists, and corrupt city hall wheeler-dealers whose lives are interconnected by botanical research, family ties, and the inevitable desires for the big payoff. His narrator is Kenneth Trachtenberg, a thirty-five-year-old assistant professor of Russian literature. Born and educated in Paris, Kenneth has moved to America and its Midwest rustbelt to be near his uncle, Benn Crader, a world-renowned botanist teaching at the same institution. Here the nation's wiliest con artists (usually in the guise of politicians, lawyers, and doctors) exhibit their amoral energy and cunning. Once more, Bellow's concern is for the sensitive individual caught up in the turbulence that is modern life and his need to focus on his own inner life—the self—and its metaphysical emanation, the soul.

Moving through his midseventies into his early eighties, Bellow published three novellas—*The Theft* (1989), *The Bellarosa Connection* (1989), and *The Actual* (1997)—as well as two notable short stories, "Something to Remember Me By" (1990) and "By the St. Lawrence" (1995). These narratives not only explore the commingling of sex and death, the therapeutic powers of memory, the nature of family bonds, and the harrowing long-range effects of the Holocaust, but they also evoke details from Bellow's own childhood and in different ways the biographical details of his major fictional protagonists. With the twentieth century winding to a close, Bellow seemed determined not to leave unfinished or unpublished any salvageable story element or fragment remaining in notebooks or files. In a move calculated to extend his "clearing–out" process and to emphasize the autobiographical nature of his writing, Bellow published, in 1994, the first collection of his essays, lectures, journalistic articles, eulogies of close friends, travel pieces, and several interviews. In effect, *It All Adds Up: From the Dim Past to the Uncertain Future* is a repository of Saul Bellow's central thoughts and mental processes through the years. Collectively, these pieces embody nearly a half century of hard thinking by a perceptive and sensitive observer of the human comedy, especially in its American forms. They essentially comprise Saul Bellow's intellectual autobiography.

A late example of Bellow's "cleaning-out" process was the appearance of his thirteenth novel, *Ravelstein*, at the start of the new century. The title character, Abe Ravelstein, is clearly based on the brilliant philosopher and historian of ideas Allan Bloom, Bellow's longtime friend and colleague at the University of Chicago, who in 1987 published the best-selling *The Closing of the American Mind*. In his mideighties, Bellow showed that he could still write vigorous prose and that friendship and intimacy were for him the very stuff of fiction. The most directly autobiographical of his novels, and therefore the most Jewish-and-death-oriented, this late narrative also provided a reminder that any friend or enemy, colleague or acquaintance, might well end up a character in one of his fictions. (He also proved

that he could do more than merely write vigorous prose. In 1999, at age eighty-four, Bellow fathered a daughter with his fifth wife, Janis Freedman Bellow, after having three sons with his first three wives.)

Ben Siegel

References and Further Reading

Atlas, James. 2000. *Bellow: A Life.* New York: Random House.

Bellow, Saul. 1994. "A Jewish Writer." *Partisan Review* 61,3: 368–378.

Breit, Harvey. 1953. "A Talk with Saul Bellow." *New York Times Book Review* (September 20): 22.

Bruckner, D.J.R. 1984. "A Candid Talk with Saul Bellow." *New York Times Magazine* (April 15).

Cronin, Gloria L., and Ben Siegel, ed. 1994. *Conversations with Saul Bellow.* Jackson: University Press of Mississippi.

Howe, Irving, with Kenneth Libo. 1976. *World of Our Fathers.* New York: Harcourt Brace Jovanovich.

Kazin, Alfred. 1956. "In Search of Light." *New York Times Book Review* (November 18).

Siegel, Ben. 1995. "Simply Not a Mandarin: Saul Bellow as Jew and Jewish Writer." In *Traditions, Voices, and Dreams: The American Novel since the 1960s*, edited by Melvin J. Friedman and Ben Siegel, 62–88. Newark: University of Delaware Press.

Weinstein, Ann. 1985. "Bellow's Reflections on His Most Recent Sentimental Journey to His Birthplace." *Saul Bellow Journal* 4,1: 62–71.

Wilson, Edmund. 1944. "Doubts and Dreams: Dangling Man under a Glass Bell." *The New Yorker* (April 1): 78, 81–82.

Wisse, Ruth. 2003. "Jewish American Renaissance." In *The Cambridge Companion to Jewish American Literature*, edited by Michael P. Kramer and Hana Wirth-Nesher, 190–211. New York: Cambridge University Press.

Joseph Bovshover (1873–1915)

Yiddish Poet and Anarchist

Joseph Bovshover, a Russian immigrant, was one of the principal Jewish proletarian, or sweatshop, poets in the United States. He became identified with anarchism soon after arriving in this country.

Bovshover was born in Libavich, Russia, to an Orthodox family of six boys and a girl. His father was a Gemarah *melamed* (instructor of the Talmud, especially the part that comments on the Mishnah—Jewish Law). Bovshover, however, did not do well in school and worked for a merchant, later moving to Riga to work as a clerk for a grain merchant. At eighteen, he immigrated to New York, joining two of his older brothers. There he worked in a sweatshop and as a salesperson, but in both cases was laid off. One of his affluent brothers opened a grocery store for him, but it soon went out of business due to poor management.

On July 8, 1892, Bovshover's first published poem, "*Kapitals a korbn*" ("A Victim of Capital"), later retitled "*Oyf'n shterbe-bet*" ("On Death-Bed"), appeared in the socialist *Arbayter zaytung* (*Worker's Newspaper*), published in New York, under the pseudonym M. Turbov. In September, he published his first short story, "*Kapital's korbones*" ("Capital's Victims"), heavily influenced by the style of David Edelshtat, a leading radical Yiddish poet. He became a contributor to the London anarchist publication *Arbayter fraynd* (*Worker's Friend*). His first poem there was "*Tsum vint*" ("To the Wind"). His poems opposed urbanization and called for a return to nature. He also composed lyrical poems.

After Edelshtat's death (October 1892), Bovshover stopped publishing in *Arbayter zaytung* for almost a year, during which time the anarchist movement was in crisis. The socialists gained influence among the workers, while the anarchist movement lost influence. Bovshover sided with the anarchists. When the anarchist *Fraye arbayter shtime* (*FAS, Free Voice of Labor*) started appearing again on March 17, 1893, Bovshover published a poem there— "*Oyfruf*" ("A Call") against the socialists. The satirical poem addressed the current difficult times in the United States: banks failed and people lost their life savings, factories and workshops closed, and millions were jobless. The Jewish socialists joined the trade unions in opening a relief station to help the needy workers and the entrepreneurs who had lost their businesses. In the poem, Bovshover calls the socialists "sycophants" and accuses them of being "exploiters of the situation" by helping businessmen in order to "buy" votes. This, however, did not stop him from continuing to publish in the *Arbayter zaytung*.

In the summer of 1895, Bovshover moved to New Haven, Connecticut, for about a year to work in a clothing business owned by an anarchist. To make ends meet, he also distributed newspapers. It is believed he enrolled in an English literature course at Yale University. In his writings he now began to display an acquaintance with the American essayist Emerson and the poets Whitman, Poe, and Markham.

In March 1896, Bovshover looked for a job at the office of the individualistic-anarchist journal *Liberty*. Although he needed work, Bovshover refused to do translations because the material did not reflect his anarcho-communist views. He did, however, submit poems to be published. Benjamin Tucker, founder and editor of *Liberty*, thought highly of his poems, later writing that his work "was indicative of genius." Bovshover published in *Liberty* two original English poems—the first being "To the Toilers" (on March 7, 1896), an English translation of his Yiddish work *Tsum folk*—under the pseudonym Basil Dahl. He published eleven poems in English under this pen name.

In 1898, Bovshover, as Basil Dahl, translated Shakespeare's *The Merchant of Venice* into Yiddish. He also wrote a critical article about poetry, "*Vegn poezye*" ("About Poetry"). On October 6, 1899, *FAS* began publishing again, after an absence of almost five years. But about three months later Bovshover's last poem "*Frayhayt vanderer*" ("Freedom Wanderer") appeared. Because his mental health was deteriorating, he was placed in a mental hospital in Poughkeepsie, New York, where he spent the rest of his life. According to Michael Cohn, a physician and a central figure in the Jewish anarchist movement, who knew Bovshover personally, he suffered from dementia praecox paranoia. His death went unnoticed, and even his family was unsure of the exact date.

Despite his short creative period, Bovshover's work became popular among Jewish and non-Jewish workers in the United States and Europe. His early writing was influenced by the other three "proletariat poets": Morris Rosenfeld, Morris Winchevsky, and David Edelshtat. He began searching for his own style after learning English and reading American poetry by Walt Whitman and others. Although he saw himself as a poet, he was unable to detach himself from the proletarian theme and remained, like Edelshtat, an agitator. His work appeared in book form only after his hospitalization. He was soon forgotten, only to be revived by the Communists, who used his poetry in their agitation.

Ori Kritz

References and Further Reading
Agurski, S. 1931. "Yosef Bovshover un zyan tzayt" ("Joseph Bovshover and His Era"). In *Geklibene lider* (*Collected Poems*), edited by Joseph Bovshover, 3–42. Moscow: Tzentraler felker-farlag fun f.s.s.r.

Cohn, Michael A. 1928. "Joseph Bovshover: His Life and His Work." In *To the Toilers*, edited by Basil Dahl, ix–xxiii. Berkeley Heights, NJ: Oriole Press.

Marmor, Kalman. 1952. *Yosef Bovshover*. New York: Kalman Marmor Jubilee Committee.

Tucker, Benjamin. 1928. "A Remarkable Young Poet." In *To the Toilers*, edited by Basil Dahl, v–vii. Berkeley Heights, NJ: Oriole Press.

David Edelshtat (1866–1892)

Anarchist and Proletarian Poet

David Edelshtat, who became an anarchist after immigrating to the United States, was a pioneer of proletarian, or sweatshop, poetry in this country. The poetry for which he is known is in Yiddish.

Edelshtat was born on May 21, 1866, in Kaluga, about 115 miles from Moscow, outside the Pale of Settlement. Most of the six hundred local Jewish inhabitants earned the right to reside there because they were retired soldiers or artisans. Edelshtat's father had been kidnapped for military service as a child and had served twenty-five years in the czar's army. After retiring, he became a policeman and later worked in a sawmill. David was the sixth of eight children. They all received private lessons in reading and writing Russian because there were no public schools in Kaluga. At fifteen he joined three of his brothers in Kiev, where he learned both about *Yiddishkeit* (Jewishness) and revolutionary ideas.

After the pogroms of May 1881, Edelshtat, like many other Jewish radicals, concluded that he would not be able to fulfill his egalitarian dreams in Russia. Therefore, he emigrated to the United States with a group of *Am Olam* (Eternal People), whose aim was to establish Jewish agricultural colonies there. When, upon arriving in Philadelphia in May 1882, they realized their plans would not be actualized, the group dispersed, and Edelshtat joined a brother already living in Cincinnati. He learned the trade of buttonhole making along with other Russian immigrants. As he mastered English and familiarized himself with local politics, in 1885 Edelshtat affiliated with the labor movement.

The Haymarket Affair led him to anarchism. On May 4, 1886, labor unions held a demonstration at Haymarket Square in Chicago. When a bomb exploded, a policeman

was killed, and many were wounded. Several anarchist leaders were arrested, some of whom had not been present. Edelshtat and his friends were shocked by the outcome of the Haymarket trial: two of the accused anarchist leaders were sentenced to life imprisonment, one to fifteen years in prison, and five were sentenced to death (one of them, Louis Lingg, committed suicide in his cell by exploding dynamite in his mouth the day before their execution on November 11, 1887). Although the bomb thrower was never identified, the defendants were charged as accessories to murder, their oral and written statements against the state and the police alleged to have inspired his crime. The dreams of the radical immigrants about the United States, ostensibly the land of freedom of speech, were shattered.

Edelshtat, who until then considered himself an unaffiliated socialist, became an anarchist. Upon his relocation to New York in 1888, he joined the Yiddish-speaking branch of the movement, *Pionere der frayhayt* (Pioneers of Liberty), established there two years earlier. On January 5, 1889, he published his first poem in Russian, "*Pesnia proletaria*" ("A Poem by a Proletarian"), in the first issue of the Russian social democratic weekly, *Znamia* (*The Banner*). On February 15, "*Tsuruf der varhayt*" ("A Call for the Truth"), his first Yiddish poem, appeared in the inaugural issue of the first Yiddish anarchist weekly in the United States, *Di varhayt* (*The Truth*). From then on, Edelshtat ceased publishing in Russian. By then, the Yiddish he had learned from the Russian Jewish immigrants was good enough to write poetry; all his subsequent poems, short stories, and essays were in Yiddish. To achieve his goals of explaining and spreading the anarchist ideology to the Jewish masses and making them aware of their oppression, he realized that he had to write in their mother tongue, because as recent immigrants they did not understand English, and most did not know Russian. By summer 1889, Edelshtat had become a well-known poet of the proletariat, writing on social injustice and the "enslaved" workers.

Having moved back and forth from New York to Cincinnati from 1887 to 1890, he settled in New York in January 1891, where he assumed the editorship of the weekly *Fraye arbayter shtime* (*The Free Voice of Labor*), established several months earlier. Edelshtat turned the unaffiliated socialist publication into an anarchist newspaper. He held this position until the summer, when he was hospitalized in a sanatorium in Denver, Colorado, where he died of pulmonary tuberculosis on October 17, 1892, at the age of twenty-six. Before his death he saw his first book of poetry, *Folks gedikhte* (*The People's Poems*), published by *Fraye arbeiter shtime*.

Despite his short literary career (1889–1892), Edelshtat became a central poet during his lifetime and a romantic legend among revolutionaries and Yiddish poets of subsequent generations. Embraced first by socialists and anarchists, after the 1920s he was also claimed by Communists for espousing revolutionary ideals. Edelshtat created powerful international revolutionary images in his poetry, effectively using subjects like the Haymarket Affair in the poem "*Der 11-ter November*" ("November Eleventh"), the Paris Commune in the poem "*Louise Michel*," or the Russian revolutionary organization *Narodnaia volia* (The Will of the People) in the poem "*Sofia Perovskaia*," which inspired the adherents of several radical movements.

Ori Kritz

References and Further Reading

Bialostotzky, B. J., ed. 1953. *David Edelstat gedenk-bukh tsum zekhtsikstn Yortsayt, 1892–1952* (*Remembrance on the Sixtieth Anniversary of David Edelstat's Death*). New York: Edelshtat Memorial Committees.

Kritz, Ori. 1997. *The Poetics of Anarchy: David Edelshtat's Revolutionary Poetry*. Frankfurt am Main: Peter Lang.

Marmor, Kalman. 1935. *Dovid Edelstadt—geklibene verk* (*David Edelshtat—Collected Work*). 2 Vols. Moscow: Emes.

Marmor, Kalman. 1950. *Dovid Edelstadt*. New York: YKUF.

Daniel Fuchs (1909–1993)

Novelist and Screenwriter

A Depression-era novelist who put a promising literary career on hold to become a Hollywood screenwriter, but never abandoned those aspirations entirely, Daniel Fuchs inhabited and wrote about two disproportionately Jewish worlds: the immigrant neighborhoods of New York and the golden ghettoes of Hollywood.

Fuchs's greatest achievement as a writer is the trilogy of novels, set in the Brooklyn neighborhood of Williamsburg, which he published during the Depression: *Summer in Williamsburg* (1934), *Homage to Blenholt* (1936), and *Low Company* (1937). Daniel's parents, Jacob and Sarah

Malkah (Cohen) Fuchs, had immigrated separately while they were still teenagers, Jacob from Russia and Sarah from Poland, and met in New York. They were living on Manhattan's Lower East Side when Daniel was born, but moved across the East River to Williamsburg in 1914, settling initially in a small Jewish section of that ethnically diverse but divided neighborhood. His father sold newspapers and eventually owned a newsstand, and Daniel's earliest literary influences were probably journalism and magazine fiction, his father's leftover wares. He majored in philosophy at City College of New York, graduating in 1930. Almost immediately, Fuchs felt trapped in his job as a substitute public school teacher and sought escape through writing, submitting a long memoir about coming of age in Williamsburg to the *New Republic*. Its editor, Malcolm Cowley, published part of the memoir in the magazine as "Where Al Capone Grew Up" (1931), but advised Fuchs to widen his scope and pursue the topic in fiction. Married in 1932 to Susan Hessen and writing furiously during his summer vacations, Fuchs produced the first two Williamsburg novels in two years.

The autobiographical origins of the Williamsburg novels are not hard to detect. In the first, *Summer in Williamsburg*, Philip Heyman, a frustrated City College student with literary ambitions, is the most prominent player in the large ensemble cast of an ambitiously literate novel. As Irving Howe noticed, "each of the characters . . . is a point of reference by which to define Philip's situation" (1948). When a neighbor commits suicide, Philip turns, in his quest for truth, to Old Miller, whose "oily side curls" and "shiny black garments" give him the appearance of Jewish Orthodoxy. But the image is all Fuchs is interested in, to establish Miller as the novel's prophet: it is neither an attack on nor an endorsement of the haredi community. Hasidim were (and still are) a prominent component of Williamsburg, and Fuchs's use of such a character as a guide for the author's fictionalized alter-ego seems neither satiric nor ironic, even if Miller's pronouncements are devoid of traditional Jewish learning and range instead from one sort of materialism to another—from "there was one truth, one meaning in life, and this was money," to "men are the sum of a million infinitesimal phenomena and experiences. [. . .] The ultimate product, man, therefore moves mysteriously, but he is a scientific outcome of cause and effect." And Miller's naturalistic philosophy gives shape to Philip's quest, when the old man tells him, "you must pick Williamsburg to pieces until you have them all spread out on your table before you, a dictionary of Williamsburg."

The problem for Philip, however, is not the truth of Miller's observation, but its artistic utility; having dissected Williamsburg and its inhabitants, at the novel's end Philip realizes he has nothing to write about. The people of Williamsburg, he ironically concludes, went "through the stale operations of living, they were real, but a novelist did not write a book about them." The Williamsburg trilogy is, of course, proof that such books do get written, and that Philip Heyman is not, finally, Daniel Fuchs; but Philip's conclusion also reveals his author's own ambivalence about the impoverished horizons of Williamsburg's teeming streets. Recalling the writing of *Summer in Williamsburg* nearly thirty years later, Fuchs explained his character's dilemma as his own: "I was trying to find a similar direction and plan to the life I had witnessed in Williamsburg. I was struggling with form. I was struggling with mystery."

In his second novel, *Homage to Blenholt,* Fuchs relied on a similar relationship for the central story, but gained much needed perspective by distancing the work from its autobiographical origins, by limiting the main characters mostly to a single family and their friends, and by elevating avarice from a piece of the puzzle to the main theme. In *Summer in Williamsburg,* Philip may be disappointed at the end to discover that his poverty frustrates his ambitions, but a grittier materialism is played out in supporting stories of how the honest and hardworking fail while ruthless gangsters succeed. In *Homage to Blenholt,* the young protagonist, Max Balkan, is obsessed with financial rather than intellectual or artistic achievement, and his mentor, his role model, is the recently deceased Blenholt of the title. Max calls him a "hero in this flat age. [. . .] A racketeer, a gangster, a grafter, a politician, anything you want to say, but a hero!" For all Max's enthusiasm, however, the essence of Blenholt's moral corruption is perfectly and succinctly captured by Fuchs, who makes him "Commissioner of Sewers." Meanwhile, Blenholt's physical corruption is the novel's main plot device: anticipating Wallace Markfield's *To an Early Grave* (1961), the author has Max spend half the novel trying to get people to accompany him to Blenholt's funeral, where the service turns into a riot and Max ends up feeling "as miserable as a man ever felt." Gabriel Miller has called *Homage to Blenholt* a "Williamsburg comedy of manners," but the end of the novel turns darker, as Max unsurprisingly fails to find happiness in material success.

Fuchs's next novel takes up where *Homage to Blenholt* leaves off—in cynicism and low spirits—making *Low Company* the most pessimistic of the trilogy, as well as the least autobiographical. And, despite the novel's epigraph from the liturgy of Kol Nidre, it is also the least concerned with Jewish characters, though a few, like Herbert Lurie and Mr. Spitzbergen, are certainly intended to be seen as Jews. Marcelline Krafchick has argued that the "epigraph prayer serves the novel thematically in at least two ways" (1988): directly, as a menu of human failings from which the author can choose ingredients for his characterizations, and indirectly, as a suggestion of the moral wasteland that they inhabit. If true, this purely secular application of a traditional Jewish prayer is consistent with Fuchs's strategy throughout the trilogy, in which Jewish themes, metaphorical or otherwise, are largely employed for psychological and artistic purposes. Indeed, Gabriel Miller has suggested that *Low Company* "can, in fact, be read as a prose 'Waste Land,'" with numerous parallels to T. S. Eliot's modern epic, including its four-part structure, with Spitzbergen as "a kind of debased fertility-god figure" (1979). The novel takes place over a three-day period, the time it takes to journey to the underworld. But this underworld is the tawdry environment of Neptune Beach (Fuchs's version of Brighton Beach, though perhaps Pluto would have been a more suitable name), where organized crime is threatening the established dishonesty of petty criminals and predatory small businessmen. When one of the latter, Spitzbergen, is murdered near the end in a botched attempt at robbery by Karty, a gambler desperate to repay money he has embezzled from his wife's violent brothers, two of Fuchs's favorite themes are sounded once again: the price to be paid for making money into one's god and the complicated calculus of human causes and effects.

As one might expect when Philip Heyman, in *Summer in Williamsburg,* receives his assignment from Old Miller "to pick Williamsburg to pieces," Daniel Fuchs's interest in things Jewish was primarily sociological. Though his characters are mostly poor, immigrant Jews and their children, their struggles are almost entirely those of class, not religion. Though Allen Guttmann argues that "Fuchs was the first to take apart the world of Sholem Aleichem's Kasrilevka and to reconstruct it on the sidewalks of New York" (1971), he certainly does not mean this in a spiritual sense. Despite his odd phrasing, Morris Dickstein is closer to the truth when he suggests that Fuchs is "notably ham-handed in portraying the religious life of the Jews" (1974). Indeed, the Williamsburg trilogy lacks even the sort of scenes involving Jewish education and ritual observance that can be found even in the works of Fuchs's more ideological contemporaries, including Henry Roth's *Call It Sleep* and Mike Gold's *Jews without Money*.

In a preface written for a 1961 reprinting of the trilogy, Fuchs recalled his disappointment at the novels' reception: "The books were failures. Nobody seemed to care for them when they came out. [. . .] The books didn't sell—400 copies, 400 copies, 1,200 copies. The reviews were scanty, immaterial. The books became odious to me." In fact, the novels received very good reviews, especially in the *New York Times*, but, like his characters, Fuchs was weighted with financial concerns, and he eventually opted for the greater monetary rewards of screenwriting in Hollywood while occasionally publishing short fiction and essays in magazines. Among his successful screenplays, Fuchs turned *Low Company* into the 1947 film *The Gangster* and won an Academy Award for best original story for the 1955 film *Love Me or Leave Me*.

About Fuchs's career choice, Irving Howe, for whom no answer but a socialist one would do, claimed, "It would be absurd to speak of his having 'sold out' to Hollywood, for Fuchs was defeated in himself before he went to Hollywood and had he not been so defeated he would most probably not have gone there." Despite such sophism, however, Howe made a telling comparison of Fuchs's two worlds, asking, "For what is Hollywood but Williamsburg in Technicolor?" (1948). And, in fact, some of the best fiction of Fuchs's later career, including the story "Twilight in California," seems to be little more than Williamsburg pessimism recast in the glitz and sunshine of Los Angeles.

Though less than laudatory, Howe's interest helped to bring Fuchs back to fiction. He published a number of stories in 1953 and 1954, after a decade of mostly silence and screenplays, and three of these were collected in *Stories* (1956), a volume of short fiction by Fuchs, Jean Stafford, John Cheever, and William Maxwell. A one-volume reissue of the Williamsburg trilogy as *Three Novels* in 1961 introduced Fuchs to a new generation of readers and won him the sort of praise and attention he had found lacking in the 1930s. A slim novel, *West of the Rockies*, followed in 1971. Though set in Palm Springs, *West of the Rockies* is a story in which the unreality of the film industry and its stars is matched by Fuchs's uncharacteristically thin narrative—

and the resulting fiction is clearly not the result of picking Hollywood to pieces and spreading them out for study.

Fuchs's final book was the 1979 collection of two dozen essays and short fiction, *The Apathetic Bookie Joint*. The title story tells the tale of a bookie so depressed by reality—and by the apparent impossibility of luck or happiness—that he takes bets only reluctantly, and who, like Blenholt before him, is called a hero, this time by the cop who releases him without arrest at the story's end. The collection also contains "Triplicate," a previously unpublished autobiographical novella about a Hollywood screenwriter, and "Twilight in California," in which Alexander Honti, like Max Balkan in *Homage to Blenholt*, dreams of making the deal that will set him up for life. For Max, the dream involves onion juice; twenty years later in Los Angeles, Mr. Honti is in the novelty business, but only the background is new in the way he ends up, toothless, on foot, and out of luck, on Mulholland Drive. Fuchs's own story concluded in more comfortable circumstances, but to the end his characters rue having opted for the sort of materialistic choices their author himself made.

David Mesher

References and Further Reading
Dickstein, Morris. 1974. "Cold War Blues: Notes on the Culture of the Fifties." *Partisan Review* 41,1: 30–55.
Guttmann, Allen. 1971. *The Jewish Writer in America*. New York: Oxford University Press.
Howe, Irving. 1948. "Daniel Fuchs: Escape from Williamsburg—The Fate of Talent in America." *Commentary* 6: 29–34.
Krafchick, Marcelline. 1988. *World without Heroes: The Brooklyn Novels of Daniel Fuchs*. Rutherford, NJ: Fairleigh Dickinson University Press.
Miller, Gabriel. 1979. *Daniel Fuchs*. Boston: Twayne Publishers.
Rubin, Rachel. 2000. "Business Is Business: The Death of the Gangster in Daniel Fuchs's Novels of the 1930s." *Jewish Gangsters of Modern Literature*. Urbana: University of Illinois Press.

Michael Gold (1894–1967)

Journalist and Fiction Writer

Michael Gold is internationally known as the author of *Jews without Money* (1930), an acclaimed fictionalized autobiography. He was also a prolific journalist for the United States Communist movement for nearly four decades, an innovative if quirky playwright, a passionate and colorful poet, an uneven but occasionally dazzling essayist on cultural affairs, and an unforgettable literary personality of the 1920s and Great Depression eras. Among the canon of Jewish American writers, Gold's legacy is unsettled due to his Stalinist politics, his association with "proletarian literature," and his failure to produce a second major work.

Gold was born Itzok Granich on the Lower East Side of New York, although he became known as Irving Granich in public school and elected Irwin Granich for his initial publications. From his parents, Jewish immigrants from Romania and Hungary, Gold inherited an ardor for the Yiddish language and literature, especially songs and theater. His father was a failed businessman who descended into poverty, illness, and suicidal despair, before dying mysteriously when Gold was eighteen. The family's impecunious circumstances impelled Gold to leave school for factory work at age twelve. At fifteen he was publishing in settlement house newspapers, and poverty was already a theme.

Both of Gold's brothers became radical activists around the time of World War I, and in 1914 Gold himself published a poem celebrating martyred anarchists in the revolutionary *Masses* magazine. Around the same time Gold pursued courses in night school to complete his high school education, studied journalism at New York University for a year, and worked for the *New York Globe* as well as suburban newspapers. In the fall of 1916 Gold matriculated at Harvard as a provisional student. Unfortunately, Gold soon suffered a mental breakdown and became morbidly obsessed with guilt over his father's death. While he struggled with his illness he continued to circulate in the anarchist movement in Boston, living in a commune and editing a journal called *The Flame*.

In 1917 Gold departed Boston to launch a career as a playwright. That year two of his plays, *Down the Airshaft* and *Homecoming*, were performed by the Provincetown Players. The former treats the kinship between a Jewish American ghetto youth and his mother, and the second is an antiwar drama about the Russian front in World War I. Under the name Irwin Granich, an early version of an episode from *Jews without Money* appeared in *The Masses*. A year later, facing the draft, Gold escaped to Mexico

where he worked as a translator and laborer, caroused, and promoted the Bolshevik revolution from an anarchist perspective.

After returning to Provincetown, Massachusetts, in 1920 for the production of his play *Money*, Gold joined the editorial board of the *Liberator* (successor to the *Masses*) under the name Michael Gold. The pseudonym was borrowed from a Civil War veteran who was a friend of Gold's father. Gold most likely joined the Communist movement at this time, although his membership may have been inconstant until the 1930s. By 1922 he was living in Oakland, California, publishing in the *San Francisco World* and working on a life of John Brown that surfaced as a pamphlet two years afterward. In 1924 a collection of his fiction appeared as *A Damned Agitator and Other Stories*, under the imprint of the Communist Party newspaper, *Daily Worker*.

Gold passed part of the mid-1920s in the Soviet Union, where he fell under the spell of the constructivist German Jewish playwright Vsevold Meyerhold, who experimented with body movements and physical structures. Relocating to the United States, Gold helped to initiate the *New Masses* magazine in 1926 and the *Liberator*, progressively leading them in the direction of unofficial affiliation with the Communist movement. Concurrently, Gold tried to launch a United States version of the Soviet constructivist theater movement. The enterprise became the New Playwrights Theater, in which Gold was allied with Jewish American playwright John Howard Lawson and novelist John Dos Passos.

For this drama group Gold drafted his most bizarre play, *Hoboken Blues*, intended to be performed by an African American cast who would don masks to play the white characters. The text was published in 1927 in *American Caravan*, a prestigious annual of avant-garde literature, but its 1928 production was a failure. A second long play, *Fiesta*, derived from Gold's Mexican sojourn, netted a more favorable reaction when performed in 1929, but the New Playwrights company collapsed soon after. Gold's only subsequent efforts at playwriting were *Battlehymn* (1936), a drama about John Brown coauthored with Jewish American novelist Michael Blankfort, and selections from a 1948 play about the life of New York Communist city councilman Pete Cacchione.

As a poet, Gold is most admired for "Strange Funeral in Braddock" (1924). It was read publicly, performed to music, and widely known in the 1930s. His literary method here involves a refunctioning of motifs from folk tales and ballads. In dirge-like rhythms, Gold narrates the story of a martyred worker named Jan Clepak. The initials suggest Jesus Christ, and the poem has the aura of a proletarian version of the crucifixion.

Gold began working on *Jews without Money* as early as 1917 in the sense of using autobiographical experiences on which to build fictional episodes. Versions cropped up in *American Mercury, Menorah Journal,* and the *New Masses.* The appearance of a heavily revised *Jews without Money* thirteen years later coincided with the onset of the Great Depression, as well as a swing to the Left among the intelligentsia. Moreover, when the book version was published, Gold was winning notoriety for his sensational October 22, 1930, attack on the writings of Thornton Wilder in the *New Republic.* Gold's strategy in this review essay was to assume the voice of the rebel opposing the genteel hegemony that he associates with Wilder's work. In particular, Gold singles out Ivy League patrician writers for vitriolic criticism. Gold's view is that everything about Wilder's artistic vision is false in regard to expressing the social reality of the United States. Gold's position is one of rejecting fanciful or introspective literature; he believes the writer of the 1930s has a mandatory commitment to address the harsh and concrete realities of working-class life. Gold is particularly irked by Wilder's style of writing; he finds an offensive contradiction between the paltriness of Wilder's themes and the solemnity with which he treats them.

At the identical moment that Gold contested Wilder, a controversy about the rise of "proletarian literature" was gaining momentum in the Left and liberal press. Although Gold's personal work record was more bohemian than proletarian, and the characters in *Jews without Money* were mostly unemployed or part of the *lumpenproletariat,* Gold was perceived as a national spokesman for the movement. In fact, Gold began to develop both a proletarian theory of art as well as his approach to literary criticism with a 1921 essay called "Toward Proletarian Art," an account of the cultural possibilities of the working class.

In an extravagant and lyrical narrative, Gold proclaims the death of the old culture as part of the apocalyptic paroxysms of the capitalist system. He then prophesizes that, out of the ashes, will ascend a new working class culture. Depicting himself as a voice for the masses, Gold asserts that art should express the experience of workers,

giving form to their daily lives and labor. Proletarian art should also trace the political development of the working class and point the way forward. By the time Gold published a follow-up essay in 1930 on "Proletarian Realism," he was persuaded that proletarian literature was a fact—a spreading worldwide phenomenon that was destined to be the art of the future. All of these contingencies in 1930—the appearance of *Jews without Money,* the radicalization of the intelligentsia, Gold's notorious critique of Wilder, and his association with proletarian literature—combined to transform Gold into one of the most notable literary figures of the early Depression. He was praised that year by novelist Sinclair Lewis in his acceptance speech for the Nobel Prize.

Jews without Money has a complex relation to Gold's life, rendering its genre ambiguous. The earlier published chapters of the previous decade were closer to Gold's factual life, yet he insisted that these excerpts were only fiction. Upon his return from the Soviet Union, Gold undertook substantial revisions of the manuscript. The result was a work with a heightened apportionment of imaginary features, but, at that point, Gold began to contend that the work was mostly nonfiction memoirs. One conspicuous change in the book version is that Gold creates a myth that his father had been a house painter injured in a fall and afflicted with lead poisoning from paint fumes. Another invention concerns a sister, Esther, supposedly one year younger than the protagonist, Mikey; she is killed by a truck while out seeking firewood on a stormy night. A third change is that Gold's earlier versions reveal an attitude toward ghetto culture as stifling and oppressive, while *Jews without Money* celebrates the glories of *Yiddishkeit,* even as Gold acknowledges its insufficiency in dealing with capitalist America. *Jews without Money,* however, is scrupulous in the depiction of Gold's mother, and in capturing Gold's own religious quest for a savior that he ultimately locates in the dream of a working-class revolution.

Gold's title, *Jews without Money,* functions as a kind of answer to the antisemitic epithets, "rich Jews" and "Jewish bankers." These appellations were part of standard right-wing ideology of his time, but the Nazi movement was promoting them most aggressively. Gold was making an ideological intervention by trying to get into circulation a different perspective on Jews. Beyond that, Gold's title affirms a legitimate terrain for proletarian literature because "Jews without money" refers to proletarian Jews—laborers, the unemployed, or insecure middle-class Jews. As a consequence, Gold is very class-conscious throughout the book, regularly counterposing two types of Jews—a Jew without money, in contrast to a Jew who has money, or is devoted to money, or is bought out by money.

Gold's proletarian outlook is also inscribed in his class view of what constitutes culture. A great proportion of the book is devoted to excavating and re-creating Yiddish or Yiddish American folk culture as justifiable material for artistic representation. Although that culture may be characterized as *shtetl* in its European origins, the rubric "Jews without money" enables Gold to fuse transplanted rural, village Jews and dwellers of the urban ghetto. Moreover, the culture valorized by Gold is an oral culture, and the site of its expression in his book is usually the family gathering or a large group of people sitting around the table listening to Gold's father, who is the storyteller.

Gold planned several book-length projects in the aftermath of this initial success, including a volume of portraits of Jewish life in Palestine and the ghettos of Europe. Yet he was incapable of sustaining his focus, in part because of the instability of his personal life, but also due to the onset of undiagnosed diabetes. Writing regular columns for the Communist press provided Gold with a small but regular income that he supplemented with speaking engagements, but his creative energies were drained from larger projects. In 1936 he married a young French woman, Elizabeth Boussus, and later that year they started a family. In 1940 he underwent hospitalization and his diabetes was diagnosed as severe.

Although a loyal Communist, Gold was initially traumatized by news of the 1939 Non-Aggression Pact between the Soviet Union and Nazi Germany. Nevertheless, he soon began publishing denunciations of writers alienated from the Communist Party by the Pact. These comprised *The Hollow Men* (1940), one of his weakest creations. In 1947, the Gold family relocated to Europe, in part motivated by the Cold War atmosphere but also to allow their children to grow familiar with his wife's side of the family in France. The Golds returned in the spring of 1950, but the Communist Party was so depleted that the *Daily Worker* could no longer afford financial support for his column. Nearing sixty, Gold tried sundry odd jobs while his literary output dwindled. Ultimately, in 1956 Gold, his wife, and their youngest son followed their older son to San Francisco. Gold spent his closing years writing columns for the West Coast Communist paper, the *People's World,* and the Yiddish Communist paper, *Freiheit.*

Alan M. Wald

References and Further Reading
Bloom, James D. 1992. *Left Letters: The Culture Wars of Mike Gold and Joseph Freeman.* New York: Columbia University Press.
Folsom, Michael. 1972. *Mike Gold: A Literary Anthology.* New York: International Publishers.
Rubin, Rachel. 2000. *Jewish Gangsters of Modern Literature.* Urbana: University of Illinois Press.
Wald, Alan M. 2002. *Exiles from a Future Time: The Forging of the Mid-Twentieth Century Literary Left.* Chapel Hill: University of North Carolina Press.

Emma Lazarus (1849–1887)

Poet, Essayist, Proto-Zionist

Emma Lazarus was born in 1849 to a distinguished Jewish family (German on her mother's side and Sephardic on her father's side) in New York City. Her mother's and father's families could both trace their presence in the city to the years before the American Revolution. By the late 1870s and 1880s it seemed that Lazarus, now viewed by many as the most important early figure in the Jewish American literary canon, might gain entrance into the elite realm of America's Protestant literary culture. Robert Browning, Walt Whitman, Henry James, and Ralph Waldo Emerson (the latter two among her many ardent correspondents) had all praised her translations of Heine as well as her own verse that appeared in *Lippincott's* and the *Century.* She published her first volume of poetry in 1866 at the age of seventeen. But she was fated to be memorialized exclusively for "The New Colossus," her great paean to (or plea for) American largesse, and by Jewish Americans for the few years of poetry, essay, and political activity dedicated to their cause. Representative of this trend, Henrietta Szold, founder of Hadassah, hailed her as the most distinguished literary figure produced by American Jewry, and possibly the most eminent poet among Jews since Heine—although Heine converted to Catholicism. In the mid-twentieth century a highly regarded Jewish scholar, Solomon Liptzin, helped secure her reputation, claiming that in the crucial years of the late nineteenth century "only a single Jewish

American Jewish poet, essayist, and proto-Zionist Emma Lazarus. (Library of Congress)

writer, the Sephardic poetess Emma Lazarus, succeeded in groping her way during solitary and tragic years from early ignorance and indifference to profound insight and prophetic vision. Phoenix-like, the tired heiress of Colonial Jewry arose resplendent in fresh vigor and heralded a heroic resurgence of her ancient people" (Liptzin 1958).

Certainly Lazarus demonstrated previously unimagined ways for a Jewish woman to participate in American public culture. Nevertheless, her achievements have been largely forgotten; late twentieth-century scholars have noted Lazarus's contribution to Jewish American history condescendingly, at best. Though Lazarus played a significant proto-Zionist role, even major studies of American Zionism ignore her. By far the most influential Jewish American literary figure of the nineteenth century, Lazarus's reflections on the status of the Jew in gentile society and on the question of the Jews' return to Palestine offer a rich literary and historical context for examining later imaginative responses to Zionism in America.

Yet Lazarus was also ambivalent about her Jewishness. Her 1871 volume, *Admetus and Other Poems*, contains no mention of Judaism and sits firmly within traditional Western culture, but a volume issued a few years before her death, *Songs of a Semite* (1882), is generally acclaimed as the birth volume of Jewish American poetry. In marked contrast to the poet's earlier silence, it deals exclusively with Jewish identity, albeit as a dormant phenomenon situated in the past, awaiting political redemption. Ironically, Lazarus often drew her discursive authority from a religious tradition from which she felt radically estranged.

Above all, Lazarus succeeded in claiming a privileged cultural position as the re-animator of a tradition and a people in decline. Her eloquent representations of ancient "Hebrews" and the suggestion that the "Holy Land" might be resurrected as a contemporary homeland paved the way for later generations of American Zionists. Although she repudiated both Reform Judaism and the old religious rituals of the persecuted Jews arriving from Eastern Europe, Lazarus seems to embrace a notion of Jewishness as thoroughly secular, enlightened, and emancipated, suggesting that ancient myths might be recast to serve as a vital wellspring for the aesthetics and politics of the Jewish present. Reading Lazarus as the harbinger of the modern American ethnic Jew, one recognizes the competing claims of an insider and outsider sensibility; her lyrics convey much about the imagination required for the journey from the humiliation of dispersal to the sense of belonging provided by Jewish and American identities.

Anticipating the cultural strategies of Horace Kallen in a later generation, Lazarus embraced ethnicity, not religion, as the key to Jewish survival. Since her time, this has proven to be the most congenial way for translating the "Jew" into terms that are palatable in the American milieu. Jewish ethnicity, if it were to have any tangible substance, would have to be linked to a discourse about distinct origins and homeland. Hence, Lazarus's prose and lyrics must be understood in relation to the commitment of nineteenth-century nationalist movements to physical boundaries as well as to linking the notion of "race" with organicity and authenticity. Lazarus's identification of contemporary Jews with popular images of a distant past was also influenced by a Christian discourse that associated Judaism not with living Jews, but with a distant time and place—the Holy Land of "Bible days."

Lazarus's poetry and prose reflected Christian America's increasing interest in Palestine in the late nineteenth century. Her works exhibit a canny awareness of (and contributed to) her age's dichotomizing tendencies, particularly in contrasting the martial Jew of antiquity to the hopelessly decadent and passive Jew of European culture. This ethos, combined with an awareness of the widely held Christian millennial dreams of a reborn Jewish nation, enabled Lazarus to create a bridge between Protestant America and the visionary politics of twentieth-century American Zionism. Lazarus's experience anticipates writers of later decades who were still beleaguered by the challenge to articulate a hyphenated identity as Americans and ambivalent about what lies on either side of the hyphen.

Ranen Omer-Sherman

References and Further Reading

Antler, Joyce. 1997. *The Journey Home: Jewish Women and the American Century.* New York: Free Press.

Friedman, Saul S. 1989. "Emma Lazarus: American Poet and Zionist." In *Women in History, Literature and the Arts: A Festschrift for Hildegard Schnuttgen in Honor of Her Thirty Years of Outstanding Service at Youngstown State University,* 220–246. Youngstown, OH: Youngstown State University Press.

Liptzin, Solomon. 1958. *Generation of Decision: Jewish Rejuvenation in America.* New York: Bloch.

Omer-Sherman, Ranen. 2002. *Diaspora and Zionism in Jewish American Literature.* Hanover, NH: Brandeis University Press/distributed by University Press of New England.

Young, Bette Roth. 1995. *Emma Lazarus in Her World: Life and Letters.* Philadelphia: Jewish Publication Society.

Ludwig Lewisohn (1882–1955)

Novelist and Literary Critic

As novelist, social analyst, literary critic, political polemicist, and Zionist leader, Ludwig Lewisohn's role in America and in Europe during the first half of the twentieth century proved immeasurable. Lewisohn was unrelenting in seeking to breathe new life into an American society suffocated by its puritanical ethos and ethnic prejudices, to deter the Western world from its march toward tyranny, both fascist and Stalinist, and to restore to the Jewish community a sense of identity and spiritual purpose.

The product of a highly assimilated Berlin Jewish family, Lewisohn was brought to a tiny South Carolina village in 1890, following the failure of his father's inherited clothing manufacturing business. His mother's brother had preceded them to the tiny backwater of St. Matthews, where a small Jewish community had resided since just before the Civil War. Two years later, following his father's second failure at running a small general store, he and his parents moved to Charleston, where Lewisohn would achieve fame as the high school valedictorian. At nineteen, he was graduated from the College of Charleston, earning both BA and MA degrees in English literature. During these years, he had lived as a Methodist, teaching Sunday school and participating in the church's youth activities. Yet, upon graduation, he failed to win a teaching position in a local private academy because of his Jewish background.

Attendance in graduate school, planned for the following year, now seemed hopeless, but after a bitter and solitary year, financial assistance from family and a few local backers enabled him to enroll in the doctoral program in English literature at Columbia University in 1902. New York's electrifying cultural mix, together with new friendships and his first sexual encounters, male and female, heightened his inner conflict over being Jewish in an unaccepting and restrictive America into which he had so desperately sought full and unambiguous admission. Repeatedly warned by his Columbia professors that, no matter how hard he tried to move past it, his identification by others in academia as a Jew offered him little chance, for "racial" reasons, of an appointment as an English instructor at an American university, Lewisohn abandoned graduate education before completing his dissertation. Lewisohn considered this determination to preserve English and American literature for the carriers of Anglo-Saxon "blood" emblematic of the closed society that needed to be changed.

Further literary disappointments and his being fired from an editorial position at Doubleday, Page for labor organizing brought him home to Charleston. Within weeks of his arrival, Mary Arnold Crocker, an occasional playwright twenty years his senior, whom he had met while his life was unraveling, followed him south and soon married the lost young Lewisohn. Their age difference, and his growing Jewish consciousness in the years ahead, ultimately doomed his relationship with his non-Jewish wife. But in the early days of their marriage, he struggled to support them both, living with his parents and teaching adult education classes at the college (which in 1914 granted him an honorary D.Litt.), all the while still trying his hand at writing plays and short stories.

Failure to achieve financial independence forced them back to New York in the fall of 1907. He had, however, recently completed a novel, *The Broken Snare.* Brought to the attention of Theodore Dreiser, it was published the following year. The story of a young woman's intellectual and emotional development, it marked for Lewisohn a declaration of war against the forbidding, still very Victorian, society whose puritanical sexual and social mores, institutionalized in its marital laws, were throttling him.

With his book harshly criticized back home as scandalous, he felt even more determined to pursue his plan to create literary works that would tear down this restrictive structure. Yet the next two years brought only poverty, despair, and frequent, albeit momentary, thoughts of suicide. Only an unexpected appointment to the German Department at the University of Wisconsin (1910), arranged by a friend, broke this cycle. Lewisohn's reputation as a writer grew when, a year after his first novel appeared, he published a one-act dramatic poem, *A Night in Alexandria,* that also received critical acclaim. By then, his list of credits included numerous (often pseudonymous) short stories in such journals as *Cavalier, All-Story,* and *Town Topics;* articles on literary topics in *Sewanee Review, Current Literature,* and *Forum;* and a third book, *German Style, An Introduction to the Study of German Prose* (1910), which brought him to the attention of the scholarly world.

After only one year at Wisconsin, Lewisohn accepted a similar post at Ohio State University. The lure of a slightly higher salary and the promise of a change that might ease the tensions that had developed between him and Mary, often exacerbated by the presence of her children, did not, however, meet his expectations. His mother's untimely death from cancer in 1914 and his father's subsequent mental breakdown, with Lewisohn now caring for him, only deepened his domestic chaos. Still, he enjoyed both teaching and writing, and he was earning a reputation as a compelling thinker and orator that would outlast his death.

In the first of the eleven volumes of the *Dramatic Works of Gerhart Hauptmann* (1912–1919), which he edited, several of which he translated, he promoted his own views on literary realism. He was determined to expose the true nature of the individual's daily struggle for sustenance and for joy in a difficult world, a subject he felt had been largely ignored by many prominent authors. In his study of the *Modern Drama* (1915), he developed his ideas

more fully, condemning the dominant puritanical morality of America even more strongly than before. He extended this critique in *The Spirit of Modern German Literature* (1916) and praised the literary realism emerging in the land of his birth.

As Lewisohn began to examine his German roots, he began to find a positive element in his Jewish past as well. Though largely cut off from it by his father's total rejection of Jewish tradition, he had learned some rudimentary practices from his mother, the daughter of an itinerant Reform rabbi. In violation of her husband's demands that she cease all such activities, each Friday evening she and her son would go to a corner of their tiny apartment to light the Sabbath candles—even though it was she who had placed him in the Methodist church as a way to Americanize him. By college, he had internalized Methodism's religious and social teachings; yet memories of these earlier days survived. Social and professional ostracism dredged them up from the depths into which he had buried them. There are already hints of this in his writings while still at college. *The Broken Snare* can be read as a Jewish-based critique of what Lewisohn identified as the Puritan ethos of America. The frontispiece, "Our soul is escaped as a bird out of the snare of the fowlers. The snare is broken, and we are escaped"—is a quote from Psalm 124, which begins, "Let Israel now sing."

The death of Lewisohn's mother brought this inner conflict to a head as his emotions, beginning in 1912, swung from liberation to confusion and back again. It took three years to get past this state, but, in 1915, he had sufficiently settled the matter of living in two worlds—one secular, centered largely in European literature, and the other focused increasingly on the Jewishness that was becoming an ever-deepening part of his identity. He soon found himself lecturing to Ohio State's nascent Menorah Society and choosing to translate David Pinski's Yiddish work, *The Treasure,* for publication.

With America's entry into the Great War in 1917, Lewisohn's academic career came suddenly to an end when he became one of many of German background who were dismissed from their posts in a surge of hyperpatriotism and war fever. Less than neutral because of his affinity for German culture, for some years he had been fighting against the forces that he feared would reject all things German and, with them, the literary realism that was central to the cultural struggle he had joined. More the internationalist than a Germanophile, he had openly opposed the chauvinism that had now overtaken America, and he paid a severe price for his opposition.

Returning to New York, he was pleased, at least, with his release from teaching responsibilities and excited to have left the Midwest with its extreme isolationism, its overly zealous patriotism, and its intolerance of difference. Still, he could not ignore the current atmosphere, and so, under intense pressure from his publisher, the study of German and French poetry on which he had been working became the *Poets of Modern France* (1918). The remainder, with additions, would appear years later as *Modern German Poetry* (1925).

Lewisohn survived by writing articles for the *Internationalist, Forum, Bookman, Smart Set,* and *The Nation,* along with translations from German and a brief stint as a Latin instructor, until Oswald Villard, publisher of *The Nation,* asked him to become its drama critic and fiction editor. Before he left *The Nation* in 1924, he had become associate editor. Among his closest associates during these years were Theodore Dreiser, Sinclair Lewis, Horace Liveright, Edgar Lee Masters, H. L. Mencken, Upton Sinclair, and Carl and Mark Van Doren. As a perceptive critic, he championed the Yiddish, black, and avant-garde theater, and he promoted European authors, some of whose works of literary naturalism he helped to bring out in translation. *The Drama and the Stage* (1922) attested to Lewisohn's significant role as a critical voice in the theater of his age.

That same year Lewisohn published the work for which he is best known, *Up Stream,* which was both greatly praised and condemned for its grating honesty as an account of American society, as seen by an outsider. While Brander Matthews, Lewisohn's former teacher at Columbia, denounced him in the *New York Times* as one of "a militant group of un-Americanized aliens, loudly proclaiming that they and they alone are Americans," the Jewish novelist and short story writer of the Lower East Side, Anzia Yezierska, found his work to be for "us newer Americans . . . not merely a book. It is a vision, revelation. It is our struggles, our hopes, our aspirations and our failures made articulate. It is the cry of young America to old America . . . a dynamic protest against the sanctification of a priestcraft in education, a revolt against the existence of an Anglo-Saxon intellectual aristocracy in a country that is the gathering together of peoples from every corner of the earth" (Yezierska 1922). As Lewisohn himself had

written, "Among the masses of our countrymen I see no stirring, no desire to penetrate beyond fixed names to living things, no awakening from the spectral delusions among which they pursue their aimless business and their sapless pleasures. But the critical spirit that is also the creative spirit has risen among us, and it has arisen, naturally and inevitably, in the form of a protest and rebellion. Life among us is ugly and mean and, above all things, false in its assumptions and measures. Somehow we must break these shackles and flee and emerge into some beyond of sanity, of a closer contact with reality, of nature and of truth" (*Up Stream* 1922).

Lewisohn's troubled marriage into which he had been locked for nearly two decades was proof enough for him of these unnatural "Puritan" constraints. Somehow, he had to break with it. *Don Juan* (1923), a novel he had worked on for some time, announced his intent to end this arrangement. In the struggle between a tyrannical legal system and personal freedom, there could be no compromise. Lewisohn's growing affection for a young woman twenty years his junior was sufficient proof of this. An aspiring opera singer, Thelma Spear had sought him out, hoping his support would help her career. He, desperate for change, infused their friendship with the unreasonable hope of renewal. Endorsing the artist's right to absolute freedom in a collection of his essays the following spring (1924), he fled with her to Europe, where they remained for a decade.

In 1922, Lewisohn began to speak openly of his Jewish identity, calling upon others to affirm their similar deepest sense of self. It was a short leap to becoming a committed Zionist, and when Chaim Weizmann, the head of the World Zionist Organization (WZO), asked him in late 1923 to conduct a secret fact-finding mission in Eastern Europe and Palestine, his hoped-for departure from Mary and the state's grip became a reality. He and Thelma left for Europe the following year. After completing his work for the WZO, Lewisohn returned to Paris, only to learn that their passports had been revoked because they had falsified their visa applications by claiming to be married. It would be ten years before he would be allowed to return to the United States, and fifteen years before Mary consented to a divorce.

The fruitful decade in Europe began soon after his return to Paris with a book entitled *Israel.* More than a summary of his findings, it was also a cry for Jewish renewal.

Still, the spiritual return for which he called was not necessarily to traditional Jewish thought and practice. Everywhere Lewisohn traveled, he had encountered looming threats to the Jewish people—whether through pogrom or assimilation. Lewisohn knew there could be no spiritual life for Jews without the existence of a Jewish community—the solitary seeker was not the paradigm of Jewish life. Thus Lewisohn included a plea for Zionism in his call for renewal.

This two-sided struggle remained the chief focus of most of Lewisohn's energy in the decades ahead. In book after book, and in article after article, he emphasized and refined these points, as time proved his fears well founded. At the center of his vision remained his critique of the Christian ethos, so unlike the more natural and healthier approach to life he found in the Jewish tradition. It was the core message of his most influential novel, *The Island Within* (1928), an attack on the urge to assimilate, which could only be counteracted by the embrace of Jewish identity and one's people.

Lewisohn again addressed contemporary threats by challenging the most negative characterization of the Jew in English literature, that of the inhuman, self-serving, greedy moneylender. Imagining the *Last Days of Shylock* (1931), he transformed Shakespeare's stereotype into a heroic figure. In *This People* (1933), a collection of short stories and essays, he provided a historical backdrop to the physical and spiritual threats facing contemporary Jews.

Throughout this period, the question of marriage remained an additional core concern for Lewisohn. Having left his Christian wife for one whose father was Jewish, and having consecrated this union in a religious ceremony in Poland (though not yet civilly divorced from Mary), he felt liberated from the strictures that had bound him. In *Stephen Escott* (1930), he contrasted Jewish with gentile marriage, finding the latter wanting in its denial of the sexual as natural. He elaborated further on this theme in *An Altar in the Fields* (1934), where a Jewish psychiatrist aids a failing Christian marriage by exposing the couple to a life of naturalism as he leads them through Africa.

Despite Lewisohn's growing disillusionment with Western civilization and his deepening commitment to Jewish life, he kept one foot in each. He participated fully in the intellectual life of 1920s and 1930s Paris, with his home becoming one of the primary salons during his decade of residence there. When he traveled to Vienna that

first year, his interest in psychoanalysis led to several sessions with Sigmund Freud, although he later embraced Otto Rank's ideas over those of the master and wrote the introduction to his new friend's *Art and the Artist* (1932). Sharing a love of German culture, he and Thomas Mann established a lifelong friendship based on artistic affinities and a mutual hatred for the growing Nazi threat. Lewisohn also became involved with James Joyce, each sharing his published work with the other. Lewisohn "wrote the initial draft of the 'International Protest,' that argued against the banning . . . of Joyce's *Ulysses* in America." "[A]fter Archibald MacLeish added a more legalistic tone," it appeared on February 2, 1927 (Melnick 1998, I).

Lewisohn's relationship with Edward Titus, the Jewish owner of the Black Manikin Book Shop in Paris and its publishing house, and the husband of Helena Rubenstein who helped finance it, proved to be the most significant of his new friendships. Titus published Lewisohn's most controversial novel, the autobiographical *Case of Mr. Crump* (1926), a retelling of his marital bondage to Mary, which Freud called "an incomparable masterpiece" and which Mann praised as "in the forefront of modern epic narrative" (Melnick 1998, I). It sold over a million copies in a host of languages.

Although long out of the academy, with his energies turned largely to social and political issues, Lewisohn had retained his scholarly interests. Thus in 1932 he published *Expression in America*, a Freudian interpretation of American culture as expressed through its literature from the colonial period to the present, which was praised by reviewers. (He had written it prior to meeting Rank.) In it Lewisohn once again detailed his critique of the unhealthy nature of American life. *Creative America*, an anthology of the works he had analyzed, appeared the next year.

Despite Lewisohn's best efforts, Thelma never succeeded in her career, and she blamed him for her failure. He chronicled the deterioration of their relationship fictionally in *Roman Summer* (1927) and *Golden Vase* (1931). But Lewisohn had long hoped for a son. So, despite the unraveling of their relationship, he and Thelma had a child in 1933, though this only deepened her ambivalence about their marriage.

Their return to the United States a year later, aided by the intercession of influential Jewish leaders, particularly that of Stephen Wise with his friend Franklin Roosevelt, eventually brought an end to the couple's relationship.

While lecturing in upstate New York in 1939, Lewisohn met Edna Manley, a journalist familiar with his work. Lewisohn left Thelma and married within the year—once Mary consented to a divorce and a cash settlement. But this marriage ended after four eventful years that included a protracted custody battle for his son (described in *Haven* [1940]), living in a small colony of writers and artists in Tucson, and working against Nazi Germany and for a Jewish refuge in Palestine, on which he wrote several books and gave innumerable lectures. While still in Europe, he had begun to send warnings home of the growing dangers in Germany. In a prophetic article in *The Nation* (1933), he had written of "Germany's Lowest Depths," only to see Germany fall deeper into its chasm of horror. And when the British continued to keep Palestine closed to Hitler's victims, he gave a full account of the disastrous voyage of the refugee ship *Struma* in a novel, *Breathe Upon These* (1944).

Although his relationship with the Zionists had cooled because of the fear that his marital problems would reflect badly on their efforts, the growing need for his eloquent and passionate voice saw his return to the ranks of their leadership, culminating in his position as the editor of the Zionist Organization of America's journal, *New Palestine,* in 1944. His four years in that role were the most crucial in twentieth-century Jewish history, and his voice a key part of the fight for Jewish survival.

In 1948, Brandeis University invited Lewisohn to become its first full professor. At age sixty-six, with an appointment in comparative literature (and later as university librarian), he found himself, for the first time, teaching the courses he had hoped to present more than forty years earlier. It was Lewisohn who helped to bring other distinguished but similarly barred Jewish faculty to the campus as well as much financial support to the fledgling Jewish university. Still, he argued for a greater emphasis on Jewishness at the school and was in constant conflict with its administration.

Never content to play a limited role in the world, Lewisohn continued his tireless schedule of nationwide lecture tours and writing, now mostly on Jewish issues. With the decimation of European Jewry, he looked to America for a rebirth of Jewish life, stressing the need for an end to assimilation through the education of the coming generations. Still the European, however, he gave what energy remained to the translation and promotion of refugee Jewish writers into English, both to help them and to bring this lost world to those who knew so little of what had been destroyed. In the midst of all this activity, he died suddenly on December 31, 1955.

Ralph Melnick

References and Further Reading
Melnick, Ralph. 1998. *The Life and Work of Ludwig Lewisohn.* 2 Vols. Detroit, MI: Wayne State University Press.
Yezierska, Anzia. 1922. "Mr. Lewisohn's *Up Stream.*" *New York Times* (April 23).

Bernard Malamud (1914–1986)

Novelist

Winner of the Pulitzer Prize and two National Book Awards, Bernard Malamud was one of the most important American Jewish writers. He disliked the "Jewish" appellation, as he felt it reductive: "I'm an American, I'm a Jew, and I write for all men" (Lasher 1991). However, his best writing focuses on Jews. When he writes of other groups—Italians, African Americans, WASPs—a certain edge is missing: consciousness of a long history, frequently laden with suffering, and the bittersweet humor and folklore that accompanied it. His Jews and Jewishness are metaphors for humanity, and he has said that the Jew is a symbol "of the tragic experience of man existentially. I try to see the Jew as universal man. Every man is a Jew though he may not know it" (Lasher 1991). Transforming selfishness into altruism and love is his central concern in what are essentially tests of morality. If a character learns correctly from suffering, what may ensue is acceptance of responsibility for others and a moral obligation to humanity. For Malamud, this is a type of secular redemption.

The Natural (1952), his first novel, provides only a limited sense of these concerns. There are no Jewish characters, and the protagonist Roy Hobbs does not possess the necessary vision to develop morally. A baseball novel, Malamud overloads the game and characters with biblical, Arthurian, fertility, Grail, hero, and kingship myths, the weight of which they are ill fitted to bear. However, his basic theme of suffering is very much present, and we can

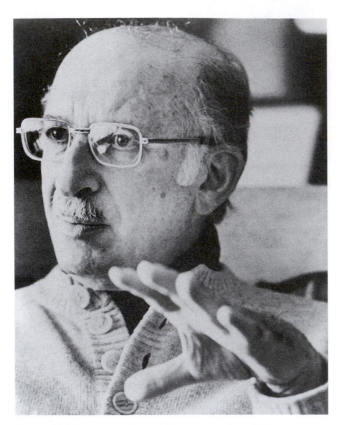

Bernard Malamud, novelist and short story writer. (Library of Congress)

see an early version of what will develop into a process of salvation for the protagonist.

The Assistant (1957) is Malamud's best novel and sets the pattern of *bildungsroman* (novels of formation and development) that would become his basic form. Morris Bober, the protagonist, has learned from suffering and is able to teach Frank Alpine the value of selflessness in life. Frank moves from petty criminality to absorbing Morris's definition of Jewish Law, which is to be honest and decent to others. However, Malamud has secularized and universalized the Jewish moral code so that being a Jew means being a moral man. That Frank, a Roman Catholic, is circumcised and becomes a Jew at the end of the novel is no surprise: in Malamud's sense he is already a Jew. The failing grocery store in which the tale is set becomes a training ground, almost a monastery, for moral development.

The novel is only partly realistic, as there are elements of fable and fantasy in the characters and the setting, a timeless poverty-stricken area. It is populated by characters distinguished by their speech patterns. Like Mark Twain's use of dialects in *Adventures of Huckleberry Finn*, this use of

largely Jewish and ethnic speech is part of the American literary tradition. There is an underlying irony that pervades the novel, heightening the sense of an unsure, perhaps treacherous, world where the obvious may not be the best, and achievement and success are not what is of most worth.

A New Life (1961) reflects Malamud's twelve years teaching at what was then Oregon State College. His first politically aware novel, the fearful effects of 1950s McCarthyism and the Cold War are seen in relation to the mythology of the American West as paradise. The protagonist, a Jew whose Jewishness is seen only in terms of his outsidedness and liberalism, learns that the beauty of the region's nature is not shared by its people, who are small-minded and suspicious of change. While Levin does not succeed in instigating major changes in the college, he does develop through love and selflessness a new life of responsibility and commitment, though in an ironically self-sacrificial form. As in *The Assistant*, Malamud presents his secular salvation as somewhat masochistic; that is, success in life is not to be seen in terms of personal comfort or even happiness, but in moral responsibility.

The Fixer (1966) was awarded both a Pulitzer Prize and Malamud's second National Book Award (the first was for his 1958 short story collection, *The Magic Barrel*). Using historical accounts of the imprisonment and trial of Mendel Beilis, a poor Jew in czarist Russia, Malamud dramatizes the slow growth in altruism, morality, and self-understanding due to the suffering of his character Yakov Bok (Bok means goat), until Bok can feel at one not only with the Jewish people but with suffering humanity. Creating Bok's thoughts in his cell, something not part of the historical record, we find that freedom here, as in the previous three novels, consists of choosing selflessness over self-centeredness and escaping from metaphorical, personal prisons more than literal ones. Bok's growth develops through his suffering, which permits him to understand the tragedies in the human condition.

Pictures of Fidelman: An Exhibition (1969), Malamud's first long comic work, is a collection comprising a short story cycle, six stories that can both stand on their own and serve as chapters of a novel. The protagonist Arthur Fidelman is a picaro, a character who must create his identity from a plethora of experiences. He learns to love and give of himself through comic experiences, largely farce and slapstick. Incompetent as an artist, Fidelman tries different forms and methods, but his lack of genuine ability condemns him to failure. For Malamud, this artistic failure is less important than Fidelman's growth in love and success as a caring human being, realizing that his real worth should not be defined in terms of artistic ability.

The Tenants (1971) treats a specific social issue, the conflict between Jews and African Americans in the late 1960s, and draws conclusions from it for the future. Each protagonist holds the stereotype that each group has of the other, with writing—art—being presented as a possible but ultimately failed way to bridge the gulf between them. Harry and Willy are tested for their ability to develop self-lessness and compassion; in the end both fail the test as neither is able to move beyond his own self-interest. Both writers hope that, if they can complete their novels, they can complete themselves; however, personal knowledge must come first, and their works, like themselves, remain incomplete. Both use art as a substitute for genuine human feeling: Harry to find love, Willy to justify himself as a black man and create an identity he can live with.

As in previous novels, the prison motif is very important here. Malamud's characters have been imprisoned by their pasts, goals, mistakes, or personality flaws. In some works there is a literal structure that has symbolized this imprisonment: the store in *The Assistant,* the cell in *The Fixer,* and the tenement in *The Tenants,* which keeps out much of the real world. For Malamud, a character must grow to understand the nature of his prison, which is the first step in breaking the bars.

The novel mixes realism with fantasy and contains three endings, Malamud having stated that one would not do, as the result of the unpredictability of black–white relations in America. It could end in reconciliation, in violence, or in each just having understanding and "mercy" for the other. The thrust of the novel is, however, toward the violent ending, Malamud's optimism being hardly visible here.

Malamud stated that, as he was approaching sixty when he began *Dubin's Lives* (1979), he asked himself what he had learned by this point; what had his life's experiences taught him? William Dubin is Jewish, but Jewishness is not important in the novel. In thematic terms, there is a continuity of theme and characterization with his previous work: the protagonist must move from self-containment to an expansion of the heart that encompasses others. He only partially succeeds in this, but does develop further than Harry Lesser in *The Tenants.*

Like Lesser, Dubin, a biographer, believes that he can learn about life by writing, in his case about other people's lives. He hopes that by writing biographies of Thoreau and D. H. Lawrence he will complete incomplete parts of himself: learn about nature, the physical and instinctual, about living life to the full and seizing the day. Again, like Lesser, Dubin is continually startled by actual life, preferring the control over life that writing gives him.

Because of what he is, Dubin's controlling mind does not permit him to benefit fully from what he learns of Lawrence's ideas, as awareness of the force of passion, spontaneity, and blood energies, largely engendered through his adultery with Fanny Bick, becomes burdened by the weight of morality. In the end, Dubin learns little and is certainly not redeemed in Malamud's secular sense.

The novel is about a failed marriage and all that flows from that. The marriage has not permitted either Kitty or Dubin to grow, and the marriages in the other novels are not presented as creating or likely to create happiness. Like the men, women in Malamud's novels frequently have personality flaws and, like Pauline's in *A New Life,* Kitty Dubin's are presented through the eyes of her husband. Fanny Bick, Dubin's mistress, does develop and provide a touchstone for judging his limitations, which include difficulty in conveying emotion. Like some characters from Malamud's previous novels, Fanny takes on the role of assistant to the protagonist, being the first female to do so, and providing a basis for Malamud's most sexually explicit novel, where sexuality is essential to full human development.

Stylistically, *Dubin's Lives* is a throwback to *A New Life* in its conventional structure, which eschews fantasy and relies on realism. One comes to it with some surprise after jungle-like apartments in *The Tenants,* Fidelman's sometimes surrealistic world, and Bok's dreams and visions in *The Fixer.* What is consistent in style is Malamud's use of a concealed third-person omniscient narrator who, while standing outside and above the action, merges with Dubin's thoughts so subtly that the transition from one voice to the other is almost seamless. In his next novel, Malamud will move firmly back into the fabulous.

In *God's Grace* (1982) Malamud returns to fantasy, in this instance to a beast fable, where monkeys speak English and face "human" issues. Previously, he used this form in two short stories, "The Jewbird" and "Talking Horse." As in the stories, the negative aspects of humanity are stressed as much as the nature of the animals. God is a character who states that He had not foreseen how evil humankind would be, so allowed humanity to destroy itself through nuclear war.

Calvin Cohn, the protagonist and last man on earth, argues with God like Job, wondering why He had to give humans such destructive traits. Free will was a great gift, but humanity is limited by its God-given constitution. Thus, Malamud discusses the theme of good and evil, with the essential nature of humanity a central issue. Will it be possible, Cohn wonders, to educate the chimpanzees in ethics so that they may create a better society than the now extinguished *homo sapiens* did? This proves illusory, as Cohn's attempts to develop in the chimps the best human qualities ignore their nature. This novel shows the level of pessimism that Malamud has reached, despite George the Gorilla, who says *kaddish* for Cohn and will carry on a Jewish code of morality. In the end, human beings are just a variety of primate, whose bestial qualities remain stubbornly resistant to change. Cohn should have listened more closely to the chimps, who at least did not destroy their own species.

Malamud wrote over fifty short stories during his lifetime, stating that he used them as laboratories for characters and ideas that would be more fully developed in novels. The short story did, however, provide a form for some of his most effective writing. Before *The Assistant*, Malamud wrote nine stories set in small, prison-like stores, in each of which it is not the goods sold that are important but the need to provide understanding and compassion for suffering human beings. The protagonists frequently grow in the course of the tales to illustrate the altruism of which humanity is capable. Those protagonists who do not develop are not "redeemed" by love.

He wrote eleven "Italian" stories, five of which appeared in the short story cycle novel, *Pictures of Fidelman*. Although the setting is not claustrophobic New York stores, the characters still suffer, need to be understood, and many must learn to "give credit" to others for their humanity. Again, these are themes that would be further developed in novels.

Some of Malamud's best short stories rely on a mixture of realism and fantasy including "The Magic Barrel," "Angel Levine," "Take Pity," "The Jewbird," "Idiots First," "The Silver Crown," and "Talking Horse." The tensions created between the commonplace and the fantastic, with the former creating an air of believability for the latter and blurring the distinctions between them, are particularly effective in elucidating Malamud's central themes of the real but almost transcendent nature of compassion, love, and selflessness.

He also wrote a few impressive realistic stories that stress sociopolitical themes: "The German Refugee" and "Man in the Drawer." Later tales written in the 1980s, toward the end of his life, they are not as effective as his earlier ones, despite his attempts at finding a new form, which he called fictive biography. This can be seen in "In Kew Gardens," about Virginia Woolf, and "Alma Redeemed," about Alma Mahler.

Considering the stories he wrote over forty-five years, one can perceive a continuity of concerns: the importance of responsibility and commitment; suffering that may spur a character to acts of selflessness; a strong moralistic tone; imprisonment of characters in past limitations; and problems of communicating deeply felt needs. Malamud was an accomplished short story writer.

His final work was published in 1989, three years after his death. He was working on chapter seventeen of a novel entitled *The People*, modeled on the history of the Nez Percé Indian tribe and Chief Joseph's failed attempts to save their lands and his people from annihilation by the rapacious white man. The Jewish protagonist Yozip, later Jozip, is kidnapped by the People and eventually becomes their chief. There are parallels with the implied destruction of the Jewish people in the Holocaust in *The Fixer*. For reasons of self-interest, the majority in both texts consider the powerless group inferior, with both Yakov Bok and Jozip having been chosen as unwilling spokesmen for the oppressed.

Because Malamud considered revision essential, this incomplete, unrevised portion of a novel cannot provide a basis for judging his artistry, although evidence of his craftsmanship is visible even here. To Malamud, since the U.S. government lacks all conscience in its relations with the Indians, only desirous of stealing their land and taking no account of them as human beings, communication between the two is impossible. This is another statement of Malamud's belief in the importance of understanding and compassion between people.

In notes Malamud left for the unwritten four chapters, we see that he planned for Jozip to go to night school, become a lawyer, and try to help the Indians, now his people, through other means. One can see possible redemption for Jozip but only catastrophe for the People. This ending reminds one of those of *The Tenants* and *God's Grace,* both of which present hope if one searches for it, but perhaps the search is too difficult and the results not entirely satisfactory.

Malamud was not in favor of suffering; however, since it exists, he felt it should be used as an aid to moral growth. His optimism lay in the belief that suffering could lead to the realization of the best that is in a character. Although his work became more pessimistic as time passed, it retained the possibility of affirmation of life for those who were able to see altruism, compassion, and love as the bases of existence.

Edward A. Abramson

References and Further Reading

Abramson, Edward A. 1993. *Bernard Malamud Revisited.* New York: Twayne Publishers.

Alter, Iska. 1981. *The Good Man's Dilemma: Social Criticism in the Fiction of Bernard Malamud.* New York: AMS Press.

Avery, Evelyn, ed. 2001. *The Magic Worlds of Bernard Malamud.* Albany: State University of New York Press.

Bloom, Harold, ed. 1986. *Bernard Malamud.* New York: Chelsea House Publishers.

Helterman, Jeffrey. 1985. *Understanding Bernard Malamud.* Columbia: University of South Carolina Press.

Hershinow, Sheldon J. 1980. *Bernard Malamud.* New York: Frederick Ungar.

Lasher, Lawrence, ed. 1991. *Conversations with Bernard Malamud.* Jackson: University Press of Mississippi.

Rajagopalachari, M. 1988. *Theme of Compassion in the Novels of Bernard Malamud.* New Delhi, India: Prestige Books.

Salzberg, Joel, ed. 1987. *Critical Essays on Bernard Malamud.* Boston: G. K. Hall & Co.

Solotaroff, Robert. 1989. *Bernard Malamud: A Study of the Short Fiction.* Boston: Twayne Publishers.

David Mamet (b. 1947)

Playwright, Screenwriter, Film Director

The Pulitzer Prize–winning playwright, screenwriter, and film director David Mamet has claimed, "I have always felt like an outsider," and it is this that his provocative work—with its focus on small-time crooks and disenfranchised

men and women—has long emphasized. His art, however, has been a search for ways to overcome this condition, which originated in "not feeling sufficiently Jewish or American, . . . a problem of reconciliation and self-worth" (Brewer 1993). But, in spite of a renewed commitment to Judaism over the last fifteen years, Mamet's aesthetic (and political) view is still one of danger and betrayal for Jews everywhere.

In a career that now spans more than thirty years, Mamet has played many roles: dramatist, screenwriter, essayist, novelist, teacher, poet, children's author, director, and *artiste provocateur* challenging the status quo. But from the beginning, his work engaged questions of Jewish identity and action. His early play *Marranos* (1975), for example, dramatizes Jewish family life in fourteenth-century Portugal as a family, unmasked as Jews, prepares to flee to Holland. Survival in a non-Jewish world is its concern: "to cope" as a Jew, the grandfather explains to his grandson in the play, "you're going to have to learn to be an actor, and you don't get a rehearsal." It is a lesson Mamet himself has followed, sidestepping persecution through an aggressive persona and often blunt language. In *Marranos* and in later works, like his play *The Old Neighborhood* and his film *Homicide,* Mamet confronts the challenges of antisemitism and anxiety over assimilation. In his prose, however, he never doubts his Jewishness—his newest work, *Five Cities of Refuge* (2003), weekly exchanges on passages from the Torah with a rabbi, reaffirming his commitment to Jewish study and life.

A good part of Mamet's career seemed accidental: "I became a playwright because I was an actor and I started directing because I wasn't a very good actor and I started writing because I was working with very young actors and there was nothing for them to do" (Schvey 2001). But in works like *On Directing Film* (1991) and *True and False: Heresy and Common Sense for the Actor* (1997), his ideas on acting, directing, and writing are vividly clear. And in his promotion of a theater practice he calls practical aesthetics, represented in *A Practical Handbook for Actors* (1986), he builds confidence in "living truthfully under the imaginary circumstances of the play," a method that has shaped the careers of William H. Macy, Joe Mantegna, and Rebecca Pidgeon, among others (Bruder 1986).

A set of dramatic tensions defined Mamet's early life, beginning with the Russian/Polish Jewish heritage of his parents that they were determined to forget, an intense family life shattered by a bitter divorce, a deep love for his mother despite her volatile temper, and admiration for his father despite his relentless criticism. Further supporting his disrupted family life was "a six-thousand-year-old Jewish tradition of a love of argument," he once declared (Gross 2001). Artistically, there were similar tensions: a desire to act but failure at acting, a need to direct forcing him to write, remarkable success with works that shock, an astonishing body of work based on obscenities and insults, an established theater career curtailed by a desire to make films.

Throughout his life, however, Mamet has found strategies for overcoming these contradictions, located in his use of language and poetic realism, which he shares with the late work of Eugene O'Neill and the plays of Tennessee Williams and Arthur Miller. His confident, if at times strident, authorial voice establishes identities that are never contested in his plays, reinforced by his characters' ceaseless reliance on indecent language. But maintaining the author's voice comes at the cost of the actor's ability to invent. This, however, is a Mamet principle, the result of his training with Sanford Meisner at the Neighborhood Playhouse in New York, where words on the page, not the actor, are important. The rhythm of dramatic speech, and nothing else, *is* the action.

Mamet's strongest feature is his unflinching indictment of cultural hypocrisy—in his dramas concerning greed (*American Buffalo*), materialism (*Glengarry Glenn Ross*), political correctness (*Oleanna*), or sexual exploitation (*Speed-the-Plow*). This is reflected with equal clarity in his films. *Homicide,* for example, condemns antisemitism through the hero/detective Robert Gold's self-discovery of his suppressed Judaism and his determination to solve a hate crime and destroy a neo-Nazi cell. In *Lansky,* a 1999 HBO film starring Richard Dreyfuss, Mamet again explores the ambiguity of Jewish identity, now linked to graft in America, which his latest film, *Spartan* (2004), exploits at the highest and lowest levels of government.

His novel *The Old Religion* (1997) treats similar themes as he challenges the bigotry and antisemitism of the Leo Frank case. Frank, falsely accused in 1913 of the rape and murder of a factory girl in Atlanta, became the focus of American antisemitism. Falsely convicted, he was condemned to death. However, after the governor of Georgia commuted his sentence to life in prison, a mob broke into the prison and lynched him. Presented as an interior monologue, the novel explores the nature of justice and the effort of Frank to comprehend his distorted world. Mamet told an interviewer that, as a Jew, the subject intensely attracted him, just as racial hatred intensely repelled him. A visit to Israel in 2002 reinforced his belief that Jews should never be ashamed of their history or their identity. In Israel, he pridefully witnessed "*actual* Jews, fighting for their country, against both terror and misthought public opinion" (Mamet 2002).

With his fierce language and uncompromising vision of modern life, Mamet has never stopped battling American complacency, presenting social questions as ethical choices, while indicting the moral bankruptcy of his nation. He is a moralist committed, like Ralph Waldo Emerson or Arthur Miller, to shine a laser through the corruption and deceit that have riven America. Judaism is the source of this indignant attitude through its ethical ideals and reliance on advocacy.

Mamet spent his early life in the South Chicago suburb of Flossmoor; at the age of eleven, however, his parents divorced. He continued to live with his mother and sister in the South Shore Highlands area, but when she remarried they moved to the suburb of Olympia Fields. From 1963 to 1965, he lived with his father, a labor lawyer, in the Lincoln Park area of the city. There he attended private school and worked as a busboy at "Second City," where he had his first exposure to professional theater, although as a child he and his sister played Jewish children on television and radio for a series produced by his uncle for the Chicago Board of Rabbis. He later worked at backstage jobs at Hull House Theatre, which produced plays by Pinter, Brecht, and Albee.

From 1965 to 1969, Mamet attended Goddard College in Plainfield, Vermont, a small, experimental liberal arts college that gave no grades and had no requirements. For his senior project, he wrote the "Camel Document," thirty-four "Second-City"–style blackouts and his first attempt at playwriting. While at Goddard, he also wrote first drafts of *Sexual Perversity in Chicago, The Duck Variations,* and *Reunion.* He spent his junior year in New York studying acting at Sanford Meisner's Neighborhood Playhouse, a formative experience because of Meisner's belief that acting should be direct and free of emotional memory, which may corrupt a part. "Acting is doing" was a frequent mantra, which Mamet has applied to his own writing and directing.

After graduating from Goddard, Mamet joined a professional theater company based at McGill University in Montreal and performed in Pinter's *The Homecoming.* A variety of theater jobs followed, including stage-managing the off-Broadway hit, *The Fantastiks.* In the summer of 1970, Mamet worked in a real estate office on the North Side of Chicago, an experience that would affect his presentation of salesmen in *Glengarry Glenn Ross.* In September that year, he became an acting instructor at Marlboro College, Vermont, and directed students in an early version of his play *Lakeboat,* about his experiences as a steward on a cargo boat on Lake Michigan. In 1971, he spent a year as Artist-in-Residence at Goddard College, where he taught acting. While there, he formed the St. Nicholas Theatre company with two students, William H. Macy and Steven Schachter, who would perform the first versions of *Duck Variations* and *Sexual Perversity in Chicago.*

Mamet returned to Chicago in 1972 where *Duck Variations* and a monologue, *Litko,* were performed at the newly formed experimental Body Politic Theatre. Chicago would be his home for the next three years. There he expanded his theater company, which soon began to give acting classes to fund productions. *Sexual Perversity in Chicago,* a satire on male behavior, opened in Chicago in 1974 and won the award for Best New Chicago Play. The company then expanded with the return of Macy and Schachter. In 1975, Mamet met Gregory Mosher, a young theater director from the Juilliard School, who would direct fifteen Mamet plays, including the premiere of *American Buffalo,* the first U.S. production of *Glengarry Glen Ross,* and *Speed-the-Plow.*

By 1976, Mamet had moved to New York, resigning his artistic directorship of the St. Nicholas Company. *American Buffalo* went with him, opening first off-Broadway, winning an Obie Award, and then going on to Broadway, where it won the New York Drama Critics' Circle Award. While teaching part-time at the Yale School of Drama, he met and then married the actor Lindsay Crouse.

By this time Mamet's plays were attracting international attention. He continued to produce shows in Chicago, becoming associate artistic director and writer-in-residence of the Goodman Theatre in 1978. Mosher had by then become its artistic director. Within three years, Mamet would complete his first screenplay, an adaptation of *The Postman Always Rings Twice* by James M. Cain. The following year, his screenplay for *The Verdict,* starring Paul Newman, would be nominated for an Academy Award. But he continued his dramatic writing, and in 1983 his startling work on American business, *Glengarry Glen Ross,* had its world premiere at the Royal National Theatre, London. The play would open in New York the following year and run for nearly four hundred performances, winning a Pulitzer Prize. A series of other major plays followed, beginning with his adaptation of *The Cherry Orchard* (1985), *The Shawl* (1985), *Speed-the-Plow* (1988), *Oleanna* (1992), *The Cryptogram* (1994), *The Old Neighborhood* (1997), and *Boston Marriage* (1999).

Mamet was equally active at this time with films, writing screenplays and then writing and directing his own work. Among his most successful were *The Untouchables* (1987), *House of Games* (1987), *Homicide* (1991), *Wag the Dog* (1997), *The Spanish Prisoner* (1997), *The Winslow Boy* (1998), *State and Main* (1999), *The Heist* (2001), and *Spartan* (2004). Multifaceted and driven, Mamet has also published three novels, the most recent being the experimental *Wilson* (2000), a combination of science fiction and history.

Mamet's essays clearly state his ideas on writing and directing. His approach is essentially to cut, and cut again: "I'm always trying to keep it spare," he told a film critic, and this is true of his playwriting and fiction as well (Corliss 1998). Samuel Beckett—and the streets of Chicago—are the likely origins of this attitude. In a short essay, Beckett wrote, "it is not a question of saying what has not been said, but of repeating, as often as possible in the most reduced space, what has already been said" (Beckett 1984). Adhering to this practice, Mamet continues to fascinate audiences, whether in theaters or movie houses, as he forcefully grapples with the contradictions of moral life. Without exaggeration, he once remarked, "if I hadn't found the theatre, it's very likely I would have become a criminal—another profession that subsumes the outsider . . . and rewards the ability to improvise" (Lahr 1997).

Ira Nadel

References and Further Reading

Beckett, Samuel. 1984. *Disjecta,* edited by Ruby Cohn. New York: Grove Press.

Brewer, Gay. 1993. *David Mamet and Film.* Jefferson, NC: McFarland.

Bruder, Melissa, et al., eds. 1986. *A Practical Handbook for the Actor.* New York: Vintage.

Corliss, Richard. 1998. "The Gamut of Mamet." *Time* (April 6).

Gross, Terry. 2001. "Someone Named Jack." *David Mamet in Conversation,* edited by Leslie Kane. Ann Arbor: University of Michigan Press.

Hudgins, Christopher C., and Leslie Kane, eds. 2001. *Gender and Genre: Essays on David Mamet.* New York: Palgrave Macmillan.

Kane, Leslie, ed. 1992. *David Mamet, A Casebook.* New York: Garland.

Kane, Leslie. 1999. *Weasels and Wisemen, Ethics and Ethnicity in the Work of David Mamet.* New York: St. Martin's Press.

Lahr, John. 1997. "Fortress Mamet." *New Yorker* (November 17): 70–82.

Mamet, David. 2002. "'If I Forget Thee, Jerusalem': The Power of Blunt Nostalgia." *Forward* (December 27).

Schvey, Henry I. 2001. "Celebrating the Capacity for Self-Knowledge." In *David Mamet in Conversation,* edited by Leslie Kane. Ann Arbor: University of Michigan Press.

Donald Margulies (b. 1954)

Playwright

The Pulitzer Prize–winning playwright Donald Margulies's core subject is the richly comic yet profoundly heartaching experience of growing up Jewish in America. "I am a second-generation American Jew," Margulies has declared; "I grew up among immigrant Jews, and I think that really has informed my world view . . . the notion of identity and questions of assimilation and where one fits in the world" (Margulies 2002). In his major plays Margulies revisits the themes that have absorbed him from the beginning, above all the troubled psyche of uprooted, unsettled Jewish artist/sons longing for some connection with the past, confronted by the ache of memory, soothing its pain with the salve of nostalgia.

Significantly, in many of Margulies's plays the "Jewish" Brooklyn of his youth looms as a sacred site of indelible memory and hazy nostalgia. "I was nostalgic for my parents' and Herb Gardner's Brooklyn ever since I was born," he confesses (Margulies 2004). Indeed, for Margulies, to be "from Brooklyn" confers an enabling identity as outsider, an empowering marginality that can seize the potential of the imagined new world *beyond* Brooklyn, beckoning over the bridge, into the city. "The Brooklynite lives on the periphery," Margulies has explained, "tantalizingly within reach of

Something Else, Something Greater, lying just across the river. It is precisely that condition that shapes personalities, fuels ambitions, and creates in some an overwhelming sense of restlessness and yearning" (Margulies 2004).

But beneath the Brooklyn boy's baby-boom nostalgia lurks the looming shadow of bent Jewish fathers—above all Margulies's own father, a Willy Loman–like figure who sold wallpaper for forty years in Pinchik's on Flatbush Avenue. Bob Margulies and his vanished world of unfulfilled dreams loom in the playwright's imagination. In this respect Margulies's play *Brooklyn Boy* (2004) represents the artist/son's way of chanting *kaddish*, a prayer (in the form of a play) offered in memory of a richly remembered world that continues to pull at the author's filial-ethnic allegiances, despite the inevitable chasms wrought by time and self-consciousness. Still *attached* to "Brooklyn," yet driven by an overwhelming desire to escape and a guilty anxiety about leaving, the artist struggles with and against the pull of parochial Jewish identity, haunted, like the famous novelist Eric Weiss in *Brooklyn Boy,* by the embittered Willy Loman–like self he might have been, indeed might have become.

Of course, Margulies is not alone in seizing the explosive potential of Jewish filiality, its fertile (if raw) mix of contradiction, ambivalence, comedy, and rage. Think of Henry Roth's harrowing *Call It Sleep* (1934), or Philip Roth's "memoirs," *The Facts* (1988) and *Patrimony* (1991), or his various "Zuckerman" novels. Margulies has acknowledged the crucial influence of Arthur Miller's *Death of a Salesman* (1949) in shaping his own often wickedly satirical imagination of middle-class Jewish life. "We aren't fancy people," the dream-obsessed mother in *The Loman Family Picnic* (1989) explains to her two sons. "We are middle-middle class, smack in the middle." In this respect Margulies's career amounts to an ongoing *midrash* (commentary) on *Death of a Salesman,* one of the foundational texts of American dreaming.

In Margulies's theater, characters are consumed with a Willy Loman–like restlessness and yearning—some even *after* they're dead, like Shirley in *What's Wrong with This Picture?* (1985; revived on Broadway in 1994), an irrepressible Jewish mother who returns, via the Brooklyn Queens Expressway, from the grave at the end of *shiva* to reclaim her domestic identity. She immediately resumes vacuuming in Flatbush, much to the bewildered delight of her grieving family.

Perhaps most brilliantly, Willy's archetypal shadow hovers fantastically over *The Loman Family Picnic*, haunting the family in their newly built "high-rise ghetto" in an alrightnik Brooklyn neighborhood ("this is modern luxury," declares Doris, the mother, without irony). Above all, Willy's troubled spirit inhabits the internally raging soul of the exhausted paint-salesman father worried about the emotional and financial costs of throwing a fancy bar mitzvah party for his son. "I go through every day with my eyes shut tight and holding my breath, till the day is over and I can come home. To what?" laments the hapless, unappreciated father, desperate that *some* attention be paid. As a creative way of coping (really dreaming), the younger "Loman" son Mitchell (the "Happy" role in *Salesman?*) conjures an inspired musical version of the dysfunctional Lomans imagined on a picnic, with the bar mitzvah boy Stewie singing a lyric while performing a soft shoe, "Dad's a little weird,/ He's in a daze./ Could it be he's going nuts?/ Or is it just a phase?"

In his later drama Margulies continues to assign "Brooklyn" even more explanatory power. In perhaps his most important play, *Sight Unseen* (1991), the globe-trotting celebrity artist Jonathan Waxman, a long way from Flatbush, seeks to fathom his current loss of creative energy (is his spiritual-aesthetic inertia also a phase, or does its source lay deeper, in his Brooklyn past?) by reconnecting with his original muse, a *shiksa* goddess/model Patricia, whose "dangerous" presence inspired him years ago, as an unknown painter still in art school. Jonathan has also just lost his father and is expecting his first child with his gentile wife; his pilgrimage to Patricia, living an ascetic life in the bleak English countryside, appears like an act of mourning, a way of sitting shiva for his own dying, spiritually lost soul.

In *Sight Unseen*'s poignant last vignette—in effect the narrative *beginning* of their fateful relationship—we witness the comic-erotic fumblings of a still innocent Jonathan, Margulies's gently satirical portrait of the provincial artist as young man (a self-portrait? Margulies studied art before he turned to playwriting). Startled by her unsettling sexual invitation, Jonathan deploys "Brooklyn" as a defense against the shiksa threat, the implied transgression *embodied* by Patricia. In a voice that shifts from honest confession to the "spritz" of an increasingly inspired comic's stand-up routine, Jonathan explains how, at least in *his* psychic universe (Jewish) geography determines character:

Look, this is hard for me. It's a major thing, you know, where I come from. . . . You got to remember I come from Brooklyn. People where I come from, they don't travel very far, let alone intermarry. They've still got this ghetto mentality: safety in numbers and stay put, no matter what. It's always, "How'm I gonna get there?" No, really. "How'm I gonna get there? and How'm I gonna get home?" "It'll be late, it'll be dark, it'll get cold, I'll get sick, why bother? I'm staying home." This is the attitude about the world I grew up with. It's a miracle I ever left the house!

At the "end" of *Sight Unseen* we witness the birth of Jonathan Waxman, the driven, self-consciously provocative artist he will later become: *from* middle-class Brooklyn by birth, but no longer (we presume) *of* middlebrow Brooklyn in imagination. But has he ever truly escaped that provincial nest? *Sight Unseen* ultimately refuses to resolve Waxman's ethnic-filial dilemma. He remains blind to his own (eventual) failures of insight and empathy, immobilized by unresolved—because uncompleted—mourning. Patricia's authentic gesture of love, deep into their relationship, despite its inappropriate timing (appearing uninvited at the end of the son's sitting shiva for his mother, she offers Jonathan sexual gratification in his childhood bedroom, an act that shocks him and results in his brutal rejection), ultimately remains "unseen," unfelt. The costs of Waxman's artistic success, Margulies seems to feel, are measured in longing and bereavement.

If in Margulies's view *Sight Unseen* "was a play about leaving Brooklyn," then *Brooklyn Boy* "would be a play about looking back" (Margulies 2004). And indeed in this play Margulies's mode is retrospective, its mood elegiac. It follows Eric Weiss (the ethnic shape-shifter/escape artist Harry Houdini's real name was Ehrich Weiss), a relatively unknown forty-something writer who has finally achieved national recognition by writing an autobiographically inflected novel titled (what else?) *Brooklyn Boy,* through a series of complicated encounters with his deep past: a dying father still bitingly critical of virtually everything the son has accomplished; a childhood friend, now religiously observant, who feels both trapped, yet identified, by the old neighborhood; a bitter, soon-to-be ex-wife who needs to banish him from sight.

In presenting such intimate conversations, *Brooklyn Boy* feels like Margulies's most personal play by far; we overhear the flow of resentment, the release of buried hurt that Eric's presence tends to dislodge in others. At the same time, with each emotionally draining ordeal by dialogue, we witness the unearthing of Eric's archaic Jewish self: the inside narrative of Rickie, the would-be nice Jewish boy who sensed the need to break away, to flee the ethnic nest to realize his literary-intellectual ambitions. Keeping faith with *Death of a Salesman*, Margulies allows Ira Zimmer, Rickie's dissatisfied, now observant boyhood friend to voice the cosmic Willy Loman question in "Brooklyn Boy:" "I had potential," Ira laments to his celebrity friend. "How did you do it?"

If Margulies casts Jonathan Waxman as a young Jewish artist who *molds* himself in unsavory ways to suit fashionable critical taste in a quest for wealth and notoriety, Eric Weiss mines memories of 1960s Brooklyn, drawing on the old neighborhood. In apparent response to his audience's needy nostalgia, the novel reaches number eleven on the *New York Times* best-seller list. Characteristically, Eric's emotionally stingy father Manny belittles the son's achievement, remarking that his son is lucky the "list" goes beyond ten. Who knew? Whatever archaic grievances have come between them, watching Eric peel an orange and feed its sections to his very sick father, we observe their unspoken but palpable love. Thus, despite all the words (explanations, recriminations, renunciations), *Brooklyn Boy* conveys its depth of affect through silent but evocative gesture.

As for Brooklyn as embracing locale, it can only nourish the seething Jewish soul so much; ultimately, as Philip Roth's alter ego Jewish son Nathan Zuckerman well knows, the self-conscious Jewish artist, in flight from smothering middle-class enclaves, needs to locate his imagination in the creatively enabling (if ethnically rootless) space of filial alienation.

In this respect Margulies's alter ego is clearly a Brooklyn cousin to Roth's Newark-born and -raised Zuckerman who, in *The Anatomy Lesson* (1983), mourns the loss of his only subject, the angst-ridden, but now exhausted story of Jewish fathers and sons: "No new Newark was going to spring up again for Zuckerman, not like the first one: no fathers like those pioneering Jewish fathers bursting with taboos, no sons like their sons boiling with temptations, no loyal ties, no ambitions, no rebellions, no capitulations, no clashes quite so convulsive again. . . . Everything that galvanized him had been extinguished, leaving nothing unmistakably his and nobody else's to claim, exploit, enlarge, and reconstruct" (Roth 1985).

In the mode of Philip Roth, *Brooklyn Boy* maps in deeply personal ways the complex emotional landscape of contemporary Jewish American experience, exploring our own mournful nostalgia for the old neighborhoods, our need to settle with the fathers. In the end, Eric achieves a spiritual breakthrough. Having fled "Brooklyn," he is now able to mourn: for his father, perhaps for himself. In *Brooklyn Boy* Margulies enacts a process of uncompleted mourning, chanting, with unfeigned love and empathy, *kaddish* for a lost soul and for an almost forgotten, now mythic territory.

Donald Weber

References and Further Reading

Coen, Stephanie. 1994. "Donald Margulies." *American Theatre* 11,6: 46–47.

Dubner, Stephen J. 1992. "In the Paint: Donald Margulies Scores with a Play about the Art Hustle." *New York Magazine* 25 (March 9): 48–52.

Margulies, Donald. 1995. *Sight Unseen and Other Plays.* New York: Theatre Communications Group.

Margulies, Donald. 2002. "On *Collected Stories.*" http://www.pbs.org/hollywoodpresents/collectedstories.

Margulies, Donald. 2004. "Brooklyn as Metaphor." *Los Angeles Times* (September 5): E37.

Roth, Phillip. 1985. *Zuckerman Bound.* New York: Farrar Strauss Giroux.

Arthur Miller (1915–2005)

Playwright

Born to a Jewish family in New York City in 1915, Arthur Asher Miller is one of the greatest American playwrights and a preeminent dramatist worldwide. When his father's clothing business declined during the Depression, the family moved to Brooklyn, where he spent his youth before making his way to the University of Michigan in 1934, after being rejected the year before. His first undergraduate play, a social drama entitled *No Villain*, won the Avery Hopwood Award at Michigan in 1936, as did his second play, *Honors at Dawn*, in 1937. After graduating in 1938, he moved to New York and wrote scripts for the Federal Theatre Project and radio plays for CBS and NBC. In 1941 he married Mary Grace Slattery, and subsequently they had two children: Jane (1944) and Robert (1947). Before begin-

Arthur Miller, major American playwright. (Hulton/Getty Images)

ning his career on the New York stage, he wrote a never-staged play, *The Golden Years,* ostensibly about the historic encounter between Montezuma and Cortez, but essentially a commentary on the failure of the West to challenge the rise of Hitler. He continued to write radio plays, authored a screenplay, *The Story of GI Joe,* and a book about army life, *Situation Normal.*

When his first Broadway production, *The Man Who Had All the Luck,* closed after four performances in 1944, he contemplated not writing again for the stage and authored a novel about antisemitism, *Focus.* When he decided to try the stage one more time, *All My Sons* (1947) won the New York Drama Critics' Circle Award and established Miller's place as a major American dramatist. In it, as in the whole body of his works, Miller addresses moral and ethical issues and examines the nature of American culture. Influenced by Greek tragedy and the dramas of Henrik Ibsen, the play explores the tragic consequences suffered by a parts manufacturer, Joe Keller, who has shipped faulty airplane parts to be used by the Army in the Pacific. Not only does he endanger the lives of American pilots, but, driven by an unrelenting guilt, he destroys his

own family, causing the suicide of his son, a pilot who blames his father for his comrades' deaths.

In this and in the major plays to follow in his long career, Miller explores the consequences of moral choices, both in the public and private arenas. Often speaking in the voice of an Old Testament prophet, he has been a voice of conscience on the American stage for some sixty years. He insists that there are inevitably consequences to choices, that only confrontation with the past can forge the hope for a meaningful future, that one must assume personal responsibility in a world seemingly bereft of a moral center.

Generally considered his greatest play, *Death of a Salesman* was produced in 1949 and won the Pulitzer Prize and Miller's second New York Drama Critics' Circle Award. Often called the quintessential American tragedy, the play from its opening has generated a lively debate about the nature of modern tragedy and, in particular, the suitability of its protagonist, Willy Loman, "the common man," as tragic hero. Compromised by counterclaims on him as a "salesman," the personification of the American dream of success, and as a father and family man, Willy ironically dies trying to sell himself by committing suicide to assure his elder son Biff's success. The part of Willy Loman has been interpreted variously in highly successful performances from Lee J. Cobb's initial touchstone depiction of a monumentally self-deluded character lost in a world of harsh reality, to Dustin Hoffman's feisty shrimp of a figure, a near adolescent drained of mythic dimension but yet a fierce fighter against an ever-widening doom, to Brian Dennehy's 1999 Tony Award–winning depiction of a towering figure casting a huge shadow across the stage, and yet a vulnerable child cowering with hands defensively folded over his head.

Miller's next major work, *The Crucible,* reflected his ever-growing involvement in social and political concerns. A direct attack on an expanding McCarthyism on the American political front, the play is set during the Salem witch trials and recounts the tragic death of an unwilling hero, John Proctor, who ultimately chooses to sacrifice his life rather than violate his integrity. The play is set in a world, the author declared, "I felt strangely at home with" because it reflects "the same fierce idealism, devotion to God, tendency to legislate reductiveness . . . [and] longings for the pure and intellectually elegant argument" Miller found in his Jewish upbringing (*Timebends: A Life* 1987).

Just three years after it appeared on Broadway, Miller refused to name names when he himself was forced to testify before the House Un-American Activities Committee (HUAC). His most performed play, *The Crucible*, has been frequently staged in the United States and across the globe.

In the same year he appeared before HUAC (1956), Miller's *A View from the Bridge* opened successfully in London, after receiving mixed reviews as a one-act play (produced along with *A Memory of Two Mondays*) at its opening in New York the year before. Originally a verse drama, the more prosaic two-act revised text intensifies quintessential Miller themes: the quest for identity, the conflict between self and society, the loss of innocence, betrayal. Set in the Red Hook district of Brooklyn where Miller grew up, the play depicts the longshoreman Eddie Carbone's violation of community values when his unacknowledged incestuous love for his niece Catherine leads him to betray her illegal immigrant lover to the authorities. Like the other early plays, *View* has generated critical debates on the nature of tragedy, but it has remained among Miller's most durable works.

After his divorce from Mary Slattery and subsequent marriage to screen goddess Marilyn Monroe in 1956, Miller did not stage a new play until *After the Fall* opened in 1964. Before that, he wrote the screenplay *The Misfits* for Marilyn Monroe in a futile effort to save their marriage. After Miller's divorce from Monroe, he married the well-known Austrian photographer Inge Morath in 1962. Their daughter Rebecca was born later in the same year. When *After the Fall* opened two years later, it generated vociferous attacks by some critics who considered it an attempt by Miller to exonerate himself from guilt in the failed relationship with Monroe, and an untoward depiction of her in the guise of the protagonist Quentin's suicidal second wife Maggie. Other critics have come to Miller's defense, but the play has remained under the shadow of the Monroe legend. Some of Miller's critics have particularly objected to his use of the Holocaust as a stage background in the play in relation to what they consider a sordid private affair, but others have argued that the play successfully integrates the enormity of the historical tragedy and the theme of self-betrayal. The play remains his most controversial work.

Miller also explored the plight of Jews in World War II in a play produced the same year, *Incident at Vichy*, which examines the destiny of nine men and a boy held by Nazi authorities in Vichy as suspected Jews. Miller had visited the Mauthausen death camp in 1964 and later the same year covered the Nazi trials in Frankfurt for the *New York Herald Tribune*. Based on a true story, the tautly constructed one-act play moves to its dramatic conclusion when the Catholic nobleman Von Berg gives up his papers to save his fellow detainee Leduc, a Jew. As in many of Miller's texts, the dialogue examines the universality of guilt and difficult moral and ethical issues in the near context of a trial.

Incident was followed by *The Price* in 1968, which includes one of Miller's best drawn characters, the Jewish Russian furniture dealer, Gregory Solomon. The play puts two brothers meeting to dispose of their deceased father's goods in a claustrophobic attic crammed with ten rooms' worth of furniture, a symbol of lives lived and lost, of choices made and suffered. A remarkable survivor of ninety years, Solomon provides the moral perspective in the play. Miller has said of him that he "has to be Jewish, for one thing because of the theme of survival, of a kind of acceptance of life" that "seemed to me to point directly to the Jewish experience through centuries of oppression" (Roudané 1987).

Miller's dramas of the 1970s and 1980s include a wide range of experimental texts that continue to treat his major themes and reflect his constant involvement in political and social causes. After failing in an attempt to write a fable, *Creation of the World and Other Business* (1972), which was later turned unsuccessfully into a musical entitled *Up from Paradise*, Miller wrote *The Archbishop's Ceiling* (1977), in part a reflection of his service as president of PEN, the international writers' association, from 1965 to 1969, when he directly supported dissident writers worldwide. Set in an East European country, it takes place under a likely bugged ceiling at the former archbishop's palace and probes the concept of causality and moral certainty as a visiting American writer returns after a four-year absence for an ostensibly friendly visit with former colleagues. The drama signals Miller's growing postmodernism, despite his continued commitment to the concept of moral choice and responsibility.

This was followed by the largely autobiographical *The American Clock* (1980), a panoramic work involving a wide range of characters, but mainly tracing the fate of a Jewish family during the Depression. It portrays the personal and public consequences of the economic collapse in tragic and comic form, which Miller saw as not unlike the tradition of Yiddish vaudeville, a juxtaposition of the epic and the private, the comic and the tragic.

In the same year Miller adapted for television Fania Fenelon's autobiography *Playing for Time.* It dramatizes Fenelon's experiences as a singer with the women's orchestra at the infamous Auschwitz-Birkenau concentration camp. Once again confronting the moral complexities of guilt and innocence, the teleplay depicts the human capacity for brutishness and murder as well as for moral restoration.

Miller's plays written during the 1980s consisted of four one-acts published as pairs of plays in two collections: *Two-Way Mirror* and *Danger: Memory!* In these often subtle works, he wrestles with the complexities, paradoxes, and ironies commonly expressed in postmodern literature without betraying his long-held optimism about the human condition. They partly signal Miller's growing sense of looking back over a long career and assessing the validity of his own canon. Like the plays of the 1990s, they are a kind of summing up of his own work.

The Ride Down Mount Morgan (1991), *The Last Yankee* (1992), and *Mr. Peters' Connections* (2000) each expresses Miller's long-stated themes, but also reveals a growing moral uncertainty, a thin line between truth and illusion, and a sustained ambiguity. *Ride,* Miller said, reflects the ethos of the Reagan years as its protagonist, Lyman Felt, embodies an unabashed self-gratification even as he undergoes a kind of self-trial on his hospital bed after crashing his car on Mount Morgan. The play embodies the dialectical forces in his life, embodied by his two wives' meeting for the first time at his bed. His bigamy exposed, he struggles with the demanding forces of memory. Trying to evade guilt, he denies closure, self-absorbed in the prison of his own psyche.

The Last Yankee similarly balances humor and the poignantly tragic, as Leroy Hamilton faces his past relationship with his wife as he visits her at a mental hospital in New England. A carpenter and descendant of Alexander Hamilton, he meets an older businessman in the waiting room as they visit their hospitalized wives. Pitting American materialism against the need for human and spiritual values, the play exposes characters caught up in the same specious mythology that entraps Willy Loman and Joe Keller in Miller's early plays. Having faced his own culpability, Leroy, like Quentin in *After the Fall,* comes to embrace a world "after the fall" and moves to a hopeful but uncertain world.

The first Miller play in the new millennium, *Mr. Peters' Connections,* is in some ways similar to *The Last Yankee* and *The Ride Down Mount Morgan,* though it is more postmodern in its exploration of the fine line between truth and illusion and its dream-like nature. It, too, addresses the essential Miller themes—the persistence of memory, the collapse of the American dream, betrayal and guilt, the nexus of the social and the personal. The elderly Mr. Peters tries to discover some residue of meaning in the borderland between dreaming and waking, life and death. Yet even in this most absurdist of his plays, Miller retains a residue of hope as Mr. Peters ends the play seeking some "connection," some union with another person as he tells his daughter Rose, "I love you, darling. I wonder . . . could that be the subject!"

In his other major 1990s play, *Broken Glass* (1994), Miller returns to the Holocaust as theme and once again juxtaposes private and corporate evil. In it Phillip Gellburg must confront his denial of his own Jewishness when his wife Sylvia experiences an unexplained paralysis upon hearing the news of Nazi atrocities during *Kristallnacht.* The paralysis symbolizes the spiritual and moral impotency that arrests all the characters and exposes the web of deceit and guilt that has bound the Gellburgs in a long and painful marriage. The drama won the Olivier award as best new play in London, even though, like all Miller's later works, it generated a mixed critical response, especially among New York critics. As Christopher Bigsby has reminded us, Miller "addressed the Holocaust to an extent that no other American dramatist would do" (Bigsby 2005).

Even in his last performed play, *Resurrection Blues* (2002), a stinging political satire set in a South American country, and *Finishing the Picture* (2004), Miller continued his penetrating analysis of the materialistic and exploitive nature of Western culture. Though his later texts appear more ambivalent in their resolve at times and suggest that an existential awareness may be the best we can hope for, Miller never wavers in his conviction that the best hope for redemption resides in the acceptance of responsibility for choice, a capacity that depends in large measure on the acceptance of guilt as the basis for moral regeneration. Often deeply rooted in the Jewish experience, his plays, like his political and theater essays, his short stories, his novel *Focus,* his wide-ranging interviews—as well as his involvement in political causes and defense of victims of political and legal abuse for all of his career—give testimony to his strong and abiding moral consciousness and assure his place as one of the truly major American writers of the twentieth century.

Terry Otten

References and Further Reading

Bigsby, Christopher. 2005. *Arthur Miller: A Critical Study.* Cambridge, UK: Cambridge University Press.

Centola, Steven R., ed. 2000. *Echoes Down the Corridor: Collected Essays, 1944–2000.* New York: Viking.

Gottfried, Martin. 2003. *Arthur Miller: His Life and Work.* New York: Da Capo Press.

Griffin, Alice. 1996. *Understanding Arthur Miller.* Columbia: University of South Carolina Press.

Koorey, Stefani. 2000. *Arthur Miller's Life and Literature: An Annotated and Comprehensive Guide.* Lanham, MD: Scarecrow Press.

Moss, Leonard. 1980. *Arthur Miller,* rev. ed. Boston: Twayne.

Nelson, Benjamin. 1970. *Arthur Miller: Portrait of a Playwright.* New York: McKay.

Otten, Terry. 2002. *The Temptation of Innocence in the Dramas of Arthur Miller.* Columbia: University of Missouri Press.

Roudané, Matthew. 1987. *Conversations with Arthur Miller.* Jackson: University Press of Mississippi.

Savran, David. 1992. *Communists, Cowboys, and Queers: The Politics of Masculinity in the Work of Arthur Miller and Tennessee Williams.* Minneapolis: University of Minnesota Press.

Schlueter, June, and James K. Flanagan. 1987. *Arthur Miller.* New York: Frederick Ungar.

Welland, Dennis. 1985. *Miller the Playwright,* 3rd ed. New York: Methuen.

Chaim Potok (1929–2002)

Novelist, Essayist, Author of Historical Works

Chaim Potok's reputation as an American Jewish writer is firmly established. In fiction and nonfiction he presents the importance of Judaism and religious belief in the modern world while also depicting the difficulties suffered by inquisitive protagonists attached to Jewish Orthodoxy. A Conservative rabbi who, unlike many American Jewish authors, has a deep understanding of Judaism and Jewish culture, he is best known for novels that present con-

frontations between Jewish and non-Jewish worlds. He referred to these as "core-to-core confrontations" between the Jewish subculture and the attractive "umbrella culture" of the wider secular society. These confrontations created characters who had insights into more than one culture but felt completely at home in no single one, a "between person" in Potok's term. In addition, many of his protagonists suffer confrontations within Judaism itself between differing interpretations of the faith. Desirous of taking account of the latest discoveries and insights of anthropologists, linguists, and biblical scholars, he desired a faith that was inclusive enough to permit new ideas. The difficulty of reconciling religious orthodoxy to the modern world is a central problem for many of his protagonists.

In *The Chosen* (1967), his first novel, two extremely intelligent adolescents, one having a photographic memory, set a pattern for many of his fictional child prodigies. The ideologies of Hasidic and Orthodox Judaism provide the bases for the novel's conflicts. Reb Saunders, Danny's father, leader of a Hasidic (ultra-Orthodox) group, and

Chaim Potok, novelist. (American Jewish Archives)

David Malter, Reuven's father, an Orthodox, highly moral, but non-Hasidic teacher of Judaism, represent the poles of opinion that test their sons' friendship. It is the quality of the characterizations that makes the novel so effective, with Potok managing to make interesting, decent people involved in important yet often parochial issues, without a stress on physical violence or sexuality.

Danny and Reuven's friendship across a sectarian divide humanizes the more esoteric aspects of the conflict between their fathers: a repressive or more liberal interpretation of Jewish law; religious, or political and emotional Zionism; reading only the Talmud or valuing secular books as well. The friendship is threatened by Reb Saunders's rigidity and insularity, and by Danny's being trapped in the seemingly non-negotiable position of his father's heir as communal leader. David Malter feels it his duty to suggest secular books to Danny that will feed his intense desire to learn about more than Talmud, although Danny finds that he can use talmudic methods to decipher Freud's writings. Danny must cope with being raised in silence, a device his father believes will give him a suffering soul to balance his intellect. These differences provide important conflicts in the novel, which, despite its highly Jewish content, was on the best-seller list for thirty-eight weeks. In the end Potok's optimism gives both boys a limitless future and supports the ideal of the American Dream that hard work will lead to success.

The novel captures the Jewish love of education, in that both boys and their fathers are involved in learning, but with moral and spiritual overtones. The fathers use different methods of teaching, and their sons move in different directions, but all remain deeply attached to Judaism, which they believe to be relevant and give meaning to their world. Unlike Hasidism, the Malters' form of Orthodoxy finds more joy and emotion in the faith—ironic, given Hasidism's beginnings. Although both boys are interested in aspects of the world beyond their narrow group, neither seems to have any of the "normal" interests of American male teenagers: sports, popular music, girls. They are studious and moral, with Danny's rebellion pivoting around his desire to become a psychologist rather than a *tzaddik* (inspired religious leader) like his father, hardly a form of juvenile delinquency. In addition to adults, the novel has been popular with both Jewish and non-Jewish teenagers, perhaps tapping into a vein of adolescent idealism or a desire for security in the presentation of worlds that, although restrictive, provide stability and surety.

The Promise (1969) continues the lives of Danny and Reuven, dramatizing the results of decisions made in *The Chosen,* though stylistically this sequel is not as effective. With Danny studying for his doctorate in psychology and Reuven for rabbinical ordination, the novel is rich in learning and teachers, and contains themes similar to those in *The Chosen:* characters committed to different interpretations of Judaism and issues of tolerance and fanaticism. Potok seems to provide some justification for Danny's having been raised in silence, as using this questionable method is effective in treating his patient, Michael Gordon. Potok shows how the lives of the three boys have been shaped by religious issues, and through this he humanizes what might be rather dry, intellectual matters.

The battles between very liberal (Abraham Gordon) and archconservative (Rav Kalman) interpretations of the tradition provide the basis for character development with, as in *The Chosen,* the latter approach being seen to harm decent people due to its rigidity. However, the conservatives are not presented as villains, but as holding their views for deeply felt reasons. David Malter, a minor character here, again takes the humanistic position, a bastion of rather hard-to-believe tolerance, given the attacks on him for his liberal approach to understanding the Talmud and his being driven from his school by ultra-Orthodox newcomers. The tensions in the novel revolve around the religious ideas of the teachers and their level of tolerance for the ideas of others, Potok stressing the need for forbearance and sufferance.

The protagonist of Potok's third novel, Asher Lev, appears in two novels almost twenty years apart. *My Name Is Asher Lev* (1972) is Potok's most accomplished novel, particularly in relation to style. Asher is another prodigy, and Potok depicts a conflict with his Hasidic world, which interprets the second commandment's restriction on worship of graven images as precluding any artistic creation. Asher's characterization stresses his inability to cease drawing and painting despite his father's and community's disapproval. This irreconcilability of art and Jewish Orthodoxy is a central theme of the novel, as Asher is forced into the world of Christian art, nudes, and secular values on account of the lack of a Jewish artistic tradition.

Asher's obsession with painting also has the effect of his putting his own needs before those of the Jewish community, while Judaism places greater stress on the survival of the Jewish people, with whom God made a covenant, than on the individual, valued as individuals are. Asher resists pressures from his father, who travels the world to create yeshivas (schools of Jewish higher learning), and from the rebbe (the communal spiritual leader), who tries to harness his gift for the service of the community, and refuses to sacrifice his painting for his people. Thus, his father is not completely incorrect when he tells Asher that adhering to the demands of his artistic gift will lead him to selfishness. However, as in the previous novels, Potok cannot bring himself to cut off his protagonist from his religious roots, and so transports him to a more sympathetic Jewish community in Paris. There, it is implied, he will be able to paint and remain a practicing Jew and a member of the Ladover Hasidic community.

Potok returned to his exiled artist in *The Gift of Asher Lev* (1990). Still living in France, Asher is now a famous artist but in an arid period when his creativity has deserted him. Moreover, he is not at ease with himself, and the novel traces his meditations on his spiritual needs and the nature of artistic creativity. With the death of his uncle, he returns to visit the Brooklyn world that he had to leave when an adolescent and is confronted by his legacy. Potok is adept at showing the slow process of the renewal of creativity in Asher, who is made whole through "giving" his son Avrumel to the rebbe, his father, and the Ladover community to become the Hasid he could not. It is as though Potok needed to "tie up loose ends," having originally allowed Asher to escape that world. As in the earlier novel, there is an impressive use of the language of art, as Asher views the world through color, shape, and texture.

The protagonist of *In the Beginning* (1975) is another very bright child and adolescent, who becomes a biblical scholar to defend the Jewish people from the denigrations of what came to be called "the higher biblical criticism," largely developed by non-Jews. Set in the 1930s and 1940s during a rise in antisemitism in Europe and America, the novel depicts David Lurie's attempts to overcome attacks by a local antisemite, while providing a historical backdrop through his father's battles against Jew-hatred in Poland during World War I and his hatred of most gentiles. Potok again describes intra-Jewish hostilities, as David is ostracized by his fellow yeshiva students and by his parents because, in order to analyze the Bible using the new largely

German scientific criticism, he will have to study with non-Jews and Jews who do not observe the commandments. He decides to fight antisemitism in his own way. Potok has frequently presented battles with authority figures seen through literal and symbolic father–son motifs. David's parallel those of Danny in *The Chosen,* Reuven in *The Promise,* and Asher, each of whom had to fight to believe in ideas other than those held by the majority of their communities. Whereas Reuven had his father's support, David, like Danny and Asher, is almost completely on his own. While David has wrestled with his conscience and loves the Torah, his brother Alex has quietly given up Orthodox belief but continues its practice while still living at home. Thus Potok sets forth the need for a modern appeal of the Bible for a new generation who may see it as only a "bunch of Sunday school stories."

Potok wrote two novels based on his experiences as an Army chaplain during the Korean War. *The Book of Lights* (1981) is impressive in its writing and scope, which ranges from kabbalah (Jewish mysticism), to cultural issues concerning Korea (a country that has never heard of Judaism), to moral issues surrounding the atom bomb. The "lights" refer to those of the *En-Sof* and *Sefiroth* of kabbalistic lore, and to those of the atom bomb. The two adult protagonists are rabbis, one a budding kabbalist, the other a physicist who has rejected science for religion because of the "death light" science has created. Important moral conflicts revolve about the poles of Judaism/paganism and religion/science. His protagonists are still teachers and students, but they engage in adult sexual thoughts and activities befitting grown men, a first for Potok. *I Am the Clay* (1992) is Potok's first and only novel in which Jews barely appear at all, Potok seemingly wishing to try to write a novel without his main ethnic group. The stress is on the fortitude of an old Korean couple fleeing the ravages of war. Their compassion is brought forth by a wounded boy discovered in a ditch, and Potok shows marked ability to create empathy in readers. While it is not as effective as his "Jewish" novels, largely because he cannot present his depth of knowledge concerning Judaism, he does manage to elicit the power of compassion within a commendable portrayal of the horror of war.

In *Davita's Harp* (1985), Potok presents his first female protagonist, who recalls the events and impressions of her life between the ages of roughly eight and fourteen, along with her attempts to achieve selfhood and to cope with life's disasters. Ilana Davita's mother is Jewish, her father

Christian, both being nonbelievers whose faith lies in communism. Potok sensitively dramatizes Davita, who is extremely intelligent and sensitive, much like Potok's previous young protagonists. Set between 1936 and 1942, he depicts her coping with her parents' ostracism and evictions due to communist activities; her awareness of fascism; the Spanish Civil War, in which her father dies; the beginnings of World War II; and the Nazi–Soviet Pact, which destroys her mother's idealism. In addition to world events, always present in Potok's novels, she must cope with being a very bright girl in an Orthodox Jewish school, who is denied the Akiva Award for the highest scholastic achievement because she is not a boy. Potok is highly critical of Orthodox Judaism, which, as previously, is presented as narrow and unquestioning, and he uses the widest range of beliefs thus far in his novels: Orthodox Judaism, Christianity, communism, and a type of humanism. One feels that Davita will move even further away from Orthodoxy than did Asher Lev, perhaps opting for the spiritual truths of literature.

In *Old Men at Midnight* (2001), Davita reappears as Davita Dinn in a trilogy of novellas. In "The Ark Builder" we find her seventeen, an English tutor for a sixteen-year-old Auschwitz survivor. Through his drawings, she brings out the repressed Noah Stremin, who relates the story of his inspiration, a builder of synagogue arks in his Polish village who commits suicide when the Nazis invade. "The War Doctor" sees Ilana Davita, now a teaching assistant in Russian studies at Columbia University, convincing a former Jewish KGB (Russian Secret Police) officer to relate his experiences during the revolution and Stalinist years. Leon Shertov is humanized by his inability to save the life of a Jewish doctor who had saved him. In "The Trope Teacher" we find Ilana, now a famous novelist, forcing out the stories of an old and famous military historian. She teaches him how to accept and so recall the important elements of his life, and he comes to realize the central importance of the man who taught him how to chant the Torah. In all three novellas, we see how the lives of individuals have been deeply changed by exposure to one person, and how Davita has become sensitized to human problems.

Best known as a novelist, Potok has also written short stories, plays, children's books, essays, and other nonfiction. Noteworthy are two historical works: *Wanderings: Chaim Potok's History of the Jews* (1978) and *The Gates of November: Chronicles of the Slepak Family* (1999). In *Wan-*

derings he is successful in using a storyteller's skill to dramatize the history of the Jews through scholarly and popular styles, a difficult balance to achieve. He depicts the effect on Judaism of the different cultures to which Jews have been exposed and shows how Judaism has affected them. He takes a nonfundamentalist approach to the development of the Hebrew Bible and treats pagan and other non-Jewish cultures with great understanding. His treatment of historical figures has a novelist's touch that humanizes them so that, for example, Moses and Jesus are seen as real people, with Potok speculating what they may have felt or thought in particular situations. Like his fictional characters—Danny Saunders, Reuven Malter, and David Lurie—Potok sees the religious sages interpreting and editing the Talmud to meet changing circumstances or make sense of a passage. Thus, attitudes that were first expressed in the novels appear again in a historical context in *Wanderings*—fiction and nonfiction supporting each other. In *The Gates of November* Potok effectively presents the true story of the Jewish Slepak family, whose members included a high-ranking communist officer and a son who was a "refusenik," disagreeing with everything his father believed. As in *Wanderings*, real people dramatize historical events. In its variety and insights, Potok's body of work provides a unique chronicle of American Jewish life.

Edward A. Abramson

References and Further Reading
Abramson, Edward A. 1986. *Chaim Potok*. Boston: Twayne.
Barkess, Joanna. 1998. "Painting the Sitra Achra: Culture Confrontation in Chaim Potok's Asher Lev Novels." *Studies in American Jewish Literature* 17: 17–24.
Kremer, S. Lillian. 1984. "Chaim Potok." In *Dictionary of Literary Biography*, edited by Daniel Walden, 232–243. Detroit, MI: Gale.
Kremer, S. Lillian. 1997. "Chaim Potok (1929–)." In *Contemporary Jewish American Novelists: A Bio-Critical Sourcebook*, edited by Joel Shatzky, 284–294. Westport, CT: Greenwood Press.
Marovitz, Sanford E. 1986. "Freedom, Faith, and Fanaticism: Cultural Conflict in the Novels of Chaim Potok." *Studies in American Jewish Literature* 5: 129–140.
Potok, Chaim, and Daniel Walden. 2001. *Conversations with Chaim Potok*. Jackson: University Press of Mississippi.
Purcell, William F. 1989. "Potok's Fathers and Sons." *Studies in American Literature* 26: 75–92.
Soll, Will. 1989. "Chaim Potok's Book of Lights: Reappropriating Kabbalah in the Nuclear Age." *Religion and Literature* 21,1: 111–125.

Sternlicht, Sanford. 2000. *Chaim Potok: A Critical Companion.* Westport, CT: Greenwood Press.

Uffen, Ellen. 1982. "*My Name Is Asher Lev:* Chaim Potok's Portrait of the Young Hasid as Artist." *Studies in American Jewish Literature* 2: 174–180.

Walden, Daniel, ed. 1985. "The World of Chaim Potok." *Studies in American Jewish Literature.* No. 4.

Zuehl-Engel, Catherine. 1997. "Modern Jewish Art and the Crucifixion: A Study in Appropriation." *Soundings: An Interdisciplinary Journal* 80,1: 133–152.

Morris Rosenfeld (1862–1923)

Yiddish Proletarian Poet

Morris Rosenfeld (Moyshe-Yankev Alter) was born on December 28, 1862, in Buksha, Poland, about a hundred miles southwest of Vilna, to a family of fishermen. His parents relocated to Warsaw, where Rosenfeld was sent to a *cheder* (a traditional Jewish school). In 1880 he married Rebecca Bessie Yavorosky and moved to Amsterdam, where he was a diamond grinder. After six months they returned home but soon immigrated to London. The couple lived there several years in great poverty, while Rosenfeld was a tailor. He joined the Yiddish anarchist Brenner Street Club and wrote proletarian poems in Yiddish. However, the London anarchist Yiddish weekly *Arbayter fraynd* (*Worker's Friend*) did not publish them.

In 1886 Rosenfeld moved to New York where he continued to work in sweatshops, first as a baster and later a presser. He became active in the labor movement and on December 17, 1886, published his first Yiddish poem, "*Dos yor 1886*" ("The Year 1886"), about the Haymarket anarchists, in the *Yidishe folktsaytung* (*Yiddish People's Newspaper*). He started publishing regularly in *Arbayter fraynd* as well. When the socialist weekly *Arbayter tsaytung* (*Worker's Newspaper*) began in 1890, Rosenfeld became its official poet. He published poems there almost every week, describing the harsh working conditions and oppression of the sweatshop.

In 1888, Rosenfeld published his first collection of proletarian poems, *Di gloke* (*The Bell*). Later, however, feeling the work did not meet his own poetic standards, he bought and destroyed all obtainable copies of the book. His second book, *Di blumen kete* (*The Flower Wreath,* 1890), contains better poetry. The quality of the language,

versification, and images in his work continued to improve, as demonstrated in his third collection of poems, *Das lider bukh* (*The Book of Songs,* 1897). His reputation spread to non-Yiddish readers after Leo Wiener, a Harvard University professor of Slavic languages, translated this book—in prose form—into English as *Songs from the Ghetto* (1898). Wiener thought highly of Rosenfeld's poetry, comparing it to Dante's *Inferno.* In 1898, Rosenfeld started giving readings of his poems in English in universities, first at Harvard, then at the University of Chicago (1890), and at Wellesley and Radcliffe Colleges (1902). He also recited or even sang his poems in gatherings, since he had a pleasant tenor voice. In 1890 he wrote theater reviews and several plays for the *Folks advokat* (*The People's Advocate*). His historic drama *Der letster kohen godl* (*The Last High Priest*) was performed in New York, but with little success. He always hoped to make enough money from his tours and writing to quit working in sweatshops, but that was never possible.

In the 1890s Rosenfeld began an editing career. In 1892 he co-edited *Di zun* (*The Sun*), though it only lasted through June and July. In 1894, he co-edited the satirical weekly *Der ashmeday* (*Asmodeus,* the king of demons). In 1900 he co-published *Der pinkes* (*The Book of Records*), a magazine on literature, history, and current issues. By then Rosenfeld had become an enthusiastic Zionist, and in 1900 was a delegate to the fourth Zionist Congress in London.

During the next decade he published in various Yiddish papers, among them the anarchist weekly *Di varhayt* (*The Truth*), *Der morgenshtern* (*The Morningstar*), and the daily *Di idishe velt* (*The Jewish World*). His popularity grew, his poems impressing Yiddish-speaking workers, who sang those that were put to music, in factories, sweatshops, and mass meetings. Yet Rosenfeld barely made a living as a writer or a presser.

In 1905, he moved on to edit the daily *New Yorker Morgenblat* (*Morning Paper*), a job that again lasted only several months. That year Rosenfeld's son Joseph, for whom he wrote one of his most beloved poems, "*Mayn yingele*" ("My Little Son"), died at fifteen. It was believed at the time that Rosenfeld's paralytic stroke and near-blindness in 1907 resulted partly from poor health due to poverty, but mostly from grief over losing Joseph. After recovering, he published biographies of Heinrich Heine (1906) and Yehudah Halevi (1907), two poets who influenced him. He became a staff writer on the *Forverts* (*Forward*), where he published not only poetry but also prose and feuilletons (generally articles on social issues) twice a week.

In 1908 Rosenfeld traveled to Galicia and Western Europe, where he was enthusiastically received. At home, however, things were not going well for Rosenfeld. He did not get along with his colleagues, and in 1913 was dismissed from his position at the *Forverts*. Wanting to continue his journalistic career, he moved on, unenthusiastically, to write for the Orthodox *Yidishes tageblat* (*The Jewish Daily Paper*). His bitterness, resulting in part from disagreements with other writers and editors, increasingly led him to write less. The quality of his writing also deteriorated, until in 1921 he was dismissed from this paper as well. Poor, sick, and lonely, he became ever more embittered. Although removed from the literary scene, he continued publishing sporadically in *Morgen jurnal* (*Morning Journal*) and *Amerikaner* (*The American*). Rosenfeld died on June 22, 1923.

Of his twenty published volumes, the most widely read were the six-volume *Shriftn* (*Writings*, 1908–1910), the three-volume *Gevelte shriftn* (*Selected Writings*, 1912), and the two-volume *Dos bukh fun libe* (*The Book of Love*, 1914).

Rosenfeld was, for a time, the leading Yiddish poet, especially in the United States. But a younger generation of Yiddish poets in the United States started new trends, in which Rosenfeld did not fit. Writing didactic, moralizing, and sentimental proletarian poetry and using poetry to propagate socialism, anarchism, and Jewish nationalism were no longer in fashion. The most dominant literary movement among Yiddish writers and critics in the United States since 1907 was *Di yunge* (*The Young*), which believed in art for art's sake. During his lifetime the quality of Yiddish poetry developed far beyond Rosenfeld's capabilities.

Rosenfeld was celebrated for his proletarian poems that depicted his sweatshop experiences and stirred the Jewish masses. They were translated into German, Romanian, Polish, Hungarian, Czech, Russian, and English. The English translations were done first by Rose Pastor Stokes and Helena Frank, *Songs of Labor and Other Poems* (1914); later by Aaron Kramer, *The Teardrop Millionaire and Other Poems of Morris Rosenfeld* (1955); by Itche Goldberg and Max Rosenfeld, *Morris Rosenfeld: Selections from his Poetry and Prose* (1964); and by M. T. Cohen, *Poems of Morris Rosenfeld* (1979).

Ori Kritz

References and Further Reading

Bialostotzky, Benjamin Jacob. 1941. *Morris Rosenfeld*. New York: Workmen's Circle.

Goldenthal, Edgar, J. 1998. *Poet of the Ghetto: Morris Rosenfeld*. Hoboken, NJ: KTAV.

Minkoff, Nochum, B. 1937. "Morris Rosenfeld." In *Yiddishe klassiker poetn* (*Yiddish Classic Poets*), 67–98. New York: Farlag Bodn.

Leo Calvin Rosten (1908–1997)

Novelist, Social Scientist, and Lexicographer

Though he achieved success as a social scientist, a screenwriter, a wartime government official, and a journalist, Leo Rosten is best remembered as a writer who celebrated the transitional culture of Jewish immigrants in the United States and who helped bring ethnic Jewish humor into the American literary mainstream.

Many read Rosten as a conservator of Yiddishkeit and Jewish traditions; yet, in many ways, they misunderstood him. Leo Rosten was, instead, an advocate of the melting pot who strove for objectivity in his writings, and who wrote about Yiddish and those who spoke it primarily as a vocabulary and a population that had been or could be assimilated into American English and society, to the betterment of all.

Perhaps because of his predilection for objectivity (which he liked to call omniscience, making it sound even more impersonal), descriptions of Rosten's upbringing and family life, both as a child and as an adult, are rare in his writing. Born in the Polish city of Lodz, Rosten was raised in a Yiddish-speaking family and arrived in the United States when he was three years old, settling with his mother and father, Ida and Samuel Rosten, in Chicago. Leo grew up in Chicago's Greater Lawndale section, which, in the decade before World War II, was home to almost half of the city's Jews. One of the few descriptions of his childhood comes in "My Father," at the beginning of his *People I Have Loved, Known or Admired* (1970), where Rosten makes a political point in recalling that his parents were "ardent trade unionists" and "loyal members" of the Workmen's Circle, even though they were shop owners. There is one tantalizing glimpse of the role that background played in Rosten's writing, when he admits to using a story about

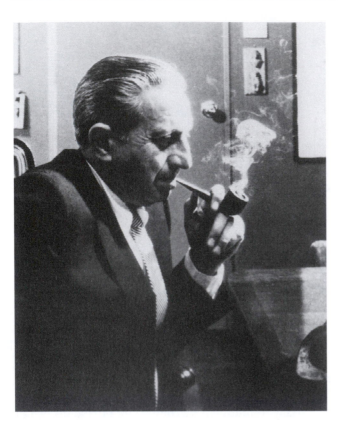

Leo Rosten, writer. (American Jewish Archives)

his father in his first novel. Otherwise, this short memoir contains little of Rosten's father and less of Rosten himself growing up in an immigrant household.

Rather than personal or emotional tales of boyhood, Rosten preferred to describe his own coming-of-age through books, a sanitized and purely intellectual process. In "A Letter to My Reader," which serves as a foreword to *The Many Worlds of L*E*O R*O*S*T*E*N* (1964), he claims, "I was addicted to reading from the time I was six." In that essay, Rosten distinguishes between his early years reading and writing fiction ("the province of those engrossed in make-believe") and his graduate school days in the social sciences at the University of Chicago, when, for "ten to fifteen hours a day [. . .] I guzzled theories of human behavior and social process; I feasted on political philosophies and sopped up economic systems." Rosten excelled at the guzzling, feasting, and sopping up, serving as both a research assistant for the prominent political psychologist Harold Lasswell, as well as a lecturer in political science in his own right. He studied briefly at the London School of Economics, before joining the Social Science Research Council in Washington, D.C., to conduct research

for a doctoral thesis on the Washington press corps, from 1935 to 1936. Also in 1935, Rosten married Priscilla Ann Mead though, as with his parents, his relationship with her and their three children receives almost no mention in Rosten's published writings.

The apparent split in Rosten's personality—the social scientist pursuing truth through methodology and the fiction writer seeking "admission to the holy order of Authors"—is nowhere more striking than with the publication of Rosten's first two books, both in 1937. One was the culmination of his research, for which he received a PhD from Chicago that same year. Entitled *The Washington Correspondents,* and widely praised by both academic and general reviewers, Rosten's study was a profile, based on the statistical evidence he had gathered, of the typical journalist covering the nation's capital at a time when such correspondents were having an increasing impact on American politics and policies.

The other book was also "omniscient," but in a literary sense: a linked collection of stories that had originally appeared in the *New Yorker* magazine, with a third-person narrator, entitled *The Education of H*Y*M*A*N K*A*P*L*A*N.* The stories are set in Mr. Parkhill's adult night-school English class—a class such as Samuel Rosten had attended as a new immigrant, and as his son Leo had taught in the early 1930s before enrolling in graduate school. And, like the stories before it, the book was published under the name Leonard Q. Ross, a pseudonym that Rosten later claimed he adopted because he was "afraid of what his professors might do if they discovered that whilst he was living in Washington on an honorific fellowship, he was spending his weekends in his secret vice—the writing of fiction" (*The Return of H*Y*M*A*N K*A*P*L*A*N*). Though Rosten never admitted it, the name may also have been designed to give an ethnically neutral quality to the persona of the supposed author, fitting into a pattern of ways in which Rosten distanced himself from his Jewish origins, even while exploiting them in his writings, early in his career.

With *The Education of H*Y*M*A*N K*A*P*L*A*N,* Rosten achieved both critical and popular success. It is full of broadly drawn humor, making fun of its title character's equally mangled English and perceptions of American life. But it also satirizes Mr. Parkhill's uninspired blandness in the face of Hyman Kaplan's irrepressible originality—one sign of which, of course, is the way Kaplan writes his name with stars between the letters. These were familiar stereotypes at the time: the dependable, sophisticated, but emotionally unresponsive Anglo-Saxon native, and the unpredictable, ill-mannered, and excitable immigrant. Rosten's humorous insights remain within the bounds of such stereotypical (but never mean-spirited) characterizations.

Significantly, in a class filled with Kaplans, Mitnicks, Blooms, Moskowitzes, and one Caravello, missing from *The Education of H*Y*M*A*N K*A*P*L*A*N* is anything Jewish beyond the Yiddish-inflected accents. Parkhill sometimes talks to himself in Latin, his lessons are filled with references to American and European history and literature (including, according to Kaplan, "Judge Vashington," "Mocktwain," and "Jakesbeer"), and, in the curiously entitled "Mr. K*A*P*L*A*N and the Magi," the class observes Christmas by presenting Mr. Parkhill with a gift. But the Jewishness of his students is only tongue-deep: there is no reciprocal use of specifically Jewish traditions, languages, or culture anywhere in the volume, as if for Rosten the secular values many Jewish immigrants held in common—including education, financial success, and liberal political views—were the most important part of their heritage.

Following the success of *The Education of H*Y*M*A*N K*A*P*L*A*N*, Rosten published *The Strangest Places* (1939), another book of *New Yorker* pieces, this time nonfiction, and two novels with journalists as the protagonists: *Dateline: Europe* (1939) and *Adventure in Washington* (1940), all three published under the pseudonym Leonard Ross or Leonard Q. Ross. Rosten also began working as a screenwriter in Los Angeles, but returned to his roots as a social scientist to produce a study of the film industry entitled *Hollywood: The Movie Colony, The Movie Makers* (1941). When World War II began in Europe, Rosten parlayed his inside knowledge of Washington and Hollywood into a series of increasingly important government jobs, often related to filmmaking for propaganda and informational purposes. After the war, he continued to write popular fiction and screenplays, while working for the Rand Corporation in Los Angeles, and then, beginning in 1950, for *Look* magazine in New York.

By the end of the 1950s, Rosten's career as a writer seemed moribund. The only books he had published for more than a decade were a pamphlet entitled *How the Politburo Thinks,* which was published by the International Ladies' Garment Workers' Union in 1951, and *A Guide to*

the Religions of America (1955), edited by Rosten and based on a series of articles that had originally appeared in *Look*. Not long afterward, Rosten published an article entitled "The Intellectual and the Mass Media: Some Rigorously Random Remarks," which appeared in a special number of the academic journal *Daedalus* (along with contributions by Hannah Arendt, Randall Jarrell, James Baldwin, T. S. Eliot, and others), and was later reprinted in *The Many Worlds of L*E*O R*O*S*T*E*N*. In it, the author defended the rise of mass media in the United States (and, by implication, his own work for *Look*) against the charges of artists and intellectuals who saw it as a sign of the debasement of American culture—or, as Rosten put it, "our latter-day intellectuals seem to blame the mass media for the lamentable failure of more people to attain the bliss of intellectual grace" (1960). This position—predictable enough from a man who seemed to celebrate all things American throughout his career—garnered Rosten notoriety in the continuing debate of that period on "masscult and midcult," to use the terms, popularized by Dwight Macdonald, in which it was usually framed.

Rosten soon returned to a more familiar kind of popular culture, with the publication of *The Return of H*Y*M*A*N K*A*P*L*A*N* (1959), the first of several successes over the next ten years that resuscitated and reshaped his career. Some of the stories in the sequel had appeared in the *New Yorker* the year after the first Kaplan collection was published, most were of a more recent vintage, but all employ the same formula of fractured language compounded by contorted logic to produce comedy and, on occasion, understanding. There are, however, some important changes: Kaplan returns with much greater diversity in his cast of supporting characters—the better to represent America's immigrant community at the end of the Eisenhower years; and Rosten's self-imposed restrictions on acceptable language and culture are relaxed enough, especially in the final story, "H*Y*M*A*N K*A*P*L*A*N, Ever Eumoirous," to allow a class discussion of English borrowings from ancient Greek to Yiddish. Remarkably, however, even here Rosten cannot bring himself to use words such as "Jew" or "Yiddish": while Greek, Latin, Russian, and even Chinese etymological roots are openly identified, the class's examples from Yiddish are described only as bearing "Israel's proud *imprimatur.*"

Rosten quickly followed up *The Return of H*Y*M*A*N K*A*P*L*A*N* with a series of successes during the 1960s.

Captain Newman, M.D. (1961), the story of an American Army psychiatrist during World War II, is Rosten's best and best-selling novel, and was made into a feature film, though it suffers both from the author's penchant for stereotyped characters and from comparisons with Joseph Heller's *Catch–22*, which appeared in the same year and explores the same theme: war is crazy. *The Many Worlds of L*E*O R*O*S*T*E*N* (1964) is mostly a recycling of published material, from selected Kaplan stories to Rosten's columns for *Look*, and *A Most Private Intrigue* (1967) is perhaps his best thriller.

Then, in 1968, Rosten published *The Joys of Yiddish*, a work that probably derives from the same impetus as the lesson on English borrowings in "H*Y*M*A*N K*A*P*L*A*N, Ever Eumoirous." *The Joys of Yiddish* mixes etymologies and vaudeville jokes with cultural observations and scholarly research. It was accepted enthusiastically by an entire generation of the children of Jewish immigrants, whose postwar lives, affluent and increasingly assimilated, were among the most upwardly mobile in America. What *The Joys of Yiddish* seemed to celebrate was their differences, their unassimilability. Although Rosten had begun as an advocate of assimilation, his post-Holocaust work reflects a revised appreciation for Yiddish and the vanished Jewish community that spoke it. Such moderation of prewar antipathy toward the perceived exceptionalism of Jews and Jewishness can, of course, be seen in the work of other writers of the time—most notably, Irving Howe—and understandably so, considering the upheavals that produced the destruction of European Jewry and the reestablishment of the State of Israel.

Nonetheless, *The Joys of Yiddish* is really less about Yiddish than about how that language has been assimilated into American English—a point suggested in the book's own description, which says it is, in part, "a relaxed lexicon of Yiddish, Hebrew and Yinglish words often encountered in English," and that is made even clearer in the subtitle of a companion volume, *Hooray for Yiddish! A Book about English* (1982). Rosten's biases can also be seen in the contents, which avoid divisiveness and controversy. For example, he gives the meaning of the Hebrew word *goy* (gentile in Yiddish) as "nation," which does not sound especially insulting, but avoids mentioning that *shaygets* and *shiksa* (Yiddish for "gentile young man/woman") are the male and female forms of the Hebrew word for serpent. Accuracy aside, Rosten's compilation of illustrative jokes and

anecdotes makes this (often by their corny predictability or sheer inappropriateness) one of the few lexicons worth reading cover to cover.

After the death of his first wife, Rosten married Gertrude Zimmerman in 1970, and continued to work on books for publication up until his death in 1997. There were further lexicographical explorations in *Hooray for Yiddish!* (1982) and *The Joys of Yinglish* (1989); several collections of his journalism; a new Kaplan book comprised mostly of stories from the earlier two; edited volumes of selections from Jewish sources, general literature, and *Look*; two books of jokes; and several potboilers, including two installments in a Jewish detective series. With his remarkable successes in a variety of fields, his unquestioned devotion to the American ideal, and his gradual appreciation of a Jewishness from which he at first sought to distance himself, Leo Rosten's story is the comic but cautionary tale of a twentieth-century American Jewish prodigal.

David Mesher

References and Further Reading
Bronner, Simon J. 1982. "Structural and Stylistic Relations of Oral and Literary Humor: An Analysis of Leo Rosten's Hyman Kaplan Stories." *Journal of the Folklore Institute* 19,1: 31–45.
Golub, Ellen. 1982. "Leo Rosten." In *American Humorists, 1800–1950. Dictionary of Literary Biography.* Vol. 11, 410–418. Detroit, MI: Bruccoli Clark Layman.
Hasley, Louis. 1984. "Hyman Kaplan Revisited." *Studies in American Humor* 3,1: 56–60.
Shiffman, Dan. 1999. "The Ingratiating Humor of Leo Rosten's Hyman Kaplan Stories." *Studies in American Jewish Literature* 18: 93–101.
Shiffman, Dan. 2000. "The Comedy of Assimilation in Leo Rosten's Hyman Kaplan Stories." *Studies in American Humor* 3,7: 49–63.

Henry Roth (1906–1995)

Novelist

Henry Roth is one of the greatest Jewish American writers, most well-known for his novel *Call It Sleep* (1934), the story of an immigrant family's encounter with urban America from the perspective of a young boy. Roth powerfully articulates the experience of Americanization in its

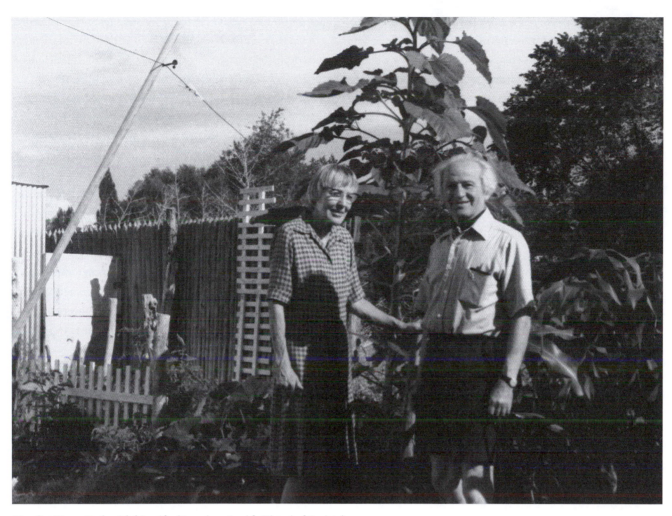

Novelist Henry Roth with his wife. (American Jewish Historical Society)

historical, social, psychological, and linguistic aspects. Roth's brilliant first novel, the history of its reception, his long literary silence, his comeback in 1994 with the first of a four-volume autobiographical fiction *Mercy of a Rude Stream*, and the extremities in his own life have made him a captivating figure on the American and Jewish American literary scenes.

Born Hershel Roth in 1906 in Tysmenitz, a small town in Austro-Hungarian Galicia, he immigrated to the United States in 1909 when his mother Leah joined Roth's father Herman, who had arrived in New York the previous year. *Call It Sleep* draws on his own early years in Brownsville and the Lower East Side, and then in Harlem, a move he portrayed as leaving behind a homogeneous Jewish neighborhood for a heterogeneous and threatening American environment. Filtered through the consciousness of the child of Eastern European Jewish immigrants, *Call It Sleep*

gives expression to the rupture with tradition and the ensuing loss of cultural, religious, and communal life often exacted by assimilation. Through David Shearl's quest for the source of power and holiness in his menacing New York neighborhood, Roth also chronicles the severing of the child from his parents and the inner struggle to stake out his new world through the English language and American culture. In this depiction of the curious child's fertile mind at work, *Call It Sleep* has often been read as a Jewish American portrait of the artist as a young boy, representative of a generation shaped by Yiddish and dedicated to English, who made great contributions to American culture.

Call It Sleep has been hailed as a great proletariat novel portraying the gritty life of immigrants in what they mistakenly assumed would be a Golden Land. It has also been read as one of the great modernist novels of the century, inspired by Joyce's *Ulysses,* a work that Roth admitted had taught him that great art could be wrought from urban squalor. The originality of Henry Roth's writing style lies in its combination of naturalism and experimental modernism, as well as its extraordinary multilingual word play, as Yiddish and Hebrew intersect with American English. Although it met with favorable reviews when it first appeared in 1934, its legendary status in American literary history dates from its record-breaking paperback edition three decades later, when the college-educated children of immigrants constituted a new and eager readership for a work in which they recognized their own childhood and when interest in ethnicity in American culture was already on the rise. Shortly after the 1964 edition appeared, it sold over one million copies in thirty printings, attaining the status of both best-seller and classic, and has assumed a place at the center of Jewish American writing as an American, Jewish, and modernist work.

Just as the reception of *Call It Sleep* illustrates the dramatic shift in linguistic and cultural identity from immigrant to ethnic Americans, the drama of Roth's literary life and career represents one of the overarching themes of his generation, severing bonds with Jewish life (the child in *Call It Sleep* is named Shearl, which means scissors in Yiddish) in order to emphatically embrace America. In *Call It Sleep,* this period in American Jewish history is portrayed as an Oedipal drama where the loving harmony with a Yiddish-speaking mother gives way to symbolic patricide and a violent yet redemptive initiation into the New World. Although his emotional attachment to Yiddish lingered throughout his life, Roth aimed for universality, which he, along with many others of his generation, believed could be attained in Communism. His attempts to write a proletariat novel divorced from Jewish content, his advocacy of Jewish assimilation into American society, and his political activism on behalf of a communist vision, were dramatically repudiated by Roth when he feared for Israel's survival in the days leading up to the Six Day War in 1967. A watershed event for Roth, the war signified a regeneration of the Jewish people that inspired him to renew his own writing efforts as he redefined himself as a Jew and a Zionist.

After many years of silence, Roth published several other works: *Shifting Landscape* (1987), a collection of his short writings (edited by Mario Materassi), and a four-volume autobiographical fiction, *Mercy of a Rude Stream.* The first two volumes appeared in his lifetime, *Mercy of a Rude Stream: A Star Shines over Mt. Morris Park* (1994) and *A Diving Rock on the Hudson* (1995); the final two were published posthumously: *From Bondage* (1996) and *Requiem for Harlem* (1998). The first volume picks up where *Call It Sleep* leaves off, in that the protagonist, renamed Ira Stigman, has already moved from the Lower East Side to Harlem, where he encounters both the vulgarity of the street and the joy of wordplay in his efforts to describe all of the nuances of his world.

His renewed Jewish identity is most evident as the author interjects his own comments, fueled by his anxieties about the Jewish people in a post-Holocaust world, concerning his character's actions and the historical events that frame the story. Addressing his computer, named Ecclesias, Roth professes views about Middle Eastern politics and history and laments his earlier abandonment of Judaism. The hindsight of the struggling elderly writer berating his younger self marks the entire *Mercy of a Rude Stream* series, along with a more liberal use of Yiddish, so extensive as to require glossaries at the end of each volume. The effect of these literary devices is to draw attention to forgetting and remembering, past and present, and autobiography as it is transformed into art.

The rebellions of David Shearl and Ira Stigman are cast as crossing boundaries that are both liberating and transgressive. In *Call It Sleep,* David's flight out of his parental home toward the city is depicted as symbolic death and rebirth, a crossing-over into the world of gentile America. In *A Diving Rock on the Hudson,* Ira's rejection of his father's tyranny is compounded by incest with his sister. The choices that are posed to his characters are exogamy and endogamy in their extremes, either abandoning home entirely or remaining at home in its most debilitating form, Jewish identity as incest. Marked by self-loathing and guilt, *Mercy of a Rude Stream* is also a nuanced document of the interwar period in New York City and a painstaking record of soul-searching, humility, and creativity as redemption. It is also a return to "the little he knew, the essential plug he had retained of his Jewishness, of Jewish tradition. . . . And when he tried to pluck it out . . . creative inanition followed" (Roth 1994).

Hana Wirth-Nesher

References and Further Reading
Baumgarten, Murray. 1982. *City Scriptures: Modern Jewish Writing.* Cambridge, MA: Harvard University Press.

Lyons, Bonnie. 1976. *Henry Roth: The Man and His Work*. New York: Cooper Square Publishers.

Kazin, Alfred. 1991. "Introduction to *Call It Sleep*." New York: Farrar, Straus, Giroux.

Kellman, Steven. 2005. *Redemption: The Life of Henry Roth*. New York: W. W. Norton.

Roth, Henry. 1994. *Mercy of a Rude Stream*. New York: St. Martin's Press.

Wirth-Nesher, Hana. 1990. "Between Mother Tongue and Native Language: Multilingualism in Henry Roth's *Call It Sleep*." (Afterword to Noonday edition).

Wirth-Nesher, Hana. 1996. *New Essays on* Call It Sleep. Cambridge, UK: Cambridge University Press.

Philip Roth (b. 1933)

Novelist and Short Story Writer

Philip Roth, novelist and short story writer. (Library of Congress)

One of the most prominent American writers of his generation, Philip Roth repeatedly inquires in his novels, short stories, and essays into the meaning of being a Jew in the United States in the late twentieth century. A second-generation Jewish American born into a largely Jewish neighborhood of Depression-era Newark, New Jersey, Roth often portrays the ambivalence felt by Jews toward assimilation into American culture. Roth's work recognizes that assimilation promises the rewards of freedom, privilege, and prosperity even as it threatens the loss of a distinctive Jewish identity and sense of community. His extravagant comic imagination and inclination to challenge proprieties have won Roth a controversial place in American letters, ever since the publication in 1959 of his first book. From *Goodbye, Columbus, and Five Short Stories* onward, he has dramatized the challenges faced by the modern Jew in maintaining an authentic selfhood in the American diaspora. Roth presents Jewish individuals who pursue their erotic and artistic desires as a means to an autonomous self only to find themselves in conflict with social constraints. Roth's Jews feel caught between loyalty to a Jewish ethos and family life and the temptations—both fleshly and material—of non-Jewish American culture.

Roth's career can be divided roughly into three phases. The early work, through the novels of the mid-1970s, generally offers realistic psychological portraits of protagonists subject to instinctual repression, for whom the question of identity hinges on the individual's tormented negotiations with a restrictive social code. Roth's midcareer fiction and nonfiction, into the early 1990s, shift toward a more liberated sense of the possibilities for identity, as they also shift toward a self-conscious, postmodern narrative mode. The protagonists in these works often engage in the process of inventing themselves, both within and outside conventional Jewish models, as they come to see selfhood as a construction analogous to storytelling. The narratives of Roth's later phase return his assimilated characters to a realistic canvas, there to face the consequences of a broadly conceived historical determinism; these individuals inevitably come to experience their identities, for good or ill, as the products of American culture.

In a 1974 essay about *Portnoy's Complaint* (1969), Roth identifies the tension governing much of his early work when he distinguishes between "the 'Jewboy' (with all that word signifies to Jew and Gentile alike about aggression, appetite, and marginality)" and "the 'nice Jewish boy' (and what that epithet implies about repression, respectability, and social acceptance)" (Roth 1985b). At stake is the postimmigrant American Jew's desire both to improve his lot and to earn a respectable position in non-Jewish American culture. Roth expresses the attendant anxiety succinctly in the 1963 essay "Writing about Jews": "What will the goyim [non-Jews] think?" (Roth 1985b).

In the novella "Goodbye, Columbus," Neil Klugman pursues a summer romance with Brenda Patimkin, whose family's suburban affluence signifies the 1950s American promise of plenitude. The Patimkin "aggression" and "appetite" are visible in the "heapings, spillings, and gorgings" of the family table (Roth 1959). The abstract temptations of Patimkin prosperity are made concrete in Neil's desire for a sexual relationship with Brenda. The virtual Garden of Eden housed in her family's refrigerator, stocked with a cornucopia of fresh fruits, tempts Neil, symbolizing both his desires and their prohibition. Neil later prays to God in the confused terms the Patimkin world has defined for him: "If we meet You at all, God, it's that we're carnal, and acquisitive, and thereby partake of You." That Neil prays in a *cathedral* suggests that, as a Jew, he has lost his spiritual compass, leading him to conceive of humans as carnal and acquisitive. The postimmigrant Jewish success story thus probes Neil's sense of who he is—and what Jews are—in this New World. When Neil attends the wedding of Brenda's brother, he witnesses the corruption inherent in the Patimkin ethic of consumption, the extravagant food "gone sticky with the hours." Neil finally bids farewell to Brenda and to his passion for her, repudiating an assimilation driven by pleasure.

The tension between New World gifts and Old World sacrifices, between sensuality and regulation by a communal order, between transgression and obedience, is played out in the other stories in *Goodbye, Columbus*. In "The Conversion of the Jews," a child challenges his rabbi over Jewish dogma. Rejecting religious authoritarianism in favor of American ideology, Ozzie Freedman subdues an awed assemblage of authority figures as, arguing for absolute freedom, he leaps from the roof of his synagogue. The middle-aged hero of "Epstein," however, is defeated in his pursuit of pleasure and self-liberation. His affair with a neighbor is exposed when he suffers a heart attack while with her; the judgment upon him is indicated by the rash that has developed on his penis, like the visible mark of Jewish circumcision requiring his return to the fold. "Eli, the Fanatic" turns a comfortably assimilated, secular American Jew's confrontation with the sorrows of the Holocaust into a search for an old world identity that culminates in his assuming the blackness of suffering that is his cultural heritage. "Defender of the Faith" exhibits a Jew exploiting his Jewishness. When Army trainee Grossbart manipulates another Jew, Sergeant Marx, for unorthodox favors, he reinforces antisemitic stereotypes. Marx, who has won through his military service a sense of power and belonging as an American, thereafter suffers from self-loathing; shamed by their shared Jewishness, he paradoxically also feels shame for the repugnance his fellow Jew inspires in him.

Roth was excoriated by many in the Jewish establishment for exposing Jews to criticism—for depicting Jews in all their humanity as lustful, neurotic, and self-absorbed. Having overturned the image of the Jew in postwar American fiction as a figure of "righteousness and restraint" in favor of narratives of "libidinous and aggressive activities" (Roth 1985b), Roth seems for a period to have drawn away from the controversy of representing Jews *as* Jews. *Letting Go* (1962) and *When She Was Good* (1967) both return bleakly to examining how the social contract demands instinctual repression. In *Letting Go*, Roth's first novel, the characters' joyless marital and erotic relationships consign their Jewishness to the background. The psychological realism, muted tonalities, and grim compulsion toward responsibility of *Letting Go* reveal Roth's debt to Henry James. *When She Was Good* witnesses the destruction wrought in a gentile family by one member's thirst for respectability.

With the controversial best-seller *Portnoy's Complaint* (1969), however, Roth breaks through to the voice of a Jewboy in high-decibel crisis, simultaneously revolutionizing the depiction of sex in American fiction. Alexander Portnoy tells his psychoanalyst of outrageous sexual transgression motivated by severe repression and punished by impotence. Hysterical in both senses of the word, Portnoy traces his dysfunction to stereotypes of Jewish family life—the man-eating mother, the father so bound up by his role as provider that he spends his home life in a struggle with constipation—and to the wider proscriptions of the code of Jewish assimilation. Portnoy lives in a "Jewish joke," repressing his desires in homage to "Jewish suffering." Desperate to "put the id back in Yid," Portnoy breaks sexual taboos against masturbation, extramarital sex, and, especially, sex with *shikses* (non-Jewish women). He hopes through sexual activity to "discover America. *Conquer* America." Failing to establish a wholly American identity, Portnoy seeks coherence in the fantasy of Israel, where everyone and everything is Jewish, only to be humiliated by a young woman from a kibbutz who diagnoses in him "what was most shameful in 'the culture of the Diaspora'":

a man "frightened, defensive, self-deprecating, unmanned and corrupted by life in the gentile world," the very complaint that constitutes his book-long lament.

Portnoy's bedevilment by *shikses* and Jewish women alike brings into focus the question of whether, as he has at times been accused, Roth offers misogynistic representations of women. He has indeed relied on comic stereotypes—the Jewish American Princess Brenda Patimkin, for example, or the castrating Jewish mother Sophie Portnoy, or even the sexually insatiable Drenka Balich of the many malapropisms, in *Sabbath's Theater* (1995)—and with rare exception (notably *When She Was Good),* the fiction almost universally details a male, Jewish perspective. Insofar as Roth is concerned with women's power over men, however, he not only at times exposes male objectification of women, but also largely portrays such a concern as the product of his male characters' culturally determined anxiety over their own symbolic masculine power. Such is the case of Portnoy, whose sexual and psychological impotence derives from the way he has come to view Jewish women as signifying the demanding Jewish ethical standards from which his guilt at his repressed desires emanates.

The primal scream that literally concludes *Portnoy's Complaint* sets the tone for the next two novels: *Our Gang* (1971), an enraged satire of the Nixon presidency, and *The Breast* (1972), a Kafkaesque parable of metamorphosis. In the latter novella, David Kepesh, who reappears in subsequent novels, wakes up one morning to find himself absurdly transformed into a six-foot mammary gland. Kepesh's agonized confrontation with his alien flesh serves as an existential metaphor for the uncertainty of selfhood driven and defined by desires. Roth next digresses into profligate comic allegory in *The Great American Novel* (1973), a book exploring the mythic status of baseball as the icon of twentieth-century American culture. Roth experiments boldly with the kind of exaggerated invention that was appearing among his contemporaries in American fiction-making, such as Thomas Pynchon, Robert Coover, and Donald Barthelme.

Roth returns to the wages of desire in *My Life as a Man* (1974), a transitional work. The writer Peter Tarnopol finds himself in psychotherapy—with Portnoy's analyst, Dr. Spielvogel—for a crisis precipitated by a disastrous marriage. Tarnopol attempts to write himself out of his trauma in two short stories. When the displacements of his biography into "Useful Fictions" prove unsuccessful, he composes "My True Story," an undisguised attempt to make sense of his sexual and romantic history. In Tarnopol's wife, Maureen, Roth returns to the deadly attractions of the *shikse* for the Jewish man. Tarnopol is torn over how to *be a man.* For him, the phrase means finding a stable self and modest satisfaction of his desires; for Maureen, who has tricked him into marriage and then damaged him with her deeply neurotic needs, it means sacrificing himself to her and to an emasculating ideal of responsibility.

In keeping with shifts in American writing at large, *My Life as a Man* looks forward to the second phase of Roth's career. First, though Roth retains his interest in psychological determinism, he places the act of writing at center stage as a means to order fragmentary experience and construct an identity. Roth draws attention to the self-conscious artifice of fiction and fiction-making, stripping the illusion of reality away to remind readers that, just as Tarnopol's "Useful Fictions" are simply inventions, so, too, is Roth's invention of Tarnopol's story. Second, *My Life as a Man* insists on the indeterminacy of identity, implicit in Tarnopol's anxious attempt to write a self; the novel thus prepares for the freer experiments in narrative self-invention that follow. Third, the novel emphasizes autobiography as the source of fiction. Having been perhaps unfairly accused of writing directly from his life in his early stories, Roth defiantly proposes to make the transformation of life into art his subject, even more so in that the tragedy of Tarnopol's marriage is drawn largely from Roth's history with his first wife, as he reveals in his autobiography, *The Facts* (1988).

The Facts quotes as its epigraph a line from *The Counterlife* that expresses a key issue in the novels of the late 1970s and 1980s: "And as he spoke I was thinking, *the kind of stories that people turn life into, the kind of lives that people turn stories into*" (Roth 1986). The interrelation of stories and lives as well as the possibility for the self to create a life story autonomously become central to Roth's concerns. *The Professor of Desire* (1977) returns to David Kepesh from *The Breast*, filling in the tale before his metamorphosis. The dilemma of second-generation Jewish assimilation is now an unspoken grounding for Kepesh's anxiety, which nevertheless takes on the inflections and conflicts of such works as "Goodbye, Columbus" and *Portnoy's Complaint*. Drawn at once to sensual excess and conscientious restraint, Kepesh feels victimized by his dual nature, represented by the sexual partners he chooses and influenced by the literature he teaches as a professor of comparative literature. The bittersweet ending of the novel, in which Kepesh seeks solace from a woman who nevertheless fails to arouse his passion, forecasts his failure to rewrite his life coherently.

For Kepesh, the notion of rewriting one's life story remains at the level of metaphor. The metaphor becomes concrete in the next series of novels, in which a Jewish writer/character, whose biography coincides in many ways with Roth's own, stands in for Roth himself. Nathan Zuckerman first appears as Tarnopol's alter ego in his "Useful Fictions." The tetralogy collected as *Zuckerman Bound* (1985)—including *The Ghost Writer* (1979), *Zuckerman Unbound* (1981), *The Anatomy Lesson* (1983), and *The Prague Orgy* (1985)—features Zuckerman centrally, as does *The Counterlife*. Zuckerman reappears as Roth's epistolary critic in *The Facts* and as the narrator in three subsequent novels: *American Pastoral* (1997), *I Married a Communist* (1998), and *The Human Stain* (2000).

Zuckerman Bound traces the story of an artist. Zuckerman finds a voice, confronts celebrity, suffers recriminations over the offenses in his work against Jews in general and his father in particular, and eventually finds his voice silenced. Having rebelled against familial and communal authority, betokened by his biological and surrogate fathers, Zuckerman travels toward remorse. He begins writing his own story in youthful confidence. In blithe disregard of historical reality, Zuckerman fantasizes grandiosely that he can be redeemed for his sins against the Jewish fathers by imaginatively reinventing an iconic Jewish figure. In his middle age, however, he is hemmed in by the recognition that a moral reality irrevocably holds sway over his inventive capacity.

The Ghost Writer presents Zuckerman as a young writer awed by his literary forefathers and in a pilgrimage to the Jewish master, E. I. Lonoff. Antagonized by his father, who deems his writing offensive to the Jews, Zuckerman has been attacked by an authority figure in his home community, Judge Wapter, in much the same language that had been leveled at Roth during a panel discussion at Yeshiva University in 1962. Wapter's list of questions for Zuckerman—concluding with "Can you honestly say that there is anything in your short story that would not warm the heart of a Julius Streicher or a Joseph Goebbels?"—encapsulates the harsh criticism many Jewish readers directed

at Roth for exposing Jewish lusts and yearnings in *Goodbye, Columbus* and elsewhere (Roth 1985c). To shake off the accusations of antisemitism, Zuckerman turns to the austere Lonoff for aesthetic encouragement, only to propose himself as Lonoff's rival for the mysterious young woman at Lonoff's rural retreat. Zuckerman fantasizes an elaborate alternative life for Amy Bellette as Anne Frank, miraculously survived, living incognito, and ripe for romance with Zuckerman himself. Since no potential mate has more impeccable Jewish credentials than Anne Frank, Zuckerman's fantasy clearly recasts his own identity to reconcile with the Jews he has affronted, even as he competes with his surrogate artistic father.

The metafictional experiment in *The Ghost Writer*—in which the narrative offers indeterminate levels of "reality" with respect to the characters' histories—is replaced by the realism of *Zuckerman Unbound*. Zuckerman's sense of his identity is unmoored by the notoriety and loss of privacy that attend the success of his novel *Carnovsky* (an undisguised reference to *Portnoy's Complaint*) and by his estrangement from his family, especially his dying father, for his repudiation of the Jews. Roth develops that estrangement into self-alienation in *The Anatomy Lesson*. Unable to write because of a mysterious back pain that he interprets as punishment for his offenses, Zuckerman embarks on an absurd switch of career that concludes with him, jaw broken, effectively silenced. *The Prague Orgy* finds Zuckerman on a quixotic quest in Eastern Europe for the lost manuscripts of a Yiddish writer, victim of the Holocaust. Here, he seems to renounce his own writing career, and the self defined through it, in order to enact the nice Jewish boy, recovering his cultural past as an offering to the Jewish fathers.

Zuckerman's efforts toward self-invention are tentative and compromised in *Zuckerman Bound*. In *The Counterlife*'s exuberant exercise in storytelling, however, Roth offers a Zuckerman so freed from the constraints of family, community, and fictional conventions that he audaciously composes a series of counterlives for himself. Five chapters present five alternative but linked fates for Zuckerman in a sequence of irreconcilably contradictory stories, all convincing but none finally definitive. As a result not only does Zuckerman's "self" appear the pure product of narrative, but also Roth playfully undermines the capacity of narrative to represent a determinate "reality." By implication, he undermines the determinacy of reality itself. Roth also returns explicitly to the problem of constructing an authentic Jewish identity in the

Diaspora. Zuckerman examines the meaning of an American Jew's *aliyah* to Israel, the effects of Zionism on Jewish selfhood, and the implications of assimilation taken to the extreme of intermarriage. The latter, an idealized condition of cultural unity, he ultimately rejects as a "pastoral," defined in terms of the literary genre that celebrates innocence, in which "everything [is] cozy and strifeless, and desire simply fulfilled" (Roth 1986). No longer fighting his fathers but preparing for fatherhood himself, Zuckerman embraces conflict to assume the place of the Jewish patriarch, insisting on circumcision as the "quintessentially Jewish" mark that "you're mine and not theirs" (1986).

Roth's work of the late 1980s and early 1990s, like *The Counterlife* itself, bridges psychological realism and postmodern self-consciousness about fictional artifice as it moves toward the third phase of his career. *The Facts* presents Roth's autobiography through his mid-thirties, when he was on the brink of commercial success. The book offers a straightforward life story, rich in its account of a Jewish American upbringing and young manhood. It is framed, however, by a correspondence between the writer and his character Zuckerman, reminding the reader that autobiography as a form relies on the conscious crafting of selfhood into narrative. More consistent in its realistic mode is *Patrimony* (1991), Roth's moving memoir of his father, focusing especially on the year of his father's dying and filling in the details of his father's post-immigrant generation for whom "the real work . . . was making themselves American" (Roth 1991). Sandwiched between the two nonfiction narratives is *Deception* (1990), an experiment in the novel as intimate dialogue, in which Roth tantalizes the reader with a central character named Philip, who bears an irrefutable resemblance to Roth himself. Like *The Counterlife* and *The Facts*, the novel works to obscure the line between fiction and reality, especially with respect to a reader's tendency to see an author's identity in the fiction he or she writes.

Roth reinforces that temptation in *Operation Shylock* (1993). The narrating central character "Philip Roth" confronts his double in Jerusalem in a story that spins into antic implausibility, engaging a devastating shikse and an Israeli spy plot along the way. The identity crisis with which "Roth" struggles, figured in his double and in his journey to Israel, centers largely on his self-conception as a Jew in the American diaspora. Going beyond *The Counterlife, Operation Shylock* proposes that Jewish identity is inescapably a historical product. "Roth's" capacity for self-invention and even fiction-making itself is finally circumscribed by his debt to his Jewish past.

The conclusion of *Operation Shylock* returns Roth not just to Jewish obligation but also to realism as a fictional mode and desire as a subject. *Sabbath's Theater* recasts the Jewboy of *Portnoy's Complaint* as an aging puppeteer—a hedonist, nihilist, and master of erotic transgression. Embracing the American individualistic ethos, Mickey Sabbath defies social convention to gain special access to the life force, most recently with his married lover. His identity is tested by his confrontation with death and disappearance—his lover's, his first wife's, his brother's—and by implication with his own mortality. *The Dying Animal* (2001) resurrects an elderly David Kepesh to face the same challenge, but in specifically erotic terms: in the disfiguring breast cancer of his former, youthful lover he meets with his own decaying flesh and failing sexual powers.

Roth replaces the determinism of mortal flesh with historical determinism in the trilogy of novels about America that follows *Sabbath's Theater*, all narrated by Nathan Zuckerman. *American Pastoral* (1997) recounts the tragic story of a Jewish golden boy. Swede Levov's successful life is destroyed by the chaos of 1960s America, largely because he is blind to the hollowness of his pastoral dream of harmonious Jewish assimilation. In Levov's futile fantasy of being a new Johnny Appleseed, Roth returns to the Edenic metaphors of *Goodbye, Columbus:* the American Jew's assimilation, signified by the real and figurative fruits of his labors, portends both his material success and his spiritual fall. Swede Levov's innocence is countered by the secret crime of Ira Ringold in *I Married a Communist* (1998), committed in response to antisemitism. Ira reinvents himself as the classic midcentury Jewish liberal, masking his violence under a politics of social conscience, only to be exposed and abandoned by the radically violent American ideology of the McCarthy era. A secret life story is likewise at the core of *The Human Stain* (2000), in which the African American Coleman Silk has passed for years as a white Jew. He becomes a victim—figuratively, of the discriminatory racial ideology he has internalized, and literally, of vengeance for his attempts to satisfy his sexual desires. In each case, a man's efforts to invent himself are doomed by the constraints American culture imposes upon its ethnically marginal citizens.

Debra Shostak

References and Further Reading

Cooper, Alan. 1996. *Philip Roth and the Jews.* Albany: State University of New York Press.

Halio, Jay. 1992. *Philip Roth Revisited.* New York: Twayne Publishers.

Halkin, Hillel. 1994. "How to Read Philip Roth." *Commentary* (February): 43–48.

Milbauer, Asher Z., and Donald G. Watson, eds. 1988. *Reading Philip Roth.* New York: St. Martin's Press.

Pinsker, Sanford, ed. 1982. *Critical Essays on Philip Roth.* Boston: G.K. Hall & Co.

Roth, Philip. 1959, 1963. *Goodbye, Columbus, and Five Short Stories.* Boston: Houghton Mifflin. (1959)/Reprint (1963). New York: Bantam.

Roth, Philip. 1969, 1985a. *Portnoy's Complaint.* New York: Random House. (1969)/Reprint (1985). New York: Ballantine Books.

Roth, Philip. 1975, 1985b. *Reading Myself and Others.* New York: Farrar, Straus and Giroux. (1975)/Revised ed. (1985). New York: Penguin.

Roth, Philip. 1985c. *Zuckerman Bound.* New York: Farrar, Straus and Giroux.

Roth, Philip. 1986. *The Counterlife.* New York: Farrar, Straus and Giroux.

Roth, Philip. 1988. *The Facts: A Novelist's Autobiography.* New York: Farrar, Straus and Giroux.

Roth, Philip. 1991. *Patrimony: A True Story.* New York: Simon & Schuster.

Searles, George J., ed. 1992. *Conversations with Philip Roth.* Jackson: University Press of Mississippi.

Shechner, Mark. 2003. *Up Society's Ass, Copper: Rereading Philip Roth.* Madison: University of Wisconsin Press.

Shostak, Debra. 2004. *Philip Roth—Countertexts, Counterlives.* Columbia: University of South Carolina Press.

Isaac Bashevis Singer (1904–1991)

Last of the Great Writers of Yiddish Fiction and Winner of the Nobel Prize for Literature

Isaac Bashevis Singer is the only Yiddish writer whose work (in translation) caught the imagination of the American public. Born in Radzymin, a town fifteen miles northeast of Warsaw, in 1904, he emigrated to America in 1935, continued to write in his native Yiddish, and produced a long succession of stories, novels, memoirs, and children's books about life in his native Poland and about his experiences as an immigrant in America. This massive body of work earned him the Nobel Prize for Literature in 1978. Singer died in Surfside, Florida, on July 24, 1991.

The tale of Singer's remarkable career is one of the most improbable in all literature. How did it come to pass that this storyteller (as Singer liked to call himself), writing in a dying language (Yiddish) about a vanished world (the Jews of Eastern Europe), not only fashioned the most successful career in modern Yiddish letters but also became a celebrated *American* writer, so much so that in September 1980 he was invited to review the troops—2,000 massed cadets—at West Point, and after his death his papers found a home in the University of Texas? "How had he begun?" asks a resentful fellow-writer of Yiddish in Cynthia Ozick's short story "Envy; or, Yiddish in America": "A columnist for one of the Yiddish dailies, a humorist, a cheap fast article-writer, a squeezer-out of real-life tales. . . . From this, how did he come to the *New Yorker*, to *Playboy*, to big lecture fees, invitations to Yale and M.I.T. and Vassar, to the Midwest, to Buenos Aires, to a literary agent, to a publisher on Madison Avenue?" Or, one might add, to the Nobel Prize for Literature, the National Book Award in 1970 and 1974, and the Gold Medal of the American Academy and Institute of Arts and Letters in 1989?

Singer's beginnings do not, at first glance, seem well-suited to a literary career at all. He was born (as Isaac Singer) into a world of almost medieval Polish Jewish Orthodoxy. His father, an impoverished rabbi and Hasid (pietist), held rigidly to the conviction that the world itself was *treyf* (unclean). It was a function of his father's unworldliness to condemn theater, the visual arts, and literature as idolatrous. Literature might be supposed less offensive than painting or the stage because it was, like the Jewish religion itself, oriented toward the word rather than the graven image. But Singer's father saw in literature, especially Yiddish literature, the most potent threat of all to a way of life in which every human activity—including cooking, eating, washing, praying, and lovemaking—was regulated by religious law. "My father," Singer recalled, "used to say that secular writers like [I. L.] Peretz were leading the Jews to heresy. He said everything they wrote was against God. Even though Peretz wrote in a religious vein, my father called his writing 'sweetened poison,' but poison nevertheless. And from his point of view he was right. Everybody who read such books sooner or later became a worldly man and forsook the traditions" (Blocker 1963).

Isaac Bashevis Singer, Yiddish author and winner of the Nobel Prize for literature in 1978. (Library of Congress)

Singer too would forsake the traditions as they are commonly understood, for he was not a religiously observant Jew, and he took up a calling that to his father made him as bad as a *meshumad* (apostate), but the father despaired prematurely. For Singer instinctively understood the literary possibilities of the intensely traditional life to which he had immediate access of a kind denied even to writers older than himself. He also understood that writers can be sustained by what they deny, and that religious faith rejected usually exercises a more powerful hold over a writer than new, "secular" faiths adopted. (Singer believed that the dream of a secular Jewish culture—with the accent on *secular*—had already played itself out by the time he arrived in America.) Most Yiddish writers, his predecessors as well as his contemporaries, could only revisit the rich social and spiritual texture of the covenant-determined religious world nostalgically or through the collection of folk materials.

No more than I. L. Peretz or Sholom Aleichem or Mendele Mocher Seforim, the classical Yiddish writers who preceded him, was Singer an unsophisticated folk artist. He recognized, as they did, that folklore is the soil in which literature grows best, and his rootedness in the old Jewish life would make his books a bridge between the assimilated Jews of America and the destroyed world of their East European ancestors. But when critics like Ozick and Irving Howe spoke of the unique recklessness with which Singer surrendered himself to the claims of the imagination, they meant something more than his ability to write about the destroyed world of European Jewry (as he did) as if it were brilliantly alive. They were also paying tribute to him as a magnificent inventor of an imagined world, not simply the curator of the artifacts of a vanished one.

It is the justified boast of Yiddish literature that it was based on a peculiarly intimate relationship between authors and readers for whom storytelling was a communal activity. When Peretz died in 1915, 75,000 people came to his funeral in Warsaw, and Sholom Aleichem's funeral the following year was attended by an even greater number in New York. Such demonstrations of popular affection were unmatched for any other modern writers. Singer never achieved the status of these classical Yiddish masters within the community of Yiddish readers, and was even looked upon with some degree of reserve and suspicion by them because of his "modernism," his keen interest in matters sexual, above all (after 1950) his writing in one language (Yiddish) with the intention of being read in English translation. Yet he too had begun by writing only, as he put it, "for people who know everything I know—not for the stranger" (Blocker 1963). He sternly resisted the uniquely Jewish form of parochialism named "universalism," that siren call that lured so many Jewish writers to the self-destructive waste of their talent in pale imitations of Western literature and endless returns to moribund Bolshevist politics.

Singer arrived in the United States in May 1935 with the help of his older brother Israel Joshua, who had become a successful Yiddish writer in New York. He got a position as a freelance writer with *Forverts* (*Forward*), thus forming an association that endured for decades. He began to learn English, but this hardly compensated for his dim view of American Jewry and the prospects of Yiddish in America. "Here in New York," he wrote to a friend a few months after arrival, "I see even more clearly than in Poland that there is no Yiddish literature, that there is no one to work for. There is a crazy Jewish people here which keeps slightly kosher and peddles . . . and awaits Marxism for the people of the world. But it doesn't need Yiddish literature" (Hadda 1997). In 1937 he published, under his favored pseudonym Bashevis (i.e., Bathsheba's son), two short stories and two literary sketches, but then he went into hiding as a fiction writer even as he continued to produce journalistic work under the pen name of Yitzhak Varshavsky (Isaac, the man from Warsaw).

A main reason why his creative work languished was what America revealed to him about the future of Yiddish:

> When I came to this country I lived through a terrible disappointment. I felt more than I believe now—that Yiddish had no future in this country. In Poland, Yiddish was still very much alive when I left. When I came here it seemed to

me that Yiddish was finished: it was very depressing. The result was that for five or six or maybe seven years I couldn't write a word. Not only didn't I publish anything in those years, but writing became so difficult a chore that my grammar was affected. I couldn't write a single worthwhile sentence. I became like a man who was a great lover and is suddenly impotent, knowing at the same time that ultimately he will regain his power (Blocker 1963).

Singer, it should be recalled, had indeed (in literary terms) been "a great lover" in Poland. He was a prizewinning author by age twenty-one, and his first novel, *Satan in Goray*, was hailed as a masterpiece when published serially in 1934 and then in book form by the Yiddish PEN Club in 1935.

Singer overcame his (creative) writer's block in 1943 with a pair of short stories and two weighty articles about the state of Yiddish in Poland and in the United States. "Problems of Yiddish Prose in America" (published in *Svive* [*Surroundings*], the March–April issue) asserts that the better Yiddish prose writers wisely avoid writing about American Jewish life because they do not want to falsify dialogue and find little interest in describing again and again "a narrow circle of old people or coarse immigrants." Singer believed that words, like people, become disoriented when they emigrate, and that the Yiddish writer who bypasses Broadway to seek his subjects in Warsaw, Vilna, Lodz, is not escaping reality, but returning to a world where people truly lived within Yiddish and not the "vulgarized" gibberish "which no self-respecting Yiddish writer could use in good conscience." This means, to be sure, that the conscientious Yiddish writer dines only on "leftovers" because "only food prepared in the old world can nourish him in the new." Of course Singer exaggerated the impulse he felt to remove Yiddish from the modern world: he would later write a great deal about America (for example, in the novel *Enemies, A Love Story*) and also about the effects of the Holocaust, which goes unmentioned in this essay.

By the time this essay appeared, Singer's creative vein had once again begun to flow. *Satan in Goray* was reissued along with five new stories, among them the powerful tales "The Destruction of Kreshev" and "Zeidlus the First." In 1945, continuing a genre in which his recently deceased brother Israel Joshua had excelled, Singer commenced the long family/historical saga *The Family Moskat,* published serially in the *Forward* through 1948 and then in book form in 1950. This great novel traces the decline of Polish Jewry and ends with the German bombardment of Warsaw on September 1, 1939, and a character observing "Death is the Messiah. That's the real truth." The novel was translated into English, with the active involvement (as would be the case in all subsequent translations of his work) of the author himself, who now had a third persona: Isaac Bashevis Singer. In 1953, Saul Bellow's publication of his English translation of "Gimpel the Fool" in *Partisan Review* gave Singer's work the imprimatur of the high priests of literary modernism, including Irving Howe, and helped to gain for it an acclaim beyond what any Yiddish writer had ever received in non-Yiddish literary circles.

From that time forward, Singer went from triumph to triumph, "set aloft," as Ruth Wisse has written, "on the wave of fame that nowhere swells so high and fast as in America" (Wisse 1979). His productivity was enormous—novel after novel, story after story—an abundance equaled among American writers of the first rank perhaps only by William Faulkner. After two decades of abject poverty, he became prosperous as well as famous, not only one of the rare Yiddish writers to make his living by writing, but (so it was reported) earning over $100,000 a year from advances, royalties, lecture fees, and motion picture and television options on his work. Yet the adulation and rewards of the world did not cause Singer to swerve from his stubborn integrity as a professional literary man determined to go his own (Jewish) way. When Singer died in 1991, the loss was more than personal. He was the last of the great writers of Yiddish fiction, so that with his death, as the critic Hillel Halkin observed, the narrative prose of a whole language had come to an end.

Singer believed that an artist must have an "address," must be "rooted in his milieu," and "not deny his parents and grandparents" (Burgin 1985). He viewed himself as an old-fashioned storyteller addressing an audience that values stories for their own sake and also as a unifying agent of shared memories. But, precisely because he was content to speak as a Jew, Singer made himself heard not only among Jews but everywhere. His writing reached a large international public and was translated into many languages. The Nobel Prize citation praised his "impassioned narratives, which, with roots in a Polish-Jewish cultural tradition, bring universal human conditions to life."

Singer often insisted that he was a writer in the Jewish rather than the Yiddish tradition, even though he always wrote in Yiddish. What he meant was that he eschewed the sentimentalism and the espousal of "social justice" that characterized much Yiddish writing. "The storyteller," he declared in his Nobel acceptance speech, "must be an entertainer of the spirit in the full sense of the word, not just a preacher of social and political ideals." In pursuit of this aim, he opened himself to older sources of inspiration in Jewish lore and thought, especially mysticism. He resisted the role of cultural spokesman for his people; instead he created a body of work that encompasses the Old World, the New World, and the next world, in both its upper and lower reaches. The supernatural pervades his writing and expresses his belief in the power of the spirit over the body. "The Higher Powers, I am convinced, are always with us, at every moment, everywhere, except, perhaps, at the meetings of Marxists and other left-wingers. There is no God there; they have passed a motion to that effect" (Blocker 1963).

Singer's boundless curiosity about the "higher powers" expresses itself in three kinds of stories: supernatural, apocalyptic, and moral. In the first group, he uses Satan or some lesser demon as a symbol, a kind of spiritual stenography. "Every serious writer," said Singer, "is possessed by certain ideas or symbols, and I am possessed by demons" (Blocker 1963). Singer's receptivity to the supernatural appears in stories (like "Jachid and Jechida" in the collection *Short Friday*) that play with the idea that we die into life, trailing clouds of glory from our divine home. Such tales suggest the tenuousness of our accepted standards and values, and the strong possibility that what we hold to be the goods of this world are really its evils and what we suppose to be its ultimate calamity, death, a release into the only true life. In Singer's symbolic geography, darkness often has positive connotations—as if he meant to suggest that virtue, like any other plant, will not grow unless its root is hidden. In his own way, he could be as anti-Enlightenment and "old-fashioned" as his Hasidic father.

Clearly related to the supernatural tales are stories of apocalypse that express Singer's guilty fascination with the messianic impulse in Jewish life and his disapproval of the modern form of that impulse: political utopianism. Here more than anywhere else Singer saw himself returning to Jewish sources that preceded the rise of secular Yiddish literature in the nineteenth century. *Satan in Goray*, set in 1648, explores the messianic longing of Polish Jews reeling from the Ukrainian Bogdan Chmielnicki's massacres, the worst that had been perpetrated against the Jewish people prior to the twentieth century. In desperation, these Jews seek explanation of their ordeal through the agency of a false messiah named Sabbatai Zevi, who encourages abomination and blasphemy as the means to redemption. Singer was both fascinated and repelled by Jewish messianism, which, by stressing the inevitability of cataclysm in the transition from historical present to messianic future, encourages fanaticism, hysteria, and disintegration. These events of the seventeenth century were to become an enduring paradigm for Singer: "To me, Sabbatai Zevi was the symbol of the man who tries to do good and comes out bad. . . . Sabbatai Zevi is in a way Stalin and all these people who tried so hard to create a better world and who ended up by creating the greatest misery" (Howe 1973). And so this novel, published in 1935 about events that took place in 1648, actually epitomizes Singer's oblique way of dealing with modern politics and the poison of totalitarian ideologies.

In Singer's moral tales the assumptions of a religious way of life he had rejected remain an imperious presence. Although Singer often declared (with feigned modesty) that "literature will never replace religion" (Burgin 1985) and that his stories are not intended to "say" something, he has just as frequently recalled that he was "brought up in the categories of good and evil. Almost nothing was neutral. Either you did a *mitzvah* (good deed) or you did an *averah* (sin)" (Burgin 1985). In the best of Singer's ethical parables, we see the lingering influence of the Hasidic ethos, which stressed deeds above good intentions and intellectual grasp. In such stories as "A Piece of Advice" (in the collection *The Spinoza of Market Street* [1961]), Singer sings the praises of Hasidism for its joy, its openness to the Jewish masses, and its moral efficacy, but ultimately there is one thing Singer cannot say of the traditional faith: that it is true.

Although Singer's tales about the conflict between faith and doubt generally imply (as in the famous love story "Gimpel the Fool") that belief of any kind, even to the point of foolish credulity, is a good in itself, it is clear that he had cast off the yoke of Rabbinic Judaism and the observance and self-discipline it entails. Yet he remains a distinctively Jewish writer, mainly because he gives uniquely powerful expression to the Jewish sense of memory. He used to say that amnesia is the only sickness from which Jews do not suffer. By this he meant not only that

Jews remember what happened in their own lifetime but that their memory stretches back through the collective experience of their people, even to its origins at Sinai. A recurrent scene in his fiction, for example, is the eve of Tisha b'Av (Ninth day of Av), when Jews mourn the destruction of the First Temple and all subsequent major catastrophes up through (at least) the expulsion from Spain in 1492.

Singer is the poet laureate of a Jewish sense of the past that is archetypal and circular rather than historical and linear. His narratives touching on the Holocaust, for example, view the Nazis as only the latest in the long succession of murderous outsiders who have obtruded themselves upon Jewish history. "Yes," sighs the narrator of *The Family Moskat* (1950), "every generation had its Pharaohs and Hamans and Chmielnickis. Now it was Hitler."

The stunning paradox of Singer's work is that, by treating all these destroyers as indistinct repetitions of one another, he is able to suggest that a nation that has been dying for thousands of years is a living nation. His most beautiful story, "The Little Shoemakers," which recounts Jewish catastrophes from the seventeenth century through the Holocaust, is at once a mourning over what has been

Drawing of Isaac Bashevis Singer by Rebecca Alexander. (Rebecca Alexander)

and a celebration of what has survived. Such hymns to the Jewish power of survival gain their special force from being built into elegies over a destroyed civilization. Singer's work continually reminds readers that the very first ancient non-Jewish document to mention Israel is the gloating report of Merneptah, king of Egypt, in 1215 BCE that "Israel is desolated; its seed is no more." Singer's fiction, written in a "dead" language about an apparently dead civilization, is, like the modern state of Israel, an expression of the Jewish capacity to make a new beginning.

Edward Alexander

References and Further Reading

Alexander, Edward. 1980. *Isaac Bashevis Singer.* Boston: Twayne Publishers.

Alexander, Edward. 1990. *Isaac Bashevis Singer: A Study of the Short Fiction.* Boston: Twayne Publishers.

Blocker, Joel. 1963. "An Interview with Isaac Bashevis Singer." *Commentary* 32 (November): 364–372.

Buchen, Irving. 1968. *Isaac Bashevis Singer and the Eternal Past.* New York: New York University Press.

Burgin, Richard. 1985. *Conversations with Isaac Bashevis Singer.* New York: Doubleday.

Friedman, Lawrence S. 1988. *Understanding Isaac Bashevis Singer.* Columbia: University of South Carolina Press.

Hadda, Janet. 1997. *Isaac Bashevis Singer: A Life.* New York: Oxford University Press.

Howe, Irving. 1966. "Introduction." In *Selected Short Stories of Isaac Bashevis Singer.* New York: Modern Library.

Howe, Irving. 1973. "Yiddish Tradition vs. Jewish Tradition: A Dialogue." *Midstream* 19 (June–July): 33–38.

Kresh, Paul. 1979. *Isaac Bashevis Singer.* New York: Dial Press.

Lee, Grace Farrell. 1987. *From Exile to Redemption: The Fiction of Isaac Bashevis Singer.* Carbondale: Southern Illinois University Press.

Milbauer, Asher Zelig. 1985. *Transcending Exile: Conrad, Nabokov, I. B. Singer.* Miami: Florida International University Press.

Ozick, Cynthia. 1969. "Envy; or Yiddish in America." *Commentary* 48 (November): 33–53.

Wisse, Ruth R. 1979. "Singer's Paradoxical Progress." *Commentary* 67 (February): 33–38.

Leon Uris (1924–2003)

Historical Novelist

Leon Marcus Uris was a popular historical novelist, who was famous for his stories of the Holocaust and the founding of Israel. The protagonists of Leon Uris's novels *QB VII* and *Mitla Pass* offer significant insight into the life of their creator. Having dropped out of college, *QB VII*'s Abe Cady declares, "YOU CAN'T LEARN TO WRITE FROM COLLEGE PROFESSORS." In *Mitla Pass* Gideon Zadok, lying wounded from battle, recalls a turbulent childhood held hostage to a father's bitterness and ideology and a mother's emotional instability. Uris himself felt the sting of the English teacher's judgment; he failed high school English three times. And he too grew up in a home run by "a father who was terribly embittered" and a mother who "was a little wacko" (Christy 1988). The United States entry into World War II provided the seventeen-year-old Leon with an opportunity to escape: lying about his age, he joined the Marine Corps, eventually serving for three years in the South Pacific and fighting in the brutal battle for Tarawa. Not only did his military experience provide him with a tight-knit, stable surrogate family and a sense of adventure, but it also gave him the material for his first book, *Battle Cry* (1953). During the next fifty years, a dozen more novels followed, many of them exploring the Holocaust and its aftermath, including the founding of Israel. The first of these explorations, *Exodus* (1958), became the biggest best-seller in the United States since Margaret Mitchell's *Gone with the Wind* and was made into a major motion picture. At the time of his death in 2003, Uris was one of the most successful American historical novelists of the twentieth century.

Leon Uris's father, Wolf, was a Communist Party organizer who also worked as a paperhanger and a shopkeeper in Baltimore, Maryland, and Norfolk, Virginia. Having emigrated from Poland by way of Palestine, Wolf took the name Uris from Yerushalmi, which means "man of Jerusalem." He quickly became disillusioned with his new country, suffering both economic hardship and religious and ethnic discrimination. His son's alienation can be attributed not only to this relative poverty and anti-semitism, but to the turbulence of his family life as well. Uris's intense patriotism and lifelong loathing for Communism also reflected his utter rejection of what he saw as his father's misguided revolutionary values.

The patriotism that characterizes much of Uris's work was born and nourished during his time in the Marines. As he recounts in *Battle Cry*, the Marines embodied camaraderie, mutual support, and respect for diversity among fellow soldiers. For him, the Marines supplanted the dysfunctional family and the antisemitic culture that plagued his youth. If Leon Uris can be said to have had a tribe, it would be the United States Marine Corps; it was during his years of service that he forged his identity as a man and an American. The profound sense of Jewish identity characteristic of much of his later work is absent in *Battle Cry*; indeed, the two characters with whom the author identifies most closely are both gentile. Danny Forrester, the teenager who enlists after Pearl Harbor, is the quintessential all-American boy, marrying his high school sweetheart while on leave and returning to establish a life with her after the war is over. Marion "Sister Mary" Hodgkiss, the aspiring writer, faithfully records the life of the platoon and offers philosophical sustenance to his comrades. Nonetheless, Uris does address antisemitism in the characters of Brooklynite Jake Levin and the iconoclast Max Shapiro, both of whom discover that the prejudice and discrimination of civilian life have carried over into military life. Both characters are portrayed as heroes who give up their lives for a squad and a country that refused to accord them equal status.

Uris's second novel, *The Angry Hills* (1955), is another mainstream American novel, this time an espionage thriller. Loosely based on the adventures of his uncle, who served in a Palestinian (Jewish) unit of the British Army during World War II, the novel focuses extensively on the horrors of Nazism as evidenced by the invasion and occupation of Greece. None of the major characters is Jewish, but readers are introduced to a sympathetic Jewish couple from Palestine who fall prey to their Nazi captors after an ill-fated escape attempt. More importantly, the author's interest in exploring his Jewish heritage and identity was born during the writing of this novel. After a brief hiatus in Hollywood, where he wrote the screenplay for *Gunfight at the O.K. Corral* (1957), Uris turned his attention to the quest for a Jewish state in Palestine. In his research for the novel that would become *Exodus* (1958), he covered 12,000 miles, interviewed more than a thousand people, and read close to three hundred books. Both the research and the dedication are evident in the resulting best-seller, a sprawling, intricate account of the establishment of Israel.

The significance of the publication of *Exodus* to American Jews simply cannot be overestimated. The numbing images of the Holocaust, while creating sympathy for its victims, did little to eliminate the subtle but pervasive antisemitism that characterized the postwar United States. Uris's epic tale, based loosely on the historical account of an overloaded cargo ship destined for postwar Palestine, transformed America's image of European Jews from victims to heroes. Perhaps more importantly, the novel's biblical undertones resonated with a population newly enamored of religion in the face of the Communist threat. The novel's primary theme, "nothing less than another chapter in the long history of Jewish fulfillment of God's promise" (Cain 1998), placed the horror of the previous decades within a powerful context. As American nurse Kitty Fremont says of the young Palmach soldiers in the novel, "These were the ancient Hebrews. These were the forces of Dan and Reuben and Judah and Ephraim!"

One of the most tormented characters in *Exodus* is the teenaged Dov Landau, who has come of age in the Warsaw Ghetto and Auschwitz, only to be "liberated" into a refugee camp in Cyprus. Dov's bitterness and hatred have been fueled by the horrors he has witnessed, horrors that Uris explored in depth in his next novel, *Mila 18* (1961). Named for the address of the actual resistance headquarters in the Warsaw Ghetto, this novel puts a human face on the Nazi outrages and the Jewish heroism that characterized the uprising. The brutality with which the Nazis torture, imprison, starve, humiliate, and murder the Jewish inhabitants of Warsaw is graphically depicted, as are the bravery and determination of the resistance fighters who hold off squadrons of the world's greatest army for forty-two days (in reality, the uprising lasted twenty-seven days). Almost as significant as Uris's depiction of life and death in the ghetto is his condemnation of the world's willful indifference to what was going on in the ghettoes and the camps. When Italian-American journalist Chris de Monti smuggles firsthand accounts of death camps to the Allied governments, the news is met with deafening silence. When the Polish Catholic Gabriela Rak attempts to recruit Church leaders to save Jewish children, the result is the same. The Nazis may be the perpetrators of the Holocaust, but, as the industrialist collaborator Horst von Epp declares as German tanks prepare to demolish the ghetto, "I'm no more guilty than . . . all the moralists in the world who have condoned genocide by the conspiracy of silence."

While Uris's next two novels, *Armageddon: A Novel of Berlin* (1963) and *Topaz* (1967), dealt primarily with the Cold War, he returned to the subject of the Holocaust in the 1970 semi-autobiographical novel *QB VII* (a reference to the British courtroom Queen's Bench 7). Uris and his British publisher had been sued for libel in 1964 by Dr. Wladislaw Dering; Uris had depicted Dering in *Exodus* as a collaborator who performed medical experiments on Jewish prisoners at Auschwitz. Dering won the suit, but the court awarded only a halfpenny in damages and ordered him to pay all legal costs. In fictionalizing the trial, Uris creates the character of Abe Cady, a prizewinning American novelist whose life closely parallels Uris's own. Perhaps more interesting, however, is Dr. Adam Kelno (a character very loosely based on Dering), whose life before, during, and after the Holocaust is recounted in great detail. Dedicating himself to underprivileged people after his release from the fictional Jadwiga camp, Kelno spends years ministering to natives in Borneo before settling in London to provide medical services in a working-class neighborhood. It becomes clear during the course of the trial that Kelno is indeed guilty of the atrocities of which he is accused, but a more complex question remains both unanswered and unanswerable. When Kelno describes conditions of concentration camp life, including backbreaking slave labor, malnutrition, and torture, even Cady is left pondering the question, "What the hell would I have done?" Indeed, writers such as Primo Levi and Tadeusz Borowksi, themselves camp survivors, often explored the ways in which the camps so degraded prisoners that all sense of compassion or morality was lost.

Nonetheless, in *QB VII* Uris also presents testimony from a host of survivors, none of whom succumbed to the dehumanizing existence of the camps. The testimony is as credible as it is horrifying; the passages in which survivors recount their experiences in Jadwiga mirror those found in historical accounts. Thus Uris's audience comes away from this book, as it does from his other books, with a degree of hope for the indomitability of the human spirit.

Readers find less hope in two subsequent novels dealing with Israel: *The Haj* (1984) and *Mitla Pass* (1988). Although told from the point of view of Arabs, *The Haj* was rightly characterized by critics as a lengthy denigration of an entire people. The novel's Arab characters are consistently portrayed as lazy, gluttonous, sadistic, and sexually depraved. *Mitla Pass*, on the other hand, focuses on a devastating battle pursued by a fanatical Israeli colonel for control of land with no military value. It is conceivable that the seemingly insoluble enmity between Israelis and

Arabs as characterized by the violence of the 1970s and 1980s had soured the author, leaving him with little of the hope that redeemed *Exodus* and *Mila 18*. After *Mitla Pass* Uris turned again to the story of Ireland's struggle for freedom, continuing the tale begun in *Trinity* (1976) with *Redemption* (1995). In 1999 he published *A God in Ruins*, the story of a presidential candidate who discovers on the eve of the election that his heritage is Jewish, and in 2003, his final novel, the Civil War tale *O'Hara's Choice*, was published posthumously.

Although all of Uris's novels published before 1995 enjoyed a wide readership, his popularity waned after *Redemption*. Neither *A God in Ruins* nor *O'Hara's Choice* received much attention, either critical or popular. Of course, critics had often been the bane of the author's existence. Gideon Zak's railing against critics in *Mitla Pass* probably reflects quite accurately his creator's attitude: Uris was consistently frustrated by the critical reception of his work. He was accused of grammatical blunders, plot-level sloppiness, wooden characterizations, and questionable treatment of historical fact. His work was often labeled melodramatic. Despite a reputation as a "critic's nightmare," however, Uris enjoyed the adulation of readers for over forty years and introduced two generations to the Diaspora. Popular American interest in the Holocaust and support for Israel can be attributed in part to the influence of his novels.

Kathleen Shine Cain

References and Further Reading
Cain, Kathleen Shine. 1998a. "Leon Uris." In *The Encyclopedia of American Literature*, edited by Steven R. Serafin, 1167–1168. New York: Continuum.
Cain, Kathleen Shine. 1998b. *Leon Uris: A Critical Companion*. Westport, CT: Greenwood Press.
Christy, Marion. 1988. "Leon Uris: His Word Is Truth." *Boston Globe* (October 26): 67, 70.
Contemporary Authors Online. "Leon (Marcus) Uris." Available at: http://galenet.galegroup.com. Accessed July 20, 2004.
Kalb, Bernard. 1953. "Leon Uris." *Saturday Review* (April 25): 16.
Lehmann-Haupt, Christopher. 2003. "Leon Uris, Author of 'Exodus,' Dies at 78." *New York Times* (June 25): A25.
Peckham, S. 1976. "PW Interview: Leon Uris." *Publisher's Weekly* (March 29): 6–7.
Reynolds, Quentin. 1961. "In the Ghetto a Battle for the Conscience of the World." *New York Times Book Review* (June 4): 5.

Morris Winchevsky (1856–1932)

Poet, Hebrew and Yiddish Socialist Writer

Morris Winchevsky (Lipe Ben-Tsien Novachovitch), pioneer of socialist poetry, was born in Yanove, Lithuania, on August 9, 1856, and grew up in Kovne. Many consider Winchevsky the grandfather of the Hebrew and Yiddish socialist press in the United States. After attending *cheder,* a traditional Jewish school, his father taught him at home, and at eleven he attended a Russian public school. In 1870 he studied at the non-Orthodox rabbinical school in Vilna, where he learned German and read Russian literature. In 1873 he moved to Oriol, Russia, to work as a bookkeeper. There he became interested in revolutionary ideologies.

Winchevsky published his first literary work in Hebrew, a social satire titled "*Tahapukhot ha'itim*" ("The Turmoil of the Times") in *Hamagid* (*The Herald*) on September 8, 1874. In August 1875 he returned to Kovne, where he worked as a bookkeeper and regularly published poems, feuilletons (articles on social issues), and satires in *Hamagid.*

At twenty-one, he relocated to Königsberg, Germany, for employment and continued to publish. That year (1877) he became the editor of the Hebrew socialist monthly *Aseyfat hakhamim* (*Assembly of the Wise*), which lasted only eight issues, until October 1878. There he published under various pen names in several genres, including book reviews and a novel in sequels, *Panim hadashot* (*New Face*). The most famous series of feuilletons, "*Hezyonot ish haruah*" ("Prophetic Visions of an Intellectual"), was signed Yagli ish haruach (Yagli the Intellectual), although his most widely known pseudonym was Ben-Netz—the name by which he is still called when referring to his Hebrew writings.

In 1877 he also published his first Yiddish feuilleton, "*Der grende firer*" ("The Grand Leader"), in *Kol La'am* (*Voice to the People*), the Yiddish addition to the Hebrew *Hakol.* Once he started writing in Yiddish, his publications in Hebrew became rare; between 1886 and 1910 he did not publish in Hebrew at all. In 1877 Winchevsky had become anti-religion and antinationalism, believing the revival of Hebrew would not succeed and was not as efficient in propagating socialism as Yiddish. Concurrently, he contributed to several German publications, such as *Königsberger freier presse* (*Königsberg Free Press*).

Between February 1878 and February 1879, he was arrested three times for his socialist activities. Yet he was able to publish an eighteen-part article in *Hakol* (1878), "*Beit nivharei ha'am be'ashkenaz*" ("The Reichstag in Germany"), explaining the German constitution and German social democracy and describing the various political parties. His aim was to teach the Hebrew reader about Western Europe.

After his last release on March 16, 1879, he was expelled from Germany. He settled in London, where he remained until 1894. In 1880, he adopted the literary pseudonym Morris Winchevsky as a political expedient. While earning his living as a bookkeeper, he became active in various socialist unions, propagated socialism among Jewish workers, and helped establish the Jewish Worker Benefit and Education Union (1880).

On July 25, 1884, he started editing the first Yiddish socialist paper in England, *Der poylisher idl* (*The Little Polish Man*). After sixteen issues its name changed to *Di tsukunft* (*The Future*) because of the controversial nature of its title. In August 1885 Winchevsky resigned because of political disagreements with the owner of the paper, Eliyahu Wolf Rabinowitz, who assumed a more nationalistic stance and accepted an advertisement from the local Jewish Liberal candidate, Samuel Montagu. Winchevsky, a committed socialist, opposed it, claiming the paper ceased to represent the proletarian cause and had surrendered to the "bourgeois."

In 1885 Winchevsky married Rebecca Harris. The couple had a boy and a girl. That year he also published his first book of poetry, *Ben-Netz's folk gedikhte* (*Ben-Netz's Folk Poems*) and helped found the socialist *Der arbayter fraynd* (*The Worker's Friend*). In this weekly he published his most famous series of feuilletons: "*Tseshlogene gedanken fun a meshugener filozof*" ("Confused Thoughts of a Crazy Philosopher"). The philosopher argues with his grandson over issues from a socialist point of view and about the upcoming social revolution. The writing style and themes popularized this character, who was nicknamed *Der zeyde* (the grandfather) by enthusiastic readers. This nickname was transferred to Winchevsky himself, and, before reaching age thirty-five, he was already considered the grandfather of the Jewish workers' movement. In September 1886, Winchevsky published his first play, a comedy, *Der mirer iluy* (*The Young Genius of Mir*).

In 1891, when *Der arbayter fraynd* became anarchist, he withdrew from the editorial board and in May founded the monthly *Di fraye velt* (*The Free World*), which lasted until November 1892, and then the socialist weekly *Der veker* (*The Wakener,* 1892), which lasted for eleven issues. All the while Winchevsky published in English journals, such as the weekly *Justice.* In 1894, already a prominent figure, he immigrated to the United States, where he edited the Boston Yiddish socialist weekly *Der emes* (*The Truth*) from May 1895 until it closed in August 1896.

On April 22, 1897, the first issue of the Yiddish daily *Forverts* (*Forward*) appeared. Winchevsky was one of the founders and a regular contributor. Several months later, however, he resigned because of political disagreements with the editor, Abraham Cahan; Winchevsky was unable to freely express his views opposing Daniel DeLeon in his articles without the editor's restrictions. He propagated socialism and led the opposition to DeLeon and the Socialist Labor Party. Nonetheless, in 1916, he returned to write for the daily. Winchevsky continuously contributed to Yiddish papers and was also involved in reviving the monthly *Di tzukunft* (*The Future*) and editing it during 1902–1903 and 1907–1909.

During these years Winchevsky also translated into Yiddish works by prominent writers, including Henrik Ibsen and Thomas Hood. In 1910 he directed a successful campaign by the Cloakmakers' Union to raise funds for a general strike. That year Winchevsky also published his famous article "*Ani Maamin*" ("Creed") in the Jerusalem weekly *Haahdut* (*Unity*). The article made an immense impression on the pioneers in *Eretz Israel* because, although it described Winchevsky's vision of a united humanity, it also envisioned a separate land for each nation to develop according to its own history and culture. He also wrote against assimilation and saw Hebrew becoming the universal Jewish language—a radical change of views after he had ceased writing in Hebrew, believing the ancient language would not be revived.

From 1918 until January 1919, he edited *Glaykhhayt* (*Equality*), the organ of the blouse and garment makers' union. Influenced by the Balfour Declaration (1917), Winchevsky's nationalism strengthened, and in 1920 he was a delegate to the American Jewish Congress in Philadelphia.

In 1922 he shifted to communism, began to write for the communist *Frayhayt* (*Freedom*) published in New York, and broke ties with many of his socialist friends. In 1924 he was invited to the Soviet Union because of his pioneering communist activities among Jews in the United States and was granted a pension. He returned to New York several months later. In 1927 he became paralyzed, remaining in poor health until his death on March 18, 1932.

To his radical socialism in the 1870s Winchevsky added nationalism in the 1880s and became a communist in the 1920s. He wrote during the transition from *Haskala* (the Jewish Enlightenment movement) to modern literature. All the while he propagated socialism in various prose genres and in poetry written in Hebrew or Yiddish, but mostly in Yiddish. His popularity lies in his simple, captivating style. Although he did not experience hard labor in sweatshops like other proletarian poets, he addressed almost all aspects of contemporary socialism.

Ori Kritz

References and Further Reading
Bick, Abraham. 1956. *Morris Winchevsky—Der troymer un kempfer* (*Morris Winchevsky—The Dreamer and Fighter*). Los Angeles: Morris Winchevsky arbiter-ring tzvayg 983.
Kharlash, Isaac. 1960. "Winchevsky, Morris." *Leksikon fun der nayer yiddisher Literature* (*Lexicon of the New Yiddish Literature*) 3: 432–443.
Winchevsky, Morris. 1927–1928. *Gezamelte verk* (*Collected Works*), edited by Kalman Marmor. 10 Vols. NewYork: Farlag Frayhayt.

Herman Wouk (b. 1915)

Novelist

Herman Wouk (born May 27, 1915) was the most popular Jewish novelist in American history. His books, beginning with *Aurora Dawn* in 1947 and continuing through *The Caine Mutiny: A Novel of World War II* (1951), *Marjorie Morningstar* (1955), *Youngblood Hawke* (1962), *Don't Stop the Carnival* (1965), *The Winds of War* (1971), *War and Remembrance* (1978), *Inside/Outside: A Novel* (1985), *The Hope* (1993), and *The Glory* (1994), sold tens of millions of copies. He also published *This Is My God* in 1959, a book of reflections on Judaism, and he wrote an introduction to a volume of letters of Jonathan Netanyahu, which appeared in 1980. *The Winds of War* and *War and Remembrance* were made into two very popular television series in the 1980s, and several of his books, including *The Caine Mutiny* and *Marjorie Morningstar,* were made into feature films.

Although Wouk won the Pulitzer Prize for *The Caine Mutiny,* literary critics derided his novels. Norman Podhoretz's review of *Marjorie Morningstar* stressed its banality, "imaginative helplessness," and the "ugliness" of its prose. Wouk, Podhoretz said, was "utterly incapable of rendering the feel of an emotion or a mood or a conversation," and his imagination pointed "vaguely into space like a blind man trying to locate an object in an unfamiliar room" (Podhoretz 1956). Pearl K. Bell described *War and Remembrance* as a "good-bad book," lacking "any daunting complexities of thought, craft, or human behavior" and suffused with a cloying sentimentality. The novel's major characters are "preposterous and irritating," and the novel "never rises above the sentimental level of best-selling romance." *War and Remembrance,* Bell concluded, is part of a subliterary genre that serious readers could ignore (Bell 1978). Paul Fussell called *The Winds of War* and *War and Remembrance* a good popular history of World War II in "the guise of a very bad novel." The "skillful historiography" is marred by "embarrassing" characters and the "vulgarity" of the plot (Fussell 1978).

One reason for this hostile reception was Wouk's acceptance of traditional middle-class morality, his conservative temperament, and his rejection of the stance of alienation popular among intellectuals. This was particularly evident in *Marjorie Morningstar.* The seduction of Marjorie by Noel Airman was accompanied by "shocks, ugly uncoverings, pain, incredible humiliation." At its conclusion, Marjorie accidentally breaks a glass, a sign of Jewish mourning. Marjorie's effort to be a "morningstar" is rather fatuous, and she ends up living in Mamaroneck, New York, with her children and husband. "You couldn't write a play about her that would run a week, or a novel that would sell a thousand copies," a former beau says of this now conventional suburban Jewish matron.

Wouk's novels are replete with undesirable deracinated intellectuals. In *Marjorie Morningstar* it is Noel Airman (né Saul Ehrmann). Airman's first name, which evokes Christmas, reflects his contempt for the Jewish religious traditions of his family, and his surname symbolizes the emptiness of his life. In *Youngblood Hawke* it is Hawke; in *Don't Stop the Carnival* it is Sheldon King; in *War and Remembrance* it is Leonard Spreregen; and in *Inside/Outside* it is Peter Quat. Wouk's most famous attack on the in-

tellectual is in *The Caine Mutiny.* A group of naval officers have just been found not guilty of mutiny against the demented captain Queeg during World War II. They hold a party to celebrate their victory and invite their Navy-appointed lawyer, Lieutenant Barney Greenwald. They are amazed when the half-drunk Greenwald attacks them for deserting their captain during his and the Navy's hour of need. Greenwald is particularly disdainful of Lieutenant Keefer, an intellectual who is writing a novel of the war. Greenwald is convinced that Keefer is "the villain of the foul-up," and he is eager to read Keefer's half-finished novel. "I'm sure that it exposes this war in all its grim futility and waste, and shows up the military men for the stupid, Fascist-minded sadists they are," he sarcastically comments. Arthur M. Schlesinger Jr. called *The Caine Mutiny* America's "great anti-intellectual novel" (Schlesinger 1956), and William H. Whyte's famous pop sociology book *The Organization Man* (1956) argued that the novel exemplified the shift in American values from the Protestant ethic of individualism and self-reliance to the social ethic of organizational life. *The Caine Mutiny,* Whyte said, "rationalized the impulse to belong and to accept what is as what should be" (Whyte 1956).

It was not by accident that in *The Caine Mutiny* it was a Jew, Barney Greenwald, who defends the Navy and the military virtues of honor, duty, and obedience. For students of American Jewish culture, the great theme of Wouk's fiction is this symbiosis of American and Jewish identities. Critics noted that *Marjorie Morningstar,* which Susanne Klingenstein called "the first truly popular American Jewish novel" (Klingenstein 1998), applauded the postwar detente of American Jewry and middle-class America. The novel, Podhoretz said, was a protest against those who have "an appetite for diverse areas of experience, an unwillingness to settle into the common routines, a refusal to surrender one's demands on the world without a fight." Wouk wrote as if Jewishness would disintegrate "if it ventures beyond the moral and spiritual confines of a Judaic bourgeois style" (Podhoretz 1956).

Wouk's desire to end any estrangement between America and Jewishness, his belief that to be a good American one must be a good Jew and to be a good Jew one must be a good American, accounts for the surprising denouement of *The Caine Mutiny* when Greenwald attacks Keefer. Greenwald declares that any novel he would write of the Navy during the war would portray Queeg as a hero.

Greenwald explains to his amazed listeners that, while they were enjoying civilian life and looking down on the military, Queeg and the other "stuffy, stupid Prussians in the Navy and the Army" were preparing to defend America from the Nazis. "Yes, even Queeg, poor sad guy, yes, and most of them not sad at all, fellows, a lot of them sharper boys than any of us, don't kid yourself, best men I've ever seen. . . . though maybe not up on Proust 'n' *Finnegan's Wake* and all."

Greenwald also has a specifically Jewish reason for defending the military. "The Germans aren't kidding about the Jews," he tells the mutineers. "They're cooking us down to soap over there. . . . I just can't cotton to the idea of my mother melted down into a bar of soap." Queeg deserved his thanks, and Greenwald feels guilt for having ruined the captain during the trial. "He stopped Hermann Goering from washing his fat behind with my mother." Greenwald then throws a glass of wine in Keefer's face and leaves the party. The mutineers realize he is right. They should have covered Queeg's mistakes, upheld military authority, and concentrated on fulfilling their ship's mission. The person who had opened their eyes, one of them says, was "an amazing Jew named Greenwald."

Three and a half decades after *The Caine Mutiny*, Wouk published the semi-autobiographical *Inside/Outside*, in which a Jew defends another seemingly disreputable character. The novel's protagonist is Israel David Goodkind (a "good kind"). Goodkind, a graduate of Yeshiva University and Columbia University, is a traditional Jew on the inside and a fervent American patriot on the outside. Yeshiva and Columbia symbolize his inner and outer identities. Wouk emphasizes the merging of these two sides of Goodkind by having him begin the seven days of mourning for his deceased father on December 7, 1941. Yet Goodkind prefers not to use his first name until the end of the book, when returning to America from Israel, he tells the El Al stewardess to "Call me Israel," an allusion to Herman Melville's line "Call me Ishmael" in *Moby Dick,* the greatest of all American novels. Goodkind now feels perfectly comfortable in being a traditional Jew in America, and any dissonance between his Jewish and American identities has disappeared.

At the beginning of *Inside/Outside,* Goodkind, a lifelong Democrat, has taken a leave of absence in 1973 from his successful New York corporate tax legal practice to become a Special Assistant to President Richard Nixon. This occurs just before the Yom Kippur War of 1973 and the Watergate scandal. Before taking the job, Goodkind tells Nixon that he will not work on the Sabbath. The president responds that Goodkind is his first Jewish associate who ever made that stipulation. "I'm impressed. Very impressed." In contrast to his family and friends, Goodkind is not a visceral opponent of Nixon, and he comes to admire the president for his commitment to peace, his struggle to preserve the authority of the presidency during the Watergate affair, and especially for his support of Israel during the 1973 war. He tells the president that the Jewish people will revere him forever if he sends arms to Israel, an American ally, to balance the arms that the Arabs are receiving from the Soviet Union. "It will honor the man who showed greatness, by rising above his own desperate political predicament and coming to the rescue of the Jewish State." Nixon, in turn, praises Goodkind for not deserting his captain during the Watergate crisis. "You've stayed aboard while some others were jumping ship. It's been appreciated." Just as in *The Caine Mutiny,* the hero is a Jew who defends the values of duty and loyalty and the stability of American institutions. Wouk's critics, by contrast, argued that Goodkind's faith in Nixon was misplaced since the president's actions undermined the presidency and caused a constitutional crisis.

This reconciliation of American and Jewish identities came naturally to Wouk. The two most important intellectual influences on him were his maternal grandfather, Rabbi Mendel Leib Levine, and Irwin Edman, a Columbia University philosopher. These two were the opposing poles of Wouk's life, "a man without a trace of Western culture and a man who is its embodiment" (Wouk quoted in Beichman 1984). Levine, an Orthodox rabbi, spent all his time immersed in the study of the Talmud. He never spoke English (although he understood it), never saw a play or movie, never went to an art gallery or heard a symphony, and never read a secular book. Levine instilled in his grandson a love of Torah, and Wouk put aside a part of every day for the study of Jewish texts. Edman, a religious skeptic and disciple of John Dewey, taught a course on comparative religion that Wouk took while a sophomore, and its effect on him was electrifying. Edman opened up for Wouk the corpus of Western learning.

The other formative influence on Wouk was his service in the Navy from 1943 to 1945 aboard two destroyer minesweepers, the *Zane* and the *Southard.* He took part in eight Pacific invasions and won four campaign stars and a unit citation. He described these years as "the greatest experience of my life. . . . In the Navy, I found out more than I ever had about people and about the United States," and the more he found out, the more he admired the Navy and his country (Wouk quoted in Beichman 1984). Since World War II, he has had a lifelong love affair with the Navy. In *This Is My God* he compared the Jew with the sailor. "I have always thought that the Jewish place among mankind somewhat resembles the position of navy men among other Americans," he wrote. "Are the sailors and officers less American because they are in the Navy? They have special commitments and disciplines, odd ways of dress, sharp limits on their freedom. They have, at least in their own minds, compensations of glory, or of vital services performed." In his introduction to *Self-Portrait of a Hero: The Letters of Jonathan Netanyahu*, Wouk paid Netanyahu the highest compliment by comparing him to Admiral Raymond Spruance, the architect of American victories in the battles of Midway and the Philippine Sea. Both men "embody—by the cast of destiny—the virtue of their whole people in a great hour."

Wouk's belief that the fate of Jews and America is intertwined is a major theme of his two volumes on the history of Israel, *The Hope* and *The Glory*. These novels span the story of Israel from its founding through the early 1980s. For Wouk, war has been the greatest phenomenon of the twentieth century, and this has certainly been true for Jews. *The Hope* chronicles the Israeli wars of 1948, 1956, and 1967, and *The Glory* discusses the Yom Kippur War of 1973 and ends with the attack by Israeli planes on an Iraqi nuclear reactor.

Wouk's account of Israel's war for independence in *The Hope* emphasizes similarities between the histories of America and Israel. A gentile woman explains to her Israeli lover why Americans are so supportive of Israel. "It's the resonance with American history," she says. "You've landed on a hostile shore, trying to bring forth a new nation conceived in liberty, haven't you? You and we both started as colonies that threw out the British. Both had early years of dangerous adversity, only yours are still going on. Almost a mirror image." Her Israeli lover agrees. "The more I come to understand things," he tells her, "the more I perceive how our miracle of the return is linked to your older miracle of America." One chapter of *The Hope* is titled "The Alamo," and it discusses the attempt to link Israeli forces to

the besieged Jews of Jerusalem. Another chapter, titled "Midway," examines the Israeli air strikes that launched the Six Day War. In *The Glory*, Anwar Sadat's visit to Jerusalem is likened to Lee's surrender at Appomattox. *The Glory* concludes with the Israeli pondering the future of Israel and the United States. "The old countries, Japan, England, Russia, worse off or better off, they just *are*. We're both trying *to be*, you the giant of the world and we the crazy little nobody in the Middle East."

A key figure in the early pages of *The Hope* is Mickey Marcus. Marcus had graduated from West Point, was a veteran of World War II, and had served as New York's commissioner of corrections. The founders of Israel believed that war with their Arab neighbors was inevitable because the Arabs would never peacefully accept a Jewish state in their midst. The Israelis asked Marcus to help train their army, and he reluctantly agreed. At one point in *The Hope*, Marcus calls David ben Gurion the George Washington of Israel, and ben Gurion responds, "And you're our Lafayette." Marcus was killed in 1948 by accident. *The Hope* has a long description of his coffin's arrival in New York and its interment in the cemetery at West Point. When the coffin is handed over to American army officers at the airport, the Israeli flag that had draped the coffin is replaced by the American flag. The Star of David is then handed reverentially to the Israeli military officer who had accompanied Marcus's body to America. The officer "could see on the tarmac, under large American and Israeli flags flapping in the brisk wind, a long line of black limousines." At the funeral at West Point, the Israeli tells Marcus's widow how her husband had once quoted to him a line by the English poet Rupert Brooke: "There is a corner of some foreign field that is forever England." Now, he says, "there's a corner of West Point that is forever Israel."

Wouk emphasizes in *The Hope* and *The Glory* the common enmity of the United States and Israel toward Communism and the Soviet Union. Israel's triumph in 1967 is portrayed also as an American victory. The most important pages in *The Glory* concern the Yom Kippur War of 1973. Wouk has Golda Meir, the Israeli prime minister, telling Henry Kissinger, the American secretary of state, that the Israelis "have been fighting America's battle in the Middle East. You and I both know it. Were it not for the Soviet encouragement of their intransigence, the Arabs would long ago have come to terms with reality and made peace with Israel." Kissinger explains to an Israeli why

Nixon so strongly supports Israel. "The President knows that if you're defeated the Russians will dominate the Middle East, the Arabs will be impossible to deal with, and the world balance will tilt against the United States."

On July 4, 1976, Israeli commandos made their dramatic rescue of Jewish hostages at the Entebbe airport in Uganda. In *The Glory,* diplomats accredited to Washington are attending a celebration of America's bicentennial on board the aircraft carrier *Forrestal* when they learn of the rescue. This comes just before the United States Marine Band begins to play "The Star-Spangled Banner." The diplomats admire Israel's boldness and believe that "America should be more like Israel in dealing with its enemies and with terrorism."

World War II was influential in the American Jews' view of themselves as Jews and as Americans. The fact that hundreds of thousands of them served in the American military forces during the war, that over ten thousand paid the ultimate price, and that Germany was the greatest enemy of both Jewry and the United States erased any lingering sense they might have had that being Jewish and being American were not fully compatible. After 1945, antisemitism appeared to Jews (and to gentiles) as not only anti-Jewish but anti-American as well. The fear that Zionism and the establishment of a Jewish state in the Middle East would call into question the loyalty of America's Jews was proven to be unfounded. As American Jews rapidly fled their psychological and geographical ghettos after 1945, they could look to Wouk's novels for reassurance. The historian Jerold Auerbach has argued that the synthesis of Judaism and Americanness was "a historical fiction" (Auerbach 1990). If so, then the historical fiction of Wouk is partially responsible.

Edward S. Shapiro

References and Further Reading

Auerbach, Jerold S. 1990. *Rabbis and Lawyers: The Journey from Torah to Constitution.* Bloomington: Indiana University Press.

Beichman, Arnold. 1984. *Herman Wouk: The Novelist as Social Historian.* New Brunswick, NJ: Transaction Books.

Bell, Pearl K. 1978. "Good-Bad and Bad-Bad." *Commentary* 66 (December): 70–72.

Fussell, Paul. 1978. "Review of Herman Wouk, *War and Remembrance.*" *New Republic* 179 (October 14): 32–33.

Guttman, Allen. 1971. *The Jewish Writer in America: Assimilation and the Crisis of Identity.* New York: Oxford University Press.

Klingenstein, Susanne. 1998. "Sweet Natalie: Herman Wouk's Messenger to the Gentiles." In *Talking Back: Images of Jewish Women in American Popular Culture,* edited by Joyce Antler, 103–122. Hanover, NH: University Press of New England.

Podhoretz, Norman. 1956. "The Jew as Bourgeois." *Commentary* 21 (February): 186–188.

Schlesinger, Arthur M. Jr. 1956. "*Time* and the Intellectuals." *New Republic* 135 (July 16): 15–17.

Shapiro, Edward S. 1987. "Torah, Torah, Torah: Inside Herman Wouk." *Midstream* 33 (January): 48–50.

Shapiro, Edward S. 1996. "The Jew as Patriot: Herman Wouk and American Jewish Identity." *American Jewish History* 84 (December): 333–351.

"The Wouk Mutiny." 1955. *Time* 66 (September 5): 48–50.

Whyte, William H. 1956. *The Organization Man.* New York: Doubleday.

American Jewish Literary Critics

Irving Howe (1920–1993)

Literary Critic, Yiddishist, Socialist Activist, and Editor

Irving Howe's career was the story of three loves: socialism, literature, and Jewishness. He began as a passionate believer in the capacity of socialism to end war and injustice but eventually was forced to acknowledge its universal failure as a political movement. Nevertheless, he transformed socialism into a myth of considerable power as an ethical instrument of social and political criticism. He was stirred belatedly into Jewishness by the Holocaust and undertook a heroic effort to save the language and literature of Yiddish, which had been consigned to destruction, along with the Jews themselves, by Nazism. Although he endowed the idea of secular Jewishness with a special twilight beauty, he could not rescue it from its inevitable demise and ceased to believe in its future long before he died. Literature proved to be the most powerful and compelling of his three loves; he defended its autonomy against Stalinists (and Trotskyists) in the forties; against "guerrillas with tenure" in the sixties; against theorists in the eighties. Among American men of letters in the twentieth century, he was the exemplar of intellectual heroism and tenacious idealism.

Howe was the son of David Horenstein, at various times a grocer, peddler, and dress factory presser, and of Nettie Goldman Horenstein, a dress trade operator. In 1934, still a student in De Witt Clinton High School in the Bronx, Howe became active in left-wing but strongly anti-Stalinist politics. In 1936 he entered City College of New York, where, though a dilatory student, he took a serious interest in literary criticism, especially that of Edmund Wilson. Although he was still Horenstein in class, he began to use the (Trotskyist) party name of Hugh Ivan and, for speeches and articles, Irving Howe. Although an English major, his degree was a Bachelor of Social Sciences.

By late 1941, married to Anna Bader and living in Greenwich Village, Howe became managing editor of *Labor Action,* the weekly paper of the Workers Party. Under Howe's leadership the paper consistently opposed American entry into and prosecution of the war against the Axis powers. But in mid-1942 Howe was himself drafted into the Army, where he did a stint of three and a half years, reaching the rank of sergeant before being discharged early in 1946. He then legally changed his surname to Howe, divorced Anna, and moved back to the Bronx. Although he resumed writing for *Labor Action* as well as for the Trotskyists' "theoretical" journal, *New International,* he began, also in 1946, to write on Jewish topics for *Commentary* and on literary ones for *Partisan Review,* whose paradoxical devotion to both Trotsky and T. S. Eliot Howe shared.

In 1947 Howe married Thalia Filias, an archaeologist, who later bore him two children. He worked for a time as assistant to Hannah Arendt at Schocken Books and to Dwight Macdonald at *Politics* magazine, where he wrote under the pseudonym Theodore Dryden. For four years, starting in 1948, he reviewed nonpolitical books for *Time*, a publication universally scorned by people of Howe's political persuasion. Moving to Princeton when his wife got a job teaching at a girls' school there in 1948, Howe became acquainted with Princeton's numerous literary inhabitants, including Delmore Schwartz and Saul Bellow.

In his first public involvement in "Jewish" issues, in 1949, Howe entered the controversy over the award of the Bollingen Prize for poetry to Ezra Pound, who had speechified on behalf of fascism and against Jews during the war. At the same time Howe was publishing (with B. J. Widick) a book entitled *The UAW and Walter Reuther* (1949). His career as literary critic burgeoned with two books on American writers well outside of his New York milieu, *Sherwood Anderson* (1951) and the pioneering *William Faulkner* (1952). Largely for financial reasons, Howe (who had no graduate degrees although he had taken some courses at Brooklyn College after the war) took up a teaching post in English at the newly formed Brandeis University (where his job interview was conducted in Yiddish). During his tenure at Brandeis (1954–1961), Howe established a reputation as a superbly gifted teacher.

Although he had abandoned Trotskyism by 1948 (and resigned from the Independent Socialist League in 1952), Howe was still a committed socialist who did not give up on Marxism until 1960. In 1954 he founded *Dissent* magazine as an instrument to promote "democratic" socialism, although more as an animating ethic than as a political program, and for the next forty years he spent two days a week (without remuneration) editing the magazine. In the very same year, he published (with the Yiddish poet Eliezer Greenberg) the first of a series of groundbreaking anthologies, adorned with scintillating introductions, that were designed as acts of critical salvage of the destroyed culture of Eastern European Jewry. *A Treasury of Yiddish Stories* (1954) was dedicated "To the Six Million." Howe had turned to Yiddish literature in belated response to the shock following the war years.

Now writing on all his three tracks—socialist, literary, Jewish—with the abundance of a major industry, Howe published in 1957 his first major collection of literary essays, *Politics and the Novel*, as well as *The American Communist Party: A Critical History* (with Lewis Coser). But his

personal life was less happy: 1959 brought divorce and the breakup of his family. In 1961 he moved to California to teach at Stanford University, a place he soon intensely disliked (partly, so it was reported, because nobody there could understand his Jewish jokes). When a job offer came from Hunter College in the City University of New York, he accepted it with alacrity and in 1963 returned to what he called his natural habitat. In 1964 Arien Hausknecht, a widow and a member of the New School (New York) faculty in psychology, became Howe's third wife.

The sixties was for Howe a decade of controversy. In 1963 he organized a tumultuous public forum to debate Hannah Arendt's *Eichmann in Jerusalem*, the book that blamed European Jews for having significantly and willingly participated in their own destruction. He became active in opposition to the Vietnam War but also to its anti-democratic New Left opponents. His critiques of the "authoritarians of the left" were collected in a volume of essays on the politics of democratic radicalism entitled *Steady Work* (1966). By now a famous, respected, and honored literary critic, Howe published in 1967 his only book-length study of an English novelist, *Thomas Hardy*.

In the seventies Howe became a sharp critic of the new generation of militant feminists and also of the professors who, in universities and professional organizations, exploited literature for partisan political purposes. At the same time, he continued his collaboration with Greenberg in establishing a canon of the essential works of secular Jewishness. *A Treasury of Yiddish Poetry* appeared in 1969 and *Voices from the Yiddish*, a collection of nonfictional writing, in 1972. In 1970 he was named Distinguished Professor at the City University of New York and in 1971 awarded both the Bollingen and Guggenheim Fellowships. Then, in 1972, with indefatigable energy and in defiance of the expectations of friends, Howe plunged into work on a massive history of the immigrant Jewish world of New York. For four years he pored over memoir literature in English and Yiddish, studies of immigrant experience, the Yiddish and American press, historical studies, personal interviews, and works of fiction, to produce a work of social and cultural history that could "lay claim to being an accurate record." *World of Our Fathers*, a masterwork of historical writing, was timed to appear in 1976 to coincide with the bicentennial celebration of American independence. Howe was proclaiming that the history of the 2 million East European Jews who came to America starting in the 1880s was a distinctly American story, a part of American history.

Noting that "cultures are slow to die," Howe asked in his book to what extent the culture of East European Jewish immigrants was still active in second- and third-generation Jews. He claims that although "a great many" suburban Jews no longer spoke Yiddish, and a growing number did not understand it, or even know what, as Jews, they did not know, nevertheless their deepest inclinations of conduct showed signs of immigrant shaping. The kinds of vocation toward which they urged their children, their sense of appropriate family conduct, their idea of respectability and its opposite—all of it, according to Howe, "showed the strains of immigrant Yiddish culture, usually blurred, sometimes buried, but still at work." Jewish socialism as such nearly vanished, but it took on a second, less vigorous life in the standard liberalism of suburban Jews. But the uglier impulses of Jewish radicalism, going back to the 1880s, also survived in the children of the Jewish suburbanites who filled the ranks of the New Left in the sixties: "A few of these young people . . . became enemies of Israel . . . ; they collected funds for Al Fatah, the Palestinian terrorist movement" (Howe 1976). This too, Howe acknowledges, had its precedent in the immigrant world, in postures of self-hatred and contempt for one's fathers that were already present in the anarchists of the 1880s.

Although the popularity of *World of Our Fathers* (which won the National Book Award for history and enabled its author to be elected a member of the American Academy of Arts and Letters in 1979) threatened to make Howe into an institution, he was determined to make a full and honest reckoning with his past. This he did in *Leon Trotsky* (1978), *A Margin of Hope* (1982), and *Socialism and America* (1985). In all three, Howe tried to tell the truth about his radical socialist past. The second was an autobiography, telling little of life and loves, but much about his career as a public intellectual. Still, its dedication told of yet another change in Howe's private life: whereas *World of Our Fathers* was dedicated to his third wife, the book of 1982 was dedicated to Ilana Wiener, an Israeli expatriate who had become his fourth.

Howe retired from the City University of New York in 1986, but he continued to write voluminously (and was named a MacArthur Fellow in 1987). For the third time in his career he went into combat against literary radicals, now called theorists, who saw little intrinsic value in litera-

ture and used it mainly as an instrument of their political ambitions. Slowed by illness in his last years, he died of a ruptured aorta in New York City in 1993.

What is Howe's legacy? He viewed his three loves as lost causes. Two of them, socialism and secular Jewishness, really were; the third, humane literary study, may yet prove to be so. But to chronicle a devotion to lost causes, forsaken beliefs, and impossible loyalties is also to chronicle a kind of heroism. Howe liked to say that "one of the arts of life is to know how to end" (Howe 1982). Taken out of context, this might seem a counsel of stoical resignation; in fact, it was the opposite. He said it when writing about the American Yiddish poets who refused, out of a sense of honor and a strength of will, to admit the bleakness of their future. However desperate, they would confront the world with firmness—and that quixotic utopianism is what Howe meant by knowing how to end.

Edward Alexander

References and Further Reading
Alexander, Edward. 1995. *Irving Howe and Secular Jewishness.* Cincinnati, OH: University of Cincinnati.
Alexander, Edward. 1998. *Irving Howe—Socialist, Critic, Jew.* Bloomington: Indiana University Press.
Alexander, Edward. 2004. "Lionel Trilling and Irving Howe: A Literary Friendship." *New England Review* 25,3 (Autumn): 20–75.
Howe, Irving. 1976. *World of Our Fathers.* New York: Harcourt Brace Jovanovich.
Howe, Irving. 1982. *A Margin of Hope: An Intellectual Autobiography.* New York: Harcourt Brace Jovanovich.
"Remembering Irving Howe." 1993. *Dissent* 40 (Fall): 515–549.
Rosenfeld, Alvin. 1976. "Irving Howe: The World of Our Fathers." *Midstream* 22 (October): 80–86.
Sorin, Gerald. 2002. *Irving Howe: A Life of Passionate Dissent.* New York: New York University Press.

Alfred Kazin (1915–1998)

Literary Critic

In the fall of 1942, Alfred Kazin, literary critic, historian, autobiographer, and all-around man of letters, burst onto the American literary scene at the age of twenty-seven with the publication of his classic study of modern American prose, *On Native Grounds*. He had already acquired the

Alfred Kazin, literary critic. (Corbis)

title of the wunderkind of American criticism as a prolific young reviewer for *The New York Herald Tribune: Books, The New York Times Book Review,* and *The New Republic.* The appearance of *On Native Grounds,* an authoritative study of the realist tradition in American literature, confirmed that a resounding new voice had entered the American literary arena. That he was educated at City College and came from the Brownsville district of Brooklyn, the son of working-class immigrant Jews, was also of interest. At a time when Jews were being slaughtered across Europe, the fact that the son of a house painter and an illiterate seamstress from the Minsk area of Russia had just published a 500-page history celebrating the democratic traditions in American letters was regarded by more than one reviewer as not just a literary, but a moral event.

On Native Grounds was an extraordinary act of *possession,* to use a favorite Kazin word. American literature was not there for the asking; it needed to be earned, as only an "outsider" felt that need. In a steady stream of essays and books—*The Inmost Leaf* (1955), *Contemporaries*

(1962), *Bright Book of Life* (1973), *An American Procession* (1984), *God and the American Writer* (1996)—Kazin would spend much of the next five decades making American literature his own. Some writers he possessed more completely than others. An "enthusiast," he needed to feel close to writers. He wrote unconvincingly about figures beyond his range of sympathy: Nathaniel Hawthorne, Henry James, Edith Wharton, Edgar Allan Poe. When he felt an intuitive kinship, however, he could be incandescent. His essays on Ralph Waldo Emerson, Herman Melville, Walt Whitman, Emily Dickinson, Theodore Dreiser, and Saul Bellow are among the finest that have been written on these writers.

But *possession* need not mean assimilation. Kazin's next major work, *A Walker in the City* (1951), is a memoir of his life growing up in the Brownsville section of Brooklyn. It describes a world of loneliness, yearning, fear, and belonging, where he often felt torn between his loyalties to his working-class Jewish parents and his desire for the world beyond the ghetto. What made his situation particularly difficult (and the book moving) is that his passion to escape Brownsville owed much of its intensity to his parents' desire for him to leave—"anything just out of Brownsville"—an event that would release them from the "shame" of their lowly, outsider status (Kazin 1951). "I was to be the monument of their liberation from the shame—of being what they were" (Kazin 1951). He could redeem them only by leaving them. Having established his reputation as an international authority on American literature, Kazin made it again in *A Walker in the City,* a recognized canonical text in Jewish American literature.

A Walker in the City would be followed by two more autobiographies: *Starting Out in the Thirties* (1965) and *New York Jew* (1978). Their setting is Manhattan, where the child's contradictory feelings about life in Brownsville return as a conflict between the rewards and the cost of "making it" in the world "beyond." These too are intensely personal works, but Kazin also sees himself representing a historical phenomenon—the movement of Jewish American writers (and Jews generally) into the American mainstream. He calls the autobiographies "personal histories"—telling his own story, he was also writing history (Kazin 1982).

In the thirties, radical politics was one route for Jewish writers into American life. Kazin's credentials as a literate socialist were important qualities for editors looking for youthful talent. But if he possessed the political and intellectual credentials, he did not share the social background of those with whom he worked. Much of the drama of *Starting Out in the Thirties* derives from its hero's struggle to find his way socially in a largely WASP world very different from his own. The rest comes from history itself, as dreams of revolution turn into the nightmare of Hitler's war.

In *New York Jew*, Kazin is no longer the outsider. He is now at the center of New York's (and America's) intellectual and cultural life. Instead of struggling with a WASP literary establishment, he finds himself wrestling with the implications of his own success and that of other Jews who, like him, had started out in the thirties. The recurring question raised in the book is how to keep faith with his sense of himself as a Jew when Jews were no longer in the working class, no longer outsiders. One way was satire directed at those Jews, arrivistes, who, having "made it" in American life, had shed their early political commitments to the poor and dispossessed and joined in the strident anti-Communist crusade cheering on "America as an ideology" (Kazin 1978). An episodic, emotionally jagged account of life in postwar America, *New York Jew* is most impressive for its vivid, sometimes loving, sometimes acerbic portraits of Kazin's contemporaries: Saul Bellow, Lionel Trilling, Hannah Arendt, Edmund Wilson, among many others.

Kazin will be remembered primarily for *On Native Grounds* and his three autobiographies. It is important to note, however, that from the mid-thirties until his death on June 5, 1998, he was one of the country's most influential reviewer-critics, with a range of interests that included modern European and American literature and history, Jewish literature, and contemporary politics and culture. He was also a notable educator and cultural ambassador, who taught and lectured at universities around the world and held sustained professorial positions at Amherst, State University of New York–Stony Brook, Hunter College, and the Graduate Center of the City University of New York. One of his favorite quotes was Issac Babel's "You must know everything." Kazin spent a lifetime in pursuit of that goal—reading, writing, teaching. On his death, the novelist Philip Roth called him "America's best reader of American literature in this century" (Hampton 1998).

Richard M. Cook

References and Further Reading

Hampton, Wilborn. 1998. "Alfred Kazin, the Author Who Wrote of Literature and Himself." *New York Times* (June 6): A13.

Kazin, Alfred. 1942. *On Native Grounds: An Interpretation of Modern American Prose Literature.* New York: Reynal and Hitchcock.

Kazin, Alfred. 1951. *A Walker in the City.* New York: Harcourt Brace.

Kazin, Alfred. 1982. *Contemporaries,* rev. ed. New York, NY: Horizon Press.

William Phillips (1907–2002)

Editor of *Partisan Review*

William Phillips was chiefly known as an editor of *Partisan Review* magazine for sixty-eight years. Commencing in an era when the literary establishment and universities placed a premium on the Anglo-Saxon heritage of literary critics and scholars, the journal was conceivably the most conspicuous venue by which several generations of Jewish American intellectuals won admittance to the centers of intellectual, cultural, and academic life in the United States. Its pages were electrified by worldly and novel ideas about modern literature, socialist doctrine, abstract art, and the role of the intelligentsia, sometimes published in the form of symposia. The publication was founded under a secular and cosmopolitan ethos that was never abandoned, even as the editors' original Marxist political militancy waned. Phillips rarely wrote on explicitly Jewish topics, although late in the history of the magazine he commented briefly on the trial of Adolph Eichmann and on the Israeli state.

Phillips's 1983 autobiography, *A Partisan View,* reveals a personal background of rootlessness and insecurity. He was born in Manhattan on November 14, 1907, to Jewish parents from Russia, Marie Berman and Edward Litvinsky. Phillips's father, trained as a lawyer but unsuccessful in his career, replaced the name Litvinsky with Phillips. During a period of marital separation, young William accompanied his mother to Kiev, where they lived for three years in the Berman household. When they returned with Phillips's maternal grandmother, the family moved to the Bronx.

Phillips's father sought escape from his occupational failures through sundry forms of spiritualism. Phillips's mother suffered from hypochondriacism, and the grand-mother was querulous too. Phillips attended the City College of New York and escaped his unpleasant home environment. There his friends introduced him to literary modernism, most notably a 1920 collection of essays by T. S. Eliot, *The Sacred Wood.* After graduating in 1928, Phillips became a graduate student at New York University, receiving an MA degree in 1930. While working as an instructor in the English department from 1929 to 1931, he read journals such as the *New Republic* and *Nation,* which moved him to the Left. He also met his first wife, Edna Greenblatt, who was an undergraduate studying literature and philosophy.

The Phillipses rapidly gravitated toward Bohemian and Communist circles in Greenwich Village. While Edna, who would become a public school teacher, joined the Communist Party, William became an activist in party cultural affairs as early as 1932. The theoretical journal of the party, *The Communist,* carried an essay of his on the philosopher Ortega y Gasset in January 1933, for which Phillips used the pseudonym Wallace Phelps. Reflecting the ultrarevolutionary party orientation of the time, Phillips characterized the Spaniard as a defamer of the Soviet Union, tool of Wall Street, and a concealed fascist. Nevertheless, in the January 1933 issue of the literary journal *Symposium,* writing under his own name, he announced himself a specialist in the technical aspects of criticism with an impressive essay, "Categories for Criticism."

By 1934, Phillips was a leader of the New York City chapter of the John Reed Club, a cultural affiliate of the Communist Party. In this capacity he made the acquaintance of a Communist Party member named Ivan Greenberg, who had been publishing criticism and poetry under the name Philip Rahv. Together they worked with party members and supporters to launch a new journal for the Club, which they called *Partisan Review.* The first issue, described as "A Bi-Monthly of Revolutionary Literature Published by the John Reed Club of New York," was dated February–March 1934 and included a review essay by Phillips. Writing as Wallace Phelps, his "The Anatomy of Liberalism" was a Marxist assessment of British literary critic Henry Hazlett.

Yet by 1936, Phillips and Rahv had become disenchanted with the Communist Party. They were disturbed by the 1935 turn of the Communist International toward the Popular Front alliance with liberal democracies, which

had produced a sea change in the party's cultural orientation, and also by the commencement in 1936 of the Moscow Purge Trials. Still adhering to a form of revolutionary Marxism, Rahv and Phillips were increasingly swayed by writings of the exiled Bolshevik Leon Trotsky, who repudiated Stalin's regime from Bolshevik principles. They stopped publishing *Partisan Review* for a year; it reappeared in December 1937 with a new editorial board of non-party members and a distinct orientation toward the modernist avant-garde in literature and art.

However, by the early 1940s Rahv and Phillips were feeling frustration with all components of the organized Left. Consequently Phillips sought to establish a surrogate foundation for *Partisan Review*'s project, one that would justify their commitment to avant-garde modernism as well as to a radical outlook. His 1941 essay "The Intellectuals' Tradition" was a substantial effort to define that alternative. In this discussion of the nature of alienated avant-garde culture, he tries creatively to walk a middle ground between cultural criticism that focuses on the individual artist and a Marxist/historical criticism that tends to emphasize historical circumstance. While Phillips still saw Marxism as an advance over earlier approaches, he was vexed by an unresolved contradiction for the Marxist critic who insists that literature has autonomous values at the same time that he or she believes the values are actually produced by social context. Phillips theorizes that modern art actually springs from the intellectual stratum of society, sections of which are often in rebellion against the reigning ideas. Thus he regards the intellectuals themselves as the foundation of a tradition that can sustain the individual artist, making him or her a more representative figure.

In Phillips's view, intellectuals have set the tone for the European creative imagination since the rise of capitalism in countries that were adequately wealthy to maintain the growth of this stratum. United States literature, however, exhibits singular problems because the native intelligentsia has not paralleled Europe in becoming a detached and self-sufficient group. This tardiness is a consequence of the modern history of the United States occurring too swiftly and expansively, with the city starting to displace the countryside only after the Civil War.

For Phillips, the whole of United States culture might be typified by Henry Adams, a New Englander desperately in search of some pivotal tradition, some feeling of synthesis. Adams thought he discovered this in a dynamic law of history, yet he ultimately came to suspect theory as inevitably misrepresenting facts. The result of this cultural heritage that strives for wholeness and then reverts to a new start is an ambivalent psyche; United States intellectuals are torn between the drive for self-rule and a tendency toward self-obliteration that produces a propensity to melt into the popular mind. The twentieth century has witnessed a regional nostalgia that was repudiated by naturalism, followed by the proletarian literary movement's aspiration to erase the bourgeois past. The disastrous pattern of the United States intellectuals perseveres—opposition followed by reconciliation, but never autonomy.

Phillips's views retained their same locus of values throughout the World War II years. In 1956 he furnished a retrospective called "American Writing Today." Here Phillips depicts the 1950s as a time when the literary intelligentsia was concentrating more on their own writing than on capacious literary and political questions. This was to some extent a backlash against the overpoliticized years of the 1930s and 1940s, but it was also a consequence of an enlarging affluence with a greater and more literate readership for books. Both imaginative authors and literary critics have narrowed, while sociologists and historians have provided much of the political thinking.

Phillips was also doubtful about recent shifts in publishing and on university campuses. Mass-market literature might simply create passive consumers, and college teaching tends to housebreak creative writers. He laments that the recent attacks on conformity in cultural spirit have mainly been against political repression from the Right. What has been ignored are intellectual conservatism and the tendency of literature to adapt to the marketplace.

Phillips published a small number of short stories after the late 1940s. Characteristic is his 1949 "Sleep No More," which features a Phillips-like protagonist named David Miller. Miller, a writer who travels in Bohemian circles, is awakened from an afternoon nap by a large man who identifies himself as being from Army Intelligence. The man is in search of a neighbor, Miss Caruso, who has moved out of the apartment complex. Miller allows himself to be questioned, although he knows little about Caruso. He recalls that she had literary pretensions, although he is unaware of her employment. Miller is desperate to know the reasons for the investigation, but the man from Army Intelligence evasively insists that his questions are routine. In the series of self-rationalizations that domi-

nate the first-person narrative, Miller tells himself that he will have no part in any political witch-hunting. Yet he also acknowledges that he would assist government authorities in helping to identify a possible spy. Although the Army Intelligence man never suggests that this is the case with Caruso, the overly loquacious Miller finds himself persisting in volunteering evidence, including the rumor that Miss Caruso is a lesbian and part Jewish.

Toward the end of the interview, Miller urges that the man from Army Intelligence confer with another tenant, Miss Johnson, as well as with the building superintendent. However, a few days later, Miller learns that neither person had been interrogated, and he becomes quite agitated. Attempting to contact Army Intelligence, Miller discovers that no such agency exists. Ultimately, Miller arranges a discussion with a military colonel who informs him that no person named Caruso has been under investigation, that the credentials that the alleged Army Intelligence man showed Miller appear to be phony, and that there have been additional reports of an imposter making the rounds. Miller is left unable to sleep and wondering what Miss Caruso would have said about Miller, had she been the one interviewed by the man claiming to be from Army Intelligence.

The story recalls the fiction of Franz Kafka in the hyperconscious self-reflexivity of the narrator and the sense of free-floating guilt hanging over him. At the same time the story blends this neurotic response to an investigator with what was probably an accurate reflection of the conflicted reaction of Phillips and his colleagues to the antiradical witch-hunt that would become known as McCarthyism. The *Partisan Review* editors wanted to do nothing to intensify the persecution of people who were simply nonconformists and heretics, yet they held that Communists were potentially dangerous to society in various ways.

Phillips's chief role on *Partisan Review* was to supervise fund-raising and the general functioning of the magazine. In 1963 he moved the magazine to Rutgers University for fifteen years, and Phillips became a faculty member in the English department. Rahv, however, grew increasingly distant from the journal, and also evolved a political and cultural perspective that Phillips did not share. Strangely, Rahv was moving back to the Marxism of his youth, while taking a much harsher view than Phillips of the cultural trends among younger writers and artists in the 1960s. In 1969 Rahv resigned, and Phillips's own public stature became elevated as he chaired the Coordinating Council of Literary Magazines (funded by the government) from 1967 to 1975. He also wrote more editorials for *Partisan Review* and participated in a greater number of the journal's symposia. In 1967 he published an essay collection called *A Sense of the Present*. However, a change in the administration at Rutgers in 1978 forced Phillips to move the journal to Boston University, where he continued editing it until he died of pneumonia in New York City at age ninety-four. Edna Phillips died in 1985, and in 1995 Phillips married Edith Kurzweil, a literary critic who briefly succeeded Phillips as editor of *Partisan Review* until Boston University closed the magazine in 2003.

Alan M. Wald

References and Further Reading
Barrett, William. 1982. *The Truants: Adventures among the Intellectuals.* Garden City, NY: Anchor Press/Doubleday.
Cooney, Terry A. 1986. *The Rise of the New York Intellectuals: Partisan Review and Its Circle.* Madison: University of Wisconsin Press.
Gilbert, James B. 1968. *Writers and Partisans: A History of Literary Radicalism in America.* New York: Wiley.
Phillips, William. 1967. *A Sense of the Present.* New York: Chilmark.
Phillips, William. 1983. *A Partisan View: Five Decades of the Literary Life.* New York: Stein and Day.
Wald, Alan M. 1987. *The New York Intellectuals: The Rise and Decline of the Anti-Stalinist Left from the 1930s to the 1980s.* Chapel Hill: University of North Carolina Press.

Philip Rahv (1908–1973)

Literary Critic

Philip Rahv was among the principal Jewish American literary critics of the generation coming of age during the Great Depression. Author of a series of brilliant essays, some of which were collected in *Image and Idea* (1949), *The Myth and the Powerhouse* (1965), and *Literature and the Sixth Sense* (1969), Rahv provided influential cultural leadership for the circle of writers known as the New York Intellectuals. From 1934 until 1969, he was, with William Phillips, a co-editor of *Partisan Review,* the chief literary organ for this group, many of whom were Jewish American.

Rahv was born Ivan Greenberg at Kupin in the Russian Ukraine, arriving in Rhode Island at age fourteen to live with an older brother. Prior to the Depression, Rahv worked in advertising on the West Coast, then moved to New York City where he joined the Communist Party in 1932. Soon he was publishing poetry and criticism in Communist Party journals as Philip Rahv, chosen because the last name means rabbi in Hebrew. In 1934 he united with Phillips and other members of the John Reed Club, a Communist-led cultural organization, to launch *Partisan Review* as its New York City publication. Two years later, however, Rahv began to reconsider his relation to the party in light of the party's turn to the Popular Front and onset of the Moscow Purge Trials.

In December 1937 *Partisan Review* reappeared, this time as a rival to the party's cultural movement and with a special focus on literary modernism. The magazine was partially identified with the ideas of the exiled leader of the Russian Revolution, Leon Trotsky, until the start of World War II. At that time Rahv fell into a dispute with two of the more left-wing editors, Dwight Macdonald and Clement Greenberg, who resigned in 1943. Thereafter the politics of the magazine became steadfastly tempered, although the literary alignment remained fixed on the high modernism associated with T. S. Eliot, James Joyce, Franz Kafka, and other Europeans.

In accordance with many Marxist-oriented Jewish intellectuals of his era, Rahv regarded his Jewish identity as a constituent of his internationalism and cosmopolitanism. However, his consistent emphasis on the need to Europeanize United States culture, and his fusing literature with a program of radical social change to overcome provincialism and insularity, may be expressions of his Jewish background. Beginning as an outsider to the cultural establishment of the United States, Rahv's upward mobility into a position of considerable influence in the 1950s more or less parallels the movement of Jewish American literature as a whole.

Among Rahv's most prominent essays is "Proletarian Literature: A Political Autopsy," a landmark renunciation of the Communist-led cultural movement of the 1930s. Rahv's mission was to debunk the literary movement of writers allied with the Communist Party. While the newness of the proletarian literary phenomenon resided in the attention that writers and critics drew to connections between art and society, Rahv reasoned that the novel movement could not be fathomed apart from the Communist Party's particular version of those connections. It was not Marxist doctrine that the critics promoting proletarian literature applied to culture, only the Communist Party's questionable redaction.

Rahv explained that objective conditions set the stage for the development of the proletarian movement. These included the catastrophe of the Depression that drew compassion for the working man; the inability of literary models of the 1920s to acknowledge the new situation in the 1930s; and the actuality of a Communist Party that gladly received a literary program that might correspond to its political aims. Moreover, the Communist Party afforded an audience and foundation, and it even offered the illustration of the Soviet Union as the quintessence of the socialist utopia. Writers were bewitched by the formula that they should confederate with the working class and admit the class struggle as the overriding fact of modern life. However, this formula said nothing about aesthetics, mixed the borders between art and politics, fell short of concretizing what the political commitment actually meant in the circumstances of the 1930s, and hid the fact that the welfare of the working class was identified with the politics of a particular party. Under these conditions, discernments of literary critics became political judgments of the apparent or veiled ideas of the literature vis-à-vis the Communist Party. The result was not revolutionary writing, but "an internationally uniform literature . . . whose main service was the carrying out of party assignments" (Rahv 1978).

The implications of Rahv's critique were not restricted to the Communist Party. After all, any literature allied with a political movement is curbed by utilitarian objectives, and the authentic literature associated with a gigantic social class expresses a variety of levels, groupings, and interests. Moreover, in the instance of industrial capitalism, it was not the proletariat but the ruling class that had the assets to command the culture, leaving the subaltern group only minor resources such as urban folklore. Rahv thus observes that even the writers formally certified as proletarian by the Communist Party are affiliated with bourgeois creative styles and techniques; their writings are unique only on a doctrinal political foundation. Further confirmation that proletarian literature was Communist Party literature can be found in its swift rise and collapse in connection with the fate and political requirement of the Party. In the second part of the 1930s,

with the appearance of the Popular Front and the Communist Party's attempt to ally with the forces of liberal capitalism, the party shifted its alignment in culture. The central question was no longer the pro-Communist ideological implications of the literary text, but the anti-fascist political stance of the artist, whose writing need not even be radical to gain approval.

Rahv's polemic embodied many substantial truths, eminently in regard to the Communist Party's identification of Marxism and the interests of the working class with its own policies. On the other hand, Rahv blundered in curtailing complex works of art to their political component; he failed to concede the central part played in the creative process by individual psychology as well as each artist's reservoir of skills. Seventy years later, many books associated with the proletarian school have been reprinted and are valued for formal and dramatic features that Rahv was either unaware of or failed to esteem.

In the summer of 1939, Rahv concurrently published in *Kenyon Review* an influential statement about the past, present, and future of United States literature, "Paleface and Redskin." His thesis was that United States writers gravitate toward two categories, usually antagonistic, resulting in overall literary careers that were asymmetrical and fractional. Some writers Rahv assessed as tragically lonely, such as Herman Melville, or as sometimes writing drawing room fiction, such as Henry James. Others were obstreperous and open-air, such as Mark Twain and Walt Whitman. In other words, one school tended toward sensibility, discipline, and theory; the other toward energy, action, and opportunity. One side is genteel and sees ambiguity in the culture; the other is rough-hewn and rejoices in it. The palefaces are regarded by Rahv as highbrow, but not to be assessed as an intelligentsia in the European sense. The rival redskins are educated, but actually lowbrow in being impulsive and passionate. James and Whitman are the farthest apart. In a memorable phrase he characterized them as "fatal antipodes," between whom one appears compelled to take sides (Rahv 1978). They occasion a cleft in literary tradition unmatched in Europe.

Rahv's 1940 "The Cult of Experience in American Writing" is an embellishment of the same proposition. James again exemplifies the paleface tradition, but this time Rahv adds that James's fiction sporadically discloses an awareness that the individual can mature only through interplay with experience. In contrast, there is once again the outstanding literary trend celebrating experience, associated with Whitman, Sherwood Anderson, and Thomas Wolfe. Yet their writings are largely denuded of ideas. In fact, even James is limited intellectually in that he searches for a means of enhancing life; this approach is distinguished from European masters—such as Tolstoy, Dostoyevsky, Flaubert, Proust, Joyce, Mann, Lawrence, and Kafka—who are characterized as focusing on life's essential quality and fate. Rahv believes that here lies the explanation for the absence of a genuine intelligentsia as characters in the American novel; there are artists, teachers, and scientists, but "not a person thinking with their entire being . . . who transforms ideas into actual dramatic motives instead of using them as ideological conventions or as theories so externally applied that they can be dispensed with at will" (Rahv 1978).

Rahv differentiates the twentieth-century novel as exhibiting a positive advance toward the acquisition of experience, whereas classic, early United States writing is more a chronicle of inexperience; that latter is mostly genteel and local, with romance as a preferred genre. Only in the writings of James did the new realist methods of Europe make an impression. The 1920s featured a drive for an even greater experience, and the 1930s witnessed an attempt to appropriate political ideas. However, when U.S. Left writers of the Great Depression are compared to European contemporaries such as André Malraux and Ignazio Silone, Rahv feels as if the former are only providing a slice of life, not depicting personalities cognizant of historical necessity. At the end of the 1930s, Rahv felt the creative capacity of the "cult of experience" to be well-nigh depleted, at the same time that a new shift was under way from national to international forces of cultural determination.

By the time of the Cold War, Rahv, despite a short blast against Senator Joseph McCarthy, appears to have become de-radicalized. After 1957 he was ensconced as professor of English and Comparative Literature at Brandeis University. Yet, in 1967, when the New Left was well under way, Rahv began to aggressively differentiate himself from the liberal anticommunists with whom he had been closely associated for nearly two decades. Declaring firmly that he was never a liberal, Rahv avowed that his views were still considerably the same as they were in the late 1930s. His ensuing exertions to persuade militant activists of the 1960s that what they required for victory was a truly revolutionary political party indicates that his reconversion in

the realm of ideology was earnest. At the same time, however, Rahv was repelled by the cultural ethos of the New Left, and he began to suspect that his co-editor of *Partisan Review,* Phillips, was capitulating to the revolution of drugs, rock music, and cult figures such as Marshall McLuhan. Thus Rahv parted from the journal and launched his own short-lived publication in 1971 called *Modern Occasions.* His personal life fared no better as he failed in a third marriage, succumbed to rages and vendettas against one-time literary allies, and drank excessively. In 1973 Rahv took a leave of absence from Brandeis to complete books on Leon Trotsky and Fyodor Dostoevsky, but died halfway through the year at age sixty-five. To the amazement of some of his radical friends, Rahv willed his fortune to the State of Israel.

Alan M. Wald

References and Further Reading
Edelstein, Arthur, ed. 1979. *Images and Ideas in American Culture—The Function of Criticism: Essays in Memory of Philip Rahv.* Hanover, NH: Brandeis University Press.
Howe, Irving. 1982. *A Margin of Hope: An Intellectual Autobiography.* New York: Harcourt Brace Jovanovich.
Rahv, Philip. 1949. *Image and Idea: Essays on Literary Themes.* New York: New Directions.
Rahv, Philip. 1978. *Essays on Literature and Politics, 1932–1972.* Boston: Houghton Mifflin.
Wald, Alan M. 1987. *The New York Intellectuals: The Rise and Decline of the Anti-Stalinist Left from the 1930s to the 1980s.* Chapel Hill: University of North Carolina Press.

Lionel Trilling (1905–1975)

Literary Critic

When Lionel Trilling died in 1975 it was generally conceded that literature had lost the most influential critic of the post–World War II era and that, in effect, a literary office had fallen vacant. Trilling was by then something more than just a critic; he was a *figure* and almost that rarest of creatures, an academic celebrity. His words carried weight: they had gravitas. He even came, in time, to be something of a standard source, a coiner of commonplaces: variousness and possibility, the tragic sense of life, the opposing self, the liberal imagination, ideas in modulation.

Lionel Trilling, literary critic and Columbia professor. (Getty Images)

Trilling enjoyed standing in both the academy and the cockpit of literary politics and polemic: New York City. He was a pivotal figure among the New York intellectuals, and a crude silhouette of his career would look like a shadow of what they all had experienced. Like others of his generation, Trilling had survived a youthful brush with Marxism, touching down briefly in the National Committee for the Defense of Political Prisoners, a radical group of intellectuals, artists, and writers associated with the Communist Party. That experience made lifelong anti-Communists of both him and his wife, Diana. Trilling shifted course in the 1930s by immersing himself in the writing of Matthew Arnold (about whom he wrote his PhD dissertation) and E. M. Forster. Indeed, Trilling's first book of essays, *The Liberal Imagination* in 1950, was a testament of conversion, and it would become the signature book by which the intellectual world would ever after judge him.

Unlike other New York intellectuals, who fancied themselves modernists, Trilling distrusted the avant-garde

and was more at ease in the nineteenth century, with its broad vistas and thick textures, its social novels with their manners, morals, and cool-eyed acceptance of fatality. He shared with the others the view of literature as the expression of history, politics, class, and the *Zeitgeist,* and he made a practice of keeping watch over the currents and eddies of what his circle called "the culture," which consisted largely of the opinions and social habits of the eastern, liberal intelligentsia. But he was also a scholar and a teacher, a historian of modern social thought whose early books on Matthew Arnold (1939) and E. M. Forster (1943) and later studies of Freud—"Freud and Literature" (1947), "Art and Neurosis" (1945)—gave him credentials in the Modern Language Association and International Psychoanalytic Association. In addition, as an editor of the Readers' Subscription, Trilling enjoyed a rare and successful venture into the commercial side of letters.

It was a matter of vital importance that he was the first Jew to gain a full-time appointment (in 1939) and to gain tenure in English (1945) at Columbia University, where for years he was looked upon as an experiment. However, as the age demanded, his Jewishness could appear abstract and occluded. Seldom did his imagination come to rest on Jewish themes—most notably in his magisterial introduction to the stories of Isaac Babel in 1955—and nothing in his personal elegance or his lucid, supple, periodic prose suggested the restlessness, vividness, and combative postures that otherwise marked the entry of Eastern European Jews into the precincts of American thought. Maybe the word that best describes Trilling ethnically is *cosmopolitan,* suggesting the internationalism and worldliness of those whom historian Isaac Deutscher famously referred to as non-Jewish Jews. And it was a regional cosmopolitanism at that. Trilling was born in New York City, taught at Columbia University on Morningside Heights, and died in New York. But then New York was an international city, and never more so than during the 1940s and 1950s when it became home to the emigré artists, writers, and intellectuals who had fled from Stalin and Hitler and who had brought the intellectual vitality of Paris, Berlin, and Leningrad to Manhattan.

Trilling began publishing in 1925 in Elliot Cohen's and Henry Hurwitz's *Menorah Journal,* the monthly publication of the Menorah Society, whose broad purpose was the formation of a nonsectarian, humanist, and progressive Jewish consciousness in America. But he deserted that magazine and its efforts at "cultivated" Jewishness in 1930 for the swifter tides of the intellectual mainstream in *The Nation* and *The New Republic,* as well as, for a brief moment, in V. F. Calverton's leftish *Modern Quarterly/Modern Monthly.* In 1944, reflecting on the depth and import of his Jewishness, he declined to waste any nostalgia on his youthful torments over his Jewish identity or to claim any influence on him of organized Jewish life. "As the Jewish community now exists," he harshly observed, "it can give no sustenance to the American artist or intellectual who is born a Jew. And so far as I am aware, it has not done so in the past. I know of writers who have used their Jewish experience as the subject of excellent work; I know of no writer in English who has added a micromillimetre to his stature by 'realizing his Jewishness', although I know of some who have curtailed their promise by trying to heighten their Jewish consciousness" (Trilling 1944).

The cosmopolitanism that Trilling adopted in place of the discarded Jewishness included a proclivity for the literature and thought of England's Victorian age. Though unique in its devotion, Trilling's Anglophilia followed certain lines of cultural force that were bound to affect a Jewish literary intellectual whose education had put him in touch with the expressive powers of the English language and the vitality of English literature, and, yes, with those gargoyles of the Anglo-Saxon imagination: the Fagins, Shylocks, Bleisteins, and Jews of Malta who haunted its dreams.

As a Victorianist, Trilling made character his touchstone; he was a Hebraist, as Arnold used the term—one who placed strictness of conscience before the sweetness and light of Hellenism. He could have been speaking for himself in claiming for George Orwell that, unlike Yeats or Eliot or Forster, he "takes his place . . . as a figure. In one degree or another they are geniuses, and he is not; if we ask what it is he stands for, what he is the figure of, the answer is: the virtue of not being a genius, of fronting the world with nothing more than one's simple, direct, undeceived intelligence, and a respect for the powers one does have, and the work one undertakes to do" (Trilling 1944). It is a claim for the undeceived intelligence that Trilling will stand on for all his literary heroes as well as for himself.

Trilling these days is best known for his resistances—his antagonism to the articles of progressive faith held dear by his own literary culture: revolutionism, social justice, the injuries of capitalism, and in later decades the fetish of

"authenticity" in the 1960s counterculture. Trilling's brand of cosmopolitanism was parochial after its own fashion, not only in its exaggerated regard for Bloomsbury mannerisms but in Trilling's general preference for defining himself against the grain of whatever garde was currently avant. His was a cosmopolitanism with a stringent sense of limits and a practice of being old-fashioned. As a writer, too, he could be studiously retro in prizing the human figure, the moral exemplum, above all else. Thus his most memorable essays from the essay collections, *The Liberal Imagination* (1950), *The Opposing Self* (1953), and *Beyond Culture* (1965), were his portraits: "Kipling," "The Poet as Hero: Keats in his Letters," "George Orwell and the Politics of Truth," "Isaac Babel," "James Joyce in his Letters," "Why We Read Jane Austen."

The actual gratifications in reading Trilling, however, are not those of coming upon insights indelibly phrased, as they are in reading, say, Edmund Wilson. Trilling was a soft stylist. His sentences generally lack a high gloss; they are plainspoken tending toward the fussy, sometimes indeed overripe with the "yet" and "but" clauses of the dialogist who happens to be conducting his most animated dialogues with himself. No, the pleasures of reading Trilling are those of watching an argument unfold, as he appears to make decisions on the fly, turning this corner or that as if weighing each implication as he writes.

But style with Trilling sometimes had a way of turning into matter. In his later books, Trilling showed a weakness for personified abstractions, like *mind, thought, the self,* and *the modern will,* which were often aliases for himself, and his continuing efforts to transcend culture, while recommending those novels in which it was most urgently recorded, exfoliated into aviaries of thought in which his positions became elusive, the dialectics hermetic, and the abstractions vaporous. *Beyond Culture* (1965) and *Sincerity and Authenticity* (1972) are troubled and troubling books whose difficulties reflect the perplexities of Trilling's own thought and the ambiguities of his own system of metaphysics and masks. The very title of his last publication in book form, the monograph *Mind in the Modern World* (1972), suggests the mental embattlement that in later years would dominate his self-conception. These later books did not exert influence comparable to that of *The Liberal Imagination,* though their prestige may grow in time when their exquisite ironies and superb balances can be better appreciated.

Ironic though it may seem, it is likely that what will keep Trilling's name and example alive into the twenty-first century is precisely the literary academy that has done all it can to erase him. Indeed, a Balkanized literary culture in which anything can be text, any text can be "theorized," and even the soundest idea can be tortured into barbarous, Latinized syntax may be the condition for recalling the lucidity and rationality for which Trilling stood. In death as in life Trilling remains the opposing self, the counter-example, the antidote to those intellectual excesses that dominate our present culture of literary study.

Mark Shechner

References and Further Reading

Krupnick, Mark. 1986. *Lionel Trilling and the Fate of Cultural Criticism.* Evanston, IL: Northwestern University Press.

Krupnick, Mark. 2005. "Lionel Trilling and the Deep Places of the Imagination" and "Lionel Trilling and the Politics of Style." In *Jewish Writing and the Deep Places of the Imagination,* edited by Jean K. Carney and Mark Shechner. Madison: University of Wisconsin Press.

O'Hara, Daniel T. 1988. *Lionel Trilling: The Work of Liberation.* Madison: University of Wisconsin Press.

Trilling, Lionel. 1944. "Under Forty." *Contemporary Jewish Record* 7 (February): 151–172.

Trilling, Diana. 1993. *The Beginning of the Journey: The Marriage of Diana and Lionel Trilling.* New York: Harcourt Brace.

American Jews and Art

Jewish American Artists and Their Themes in the Twentieth Century

The underlying question for Jewish American artists in the twentieth century is where their art fits into Western art, which has been essentially Christian during most of the past seventeen centuries. Interwoven with this question is an array of social, religious, and aesthetic issues reflecting on the matter of being Jewish and American.

The theme of art as a commentary on the ills of the world—which helps to correct these ills by causing the viewer to consider them—has engaged many Jewish American artists. Ben Shahn (1898–1969) traced the sociopolitical concerns of his Social Realism to his Jewishness and to the heritage derived from the biblical prophets. Raphael Soyer and Jack Levine followed a similar Social Realist course. Soyer's brooding, lonely dark-eyed figures—whether his immigrant parents, struggling to adjust to the New World, or children on a New York City street—are steeped in existential isolation. Levine's imagery is often politically charged. *Feast of Pure Reason* (1937) shimmers with a gauze-like light that illuminates the well-fed look of officials who have grown fat leeching the People.

Joyce Ellen Weinstein taught for years in a mostly African American high school, where a number of her pupils did not make it through school alive. In 1988 she began a series that memorialized *The Bold Dead Boys*, working on it through the mid-1990s (Soltes 1996). Sixteen portraits and eight smaller details were done with charcoal on paper and dripping red oil paint. The colors of purgatory—but leading to no salvation—the colors of death and blood, depict Malcolm, Kevin, Robert, and other young men. Their birth and death dates—none older than twenty-one—require no further words. Their blood cries out, but society is deaf to those cries.

Within this context of social concern, one of the most frequent reference points for Jewish artists, especially in the last quarter of the twentieth century, has been the Holocaust. From Ben-Zion's series *De Profundis* (1943) and Leon Golub's *Charnel House* (1946) to Marty Kalb's *They No Longer Cry* series (1993), scores of Jewish artists have responded in a manner representational enough for there to be no question as to the horror that inspired them. The work of others, like survivor Kitty Klaidman, falls on the border between the representational and the abstract. The titles and/or the viewer's awareness of this period in her life clarify the subject. In her 1992 *Abstracting Memory* series, she reduced the joists and beams of an attic space to a Chromaticist exploration of verticals, horizontals, and diagonals filled in with flattened pigment. The attic was the place in which she, then three, together with her brother and parents, was hidden by a Slovakian family. She began to wrestle that subject onto the canvas only after a forty-four-year hiatus that ended with a trip to Slovakia and the farmhouse where her memories were hidden (Soltes 2003).

Some American Jewish artists have developed their own vocabulary for reflecting on the Holocaust. For RB Kitaj, the crematorium chimney became a recurrent motif in the 1980s: for him it is *the* Jewish symbol. Others have found resonance in other images. Railroad tracks lead, ladder-like upward—to nowhere except the oblivion beyond the canvas, as in work by Alice Lok Cahana, Hungarian survivor—or converge to a vanishing point deep within the picture plane. Suitcases, particularly piled up alongside attenuated figures, are a Holocaust symbol in the hands of artists like Michael Katz. They connote the Jewish experience of *aloneness*—waiting, suitcase in hand, on the railroad platform, on the way to the concentration camp—joined to the universal idea of the loneliness experienced by *any* traveler in an alien setting (Soltes 1995).

In the last two decades, Jewish American artists' focus on the Holocaust has expanded exponentially, in terms of both the symbols and the range of media and style. In Judy Herzl's *Forest of Witnesses* and *I Question* (1990), leaves, the trees from which they have been stripped, and the forest are multiply evocative of the Holocaust. They call out for those marched into the woods and executed without human witnesses. But the trees themselves *were* the witnesses, standing silently, passively—as silent and passive as so many humans beyond those forests were. Forests were also redemptive witnesses, hiding those fleeing from or fighting against the Nazis.

Parts of Judy Chicago's *Holocaust Project* deconstruct the world and put it back together in a geometrically skewed fashion. Combining photography by her husband Donald Woodman with her painting and drawing, together with an eighteen-foot tapestry and stained-glass work, her team produced a 3,000-square-foot compendium of darkness and hope. An array of details connects the Holocaust to larger Jewish—and human—issues, including the other twentieth-century genocides and the threat of nuclear annihilation. In manipulating combined media to produce its imagery, the *Project* plays on the power of manipulation. The conceptually seminal image in the series is *Four Questions,* in which each triangularly—triunely—faceted edge thrusts out at the viewer, asking unanswerable questions regarding God's presence or absence and the human role, active and passive, in the Cata-

strophe. *Four Questions* traditionally alludes to the questions asked at the Passover table, the answers to which form the narrative that shapes the seder. If the theme of the seder is God's redemptive power, turning the Four Questions toward the Holocaust induces the viewer to wonder where that redemptive right arm and outstretched hand were half a century ago (Chicago 1993).

Dorit Cypis's photographs offer analogous visual questions, directed at humans, not God. Her *Aesthetic Lessons* series is a group of abstract plays with line and form, and dark/light contrasts. Slowly the viewer realizes that these are piles of hair and eyeglasses, suffused with a familiar horror. They can only be piles gathered and stored in the Nazi extermination camps and displayed half a century later. Cypis's *Hybrid Eyes* series is an eerie play on revisioning familiar elements in unfamiliar combinations (one blue, one brown, for instance) that have as their visual purpose to make us look and look again, to question whether our first vision was true or false. In the context of the experiments with eyes, as with other body parts, in the Nazi camps, these enormous off-eyes are *disturbing.*

Contrary to general critical assumption, the Chromaticist Abstract Expressionists who dominated the New York art scene in the 1950s—Mark Rothko, Barnett Newman, and Adolph Gottlieb—were not merely focused on aesthetics. They engaged in long discussions, asking what, if anything, their art had to do with their Jewishness, and how their art might be an instrument of response to the Holocaust (Soltes 2003). Their large, unframed canvases became part of the answer. One's eye is drawn toward the *center* of a Rothko or a Newman; chaotic forms are framed in a unifying white in Gottlieb's canonical works. Newman wrote about their discussions, including references to the sixteenth-century kabbalist Isaac Luria; Newman also often offered titles suggesting his beyond-mere-aesthetics agenda. They suggest the Lurianic goal of *tikkun olam* (repairing the world).

In Newman's "zip" paintings, a central element emerges from behind the larger fields of color that flank it, which are being driven apart by it (as in *Genesis,* when the ordering process leads from light to the separation of the waters above from those below by a firmament). But the central element also draws the viewer's eye *toward* it, symbolically restoring order by reunifying the world blown apart by the events of midcentury. The title of the *Covenant* series specifically alludes to the agreement be-

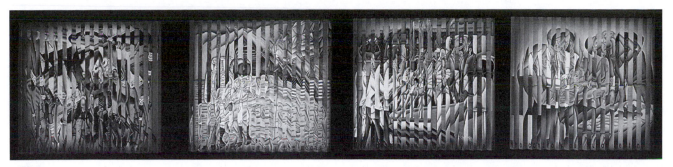

The Four Questions *by Judy Chicago, from her series* The Holocaust Project. *(© 2005 Judy Chicago/Artist Rights Society [ARS]/New York)*

tween God and the Israelites at Sinai. The Covenant carried with it promise and responsibility for those who practice the moral behavior set forth by the Covenantal text (the Torah). Works such as this express the hope for the restoration of moral order in a moral covenant of humans with humans.

It is not only the work of the Chromaticist Abstract Expressionists that combined aesthetic and other concerns. Some claim that Morris Louis's first group of canonical paintings, the *Veils II* series (1958–1959) of rich yet delicate overlapping pigments, offers a mystical quality (Preston 1959). Frequently traveling to New York from Baltimore, Louis sat in on the kabbalistic discussions of Newman and the other Chromaticists. Some of the issues they raised must have influenced Louis. The veils are not merely veils of color, but reflections on the Jewish mystical notion that veils, however infinitesimally thin, remain between God and the mystic.

Louis's second canonical series, the *Unfurleds* (1960–1961), offers a translucence analogous to the *Veils,* but the pigment flows along the *sides* of the canvas, leaving a vast, open space as the center. That center is not merely unpainted, it is also unprimed, as empty as a stretch of canvas could possibly be. In art historical terms, the area that is traditionally positive is negative; the outer edge that would frame the subject is all that is painted, which one might call a subject. In traditional and certainly in Christian art, that central area might be expected to depict and/or address divinity and its concomitants. In Louis's *Unfurleds,* that space—devoid of color, yet in being white, actually filled with the totality of color—may depict the subject that it appears not to depict and that it cannot depict, in Jewish terms.

Louis's canvases reorder the universe in microcosmic terms, and they comment on the absence of the Supreme

Orderer when humans were so overwhelmingly destructive of one another in the generation preceding these works. The end of that era initiated a period of nuclear experimentation and terror in the context of the Cold War. The downward drip of the side pigments pushes to the canvas edge, as if contouring a mushroom-shaped flash of blinding light. The nuclear reality of the Kennedy-Krushchev-Cuban missile crisis is analogous to the chaos in the era of Noah and the Flood. Is it mere coincidence that those colorful *Unfurleds* side elements bear a strong resemblance to rainbows (Soltes 2003)?

Jewish American artists have focused variously on "Jewish" subject matter. Tobi Kahn's paintings—landscape-like abstractions, which in their luminous spiritual quality evoke Mark Rothko and in their biomorphic contours recall Arthur Dove and Georgia O'Keefe—are richly sculptural. Whole groups of his sculptures—the "shrines," in which carved pieces of wood, cast in bronze, are placed in architectural settings—suggest liturgical art without being liturgical art. He has been creating these for years in all sizes; they simultaneously evoke Greco-Roman *aedicula,* Christian reliquaries, and—not least—the *mishkan* (tabernacle) itself in the Jewish tradition. He creates Jewish ceremonial objects with a newness of style and method that recalls his paintings and sculptures. His Judaism and his art are subtly interwoven strands in one tapestry.

Archie Rand's work, though more obviously Jewish, will not fit into a particular box of Jewishness. Rand's painting consistently expresses the conviction that art can be contemporary—even abstract—and bear overtly Jewish content. A frequent feature of his work is text—the ultimate Jewish tradition—but invariably superimposed over visual elements that invoke Chromaticist Abstract Expressionism. From his overrunning the walls of the B'nai Yosef synagogue in Brooklyn (1974–1977) with murals that recall the mid-third-century synagogue at Dura Europus, to his 1994 series of paintings, *The Eighteen: Blessings at the Heart of Jewish Worship*, Rand synthesizes traditional Jewish visual imagery with features—like Abstract Expressionist features—customarily thought to eschew a religious connection.

In *The Eighteen* one can observe four distinct elements that, in each of the panels, offer a synthesis of visual thinking. The general tenor is that of a Chromaticist painting, but within it symbols significant to Jewish visual history, such as the seven-branched candelabrum or the ancient synagogue's Syrian gable, share the foreground with multicultural elements that range from Ionic/Aeolic column capitals to infinitizing Islamic patterning. The center offers the sweep of the Hebrew benediction; text and image thus interplay in eighteen particular forms that not only refer to those benedictions, but are a pun on the number eighteen as representing life. (Eighteen is the numerical value of the two letters that comprise the Hebrew word for life.) Rand's work is about making "an art that was not *about being Jewish* but that *was Jewish*" (Rand 2003).

The matter of textuality—*how* are Jews the People of the Book—has also flourished in late twentieth-century art by Jewish Americans, particularly as letters and deconstructed words relate to Jewish mysticism. Jane Logemann's work is layered with text: rows of letters and words over which subtle pigments are washed. They may be viewed as abstractions and, at the same time, read literally in terms of their content and message. The word has become the image: the repetition of a word, run together so that its beginning and end points are not apparent, implies that it is the letters, not the words, that are repeated endlessly. This suggests the patterns of sound-and-syllable repetition prescribed for the Jewish mystic in some kabbalistic systems. The *sense* of the words is lost in the patterns that carry the mystic toward union with the realm of *non*-sense. But the ongoing rhythmic patterns also recall contemporary music (Philip Glass, for instance), ancient Byzantine mosaics, and Islamic art—thereby embedding Jewish foci within universal ones.

This screw is twisted backward in the work of Diane Samuels. *Letter Liturgy (for Leon)* (1995), an installation centered on a "book" written with both real and imagined alphabets, reflects on an old Hasidic story regarding what God accepts as piety: not book-learned knowledge of the prayer book or the Torah, but the purity of the heart's intention, symbolized by the illiterate Jewish peasant who cannot read the prayers but keeps reciting the letters of the Hebrew alphabet, which God combines into words. Samuels plays on the arbitrariness of letters as symbols that, in combination, represent words and ideas. Do prayers require well wrought words or, for a textual people like Jews, well shaped letters? With what instruments—words? melodies? gestures? images?—does one most effectively address God? Is God listening and looking—and interested—anymore?

Mel Alexenberg's work insists that God *is*. He repeatedly draws from the Jewish tradition and/or his thinking about it. Even the method of much of his work, computer generation, is inherently Jewish. The circular structure characteristic of computers and their chips is analogous to the circularity that is at the heart of Jewish thinking, as opposed to linear, Greek-based Western thinking. The Torah is a double scroll; it is read from beginning to end again and again ad infinitum, so there is no end to its study; the *midrash* (its primary forum of study and discussion) is circular in its thought patterns. Alexenberg often uses the images of angels (which he computer-generates), based on those in Rembrandt's version of *Jacob's Dream*, superimposed over, or in conjunction with, banal advertisements for food. He intends to suggest art as a connector between heaven (angels) and earth (food), by way of wordplays in Hebrew (for the root of all three words—*food, art,* and *angel*—is the same in Hebrew).

Susan Schwalb's *Creation* series of the early 1990s is a series of triptychs. But the artist has redefined that most Christian form of visual expression, with its triune symbolism, as many Jewish artists have, in Jewish terms. Her technique revives the Renaissance penchant for silver and copper point and weds it to the medieval use of gold leaf—but in abstract compositions inspired by the opening images in the *Sarajevo Haggadah*. In most of the works in Schwalb's series, six small circles and a significantly larger seventh circle swirl in silverpoint against an earth-brown and/or a dark or light (night or day) sky-blue background, the whole edged by a white gold leaf frame. Creation has been revisioned in the abstract geometry of the circle. "When I first came across the *Sarajevo Haggadah* I was powerfully stirred to find images of arc and circle. . . . Unlike familiar Christian portrayals of the creation, the image of God is not represented," she wrote (Soltes 1993).

Many works in Schwalb's *Creation* series add to the arc-circle configuration a downward-pointing triangle with vertical line from midbase to apex—a symbol of femaleness traceable back to Neolithic art. The issue of long suppressed female artistic creativity is interwoven with that of Jewish visual creativity in the very textures of the silverpoint surface she works. Thousands of fine lines engender an active energy—flesh-like, water-like, sky-like—within the static confines of the framing forms. The watery, wave-like lines of the silverpoint surface in the tumescent frame suggest the amniotic fluid of the womb that connects the birth of humans to the birth of art and Jewish art and the birth of the universe.

Susan Ressler has synthesized the triptych form to the visual investigation of a particular Jewish holiday and to specific questions regarding the role of women in her *Vashti's Tale: A Modern-day Bestiary*. Vashti is the queen disposed of by Persian King Ahasuerus when she refuses to entertain him and his pals in the midst of a monthlong drinking party; her demise clears the way for the heroine, Esther, to appear on the stage. The artist is transfixed by how to understand both Vashti (as a feminist heroine) and Esther (as the first diasporatic crypto-Jew)—and the interweave of politics and spirituality in the text of the Book of Esther.

Devorah Neumark's work focuses on the two edges of Jewish married life—wedding and divorce—with irony and wit. "*Harrei At Mutteret . . .*" ("Behold you are released . . .") are words of divorce, echoing the words spoken by the groom, as he places a ring around the bride's finger. Neumark's installation follows women through the passage between marriage and nonmarriage, a metaphor for the passage between entitlement and nonentitlement. Framed transparencies of historic illustrations by unknown and well-known artists (not Jewish, like Rembrandt, and Jewish, like Moritz Oppenheim) depict the joy of the Jewish wedding. There are ten of these photo boxes, as if we are observing a women's *minyan*; each is surmounted by a wine goblet—wine being a traditional Jewish symbol of joy. Seven of the goblets (the number of blessings recited at the wedding and the number of times the bride walks around the groom) are inscribed with the Hebrew words of release. Scores of goblets complete the installation, stacked and pulling from the wall in a semicircle. The shattered forms ("to remember the destroyed Temple") of some recall the relative ease of divorce in Judaism (compared to the Christian tradition), and yet its difficulty, indeed impossibility, should the husband not desire it.

Also rich with paradox is Helene Aylon's *The Book That Would Not Close*, whose five open volumes revision the beginnings of Judaism through revisioning Judaism's textual foundation, the Torah. In *her* texts she has singled out and deleted or highlighted passages that reflect negativity toward women. In this the artist highlights her own struggle (she comes from an Orthodox background) to reconcile her religious and gender identities as she reshapes what is traditionally understood to be the word of God into a more female-inclusive form. Can God have uttered the words that she has excised, or do they derive from God's male conduits and interpreters?

Israel has also been a focus of Jewish American artists. Photographer Judy Moore-Kraichnan blends images taken at different times as "a way of bringing time into an otherwise static medium" (Soltes 2005). Both *Hebron Road* and *Western Wall and Tunnel* merge the past and the present—continuity and change—in the context of Jerusalem, as seen between 1849 and 1917 and again between 1993 and 1998. In the first image, an 1895 photograph with a caravan of camels is implanted within the 1994 photograph by Moore-Kraichnan: automobiles seep from the newer image into the older. In the second, the double-exposure effect yields a play on the idea of perspective: our eyes move into the picture toward the vanishing point, and thus the notions of reality and illusion—central to the very air of Jerusalem, thick with the claims of diverse religious groups and crawling with both tourists and would-be prophets—overwhelm the viewer's eye and mind.

Jews reaching out from America and Jews flowing into America are part of an enduring theme. In a series of collage-paintings—*Where Did They Go When They Came to America?* (1989–1994)—Marilyn Cohen presents the stories of one immigrant Jewish family in each of the fifty states. Based on oral histories and old photographs, these reflect more than a century of everyday life. *Aloha Gothic* depicts Nachman ben Joseph Usheroff, who migrated from czarist Russia to Harbin, China, in 1905 and eventually to Hawaii in 1928, where his wife and daughter joined him two years later—as part of the *Chinese* immigrant quota. We see the couple—in a pose echoing Grant Wood's famous *American Gothic*—among the flowering trees and the red-and-white-American-flag-striped awning of their Oahu home. There, on that edge of America, the strapping blacksmith made ironworks for the Dole Pineapple Company, for the Royal Hawaiian Hotel, for the

Oahu prison—and for the *mikvah* (ritual bath) in his backyard.

At the end of the twentieth century, once again a substantial number of Jews poured onto American shores. Among these are Vitaly Komar and Alexander Melamid. While still in the Soviet Union, they were known for their 1972 creation of *SotsArt,* an allusion to American Pop Art and a satire of socialist (*Sots*) propaganda and its art. Since their arrival in America six years later, they have captured the interest of the art public with their clever visual commentaries on the icons of Soviet and Euro-American history and art history. Ironically, Komar and Melamid were invited to represent Russia at the 1999 Venice Biennale. During this same recent period, they have also redefined themselves—not as Russians or Soviets or Americans. "We realized that we are, when all is said and done, Jews, as we migrate from one place to another and take root in one culture after another" (Conversation with Soltes, 1999). Their most recent large project is an exploration of the relationship between the Star of David and other visual forms, ranging from the Ouroboros to the broken cross (the swastika). Called *Symbols of the Big Bang,* the vast series of drawings and paintings wrestles with the origins and changing meanings of familiar symbols and the synthesis of visual ideas. But its centering point is the artists' reflection on their identity through imagery that forms an edge between the national/ethnic and the universal. It is the sort of reflection that repeats itself in myriad variations among Jewish American artists in the twentieth century.

Ori Z. Soltes

References and Further Reading
Chicago, Judy. 1993. *Holocaust Project: From Darkness into Light.* New York: Penguin.
Preston, Stuart. 1959. "Sculpture and Paint." *New York Times* (April 26).
Rand, Archie. 2003. Letter to Soltes (April 3).
Soltes, Ori Z. 1993. *Everyman a Hero: The Saving of Bulgarian Jewry/Susan Schwalb: The Creation Series.* Exhibition catalogue. Washington, DC: B'nai B'rith Klutznick National Jewish Museum.
Soltes, Ori Z. 1995. *The Contents of History: Works by Janis Goodman and Michael Katz.* Exhibition catalogue. Washington, DC: B'nai B'rith Klutznick National Jewish Museum.
Soltes, Ori Z. 1996. *A World of Family: The Work of Joyce Ellen Weinstein.* Exhibition catalogue. Washington, DC: B'nai B'rith Klutznick National Jewish Museum.
Soltes, Ori Z. 2003. *Fixing the World: Jewish American Painters in the Twentieth Century.* Hanover, NH: University Press of New England.
Soltes, Ori Z. 2005. *Jewish Artists on the Edge.* Santa Fe, NM: Sherman Asher Publishing.

Jewish American Artists and the Holocaust

Because very few visual resources were available during World War II that depicted the roundups, life in the ghettos, or the concentration and death camp conditions, artists either imagined such scenes or found alternate subject matter to express their horror at the events as they unfolded. These included the use of Christian subjects such as the Crucifixion and imagery based on ancient mythology. For a few years after the war's end in 1945, a bare handful of artists employed Holocaust themes or alluded to it in their work. By 1950, such imagery largely disappeared, the immediate revulsion to the Holocaust having apparently subsided, and perhaps memories of it had become too unpleasant to contemplate. But beginning in the 1970s, such themes became popular again and retain their popularity today. Artists often based their work on documentary photographs of the camps and on biblical scenes that had Holocaust resonances. In the early twenty-first century, its hold on artists' imaginations constant, the Holocaust remains one of the most popular subjects among Jewish American artists of all ages.

By the late 1930s, artists were well aware of the horrific and soon to be catastrophic plight of Europe's Jews. Within weeks of Hitler's ascent to the chancellorship of Germany in 1933, American art magazines began to record his economic and physical assaults on Jewish artists and art dealers. By the middle 1930s, refugees from Germany made their presence felt in larger cities, especially New York. At the end of the 1930s, artists such as Marc Chagall and Jacques Lipchitz, as well as American expatriates, including Abraham Rattner and Man Ray, fled German-occupied France, most settling in New York, with some, like Chagall and Lipchitz, invited to exhibit immediately.

By 1937, in response to the events taking place in Europe, artists, including the Soyer brothers (Moses and Isaac), William Gropper, and Max Weber, began to create two distinctive types of images, the first illustrating German militarism and brutality, the other portraying refugees. From their clothing, we know that the refugees could be victims either of the Spanish Civil War (1936–1939) or Eastern European Jews (especially in paintings made after 1938), presumably escaping from the Germans.

By 1940, New York was the artistic center of the free world and the gathering place for more Jewish artists than any other city in the world. By late 1941, probably all knew through conversations, listening to radio reports, reading Yiddish- and English-language Jewish magazines, as well as the daily American press, that most European Jews were living in squalid conditions in ghettos and camps and that the Germans intended to kill every Jew in the world. But because of the period from Hitler's takeover of Germany in 1933 to the commencement eight years later of the so-called Final Solution in 1941, and the blackout of visual documentation of the subsequent murders of six million Jews between 1941 and 1945, artists could not develop a coherent set of styles or images with which to depict the ongoing tragedy, and they had no readily available precedents to rely on. They were largely alone physically and emotionally in their studios, and each responded in his or her own way.

Some, especially those born in Eastern Europe and who had orthodox religious training, painted traditional, easy-to-read images. Interviewed years later, Max Weber (1881–1961) remembered certain works he had created just after *Kristallnacht* (Night of the Broken Glass) in November 1938, when Germans destroyed synagogues, Jewish business establishments, and attacked and bloodied numerous Jews. "When I heard of Hitler . . . and when I heard he was beginning to break the Jewish shops in Berlin and all that, I walked around in this studio quite hurt, disturbed. I could see what an anti-Semite could do when he's bloodthirsty and fanatic and crazy . . . Oh, where are the people going to go now? What are these Jewish people in Germany going to do . . . ? And I painted a large canvas of two Jews called *Whither Now?* [1938]" (Baigell 2002). The painting shows two men standing in a synagogue or study hall dressed in old-fashioned East European clothing. Their faces and long coats appear through transparent washes of color as if they and what they represent had already become disembodied and had begun to disappear before our eyes.

Other works Weber created at that time record ceremonial and religious activities of generations of pious

Jews, including *Hassidic Dance* (1940) and *Adoration of the Moon* (1944). Based on memories of his childhood in Bialystok, Russia, these works reveal Weber's deep concern for the continued presence of traditional Jewish culture as it was being physically destroyed in Europe and assimilated into mainstream American life.

Hyman Bloom (b. 1913), from Latvia, created in 1940 a multi-figured scene of a Yom Kippur service entitled *The Synagogue*. In the center of the painting, the cantor, chanting from the liturgy, is surrounded by youngsters (the future), elders holding Torah scrolls (tradition), and the congregational community (the present). It is as if, given the year in which the work was created, Bloom was welcoming all those who no longer had a place to worship to join him. Although painted on the American side of the Atlantic Ocean, *The Synagogue* can be read as an act of defiance against all those who wanted to put an end to the worshippers and their worship.

Ben-Zion (1897–1987) from Ukraine must have felt the same way as Bloom. He made several paintings during the 1940s of cantors holding up Torah scrolls to the viewer, recording that moment in the service when the entire congregation chants or says that this is the Torah God gave to Moses. The last lines chanted, "Renew our days as in the past," must have had great resonance at the time, especially for Ben-Zion who, of all the artists, remained closest to his Eastern European roots.

Ben-Zion also created one of the first series of works based directly on the Holocaust. Entitled *De Profundis* (1944–1946), each of the fourteen works shows the torsos of old men piled one on top of the other, their heads covered by prayer shawls, confined within circles of barbed wire. He chose these figures because, as he said, "The patriarchic type of Jews dominated my conceptions . . . because they were the backbone of the nation and its cultural source" (Baigell 2002).

William Gropper (1897–1977) also used the title, *De Profundis,* for one of his paintings. Created in 1943 to commemorate the failed Warsaw Ghetto Uprising, it reveals an ancient man, wearing phylacteries and his head and upper body covered by a prayer shawl, looking up with blinded eyes presumably to God, intoning similar lines from either Psalm 130 or Lamentations 3:55, in which the supplicant calls to God from the depths of his or her own being. Gropper is probably better known, however, for the many anti-German cartoons he made during the 1930s and

1940s, many of which illustrated directly the murder of Jews. In fact, during the first half of 1940, he, more than any other artist, provided a means by which viewers could conjure up images of events then taking place. These included grisly scenes of piles of bodies, random murders, looting, executions by firing squads, and hangings.

Not all artists limited themselves to scenes of everyday life such as Weber, Bloom, and Ben-Zion, or to imaginative works portraying the ongoing destruction such as Gropper. Several American artists also painted Crucifixion scenes, perhaps in emulation of Marc Chagall, who, while in New York, painted several scenes of Jesus as a Jew on the Cross—Jesus not as the redeemer of humankind but as a Jew who was murdered. In Chagall's paintings, Jesus wears a prayer shawl as a loincloth, and around him are images of ghettos burning, people fleeing, and open Torah scrolls with no words, signifying the absence of God. One artist, Abraham Rattner (1895–1978), concentrated just on images of Jesus on the cross and often wrote that he identified both himself and the Jewish people with Jesus because of all the suffering both he and they had endured as a result of antisemitism. Although some objected to the use of the Crucifixion to convey Jewish tragedy, others held that Christians might better understand and be more sympathetic to the Jewish plight with such a familiar image. Furthermore, it was virtually impossible to find appropriate images in the Hebrew Bible to convey the full force of the Holocaust. The story of Abraham and Isaac was about sustaining, not destroying, life. Job was ultimately redeemed, something that did not take place in the ghettos and camps, and neither Joshua's victory at Jericho nor Elijah's prophecy of the resurrection of the dry bones and the return of the Israelites to Israel had much currency in much of the 1940s.

But one artist, Mark Rothko (1903–1970), did find in Christian iconography, the lamentation over the dead body of Jesus, an image that perhaps better than any other caught the horror of and subsequent grief caused by the Holocaust. Rothko's style, modified by Surrealism, was not as realistic as those of Chagall and the others. But, as in Chagall's works, Jewish elements appear. In a group of works painted in the middle 1940s, one sees a horizontal form (the body) lying on the laps of vertical figures (the mourners). In probably the last version, *Entombment*, painted in 1946, after Rothko would have seen documentary photographs of the piles of bodies in the just liberated

concentration camps, there appears for the first time a transparent, horizontal form that hovers in front of the heads of the vertical figures. The significant Jewish elements in this work are these. The lower horizontal figure, lying on the laps of the vertical figures, also lies either on straw, an old Jewish custom as part of the burial procedure, or on a shroud in which Jewish men were and still are buried. Since Rothko had religious training as a youth in his native Latvia and taught art in New York from 1929 to 1946 in a building that housed a conservative congregation, he probably was aware of the belief that a Jewish person's soul would never find rest or entirely leave the body if improperly buried or desecrated in any way. Certainly, proper burials did not take place in the camps or in communities where Jews by the hundreds and thousands were murdered. The transparent, hovering form in Rothko's painting, then, might symbolize the collective soul of the six million who were not buried properly in the Holocaust and who would never be remembered in annual ritual observances because their families, too, had been murdered. Thus, he too transformed a Christian theme into a Jewish subject.

Among the artists born around 1900, Barnett Newman (1905–1970) made the most radical visual statement that can be associated with the Holocaust. Beginning in 1948, he made the first of many paintings consisting of a single stripe or a few stripes running vertically from the top of a canvas to its bottom. Based on the teachings of the kabbalist, Rabbi Isaac Luria (1534–1572) of Safed, now in Israel, who was concerned with the creation of the world, the single stripe was, as Newman explained, the artist acting as the Creator marking the stripe as the first act of creating a new world out of chaos (Hess 1971). The first of these paintings was probably made between the time the United Nations began discussing the partition of Palestine into Jewish and Arab states and the declaration of Israel as an independent country. Thus Newman's stripe paintings can be read as a rejection of God and Western society that had done very little to aid Jews, and as Newman's raw assertion of the self against that society and of a new beginning for Jews in their own newly created country.

The sculptor Seymour Lipton (1903–1986), in the middle and late 1940s, also found veiled ways to refer to the Holocaust. Pre-Columbian sculpture provided him with a source to create works with jagged and menacing abstract forms that suggested the predatory and destructive. Lipton thought that such forms revealed the tragic condition of humankind and, as he said, "the dark inside, the evil of things" (Elsen 1974). To make his point clear, he gave the name *Moloch*, the biblical figure to whom children were sacrificed, to a group of works in the middle 1940s. Like other artists of his generation, with the exception of Gropper, he did not refer to the Holocaust directly in his art or, if it was mentioned in a statement or interview, it was done in veiled and guarded language. Rather, Lipton and others hid their anger in religious imagery, in scenes of Jewish life, or in works derived from the art of other cultures. Perhaps they were overwhelmed and could find no adequate visual language to express their feelings, or they felt too vulnerable and embarrassed by their helplessness to address the event directly, or perhaps they thought that such work would not be marketable. Whatever the reasons, their responses were very tempered and allusive rather than direct and angry (Baigell 1997).

But at least two artists of the next generation, Leon Golub (1922–2004) and Harold Paris (1925–1979), expressed their rage quite openly. Both had served in the military, and the latter had seen the Buchenwald concentration camp shortly after its liberation. Of works such as *Charnel House* (1948), composed of writhing figures vaporizing in flames, Golub said that they were concentration camp scenes as well as works about individual identity and lack of power (Baigell 1997). But in the *Burnt Man* series of the early 1950s, composed of figures with flayed skin and mangled limbs, Golob, like other artists, often conflated the effects of atomic warfare with those of the Holocaust, thus compromising the latter's singular and unique significance, perhaps, like artists of the previous generation, revealing a fear of being considered too Jewish or Jewish at all.

Not so Harold Paris, whose anger culminated in 1972 in his *Koddesh-Koddashim*, a sealed room based on the small interior space called the Holy of Holies in the ancient Temple in Jerusalem, a space that the high priest could enter only once a year on Yom Kippur. When asked what his interior looked like, Paris answered, "Like the inside of my soul." And when asked what is inside, he answered, "All my dreams of the outside." In short, Paris could find no visual or verbal language to articulate his feelings that were figuratively and literally locked up in that sealed room (Selz 1969).

Very few artists seem to have been attracted to Holocaust-derived images through the 1960s, but works by Ruth Weisberg (b. 1942) and Audrey Flack (b. 1931) in the 1970s signaled the revival of interest in this subject matter. One of Weisberg's first works on this theme, a set of nine prints entitled *The Shtetl: A Journey and a Memorial* (1971), portrayed with great empathy the apprehensions that inhabitants felt in the weeks before the destruction of their community and the loss of their own lives. Weisberg said, "I am a branch, a resting place for their souls. This book is my life's journey in place of theirs" (Baigell 1997). Flack derived her *World War II (Vanitas)* (1976–1977) from Margaret Bourke-White's famous photograph of prisoners just liberated from Buchenwald who posed for her behind a barbed wire fence.

Their work also signaled three trends: first, the emergence of women artists who in increasing numbers portrayed such scenes; second, the lessening of interest in religious imagery as a means to comment on the Holocaust; and, third, the growing popularity of documentary photographs as source material. Several factors probably account for the revival of interest in Holocaust-related themes: Israeli successes in the wars of 1967 and 1973, a newfound pride in one's own Jewishness encouraged by contemporary feminist and black power movements, and the realization that survivors were beginning to age and die. Some artists also hoped that calling attention to the Holocaust would prevent such an event from ever happening again, thus contributing to a sense of *tikkun olam* (the kabbalistic notion of repair of the world). By 1980, the "silence" had ended, and artists all over the country began to create and exhibit Holocaust-related works. A few began to devote their entire careers to this subject; others turned to it occasionally. Some artists were victims of antisemitic acts in Europe in the 1930s or survivors of the camps, some were children of survivors, and some, born after World War II, had no personal connection to the events of the 1940s. What they all shared, however, was the desire to record, memorialize, and act as witnesses to the Holocaust.

Perhaps the most famous work to emerge since 1980 is the multifigured sculpture, *The Holocaust* (1983), by George Segal (1924–2000), composed of a pile of bodies lying on the ground and one figure standing behind barbed wire. Although Segal arranged some bodies to form a six-pointed Jewish star as well as a female figure with an apple (representing Eve) and a father protecting his son

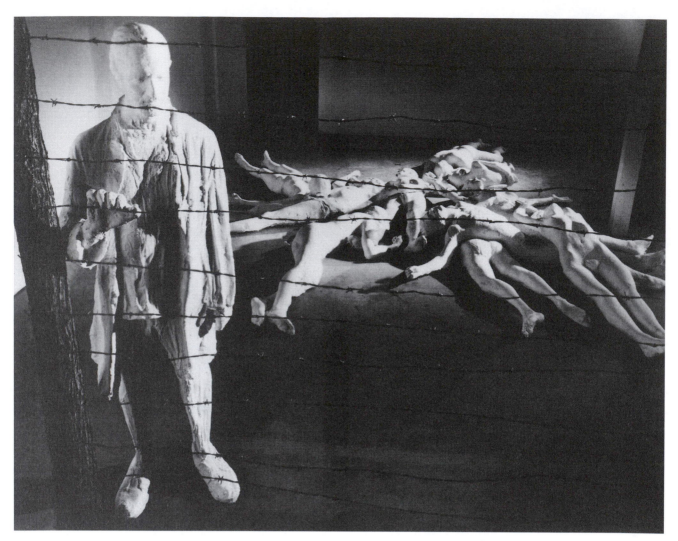

The Holocaust *by artist George Segal, 1983. (Segal, George [1924-2000] © VAGA, NY)*

(recalling the story of Abraham and Isaac), his sources obviously lie in the many documentary photographs published when the camps were liberated.

Like much Holocaust-related art, Segal's work reveals more sorrow than anger in its commemoration of the dead. Yet many artists responded with anger and rage. They also felt that mythic and religious images were not adequate to confront the Holocaust directly. For example, Murray Zimiles (b. 1941) created a series, *The Fire Paintings* and *The Book of Fire* in 1986, depicting the burning of Polish synagogues, which symbolized the destruction of the Jewish past. Marty Kalb (b. 1941) and Howard Oransky (b. 1955) have painted portraits of those murdered in the camps as a way to reestablish their individuality and identity. Jerome Witkin (b. 1939), in his paintings of the 1980s and 1990s of murdered and butchered victims, has, as he

has said, "a need to open heavy, dark doors" (Baigell 1997). And Gerda Meyer-Bernstein, who witnessed *Kristallnacht* in 1938, began around 1980 to make works that force confrontation with the experiences of the victims. One such work, *Block 11* (1989), an installation containing hundreds of pieces of luggage on which she has painted names, birthdates, and concentration camp numbers of those incarcerated, is always exhibited in small, narrow spaces so that the viewer is forced to walk around the luggage and to think about who has been murdered, about the generations lost, and about what they might have contributed to humanity.

All hope that their work—because it witnesses and calls attention to the Holocaust—will also contribute to lasting peace. To that end, Edith Altman (b. 1931), born in Germany, has created an installation that is part of her search for and contribution to universal healing, or tikkun olam. Her *Reclaiming the Image/The Art of Memory* (1988–1992) might very well lay claim to being the late twentieth-century talismanic image of Holocaust art by an American artist. In this installation, she creates forms based on Jewish mysticism and the Nazi swastika, also invoking her own experiences. The work includes a golden swastika placed on a wall in its pre-Nazi configuration, symbolizing growth and the triumph of good over evil. Its black reflection on the floor, symbolizing the lower physical world, is configured in the Nazi way. Several objects based on kabbalistic references to base matter transformed into spiritual presences are placed on the floor and on the other walls. Altman said that she wanted to face the hated symbol directly and subdue the residual fears it still evokes in her and others so that it can be invested once again with mythic meanings (Baigell 1999). In effect, then, *Reclaiming the Image* lends itself to religious-mystical interpretation, to direct confrontation with the most obvious symbol of the Holocaust, and to personal memory.

Several artists born in the 1940s and after have described the Holocaust as the major historical event of their lifetime and have stated the impossibility of avoiding it in their art. All, by admitting its importance to their art, reject those aspects of post-modernism that are characterized by irony, the denial of authorial responsibility, and the willful manipulation of subject matter and materials. Natan Nuchi (b. 1951), who through the 1980s and 1990s created a series of emaciated nude forms floating in space as if suspended between life and death, found that much postmodern art exhibited a kind of mental fatigue (Baigell 1997). Instead, he and others carefully choose their subject matter, certainly accept responsibility for it, give it moral resonance, do not revel in ambiguity, and see their art as fulfilling an important purpose.

With earlier artists such as Weber and Bloom, Nuchi and all the others were or are engaged in honoring the victims of the Holocaust and of identifying as Jews and with other Jews, in the hope that their images will become part of the heritage that is passed on to future generations.

Matthew Baigell

References and Further Reading

Amishai-Maisels, Ziva. 1993. *Depiction and Interpretation: The Influence of the Holocaust on the Visual Arts.* New York: Pergamon Press.

Baigell, Matthew. 1997. *Jewish American Artists and the Holocaust.* New Brunswick, NJ: Rutgers University Press.

Baigell, Matthew. 1999. "Kabbalah and Jewish-American Artists." *Tikkun* 14 (July/August): 59–61.

Baigell, Matthew. 2002. *Jewish Artists in New York: The Holocaust Years.* New Brunswick, NJ: Rutgers University Press.

Elsen, Albert. 1974. *Seymour Lipton.* New York: Harry N. Abrams.

Feinstein, Stephen, ed. 1995. *Witness and Legacy: Contemporary Art about the Holocaust.* St. Paul: Minnesota Museum of American Art.

Hess, Thomas B. 1972. *Barnett Newman.* New York: Museum of Modern Art and Schocken Books.

Selz, Harold. 1969. "The Final Negation: Harold Paris' Koddesh Koddashim." *Art in America* 57 (March–April): 62, 66.

Jewish and Christian Symbols in the Work of Jewish American Artists

Prior to emancipation, it was inconceivable that Jewish artists or craftspeople might refer to Christian symbols—images of Jesus, the Virgin Mary, and the like—both because Jews were outside mainstream art and because such images represented oppression and persecution. But by the late nineteenth century, American Jewish artists in particular began to examine Christian symbols and to transform them, both overtly and subtly. At the same time, a new vocabulary of Jewish visual symbols was emerging. In concert, newly shaped Christian and Jewish symbols address layered questions of how Jewish artists fit into the world of Western art.

With the reconfiguration of the Western Christian world by the end of the eighteenth century, emancipated Jews found it possible to enter the cultural mainstream. And by the late nineteenth century, American Jewish sculptor Moses Jacob Ezekiel (1844–1917) was exploring surprising new possibilities in self-expression in his depictions of Jesus. One is a torso with just the beginnings of the extended arms of the crucified Christ, the crown of thorns jammed onto his head. A second depicts Jesus laid in the tomb as if in peaceful sleep. A Jewish prayer shawl, a *tallit*, is wrapped around his head. Ezekiel's contemporaries were stunned both that a Jew would depict Jesus and that the image was so sensitive and sympathetic. For Ezekiel, Jesus is no longer a symbol of Christianity and its antagonistic relationship with Judaism. Nor is the image similar to the thousands of Christian portrayals of the long-suffering, self-sacrificing Savior. He is simply a quiet symbol of noble, peaceful possibilities. Christians can view him through religious eyes, but both Jews and Christians can see him through secular humanist eyes.

Through Ezekiel, the legacy of emancipation arrived in the twentieth century, with its question of where Jewish artists fit within Western art, which had been so obviously Christian during most of the past seventeen centuries. Ezekiel's implicit response was to engage a traditional Christian subject from a new perspective. By the 1920s and 1930s, subtler angles were visible in the Social Realism of Ben Shahn (1898-1969), who traced his sociopolitical concerns to the Biblical prophets. Hence his interest in the miscarriage of justice that led to the deaths of the Italian-American immigrants Sacco and Vanzetti. He viewed the event as a contemporary equivalent of the Crucifixion and used Christian symbols in his paintings of them (Pohl 1993). In *The Passion of Sacco and Vanzetti* (1932–1933), white lilies held by two members of the Lowell Committee refer in traditional visual terms to the purity of the Virgin Mary. They become a sarcastic comment on the impurity of those holding the lilies, underscoring the moral bankruptcy of the Committee's bluebloods, whose claim was to save America from the satanic evils of unwashed, unlettered immigrant anarchists—but actually martyring two Christ-like innocents.

Shahn's work was produced on the eve of Hitler's rise to power. Respondents to that era of horrors include the Jewish Chromaticist Abstract Expressionists who dominated the New York art scene in the 1950s (Soltes 2003). Barnett Newman wrote of gathering in each other's studios to discuss art. Among the discussion topics was *tikkun olam*—repairing the world—by putting it back together on the canvas. Newman's painting titles often offer explicit evidence of his beyond-mere-aesthetics agenda—of the intention of symbolic tikkun olam.

In *The Name II* (1950), Newman joins the issue of unifying the canvas as a symbolic statement of fixing the world to both a Jewish art historical question and a post-Holocaust theological question. The all-white canvas offers both the absence and the totality of color: white, symbol of light, contains all the colors within it, while it appears to be devoid of color. This is an image of nothing and everything in the coloristic terms of traditional painting. Moreover, the canvas is divided into three parts by a pair of vertical lines. So it is a sort of triptych, that most traditional of Western—Christian—forms of visual self-expression. In Christian terms, triptychs symbolize the Trinity, and the center is typically occupied by a crucified Christ or the Virgin and Child—images of God as Christianity understands It. But the Jewish view of God is that It is invisible. Then how might a Jew represent God through the visual medium so essential to most religions from time immemorial: where *does* a Jewish artist fit into Western, Christian art?

Newman responded by appropriating the Christian form and radically transforming it. His triptych is filled with the image of the imageless God, Who is both absent and present, like the invisible yet present colors on the canvas. The name of the painting confirms this as part of the artist's intention, for traditional Judaism never uses the word "God" other than in prayer; the circumlocution customarily used is *HaShem*—Hebrew for the Name. Verbal circumlocution is expressed by visual circumlocution.

The painting also offers a response to a theological question raised by the Holocaust. Where was the all-powerful, all-loving God during those horrors? The answer, like the image, is paradoxical: God was both present and absent, as human action was both moral and immoral. The question of how to be a Jewish artist in a world of Christian art is wedded to the question of how both Jews and Christians can understand God. The notion of restoring—reordering—the post-Holocaust world is embedded in the whiteness as a cognate to light. For light is the element called into existence by God at the outset of the world—the beginning of ordering empty, chaotic preorder.

Samuel Bak uses a rich vocabulary of Jewish symbols to address the matter of the Holocaust. Born in 1933, he was six when World War II began and not much older when it arrived in Lithuania, his childhood left buried in the ashes of Vilna. In Bak's *Otiyot* (*Letters*), the Ten Commandments disintegrate in midair, as they float in their stony weight. The letters, symbols of the commandments, peel off the crumbling surfaces and float upward—reminiscent of the Hasidic story of the righteous illiterate, who simply recited the letters of the alphabet that, floating toward heaven, were gathered by God and formed into words of prayer. But we wonder if the Gatherer is still there—or if what is absent is our memory of how to adhere to the

Commandments. The sixth letter, *vav,* is the only one not fully visible. Its prominence is found both in its absence and its accentuation by means of its replacement with the number six—which is also the number of points on the Star of David, and the number of Jewish millions killed in the conflagration beginning by the time the artist was six years old, and the number of the disintegrating commandment "Thou shall not murder."

The Star of David also rises repeatedly from rough-hewn, barren, and empty landscapes, or floats like numberless paper kites in skies crowded with purple and gold light—or, in *Alone III,* appears as a cracked and ruined island surrounded by a vast night-lit sea. The symbol that, in the twentieth century, has become universally recognized as representing Judaism reaches out in the six directions—east, west, north, south, up and down—for help, for humanity, for contact, for Covenant. And the spaces around it respond with an infinite silence, recalling Balaam's prophecy (Numbers 23:9) that the Israelites would dwell alone. It turns on its ear John Donne's claim that "no man is an island," for in the vast, stormy seas of history and of the Holocaust, Jews have often been precisely that.

Judy Chicago's enormous *Holocaust Project* (1987–1992) includes a search for new *methodological* ground, combining photography by her husband Donald Woodman with her painting and drawing, together with an eighteen-foot tapestry and stained-glass work. (Ironically, the material that could most effectively sustain this combination, photolinen, was available only from Germany at the time of her project.) The 3,000-square-foot result is a compendium of darkness and hope, culminating in a triptych, *Rainbow Shabbat.* This is a light-and-color-filled stained-glass composition, drawing as a medium—not only in its structure—from the medieval Christian heritage. The precision of geometric lineation contrasts with the gentle irregularities of human form. Those gathered around the table to celebrate God's completion of the physical ordering of the world—leaving to us the task of completing its moral and ethical order—have arrived from around that world: diverse faiths, races, ethnicities, nationalities, and both genders are included among the twelve figures seated, arm on shoulder, at the Sabbath Eve Table marked by a postdeluge rainbow. This is the number of Israelite tribes who subscribed to the Covenant at Sinai and the number of Apostles who carried the word of Jesus into the world. The culmination of a dark project asks for healing between Christians and Jews—and all religions and races—and a journey into light.

Sy Gresser's *Tribal Faces (Menorah)* seeks that journey by means of the most consistent of Jewish symbols in art: the seven-branched candelabrum. His 1996 steatite sculpture is a not-quite-complete circle, in which faces extend from the stylized menorah form. The faces represent different races and ethnic types, held together by that symbol. With one eye open, the other closed, they have both outer and inner vision. The unfinished circle suggests an unfinished world that needs fixing; the work symbolizes tikkun olam in process.

Like Newman and Chicago, Susan Ressler has revisioned the triptych form in her *Missed Representations* series. In *Expulsion,* the middle panel is a detail from the early fifteenth-century Florentine Masaccio's *Expulsion.* Adam and Eve leave the Garden of Eden in an anguish conveyed in part by the dark, pained eyes of Eve, who is perceived as the primary perpetrator of the expulsion-inducing crime most emphatically by the Christian branch of the Abrahamic tradition. Ressler has flanked this with two images of contemporary models in bathing suits (whose body language echoes that of Masaccio's Eve), one with a design offering a snake (Satan personified) slithering around her torso. The models are all but unidentifiable as people: they are advertising armatures for the bathing suits and/or enticing sexual objects. So an icon from the Western and the (Judaeo)-Christian theological tradition (Masaccio's painting) is synthesized to an icon from the modern visual world (bathing suit advertisements) and the art historical pattern of objectifying women.

The issue of the woman in the Jewish tradition—not permitted to read from the Torah, to be part of a *minyan,* to lay *tefillin* (phylacteries)—is embedded in many works by Jewish American artists toward the end of the twentieth century. Not only women, but occasionally men have addressed this. Geoff Laurence's triptych, *T'fillah* (1999), intertwines Christian and Jewish symbols. Like Ressler's, it offers pieces and parts of a woman's body, in this case broken into three discontinuous segments, around each of which is wrapped a leather phylactery thong. Pious Jewish males wrap the phylactery around their arm and forehead for morning prayers, fulfilling the Torah injunction to "bind it for a sign upon thy hand and place it as a frontlet between thine eyes." Those prayers include words thanking God "that He did not make me a woman." The issues of women as commodities (body parts) and the exclusion of women or negativity toward them are interwoven with the suggestion of contemporary sexual mores: a nipple ring suggests that the leather thongs play a role in sexual bondage, which then becomes a pun regarding gender bondage and "binding it . . . upon thy hand" in traditional Jewish settings: bind versus bound (Soltes 2003, 2006). The Christian triptych form has been turned literally on its side—and the three pieces together assume a cruciform, since the middle one is wider than the upper and lower ones—to address an internal, not an external Jewish question.

Marilyn Cohen transforms icon imagery in her 1995–1997 collage series, *Teach Me the Songs My Mothers Sang*. The artist depicts an array of women who have defined aspects of the American past. There are eighteen women, each in her own frame. (The Hebrew-language symbolism of the number eighteen, meaning life, suggests these women as expositors as well as givers of life.) Among the women is Annette Retablo: Our Lady of the Convoy. Annette volunteered for a humanitarian mission to Central America in 1989. That put the seventy-two-year-old Jewish grandmother behind the wheel of a fourteen-year-old Mercedes bus carrying supplies into the unpredictable landscapes of Mexico, Guatemala, Honduras, El Salvador, and Nicaragua, to women and children in refugee camps and union halls, in orphanages and cornfields. We see her as the sort of saint whose image would be venerated by Catholic populations in those countries: a *santera*, Central American Gothic. For she is rendered as an icon clothed in the blood red of self-sacrificing involvement, surrounded by the attributes of the worlds whose borders she has traversed, surmounted by the sort of angel-held banner that would affirm her actions as a *santera*.

The allusions to Christian art can be more oblique. Shirley Klinghoffer's untitled slumped glass installation (1999) is a tribute to women who have survived breast cancer. Each piece is molded on and from the torso of one of these women. The work is in part inspired by the small images of breasts offered to Saint Agatha by Christian women who have survived breast-related maladies. But these are life-sized actual molds, not miniature symbols. And there are precisely eighteen of them, symbolizing *life*. So the Christian allusion interweaves Jewish symbolic numerology to offer a statement of the triumph of life over death.

Annette Retablo: Our Lady of the Convoy *by Marilyn Cohen, part of her series* Teach Me the Songs My Mothers Sang *(Marilyn Cohen)*

At the end of the twentieth century, a substantial number of Jews poured onto American shores from the crumbling Union of Soviet Socialist Republics (USSR). Among the arrivals were artists Vitaly Komar and Alexander Melamid. They first went to Israel where, in 1978, the stage setting they erected in Jerusalem as the *Temple for the Third Exodus*—in which they performed the "sacrifice of the Russian suitcase"—ended up as burnt fragments. They composed a narrative of their journey with a series of illuminations in which they turned the Russian icon on its ear. In each of the "icons" the artists appear, attired and adorned with halos, like saints. Their pairing evokes Cyril and Methodius, bringers of Christianity to the Slavs. But Komar's glasses and the expressions on both their faces suggest the wryness that was shaping their own journey.

The Remains of the Temple is a crushed compendium of the identity that they took—or did not take—with them from Russia to Israel to the United States. What *is* (or *was*) that identity? In the USSR they were viewed as Jews, not Russians; here they are viewed as Russians. What identity should they embrace once they are here, but not yet *American*—and how long does it take to *become* American? The pieces of their identity cannot be contained in a burnt suitcase. Their most recent joint project (2002) was an exploration of the relationship between the Star of David and other visual forms, from the Ouroboros to the broken cross (the swastika). The extensive series wrestles with the origins and changing meanings of familiar symbols and the synthesis of visual ideas. What have become Jewish or Christian—or Nazi—symbols did not necessarily begin that way (Soltes 2002–2003).

Thus as intensely as anywhere and anytime in the history of art, symbols in the hands of American Jewish artists from Ezekiel to Komar and Melamid—particularly symbols that allude to the Christian and Jewish religious traditions—have repeatedly articulated the unanswerable question of how to define one's self in a world that prefers the simple definitional boxes into which the Jewish experience will not readily fit.

Ori Z. Soltes

References and Further Reading
Pohl, Frances K. 1993. *Ben Shahn*. San Francisco: Pomegranate Artbooks.
Shahn, Ben. 1957. *The Shape of Content*. Cambridge, MA: Belknap/Harvard University Press.
Soltes, Ori Z. 2002–2003. "Komar and Melamid, Jewish Questions and Art." In *Komar and Melamid: Symbols of the Big Bang*, 66–99. Exhibition catalogue at Yeshiva University Museum. New York: Center for Jewish History.
Soltes, Ori Z. 2003. *Fixing the World: American Jewish Painters in the Twentieth Century*. Hanover, NH: University Press of New England.
Soltes, Ori Z. 2005. *Jewish Artists on the Edge*. Santa Fe, NM: Sherman Asher Publishing.
Soltes, Ori Z. 2006. *The Ashen Rainbow: Essays on the Arts and the Holocaust*. Washington, DC: Eshel Books.

Clement Greenberg (1909–1994)

Art Critic

Clement Greenberg was probably the most important art critic in American history. His two basic theses were that avant-garde art represented the best and most forward-looking aspect of modern culture and that each art medium should be concerned only with its own particular possibilities. A painting, for example, should be abstract and concern itself with the flatness of the canvas surface, texture, color, and form, but not with depth, the third dimension, or with narrative content. Put forth in a series of articles beginning with "Avant-Garde and Kitch" in 1939 and developed definitively by 1960 in "Modernist Painting," Greenberg's theories dominated American art making and art writing during the last half of the twentieth century (O'Brian 1986).

In "Avant-Garde and Kitch," his first important essay, Greenberg pitted avant-garde culture against popular and commercial art, which he called kitch. The former, he held, could keep high culture moving forward; the latter, whose products were debased forms of high culture, could destroy it. Kitch was the culture of the masses, which Greenberg associated with the culture of fascist countries such as Germany and Italy. In effect, Greenberg sought to maintain culture as an elite function, impregnable to compromise and adulteration. As a result, he contributed to the important shift in thinking in the 1940s whereby avant-garde activity, the development of new styles based on the possibilities within a particular medium, replaced art with political subject matter as the most advanced form of art making. Greenberg held that modernism was the vehicle to preserve high culture and that abstract art was the most important art of our time. In effect, he explained how artists could now involve themselves with art problems to the exclusion of all else, the overriding importance of aesthetic matters replacing political ones. This attitude helped create a climate of opinion receptive to the development of the Abstract Expressionist art movement of the mid-1940s. In fact, Greenberg, who had an uncanny eye for identifying the most important young artists, was instrumental in calling attention to such ultimately major figures as Jackson Pollock, the artist famous for his so-called drip paintings. As a result, Greenberg was among those who helped popularize the notion that American rather than European artists were now in the forefront of avant-garde developments, building on the pictorial inventions of the Impressionists and of figures such as Paul Cézanne and the Cubists.

But his commitment to a concept of avant-garde art that was removed from interaction with contemporary life insulated it from further development. Only Color-Field painting in the 1950s, a style characterized by surfaces awash in loosely defined areas of colored pigment that contained little depth and no apparent content, appealed to him. His favored painters became, within the Abstract Expressionist generation, the color- rather than expressionistically oriented Barnett Newman, Mark Rothko, and Clyfford Still, and in the subsequent generation, Jules Olitski. By the mid-1950s, his once forward-looking theories, which he asserted with practiced authority and assurance, had grown conservative and maintained value only as theories against which to react. In the late 1930s, Greenberg emerged from left-wing Jewish (but not exclusively Jewish) intellectual circles in New York that included figures such as Irving Howe, Harold Rosenberg, and Meyer Schapiro, in which ideas about art and politics mixed easily. Among the various positions he held, Greenberg served as managing editor of *Contemporary Jewish Record* from 1944 to 1945 when it was incorporated into *Commentary,* for which he was associate editor until 1957. Despite his search for universal truths and unchanging criteria, his art and literary criticism, therefore, has often been considered and explained within a Jewish context.

For example, since there is little place for individual personality or idiosyncrasy in his theories, it has been suggested that this reflected his desire, like others of his generation, to escape his parochial Jewish background and reinvent himself (and modern art) with a selective pedigree of his own invention. But several of his critical observations indicate the impossibility of this task and the inner conflicts it created. He wanted to feel integrated in society, but, realizing his sense of alienation, blamed it more on the effects of modern capitalism than on his outsider status as a Jew. On one occasion, he said that he had hardly any awareness of his Jewish heritage, yet "a quality of Jewishness is present in every word I write" (O'Brian 1986, I). That quality, which characterizes much of his criticism, he identified as a bias for the abstract rather than for the immediate experience of everyday life.

He was also upset by the helplessness and powerlessness of East European Jews, who, by confining themselves to their religious culture, refused to confront the reality of antisemitism until it was too late. At the same time he was disturbed by those who, in joining the gentile world, lost a certain sense of self that had been sustained by traditional Jewish culture (O'Brian 1986, II). Greenberg found in the Czech author, Franz Kafka, a unique Jewish vision of reality that reflected what it meant to be a Jew in the early and mid-twentieth century. Kafka understood the dilemma of searching for security and of not being able to find it, of

understanding the gentile threat to Jews. He therefore, according to Greenberg, established a zone of safety for emancipated Jews, a secular version of the Jewish rules of conduct known as *halacha,* that provided a sense of orderliness and middle-class routine as well as explanations for inexplicable activities. But in the end this did not alleviate personal anxiety because Kafka's stories and novels had no resolution or closure (O'Brian 1986, II, III; Greenberg 1961).

Greenberg acknowledged his own Jewish self-hatred and wanted a new Jewish consciousness that liberated rather than organized Jews into new configurations. In desiring Judaism to become a non-issue, he found the extremes of overassimilation and Jewish nationalism to be equally egregious. He wanted to accept "my Jewishness more implicitly, so implicitly that I can use it to realize myself as a human being in my own right, and *as a Jew in my own right.*" In connection with the Jewish community, he held that Jews will persist "as long as Jewishness remains essential to our sense of our individual selves, as long as it is the truth about our individual selves" (O'Brian 1986, III). By holding to this position, Greenberg defined and dated himself as a child of the immigrant generation whose sense of Judaism came, as he said, "through mother's milk and the habits and talk of the family" (O'Brian 1986, I). Of course, future generations would lose their sense of Jewishness unless efforts were made to sustain it. Likewise, his criticism can be dated to the outlook of his generation who knew where they came from, but did not want to remain there.

Matthew Baigell

References and Further Reading

Greenberg, Clement. 1961. *Art and Culture: Critical Essays.* Boston: Beacon Press.

Kuspit, Donald B. 1979. *Clement Greenberg: Art Critic.* Madison: University of Wisconsin Press.

O'Brian, John. 1986. *Clement Greenberg: The Collected Essays and Criticism.* 4 Vols. Chicago: University of Chicago Press.

Harold Rosenberg (1906–1978)

Art Critic

One of the most important American art critics to emerge in the late 1940s, Harold Rosenberg stressed the importance of the creative act itself in the art-making process. Thus he helped to popularize such action-oriented artists as Jackson Pollock and Willem DeKooning, as well as subsequent art movements such as Process Art, in which the subject of the artwork is the record of its own creation. In his most famous essay, "The American Action Painters" (1952), Rosenberg emphasized the idea that a canvas surface was "an arena in which to act—rather than as a space in which to reproduce, re-design, analyze or 'express' an object real or imagined." The image produced was "the result of this encounter." To a greater or lesser degree, each work, even each brushstroke, marked a new beginning, a type of creativity that grew directly from the artist's inner being, free from external restraint, politics, European art traditions, morals, and values. In effect, each brushstroke, mark, or drip was made in response to the previous one and to nothing else (Rosenberg 1961).

Before developing this aesthetic philosophy, Rosenberg was active in left-wing political circles in New York during the 1930s as a poet and a writer. By the early 1940s, disenchanted by leftist dogma, he absorbed the Surrealist interest in the importance of creative processes. In addition, like others at the time, he accepted the idea that artists were alienated from society. Cut off from any grounding in tradition and community, artists could therefore develop their personal essence in isolation. Rosenberg found this beneficial in that, by annihilating the past, artists could, in effect, create new worlds. Art became a form of self-discovery. This attitude, according to Rosenberg, prompted artists of his generation, many of whom were born abroad or were the children of immigrants, to create a new American art free from inherited attitudes and different from older art-making traditions that emphasized design, craft, and technique. This attitude also provided a way for artists to replace ethnic and political issues with an aesthetics of the self, which became so important in the 1940s. It encouraged artists to develop their art as singular individuals, whatever their particular backgrounds.

But in the years during and after World War II, Rosenberg also wrote several articles attentive to Jewish issues, ranging from an explanation of how modern, nonreligious Jews substituted secular leftist politics for old-fashioned religious messianism (Marx replaced the Messiah) to a brilliant critical analysis of French philosopher Jean-Paul Sartre's book, *Anti-Semite and Jew* (1948), in which Rosenberg pointed out Sartre's own misguided antisemitism

(Rosenberg 1973). Rosenberg also addressed the issue of Jewish identity and freedom in the postwar world. Because Jewish origins no longer established commonalities among Jews, each Jew could reinvent or redefine him- or herself in different ways, based on whatever or however much of the Jewish past the individual invoked. Like contemporary artists, individuals could also begin their own voyage of self-discovery, each person hopefully secure in his or her own worth. As in Existential philosophy, each person, Rosenberg hoped, could become somebody "through the acts by which he projects himself into the future." That is, each person had the potentiality to choose the self he or she could become (Rosenberg 1973).

Rosenberg believed that the issue of identity was a modern problem, not just a Jewish one. But since Jews were often alienated from other Jews as well as from mainstream society, it was a particularly Jewish problem. To surmount this problem, Jewish artists, Rosenberg held, had begun "to assert their individual relation to art in an independent and personal way." By so doing, they were involved in two activities at the same time—creating a genuine American art and indulging in a profound Jewish expression of self-identification (Rosenberg 1973). In truth, this is the reasoning of a person who wants to escape his or her background without necessarily denying it entirely, for Rosenberg turned the modern search for self-identity in an alienated world into a Jewish quest for identity, but one without Judaism. Those who wanted to identify as Jewish had to look elsewhere.

Is there, then, a Jewish art? Rosenberg answered this question in the negative. He surmised that without common experiences there could be no unifying style. Lacking a singular style, there was no identifiable Jewish art, although there were obviously Jewish artists who employed Jewish subject matter. Like others of his generation who asked this question, he looked for an all-embracing definition that could encompass male and female, rich and poor, rural and urban, religious and secular, as well as European- and African-descended Jewish artists. Of course, the answer had to be in the negative. But the interesting point is that, even as Rosenberg encouraged artists to find their own individual identities, he still thought of Jews as a near monolithic group, or else why ask about the nature of Jewish art (Rosenberg 1973, 1985)?

Rosenberg acknowledged the necessity of possessing the moral courage and inner stability to engage in the adventure of self-discovery because it might involve a kind of existential agony. On the one hand, there was no firm starting point, and, on the other, a separation from one's own past. The problem was to bridge the distances between one's Jewish self, the self as Other (as others viewed the individual), and the self that wanted to emerge. This was no easy task, but one Rosenberg thought to be well worth the effort as one came to terms with the modern world.

Matthew Baigell

References and Further Reading
Rosenberg, Harold. 1961. *The Tradition of the New*. New York: Evergreen.
Rosenberg, Harold. 1973. *Discovering the Present: Three Decades in Art, Culture, and Politics*. Chicago: University of Chicago Press.
Rosenberg, Harold. 1985. *Art and Other Serious Matters*. Chicago: University of Chicago Press.

Meyer Schapiro (1904–1996)

Art Historian

Meyer (originally Meir) Schapiro, distinguished art historian, was born in Siauliai, Lithuania (near Vilna) in 1904, immigrated with his family to the United States in 1907, and died in New York City in 1996. A descendant of Talmudic scholars, his father, Nathan Menachem Schapiro, abandoned Orthodox Judaism early in life and, influenced by Haskala, an East European derivative of the West European Enlightenment, became a secular Jew. Nathan was also involved with the Jewish Socialist Bund, which influenced Meyer's leftist activism, evident in his writing for *Marxist Quarterly, New Masses, Nation,* and *Partisan Review,* and more generally, in his humanist concerns. Yiddish was Schapiro's first language, and it was at the Hebrew Settlement House in Brownsville, Brooklyn, where he first seriously engaged art, as a student in an evening studio class with John Sloane, the leader of the so-called Ashcan School. While gaining prominence as an art historian, Schapiro made art throughout his career and influenced numerous contemporary artists, among them Jacques Lifschitz and Robert Motherwell.

Schapiro applied for graduate study at Princeton University, which turned him down—he believed in part because he was a Jew—but went on to receive his doctorate in art history from Columbia University (1929), where he taught for almost a half century (1928–1973). His dissertation on Romanesque sculpture remains the basic work in the field. He continued to do major work in the area of early Christian and medieval art. In a breathtaking essay, "On the Aesthetic Attitude in Romanesque Art" (1947), Schapiro argued that "a new sphere of artistic creation without religious content [had emerged] in Western Europe within church art," and that its "values of spontaneity, individual fantasy, delight in color and movement, and the expression of feeling . . . anticipate modern art" (Schapiro 1977). In a sense, Schapiro spent the rest of his career demonstrating this. He moved effortlessly between Romanesque and modern art (ca. 1000–1150 and ca. 1838–1973, respectively), writing about the sculptures of Moissac, Silos, and Souillac as well as the paintings of Van Gogh, Cézanne, Mondrian, and Picasso, among other artifacts and artists. He was one of the earliest defenders of Abstract Expressionism, suggesting that it was the climactic realization of the values of Romanesque art.

Writing on the "Nature of Abstract Art" (1937), he argued that it was a mistake to think that it was simply "an art of pure form without content" and thus "independent of historical conditions" and "subjective conditions" (Schapiro 1978). Again and again he proceeded to show how those conditions influenced artistic innovation in the Romanesque and modern periods, perhaps most famously in his analysis of the effect of the industrial revolution on the development of nineteenth-century French painting. Schapiro's humanistic perspective is at its clearest in his essays on "Chagall's Illustrations for the Bible" (1956) and "The Humanity of Abstract Painting" (1960). The artists who most captured Schapiro's intellectual imagination were those who went against the grain of established opinion (like Schapiro himself), and Chagall was among the most daring of them, for he went against established avant-garde opinion. As Schapiro writes, modern painters "prefer the spontaneous, the immediately felt, and often discovered their subjects on the canvas while at work," but Chagall took as his subject the "set theme[s]" of the Old Testament, "a living book because of our open interest in the moral, the social, and the historical, whatever our beliefs. . . . A striving toward right in purity of spirit, a feeling of commitment and fulfillment, pervade the book" (Schapiro 1978). To Schapiro, Chagall is the morally exemplary modern artist, for his work successfully integrates modernist and humanistic concerns, that is, presents Old Testament scenes in a spontaneous, immediately felt way, as though they were freshly experienced.

From his essay "On Geometrical Schematism in Romanesque Art" (1932) through his essay on "Style" (1953) to his essay "On Some Problems in the Semiotics of Visual Art: Field and Vehicle in Image-Signs" (1969), Schapiro remained concerned with aesthetic structure as such, indicating that he was not the one-sided humanist he has sometimes been understood to be. He also wrote tellingly about Jewish matters, perhaps most notoriously in his critique of "Mr. [Bernard] Berenson's Values" (1961). In a sense, the essay is an examination of the path not chosen and, as such, subliminal self-analysis, all the more so because Berenson was also born in Vilna. Unlike Schapiro, who never changed his name and religion, Berenson changed his name and became Protestant and then Catholic. But Schapiro admired his survival skills in an alien world—fascist Italy as well as Brahmin Boston—and his power over the wealthy Christians who sought him out for his expertise about Renaissance art. He became as wealthy as many of them.

Berenson and Schapiro were prominent, innovative art historians and thinkers who dealt, in radically different ways, with the problem of being Jewish in a world that was prejudiced against Jews, although they had their uses. Schapiro never forgot his Jewishness, although he rarely made a point of it, while Berenson tried to forget it, and in fact made remarks that have been interpreted as antisemitic, or at least suggestive of his indifference to Jewishness. But Berenson never did forget his Jewishness, as Schapiro convincingly argues, suggesting that, however dissimilar, he and Berenson shared a sense of Jewish identity and destiny. Both were at once assimilated and alienated, as indicated by the fact that Schapiro was drawn to art that, at the time, was considered marginal and noncanonical, and Berenson significantly revised the understanding and canon of Renaissance art, once considered the apogee of Western art.

Schapiro wrote a great deal about Christian religious art but not much about Jewish religious art. Is this because the latter, unlike the former, was not mainstream and did not have much influence on the history of art, and in fact seems derivative of Christian religious art in its form if not content? No, there is likely a deeper reason. Modern times are not religious times—not dominated by religious thinking as medieval times were. Chagall was religious, but he was a rarity. Nonetheless, Schapiro thought it was possible to make convincing religious art in modern times. His belief that Romanesque art and modern art share the same spiritual values suggests as much. "On the Aesthetic Attitude in Romanesque Art" makes his position clear. Schapiro writes: "Hegel said very justly that in an age of piety one does not have to be religious in order to create a truly religious work of art, whereas today the most deeply pious artist is incapable of producing it. This discrepancy between the personal religious aim and the present condition of art was expressed in another way by Van Gogh, a man of passionate Christian insight, when he wrote that one could not paint the old religious subjects in an Impressionist style." If Van Gogh's art is implicitly religious if not explicitly Christian, then Schapiro believed that modern art could convey religious values through its style and atmosphere. As he wrote, Gorky's "beautifully made . . . delicate style" and "primitive, visceral and grotesque . . . atmosphere" conveyed "feelings of love and fragility and despair," the contradictory substance of religious feeling (Schapiro 1977). As Schapiro argues, dogmatic religion, whether Christian or Jewish, is beside the point of human feeling at its most intense and deep, which is what the best art, be it officially Christian, Jewish, or secular, conveys, often through the same stylistic features. For Schapiro, it seems, Jewish art, with a few rare exceptions, such as Chagall's, stood apart from the new sphere of art, with its spontaneity and fantasy, which began with Romanesque art and climaxed in modern art. Perhaps this is because he thought that Jewish art had more to do with religious conformity than with the "inner freedom," as he called it, of art at its most authentic, and thus was too creatively inhibited to be aesthetically innovative.

Schapiro was the Charles Eliot Norton Professor at Harvard in 1966–1967 and the Slade Professor for Art History at Oxford University in 1968. In 1975 he received the Alexander Hamilton Medal (awarded to distinguished alumni) from Columbia, and in 1976 he was elected to the National Institute of Arts and Letters. Four volumes of his *Selected Papers* have been published, spanning the history of art, except, surprisingly—was there no spontaneity, individual fantasy, delight in color and movement, and expression of feeling in it?—the art of the High Renaissance. (But Berenson dealt with that.) The volume on Modern

Art won the National Book Critics Circle Award in 1978 and the Mitchell Prize for Art History in 1979. The Brooklyn Museum has a large exhibition space dedicated to Schapiro and his brother Morris, and Columbia has inaugurated the Meyer Schapiro Professorship.

Donald Kuspit

References and Further Reading

Schapiro, Meyer. 1977. *Romanesque Art.* Vol. I of *Selected Papers.* New York: George Braziller.

Schapiro, Meyer. 1978. *Modern Art.* Vol. II of *Selected Papers.* New York: George Braziller.

Schapiro, Meyer. 1994. *Theory and Philosophy of Art: Style, Artist, and Society.* Vol. IV of *Selected Papers.* New York: George Braziller.

Jack Levine (b. 1915)

Artist

Jack Levine is an American artist known for his social realist commentary, and his paintings and prints of biblical figures and Jewish sages. A painter and printmaker of Jewish figures in an abstract art world, he has defied the conventions of mid- to late twentieth-century American art. He aims, in his words, "to develop some kind of iconography about my Jewish identity" (Levine 1989).

Born January 3, 1915, in Boston's South End, Levine was the youngest of Lithuanian immigrants Mary and Samuel Levine's eight children. A poor shoemaker and Hebrew scholar, Samuel enrolled his son in children's art classes at a Jewish Community Center, and later at a settlement house in Roxbury. There Levine met Harold Zimmerman, who became his first mentor, and Hyman Bloom, who also went on to become a painter of Jewish subjects.

At fourteen, Levine became acquainted with Denman Waldo Ross, an art professor at Harvard University. Ross provided financial assistance for Zimmerman, Levine, and Bloom, and arranged Levine's first public exhibition, a small showing of his drawings at Harvard's Fogg Art Museum in 1932 when Levine was only seventeen.

While as a child Levine created a chalk drawing titled *Jewish Cantors in the Synagogue* (1930, Fogg Art Museum, Harvard University), he first explored Jewish subjects in earnest, specifically biblical subjects, in 1941 when he painted *Planning Solomon's Temple,* a small, 10-by-8-inch homage to his recently deceased father (Israel Museum, Jerusalem).

Hundreds more biblical kings and Jewish sages followed, from well-known figures such as *King David* (1941) to the lesser-known *King Josiah* (1941). In 1942, Levine's work was interrupted by three and a half years in the Army. In 1946 he married the Ukrainian-born artist Ruth Gikow. During his time in the service, in 1943, the Metropolitan Museum of Art purchased *String Quartette* (1936–1937), a boldly colored tempera and oil image of four musicians.

Returning to New York in 1946, Levine continued the social realist work for which he had been known. Levine's unique, expressionistic style complemented his satirical eye, which recorded corrupt politicians, crooked cops, and social and political injustices on canvas and paper. Among his best-known works in this genre is *The Feast of Pure Reason* (1937, Museum of Modern Art, New York)—the title derived from James Joyce's novel *Ulysses*—a painting completed while Levine was employed by the Works Progress Administration's Federal Art Project.

In the fifties, Levine once again became engaged with Jewish kings and learned men, painting, among others, *King Saul* (1952), *King Asa* (1953), and the sages *Maimonides* (1952) and *Hillel* (1955).

In 1969 Levine created a lithograph, *Cain and Abel II.* While in an earlier print (1964) Levine used the theme "to capture the male mood in action" (Prescott 1984), the second version employed the Cain and Abel story as an allegory for the Holocaust (an oil painting of this subject is in the Vatican Museum's Gallery of Modern Religious Art). The lithograph was published by the Anti-Defamation League, to whom Levine donated the print to assist with fund-raising. Here Levine explores the symbolism of the Holocaust by showing the brothers' legs intertwined to form a swastika.

Levine has shown his work in numerous venues, including his first retrospective exhibition at the Institute of Contemporary Art in Boston (1952–1953), a show that traveled to five other museums, including the Phillips Collection in Washington, D.C. (1953), and the Whitney Museum of American Art (1955). Another retrospective was organized by the Jewish Museum in New York, which subsequently traveled to five other U.S. cities (1978–1980). He

Feast of Pure Reason *by Jack Levine, 1937 (©The Museum of Modern Art/Licensed by Scala/Art Resource, NY)*

has works in the permanent collections of the Smithsonian American Art Museum, the Whitney Museum of American Art, the Metropolitan Museum of Art, and the Museum of Modern Art in New York.

Samantha Baskind

References and Further Reading
Getlein, Frank. *Jack Levine.* 1966. New York: Harry N. Abrams.

Levine, Jack. 1989. *Jack Levine,* compiled and edited by Stephen Robert Frankel, introduction by Milton W. Brown. New York: Rizzoli.

Prescott, Kenneth W., and Emma-Stina Prescott. 1984. *The Complete Graphic Work of Jack Levine.* New York: Dover Publications.

Man Ray (1890–1976)

Dadaist Artist

Man Ray (born in Philadelphia 1890, died in Paris in 1976) was a major avant-garde Dadaist artist, one of the founders of New York Dada. Man Ray was an ingenious inventor and all-around artist: painter, photographer, filmmaker, and a Dadaist creator advocating the use of the "ready-made" (found objects) in unexpected combinations. His artistic language questioned the relationship between the verbal and the visual by means of his unique blend of irony, puns, subterfuge, and uncanny images. As a photographer, he was

Man Ray, avante-garde Dadaist. (Library of Congress)

known for his innovative technique of camera-less direct contact photography—named rayograph (after its inventor)—made by placing objects of various opacities on light-sensitive paper and exposing them to light. In many of these rayographs, the effect is the de-materialization of the objects.

Throughout modernism, Man Ray's art was read exclusively in universal terms. Viewed from a postmodern perspective, however, which credits minorities for their contributions to culture, the hidden Jewish American background of Man Ray's avant-garde universal persona emerges.

In the beginning of his artistic career in New York, Man Ray attended night classes at the Art School of the Francisco Ferrer Social Center (1910–1911), where *Tapestry* (1912) was shown—a patchwork of fabric scraps, whose center might be read as an abstract shape of a human figure (Man) with raised hands. His early exposure to photography and modern art took place in Alfred Stieglitz's "Gallery of the Photo-Secession, 291." Influenced by the Armory Show exhibition (1913) that served as an introduction to modernism, Man Ray joined the Ridge-

field community, where he met his first wife, Adon Lacroix, and two years later, his artistic soul mate, Marcel Duchamp. Whereas Duchamp went to New York to free himself from the confinement of old Europe and exhibited his famous *Fountain*/urinal in the Armory Show (later returning to Paris), Man Ray sought freedom in Paris. There he developed his artistic persona. Paris became his adopted city from 1921 to 1940, returning there in 1951 after spending the World War II years in Los Angeles, where he met his second wife, Juliet Browner.

In Paris, Man Ray also became a photographer of haute couture (high fashion), as in the photo of Coco Chanel in a little black dress, smoking a cigarette, the prototype of the *New Woman* (1935). Artistically, in the sophisticated use of the ready-made as well as in the subversive artistic language he used, this brilliant vanguard artist-provocateur was close to Duchamp, whom he photographed in his female persona as *Rose Sélavy* (*Rose c'est la vie*, phonetically), appearing in a woman's attire. Man Ray's relationships with women were a source of artistic inspiration and express the white male's dominant gaze. Women's nude bodies are turned into objects of merchandise as in his sculpture of Venus's nude torso, tied up with a string (1937/1971). Women were photographed as nudes, as torsos, or in full body length, focusing on the heads in unique combinations, as in his 1926 *Noire et blanche* (*Black and white*). Here, the oval white head of his lover and model Kiki de Montparnasse is juxtaposed to an African mask, also printed in a negative version. The elongated neck and classic beauty of Lee Miller was captured in her elegant profile (1930). However, Man Ray commemorated the termination of their relationship with a Dadaist ready-made, *Object to Be Destroyed* (1922–1923), later called *Indestructible Object*, in which a photograph of her beautiful blue eye was clipped to a pendulum. Here, irony and humor are used to overcome their separation, the change of title signifying the failure of the attempt. The eye, both the artist's and the spectator's gaze, is emphasized in the portrait of *La Marchesa Casti* (1922), in which two pairs of eyes appear one above the other, causing movement and a mesmerizing effect.

Man Ray's photographs of pivotal modernist artists have become classics. These include Tristan Tsara (who was the first to appreciate Ray's rayographs), the Surrealist group (André Breton, Max Ernst, Salvador Dali, Alberto

Giacometti), and many others. Man Ray himself was the subject of many photographs. In a series of photographed self-portraits done in the 1920s, he presents himself as different personae: a Far Eastern fakir, an intellectual with a beard and spectacles, a Parisian with a black beret, the latter being his most desired persona. In his *Self-Portrait* (1924), a self-photograph in ¾, the artist in suit and tie is seen on the background of the blurred image (achieved by long exposure) of the tools of his métier. The intense expression of his enlarged widely open eyes is that of a magician, hypnotizing and being hypnotized. This modern alchemist also mystifies the process of photography, undermining its factual, naturalistic function. But he mystified more than the function of his art. Throughout his mature life, he was engaged in creating a mystery of his own family background. His 1924 *Self-Portrait,* signed and dated by the artist, attributes to his profession the ability to create his own chosen world.

Man Ray, an acronym for Emmanuel Radnitzky, was born to Manya Louria (or Lourie), who grew up in Minsk (Russia), and Melech (Hebrew for "king") Radnitzky, who emigrated to the United States to avoid the draft. The family settled in Philadelphia and later in Brooklyn, New York (1897), earning their living as tailors. In this respect they resembled many other Jewish Eastern European immigrants (and artists, such as William Gropper, Hugo Gellert, and Max Weber), who shared the memories of the sweatshop experience. As a young child, Emmanuel took part in the family enterprise as a delivery boy. However, in Man Ray's autobiography, *Self Portrait* (1963), there is neither mention of his family's occupation nor of the fact that he was born a Jew. He chose rather to ignore his socioeconomic and ethnic background, wishing to detach himself from his Jewish origins through a change of name and place, inventing his own biography.

Apparently, Man Ray was unable to rid himself of that background, as can be seen in various images in his art that are related to the sweatshops. Needle and threads, pins, coat hangers, photographs of shirts next to zebras (the only animals "wearing" clothes), as well as sewing machines and flatirons populate his art. In a compulsion to repeat, many of these images reappear in his art, becoming leitmotifs. Man Ray's struggle with his identity is exemplified by a recurrent image of major importance in the avant-garde art, *The Enigma of Isidore Ducasse,* done in New York in 1920 before leaving for Paris.

The assemblage pays tribute to Comte de Lautréamont's (alias Isidore Ducasse) famous statement, "Beautiful as the chance meeting of a sewing machine and an umbrella on a dissecting table." In this work, one of the most radical Dadaist pieces, Man Ray achieves an eerie integration of visual and verbal effects. The viewer sees a mystifying, sinister image of a coarse opaque blanket, covering a vaguely anthropomorphic form and tied with a rope. In the relationship between the verbal and the visual, the artist engages the viewer in a sophisticated game of hide-and-seek. The enigma is the enigma of Man Ray, or of Emmanuel Radnitsky. For Man Ray, sharing with Lautréamont the need to conceal his identity, sends us through the hidden sewing machine to the world he wished to leave behind.

Soon after his arrival in Paris (1921) Man Ray produced a more overtly aggressive "assisted" ready-made, *Cadeau* (gift), a flatiron bristling with nails, obviously suggesting the tearing up of cloth rather than ironing it smoothly. Although this was what he would have wished to do, his art reveals how agonizing this "tearing" of (or tearing himself away from) the past proved to be. His reiteration of specific themes provides evidence of his compulsive confrontation with the milieu from which he had fled. The iron—with or without nails—is one such recurrent motif. In *Lingerie* (1931), a rayograph, the iron is manipulated through the process of dematerialization. And in *The Red Iron* (1966), the red hot iron continues to convey a sense of danger. The *Enigma* also became a leitmotif: in one version the sewing machine is uncovered (1933); however, two years later, the bundle of objects was put into a paper bag, tied with a string, with the suggestion that in case of need, it is already wrapped up, as indeed happened when Man Ray had to flee Paris during World War II. The *Enigma* and the *Cadeau* are related and bring new insight into the artist's world—existentially as well as artistically—and call for an awareness of the hidden "Jewish problem" underlying Man Ray's avant-garde art.

In his Dadaist films there were also instances in which he explored his highly ambivalent relation to the past, as in the film *Emak Bakia* (*Leave Me Alone* in Basque), produced in 1926. Here, the artist presents the metamorphosis of a dozen stiff white collars by ripping them apart and shooting their dance-like passage through revolving and deforming mirrors. Following this exhilarating pirouette to freedom, the sequence is rewound, so that at the end the torn collars become whole again.

His seemingly naive playful art objects, such as the mobile *Obstruction* (1920/1947), also convey Man Ray's grappling with the past. This graceful aerial sculpture is made of coat hangers. The artist's idea was to add more and more hangers, eventually obstructing the whole universe. In the early version he reached the total of 117, obstructing the whole space of the studio. The form itself is associated with a family tree—but one in which the branches (the hangers) are getting in each other's way (that is, obstructing one another). In fact, he is "hanging" them with their own working tools. Thus, by means of black humor and double entendre, Man Ray strove to cast off the burden of the past, ironically continuing to cull his images from the very world he wished to obliterate.

Although Man Ray distanced himself from his family, never attending his mother's or his father's funeral, the slender image of his mother, based on an 1895 cropped photograph, appears in a witty drawing, *Needle and Thread* (1937). The thread delineates the mother's silhouette, while the needle pierces the center of her spine. Here is an attempt to exorcise the magic spell she had on him through the combination of both his and her professions. From another perspective, Man Ray himself has become a tailor.

Man Ray, who was also a painter, known for the lovers' fragmented red lips hovering in the sky, symbolizing two bodies joined together, as in the 1934 *Les amoureux* (*The Lovers*), claimed that he painted what cannot be photographed and vice versa. It is therefore significant that the last version of the bundle of tied-up objects resembling the original *Enigma*, done after World War II, was a painting rather than an assemblage or photograph. Its title, *Rue Férou* (1952), was the name of the street of the artist's studio in Paris. This work also differs from the ironic stance and emotional aloofness typical of many of his Dadaist works. Here we see a shadowlike, dwarfish man with a cap, seen from behind as he pulls a loaded cart containing the tied-up bundle. He is moving down a narrow, empty cul-de-sac. The lonely figure comes to impersonate the Jewish peddler destined to roam forever from place to place—a modern version of the age-old theme of the Wandering Jew. It is a rare moment of Man Ray's coming to terms with his past and with the fate of the Jewish people, which seems to be a consequence of the war. Yet, on the manifest level, Man Ray refrained from referring to the Holocaust and continued to claim that "race, or class become irrelevant."

The collector and art critic Arturo Schwarz donated his Dada and Surrealism Collection of art objects as well as documentation to the Israel Museum in Jerusalem. Many of Man Ray's photographs and Dadaist objects, the *Enigma* and flatiron included, are housed there.

Milly Heyd

References and Further Reading
Baldwin, Neil. 1988. *Man Ray*. London: Hamish Hamilton.
Heyd, Milly. 2001. "Man Ray/Emmanuel Radnitsky/Who Is Behind the 'Enigma of Isidore Ducasse'?" In *Complex Identities: Jewish Consciousness and Modern Art*, edited by Matthew Baigell and Milly Heyd, 115–142. New Brunswick, NJ: Rutgers University Press.
Ray, Man. 1963. *Self-Portrait*. Boston: Little, Brown and Company.
Schwarz, Arturo. 1977. *Man Ray: The Rigour of Imagination*. London: Thames and Hudson.

Larry Rivers (1923–2002)

Artist and Musician

An artist and musician, at times Larry Rivers made Jewish concerns the subject of his work, including a monumental triptych, *History of Matzah* (*The Story of the Jews*). Although sometimes these images were created tongue-in-cheek, as was typical of his art, he also reserved rare serious moments for his Jewish imagery.

Born Yitzroch Loiza Grossberg in the Bronx to Jewish immigrants from the Ukraine, Rivers initially made his reputation as a jazz saxophonist. After a brief stint in the U.S. Army Air Corps during World War II (1942–1943), he studied music theory and composition at the Juilliard School of Music (1944–1945). During this time he discovered the fine arts and in 1945 he began painting. Although working in an art world dominated by abstraction, Rivers retained the figure and explored historical and personal subjects. He was among the first to use popular imagery in his paintings, making him a forerunner of the Pop Art movement.

In the early fifties, when he might have made a transition to abstraction, Rivers began to paint autobiographical themes in works such as *The Burial* (1951, Fort Wayne Museum of Art, Indiana), a canvas inspired by the memory of his grandmother's funeral, and *Europe I* (1956, Minneapolis Institute of Arts) and *Europe II* (1956, private collection, New York), the latter based on a formal portrait of Polish relatives.

Bar Mitzvah Photograph Painting (1961, private collection, New York) more specifically addresses Jewish identity issues. Here two minimally rendered children, Rivers' first cousins, are flanked by their mother and father in this family portrait. Based on a studio photograph, Rivers retains the essence of the photograph as a proof: stenciled diagonally across the canvas are letters spelling "rejected." Avram Kampf argues that Rivers parodies the diluted Bar Mitzvah ceremony, a social rather than a spiritual ritual as practiced in America (Kampf 1990).

Indeed, parody is an important facet of Rivers' work. In *Washington Crossing the Delaware,* for example, a canvas mocking the grand heroics of nineteenth-century American history painting, Rivers appropriates the imagery of Emanuel Leutze's iconic painting of the same name. In 1951, Rivers' version was acquired by the Museum of Modern Art in New York, his first painting to enter a major public collection.

Parody also pervades *History of Matzah (The Story of the Jews),* an ambitious project that attempts to tell the nearly four-millennia story of the Jews. Painted by commission from Rivers' frequent patron, the art dealer Jeffrey Loria, *History of Matzah* was completed over a two-year period (1982–1984). Created in a collage-like form—superimposed on a painted rendering of flat, dry matzah, the unleavened bread that resulted from the Jews' haste when fleeing Egypt—images and stories overlap on three 9-by-14-foot canvases in Part I, titled *Before the Diaspora;* Part II, *European Jewry;* and Part III, *Immigration to America.*

History of Matzah sustains Rivers' plays on the masters, as he manipulates biblical history through the appropriation of common imagery, including Leonardo's *Last Supper* and Michelangelo's *David.* In each appropriation, Rivers returns the iconic figures to their Jewish origins. For instance, *David* appears with a Semitic nose and circumcised. Each commentary is an attempt by Rivers to express his Judaism, an identity that he previously suppressed; *History of Matzah* stands as a recuperative painting in which Larry Rivers/Yitzroch Grossberg affirms his presence as a Jew and a Jewish artist (Baskind 1999).

Other works influenced by Rivers' Jewish identity include a large mural, *Fall in the Forest at Birkenau* (1990), hanging in the United States Holocaust Memorial Mu-

seum, three posthumous portraits of the Holocaust memoirist Primo Levi (1987–1988, Collection La Stampa, Turin, Italy), and the illustrations for a Limited Editions Club publication of Isaac Bashevis Singer's short story "The Magician of Lublin" (1984).

The multi-talented Rivers also designed sets for the play *Try! Try!* (1951), written by Frank O'Hara, as well as plays by LeRoi Jones (1964) and Stravinsky's *Oedipus Rex* (1966). In 1954 Rivers wrote a play, *Kenneth Koch: A Tragedy,* with O'Hara; in 1957 he began making welded metal sculpture. He also wrote poetry and performed in plays, including Koch's *The Election* (1960).

Rivers' art hangs in many venues, including the National Gallery of Art, the Hirshhorn Museum and Sculpture Garden, and the Tate Gallery in London. He has had several retrospective exhibitions, including a show at the Museo de Arte Contemporáneo in Caracas, Venezuela (1980) and the Corcoran Gallery of Art in Washington, D.C. (2002).

Samantha Baskind

References and Further Reading

Baskind, Samantha. 1999. "Effacing Difference: Larry Rivers's *History of Matzah (The Story of the Jews).*" *Athanor* 17: 87–95.

Hunter, Sam. 1989. *Larry Rivers.* New York: Rizzoli International Publications.

Kampf, Avram. 1990. *Chagall to Kitaj: Jewish Experience in 20th Century Art.* New York: Praeger Publishers.

Levy, David C., Barbara Rose, and Jacquelyn Days Serwer. 2002. *Larry Rivers: Art and the Artist.* Boston: Little, Brown and Company and Corcoran Gallery of Art.

George Segal (1924–2000)

Sculptor

George Segal, a major Jewish American sculptor, was one of the most innovative sculptors of the second half of the twentieth century. Known as the mythologizer of urban existence, Segal was associated in the initial stages of his career with Pop Art (1960s). Originally a second-generation Abstract Expressionist painter, Segal turned to sculpting by casting plaster bandages directly on the human body. Since casting does not end with the protagonist's physical boundaries, this kind of art captures the human being's

George Segal, sculptor. (Hulton/Getty Images)

spiritual essence. The sculptures that bring inner reality to the surface embody that which is quintessentially human. Psychological relations between people and modern urban life are explored. Most of the bandaged figures are white, but Segal occasionally used black as well as primary colors monochromatically.

Plaster is juxtaposed to objects from daily life. Although the human figures, usually people to whom the artist was close (his wife and friends), are individualized, the white color neutralizes their personal features, endowing them with an apparition-like, decontextualized appearance. Daily objects, such as a red refrigerator (in *The Gas Station,* 1964), a green table (in *Alice Listening to Her Poetry and Music,* 1970), a bench (in *Gay Liberation*), street signs (in *Times Square at Night,* 1970), a bath (in *Woman Shaving Her Leg,* 1963), add a contrasting color and texture and contribute to the dissonance.

In Segal's sculptural world, introverted participants are enclosed within their inner worlds, making no eye contact or any other form of rapport with one another. The white figures are associated with alienation in the modern city, hence resemble Edward Hopper's cityscapes, portray-

ing people as loners. Anonymity, the magic of street signs, and the tension within the body are explored in *Walk— Don't Walk* (1976), focusing on three people trying to cross the street. The protagonists' position and body language can be read as posing an existential question of "being" and "nonbeing."

However, there is also a political dimension. Segal's *The Bus Riders* (1962) carries more than a one-to-one relationship to the politics of the civil rights movement. His sculptural environments are imbued with ambiguities: between figure and environment and between the actual identity of the protagonists and their unnatural white casting. The political dimension adds another layer to the intricate staging of Segal's environment. In *The Bus Riders* three white cast figures occupy the bus seats, while a fourth seat remains vacant, although a man is standing behind it, raising the question, Why is he standing? Segal's sculpture is his tribute to the background of the Montgomery bus boycott that began in December 1955, after Rosa Parks's refusal to move to the back of the bus. It was his way of opposing racism and segregation. In this respect, his work is compatible with other Jewish American artists who were engaged in the black cause before and during the civil rights movement. (The long list includes Jack Levine, Raphael Soyer, Ben Shahn, Chaim Gross, and many others.)

Segal's universality does not exclude involvement with the fate of Jews, as in his *Holocaust Memorial* (1983) at the Jewish Museum, New York, where a pile of white emaciated bodies is seen in juxtaposition to a contemplative survivor fenced by a barbed wire. Martin Weil, the director of the Israel Museum, himself a survivor, was the model for this image. In addition, Jewish biblical texts were a source of inspiration, as can be seen in installations dedicated to biblical themes such as *Lot and his Daughters* (1958), *The Sacrifice of Isaac* (1973 and 1978), as well as *Abraham's Farewell to Ishmael* (1987). Rather than depict the world of classic mythology to stage archetypal moral dilemmas, Segal found himself closer to dramatic situations in the Hebrew scriptures.

Some sociohistorical background on Segal's family in general and on George Segal in particular provides a means for contextualizing his work from a Jewish American perspective. George was born to Jacob Segal and Sophie Gerstenfeld. The artist's father emigrated to America in 1922 from a village near Kiev, Ukraine. Having survived

World War I, Jacob left to avoid being drafted into the army. He settled in the Bronx, New York, where he owned a kosher butcher shop. In 1940 the family moved to South Brunswick, New Jersey, where the father embarked on chicken farming. There George met his future wife, Helen Steinberg, the daughter of a neighboring farmer. In 1949, after graduating from Cooper Union and Rutgers University, George Segal bought a chicken farm across the road from his family. The chickens were sold in 1958, and the coop was converted into an artist's studio.

The family's transition from the city to a rural area was part of a larger movement of some Eastern European Jewish immigrants from the big cities to rural America. This transition had to do with revolutionary and socialist ideology. The new way of making a living had its ups and downs. Whereas between 1940 and 1955 there was a vast increase in the demand and supply of poultry, after that the industry collapsed, and the farm was turned into a place where Segal's sculptures were made.

A process of three stages in the Segal family's history of acculturation in America has its resonance in George Segal's art. It involves a transition from urbanization (Bronx), through agriculture, to sublimation into art. The installation *The Butcher Shop* (1965) commemorates the first stage, and it relates to the family shop on 174th Street in the Bronx. Done six months after the father's death, the installation is inscribed "Kosher Butcher." A number of white casts of chickens are lying there next to hooks behind a glass window. On an authentic butcher's table, the white cast of the artist's mother, a knife in her hand and in a ritualistic pose, is in the process of chopping off a chicken's head. The chicken played a role in one of Segal's early paintings representing the farm period, *A Man with a Dead Chicken* (1957). Here the dead fowl is closely attached to a nude man's chest, becoming part of him, its whiteness contrasting with his bleeding red color. Segal draws an analogy between himself and the dead animal, as if he himself has been sacrificed. The artist was aware of the eve of the Day of Atonement ritual, in which a fowl is encircled around the head as a scapegoat (substituting for the sacrificial goat in the biblical Temple). Indeed, as a child Segal was in charge of cleaning the blood in his father's shop before the Sabbath. The place itself was maintained according to the Jewish dietary laws, which forbid eating blood, which has to be drained from the meat before cooking.

Hence it is significant that George Segal (unlike Chaim Soutine, who preferred to be drenched in blood) opted for white in many of his sculptures, as if whiteness is all. Moreover, for his conception of *The Butcher Shop*, blood is conspicuously absent. In his white sculptures Segal is continuously exorcising the blood that was part of his childhood experience, as if he were washing that blood away. In this respect, a pure white sculpture can be seen as a disembodied spirit.

In later assemblages, such as *Still Life with Shoe and Rooster* (1986), the rooster stands for the third stage of acculturation. Here it is part of a Cubist assemblage rather than placed on the body, as in *A Man with a Dead Chicken* or in *The Butcher Shop*. In other words, the concrete context has been eliminated, removing the rooster from the original experience. The use of Cubism as a universal language shows the change that has taken place since the days in the Bronx, immortalized in *The Butcher Shop*. The assemblage symbolizes the process of sublimating the past into art. In terms of the history of the Jewish immigration to America, Segal's family history can represent some aspects of the Jewish experience: the city, the farm, and art.

George Segal created two versions of *The Sacrifice of Isaac*. The early one was done in Israel in 1973 when the place itself triggered the artist's sense of identification with the biblical drama in the period following the Yom Kippur War. Under the impact of his reading of Søren Kierkegaard's *Fear and Trembling*, Segal speculated on the moral options Abraham had to face on the way to killing his son. In his white plaster image an intergenerational struggle takes place with neither God nor ram (deviating from the biblical story and artistic prototypes, such as Rembrandt's). The conflict had to be resolved between father and son, between youth and old age. Indeed, the scene is very charged erotically. The older man, whose bust is bare, is standing above a beautiful young boy, lying exposed on a rock. Although Abraham is holding a real knife (found in Jaffa's Arab market), he is not pointing it toward his son but rather in a reverse direction. The plaster was cast on the Israeli artist Menachem Kadishman and his son Ben (meaning son in Hebrew). Kadishman, a big, heavy, bearded man, was a shepherd, and he is conceived as a patriarchal figure. Segal is constantly engaged in the theme of Isaac's sacrifice in the context of Israeli wars, which has become a leitmotif in Israeli art and literature in general.

In producing two versions of the *Sacrifice of Isaac*, as well as *Abraham's Farewell to Ishmael* (1987) (in Hebrew, God will hear), George Segal deployed two parallel narratives of sacrifice. If in the first case Segal identified with the fallen Israelis, in the second he also identified with the position of the rejected son. In the two stories Segal saw the correspondence between Moslems and Jews. Four figures take part in the moral dilemma of sending Hagar and Ishmael away. There is a close embrace between father and son (Abraham and Ishmael), while the two women, the young beautiful Hagar and the old Sarah, are excluded from the intimacy. Hagar hugs herself, while Sarah, who stands behind, austerely clad like a monk, stares harshly on her rival. Whereas in the Bible there is neither a description of facial features nor a clue to internal emotions, Segal's biblical drama centers on feeling, depicting physical gestures in expressive body language. Hence the biblical narrative is psychologized and applied to modern situations of relatedness and separation.

The second version of the sacrifice was done in bronze in memory of May 4, 1970: *Kent State University* (1978). Segal was commissioned to do a monument. Because he would not do a soldier with a rifle, Kent State rejected the sculpture. His sculpture was eventually installed on the Princeton campus. It commemorates the killing of four university students by the National Guard during the Vietnam War demonstrations. Two adults confront one another: the young one, Isaac, on his knees with his hands tied. Abraham towers in front of him, yet it is clear that, if Isaac rose, he would be taller than his father. The notion of Isaac's adulthood is obviously in accordance with the Kent State situation, but it also emphasizes his accountability and the threat he poses as a rising power. There are, in fact, versions in rabbinical chronologies conceiving of Isaac as an adult. The sculpture itself is a concentrated moment of love and hate, depending on the spectator's position. It can be seen with or without a knife, portraying an intense stabbing or an intense longing. Moreover, one is not sure whether the knife will stab the youth or cut his bonds and free him.

George Segal, a proud Jew, well read in Jewish matters, emphasized that the luckiest stroke in his life was that he was born in the United States. It is therefore very appropriate that he was chosen to be one of the artists commemorating the Franklin Delano Roosevelt Memorial in Washington, D.C. The cycle of three works—which sum-marized Roosevelt's presidency: *Fireside Chat*, *The Breadline* (referring to the Depression years), and *The Rural Couple*—was done out of empathy and social consciousness, befitting the great humanist that Segal was.

George Segal was represented by the Sidney Janis Gallery, New York City, where he had solo exhibitions from 1965 through 1993.

Milly Heyd

References and Further Reading
Baigell, Matthew. 1983. "Segal's Holocaust Memorial." Interview. *Art in America* 71 (Summer): 134–136.
Heyd, Milly. 1997–1998. "George Segal: The Multifaceted Sacrifice." In *Jewish Art*, edited by Bianca Kühnel, 617–628. Vols. 23–24.
Hunter, Sam, and Don Hawthorne. *George Segal.* 1984. New York: Rizzoli.
Segal, George. 1997–1998. "Reflections on My Work While in Jerusalem." In *Jewish Art*, edited by Bianca Kühnel, 600–616. Vols. 23–24.
Van der Marck, Jan. 1968. *George Segal.* Chicago: Museum of Contemporary Art.

Raphael Soyer (1899–1987)

Realist Artist of the American Scene

Raphael Soyer has sometimes been considered the quintessential painter of the Jewish American experience.

Soyer, active throughout a great part of the twentieth century, retained the human figure even if the American art world was concerned with more abstract ideals. His body of work includes several images that employ overt Jewish iconography, as well as art that was influenced by his Jewish identity even while not engaging obvious Jewish subjects (Baskind 2004).

Soyer was born on December 25, 1899, in Borisoglebsk, Russia. The first of six children, Raphael was one of four sons, three of whom—Raphael, his twin brother Moses, and Isaac—became artists. In 1912, when the family was forced to leave Russia because their Right to Live permit was revoked, they embarked for the United States, settling in the Bronx.

After taking drawing classes at the Cooper Union Art School from 1914 to 1917, Soyer spent four years at the National Academy of Design beginning in fall 1918, and

Raphael Soyer painting in his studio in 1940. (Time Life Pictures/Getty Images)

completed his artistic schooling at the Art Students League intermittently from 1920 to 1926. Soyer held his first one-man show at New York City's Daniel Gallery in 1929. It was there that his 1926 painting *Dancing Lesson* (Collection Renee and Chaim Gross, New York), often understood as the exemplar of Jewish American art, was first exhibited publicly. The painting is reproduced in almost all Jewish art books. It adorned the cover of *Painting a Place in America,* a catalog compiled in celebration of the hundredth anniversary of the Educational Alliance, even though it was Moses, not Raphael, who took classes at the Alliance. The image is also reproduced on the cover of a volume of Jewish American poetry and employed as a visual example of "Jewish acculturation in the New World" in a book on modern Jewish politics.

Dancing Lesson depicts the artist's sister Rebecca teaching Moses to dance. The crowded canvas, which measures only twenty-four by twenty inches, also shows three figures packed on a couch watching the dance scene. Raphael's youngest brother, Israel, plays the harmonica on the right side of the sofa, his father and grandmother survey the scene from the couch, and his mother sits on an armchair

holding a copy of the Yiddish daily newspaper *Der Tog,* inscribed with Hebrew lettering. A portrait of family ancestors in traditional attire hangs on the wall above the sofa.

Throughout his career, Soyer was interested in Social Realist themes, which he both painted and made into prints. During the Great Depression he often created compassionate renderings of the down-and-out. Samantha Baskind argues that it may be because of the influence of Judaism's teachings about the importance of *tikkun olam* (repairing the world) that Soyer rendered the homeless in such detail (2004). Soyer's work was also shaped by his affiliation with Communist organizations in the thirties, including the John Reed Club.

Overwhelmed by increased traffic after the construction of the East and West Side Highways, Soyer retreated into his studio. Indeed, self-portraits at his easel and studio scenes of female nudes comprise Soyer's artistic interests through the forties. At this time Soyer also began a series of portraits of his artist friends as well as artists he admired. In a 1941 one-man show at the Associated American Artists Gallery, twenty-three of Soyer's artist portraits were exhibited in a section entitled "My Contemporaries and Elders." Among the paintings displayed were portraits of Philip Evergood and Abraham Walkowitz. In the late 1950s Soyer started to paint outdoor scenes again, most of which were large canvases, such as *Farewell to Lincoln Square* (1959, Hirshhorn Museum and Sculpture Garden, Washington, D.C.). Inspired by Soyer's eviction from the Lincoln Arcade Building, where he kept a studio for fourteen years, torn down because of the construction of Lincoln Center, the painting measures sixty by fifty-five inches.

Soyer remained a representational artist in an abstract art scene, proudly declaring his desire to paint "man and his world" on many occasions, including in *Reality: A Journal of Artists' Opinions,* a periodical Soyer founded to declare the importance of representational art (published annually from 1953 to 1955). The large-scale canvases of the fifties may have been a reaction to the ascension of Abstract Expressionism, whose artists favored large canvases (Baskind 2004).

After meeting the Yiddish writer Isaac Bashevis Singer in the elevator of his New York apartment building, Soyer began several projects with him late in life. Soyer illustrated a Limited Editions Club publication of two Singer stories, "The Gentleman from Cracow" and "The Mirror" (1979), and the second and third volumes of Singer's memoirs, *A Young Man in Search of Love* (1978) and *Lost in America* (1981).

Soyer chronicled aspects of his life in four autobiographies and many interviews. Among other venues, his works reside in the permanent collections of the Smithsonian American Art Museum, the Whitney Museum of American Art, the Metropolitan Museum of Art, and the Hirshhorn Museum and Sculpture Garden.

Samantha Baskind

References and Further Reading

Baskind, Samantha. 2004. *Raphael Soyer and the Search for Modern Jewish Art.* Chapel Hill: University of North Carolina Press.

Cole, Sylvan, ed. 1978. *Raphael Soyer: Fifty Years of Printmaking, 1917–1967,* rev. ed. New York: Da Capo Press.

Goodrich, Lloyd. 1972. *Raphael Soyer.* New York: Harry N. Abrams.

Heyd, Milly, and Ezra Mendelsohn. 1993–1994. "'Jewish' Art? The Case of the Soyer Brothers." *Jewish Art* 19–20: 194–211.

American Jews and Music

The Cantorate in America

The cantor (*hazzan* in Hebrew) musically leads prayers and other ritual activities in the synagogue and presides at Jewish life-cycle events. The cantorate emerged around 800 CE and became a part of synagogue life in the Medieval period. During the Enlightenment, the cantorate became a profession that sought parity with the rabbinate. In both the Ashkenazic and the various Sephardic traditions, cantorial music adapted the melodies and musical aesthetic of the surrounding cultures. The Ashkenazim and Sephardim who immigrated to America transplanted the musical styles of their countries of origin, which varied widely. The synagogue was initially a place to hold onto premigratory traditions. Over time, however, American popular music, Broadway, folk, and rock styles significantly influenced the cantorate. The current challenge is to fashion a role that adheres to the cantorial tradition with its European roots while singing in a liturgical style that appeals to American Jews. At the beginning of the twenty-first century, no style predominates; the diversity is vast.

During the first centuries after the destruction of the Second Temple in Jerusalem in 70 CE, prayer in the Jewish tradition was not systematized. In this period, however, Rabbinic Judaism established a tradition of prayer, with the first prayer book created in the Geonic period (eighth–tenth centuries CE). Prior to this time the text of

prayer was not mandated. A member of the congregation—called the *shaliach tzibur*—led prayers expressing personal and communal requests. As this role developed and became standardized, the term *hazzan* was applied to the leader. The term likely derives from Aramaic, because it is not found in the Bible. The hazzan musically recited the prayers.

In the second millennium the role of the cantor became established in Jewish ritual and was much discussed by rabbis. In the Medieval period the hazzan often traveled to different communities, bringing a supply of new melodies. Written descriptions and iconographic sources show the *meshorerim* practice (assistant singers) consisting of a hazzan with two assistants: a male bass and a boy soprano. As a trio they sang with lengthy melodic elaborations in synagogue services, much to the scorn of some observers and rabbis. In the Enlightenment, cantors sought to change the nature of prayer and melodies.

The most significant development in Central European cantorial and synagogue music resulted from the liturgical and aesthetic changes introduced by the Reform movement. Although changes began in the late eighteenth and early nineteenth centuries, it was in the mid-nineteenth century that they assumed an established form. Israel Jacobson (1768-1828), a merchant by profession, introduced various reforms in the synagogue service. These included the elimination of the hazzan, the use of

Protestant hymns with Hebrew words, sermons in German, confirmation for boys and girls, and the reading, not cantillation, of the Bible. With the exception of the elimination of the hazzan, most of his changes were incorporated into the Reform service later in the nineteenth century and thereafter. Many congregations replaced traditional Jewish music with hymnal singing in the Protestant style, and in some cases they literally translated German Protestant hymns into Hebrew. Jacobson introduced the first organ into services in Seesen in 1810. Although it was short-lived there, the practice was continued in Hamburg in 1818, which became an important city for the advancement of reforms. At the time many Jews considered the musical changes radical and extreme.

Salomon Sulzer (1804–1890) introduced musical innovations that had a lasting impact. From 1926 he officiated at the New Synagogue in Vienna. He elevated the office of cantor with his fine musicianship. Indeed Franz Schubert and Franz Liszt admired his singing. Sulzer's lasting contribution is his two-volume *Shir Zion* (vol. 1, 1840; vol. 2, 1866), a collection of his compositions and those of others that he commissioned. Sulzer preferred a straightforward lyrical melodic setting of a text and the refinement of traditional melodies. In addition, Sulzer sought to harmonize melodies within the prevailing rules of musical art of his time. Sulzer wrote out the music for the cantor and choir, with no improvisation or congregational singing allowed. He gained wide respect throughout Central Europe, and many cantors came to study with him. His impact on synagogue music was unprecedented and long lasting. He was the first to take the title *cantor*—the German title introduced in the eighteenth century by J. S. Bach—which replaced the word *hazzan*.

Louis Lewandowski (1821–1894) refined Sulzer's efforts. A choral director and composer, he served as the music director in Berlin at the Old Synagogue in the Heidereutergasse and after 1866 at the New Synagogue. His musical compositions appear in two well-known publications: *Kol Rinah U'T'fillah* (1871) for one and two voices; *Todah W'simrah* (1876–1882) for four voices and soli, with optional organ accompaniment. Lewandowski arranged traditional melodies and also wrote unique compositions both with and without *nusach* (musical modes of traditional Jewish prayer). His music had a major impact on both Reform and traditional synagogues throughout Central Europe and America from the nineteenth century well into the twentieth century.

The East European cantorial style, however, remained traditional. Few East European synagogues incorporated the reforms commonly found in Central Europe. Traditional melodies and nusach remained pervasive in the region. Still, some cantors came to Vienna to study with Sulzer and incorporated his musical innovations in a style appropriate for the East European region. Nissan Blumenthal (1805–1903) was born in the Ukraine and introduced German-style music at the Brody synagogue in Odessa. He founded a choir school in 1841 and developed choral singing in four voices. Eliezer Gerovich (1844–1913), a student of Blumenthal, began as a hazzan at the Choral Synagogue in Berdichev. Students of these cantors and others immigrated to America in the early twentieth century.

The hallmark of the East European style is the use of recurring melodic fragments intent on conveying a deep emotional feeling to the congregation. Ornate musical embellishments were used to transport the listener into a spiritual realm. Word repetition was not uncommon. The nicely patterned Central European phrases came to be known as *hazzanut ha-seder*—orderly hazzanut—whereas the free and ornate East European style was known as *hazzanut ha-regesh*—emotional hazzanut. This latter style became the foundation for the Golden Age of the cantorate, which took hold in America during the first few decades of the twentieth century. Although distinct styles, hazzanut ha-seder and hazzanut ha-regesh were also intermingled.

By the mid-nineteenth century, Reform synagogues in America used the music that was current in Europe, predominantly that of Sulzer and Lewandowski, as well as the music of American composers. The new music by nineteenth-century American synagogue composers included that of Sigmund Schlesinger (1835–1906) and Edward Stark (1856–1918), whose music was devoid of traditional prayer modes. Schlesinger was an organist at a synagogue in Mobile, Alabama, who used operatic excerpts from Bellini, Donizetti, and Rossini in synagogue services, although he changed the words. Stark, a cantor at Temple Emanu-El in San Francisco, used some traditional melodies but his compositions were unsophisticated. Hungarian-born Alois Kaiser (1840–1908), an apprentice to Sulzer, after serving communities in Vienna (1859–1863) and Prague (1863–1866), immigrated to America in 1866 and became the cantor for Congregation Ohab Shalom in

The opening of the Hebrew Union School of Sacred Music in New York, 1948. (American Jewish Archives)

Baltimore. His collections of synagogue music include hymnal compositions, melodies with four-part chorale settings, following the Lutheran model of J. S. Bach.

Isaac Mayer Wise (1819–1900), the progenitor of American Reform Judaism, coined the term *Minhag Amerika* to refer to the American modification of Jewish traditions. Originally the title of a prayer book published in 1857, the term now refers more generally to the Americanization of European Jewish traditions. Wise and other rabbis of his era believed that communal hymn singing was the quintessential religious experience. In 1892 the Central Conference of American Rabbis (CCAR) resolved to adopt Wise's hymnbook as the official one of American Jewish Reform Congregations. In discussing the resolution, rabbis commented that they sing a good deal of non-Jewish music out of necessity because few Jewish composers value

hymns. Rabbi Adolph Guttman (1854–1927), of Syracuse, New York, recognized the power of Christian worship to be the communal singing of hymns. By 1912 the first edition of the Wise hymnal had been deemed a failure, since the hymns did not contain traditional Jewish melodies, and rabbis encouraged cantors to create a more effective one. Although hymn singing remained a part of many Reform congregations through the 1950s, it fell out of fashion as worship styles changed to include cantorial and choral singing.

Resettlement and the rising tide of secularism posed strong challenges to the religious life of Jewish immigrants. The period between the World Wars was a time of reorientation, as rabbis sought to craft a role for the synagogue that would be relevant to American Jewish life. Similarly, composers sought to make the music in American synagogues a viable religious experience. They gave much attention to preparing new compositions for the synagogue, as well as to teaching and writing about Jewish music. The Jewish Music Forum (1939–1962) addressed many musical and liturgical issues and encouraged a range of musical activity, from the gathering of composers for discussion to conferences, concerts, and compositions. This organization fueled the development of American cantorial schools in each of the major denominations: Reform, School of Sacred Music at Hebrew Union College–Jewish Institute of Religion in 1948; Conservative, the Cantor's Institute at the Jewish Theological Seminary in 1950; Orthodox, Yeshiva University's program in 1954. Graduates of these training programs formed professional cantorial societies: Reform, American Conference of Cantors; Conservative, Cantor's Assembly; Orthodox, Cantorial Conference of America. The goal of each movement was to create a new form of Jewish liturgical music that was distinct from that of the previous century.

The period 1880 to 1930 is considered the Golden Age of the cantorate. The cantors associated with the Golden Age were born and trained in Eastern Europe, and came to America after the turn of the century. Some had regular pulpits for the entire year and others were engaged only for the High Holidays, when they commanded large fees. This musical liturgical artistry proliferated through radio broadcasts, 78-rpm recordings, and concerts. Great cantors include Yossele Rosenblatt (1882–1933), Leib Glantz (1898–1964), Mordecai Hershman (1888–1940), Leibele Waldman (1907–1969), Pierre Pinchik (1900–1971), and Moshe Koussevitzky (1899–1966) and his brother David. So admired were these cantors that people came from long distances to hear them sing at concerts and services. The Golden Age of the cantorate uniquely fused vocal artistry and impassioned prayer in a distinctive style that, for many, has become the definitive form of hazzanut.

By the early 1960s the growth of Jewish institutions had a direct effect on contemporary Jewish music and on the role of the cantor. Paradoxically, up to the 1950s, and even more so since, the role of the cantor increased in status, but the musical artistry of hazzanut decreased. The cantor became prayer leader, musical expert, music teacher, facilitator, educator, pastoral counselor, and administrator. The hazzan as star performer came to an end. The cantor who just sang artistic renditions of liturgical music became increasingly less common. The changed musical role of a cantor reflected the needs of American

Judaism for a more accessible music that engenders participation in a familiar—and less European—aesthetic. As cantors assumed pastoral responsibilities as counselors and chaplains, they gained recognition in the Reform and Conservative movements as co-clergy, even officiating at life-cycle events.

In the last two decades of the twentieth century, women entered the cantorate. Women now led services and were accepted as clergy. In the mid-1970s the Reform movement invested the first female cantor, and in the mid-1980s the Conservative movement did the same. The Orthodox movement does not allow women to be cantors or clergy. By 2005, women comprised 52 percent of the membership of the Reform movement's American Conference of Cantors. Women now serve in leadership positions and hold half the senior cantorial positions in large congregations. Women comprise 30 percent of the members of the Conservative movement's Cantor's Assembly. Participating for two decades, they occupy mostly midsized and small congregations, and have limited leadership positions.

During the second quarter of the twentieth century, composers sought to make the music of the synagogue more compatible with contemporary musical styles. Composers such as Abraham Binder (1895–1966), Isadore Freed (1900–1960), and Lazare Weiner (1897–1982) sought to adapt traditional cantorial melodies, melodic style, and harmonies to a more modern musical framework. In 1933 Ernest Bloch (1880–1959), a well-known American composer, premiered his *Avodath Hakodesh* (Sacred Service) for cantor, choir, orchestra, and narrator to much acclaim, elevating this work of Jewish liturgy to the status of an oratorio. Toward the middle of the twentieth century, Max Helfman (1901–1963) and Max Janowski (1912–1991) wrote compositions that are commonly sung in American Reform and Conservative congregations for the High Holidays: Helfman's *"Sh'ma Koleinu"* and Janowski's *"Avinu Malkeinu."*

During the second half of the twentieth century, composers such as Michael Isaacson drew from a variety of musical styles, both classical and contemporary, for their synagogue compositions. They are also influenced by folk, popular, and Israeli-style songs. Debbie Friedman, whose popularity increased in the 1980s and 1990s, is representative, drawing her music from folk and soft rock styles. Today cantors in Reform synagogues use all these diverse musical styles.

The approach to music in Conservative synagogues is similar. Traditional melodies may be more common in Conservative synagogues, but these melodies are, in fact, less than a hundred years old. Abraham Goldfarb (1879–1956) arrived in the United States in 1893 from Poland and studied at the Jewish Theological Seminary. He produced many books and pamphlets of synagogue melodies that are regularly sung in synagogues and home rituals at the beginning of the twenty-first century. The *havurah* movement began in the 1970s, seeking to empower the laity to participate in services and further their knowledge and education about Judaism. The result has been an increase in congregational involvement throughout the service. The cantor often functions as an educator and facilitator for congregational participation. But, particularly on the High Holidays and for special events, liturgical music can be heard that combines the artistry of cantorial recitatives, taken from or inspired by the Golden Age of the cantorate, compositions based on the traditional use of prayer modes, and liturgical chants. Volunteer and professional choirs are also used.

In Orthodox synagogues, music serves a more functional purpose. Although a paid professional cantor is common in Reform and Conservative synagogues, it is rare in these synagogues. The prayer leader in an Orthodox synagogue keeps vocal embellishments to a minimum. Congregational involvement is interspersed throughout the service. As in the other branches of Judaism, traditional melodies are more commonly heard on the High Holidays. In many Orthodox synagogues a hazzan may only be employed during the holidays; on the other days a congregant serves in this role. Orthodox congregations also differ in their use of nusach. Some prefer Israeli melodies or tunes from songs popular in the Orthodox community for the highlighted portions of the prayer, such as the *kedusha* in the Sabbath morning service. Rabbi Shlomo Carlebach (1925–1994) combined the participatory ease of folk music, the energy of the new music from Israel, and the religious fervor of the Hasidic *niggun* (melody), and succeeded in moving liturgical music out of the synagogue into a wide range of other settings. The "Carlebach Synagogue" in New York, where he served as rabbi from his father's death in the 1970s to 1994, is known for lengthy services with much singing. Since Shlomo Carlebach's death, services deriving from this style have spread throughout America and to Jewish communities across the world.

The three major denominations of American Judaism all have similar concerns with respect to new music in the synagogue. At issue is both the role of the cantor as prayer facilitator and the participation of the congregation. The rhythmically precise Central European and the rhythmically free East European traditions have been combined in varying ways in American congregations. Whereas Reform synagogues were once the source of artistic innovation, this trend has diminished in favor of participatory services. Trained cantors and some congregants desire to utilize music that draws on the rich musical history of the Jewish tradition. Other congregants choose a more accessible musical service that facilitates their participation in an idiom they prefer. Although the Jewish musical tradition from which they draw includes Hasidic and Israeli melodies, folk and popular styles predominate.

While some decry the lack of artistry in the continual popular influence on liturgical music, others have embraced it as a way to encourage synagogue attendance. The popular trends reflect the influences of, and the gradual adaptation to, American culture. The process of adapting musical influences to the surrounding culture has long been a part of synagogue music's history.

The non-Ashkenazic communities in America, though few in number, provide a contrast with the Ashkenazim. Sephardic Jews, commonly defined as the Jews from Spain and their descendants in various areas of relocation, differ in their traditions because they have been influenced by many distinct cultures. Although the Sephardim who arrived in America in the seventeenth century were originally from Spain or Portugal, those who immigrated in the late nineteenth and early twentieth centuries came from Morocco, Turkey, Syria, Iran, Iraq, Bukhara, and Yemen. In general, their synagogues followed the prayer style of their country of origin. In the years after migration, however, the communities varied in their degree of adherence to premigratory customs. The traditional liturgical melodies of early immigrants were regularly maintained in these communities. Recently, some Sephardic congregations—for example, Syrian synagogues in Brooklyn and Turkish synagogues in Seattle—have employed a professional, paid cantor. Most congregations, however, are led by a lay cantor. Sephardic communities, like American Ashkenazic congregations, struggle to hold onto the past, even as they innovate in the present.

Mark Kligman

References and Further Reading

Binder, A. W. 1971. *Studies in Jewish Music: Collected Writings of A. W. Binder,* edited by Irene Heskes. New York: Bloch Publishing Company.

Heskes, Irene. 1994. "Three Hundred Years of Jewish Music in America." In *Passport to Jewish Music: Its History, Traditions, and Culture,* 177–226. Westport, CT: Greenwood Press.

Kligman, Mark. 2000. "Music." In *The Jews of the Middle East and North Africa in Modern Times,* edited by Reeva Simon, Michael Laskier, and Sara Reuger, 224–234. New York: Columbia University Press. (Compact disc of musical examples discussed in this chapter accompanies the book.)

Landman, Leo. 1972. *The Cantor: An Historic Perspective.* New York: Yeshiva University.

Pasternak, Velvel, and Noah Schall. 1991. *The Golden Age of Cantors.* Cedarhurst, NY: Tara Publications.

Schleifer, Eliyahu. 1995. "Current Trends of Liturgical Music in the Ashkenazi Synagogue." *The World of Music* 37,1: 59–72.

Slobin, Mark. 1989. *Chosen Voices: The Story of the American Cantorate.* Urbana: University of Illinois Press.

Walton, Janet, and Lawrence Hoffman, eds. 1992. *Sacred Sound and Social Change: Liturgical Music in Jewish and Christian Experience.* Notre Dame, IN: University of Notre Dame Press.

Jews in Rock 'n' Roll

At first glance, Jews in rock 'n' roll seems to be only a slightly more promising subject than Jewish sumo wrestlers. Derived—or stolen—from rhythm and blues (R&B) and country music, rock 'n' roll attracted African Americans and Southern whites as its greatest performers throughout the 1950s. The music of Chuck Berry, Little Richard, Elvis Presley, and Jerry Lee Lewis was not designed by (or for) the stereotypical Jewish sensibility. Rock 'n' roll, E. Anthony Rotundo has suggested, appeals more to feelings than to ideas, more to the beat than to the lyrics; it is more passionate than ironic, more spontaneous than studious, more libidinal than sublimating. Consequently, Rotundo asserts, Jews have had less influence on rock 'n' roll than on any other form of popular entertainment (1982). And yet, the impact of Jews on rock 'n' roll from the 1950s into the twenty-first century has been significant. In the 1950s Jews provided the capital to produce and distribute the music and played a pivotal role in injecting rock 'n' roll into the white mainstream. In the 1960s and 1970s, as rock became more socially and politi-

cally conscious, Jewish musicians and singers proliferated while Jewish producers and promoters remained active off stage. Since then, as Jews in the United States have challenged some of the characteristics attributed to them, Jewish performers have strummed, strutted, screamed, and smashed their way to stardom in heavy metal, punk, grunge, rap, hip hop, and virtually every other incarnation of rock music.

Although country and rhythm and blues had found a niche in some theaters, jukeboxes, and radio stations by the early 1950s, the major record companies—Capitol, Columbia, Decca, Mercury, MGM, and RCA—stuck with the romantic ballads of established stars such as Frank Sinatra, Perry Como, Bing Crosby, and Nat King Cole. As they had in many other businesses, Jewish entrepreneurs seized an opportunity that others thought marginal and, given the "smutty" lyrics sung by African Americans, rather tawdry as well. They aimed initially at Southerners and the substantial number of blacks who had migrated to cities in the North after World War II. Between 1948 and 1954, a thousand independent record labels were established, many of them specializing in R&B. "I looked for an area neglected by the majors," acknowledged Art Rupe (born Arthur Goldberg), the founder of Specialty Records in Los Angeles, "and in essence took the crumbs off the table in the record industry" (Altschuler 2003). Not every owner of an important "indie" was Jewish. Vee Jay in Chicago, and Peacock and Duke Records in Houston, for example, had black owners. But the vast majority were. In addition to Rupe, Jewish producers included Phil and Leonard Chess, whose name is known to all blues fans; Syd Nathan, a pawnbroker, amusement park concessionaire, and wrestling impressario in Cincinnati whose King and Federal labels featured country and R&B; Leo, Edward, and Ida Messner, whose Aladdin Records had a brief run of R&B hits; and Herb Abramson and Jerry Wexler, partners of Ahmet Ertegun (the son of a Turkish ambassador) at the soon-to-be-legendary Atlantic Records.

Bottom-line businessmen, indie owners ruthlessly cut costs to stay afloat. In the 1950s high-quality recording equipment was relatively inexpensive, and they discovered that they could pay composers and performers as little as $10 and a case of whisky per song while assigning copyright to themselves. "The way an 'indie' survives," claimed Herman Lubinsky, the owner of Savoy Records, "you don't pay anybody" (Lisheron 1997). Little wonder, then, that breakeven for a record could be reached with a sale of 1,500 units. Little wonder, too, that Jewish owners acquired a reputation for exploiting rock 'n' roll artists. The owners subsequently insisted that they were using practices common in the industry and were no more exploitative than non-Jewish indie producers or, for that matter, the major record companies. "People forget these Jewish fellows in the business were entrepreneurs who spent their money to make hit records," said Art Sheridan, who ran Chance Records in Chicago. "There wasn't any altruism at the time any more than there is today in the music business. The singers wanted to be heard. They wanted to sell records. There were just as many artists who ran out on their contracts or who borrowed against their appearance fees as there were record executives who took advantage of the artists" (Lisheron 1997).

These disclaimers notwithstanding, many producers justified Bo Diddley's charge that R&B really meant "Ripoffs & Bullshit." Nonetheless, the Jewish owners should not be dismissed simply as parasites. With a few exceptions, they exhibited a genuine, if paternalistic, affection for the African Americans with whom they worked and a commitment to toleration and equal opportunity born of their own experience with bigotry. Rupe recalled that the neighborhood he grew up in near Pittsburgh had so many blacks he looked "like a sugar cube in a coal bin" in his class picture: "What bonded us was to a culture shaped by our similar status, not our ethnicity." In 1950, Rupe recorded Percy Mayfield's R&B hit, "Please Send Me Someone to Love," a plea for an end to prejudice, "this damnable sin" (Lisheron 1997). So tyrannical that singer James Brown called him Little Caeser, Syd Nathan always insisted, "We pay for ability and ability has no color, no race, no religion" (Lisheron 1997). Nathan made sure that King Records was integrated, from the factory floor up to the offices of middle managers. Leonard Chess, according to his son, saw blacks as fellow immigrants who wanted what he wanted: freedom and money. He could be stingy with royalties, but also assisted performers when they were on dope or down on their luck. The relationship between Jewish producer and African American performer, then, was complicated. The owners often deprived performers of the financial rewards to which they were entitled, but in a racist society where economic options for blacks were limited, they helped talented artists find their audiences and advance their careers.

Many of the owners had little affinity for the music they produced. When Syd Nathan heard James Brown's "Please, Please, Please," he thought the singer was stuttering. Expecting a "big band sound expressed in a churchy way," Art Rupe hesitated to distribute Little Richard's "Tutti Frutti" (Altschuler 2003). But one of the Jewish producers, Jerry Wexler, made a significant and lasting impression on the aesthetics of rock 'n' roll, combining the soul of Southern gospel with the sounds of Southern country music. Born and raised in Manhattan, Wexler was the son of a Polish immigrant, who eked out a living as a window washer. Saddled with a bearded Hebrew teacher, who smelled from garlic and used his ruler to discipline wayward students, he rejected the Orthodox Judaism of his parents. Wexler discovered rhythm and blues, and he journeyed to Harlem where he would "sit and drink and watch the smoothest, most spectacular dancers pulsate to the smoking beat" (Lisheron 1997). After a stint in the Army and a degree in journalism at Kansas State, he landed a job with *Billboard* magazine, making a name for himself by changing the title of the publication's "Race Music" charts to "Rhythm & Blues." The latter phrase, he argued, was "more appropriate to more enlightened times" (Lisheron 1997). In 1951, Wexler left *Billboard* for MGM; he moved to Atlantic in 1953 and built a reputation for discovering new talent and coaxing superior performances out of veterans. He encouraged Ray Charles to sing the blues as he would in church, providing him with a female choir to respond to "Hallelujah I Love Her So." He produced four classics by the Dominoes, who in other hands would pretty-up and water down their sublime gospel harmonies. And he helped breathe new life into the career of Big Joe Turner, an R&B shouter from Kansas City, who recorded "Shake, Rattle, and Roll" and "Corrine, Corrina" for Atlantic.

Wexler's greatest contribution to rock 'n' roll came in the 1960s. Working with Aretha Franklin, Wilson Pickett, and Sam and Dave, he helped make possible the rise of soul music. With these artists, as with Ray Charles, Wexler encouraged a return to blues and gospel roots, producing Aretha's "Do Right Woman" and "(You Make Me Feel Like) A Natural Woman." In presenting him with a lifetime achievement award for the Blues Foundation in 1995, Al Bell of Stax/Volt Records, the legendary Memphis label, called Wexler "the mother and father of what became known as R&B and then soul music. He heard it, he loved it, he respected it and he taught America and then the world to love and respect it" (Lisheron 1997). In the last third of the twentieth century, Wexler remained active and influential, working with, among many others, the Rolling Stones, Bob Dylan, Willie Nelson, and Dire Straits.

In the early 1950s, the Jewish producers helped introduce rhythm and blues to new audiences, especially white teenagers who listened to it late at night on local radio stations and journeyed to neighborhoods whose theaters presented a multicultural musical fare. But the indies had neither the capital nor the clout to make the music a mass culture phenomenon. In 1953 R&B records still accounted for a small fraction of total record sales. Elvis Presley, Chuck Berry, Little Richard, and Bill Haley changed all that. Wildly popular in live concerts, they made radio, television, and the major record companies sit up and take notice.

Integral to this process as well was a Jewish disc jockey, Alan Freed, the man who gave rock 'n' roll its name. Born near Johnstown, Pennsylvania, in 1921, Freed commenced his love affair with broadcasting while a student at Ohio State. He spun platters in Akron, moving on to WJW radio in Cleveland in 1950. When Leo Mintz, the Jewish owner of Record Rendezvous, located near Cleveland's black ghetto, told him that white kids were flocking to his store in search of R&B records, Freed began to feature the music on his show. Although some adults complained he was a "nigger lover," Freed had made a shrewd choice. Since few stations hired African American disc jockeys, Freed had few on-air R&B rivals. Billing himself as the King of the Moondoggers, Freed rang a cowbell, slammed his hand on a telephone directory in time with the beat, and imitated a black patter. Black and white teenagers, in the city and the suburbs, tuned in, making the Moondog House the hottest show in town. The first white DJ in Cleveland to play "Crying in the Chapel" by the Orioles, Freed got the credit when 30,000 fans bought records of the song the next day.

In 1954, Freed moved to New York City, with a show in prime time on WINS radio. Callers bombarded the station, eager to know whether he was black or white. The advertising revenues of WINS skyrocketed. But in November, trouble found Freed, in the person of Thomas Louis Hardin, a blind street musician and composer, who often stationed himself near Carnegie Hall, with triangular drums he called trimbas, dressed like a Viking, asking

passersby for their loose change. Hardin had used the name Moondog for years and sued Freed for infringement. That Freed had, in fact, played Hardin's composition, "Moondog Symphony," on his show clinched the case. Judge Carroll Walter barred the disc jockey from using the name on his show.

Freed made a virtue of necessity. "Moondog House" became "Rock 'n' Roll Party." A black euphemism for sexual intercourse and for hot, danceable music, the term *rock 'n' roll* had been used in R&B songs for decades. Thus, Freed's claim that the phrase came to him in an inspirational flash is as dubious as his assertion that he used it to get rid of the racial stigma of rhythm and blues. Whatever his intentions, Freed hit the jackpot. Freed and WINS scrambled to copyright it, but the very ubiquity of the phrase made a copyright unenforceable. As if by magic, the new name enabled producers and promoters to market the music to a much broader audience. African American performers made a compelling case that rock 'n' roll was nothing more than a white adaptation of rhythm and blues. But by giving rock 'n' roll its name, Alan Freed invited millions of whites to believe in an immaculate conception of a distinctive, not a derivative, musical form.

Freed's career came crashing down at the end of the decade. Accused of taking "payola" in exchange for radio play, Freed lost his job. He stumbled on, often in an alcoholic haze, until his death in 1965. By then, rock 'n' roll disc jockeys, many of them Jewish, were filling the airwaves in New York. WINS replaced Freed in 1959 with Murray "The K" Kaufman, who was soon acclaimed as the best rock DJ in the city. Kaufman and "Cousin Brucie" Morrow, a Jewish DJ born in Brooklyn, were early promoters of the Beatles, helping extend the reach of rock 'n' roll into a new decade.

As a mass culture phenomenon, rock 'n' roll attracted many white performers. Their backgrounds varied, ranging from Pat Boone, a Southerner, to "schlock rocker" Fabian Forte, an Italian heartthrob from Philadelphia. Still, few Jews applied. Entrenched in Tin Pan Alley, which continued to churn out melodic, romantic ballads, Eddie Fisher, Steve Lawrence, and Edie Gormé had no incentive to experiment with a genre as controversial—and, they thought, faddish—as rock 'n' roll. In the decades to come, Neil Diamond, Barbra Streisand, Barry Manilow, Billy Joel, and Michael Bolton also took the path more traveled by. On occasion, as with Neil Sedaka, who reached the charts with "Oh! Carol," "Happy Birthday Sweet Sixteen," and "Breaking Up Is Hard to Do," a Jewish singer recorded a song best characterized as "rock light." Baby-faced, with a high-pitched voice, Sedaka had been selected by Arthur Rubinstein as one of the best pianists among high school students in New York City. A likely rock 'n' roll icon he was not.

Significantly, Sedaka was a songwriter as well. For better or worse, Jewish songwriters helped bring rock 'n' roll into the mainstream by turning out softer, more harmonic compositions, sometimes backed by lush orchestration, with lyrics exploring teenage love and angst. In the 1950s, "Doc" Pomus and the team of Leiber and Stoller parlayed their knowledge of R&B into songs with crossover appeal. Born Jerome Solon Felder in Brooklyn in 1925, Pomus found his calling as he listened to Big Joe Turner. Changing his name to hide his profession from his parents, who wanted him to become a doctor or an accountant, Pomus wrote songs for Turner and Ray Charles and, with Mort Shuman, more than twenty singles for Elvis. Pomus's biggest hits, sung by the Drifters, were the love songs "This Magic Moment," "Sweets for My Sweet," and the poignant "Save the Last Dance for Me." Explaining his shift to a more frothy fare, Pomus said, "Sometimes the superego has to take a holiday" (Billig 2001). Before he died in 1991, Pomus had written over a hundred Top Ten singles, for the likes of the Beatles, Bob Marley, Dolly Parton, Bruce Springsteen, Elvis Costello, and Andy Williams.

Jerry Leiber and Mike Stoller were both born in 1933, Leiber in Baltimore, Stoller in Belle Harbor, New York. Before they reached their teens, Leiber and Stoller were African American wannabes. Leiber's Irish and Polish friends fought with him, but the blacks remained loyal, each recognizing in the other an underdog. Stoller's life changed when at a camp in Hacketstown, New Jersey, he heard a black youngster play boogie-woogie piano. Stoller invited a black girl from Brooklyn to his prom at Forest Hills High School. "Blacks were warmer. They were sharper," he recalled. "Everything about them was somewhat heightened" (Lisheron 1997). Leiber and Stoller met after their families moved to Los Angeles and they decided to write "black songs" together. Unlike Pomus, they did not adopt less Jewish-sounding names. On the credits for "Dance with Me," in fact, they identified themselves as Louis Lebish and Irv Nathan. Leiber and Stoller hit paydirt with "Kansas City" for Wilbert Harrison, "Saved" for La-

Verne Baker, and, of course, "Hound Dog," for Willie Mae "Big Mama" Thornton (later covered by Elvis Presley). They were acclaimed for an uncanny ability to write in a black idiom and for writing about the street life of African Americans when few other songwriters dared to. But Leiber and Stoller also capitalized on—and reinforced—a more mainstream sound. "Yakety Yak" and "Charlie Brown" were novelty songs with mass appeal, and the team wrote or cowrote the ballads "There Goes My Baby," "On Broadway," and "Stand by Me."

In the late 1950s, Leiber and Stoller relocated to the Brill Building, 1619 Broadway in Manhattan, which housed a stable of songwriters, most of them Jewish. Although, for a time, as Michael Billig argues, rock 'n' roll "was coming from elsewhere" (Billig 2001), the move put an exclamation point on the convergence of Tin Pan Alley, pop, and rock 'n' roll in New York City. Working at the Brill Building (or at a branch office in Los Angeles), at one time or another, often for Jewish rock impresario Don Kirshner, were Sedaka, Al Kooper, Lou Adler, Barry Mann, Cynthia Weil, Carol King, Gerry Goffin, Herb Alpert, Hal David, and Burt Bacharach. Their output of soft rock 'n' roll hits was phenomenal. King and Goffin, for example, combined rhythm and blues with a classical sound to produce "Will You Still Love Me Tomorrow?" for the Shirelles, "Up on the Roof" for the Drifters, and the dance record, "Loco-Motion."

Another Brill alumnus was Phil Spector. Born in the Bronx in 1940, Spector wrote a million seller—the hummable, singable "To Know Him Is to Love Him"—when he was eighteen. The title phrase came from the inscription on his father's headstone in Beth David cemetery on Long Island. A brilliant and bizarre man, as well as an obsessive and controlling producer, Spector created the legendary "wall of sound" in the early 1960s for the Crystals, the Ronettes, and the Righteous Brothers. In what Spector grandiloquently called a "Wagnerian approach to rock and roll" (Billig 2001), the lyrics did not matter much. Through dubbing and mixing, horns, strings, and percussion were layered and blended, track on track, instrument on instrument. Spector is generally credited with revolutionizing the techniques of rock 'n' roll recording. In 1963, he added to the assimilation of rock 'n' roll into the musical mainstream (and, by implication, declared himself an assimilated Jew) by producing the rock album, *A Christmas Gift to You.*

With Elvis in the Army, Chuck Berry in jail, Little Richard in the ministry, Jerry Lee Lewis in disgrace, and Buddy Holly, the Big Bopper, and Ritchie Valens dead, rock 'n' roll languished between 1958 and 1963. The Beatles, the advance guard of the British Invasion, sparked American rock 'n' rollers to reinvent themselves. Jewish promoters helped bring the Fab Four to the United States. Brian Epstein stumbled across the group in a Liverpool club in 1962. Although he had no experience in the business, Epstein became the Beatles' manager. A year later, Sid Bernstein, an executive with General Artists Corporation, who had been reading British newspapers to stay abreast of musical trends, tracked down Epstein and hammered out a deal to bring the Beatles to the United States.

Opening for the Beatles in their first concert held in Washington, D.C., was Jay and the Americans, a "rock light" band composed of five Jewish vocalists. As a teenager in Brooklyn, Jay Black (born David Blatt) was inspired by African American "do-wop" groups "in a way that made me crazy, in an emotional way" (Benarde 2003). The band's hits included "Come a Little Bit Closer." Although they adopted a Broadway sound by 1964, with "Only in America" and a recording of "Some Enchanted Evening" from the musical *South Pacific*, Jay and the Americans were on the bill with the Rolling Stones during their tour of the United States in 1965.

Spurred by the civil rights movement and anti–Vietnam War protest, rock 'n' roll became more political in the 1960s and 1970s. As lyrics relevant to the issues of the day became *de rigueur*, Jews found their way to the stage. Given the traditional commitment of Jews to civil rights and social justice, this may have been inevitable, but, as Jakob Dylan, leader of the alternative rock group, the Wallflowers, has observed, "maybe it took the guts of one Jewish kid from Minnesota to stick the smug face of Brando to the ferocious danger of the faraway south" (Oseary 2001). He was referring, of course, to his father, Bob Dylan.

Robert Zimmerman was an outcast as a kid, who took Elvis as his model. His first incarnation as Bob Dylan, however, was as a folk singer, militant in his opposition to racial injustice and the Vietnam War. Famous for the exquisite "Blowin' in the Wind," Dylan stunned his fans in 1965 when he appeared in a black leather jacket and sang "Like a Rolling Stone," backed by an electric band. Initially booed for betraying folk music with a harsh and unnatural sound, Dylan soon gained an even larger following, placing several albums in the Top Ten. In subsequent years, he transformed himself musically several more times, and in the late 1970s he declared himself a fundamentalist Christian. But he left in his wake a musical legacy: "folk rock," consisting of gentle harmonies, sometimes attached to cultural and political messages, amplified by electric strings and drums in a rock backbeat.

Folk rock flourished in the mid-1960s, with Jews among its most accomplished performers. Behind singers Cass Elliot (born Ellen Naomi Cohen) and Michelle Phillips (born Holly Michelle Gilliam), for example, the Mamas and the Papas, dressed in tie-dyed outfits, produced a breezy, West Coast sound, climbing the charts with "Monday, Monday," "Dedicated to the One I Love," and "California Dreamin'." Zal Yanofsky, a Canadian Jew who was fluent in Hebrew and Yiddish, was the cofounder, guitarist, singer, and songwriter for the Lovin' Spoonful. The group blended folk, blues, and rock in what was dubbed "good time" music. Their hits included "Do You Believe in Magic?" "Did You Ever Have to Make Up Your Mind?" and "Summer in the City."

Next to Dylan, the most important Jewish folk rockers were Paul Simon and Art Garfunkel. Raised in Queens, New York, they teamed up as Tom and Jerry (two cartoon characters), scored a modest hit in high school, went their separate ways, then reunited as folk singers in Greenwich Village. Mindful of Bob Dylan's success, producer Tom Wilson took "The Sound of Silence," written by Simon and recorded in 1964, overdubbed an electric guitar, bass, and drums, and re-released it a year later as a single. Number one on the charts, the song made Simon and Garfunkel famous. Although his music lacked an insistent beat, Simon's themes of alienation and missed communication resonated with fans of rock as well as folk. Before Dylan, folk music had a middle-American Protestant provenance, identified with the likes of Woody Guthrie, Pete Seeger, and Burl Ives. Simon and Garfunkel opened the genre to a suburban, Jewish sensibility. With Garfunkel's crystalline countertenor voice and Simon's tunes, lyrics, and arrangements, the pair recorded hit after hit over the next five years, winning five Grammy awards. "Homeward Bound," "I Am a Rock," "America," "Scarborough Fair," "Mrs. Robinson," and "Bridge over Troubled Waters" became pop classics.

In 1970, Simon and Garfunkel split up. While Garfunkel had modest success as an actor and singer, Simon became one of the premier singer/songwriters in the United States, with eclectic and shifting interests in reggae, gospel, jazz, and the music of South Africa and Brazil. His solo albums drew on the musical structures of rock 'n' roll more than his work with Garfunkel had in the 1960s.

Jews were visible in "acid rock" bands of the 1960s and 1970s as well. All five of the original members of Country Joe and the Fish were Jewish. Formed in San Francisco in 1965, the band had one of the most overtly political, antiwar acts of the era. "The Jewish experience is unique," said band member Barry Melton only half facetiously, "in that you're able to engage in social commentary because you don't have a country. You're always ready to move. I wouldn't be here if some people had not been smart enough to move" (Benarde 2003). In most of their concerts, the Fish led the audience in chanting a famous four-letter word. Arrested for inciting audience lewdness in Worcester, Massachusetts, Country Joe McDonald asked a half million people in Woodstock, New York, to join him in the very same chant less than a year later. Other standout Jewish rockers of this era are singer/songwriter Laura Nyro (born Laura Nigro), Donald Fagen and Walter Becker of Steely Dan, Peter Green (born Peter Greenbaum) of Fleetwood Mac, Robbie Krieger of the Doors, Steve Katz and Al Kooper of the Blues Project and Blood, Sweat, and Tears, Peter Wolf and Seth Justman of the J. Geils Band, and Mickey Hart, drummer for the legendary Grateful Dead.

The Dead's preferred concert promoter was the almost equally legendary Bill Graham (born Wolfgang Grajonca). He was born in Berlin, Germany, in 1931, two days before his father died in a construction accident, and was placed in an orphanage so that his mother could work. When war broke out in 1939, Wolfgang was in Paris on an exchange program. After two harrowing years, the Red Cross brought the youngster, who weighed forty-four pounds and did not speak a word of English, to New York City. His mother died in a Nazi concentration camp. He became an American citizen in 1949 and changed his name to Graham. Not surprisingly, of all the Jews in rock 'n' roll, Graham was the most publicly committed to Judaism (he founded the Bill Graham Menorah Project to recognize Hanukkah in San Francisco) and one of the most politically engaged.

Winner of a bronze star and a purple heart during the Korean War, Graham returned to New York, completed his degree in business administration at City College, worked as an aspiring actor, then drifted to California where he became a business manager and concert organizer. By 1965, his knack for dealing with square politicians and decidedly less symmetrical rock musicians (despite a famously bad temper) made him the impresario of Fillmore Auditorium in San Francisco—and, a short while later, of Fillmore East in New York City. Every important rock act, it seemed, wanted to work with him, including Jefferson Airplane, the Doors, the Who, and the Dead. Graham provided superior lighting and sound equipment, treated creative artists with respect, and insisted that audiences get their money's worth.

In 1971, citing the escalating fees of performers, agents who forced promoters to take inferior acts to get a headliner, and the deteriorating taste of audiences, Graham closed Fillmore East and Fillmore West. He continued to book shows, often at Winterland in San Francisco, organized concert tours (taking Bob Dylan across America in 1974 and putting on "The Last Waltz" of the Band two years later), started record labels, founded an advertising company called Chutzpah, and built a rock merchandising company that grossed more than $100 million dollars a year.

Graham continued to enlist rock in progressive political causes. He organized a peace concert in the Soviet Union and two Amnesty International tours, enlisted marquee rockers to perform for Live Aid, and raised money for AIDS research and the Haight-Ashbury Free Medical Clinic. "What the fuck are you doing for human rights?" he would scream at performers, friends, and reporters. Graham died in a helicopter crash in 1991. After he played "I Love You Much Too Much," a 1940s tune Graham loved, for the 2,000 mourners packed into Temple Emanu-El in San Francisco for the funeral, guitarist Carlos Santana recalled Graham as "a true lion of Judah. He walked like a lion, and he lived like a lion" (Goldberg 1991).

In 1982, E. Anthony Rotundo speculated that as the baby boomers aged, acid rock might give way to a softer, smoother sound, with increasing emphasis on lyrics. With their traditions of study, storytelling, and social commitment, Jews would then gravitate toward rock in much larger numbers, as performers as well as producers. With lyrics "more prominent and contemplative," Jewish songwriters would flourish in rock, too (Rotundo 1982).

Jews have, indeed, remained influential as producers of rock 'n' roll. David Geffen is the paradigmatic example.

Born in Brooklyn, the son of a corset maker and a Western Union telegraph operator, Geffen was a college dropout who worked his way up from the mail room of the William Morris agency in Los Angeles to booking agent to multimedia mogul. In his twenties, Geffen helped catapult Laura Nyro and Jackson Browne to stardom, and encouraged Crosby, Stills, Nash, and Young to join forces. His Asylum Records, established in 1970, released hits by Joni Mitchell and Linda Ronstadt. Following the sale of Asylum and a misdiagnosis of cancer, Geffen started Geffen Records in 1980. Guns N' Roses, Aerosmith, Whitesnake, and Nirvana helped make it one of the premier labels in the music industry. As the 1980s ended, he sold out to MCA for more than $500 million.

Although a softer, "California" sound did not dominate rock in the 1980s, and lyrics were neither more prominent nor more contemplative, a substantial number of Jewish rockers did emerge. With the sexual revolution, mounting pride among "unmeltable ethnics," the victory of Israel in the Yom Kippur War, and the airing of the TV miniseries *Holocaust* in 1978, the sense of self among many young American Jews was changing. Jews were more willing to call attention to themselves as Jews, to be more physical, more libidinal, more assertive in public. While a relatively small number joined Meir Kahane's Jewish Defense League, many more American Jews resolved that "never again" would they fail to resist anyone who sought to harm the Jewish people. "Americans," said Pete Brown, Jewish songwriter for the rock group Cream, "are much less afraid of being Jewish; they hide it less" (Benarde 2003). Truer in the 1960s, when rock singer and guitarist Michael Bloomfield recorded "I'm Glad I'm Jewish," than in the 1950s, Brown's observation is particularly apposite for the contemporary United States.

Jews, then, were ready to strut their stuff in "heavy metal music," the dominant rock genre of the 1980s. Also known as "cock rock," heavy metal is masculine, aggressive, boastful, physical: bodies are on display, mikes and guitars are explicitly phallic, females are degraded in the lyrics and the videos, and the music is loud, amplified and distorted, and rhythmically insistent, suggesting arousal and release. Several Jews played important roles in creating heavy metal. As manager and songwriter for Blue Öyster Cult in the 1970s, Sandy Pearlman used laser lights on stage, soon to be a staple in concerts, and created a stage persona, Buck Dharma, for guitarist David Raeser that was not unlike

David Bowie's character Ziggy Stardust. With his heavy makeup, tattered clothing, leather pants, and rainbow-colored mop of curly hair, Dee Snider, the Long Island–born lead singer of Twisted Sister, inspired the terms *Hair Band* and *Hair Metal*. Interestingly, the group's biggest hit was entitled "We're Not Gonna Take It." Scott Ian (born Scott Rosenfeld) of Anthrax, whose song "I'm the Man" went platinum, Slash (Saul Hudson), guitarist for Guns N' Roses, Marty Friedman, guitarist for Megadeath, and the Cavalera brothers, Max and Igor, of the Brazilian band Sepultura were other Jewish heavy metal "bad boys."

Jewish performers could also have it both ways, mocking the over-the-top masculinity they were displaying. Gene Simmons (born Chaim Witz) and Paul Stanley (born Stanley Harvey Eisen) have flourished for decades as KISS, the heavy metal band "without a face," whose performers cavorted on stage in sequined black and silver outfits and sparkling makeup, presiding over an elaborate pyrotechnic show. With an action comic book by Marvel and an animated TV special to their credit, KISS has sold more than 70 million albums. With the band Van Halen, and then as a solo performer, David Lee Roth has also winked at and capitalized on a heavy metal sound. With a long mane of blond hair, skintight spandex pants, and a reputation as a party animal, Roth was the master of the music video. In "Jump," for example, during his acrobatic leaps, the camera lingered on the generative component of his anatomy. Fans variously thought Roth a stud, androgynous, or a put-on.

Well represented in heavy metal, Jews have also had a substantial impact on punk rock, a strident, sometimes discordant music, driven by disturbing, despairing, and violent lyrics. Malcolm McLaren, a Jew, was punk's founding father. Born in London, England, in 1946, McLaren attended art school in the 1960s, where he encountered the work of Internationale Situationist, a Marxist/Dadaist group that advocated staging events that would help persuade working men and women to "demand the impossible." Proprietor of Let It Rock, a shop in London that sold modish clothing, McClaren became manager of the band the New York Dolls, organizing their Better Dead Than Red Tour before returning to England as the owner of Sex, a store featuring S&M paraphernalia. From his young, urban customers, he selected members of the Sex Pistols. With lead singer Johnny Rotten, who swore, spat, scratched his face with needles, butted out cigarettes on his arm, and screamed "I hate you" at the audience, the Sex Pistols were a sensation on both sides of the Atlantic in the mid-1970s. Following the all-too-real-violence of band member Sid Vicious, the Sex Pistols disintegrated, but McClaren stayed active, with a film, *The Great Rock 'n' Roll Swindle,* a new group (Bow Wow Wow), a mercifully brief career as a singer, a stint as adviser to singers Adam Ant and Boy George, and as a promoter of hip hop.

But before the Sex Pistols burst on the scene, Lou Reed was acquiring a reputation that would make him the God-father of Punk in the United States. A native of Freeport, Long Island, Reed was the son of a stay-at-home mom and an accountant, who changed the family name from Rabinowitz. At Syracuse University, he became friends with the poet Delmore Schwartz, who encouraged him to bring a literary sensibility to rock 'n' roll. As his song "I Wanna Be Black" indicates, Reed used rock music to break with the middle-class Jewish culture of his parents. With John Cale, he founded the Velvet Underground, serving as singer, songwriter, and instrumentalist. At a time when folk rock and the "California sound" were popular, the Underground played a loud, electronic, dissonant music, behind narratives about the seamy, menacing side of urban life. "I'm Waiting for the Man" and "Heroin," for example, explored the drug underworld. A bit ahead of its time, the Velvet Underground did not have great commercial success and disbanded in 1970. Reed then launched a solo career. He continued to explore street life, prostitution, and sexual transgression in "Walk on the Wild Side," which has become a rock classic, and held fifteen-minute "fuzz sessions," reminiscent of his days with the Underground. He has had many other musical incarnations as well, some of them parodic, ranging from hillbilly to pop metallist, replete with bleached hair and painted fingernails.

The non-Jewish Sex Pistols, Patti Smith, Iggy Pop, and David Bowie established punk as the edgy, arty, and trendy music of the mid-1970s. But Jews added fuel to the fire. In 1976 Jeffrey Hyman, a Jew from Forest Hills, New York, drummer, singer, and songwriter, became Joey Ramone, forming a group that assumed his new surname. Featuring fast, loud songs, invariably less than three minutes long with no solos, the Ramones became an underground phenomenon in the United States and the United Kingdom. In the late 1970s, with Jewish guitarist Mick Jones, the Clash emerged as the most politically conscious band of their era, exploring race relations, unemployment, police violence, and Arab–Israeli relations in "White

Riot," "Career Opportunities," "Know Your Rights," and "Rock the Casbah."

One of the most successful groups to come out of punk rock is Beastie Boys. All three Beastie Boys—Mike D (born Michael Diamond), MCA (born Adam Yauch), and Ad-Rock (born Adam Horovitz)—are Jews, raised in middle-class families in New York City. Immersed in the punk culture of the city as teenagers, Diamond and Yauch formed a band in 1981. Two years later, Horovitz, a former member of the Young and the Useless, became the third Beastie Boy. Almost immediately the trio began experimenting with a rock-inflected style of rap. The result in 1983 was "Cookie Puss," a rap record based on a prank phone call they had made to a Carvel Ice Cream store. The single was a hit among rap connoisseurs in New York. Ever the punk bad boys, they showered audiences with obscenities as the opening act for the Virgin Tour of Madonna.

With the release of *License to Ill* in 1986, Beastie Boys became an attraction in their own right, their single, "Fight for Your Right (to Party)," a crossover blockbuster. Making use of street beats and metal riffs, *Licensed to Ill* sold 750,000 copies in six weeks, the fastest selling album in the history of Columbia Records and, eventually, the most popular rap album of the 1980s. With fame came controversy. Although the Animal House antics Beastie Boys manifested and sang about were partly parodic, the lyrics, critics claimed, incited crime, violence, and sexism, all the more when accompanied in concerts by a massive inflatable penis and female members of the audience dancing in go-go cages. More than once during their national tour in 1987, conservative groups sued Beastie Boys or had them arrested. As the first white rappers with mass appeal, they were accused of another crime as well, cultural piracy, the theft of the music of African Americans.

As the parody wore thin, Beastie Boys tried to change their image. Using their own record label, Grand Royal, Diamond, Yauch, and Horovitz mixed musical genres, including hip hop, retro-funk, and punk, and produced songs soaked with references to contemporary popular culture. After their second album flopped, a re-release of their early punk recordings and two albums, with the singles "Jimmy James," "Pass the Mic," "Sabotage," and "Sure Shot," were popular on college campuses and alternative and rap radio stations. The band was back, close to the top of the charts. In the late 1990s, Beastie Boys devoted their time and resources to political causes as well, helping sponsor, for example, a two-day festival devoted to ending the persecution against Tibetans by the government of China.

As a new millennium began, many Jewish performers exhibited this same audacity and cut-and-paste musical eclecticism. In their version of multiculturalism, artists could—and should—rejoice in their Jewishness while appreciating, adapting, and appropriating the musical treasures of any and every ethnic group. One did not have to be an African American to play rock, rap, or hip hop any more than one had to be Jewish to love Levy's rye bread. Nor did a rock performer have to abandon a Jewish-sounding name. "A previous member wanted us to change the band name," recalled David Fagin, leader of the Rosenbergs, "so we changed him" (Benarde 2003). The choices made by four contemporary groups underscore the distance Jewish performers have traveled fifty years after rock 'n' roll got its name.

Peretz Bernstein, a native of Queens, New York, worked with his father in the diamond district of Manhattan before migrating to California. Employed as an exotic dancer, he used the stage name Perry Farrell (playing on the word *peripheral*). In 1985, with bassist Eric Avery and guitarist Dave Navarro, Farrell founded Jane's Addiction, a band whose blend of hard rock, punk, and pop became the paradigm for the powerful but ambiguous force dubbed "Alternative Rock." In 1991 Farrell helped launch Lollapalooza, a traveling carnival of rock, which became a rock 'n' roll institution for the rest of the decade. After Jane's Addiction broke up, Farrell achieved some success fronting for a new group, Porno for Pyros. A heroin user, occasionally paranoid and violent, who was nude during the final concert of Jane's Addiction, Farrell found his Jewish roots in the late 1990s, with the help of friend and collaborator Aaron Cohen. And his faith informed his art. His album, *Song Yet to Be Sung*, was rich with Jewish themes and sounds. It included the songs "Happy Birthday Jubilee," an examination of the Israelites' annual celebration of debt forgiveness and liberation from Egypt, and "Shekina," an exploration of Jewish notions of God's female presence. In 2002, along with U2's Bono and Live Aid founder Bob Geldof, he called for forgiveness of the debt of developing countries as part of the Jubilee. Reunited with Jane's Addiction, the tattooed singer now uses his Hebrew name, Peretz. According to journalist Dan Pulcrano, he may be the first self-consciously Jewish rock superstar (Pulcrano 2003).

For more than a decade Beck (born Beck David Campbell) has been one of the most prolific and critically acclaimed rock stars. Born in Los Angeles in 1970, the son of David Campbell, a conductor and string arranger, and Bibbe Hansen, who appeared in Andy Warhol's film *Prison*, Beck dropped out of school in the tenth grade, playing acoustic blues and folk music on the streets. In 1993, Beck blended rap lyrics, a drum-machine track, and a bluesy slide guitar on the single, "Loser." The song became a catchphrase and a manifesto for the 1990s "slacker generation." Thanks to a deal worked out by David Geffen, Beck continued to make low-budget indie recordings while reaching the Top Twenty with three albums, *Mellow Gold*, *Odelay*, and *Mutations*, produced for major labels. Beck, too, was a musical synthesist, drawing on pop, folk, hip hop, country, blues, R&B, rock, jazz, and Brazilian music. Unlike Perry Farrell, Beck reveals no hint of his Jewish heritage in his songs, except, perhaps, when he implies that no one should take his lyrics all that seriously.

In choosing the name for his band, poet, songwriter, singer, and guitarist David Berman made a public proclamation of his Jewishness. Born in Virginia in 1967, Berman was raised in Dallas, Texas. In both places, he felt like an outsider. When he moved to New York, with Steven Malkmus and Bob Nastanovich, two non-Jewish friends from the University of Virginia, Berman rode on the subway, across from a passenger wearing a yamulke and decided to call the group the Silver Jews. Jew "should be a beautiful word," he said, "but Jews themselves have wondered how you can say the word. If you use the wrong tone of voice, it's a slur. . . . I'm interested in cutting off the associative baggage around it" (Sohn 1998). Silver Jews are blond-haired Jews, outsiders among the outsiders. Convinced that "rock 'n' roll started when the lessons were ripped up and burned," Berman has experimented with new musical concepts. Recording with Malkmus and Nastanovich and on his own, he mixed angular pop and acoustic ballads, anchored in a sardonic worldview. He is credited with helping to create an "alternative country" musical subgenre. Pavement, a band that grew out of the Silver Jews, was one of the most influential indie bands of the 1990s.

While scarcely a force in the music industry, Hebrew hip hop is enough of a phenomenon to attract the attention of radio and television commentators. Jewish hip hop groups tackle serious subjects, like the Holocaust, and use humor to deconstruct ethnic stereotypes. Hip Hop Hoodios, Josh Norek's band, sing in three languages: English, Spanish, and Hebrew. Claiming an openness to multiculturalism as the band's goal, Norek, who also uses the pseudonym Josue Noriega, defends the song "Kike on the Mic" and the band's references to large noses. Only a few listeners, usually Orthodox Jews, he asserts, fail to note the irreverent tone. "Havana Nagila" announces that Jews are for Allah and Jesus, as well as Adonai, Norek adds, "to bring people together, not to divide them." Hebrew hip hop, concludes Rabbi Jack Gabriel, music editor for the Jewish magazine *Tikkun*, "reflects the integration of Jews in America over the last fifty years." Jewish performers can use their own culture, much of it now "part of the American consciousness," to examine the familiar and exotic. And they add to the mix cultural and musical traditions not their own, with reasons to be confident that they can reach mainstream audiences (Osgood 2004).

Glenn C. Altschuler

References and Further Reading

Altschuler, Glenn C. 2003. *All Shook Up: How Rock 'n' Roll Changed America.* New York: Oxford University Press.

Benarde, Scott R. 2003. *Stars of David: Rock 'n' Roll's Jewish Stories.* Hanover, NH: University Press of New England.

Billig, Michael. 2001. *Rock 'n' Roll Jews.* Syracuse, NY: Syracuse University Press.

Bockris, Victor. 1994. *Transformer: The Lou Reed Story.* New York: Simon & Schuster.

Goldberg, Michael. 1991. "Rock's Greatest Showman." *Rolling Stone* Nos. 619–620 (December 12).

Helander, Brock. 1998. *The Rockin' 50s.* New York: Schirmer Books.

Helander, Brock. 1999. *The Rockin' 60s.* New York: Schirmer Books.

Herbst, Peter, ed. 1981. *The Rolling Stone Interviews: Talking with the Legends of Rock & Roll, 1967–1980.* New York: St. Martin's Press.

Hoberman, J., and Jeff Shandler. 2003. *Entertaining America: Jews, Movies, and Broadcasting.* Princeton, NJ: Princeton University Press.

Jackson, John A. 1991. *Big Beat Heat: Alan Freed and the Early Years of Rock & Roll.* New York: Schirmer Books.

King, Tom. 2000. *The Operator: David Geffen Builds, Buys, and Sells the New Hollywood.* New York: Random House.

Kingston, Victoria. 1998. *Simon and Garfunkel: A Biography.* New York: Fromm International.

Lisheron, Mark. 1997. "Rhythm and Jews: The Story of the Blacks and Jews Who Worked Together to Create the Magic of R&B." *CommonQuest: The Magazine of Black-Jewish Relations* 2,1 (Summer): 20–33.

McCormick, Carlo, and Paul D. Miller. 2001. *Pass the Mic: Beastie Boys, 1991–1996.* New York: Powerhouse Cultural Entertainment.

Oseary, Guy. 2001. *Jews Who Rock.* New York: St. Martin's Press.

Osgood, Charles. 2004. The Osgood File (CBS Radio Network). January 2.

Palmer, Robert. 1978. *Baby, That Was Rock & Roll: The Legendary Leiber and Stoller.* New York: Harvest.

Pulcrano, Dan. 2003. "Perry's Jubilee." *Metro, Silicon Valley's Weekly Newspaper.* Metro Publishing.

Quantick, David, ed. 2003. *Beck.* New York: Thunder's Mouth Press.

Ribowsky, Mark. 1989. *He's a Rebel.* New York: Dutton.

Romanowski, Patricia. 1995. *The New Rolling Stone Encyclopedia of Rock & Roll,* edited by Holly George-Warren. New York: Rolling Stone Press.

Rotundo, E. Anthony. 1982. "Jews and Rock and Roll: A Study in Cultural Contrast." *American Jewish History* 72,1 (September): 82–107.

Sohn, Amy. 1998. "Not Mad about You." *New York Press* 41 (October 14–20): 21.

Sounes, Howard. 2001. *Down the Highway: The Life of Bob Dylan.* New York: Grove Press.

Talevski, Nick.1998. *The Unofficial Encyclopedia of the Rock and Roll Hall of Fame.* Westport, CT: Greenwood Press.

Unterberger, Richie. 1998. *Unknown Legends of Rock and Roll.* New York: Backbeat Books.

Wexler, Jerry, and David Ritz. 1993. *Rhythm and the Blues: A Life in American Music.* New York: Alfred A. Knopf.

Zollo, Paul. 2003. *Songwriters on Songwriting,* 4th ed. New York: Da Capo Press.

Contemporary Jewish Music in America

The growth of American Jewish music over the last several decades of the twentieth century has been staggering. At the beginning of the twenty-first century over 2,000 recordings of Jewish music are available, and close to 250 more are released each year. The new Jewish music encompasses a wide range of artistic and popular styles, and it has been created and performed by groups throughout the Jewish community: secular Jews, Yiddishists, and Jews in religious communities—Orthodox, Conservative, Reform, and Renewal. There has also been a revival of *klezmer,* the music of Eastern European Jews that was part of life-cycle events, such as weddings. All this musical ferment reflects the development of a new American Jewish sensibility

New forms of American Jewish music began as vehicles for a new generation to distinguish itself from the immigrant cohorts. The Golden Age of the cantorate, Yiddish theater, and Yiddish cinema (1880–1940) had been a fertile period of music for resettling Jews. As American Jews acculturated, however, the music of the immigrants waned. New generations of American Jews, who came of age after World War II, and especially after the Arab–Israeli Six Day War (1967), created their own Jewish music, distinct from the past.

With the general turn to ethnic pride in the 1960s, fueled by the civil rights movement, public, cultural, and artistic expressions of Jewishness increased considerably. However, the Borschtbelt music of the 1950s and 1960s, the Yiddish shtick of Mickey Katz, and the Yiddish, Israeli folk songs of Theodore Bikel did not resonate with many Jewish baby boomers. Neither the Yiddish language nor the subjects or sentimentality of the songs appealed to English-speaking American Jews. They created a new Jewish music that would take hold in synagogues, summer camps, community centers, concert halls, and nightclubs. Today Jewish music can be found in many additional contexts. For decades Jewish musicians performed largely at local synagogues, schools, and community centers. In New York, their venues now range from college campus auditoriums to concert halls, including Carnegie Hall and Lincoln Center. Since the 1960s recordings of Jewish music have been widely available on LP, cassette, and recently CD. Since the mid-1990s, the recordings display a more sophisticated production quality, with higher fidelity standards and artistic cover designs.

New Jewish music developed in religious contexts—Orthodox, Reform, and Conservative—and simultaneously, as a cultural expression, is manifest both in the revitalization of klezmer music and Yiddish singing. It could be heard in the concert hall—art music—and in nightclubs. Musical styles include folk, pop, rock, middle-of-the-road, soft rock ballad, blues, and jazz. Reflecting the larger trend of American popular music, in the 1990s styles blended into various hybrids. Although no one style defines contemporary Jewish music, some trends can be identified: East European, or "traditional," Jewish influences are minimal, Israeli and Middle Eastern styles are common, American popular musical styles are an ongoing influence, and the texts of the songs are in English or from recognizable passages of the *siddur* (prayer book) and the Bible.

Music in the Orthodox community is by far the most prolific. The Orthodox community is generally divided into two larger communities: Modern and Ultra (*Haredi*) Orthodox. Hasidic Jews are considered part of the Ultra Orthodox community. While many Modern Orthodox Jews are college-educated professionals and are involved in the contemporary, secular world, Ultra Orthodox Jews keep their distance from it. Paradoxically, the newly created Jewish music, incorporating a variety of popular music styles, is mainly found in the Ultra Orthodox, not the Modern Orthodox, world. This is because secular entertainment—television, movies, recordings—is forbidden for Ultra Orthodox Jews. For the Ultra Orthodox, Jewish music is the only acceptable music. Modern Orthodox Jews also create and consume a new form of Jewish music, but they are not bound exclusively to it. Their musical world includes popular as well as classical and other musical styles. In the densely populated Orthodox neighborhoods in Brooklyn and Queens, New York, bookshops and electronics stores mainly feature the music of the Ultra Orthodox Jews.

The new music of the Orthodox community emerged in the 1960s, but entered a new era in the 1970s. Shlomo Carlebach (1925–1994), often labeled the father of the new Jewish music, combined participatory folk music with the energy of new music from Israel and the religious fervor of the Hasidic *niggun* (melody). The Rabbi's Sons, Mark III, Ruach, Simchatone, and, later, D'veykus followed in his style. Since the 1970s, Mordechai Ben David has had the most significant impact on music in the Orthodox community. His repertoire consists of songs in Yiddish, Hebrew, and English. His English songs, which are among his most popular, convey a strong religious message, such as "Just One Shabbes," "I'd Rather Pray and Sing," and "Someday We Will All Be Together." Along with Ben David, Avraham Fried is a superstar in the Ultra Orthodox community, and both perform before large audiences throughout the United States, in Israel, and around the world. Another prominent group, the Miami Boys Choir, with Yerachmiel Begun, has recorded and performed for over two decades. Journeys, Dedi, and Shwecky are also well-known. Only since the 1990s have groups in the Modern Orthodox community created music geared specifically for it. The messages of the English songs of groups like Soul Farm and Blue Fringe reflect their experiences and incorporate more eclectic musical styles. The ballad "Flippin' Out" by Blue Fringe (2003) expresses the experience of spending a post–high school year in Israel.

Beginning in the 1960s, music for Reform Jews, centered in the temple, changed significantly. The mainstay of Reform synagogue music consisted of the cantor accompanied by an organ, with a choral in a formal, classical musical style. But during the 1960s a younger generation found this music too formal and turned instead to folk and popular styles. The impetus for change was the summer camp, an increasingly common experience for youth in these years. In this isolated setting, young Reform Jews embarked on creating a joyful form of worship, reflective of their experience and aesthetic. They brought their camp music back to the temple with them. This led to folk/rock services such as Ray Smolover's *Edge of Freedom* (1967) and *Gates of Freedom* (1970), and Michael Isaacson's *Songs NIFTY Sings* (1972). Debbie Friedman, a well-known songwriter and performer, and the duo Daniel Freelander and Jeffrey Klepper (who together form the group Kol B'Seder) are prolific creators of new Reform music in a folk style. Folk singers Pete Seeger; Bob Dylan; Tom Paxton; James Taylor; Peter, Paul and Mary; Joan Baez; Judy Collins; and Melissa Manchester were their musical models. The guitar playing and folk singing facilitate participatory worship. With over a dozen recordings and three concerts at Carnegie Hall, Debbie Friedman exemplifies the success of the new music in Reform Judaism. Many of her songs are mainstays in Reform congregations: "Not by Might," "*L'chi Lakh*," "*Mi Shebeirach*," "Miriam's Song," and "Devorah's Song."

During the 1960s congregations expressed a growing desire for the participatory mode of worship, which clashed with the earlier formal, traditional style. The tension remains largely unresolved. Some services blend lyrically composed synagogue songs with singable refrains. In recent decades composers of synagogue music, including Michael Isaacson, Ben Steinberg, Simon Sargon, Benjie-Ellen Schiller, and Rochelle Nelson, have incorporated a myriad of musical styles, drawing from art music and popular songs with acoustic accompaniment.

In the Conservative movement, as in Reform Judaism, a younger generation wanted to carry on their camp experiences with new Jewish music, but the synagogue has not committed itself to change. As with the Orthodox, new music is heard on recordings and in concerts in Conservative settings, where it serves as entertainment. The group Safam and individual performers Paul Zim, Sol Zim, and Craig Taubman have contributed significantly to this music. Safam, an all-male group, has performed since 1974, producing ten albums. Their songs synthesize Jewish elements, such as cantorial and Hasidic music, with rock, pop, or Latin and reggae rhythms. "Leaving Mother Russia" became an anthem at rallies for Soviet Jewry in the 1980s; other songs, like "*Yismechu*," are heard in synagogues. Craig Taubman has released fifteen albums of Jewish music, with *Friday Night Live* (1999) and *One Shabbat Morning* (2002)—both from services he created for Los Angeles congregations—having a significant impact. Many congregations create monthly services based on his music. Each recording of Taubman's *Celebrate* Jewish music series is a collection of songs for a particular holiday or of a particular genre of Jewish music. Several cantors, such as Sol Zim, cater to Conservative settings. Over thirty years, Zim has released more than twenty recordings, in a variety of Jewish styles: cantorial, Hasidic, and Yiddish. His most recent efforts are devoted to music for children, including holiday recordings. Still, the new music is not as established in Conservative settings as in Reform.

Adherents of the music of the Renewal movement seek a renewed encounter with G-d through the prayer experience, with body movements, dance, and repetitive chants. Rabbi Shefa Gold, one of the most influential contributors, synthesizes a variety of Jewish and non-Jewish spiritual experiences in her worship, which is reflected in her music. *Chants Encounters* (1994) and *Chanscendence* (1997) are her most well-known recordings. Other renewal artists are Linda Hirschorn, Aryeh Hirschfield, and Michael Shapiro. The music of the Renewal movement has had a more local or regional impact than that of other movements.

For Jews who want to be connected to Judaism through the cultural dimension of Jewish life, without religious obligations, secular Yiddish and Israeli culture became viable alternatives. For others, art music in a concert hall and music performed at a nightclub are venues for the expression of their Jewishness. Music in the concert hall and nightclubs varies from a cappella choral music to orchestral and synthesized renditions of popular and folk styles. The rise in popularity of klezmer music, Yiddish songs, and the Hebrew songs of Israel reflected the increasing desire of those who wanted to be connected to Judaism, but not through religion. From the 1950s through the 1970s, Israeli music was integrated into the liturgy in American worship, and it became an important staple of the repertoire of day schools and summer camps. Israeli musical influence is limited, however, because most American Jews do not know Hebrew well enough to understand the lyrics. Since the 1990s, the influence of Israeli music has declined.

Although new Orthodox, Reform, and Conservative music began in the late 1960s, and in earnest in the 1970s, klezmer music experienced a revitalization only in the late 1970s. The klezmer style is similar to that of Romanian, Moldavian, and other Eastern European folk music. Immigrant Jews brought this music with them to America, and it was recorded on 78-rpm disks in the 1920s. By the 1950s interest in klezmer was declining, while the popularity of Israeli and American music rose. The klezmer revival began with the re-creation of the music from the 78-rpm recordings, and it spread quickly in the 1980s. The four revival bands of the 1970s were the Klezmorim, Kapelye, the Klezmer Conservatory Band, and Andy Statman Klezmer Orchestra. These new klezmer performers, unlike performers in the religious community, have approached Jewish music as a challenge to sharpen their virtuosic skills and deepen their understanding of another musical system.

In the late 1980s klezmer music changed as groups moved away from the traditional repertoire, creating new music and combining it with pop, jazz, and other styles. The four most prominent klezmer bands at the beginning of the twenty-first century are the Klezmer Conservatory Band, Andy Statman, Brave Old World, and the Klezmatics. Adrianne Cooper and Zalman Mlotek have popularized Yiddish songs. The Klezmatics are eclectic, weaving popular and world music styles, with new lyrics on many social issues. They have branched out into a variety of ventures including *Possessed* (1997), a score for Tony Kushner's adaptation of Anski's *A Dybbuk; The Well* (1998), new Yiddish songs in which they are joined by Israeli singer Chava Alberstein; and Woody Guthrie's *Happy Joyous Hanuka: A Hanuka Feast* (2003). The Klezmatics frequently perform at nightclubs and reach a broad audience. They seek to move beyond the playing of nostalgic melodies.

The new Jewish music also includes the music of non-Ashkenazic Jews. Traditional Judeo-Spanish/Ladino songs have a devoted audience. Performers and groups include Judy Frankel, Judith Cohen, Voice of the Turtle, and Alhambra. Like the klezmer revival bands, the Sephardic artists have incorporated a variety of European and Middle Eastern styles in their music. The Zamir Chorale of Boston has been the impetus for a renewed interest in choral music. The North American Jewish Choral Festival is held for one week during the summer in the Catskills, and many colleges now have a cappella choirs. Another smaller musical community is the Jewish music corner of New York Avant-Garde Jazz. Klezmatics trumpeter Frank London, with saxophonist Greg Wall, released several albums with the group Hasidic New Wave: *Jews and the Abstract Truth* (1997), *Psycho-Semitic* (1998), *Kabalogy* (1999), and *From the Belly of Abraham* (2001). John Zorn has also moved into this arena with his Masada project.

Many other groups serve a variety of interests. In the concert hall, composers of Jewish heritage have drawn on traditional sources for inspiration. David Diamond (1915–2005) wrote vocal works based on Jewish texts and synagogue services since the 1930s, including *Mizmor L'-David*, Sacred Service (1951). With just over a dozen works expressing his Jewishness, his recent *Kaddish for Violoncello and Orchestra* (1987–1989), written for and premiered by Yo-Yo Ma, draws on his own conception of Jewish music. Another example is Steve Reich, born in 1936, long associated with the minimalist movement. His *Tehillim* (1981) is based on Psalm texts and cantillation, the result of several years of exploration of Judaism. Recordings of Jewish art music appear on the Naxos label, part of its American Classics series sponsored by the Milken Archive of American Jewish Music, an ambitious project consisting of dozens of recordings. Well-known American recording artists have also explored aspects of Jewish music: Itzhak Perlman's *In the Fiddler's House* (1995), selling over 200,000 copies; Mandy Patinkin's *Mamaloshen* (1997); Barbra Streisand's recording of Max Janowski's "*Avinu Malkeinu*" on *Higher Ground* (1997); and Kenny G's *Jazz Service* (1986).

Contemporary Jewish music in America reflects the diversity of American Judaism, not only as a religion but a culture. Beginning in the 1960s and 1970s, as younger generations desired to express their American Jewish heritage, folk and soft rock were the primary musical approaches. By the 1980s, artists gained prominence, and concerts and performances became more common. In the 1990s, production, promotion, and distribution were increasingly institutionalized and often formulaic. Many critics complain that the music is increasingly shaped by a desire for commercial success rather than a commitment to explore the essence of Jewish music (Sears 1997), and they protest the lack of imagination in new synagogue music (Adler 1992). As the baby boomer creators of the new Jewish music age, a younger generation is ready to make its mark in American Jewish music.

Mark Kligman

References and Further Reading

Adler, Sam. 1992. "Sacred Music in a Secular Age." In *Sacred Sound and Social Change: Liturgical Music in Jewish and Christian Experience,* edited by Lawrence Hoffman and Janet Walton, 289–299. Notre Dame, IN: University of Notre Dame Press.

Gottlieb, Jack. 1980. "Symbols of Faith in the Music of Leonard Bernstein." *Musical Quarterly* 66,2: 287–295.

Kligman, Mark. 1996. "On the Creators and Consumers of Orthodox Popular Music in Brooklyn, New York." *YIVO Annual* 23: 259–293.

Kligman, Mark. 2001. "Contemporary Jewish Music in America." *American Jewish Year Book* 101: 88–141.

London, Frank. 1998. "An Insider's View: How We Traveled from Obscurity to the Klezmer Establishment in Twenty Years." *Judaism* 47,1: 40–43.

Rogovoy, Seth. 2000. *Essential Klezmer: A Music Lover's Guide to Jewish Roots and Soul Music, from the Old World to the Jazz Age to the Downtown Avant-Garde.* Chapel Hill, NC: Algonquin Books.

Schreiber, Gitta. 1989. "Shlomo Carlebach: An Exclusive Interview." *Country Yossi Family Magazine* 2,4 (November): 30–34.

Sears, Dovid. 1997. "Who Took the 'Jewish' Out of Jewish Music?" *Jewish Observer* 29,10 (January): 12–16.

Irving Berlin does a rendition of "Oh! How I Hate To Get Up in the Morning." (Library of Congress)

Irving Berlin (1888–1989)

Songwriter

Irving Berlin was Tin Pan Alley's most successful songwriter during the first half of the twentieth century. In the context of American Jewish history, Irving Berlin's career epitomized two paradigmatic aspects of the American Jewish experience: one, a rags-to-riches story of financial success; the other, the central importance of the entertainment industry within the larger saga of cultural assimilation and social transformation.

Berlin, the son of Moses Baline, a cantor, was born Israel Baline, on May 11, 1888, probably in the town of Tyumen, in western Siberia. The uncertainty about his birthplace arises from the fact that the family's home in

Mohilev (now in Belarus) was destroyed in a pogrom, probably in 1892. According to Berlin's daughter Mary Ellin Barrett, who has written a memoir of her father, the family subsequently managed to return to Mohilev, in the Russian Pale of Settlement, before emigrating to America in 1893. Because the history of Russian Jewish communities outside the Pale is difficult to document, some biographers have concluded that Mohilev, which Berlin listed as his birthplace on his application for American citizenship, is indeed where he was born (Bergreen 1990). But regardless of his place of birth, Izzy (as he was called as a child) grew up in New York City, on the streets of the Lower East Side and the Bowery, and his early years were spent in grinding poverty.

From the age of five until shortly before his fourteenth birthday, Izzy lived with his family in a Cherry Street tenement. However, after his father's death in 1901, Berlin left home, "went on the bum," and began supporting himself as a busker, singing for tips and handouts in the saloons of the Bowery (Woolcott 1925). By the time he turned seventeen he had found full-time employment as a singing waiter at the Pelham Café, located on Pell Street in New York's Chinatown. The proprietor of the Pelham Café was himself a Russian Jewish immigrant, Mike Salter. When Salter died in 1922, the *New York Herald* reported that "of the legion of notables who once found it pleasant to boast of Mike's friendship and familiarity with his notorious dive," only Berlin appeared at the funeral. As recounted a few years later by Berlin's first biographer, Alexander Woolcott, the story had already become emblematic of Berlin's essential honesty about who he was and where he came from (Woolcott 1925).

Berlin's first published song, "Marie from Sunny Italy" (1907), for which he wrote only the lyrics, was cowritten with Mike "Nick" Nicholson, the piano player at the Pelham Café, who composed the music. It was for this publication that Berlin selected his pen name, which appears as "I. Berlin" on the sheet-music cover. It was published by Joseph W. Stern & Co., a leading Tin Pan Alley firm.

The Tin Pan Alley era of the American popular music industry began in the 1880s, when several music publishers were clustered in the entertainment district around 14th Street in New York City. In the 1890s, the center of music publishing moved uptown to West 28th Street, dubbed Tin Pan Alley by Monroe Rosenfeld (1862–1918), a journalist and songwriter in his own right. As Charles Hamm has emphasized, the history of popular music in America neither begins nor ends with Tin Pan Alley. Rather the term refers to the popular music industry at a particular time—the 1890s through the 1940s—and in a particular place—New York City. As Hamm states, this era "was dominated by Jewish Americans, and represents one of the first great contributions to American culture by the New York Jewish community" (Hamm 1979).

The fact that Berlin's first published title had an ethnic slant was not coincidental. Ethnic stereotyping was a staple of the vaudeville stage as well as a fact of life in urban New York. "Marie from Sunny Italy" belongs to a genre of popular song known as the ethnic novelty song. Although published in sheet music form for home consumption, such songs were composed with vaudeville in mind, and with an implicit suggestion of comic action. Berlin's ethnic novelty songs include stereotyped depictions of Italians, Germans, Irish Americans, and rural American "rubes," not to mention Jews and African Americans (Hamm 1997).

As the original copyrights on Berlin's earlier songs have begun to lapse (his later songs are still under copyright), many of these ethnic songs are now back in print. Berlin's first Jewish novelty song was "Sadie Salome (Go Home)" (1909), which capitalized on the topical notoriety of the "Dance of the Seven Veils" in Richard Strauss's opera *Salome:* "Don't do that dance, I tell you Sadie,/ That's not a bus'ness for a lady!/ 'Most everybody knows/ That I'm your loving Mose,/ Oy, oy oy, oy,/ Where is your clothes?" (Berlin n.d.). "Yiddle, On Your Fiddle, Play Some Ragtime" (1909) begins with the opening musical phrase of Hatikvah, to which the following words are set: "Ev'ry one was singing, dancing, springing,/ At a wedding yesterday,/ Yiddle, on his fiddle played some ragtime . . ." (Berlin n.d.). In *World of Our Fathers,* Irving Howe situates these dialect songs in the broader context of Jewish humor. On the one hand, Howe recognizes the significance of Berlin's songs and other Jewish humor in furthering the immigrant generation's "journeys outward" into the mainstream of American life. On the other hand, Howe quotes a letter from Berlin to Groucho Marx, written in the 1950s: "Frankly, there are songs that I would be tempted to pay you not to do. For instance, 'Cohen Owes Me $97' [1915] would not be taken in the same spirit as it was when I wrote it for Belle Baker when she opened at the Palace many, many years ago" (Howe 1976).

Berlin's black dialect songs are especially problematic. Perhaps a dozen of them can be classified as "coon" songs. These belong to the most notorious subgenre of the ethnic novelty song, in which not only the lyrics, but also the sheet music covers, often portrayed African Americans in grotesque and offensive caricature. Others are "about" black musicians (in the sense that "Yiddle" is "about" a Jewish klezmer); still others simply appropriate or capitalize on the ragtime idiom that was created by, and associated with, African American musicians (Hamm 1997). "Alexander's Ragtime Band" (1911), which sold over 2 million sheet music copies and earned Berlin $30,000 in royalties, belongs to the latter category. A useful starting point for unraveling this musical and cultural nexus is Jeffrey Melnick's essay, "Tin Pan Alley and the Black-Jewish Nation"; Melnick writes: "The musical work of Tin Pan Alley . . . resulted in some fascinating contradictions. . . . [I]t situated African American music at the heart of American popular song even though the rewards went almost completely to white composers" (Melnick 2001).

In November 1911, Berlin legally changed his name to Irving Berlin, and in December, he was made a partner in Waterson, Berlin & Snyder, the company that had published "Alexander." In February 1912, already financially secure, Berlin fell in love with and married Dorothy Goetz, an aspiring singer and the younger sister of E. Ray Goetz, a (non-Jewish) songwriter with whom Berlin collaborated on several songs. The couple honeymooned in Cuba, but their time together was tragically brief. Within a few months, Dorothy had contracted typhoid fever, and she died of pneumonia in July.

In 1913, Berlin took another symbolic step in his journey outward from the Lower East Side, when he bought a house in the Bronx for his mother. Two years later, in September 1915, he filed his Declaration of Intention to apply for American citizenship. On February 6, 1918, he swore his oath of allegiance to the United States, and that spring he was drafted into the United States Army. While stationed at Camp Upton, in Yaphank, Long Island, he wrote "Oh! How I Hate to Get Up in the Morning." A short time later, he was promoted to the rank of sergeant and began work on *Yip! Yip! Yaphank,* a vaudeville-style review featuring the troops at Camp Upton. As World War I was drawing to an end, the show had a short but successful Broadway run as an Army benefit.

In 1921, Berlin established a permanent presence on Broadway in his own right, as co-owner of the new Music Box Theater. He wrote and produced four successive *Music Box Revues* for this venue. Two deaths framed the second *Music Box Review,* which opened in October 1922: Berlin's mother Lena (born Leah) died in July at the age of seventy-two, and his first employer, Mike Salter, died in December, at the age of fifty-four. The third *Music Box Revue* opened in September 1923. In February 1924, at a fashionable society dinner party, Berlin met the woman who would become his second wife, Ellin Mackay.

Ellin Mackay can be characterized objectively as the love of Irving Berlin's life, but her place in history is very much her own. By birth, she was heiress to the fortune of her grandfather, John William Mackay, an Irish immigrant who had made a fortune in silver mining from the legendary Comstock Lode. Ellin herself was brought up in New York City by her father, Clarence Mackay, the billionaire owner of the Postal Telegraph Company and pillar of New York society. At the age of twenty-one, by virtue of her own talents and insights, she became a published contributor to the *The New Yorker* magazine as the author of a piece much admired by its editor, Harold Ross: "Why We Go to Cabarets: A Post-Debutante Explains."

Ellin's father Clarence was virulently antisemitic, and he did everything in his power to prevent the marriage. In September 1924, he made arrangements for Ellin to take an extended tour of Europe and the Middle East, accompanied at first by Clarence himself and later by appropriate chaperones. The trip lasted a full year, but it did not weaken Ellin's resolve. In December she began appearing in public with Berlin, and on January 4, 1926, she married him in New York's City Hall.

Mary Ellin Barrett, Berlin's oldest daughter, although a child of intermarriage, quotes a letter that she wrote to him when he turned seventy, in 1958: "In an age and in a world where broken families were the rule, you gave us a sense of the family unit and the continuity of family life" (Barrett 1994).

Through the 1930s and 1940s, Berlin's creative powers remained undiminished. Since the hits are literally too numerous to list, one is forced to speak in generalities. Nevertheless, two songs from these decades, "God Bless America" (1938) and "White Christmas" (1942), require individual discussion.

Berlin had sketched out the lyrics and melody for "God Bless America" back in 1918, in his Camp Upton days, but felt at the time that it was too serious in tone for *Yip! Yip! Yaphank.* In 1938, with the Great Depression dragging on and with the Anglo-German Munich Pact offering the illusory hope that another world war could be avoided, Berlin felt the time was right to release the song for performance and publication. As is the case with most Tin Pan Alley standards, the familiar chorus of "God Bless America" is preceded by a verse, which establishes a context for what follows: "While the storm clouds gather far across the sea,/ Let us swear allegiance to a land that's free./ Let us all be grateful for a land so fair,/ As we raise our voices in a solemn prayer." As sung by Kate Smith (1907–1986) in a legendary Armistice Day radio broadcast on November 11, 1938, the song evoked a tremendous response. While some went so far as to propose that it officially replace "The Star Spangled Banner" as America's national anthem, others attacked it as the work of a foreign-born Jew (Furia 1998). Remarkably, its status as an *unofficial* national anthem was ratified following the terrorist attacks of September 11,

2001, when a group of senators sang it on the steps of the United States Capitol.

Berlin sketched out some ideas for a "White Christmas" song while he was working in Hollywood in December 1937, thus explaining the dreamlike appeal of "sleigh bells in the snow." The song was first presented to the public in a Kraft Radio Broadcast by Bing Crosby in December 1941, and its official release came in the movie *Holiday Inn,* starring Bing Crosby and Fred Astaire, which premiered in New York City in August 1942. By the end of October, Crosby's 78-rpm single had reached number one on the pop charts. The record has sold an estimated thirty million copies and remained the largest-selling single record ever for over fifty years. (It has been surpassed only by Elton John's 1997 tribute to Princess Diana, "Candle in the Wind.")

Musical and sociological analysis can go only so far in accounting for this kind of appeal. Jody Rosen, who has devoted an entire book to the subject of "White Christmas," argues persuasively that it was this very song that, as Christmas 1942 approached, made Christmas not just a religious holiday, but *the* American national holiday (Rosen 2002). Working within a fictional context, Philip Roth suggests that, in excising the religious significance from Christmas—and from Easter, in "Easter Parade" (1933)—Berlin not only secularized these holidays, but epitomized the strategy of assimilation at its logical extreme: "Easter turns into a fashion show and Christmas into a holiday about snow" (Roth 1993). But Mary Ellin Barret, who was sixteen when "White Christmas" became a hit, remembers it simply as "a song boys and girls on the home front danced to, fell in love to, adopted as 'their' song. However seasonal the words, we didn't hear it as a Christmas carol, we heard it as a ballad that Bing Crosby had sung to a blonde in a movie" (Barrett 1994).

As the 1940s drew to a close, it was not yet clear that the golden age of Tin Pan Alley was also coming to an end. In fact the 1950s began auspiciously for Berlin, with the successful Broadway run of *Call Me Madam,* starring Ethel Merman. Nevertheless, as the era of rock 'n' roll began in the mid-1950s, the Tin Pan Alley culture that had allowed Irving Berlin to speak so directly to American "boys and girls" became a part of history.

Over time, Berlin became increasingly withdrawn, and, by most biographical accounts, he was clinically depressed in his late years. Since he lived to such extreme old age, this is not surprising. Indeed, both the individual and paradigmatic aspects of Irving Berlin's extraordinary life seem to persist all the way to his hundredth birthday and beyond. As he approached the end of his life, his daughter described him: "In his liquid-eyed youth, he looked Italian; now he was a very Jewish looking, very old man, reunited with his forebears" (Barrett 1994). Another stereotype, to be sure, but a convincing one. In his songs and in his family, the Berlin legacy remains very much alive.

David M. Schiller

References and Further Reading
Barrett, Mary Ellin. 1994. *Irving Berlin: A Daughter's Memoir.* New York: Simon & Schuster.
Bergreen, Laurence. 1990. *As Thousands Cheer: The Life of Irving Berlin.* New York: Viking.
Berlin, Irving. No date. *The Songs of Irving Berlin,* Vol. 1. Boca Raton, FL: Masters Music Publications.
Furia, Philip. 1998. *Irving Berlin: A Life in Song.* New York: Schirmer Books.
Hamm, Charles. 1979. *Yesterdays: Popular Song in America.* New York: W. W. Norton.
Hamm, Charles. 1997. *Irving Berlin: Songs from the Melting Pot: The Formative Years, 1907–1914.* New York: Oxford University Press.
Howe, Irving. 1976. *World of Our Fathers.* New York: Harcourt Brace Jovanovich.
Jablonski, Edward. 1999, *Irving Berlin: American Troubadour.* New York: Henry Holt.
Melnick, Jeffrey. 2001. "Tin Pan Alley and the Black-Jewish Nation." In *American Popular Music,* edited by Rachel Rubin and Jeffrey Melnick. Amherst: University of Massachusetts Press.
Rosen, Jody. 2002. *White Christmas: The Story of an American Song.* New York: Scribner.
Roth, Philip. 1993. *Operation Shylock.* New York: Simon & Schuster.
Woolcott, Alexander. 1925. *The Story of Irving Berlin.* New York: G. P. Putnam's Sons.

Leonard Bernstein (1918–1990)

Renowned Composer and Conductor

Leonard Bernstein was the composer of the musical score of *West Side Story* (1957) and the principal conductor of the New York Philharmonic Orchestra from 1958 to 1969. These two signal achievements epitomize his remarkable double career as a conductor and as a composer. In both

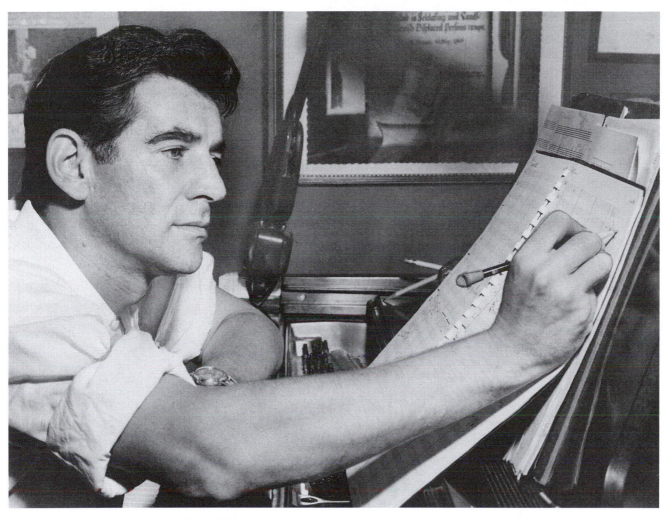

Leonard Bernstein, composer and conductor. (Library of Congress)

arenas, as composer and conductor alike, he actively sought—and frequently found—opportunities to affirm a strong sense of Jewish identity. Over the course of half a century, from the 1940s through the 1980s, Bernstein became the world's best-known classical musician, and the gap between his public and private lives shrank accordingly. His Jewishness was both a basic element of his ethos and a highly visible aspect of his public persona.

Bernstein was the child of immigrant parents whose roots were in the Russian Pale of Settlement. His father, Samuel (originally Shmuel Yosef), was born in Beresdov in 1892 and emigrated to America in 1908, finding his first employment in New York City's Fulton Fish Market. His mother, Jennie (originally Charna), was born in Shepetovka in 1898 and came to America in 1905. The couple met in Lawrence, Massachusetts, where Jennie was employed as a mill worker. They were married in 1917, and

their first home was in the then-Jewish Mattapan section of Boston. Leonard was born in 1918, followed by Shirley (b. 1923) and Burton (b. 1932).

Bernstein's childhood reflects the fulfillment of the immigrant dream: for Samuel, financial success in the beauty-supply business and membership in Boston's historic Conservative synagogue Mishkan Tefila; for Leonard, the best possible education, first at Boston Latin School and then at Harvard. *Family Matters,* a short but richly textured memoir by Leonard's brother Burton, vividly describes the dynamics of their family life. As second-generation Americans, the children were often uncomfortable with their parents' Old World ways; nevertheless, Burton writes, "To our credit, we never denied or apologized." Recounting his own adolescent rebellion against the practice of Judaism, Burton records that "even rebellious Lenny had been faultless in that department" (B. Bernstein 1982).

Leonard Bernstein's "rebellion" had two aspects. Its public aspect was his uncompromising insistence on a career as a professional musician, his father's disapproval notwithstanding. The private but by now equally well-documented aspect was his bisexuality. But even the word *bisexual* is inadequate to describe the realities of Bernstein's life, for he was both openly gay and, at the same time, deeply in love with and committed to his wife Felicia Montealegre (1922–1978), whom he met in 1946 and married in 1951.

Bernstein's musical career began in earnest in 1939, when he enrolled as a student at the Curtis Institute of Music in Philadelphia. At Harvard he had already performed Ravel's Piano Concerto in G with a professional orchestra, composed and conducted the music for a modern adaptation of Aristophanes' *The Birds,* and directed a fully staged production of Marc Blitzstein's *The Cradle Will Rock.* He had also gotten to know the conductor Dimitri Mitropoulos and the composer Aaron Copland, both of whom recognized and encouraged his talent. At Curtis, he embarked on a rigorous course of training for a professional career in music. There he continued his piano studies and honed his conducting skills under the tutelage of Fritz Reiner. In the summer of 1940 and again in the summer of 1941, he studied with Serge Koussevitzky, conductor of the Boston Symphony Orchestra, at the Berkshire Music Center at Tanglewood, Massachusetts. Nevertheless, the 1941–1942 concert season found Bernstein again living at home, severely underemployed and still financially dependent on his father. In the late summer of 1942, he moved to New York and began supporting himself as a commercial music arranger. In December, he completed his first symphony, *Jeremiah.*

Jeremiah is in three movements, respectively entitled Prophecy, Profanation, and Lamentation. The last movement, for mezzo soprano soloist and orchestra, sets a text from the book of Lamentations, beginning with the opening verse, "How lonely sits the city that was full of people." Bernstein had a good command of Hebrew and was familiar with the traditional chant associated with the Tisha B'Av liturgy, which commemorates the destruction of the Temple. Without resorting to literal quotation, he incorporated into his symphonic setting the characteristic cadence formulas and declamatory rhythms of Jewish worship. By the time it premiered in January 1944, the symphony had begun to acquire the status of a response to the tragedy of the Jews in Europe, both in Bernstein's mind and in the press. In an interview published shortly before the premiere, he stated, "How can I be blind to the problems of my own People? I'd give everything I have to be able to strike a death blow at Fascism" (Burton 1994).

In the meantime, in the summer of 1943, Bernstein had also gotten the conducting opportunity he had been preparing for, when Artur Rodzinski, music director of the New York Philharmonic, hired him as his assistant. On November 14, substituting for Bruno Walter, who was sick with the flu, Bernstein conducted the New York Philharmonic in concert for the first time. The concert, which was broadcast live, has acquired legendary status in the annals of American classical music. The *New York Times* reported, "Mr. Bernstein had to have something approaching genius to make full use of his opportunity. The warm friendly triumph of it filled Carnegie Hall and spread over the airwaves" (Burton 1994).

With his credentials as a conductor and as a classical composer established, Bernstein turned his attention to Broadway. In 1943 he had accepted a commission to compose the score *Fancy Free,* a ballet about three sailors on shore leave in New York City. Choreographed by Jerome Robbins, the ballet premiered in April 1944, and its success inspired plans for a Broadway musical, entitled *On the Town.* To complete the creative team, Betty Comden and Adolph Green, who were still in the very early stages of their own careers, were hired to write the book and lyrics. The show opened on Broadway in December 1944, and it too was both a critical and financial hit.

Paradoxically, it was the success of *On the Town* that led Bernstein to rededicate himself to his conducting career. Koussevitzksy had come to believe in Bernstein's true greatness as a conductor, and he hoped that Bernstein might even succeed him as conductor of the Boston Symphony. More importantly, Bernstein had come to believe in himself. In January 1946, he wrote to Koussevitzky, "Every time I lift my arms to conduct I am filled with a sense of wonder at the great insight that has flowed from you to me. It is the realization of an old and beautiful power, as if fashioned in heaven" (Burton 1994). As this commitment assumed the dimensions of a religious vocation, it required the subordination of Bernstein's work as a classical composer and, for a time, something approaching total renunciation of his Broadway ambitions.

For three concert seasons, from 1945 through 1947, Bernstein served as the principal conductor of the recently established New York City Symphony (unrelated to the New York Philharmonic) and made numerous guest appearances with major orchestras in Europe and the United States. In April 1947, he accepted an invitation to conduct the Palestine Symphony Orchestra.

Bernstein traveled to Palestine with his father and his sister, Shirley. He conducted concerts in Tel Aviv, Jerusalem, Haifa, and at the Ein Harod kibbutz, including his own *Jeremiah* symphony in the programs. A letter Bernstein wrote to his personal assistant, Helen Coates, attests to the impact of the experience: "Palestine opened on us like a fresh sky after the storm. We were met, taken care of, calmed. Daddy is in Paradise—he loves every minute. . . . The situation is tense and unpredictable, the orchestra fine and screaming with enthusiasm (first rehearsal this morning). I gave one downbeat today to the accompaniment of a shattering explosion outside the hall. We calmly resumed our work. That's the method here" (Burton 1994).

In October 1948 Bernstein returned to the now independent but war-torn nation of Israel to conduct the renamed Israel Philharmonic Orchestra. While there he completed and performed the slow movement of *The Age of Anxiety,* his second symphony. The concert, in Tel Aviv, marked the first anniversary of the United Nations resolution that had ended the British mandate and called for the establishment of independent Jewish and Arab states. Bernstein's symphony was inspired by a long poem of the same title by W. H. Auden. In his prefatory program note for the symphony, completed in 1949, Bernstein wrote, "The essential line of the poem (and of the music) is the record of our difficult and problematical search for faith" (Gottlieb 1980). In the poem, the character who most clearly enunciates her faith is a Jewish woman, Rosetta, who recites the Shema Yisroel. The composer, Jack Gottlieb, who served as Bernstein's musical assistant and who is an authority on his music, has identified a four-note trumpet motive as Bernstein's programmatic representation of the affirmation of faith.

Following the death of Serge Koussevitzky in June 1951, Bernstein again found himself drawn to composing for the Broadway stage. *Candide,* which exists in both Broadway and operatic versions, opened on Broadway in December 1956. The universally acknowledged masterpiece, *West Side Story,* opened on September 26, 1957.

According to Bernstein himself, *West Side Story* had been many years in the making. His principal collaborators on the project were choreographer Jerome Robbins, playwright Arthur Laurents, and fellow composer Stephen Sondheim, who actually wrote the song lyrics. Bernstein dates his own first involvement in the project to January 1949 and credits Jerome Robbins with the original idea: "Jerry R. called today with a noble idea: a modern version of Romeo and Juliet set in the slums at the coincidence of Easter-Passover celebrations. Feelings run high between Jews and Catholics. Former: Capulets; latter: Montagues. Juliet is Jewish. Friar Lawrence is a neighborhood druggist. Street Brawls, double death—it all fits" (Bernstein 1982). Although the setting was eventually moved from the East Side to the West Side, and the religious conflict reimagined as ethnic tension between white ethnic and Puerto Rican street gangs, the tragedy remained timeless, universal, and profound.

Bernstein's appointment as music director and principal conductor of the New York Philharmonic in 1958 was a milestone in American Jewish history not because of his religion, but because of his American nationality. Since the beginnings of political emancipation in Europe, many European Jews had achieved distinguished careers in classical music. During the nineteenth and twentieth centuries, many emigrated to the United States, where they were well represented in American musical life. A glance at the other orchestras that, together with the New York Philharmonic, comprise the traditional "big five" reveals that all of Bernstein's peers at the time of his appointment—Eugene Ormandy in Philadelphia, Fritz Reiner in Chicago, George Szell in Cleveland, and Charles Munch in Boston—were European-born, and all except Munch were Jewish. The cultural distinction is that, for the European generation, a career in classical music, historically associated with emancipation, was also a sign of assimilation. For Bernstein, as an American Jew, affirming his Jewish identity was part of his artistic agenda.

Bernstein's Symphony No. 3, *Kaddish,* is the most significant work he composed during the Philharmonic years. He worked on it intermittently from the summer of 1961 to November 1963. The period of its composition thus encompassed the trial and execution of Adolf Eichmann, the Cuban missile crisis, and the assassination of John F. Kennedy, to whose memory it is dedicated. The spoken English text of *Kaddish,* which

Bernstein authored, provides a dramatic framework for the traditional prayer. Bernstein's text refers to the imminent threat of "total and ultimate death" by man's "new found fire." The metaphor can be interpreted topically as a reference to the nuclear threat during the Cold War period, or retrospectively as a reference to the Holocaust, especially as it was assimilated in American Jewish consciousness during the Eichmann trial. Although the symphony reflects the broad social trends of its time, it is also a highly personal statement. Kaddish's speaker, originally gendered female (as is the people *Israel* in traditional Jewish hermeneutics), mourns for an abandoned patriarchal deity and also for herself, a private, feminine self that Bernstein could best express publicly through his art.

Two more major works, *Chichester Psalms* (1965) and *Mass: A Theatre Piece for Singers, Players and Dancers* (1971), are religiously inspired. *Chichester Psalms* was commissioned by the dean of Chichester Cathedral for an annual choral festival that brings together the choirs of Chichester, Winchester, and Salisbury Cathedrals. It is a joyous and affirmative work in three movements. The first movement joins the second verse of Psalm 108 ("Awake, psaltery and harp") with Psalm 100 ("Make a joyful noise unto the Lord"); the second movement contrasts a simple, folklike setting of Psalm 23 ("The Lord is my shepherd") with the urgent question of Psalm 2 ("Why do the nations rage?"). The final movement progresses from Psalm 131 ("Lord, my heart is not haughty") to Psalm 133 ("Behold how good and pleasant it is for brethren to dwell together in unity"). Employing choral textures inspired by the great English cathedral choirs, syncopated rhythms inspired by American jazz, and texts sung entirely in the original Hebrew, Bernstein weaves three cultures into a unified aesthetic.

Mass: A Theatre Piece for Singers, Players and Dancers (1971) is a more complex work. Its contents range from the relatively straightforward settings of Catholic liturgical texts to angry dramatizations of the loss of faith. Because the roots of the Western classical music tradition are historically embedded in Gregorian chant, and because works like Bach's *B Minor Mass* and Beethoven's *Missa Solemnis* have acquired canonical status, musical settings of the mass may aspire to a universality beyond their explicit religious content. In Bernstein's *Mass*, the Jewish perspective makes itself felt especially in the *Sanctus* movement, into which Bernstein interpolates its Hebrew antecedent, the *Kadosh*.

In what has been publicized as Bernstein's last interview for publication, he pointedly recalled the association of the Hebrew word *Kadosh*, not only with the Catholic *Sanctus*, but also with his own *Kaddish* symphony. Discussing his long and fruitful association with the Vienna Philharmonic, which he brought to Israel in 1988, he describes it as "an all-Catholic orchestra." Bernstein comments:

> Once when the players were rehearsing my work "Kaddish" for the first time, they stopped the rehearsal of their own accord to ask me what 'kaddish' meant. I said that it was related to the word "Sanctus," "kadosh." . . . People ask me how I can go to Vienna and conduct the Philharmonic. Simply, it's because I love the way they love music. And love does a lot of things (Cott 1990).

By birth a child of Eastern European Jewry and by talent and cultural choice an heir to the rich musical tradition of Central Europe, Bernstein became the quintessential American musician; yet he remained acutely aware of his European and Jewish heritage. As he traveled back and forth between Europe, Israel, and the United States, he traced and retraced the trajectories of nineteenth- and twentieth-century Jewish immigrants, emigrés, and refugees. His legacy is a strikingly original solution to the "problem" of Jewish identity in the twentieth century.

David M. Schiller

References and Further Reading

Bernstein, Burton. 1982. *Family Matters: Sam, Jennie, and the Kids.* New York: Summit Books.

Bernstein, Leonard. 1982. *Findings.* New York: Simon & Schuster.

Burton, Humphrey. 1994. *Leonard Bernstein.* New York: Doubleday.

Cott, Jonathan. 1990. "Leonard Bernstein." *Rolling Stone* Interview. (November 29): 70–93.

Gottlieb, Jack. 1980. "Symbols of Faith in the Music of Leonard Bernstein." *Musical Quarterly* 66,2: 287–295.

Gradenwitz, Peter. 1987. *Leonard Bernstein: The Infinite Variety of a Musician.* Leamington Spa, UK: Berg Publishers.

Peyser, Joan. 1998. *Bernstein: A Biography,* rev. ed. New York: Billboard Books.

Schiller, David M. 2003. *Bloch, Schoenberg, and Bernstein: Assimilating Jewish Music.* Oxford, UK: Oxford University Press.

Marc Blitzstein (1905–1964)

Composer

Marc Blitzstein, an ardent searcher for a uniquely American voice in music, composed in diverse styles, but achieved public renown for his socially conscious works. In the 1930s, his musical style changed from abstract, neo-classical to agit-prop—agitation-propaganda—and his skill in American vernacular speech became its crowning glory. His best-known works, such as *The Cradle Will Rock*, bring together blues, pop, speech patter, parody, and satire.

Born in Philadelphia on March 2, 1905, Marc Blitzstein lived in the Society Hill district. Descended from assimilated Russian Jews, he went to the Ethical Culture Sunday School and programs sponsored by the Socialist Literary Society. At age seven he gave his first public performance, a reading of Mozart's *"Coronation" Concerto*, K.537, with his teacher Constantine von Sternberg at the second piano. By nine, he had skipped two grades, his academic precocity paralleling his remarkable musical talent. After his parents separated, he moved with his mother and sister to Venice, California. There he continued his piano studies with Katherine Montreville Cocke and Julian Pascal. Performing at charitable concerts, he basked in the attention of society writers. When his mother returned to Philadelphia in 1917, he entered West Philadelphia High School for Boys. At thirteen, he reestablished a warm relationship with his philandering father, with whom he attended theatrical productions and concerts. It was perhaps a recital by Vladimir Horowitz that turned him to composition.

In 1920, Blitzstein's parents divorced and his mother remarried. After her husband's death two years later, she returned to relatives in California, but Blitzstein and his sister entered the University of Pennsylvania. When his scholarship was rescinded because of frequent absences from physical education classes, he began a three-year period of study with the Russian pianist Alexander Siloti, commuting to New York for his lessons. In 1924 he went on a two-week European trip with the conductor Alexander Smallens, eighteen years his senior. After their brief affair, his homosexual orientation solidified.

Upon returning to Philadelphia, he entered the newly formed Curtis Institute of Music, where he studied composition with Rosario Scalero, whose other pupils included Menotti, Barber, and Foss. He composed salon-styled piano pieces and songs to texts by Housman and Whitman. He performed Liszt's *Concerto in E-flat major* with the Philadelphia Orchestra (July 13, 1926) for $300. In October he went to Europe to round out his musical education and find more direction as a composer. Following a long line of predecessors, beginning with Aaron Copland, he studied for a few months with Nadia Boulanger. Smitten with Walt Whitman's imagery, he completed "O Hymen! O Hymenee!" and "Gods." The former employs bitonal relationships, while the latter is a tonal piece with frequent changes in meter, key, and rhythm. In February, he went to Berlin, where he studied with Arnold Schönberg at the Akademie der Kunste. As he immersed himself in the principles of twelve-tone composition, he grew increasingly antipathetic toward this approach to musical creation. He also disliked his mentor's German chauvinism. His own creations centered on more settings of Whitman texts, which he later called "Songs for a Coon Shouter" because of their theatrical style. Their themes, however, were universal, and there were the by-now familiar homosexual overtones.

By fall 1927, he was back in Philadelphia, seeking ways to develop a career. He spent June 15–August 1, 1928, at the MacDowell Colony in Peterborough, New Hampshire, where he met Eva Goldbeck, a novelist, translator, and book reviewer. Although she recognized his sexual orientation, they formed a relationship and married in 1933. He continued to set Whitman texts, "I Am He" and "Ages and Ages," both of which focus on homoeroticism, Blitzstein's recurring leitmotif. With their blues-oriented harmonies, the songs suggest the commonality of jazz and primal sexuality. Together with "O Hymen! O Hymenee!" and "As Adam," they were premiered on December 30, 1928, at a Copland-Sessions concert in New York. The African American baritone Benjohn Ragsdale was the vocalist, chosen both to render the "coon shout" flavor and to make a political statement. Blitzstein had always championed equality for minorities, and this theme, along with homosexuality, led to the public's often negative response to him. The *Piano Sonata* was heard several times in 1929, the same year his *Percussion Music for the Piano* was introduced at a League of Composers' concert. Inclusion in the latter of *sempre forte* markings for the slapping, shutting, and opening of the piano lid brought more notoriety. The one-act opera *Triple-Sec* premiered in Philadelphia on May 6, 1929;

its chief character, Lord Silverside, played at Blitzstein's suggestion by black singer Albert Mahler, has a love scene with a white woman. Challenging public sensibilities reinforced Blitzstein's association with advanced musical circles and leftist political ideology.

For the next several years, Blitzstein traveled in Europe and America, composing in diverse styles. *Parabola and Circula*, although set in a cubist world of forms and with a story line replete with symbolic abstraction, contains music that is melodious and conservatively written. The ballet *Cain* is mildly dissonant, occasionally polytonal, but largely modal; its biblical subject fostered a directness of expression. Songs set to texts by e.e. cummings, such as "Jimmie's got a goil," amused audiences in a conventional manner. *The Harpies*, with its Thracian setting and satirization of Gluck-style mythologizing, Wagnerian Valkyries, and Mozartian genies à la *Zauberflöte*, mixed with Broadway musical gimmicks, suggests a neoclassical tilt toward Stravinsky via the Boulangerie. *The Condemned*, an opera based on the Sacco and Vanzetti trial, broke new ground in that each of its four roles is assigned to a chorus.

In the early 1930s, Blitzstein tried to come to grips with the personal demons and sociopolitical issues that consumed him and his wife. Their marriage survived in part because of their shared support of the Communist movement. Eva suffered from cancer, but her death on May 26, 1936, resulted from a mental illness that led her to starve herself. After her death, Blitzstein no longer disguised his sexual proclivities.

Influenced by Hanns Eisler's 1935 lectures at New York's New School for Social Research, Blitzstein entered the camp agitating for music that addressed social concerns, attacked society's enemies, and conveyed its message in an accessible, vernacular musical language. The "new" Blitzstein turned to a tonal approach to the musical art, characterized by a popular song style, sardonic references to earlier styles, and parodies of art music. He wrote for "red" journals such as *New Masses* and served leftist groups such as the Composers Collective of New York.

Finding the anti-establishment, pro-union theme of *The Cradle Will Rock* too controversial, the Federal Theater Project canceled its premiere. It was then produced independently by John Houseman and Orson Welles at the Mercury Theater in New York (1936). It became the most celebrated composition of its genre in America. With

satiric quotations from music by Bach and Beethoven joined with patter, jazz, and musical revue styles, it symbolizes the musical incarnation of Bertolt Brecht's "epic theater." *I've Got the Tune* (1937), a radio song-play that picked up where *Cradle* left off, and in which Lotte Lenya made her American radio debut, made Blitzstein the favored composer of the Communist movement. *No for an Answer* (1937–1940) focuses on the hardships faced by unemployed and nonunionized Greek immigrants. Guggenheim fellowships (1940–1942) helped support Blitzstein's efforts. Scores for the films *Valley Town* and *Native Land*, concerned with unemployment and fascistic elements in capitalistic society respectively, increased Blitzstein's notoriety. J. Edgar Hoover's FBI began an investigation of his ties to the American Communist Party.

Although Blitzstein derided Army training in *The Cradle Will Rock*, in August 1942 he became Private (later Corporal) Blitzstein, attached to the Eighth Air Force in London. In 1941, after Germany invaded the Union of Soviet Socialist Republics and Russia became an ally, Blitzstein concluded that the war was just. He now composed music that pleased the military and his social conscience. He wrote *Freedom Morning* for orchestra and a chorus of black enlistees, the *Airborne Symphony* (commissioned by the Eighth Air Force), and a score for Garsin Kanin's documentary film, *The True Glory*, now lost.

After the war, he resumed writing for the stage. He created *Regina* (1950), a three-act opera with spoken dialogue, based on Lillian Hellman's *The Little Foxes* and *Another Part of the Forest*, a study of Southern mores near the end of the nineteenth century, which melded the styles of the spiritual, ragtime, blues, and traditional operatic conventions. Once again, the Negro is elevated to near-equality. *Reuben, Reuben* (1955) concerns a war veteran who suffers from aphonia, an inability to speak. The earthy New York Italian setting highlights an array of social misfits.

Blitzstein also translated and adapted *Die Dreigroschenoper* by Brecht and Kurt Weill. Its production in 1952 and subsequent revisions (a 1954 production starred Weill's fifty-five-year old widow, Lotte Lenya) brought him the fame he sought, and the seven-year run brought a financial bounty. Through Weill's inspiration, which Blitzstein once discounted, his own vision of a populist art form was realized. In 1959, Blitzstein was honored with membership in the National Institute of Arts and Letters.

Despite his reputation as an advocate for leftist causes, the Ford Foundation commissioned him to write an opera. Returning to the subject of his early choral opera, *The Condemned,* he incurred the wrath of right-wing journalist George E. Sokolsky, who excoriated the Foundation and the composer. While working on his new treatment of the Sacco-Vanzetti trial, in 1962 he served as John Golden Professor of Playwrighting at Bennington College (Vermont). There he formed a friendship with Bernard Malamud and began to set his short stories "The Magic Barrel" and "Idiots First." On November 1, 1963, he went to Martinique for work and rest. On January 22, 1964, he died there, the result of a beating by three sailors he met in a waterfront bar.

David Z. Kushner

References and Further Reading

Brant, H. 1946. "Marc Blitzstein." *Modern Music* 23,3 (Summer): 170–175.

Dietz, R. J. 1970. *The Operatic Style of Marc Blitzstein.* PhD dissertation, University of Iowa.

Gordon, Eric. 1989. *Mark the Music: The Life and Work of Marc Blitzstein.* New York: St. Martin's Press.

Kushner, David Z. 1993. "Marc Blitzstein: Musical Propagandist." *Opera Journal* 26,2 (June): 2–20.

Oja, C. 1989. "*The Cradle Will Rock* and Mass-Song Style of the 1930s." *Musical Quarterly* 73,4: 445–475.

Talley, P. M. 1965. *Social Criticism in the Original Theatre Librettos of Marc Blitzstein.* PhD dissertation, University of Wisconsin.

Ernest Bloch (1880–1959)

Composer and Conductor

Ernest Bloch was widely known in America for his works based on Jewish subjects, notably those that comprise the "Jewish Cycle" (1912–1916). He also delved into nationalism with such creations as *Helvetia,* a homage to his native land, and *America: An Epic Rhapsody,* whose thematic content is drawn from tunes related to the history and cultures of his adopted country. It was, however, his concept of a Judaism that could attain universalism via his *Avodath Hakodesh* that enlarged his reputation and brought him a diverse audience. Although he did not found any school of composition, he molded a plethora of musical ingredients into a distinctive style. For his many contributions, he was honored with some of music's most distinguished awards. His artistic integrity was such that he attracted many notable students, among them Roger Sessions, Douglas Moore, Bernard Rogers, Theodore Chanler, Frederick Jacobi, Quincy Porter, Herbert Elwell, and Leon Kirchner.

Ernest Bloch was born in Geneva, Switzerland on July 24, 1880, to Maurice Bloch, a purveyor of tourist goods, and Sophie Braunschweig Bloch. He was reared in an Orthodox Jewish environment. His early musical studies were with Albert Goss and Louis-Étienne-Reyer (violin) and Émile Jaques-Dalcroze (solfège and composition). The violinist Martin Marsick suggested that he broaden his musical training by moving to Brussels. There he studied violin with Eugène Ysaÿe, composition with François Rasse, and violin and chamber music with Franz Schörg, living in Schörg's home from 1896–1899. Seeking a change from the Franco-Belgian musical climate, he moved to Frankfurt, studying with Ivan Knorr (1899–1901), and then to Munich, where he worked with Ludwig Thuille (1901–1903). A year in Paris completed his training. During these years, his efforts reflected the tastes of his mentors and the milieus in which he lived. The effusively romantic *Vivre–Aimer* and the extravagantly orchestrated *Symphony in C-sharp minor* are products of German culture. The *Symphony,* a four-movement formally constructed work, reveals the influence of Richard Strauss. The fugue that opens the fourth movement reflects the academic formalism of his composition teachers. However, *Hiver-Printemps,* with its impressionistically tinged orchestral color, reveals the shift in France from the Franck school to the understated style of Claude Debussy, with whom Bloch established a relationship.

Returning to Geneva, Bloch married Margarethe Augusta Schneider, a pianist, in 1904 and entered his father's business. He composed sporadically, conducted orchestral concerts in Neuchâtel and Lausanne (1909–1910), and lectured on aesthetics at the Geneva Conservatory (1911–1915). He composed *Macbeth,* his only complete opera, which established his credentials as a dramatic composer. Premiering on November 30, 1910, at the Opéra-Comique in Paris, it drew together elements from such disparate sources as the Wagnerian music drama, Debussy's *Pelléas et Mélisande,* and Mussorgsky's *Boris Godunov.* He added characteristics that came to be associated with his style: frequent changes in meter, tempo, and tonality/modality; melodic use of the perfect fourth and augmented second at critical moments; a darkly hued instrumentation; repeated note patterns; ostinati; pedal points; and cyclical formal procedures.

In 1916 Bloch came to the United States to be the conductor for the Maud Allan dance company. When the tour failed, he taught theory and composition at the newly formed music school of David Mannes in New York (1917–1920). He brought his family, which included three children, to the United States. The successful premiere of his *String Quartet No. 1* by the Flonzaley Quartet in New York on December 31, 1916, established Bloch as a composer of consequence.

His quest to establish his own musical personality found fulfillment in a series of biblically inspired epics, known collectively as the "Jewish Cycle." They include settings of *Psalm 137* and *Psalm 114* for soprano and orchestra (1912–1914) and *Psalm 22* for baritone and orchestra (1914), the symphony *Israel,* with five solo voices (1912–1916), and *Schelomo,* a Hebraic rhapsody for cello and orchestra (1915–1916), in which the quarter tone makes its debut in his oeuvre. In these emotive utterances, he painted sweeping musical canvases with a richly colored orchestral palette. The quasi-Hebraic character of this music is intensified by the augmented intervals, melismatic treatment of melody, loosely metric repeated-note patterns, and coloristic orchestration. The Scotch-snap rhythm and its variants are so pervasive that it is called the "Bloch rhythm." Authentic Hebraic material occurs only occasionally, for example, in the quotations from the *Song of Songs* in *Israel* and the *gemora nigun* in *Schelomo.* The many repeated notes and the perfect and augmented fourth intervals in the *Psalms* and *Schelomo* evoke the call of the *shofar* on the High Holy Days, while the unfettered rhythmic flow suggests the melismas of Hebrew chant. The frequent accents on the final or penultimate beat of a bar have analogies in the Hebrew language.

At the invitation of Karl Muck, Bloch conducted the premiere of his *Trois poèmes juifs* with the Boston Symphony Orchestra on March 17, 1917. On May 3, 1917, he conducted the premieres of *Israel* and *Schelomo,* the latter with Hans Kindler as soloist, in New York. He conducted a program of his Jewish works with the Philadelphia Orchestra on January 25 and 26, 1918. G. Schirmer, Inc. signed him to a contract and published the "Jewish Cycle" with the logo that became his trademark, the Star of David with the initials EB in the center. This imprimatur

firmly established Bloch as *the* Jewish composer in the public's mind.

Comfortable with nonprofessionals, in 1919 Bloch conducted a People's Chorus of untrained singers at the Manhattan Trade School. The repertory was mainly Renaissance choral music. The same year he taught music fundamentals to youths in Joanne Bird Shaw's experimental summer school in Peterboro, New Hampshire. He produced the *Suite for viola and piano,* also in an orchestral version, which won the Coolidge Prize and quickly earned a place in the viola repertory.

From 1920 to 1925, Bloch was founding director of the Cleveland Institute of Music. He conducted the student orchestra, taught composition, established master classes and courses for the public, and proposed reforms such as abandoning traditional examinations and textbooks in favor of direct musical experience, that is, studying the scores of master composers of different eras. The trustees had reservations about this innovation and, along with other disagreements concerning Bloch's administrative decisions and priorities, created an environment that led to the composer's resignation. The compositions of this period represent a wide assortment of styles, genres, and performance media. A broadly neoclassical bent is exemplified in his *Quintet No. 1* for piano and strings, and in the four-movement *Concerto Grosso No. 1* for string orchestra with piano obbligato. Referential materials, however, are revealed even in these abstract works. In the *Sonata No. 2* for violin and piano, also known as *Poème mystique,* there is reference to the Gregorian mass, *Kyrie fons bonitatis.* A residue of overt Jewish expression is evident in *Baal Shem,* or *Three Pictures of Chassidic Life,* for violin and piano (orchestrated in 1939), and *From Jewish Life* for cello and piano, among others. But in these comparatively small-scaled works, the Jew of the Eastern European ghetto replaces the towering majesty of biblical heroes, monarchs, or prophets. His eclecticism is evident in *Poems of the Sea,* a piano cycle in three movements (*Waves, Chanty, At Sea*) inspired by Walt Whitman verses, which includes a mixture of impressionism, modality, and Hebrew *shtaygers.*

Following the upheaval in Cleveland, Bloch was appointed director of the San Francisco Conservatory of Music, remaining for five years. Now a U.S. citizen, Bloch's major work from the San Francisco years is *America: An Epic Rhapsody,* a three-movement program symphony with a closing choral anthem, intended for the audience to sing. Dedicated to the memory of Abraham Lincoln and Walt Whitman, the work is replete with quotations from American Indian melodies, English chanteys, Civil War tunes, African American spirituals, and references to the mechanization of America in the form of automobile horns and the suggestion of factory noises. *America* received first prize in a contest sponsored by Musical America, whose judges were Walter Damrosch, Leopold Stokowski, Frederick Stock, Serge Koussevitzky, and Alfred Hertz. Apart from the $3,000 prize, the work premiered under Damrosch's direction of the New York Philharmonic on December 20, 1928.

During the 1930s Bloch was again in Europe, based initially in Roveredo-Capriasco, Ticino, where he created his monumental *Avodath Hakodesh,* or *Sacred Service,* based on texts in the Reform Jewish prayer book. He taught himself Hebrew for this project, assisted in this and in the layout of the text by Cantor Reuben Rinder of San Francisco's Temple Emanu-El. The world premiere, which he conducted, was in New York on April 11, 1934. Upon returning to Europe, an all-Bloch concert held at Milan's La Scala proved disappointing due to public resentment that a foreigner was accorded the honor of opening La Scala's symphonic season, along with the unfortunate scheduling of the concert on Friday evening, the beginning of the Jewish Sabbath.

Between 1934 and 1938, Bloch created many important works in diverse styles, including his only *Piano Sonata; Voice in the Wilderness,* a six-movement meditative musing for cello and orchestra; *Evocations,* an atmospheric and exotic orchestral work (the second movement is titled *Houang Ti, God of War*), with pentatonic scales and coloristic orchestration; and the *Violin Concerto,* with its American Indian motto. Major festivals of his work were held in London in 1934 and 1937, the latter in conjunction with the founding of an Ernest Bloch Society, with Albert Einstein as honorary president and Alex Cohen as secretary. On March 5, 1938, *Macbeth* was revived in Naples in an Italian translation by Bloch's first biographer, Mary Tibaldi Chiesa, but Hitler's impending visit to Italy caused it to be canceled after three performances. Because of antisemitism and because he wished to retain his American citizenship, Bloch returned to the United States.

In 1940, Bloch became a professor at the University of California, Berkeley, where he taught summer classes until his retirement in 1952. Because his son Ivan lived in Port-

land, Bloch purchased a home at Agate Beach on the Oregon coast and commuted to Berkeley. Bloch offered courses on The Fugues of the Well-Tempered Clavier, The Third Symphony of Beethoven, Toward an Understanding of Music, and The Musical Language.

The compositions of the Oregon years represent an amalgam of Bloch's best creative impulses. The *Concerto Grosso No. 2* for string quartet and string orchestra and the *String Quartets Nos. 2–5,* with their formal design and abstract quality, are neoclassical. Similarly, the passacaglias and fugues of the *Suite symphonique* for orchestra and the *String Quartet No. 2* reflect a return to the techniques and formal procedures of the early masters whose technical polish Bloch so admired. However, the *Concerto symphonique* is a large-scaled piano concerto endowed with the sweeping gestures and virtuosity associated with the Romantics. Jewish associations reappear in the *Symphony for Trombone and Orchestra* and the *Suite hébraïque* for violin or viola and orchestra. Pictorialism and referential practices are largely eschewed. The kaleidoscopic and rhetorical gestures of the "Jewish Cycle" have been supplanted by a new objectivity, serenity, and control.

The musical world did not forget Bloch during his reclusive years at Agate Beach. In 1947, the Juilliard School and the League of Composers presented three concerts featuring his work. The American Academy of Arts and Letters bestowed on him its first Gold Medal in Music, for *String Quartet No. 2.* A six-day Blochfest was held in Chicago in 1950 with Bloch and Rafael Kubelik sharing the conductorial duties. The New York Music Critics' Circle Award in 1953 stands out because Bloch received this honor in both chamber music, for the *String Quartet No. 3,* and symphonic music, for the *Concerto Grosso No. 2.* Although Bloch was widely honored in his lifetime, only recently have many works from his final years received the recognition they deserve. Even during his final struggle with cancer, Bloch continued to create vigorously. His *Two Last Poems* for flute and orchestra (1958) are inscribed, respectively, "Maybe . . ." and "Life Again?" He died in Portland, Oregon on July 15, 1959.

David Z. Kushner

References and Further Reading
Bloch, Ernest. 1933. "Man and Artist." Translated by Waldo Frank. *Musical Quarterly* 19 (October): 374–381.

Bloch, Suzanne, with Irene Heskes. 1976. *Ernest Bloch: Creative Spirit.* New York: Jewish Music Council of the National Jewish Welfare Board.

Kushner, David Z. 1988. *Ernest Bloch: A Guide to Research.* New York: Garland Publishing.

Kushner, David Z. 2002. *The Ernest Bloch Companion.* Westport, CT: Greenwood Press.

Plavin, Zecharia. 1997. *Ernest Bloch (1880–1959) and a Comparative Analysis of His Jewish-Titled and General Compositions.* PhD dissertation, Hebrew University of Jerusalem.

Schiller, David M. 1996. "Assimilating Jewish Music: *Sacred Service, A Survivor from Warsaw, Kaddish.*" PhD dissertation, University of Georgia.

Strassburg, Robert. 1977. *Ernest Bloch: Voice in the Wilderness.* Los Angeles: California State University.

Weisser, Albert. 1980. "Jewish Music in Twentieth-Century United States: Four Representative Figures." DSM dissertation, Jewish Theological Seminary of America.

George Gershwin. (Library of Congress)

George Gershwin (1898–1937)

Composer and Musician

In his songs, Broadway shows, and film scores, in *Rhapsody in Blue,* and in the opera *Porgy and Bess,* George Gershwin achieved an unprecedented (and as yet unequaled) synthesis of jazz, classical, and popular music styles. His place in the history of American music can be located most accurately by situating him among three of his closest contemporaries: Duke Ellington (1899–1974), Louis Armstrong (1901–1971), and Aaron Copland (1900–1990). Among this remarkable quartet, comprised of two Jews and two African Americans, Gershwin was both an innovator and a synthesizer. His location at this historical nexus also informs his significance in American Jewish history, for it places him at the center of what Jeffrey Melnick has called the "Black–Jewish Nation." A blend of myth and fact, "of real and imagined meetings of African Americans and Jews in the modern city," the Black–Jewish nation shaped American music in the first half of the twentieth century (Melnick 2001).

George Gershwin was the second of four children born to Rose (Rosa) Bruskin and Morris (Moishe) Gershowitz (later Gershwin). Before emigrating, Morris and Rose lived in St. Petersburg, Russia; they arrived separately in New York in the early 1890s, and married in 1895. Ira (Israel, or Izzy) Gershwin, George's older brother and musical collaborator, was born on December 6, 1896, and George (Jacob) on September 26, 1898.

Morris Gershvin was entrepreneurial by temperament and reasonably successful as a leather worker, foreman in a shoe factory, owner of a Turkish bath, and restaurant owner. George's relative lack of formal education (he completed two years of high school) can be attributed not to a lack of opportunity (Ira attended City College), but to his personality and temperament. As Irving Howe put it, "Between Jewish immigrant parents and the world of the streets, there was a state of battle," and George was drawn to the streets (Howe 1976).

At the age of ten, Gershwin heard the eight-year-old violin prodigy Max Rosenzweig (professional name Max Rosen, 1900–1956) play Dvořák's *Humoresque* at a school assembly. Gershwin, who had been playing hooky, heard the concert from outside the auditorium, but nevertheless experienced the music "as a flashing revelation of beauty" (Wyatt and Johnson 2004). By the time his family bought a piano in 1910, Gershwin could already play popular songs by ear or, as he claimed, by following the motion of the keys on a player piano. He took lessons with local teachers for two years, and in 1912 began piano studies with Charles Hambitzer (1878–1918), a distinguished and gifted teacher. From about 1919 to 1923, Gershwin studied theory and harmony with the composer and violinist Edward Kilenyi (1884–1968), who had a PhD from Columbia University. In the early 1930s, Gershwin studied composition with the influential composition teacher Joseph Schillinger (b. Kharkov, Ukraine, 1895; d. New York, 1943). As these influences suggest, Gershwin actively sought out and obtained a substantial grounding in classical music studies, notwithstanding his lack of formal conservatory training.

Gershwin's professional musical career, however, was firmly rooted in Tin Pan Alley. In 1914, at the age of fifteen, he dropped out of school and was hired as a "piano pounder" by the J. H. Remick Company. He played their new sheet music releases for potential customers during the business day and earned additional income on the vaudeville circuit at night. The following year he got into the business of recording piano rolls for the popular player-piano market. While these recordings were originally made for purely commercial purposes, they have proven to be of great historical worth. Included among Gershwin's 1916 piano roll releases were two popular songs of Yiddish theater origins: "*Das Pintele Yud*" ("The Jewish Spark"), the title song of a play by Boris Thomashefsky, with words by Louis Gilrod, and music by Arnold Perlmutter and Herman Wohl; and "*Gott un Sein Mishpet Is Gerecht*" ("God and His Judgment [Are] Just") by David Meyerowitz. A recent biography of George Gershwin notes that both George and Ira must have understood "some Yiddish. Their parents often played cards with Boris Thomashefsky, the founder of the Yiddish theater on Second Avenue" (Hyland 2003).

Gershwin's first published composition was the novelty song "When You Want 'Em, You Can't Get 'Em, When You've Got 'Em You Don't Want 'Em" (1916), with lyrics by Murray Roth. By March 1917, he had enough confidence in his own talents to quit his job with Remick to pursue more creative opportunities as a pianist and songwriter.

At this point, a well-documented relationship between Gershwin and an African American musician, Will Vodery (1885–1951), assumes real significance in Gershwin's artistic development. Like Gershwin himself, but a generation earlier, Vodery had acquired a solid classical training outside the standard conservatory route. By 1913 he was one of the most respected musical theater professionals in New York and had begun a long-term association with Florenz Ziegfeld's *Follies;* as Duke Ellington put it, Vodery was "Ziegfeld's Number One orchestrator" (Tucker 1996). When Gershwin left Remick, he sought Vodery's help in finding new employment. Five years later, when Gershwin completed *Blue Monday* (1922, later retitled *135th Street*), a one-act music drama set in a Harlem bar, he turned to his friend Will Vodery for its orchestration.

In 1919 Gershwin composed the music for the song "Swanee," with lyrics by Irving Ceasar. Performed in blackface by Al Jolson in the show *Sinbad*, "Swanee" became the first Gershwin hit and has retained its status as a standard. Although the lyrics are not overtly racist, the song does draw on minstrel-show stereotypes in its melody as well as in its lyrics, which at one point quote directly from Stephen Foster's "Old Folks at Home" (1851).

Charles Hamm has argued persuasively that the renewed vogue for such "Back-to-Dixie" songs in the nineteen-teens reflected white anxieties about the ongoing migration of African Americans from the rural South to the cities of the North (1997). These imaginary projections of blackness remained in circulation as stereotypes, even as new possibilities for real inspiration and collaboration were beginning to emerge. As the migration of African Americans from the rural South to the cities of the North continued, Harlem became "home to black jazz musicians, many of them Gershwin's friends. 'Uptown' was where he could hear Bessie Smith or Louis Armstrong at Connie's Inn, or Duke Ellington at the Cotton Club" (Hyland 2003).

Both the commercially successful "Swanee" and the ambitious but relatively obscure experiment of *Blue Monday/135th Street* helped to set the stage for *Rhapsody in Blue*. On February 12, 1924, Paul Whiteman (1890–1967), leader of the most successful commercial dance orchestra of the era, presented the legendary concert that he publicized as an Experiment in Modern Music. As David Schiff summarizes, "All the elements of new music were there; jazz rhythms and colors, pop tunes, modern harmonies, virtuosic instrumental playing, lowdown fun and high-toned uplift. But only Gershwin produced a synthesis which placed these elements in a new relation" (1997). Perhaps the most telling recognition of *Rhapsody in Blue*'s jazziness came from Louis Armstrong, who brilliantly interpolated one its memorable themes into his classic 1929 recording of Fats Waller's "Ain't Misbehavin'" (Melnick 2001).

Among George Gershwin's Tin Pan Alley songs, those written in collaboration with his brother Ira retain a special resonance. In *The American Popular Ballad of the Golden Era* (1995), Allen Forte, an influential theorist of modern classical music, lists Gershwin, along with Jerome Kern, Irving Berlin, Cole Porter, Richard Rodgers, and Harold Arlen, as the Big Six of Tin Pan Alley composers. Of the Gershwin songs that Forte selects for analysis on the basis of musical merit—"Somebody Loves Me" (1924), "Someone to Watch Over Me" (1926), "How Long Has This Been Going On" (1927), "Embraceable You" (1930), "A Foggy Day" (1937), and "Nice Work If You Can Get It" (1937)—only the first (with lyrics by Buddy Desylva and Ballard Macdonald) does not have lyrics by Ira Gershwin. Edward Jablonski, whose 1987 biography of Gershwin remains standard, states succinctly that "George needed Ira" (Jablonski 1987).

"Embraceable You" comes from the Broadway show *Girl Crazy* (1930), which provides a useful reference point on the road to *Porgy and Bess*. Its most memorable song was "I Got Rhythm." Sung by Ethel Merman in her Broadway debut, it became an instant hit and made her a star. The song's afterlife, however, is equally remarkable. "I Got Rhythm" is in standard Tin Pan Alley song form: a repeated musical phrase (AA) is followed by a contrasting phrase (B), and then by a return of (A), the whole lasting a predictable thirty-two measures. Together with twelve-bar blues form, AABA song form provides one of the classic structures for jazz improvisation. In the case of "I Got Rhythm," the chord changes that Gershwin composed took on a life of their own as "Rhythm Changes," a harmonic structure that continues to provide the basis for countless jazz improvisations and compositions, including classics by Count Basie, Duke Ellington, Charlie Parker, Dizzy Gillespie, and Thelonious Monk.

The opera *Porgy and Bess* (1935) is Gershwin's masterpiece. It is based on the novel *Porgy* (1925) by DuBose Heyward (1885–1940), a white South Carolinian. Heyward's ancestry was aristocratic, but he had nevertheless experienced a poverty-stricken childhood. He was no stranger to the black community of Charleston that he depicted in *Porgy,* and he was a talented writer. Still, he wrote from the perspective of a white observer, albeit a sympa-

thetic one, and even the novel's positive characters are essentialized black stereotypes. The novel was adapted for the Broadway stage by DuBose's wife Dorothy Heyward, and it was successfully mounted, with an all-black cast, in 1927. The high quality of the acting worked to temper the stereotypes, and the show's success expanded the range of opportunities available to black actors and actresses. The opera, too, was performed by an all-black cast, including Todd Duncan (1903–1998), a Howard University music professor, as Porgy and Anne Wiggins Brown (b. 1912), a Juilliard student, as Bess. Wrestling with doubts about the integrity of a "Negro" opera composed by a white composer, the distinguished black composer Hall Johnson (1888–1970) saw the show four times before concluding, "I am now certain that I do like it," and he credited the cast with giving the show a degree of verisimilitude it might otherwise have lacked (Alpert 1990).

In fact, no opera can live without great performances, and the tradition of all-black casting of the lead roles of *Porgy and Bess* continues to be honored. For many opera aficionados, the production of 1952 starring Leontyne Price (b. 1927) as Bess and William Warfield (1920–2002) as Porgy remains the gold standard, but, as *Porgy and Bess* has entered its eighth decade in the repertory of the world's great operas, it continues to inspire new interpretations and to take on new layers of meaning and resonance.

In 1936, George and Ira relocated to Los Angeles to pursue opportunities in the movie industry. The movie *Shall We Dance,* starring Fred Astaire and Ginger Rogers, which included the songs "Let's Call the Whole Thing Off" and "They Can't Take That Away from Me," was released in May 1937. But Gershwin's health was failing. His symptoms—mood swings, severe headaches, weakness, and fatigue—resisted diagnosis. Abruptly, in July, he was found to have a brain tumor, and he died on July 11 after an unsuccessful surgery. In November, *A Damsel in Distress,* starring Fred Astaire and Joan Fontaine, was released; it includes two of the late classics cited by Forte: "A Foggy Day" and "Nice Work If You Can Get It."

George Gershwin's posthumous reputation has been debated for almost seventy years. At this point a consensus has been reached as to his distinguished place in the Black–Jewish nation of popular music. Paradoxically, his place among "classical" composers (of Jewish origin or not) is harder to define. His contemporary Aaron Copland, who followed a different musical path, did not consider

Gershwin a classical composer (Hyland 2003), and Leonard Bernstein, a younger contemporary, shared Copland's view. On the other hand, Arnold Schoenberg, whose life trajectory intersected Gershwin's when they met in Los Angeles in 1936, wrote (on the occasion of his own seventieth birthday) that "here [in America], I am universally esteemed as one of the most important composers: alongside Stravinsky, Tansman, Sessions, Sibelius, Gershwin, Copland, etc." (Schoenberg 1964). Respected as a fellow composer by Schoenberg and as a fellow musician by Armstrong and Ellington, Gershwin occupies a unique place in American Jewish history.

David M. Schiller

References and Further Reading

Alpert, Hollis. 1990. *The Life and Times of Porgy and Bess: The Story of an American Classic.* New York: Alfred A. Knopf.

Hamm, Charles. 1997. *Irving Berlin: Songs from the Melting Pot: The Formative Years, 1907–1914.* New York: Oxford University Press.

Howe, Irving. 1976. *World of Our Fathers.* New York: Harcourt Brace Jovanovich.

Hyland, William G. 2003. *George Gershwin: A New Biography.* Westport, CT: Praeger.

Jablonski, Edward. 1987. *Gershwin.* New York: Doubleday.

Melnick, Jeffrey. 2001. "Tin Pan Alley and the Black-Jewish Nation." In *American Popular Music,* edited by Rachel Rubin and Jeffrey Melnick. Amherst: University of Massachusetts Press.

Schiff, David. 1997. *Gershwin: Rhapsody in Blue.* Cambridge, UK: Cambridge University Press.

Schneider, Wayne, ed. 1999. *The Gershwin Style.* New York: Oxford University Press.

Schoenberg, Arnold. 1964, 1987. *Letters,* edited by Erwin Stein. Berkeley: University of California Press. Reprinted (1987).

Tucker, Mark. 1996. "In Search of Will Vodery." *Black Music Research Journal* 16,1 (Spring): 123–182.

Wyatt, Robert, and John Andrew Johnson, eds. 2004. *The George Gershwin Reader.* New York: Oxford University Press.

Benny Goodman (1909–1986)

Jazz Clarinetist and Band Leader

Benny Goodman, a superb jazz clarinetist and innovative band leader, was—and remains—the King of Swing. His place in American Jewish history can be understood in terms of two intersecting narratives: the story of Chicago in the early history of jazz, and the story of swing in the history of popular music in America. While encounters between black and Jewish musicians in New York were mediated through the worlds of Tin Pan Alley and musical theater, Chicago in the early 1920s was the center of the jazz world, and Goodman grew up with jazz. He began hearing it "as an impressionable youngster, . . . and very quickly he decided that this was the music that he wanted to play" (Collier 1989). *Swing* refers to the rhythmic feel of jazz itself, but also to a particular style of jazz that was just beginning to catch on in the mid- to late-1920s. Played by bands that were larger than the traditional Dixieland ensembles of earlier New Orleans and Chicago jazz, swing was jazz adapted for dancing. It was this convergence of jazz and popular music in the swing dance craze of the 1930s that made it possible for a jazz artist like Goodman also to become an entertainment idol to thousands of adoring fans.

Benny's father, David Goodman, had emigrated from Warsaw and his mother, Dora Rezinsky Goodman, from Kovno. They met and were married in Baltimore in 1894. In 1903 the family moved to Chicago, where Benny (Benjamin David) was born on May 30, 1909, in the old Maxwell Street area; he was the ninth of twelve children. When Benny was nine years old, the family moved to the Lawndale area, which was already becoming the center of the Jewish community. Goodman remembered it as "a pretty hopeless neighborhood, the Ghetto of Chicago that corresponded to the East Side in New York except that there were a few trees in the streets and we were a half-block from Garfield Park" (Goodman 1939). His lack of sentimentality grew out of his experience of poverty.

When Benny was ten, his father enrolled him and two of his older brothers in a program at the Kahelah Jacob Synagogue, in which children could take music lessons and play in a band. When that program ended, the three Goodman brothers joined the Boys' Band at Hull House, the famous Chicago settlement house founded by Jane Addams. There Benny continued to play under the direction of James Sylvester, a dedicated and talented music educator. Around the same time he began private lessons with a distinguished teacher, Franz Schoepp. By thirteen, he had a solid foundation in classical technique and the ability to play by ear whatever traditional jazz he heard on records, and to improvise in the then-current Dixieland style.

Musicians Benny Goodman (left) and Gene Krupa (right) in the studio in 1938. (Library of Congress)

While still attending school, he joined the musicians' union and began playing professionally.

In 1923, at fourteen, Goodman quit school and became a full-time, professional musician. At the same time, the finest black musicians from New Orleans, the creators of jazz, were playing the clubs on Chicago's South Side. In his memoir, *The Kingdom of Swing*, Goodman recalls one occasion when the band he was playing in appeared on a double bill that also included Lillian Hardin-Armstrong (1898–1971) on piano, George Mitchell (1899–1972) on trumpet, Warren "Baby" Dodds (1898–1959) on drums, and Johnny Dodds (1892–1940) on clarinet: "One set and they had played us kids right off the band stand. As I recall, it was the first time I had heard Johnny and I was satisfied to stand around and listen" (Goodman 1939). This musical environment, where the first generation of New Orleans jazz musicians was a constant source of both inspiration and competition, was Goodman's milieu.

Benny Goodman's career spanned seven decades, and during this time he was constantly in motion, performing all over the world with big bands and small ensembles. In

the first edition of a meticulously documented bio-discography of Goodman, D. Russell Connor developed a nine-chapter chronology, reliably based on the evidence of Goodman's recordings (Connor and Hicks 1969). By the time Connor revised his discography for the definitive 1988 edition, two more chapters had been added (Connor 1988). For a brief summary, however, one must fall back on a tripartite scheme of early Goodman (1923–1933), middle Goodman (1934–1945), and late Goodman (1945–1986), with the understanding that middle Goodman is synonymous with the swing era itself, while the long late-Goodman era includes work ranging from bop, to classical, to historic legacy concerts.

In the early era, Goodman developed his skills as a sideman and soloist, first in other leaders' bands, and then with his own band. From 1925 to 1929, he worked primarily with Ben Pollack. Goodman recalls one of their engagements at the Southmoor Hotel in Chicago, in 1926. "The Victor people were . . . interested in having us make records, and sent around an agent to hear the band. Unfortunately we didn't know what night he was coming, and it was particularly bad since he pieced out Yom Kippur, when all the Jewish Boys in the band—Gil [Rodin, sax], Green [Harry Greenberg, trumpet], Harry [Goodman—Benny's brother, tuba], myself and one or two others were away" (Goodman 1939). Fortunately, the agent returned, and a recording session with Ben Pollack and His Californians later that year resulted in Goodman's first appearance on a commercially released record.

The repeal of Prohibition in 1933 provides the most visible point of demarcation between the early jazz and the swing eras. As the speakeasies gave way to spacious music halls, with proportionately large dance floors, musicians began the process of transforming the intimate jazz ensembles of the 1920s into jazz "bands" and dance "orchestras." For Goodman, this transition was facilitated by his relationship with the visionary jazz impressario and producer John Hammond (1910–1987). An independently wealthy heir of the Vanderbilt fortune, Hammond was devoted to jazz as an art form, and he understood the music's African American roots. Although bands were still rigidly segregated in their public appearances, Hammond encouraged Goodman to begin making studio recordings with African American jazz artists. Goodman writes: "Nobody had to convince me, with my background in Chicago, about their ability. It just happened that in working along as I had during those seven or eight years, I had gotten out of touch with them, except for hearing some band in a night club or on records" (Goodman 1939).

Hammond, on the other hand, excelled in keeping in touch with established stars and discovering new ones. In Teddy Wilson (1912–1986), Hammond was sure that he had discovered the perfect talent to complement Goodman's: "I saw in Teddy Wilson the only piano player I could conceive of with the same technical facility Benny had—and who thought and was cool in the same way" (Firestone 1993). With Hammond's backing, Goodman began working with Wilson, first in the recording studio, and, in a historic concert of April 12, 1936 (Easter Sunday), in front of an enthusiastic audience at the Congress Hotel in New York City. In September 1937, now joined by Lionel Hampton on vibraphone as well, the Benny Goodman Orchestra presented the first integrated jazz concert in the South, at the Pan American Casino in Dallas, Texas.

For his big band arrangements, Goodman turned to another consummate African American musician (and another John Hammond contact), Fletcher Henderson (1897–1952). The title of a recent book by Jeffrey Magee names Henderson "the Uncrowned King of Swing," but Henderson and Goodman were not rivals; they were two faces of the same reign. As Benny Goodman and His Orchestra continued to turn out one hit after another, many arranged by Henderson, Goodman came to think of Henderson's arrangements as an essential element of his own musical identity and legacy. Magee writes: "No musician carried the torch for Henderson more than Benny Goodman, who continued to perform his arrangements for the rest of his life" (Magee 2005).

At the same time that Goodman was involved in these innovative musical collaborations, swing was reaching the apex of its appeal as popular entertainment. The initial series of "Let's Dance" radio broadcasts, which aired weekly on NBC from December 1934 through May 1935, created "a virtual ballroom where all listeners heard the same music, as in a real ballroom, but danced in their homes. It became the ideal format for listening and dancing to music during the Depression" (Magee 2005). In August 1935, the Goodman Orchestra appeared live at the Palomar Ballroom in Los Angeles. As Goodman recalled that night, the band started with some "sweeter tunes" and "softer arrangements," but the crowd did not seem to be respond-

ing very enthusiastically. Then, Goodman writes: "I called out some of our big Fletcher [Henderson] arrangements for the next set, and the boys seemed to get the idea. From the moment I kicked them off, they dug in with some of the best playing I'd heard since we left New York. To our complete amazement, half of the crowd stopped dancing and came surging around the stand. It was the first experience we had with that kind of attention, and it certainly was a kick" (Goodman 1939). In March 1937, at the Paramount Theater in New York, the sellout, mostly teenaged crowd responded with roars of approval and dancing in the aisles. At the time, from the perspective of the entertainment trade journal *Variety*, the response was "tradition-shattering in its spontaneity" and "in the child-like violence of its manifestations" (Firestone 1993).

In retrospect, the Paramount Theater concert remains a milestone in the history of American youth culture, anticipating the Sinatra phenomenon of the 1940s or that of Elvis in the 1950s. In one way, however, swing's appeal was even broader, since it was embraced by sophisticated adults and teenaged fans alike; it was even accepted in venues traditionally associated with classical music. On January 16, 1938, the Benny Goodman Orchestra scored another historic triumph in a sold-out concert at Carnegie Hall. Much as the Paramount Theater show has come to epitomize swing's triumph in the popular arena, the Carnegie Hall concert symbolized its acceptance as art. In the preface to his study of Goodman and the swing era, James Lincoln Collier states bluntly: "This was my generation. I am therefore perhaps biased when I say that the popular music of that time, swing, was better—more sophisticated, more genuinely musical—than virtually any popular music before or since" (Collier 1989).

A dramatic convergence of personal factors and historical trends marked the transition to the post-swing—or late-Goodman—era. In March 1942, Goodman married Alice Hammond Duckworth, the older sister of John Hammond. Paradoxically, Goodman's relationship with John Hammond had run its course; according to Jimmy Maxwell, "Benny in many ways was indebted to John, and he resented it. John also rode on Benny's coattails a great deal, and *he* [John] resented that" (Firestone 1993). When Benny Goodman and His Orchestra again played the Paramount in December 1942, he shared the bill with Frank Sinatra, the new teen idol and future of popular music. In addition, the new language of jazz, bebop, was being created at Minton's, a Harlem night club. In short, the swing era was in decline.

The bebop style, with its offbeat rhythms, asymmetrical phrases, and adventurous harmonic innovations, was *not* designed for dancing or, for that matter, for mass appeal. It was jazz created by black musicians for whom creative control and artistic independence were of paramount importance, and it was geared toward an in-group of musically sophisticated listeners. Goodman made no sustained attempt to master the bebop idiom, but he did make appearances and cut records with tenor saxophone player Wardell Gray (1921–1955) and other bebop innovators. In 1949, Goodman took a renewed interest in classical clarinet technique and music, studying with the English virtuoso Reginald Kell. Among Goodman's memorable classical performances is a 1956 recording of the Mozart *Clarinet Concerto* with the Boston Symphony Orchestra. It was re-released on CD in 1997 and remains available.

By the mid-1950s, Benny Goodman's legacy was secure. A Hollywood biopic, *The Benny Goodman Story,* with Steve Allen in the title role, was released in 1956. An embarrassing amalgam of stereotyped characters and clichéd dialogue, it includes Berta Gersten as "a grossly caricatured Jewish mother" (Firestone 1993). By far, Goodman's most important contribution to the cultural history of this period was his visit to the Soviet Union during the short-lived and tentative thaw of 1962. Khrushchev, though no fan of jazz, showed up on opening night in Moscow and later met with Goodman and the band at the American embassy.

Goodman continued to practice and perform until the day he died, June 13, 1986. Just three days before, he had visited Yale University, along with his friend William F. Hyland, a co-executor of his musical estate, to review the arrangements for the Benny Goodman archives that were to be established there after his death. On June 12, he called Hyland "to report with great satisfaction that the August 'Mostly Mozart' concert [at Lincoln Center] was sold out and that he had been asked to play another concert in that series in July" (Connor 1996). He was practicing for that concert when he died of a heart attack.

David M. Schiller

References and Further Reading

Collier, James Lincoln. 1989. *Benny Goodman and the Swing Era.* New York: Oxford University Press.

Connor, D. Russell. 1988. *Benny Goodman: Listen to His Legacy.* Metuchen, NJ: Scarecrow Press.

Connor, D. Russell. 1996. *Benny Goodman: Wrappin' It Up.* Lanham, MD: Scarecrow Press.

Connor, D. Russell, and Warren W. Hicks. 1969. *BG on the Record: A Bio-Discography of Benny Goodman.* New Rochelle, NY: Arlington House.

Firestone, Ross. 1993. *Swing, Swing, Swing: The Life and Times of Benny Goodman.* New York: W. W. Norton.

Goodman, Benny, and Irving Kolodin. 1939. *The Kingdom of Swing.* New York: Stackpole Sons.

Hammond, John. 1977. *John Hammond on the Record.* New York: Summit Books.

Magee, Jeffrey. 2005. *The Uncrowned King of Swing: Fletcher Henderson and Big Band Jazz.* New York: Oxford University Press.

Steve Reich (b. 1936)

Musical Creator

One of the central musical creators of the late twentieth and early twenty-first centuries, Steve Reich's work is informed by diverse musical traditions: Western and non-Western, classical and popular, acoustic and electro-acoustic, taped and videotaped. Although Jewish themes are the subject or inspiration for some of his most well-known compositions, the cultural diversity of his work has earned him an unusually large following among both the public and cognoscenti.

Steve Reich was born in New York City on October 3, 1936. Although he was taught piano as a child, in early adolescence he began to study drumming with Roland Kohloff, a timpanist. However, Reich's intellectual interests extended far beyond music. At Cornell University he studied philosophy, but he also worked with musicologist William Austin. After graduating in 1957, he returned to New York City, where he studied composition with Hall Overton, Vincent Persichetti, and William Bergsma, the latter two at the Juilliard School of Music. He received a master's degree in composition from Mills College in Oakland, California, where, in contrast to the conservative approach of his three previous instructors, he studied under the avant-garde master Luciano Berio.

After his graduate studies, Reich settled for a time in San Francisco, where he composed the first work that brought him fame and acclaim, *It's Gonna Rain* (1965). In it, he espoused a musical philosophy centered on phasing, a technical feature in which the same musical materials move in and out of synchronization with each other by slightly altering their speed. Reich was also particularly interested in process—the way in which the music gradually unfolds. He often mixed taped speech and sounds with instruments and voices in unique combinations.

Believing the roles of composer and performer should merge, while in San Francisco Reich formed a quintet, of which he was a member, and spent several months in improvisatory jam sessions. In 1965, he returned to New York, forming a trio a year later—Art Murphy, piano; Jon Gibson, woodwinds; and Reich, piano. This group remained more or less intact until the composition in 1970 of *Phase Patterns* for four electric organs and *Four Organs* for four electric organs and maracas, and the creation of *Drumming* in 1971. Reich had studied African drumming at the University of Ghana in 1970. As a result of numerous repetitive patterns, *Drumming*, which takes about eighty minutes to perform, brought its composer under the canopy of minimalism, a major movement of the late twentieth century. In *Drumming*, a work for eight small-pitched drums, three maracas, three glockenspiels, piccolo, and voices, the expanded core of artists called itself *Steve Reich and Musicians*. As the performers changed—often depending on the venue of the performance—new patterns emerged in a composition. This allowed performers a role in the ongoing re-creation of the work.

Reich's world of sound was always eclectic, as evidenced in his *Clapping Music* for two pairs of hands (1972), *Six Pianos* (rearranged as *Six Marimbas*), and *Music for Mallet Instruments, Voices and Organ* (1973). In Seattle, Reich had worked with musicians from Bali, and the exotic effects in the latter, as well as many subsequent, compositions, reflect their influence.

In the mid-1970s, Reich moved from "exotic" musical traditions to his own Hebrew culture. He saturated himself in Hebrew language, Torah, and chant, with special attention to Sephardic singing, the latter in Israel. *Tehillim* (*Psalms*) sets verses from various psalms. To conjure up associations with biblical times and practices, he used tambourines bereft of the jingles, an instrument somewhat akin to the *tof*, a small drum mentioned in *Psalm 150*, and hand clapping, rattles, and small cymbals. Because the oral tradition for psalm singing has been lost,

Reich created his own melodies, without preconceived notions of the original sounds. Canons and variations, rather than the brief repetitions found in his earlier works, make *Tehillim* somewhat closer to Western practices. However, the rhythm, which derives from the rhythmic accents of the Hebrew words, is in constant flux. It also includes word painting, another Western tradition, so that in verses 13–15 from *Psalm 34* the words "turn from evil, and do good" feature a descending melodic line (evil) followed by a clearly rising line (good).

Different Trains (1988), scored for string quartet and tape, is autobiographical. Its impetus came from the years in Reich's childhood, 1939–1942, when he frequently traveled with his governess between New York and Los Angeles, the result of his parents' separation, with his father living on the East Coast and his mother on the West Coast. He was prompted to create this work when he reflected on the vast differences between his train journeys and those of the European Jews in the Holocaust at the same time. For this work he taped the voices of his governess, Virginia; a retired Pullman porter, Lawrence Davis, who worked on the New York–Los Angeles run; and three Holocaust survivors. He added the taped sounds of American and European trains of the third and fourth decades of the twentieth century. Small speech segments were provided with specific pitches and rhythms, and these were imitated by the strings. The three movements (*America—Before the War, Europe—During the War,* and *After the War*) suggest a musical documentary.

Building on the docudrama concept, Reich and his wife, Beryl Korot, joined forces for *The Cave*, which brings the biblical past to contemporary Israel and Palestine. The cave is the Cave of Machpelah, which is now in Hebron. It is where Abraham and his family are said to be buried, and where oral tradition suggests that Adam and Eve and the Garden of Eden were located. In three acts, the work asks contemporary Israelis, Palestinians, and Americans who they think Abraham, Sarah, Hagar, Ishmael, and Isaac are. Voices are taped speaking in Hebrew, Arabic, and English, and chanting from the *Torah* and the *Koran*. The biblical cave is the point of convergence for the two ancient peoples. As a stage production, the visual aids flashed on a screen help the audience understand the narrative; however, even when someone is just listening to the work, the mesmerizing music enhances the story line.

In addition to his Jewish-themed creations, Reich moved in a variety of other directions. He wrote works for solo instrument and tape for specific artists, such as Ransom Wilson, flutist (*Vermont Counterpoint,* 1982), Richard Stoltzman, clarinetist *(New York Counterpoint,* 1985), and Pat Metheny, electric guitarist (*Electric Counterpoint,* 1987*)*. In these works the soloist performs with prerecorded tapes he has made, thereby exploring the varied timbres, textures, and sonorities that each instrument is capable of producing. Reich's other innovative ventures include *City Life* (1994), an effort to portray his home and environs through taped spoken phrases, hissing steam emitted from the street, a fog horn, and the like. In the neo-medieval *Proverbs* (1995), drones and repetitive contrapuntal patterns exploit a single melodic idea. *Triple Quartet* (1999) contains aspects of *Different Trains,* and the *Counterpoint* pieces reveal the influence of Bartók's string quartets and include the modal flavoring associated with Jewish sources. The documentary digital video opera, *Three Tales* (1998–2002), another Reich-Korot creation, concerns three significant events of the early, middle, and late twentieth century, reflected in the movement titles: *Hindenburg, Bikini,* and *Dolly.* The work is an advanced form of musical theater in which the raw materials are created on a computer, videotaped, and projected onto a thirty-two-foot screen. The musicians—sixteen instrumentalists and singers—perform on a stage below the screen. The fusion and diffusion of multiple styles suggest that Reich's oeuvre is best described as eclecticism.

David Z. Kushner

References and Further Reading

Duckworth, William. 1995. *Talking Music.* New York: Schirmer Books.

Dufallo, Richard. 1989. *Trackings: Composers Speak with Richard Dufallo.* New York: Oxford University Press.

Mertens, Wim. 1991. *American Minimal Music: LaMonte Young, Terry Riley, Steve Reich, Philip Glass.* London: Kahn & Averill.

Potter, Keith. 2000. *Four Musical Minimalists: LaMonte Young, Terry Riley, Steve Reich, Philip Glass.* New York: Cambridge University Press.

Reich, Steve. 1974. *Writings about Music.* New York: New York University Press.

Strickland, Edward. 1991. *American Composers: Dialogues on Contemporary Music.* Bloomington: Indiana University Press.

Strickland, Edward. 1993. *Minimalism: Origins.* Bloomington: Indiana University Press.

Arnold Schoenberg (1874–1951)

Composer

Arguably the most influential composer of the first half of the twentieth century, Arnold Schoenberg (originally Schönberg) was born in Vienna. His original approach to composition, which he called the "method of composing with twelve tones," is a cornerstone of the modernist aesthetic in twentieth-century art music. In the 1920s, Schoenberg achieved considerable prominence and success in Europe, and in 1925 he was appointed professor of composition at the Prussian Academy of the Arts in Berlin. In 1933, the Nazi authorities demanded that the Academy be cleansed of Jewish influence, and Schoenberg chose to resign immediately. He left Berlin with his family in May and in October arrived in the United States, where he lived the rest of his life.

Schoenberg's significance for American Jewish history is thus inextricably bound to the rise of Nazism. As with his musical thinking, however, Schoenberg's understanding of Judaism and Jewish history underwent several transformations.

Schoenberg's musical oeuvre can be divided into three style periods. His early works, exemplified by the programmatic string sextet *Verklärte Nacht (Transfigured Night),* are in a lush, post-Wagnerian idiom. In 1908, he began to compose in a much more dissonant style, known as free, or atonal, expressionism. *Pierrot Lunaire* (1912), a cycle of songs for soprano and chamber ensemble, is a celebrated example of this style. Schoenberg developed his mature style, the method of composing with twelve tones, from 1915 to 1923.

In the twelve-tone method, the composer uses all twelve pitches of the chromatic scale in a predetermined order, or row, which is maintained, subject to various transformations, throughout the piece. As developed by Schoenberg himself and subsequently by his students and followers, the twelve-tone method evolved into the influential school of composition known as serialism. Schoenberg's twelve-tone works include the *Variations for Orchestra* (1927–1928), the opera *Moses und Aron* (1930–1932; third act unfinished), and the cantata *A Survivor from Warsaw* (1947).

With respect to his religious development, Schoenberg, whose parents were both Jewish, had converted to

Protestantism in 1898. Nevertheless, in the summer of 1921, when he arrived on vacation with his family at the resort town of Mattsee, Austria, Schoenberg was confronted with an organized and officially sanctioned antisemitic campaign that forced them to depart abruptly. This event precipitated a strong sense of re-identification with his Jewishness in both its religious and Zionist dimensions. Furthermore, the fact that this incident occurred at a critical juncture in Schoenberg's musical evolution had a direct influence on his subsequent compositions.

Schoenberg's formal return to Judaism took place in July 1933. Having fled Berlin some weeks before, Schoenberg met with Rabbi Louis-Germain Lévy of the Union Libérale Israélite in Paris "to express his formal desire to re-enter the community of Israel" (Ringer 1990). In the presence of two additional witnesses, one of whom was Marc Chagall, Lévy wrote out the declaration, and Schoenberg signed it. It must be emphasized, however, that Schoenberg regarded this formal procedure only as ratifying a decision made much earlier. In a letter to his friend and former student, Alban Berg, he wrote:

> [M]y return to the Jewish religion took place long ago and is indeed demonstrated in some of my published work ("Thou shalt not . . . Thou shalt") and in "Moses and Aaron," of which you have known since 1928, but which dates from at least five years earlier; but especially in my drama "Der biblishe Weg" which was also conceived in 1922 or '23 at the latest, though finished only in '26–27 (Schoenberg 1964).

"Thou shalt not . . . Thou shalt" ("*Du sollst nicht, du musst*") is the second of Schoenberg's *Four Pieces for Mixed Choir,* op. 27 (1926). Its text, written by the composer himself, begins with a paraphrase of the second commandment, "Thou shalt not make unto thyself any graven image," and concludes with a command to believe in a limitless God. *Der biblishe Weg* (*The Biblical Way*) is a spoken drama about the establishment of a Jewish state, not in Palestine, but in a fictional setting modeled on Theodor Herzl's Uganda proposal, which had been debated in the Zionist congress of 1903 and rejected in the seventh Zionist Congress of 1905.

In his most comprehensive statement on the Jewish situation, "A Four-Point Program for Jewry" (1938), Schoenberg explained his decision to settle in the United States as follows: "It was my desire to come to America and start here that movement which in my belief offers the only way out of our problems" (Ringer 1990). The movement of which Schoenberg conceived was that of a unified Jewish party committed to the rescue of the Jews of Europe as a first priority, and as a corollary, to the earliest possible creation of a Jewish state, not necessarily in Palestine. As these priorities diverged from the Zionist movement's primary objective of a Jewish homeland in Palestine, Schoenberg's political hopes were doomed to failure.

Schoenberg's most lasting contribution to American Jewish culture can be found in several late works that epitomize his mature understanding of Judaism and Jewish history. *Kol Nidre* (1938) takes the form of a twelve-minute cantata for narrator, mixed chorus, and orchestra. In this work, Schoenberg adhered neither to the traditional melody nor the traditional text of the Yom Kippur petition. Rather, he took from its musical motives, its language, and its historical associations a framework on which to construct his own creative response to the themes of transgression and return: "In the name of God: We solemnly proclaim that every transgressor, be it that he was unfaithful to our people because of fear, or misled by false doctrines of any kind, out of weakness or greed: We give him leave to be One with us in prayer tonight" (Schiller 2003). *A Survivor from Warsaw* (1947), a cantata for narrator, male chorus, and chamber orchestra, depicts the deportation of the Jews of Warsaw to the death camp of Treblinka in the summer of 1942, through the eyes of a "survivor" who witnesses their singing of the *Shema Yisroel*. The piece ends with the powerful setting of the *Shema*.

Three final choral works, which Schoenberg grouped together as his fiftieth opus, bring together his understanding of the Jewish experience and his individual spirituality. Opus 50a, *Dreimal Tausend Jahr* (*Thrice a Thousand Years*), acknowledges the establishment of Israel in a setting of a poem by a fellow emigré, the Rumanian-born and Viennese-educated writer and publisher Dagobert Rune. In 1951, Schoenberg was asked to serve as honorary president of the Israel Academy of Music, and his letter of acceptance, written less than three months before his death, leaves no doubt that Israel had indeed come to represent the fulfillment of his own "most ardent wish" (Ringer 1990). Opus 50b, written in response to an invitation by

Chelmo Vinaver, is a setting of the Hebrew text of Psalm 130. Opus 50c, which Schoenberg entitled *Moderne Psalm,* sets his own text and remains incomplete.

David M. Schiller

References and Further Reading
Reich, Willi. 1971. *Schoenberg: A Critical Biography,* translated by Leo Black. New York: Praeger.

Ringer, Alexander L. 1990. *Arnold Schoenberg: The Composer as Jew.* Oxford, UK: Oxford University Press.

Schiller, David M. 2003. *Bloch, Schoenberg, and Bernstein: Assimilating Jewish Music.* Oxford, UK: Oxford University Press.

Schoenberg, Arnold. 1964, 1987. *Letters,* edited by Erwin Stein. Berkeley: University of California Press. Reprinted (1987).

Stuckenschmidt, H. H. 1977. *Schoenberg: His Life, World, and Work,* translated by Humphrey Searle. London: Calder.

American Jews and the Social Sciences

American Jews and Psychology

Jews have made substantial contributions to many areas of psychology since the field emerged as an academic discipline late in the nineteenth century. By 1900, Hugo Münsterberg and Joseph Jastrow had become prominent publicizers of the new science and served as presidents of the American Psychological Association (APA). After 1900, Jews trained in academic psychology increased in number and diversity. As the first sizable sociocultural minority group who sought careers in the field, Jewish psychologists faced increasing barriers to employment during the early decades of the twentieth century, with discriminatory practices in many academic disciplines reaching a high point in the 1920s and 1930s.

During this period, many Jewish psychologists who could not secure academic appointments sought additional training in medicine or worked in applied positions in clinical or industrial settings, social work agencies, or businesses. Among psychologists who continued to conduct research, several questioned the nativist claims of "race psychology" and made important contributions to the study of prejudice and other social problems. After World War II, the decline of antisemitism and increasing needs for faculty in colleges and universities resulted in a dramatic increase in the number of academic appointments for Jews in psychology, as in many other disciplines.

At the same time, the rapid postwar expansion of clinical psychology created new academic positions for Jewish psychologists who had begun their professional careers in applied settings.

By 1969, Jews were highly represented among faculty in clinical, experimental, and social psychology; today, many Jewish psychologists are known as eminent contributors to all areas of the discipline. The work of many Jewish psychologists has reflected their concerns with promoting intergroup tolerance. However, the professional activities of Jewish psychologists have varied along with several dimensions of diversity among Jews—their generation, their national origins, their orientations to Jewish ethnicity and to Judaism, and their degree of assimilation or resistance to assimilation.

Before 1900

Two psychologists of Jewish background, Hugo Münsterberg (1863–1916) and Joseph Jastrow (1863–1944), held academic positions in the United States before 1900. A third, Boris Sidis (1867–1923), who immigrated to the United States from Russia in 1887 and earned a PhD in psychology at Harvard in 1897, sought further training in medicine and opened a psychiatric institute in Portsmouth, New Hampshire. Münsterberg and Jastrow became well-known both as academic psychologists and as popularizers of psychology. Münsterberg, born in Germany, came to the United States in 1892 at the invitation of William James to head the Psychological Laboratory at Harvard University. Münsterberg had converted to Christianity while still in Germany, most likely to enhance his job prospects. He identified as a German and rarely mentioned Jewish issues in his work. Münsterberg contributed to the development of applied psychology, writing on such topics as psychotherapy, industrial psychology, eyewitness testimony, and film.

Joseph Jastrow, son of a prominent Prussian rabbi, was raised in Philadelphia after immigrating to the United States in 1866. At Johns Hopkins University in 1886, he earned the first PhD from the first formally organized American doctoral program in psychology, under G. Stanley Hall. Jastrow joined the faculty at the University of Wisconsin in 1888 and founded a psychology department with a laboratory. In addition to his research on psychophysics (the study of functional relationships between physical stimuli and sensory processes) and hypnosis, Jastrow published popular books based on his newspaper column, "Keeping Mentally Fit." Münsterberg and Jastrow organized the psychology pavilion at the Chicago World's Fair (the Columbian Exposition) in 1893. Both men were charter members of the APA, founded in 1892, and both served as presidents of the association, Münsterberg in 1898 and Jastrow in 1900.

1900–World War II

Between 1900 and 1940, Jewish psychologists as a group grew both in number and in internal diversity, as recent immigrants from Eastern Europe joined American-born Jews in pursuing graduate study. As in many other academic disciplines, faculty positions were generally limited to a small number of Jews from "acceptable" backgrounds—those from established American families who were relatively assimilated or those who were strongly recommended by sponsors as "courteous" and as "not insisting on [their] Jewishness" (Feuer 1982). For example, Samuel Fernberger (1887–1956), a Son of the American Revolution born into a prosperous Philadelphia family, earned a PhD at the University of Pennsylvania in 1912. After teaching at Clark University for several years, he joined the faculty at the University of Pennsylvania in 1920. Fernberger edited several major psychological jour-

nals and served as secretary and as treasurer of the APA. His research focused on problems of psychophysics and did not address minority issues.

Even American-born Jewish psychologists from "acceptable" backgrounds faced discrimination, and many who did not find faculty positions shifted to other fields. After earning a PhD in psychology at Harvard in 1910, Edmund Jacobson (1888–1983), a native of Chicago, sought training in medicine and became a psychiatrist well known for developing the technique of progressive relaxation. Samuel Kohs (1890–1984), who earned his doctorate at Stanford in 1919, worked in Jewish social welfare agencies; his nonverbal Block Design Tests of intelligence are still widely used. Some Jewish psychologists who did secure academic appointments did not identify as Jewish or mentioned their Jewishness only in private. Some changed their names to enhance their job prospects, and some found positions only with help from a mentor. When Josiah Morse (1879–1946), formerly Josiah Moses, accepted a position at the University of South Carolina in 1911, university president Samuel Mitchell, his former professor, had to quash a faculty protest. Morse changed his name in 1907, during a period of unemployment that inspired him to publish apparently the first article on prejudice by an American psychologist, some twenty years before the topic became popular in the psychological literature. Jewish immigrants generally had more difficulty finding academic positions than Jews born in the United States; many shifted to other fields, such as journalism or secondary education, or sought applied positions in industry or business.

Heightened xenophobia and antisemitism, coupled with a shortage of academic positions around World War I, exacerbated the difficulties of Jewish psychologists. Several of those who did not find faculty appointments managed to contribute to the field despite their marginal positions. For example, Gustave Feingold (1883–1948), who worked in a public high school, published research comparing intelligence test scores of children of immigrants and American-born parents to contest the nativist claims of immigration restrictionists. A. A. Roback (1890–1965) wrote popular and scholarly works on character and personality and published the first history of modern American psychology. Barriers to employment reached a peak in the 1920s and 1930s. As in many other academic disciplines, letters of recommendation routinely described Jewish candidates either as showing "objectionable" characteristics identified with Jews or as exceptions to these stereotypes (Winston 1996). Some Jewish psychologists found positions at new or less prestigious institutions or at historically black colleges; others held a series of temporary positions as instructors or researchers until the demand for faculty increased in the mid- to late-1940s.

Like Feingold, many researchers from Jewish and other ethnic minority backgrounds contributed to a thematic shift between 1920 and 1940 from "race psychology" to "studies in prejudice" (Samelson 1978). These researchers challenged claims of inherited racial and ethnic differences in intelligence and conducted studies on prejudice as a social problem. Jewish psychologists who contributed to the shift included Morris Viteles (1898–1996), who also became a pioneer in industrial psychology; Otto Klineberg (1899–1992), a former student of anthropologist Franz Boas (1858–1942); Daniel Katz (1903–1998); and Eugene Horowitz (1912–2002) and Ruth Horowitz (1910–1998), who became Eugene and Ruth Hartley during World War II. Several of these researchers focused primarily on the origins and effects of prejudice toward African Americans. Others, like Max Meenes (1901–1974) at Howard University, also studied antisemitism, as did Kurt Lewin (1890–1947) and Else Frenkel-Brunswik (1908–1958), who emigrated to the United States from Europe in the 1930s.

Of the large group of Jewish emigré psychologists who arrived in the United States before World War II, several of those who found faculty appointments played important roles in shaping American psychology. For example, Max Wertheimer (1880–1943) and Kurt Koffka (1886–1941) brought the influence of Gestalt psychology to the study of topics as diverse as perception, learning, development, memory, emotion, and personality. Heinz Werner (1890–1964) made important contributions to developmental psychology. Kurt Lewin's pioneering efforts in group dynamics and action research have had an enduring impact on social psychology.

During the 1920s and 1930s, many Jewish psychologists found employment in clinical settings where they developed training techniques, designed tests, and conducted experimental research in psychopathology (Winston 1998). David Wechsler (1896–1981), who began his career in the applied areas of guidance and testing in the early 1920s, became well known as the developer of the Wechsler Intelligence Scales; he joined the faculty of the New York University College of Medicine in 1942. Like many other Jews who made substantial contributions to clinical psychology, David Shakow (1901–1981) and Saul Rosenzweig (1907–2004) conducted research in hospital settings in the 1930s before moving into faculty positions during the postwar expansion of clinical psychology.

The Postwar Period

After World War II, the reduction of antisemitism in academia, the demand for faculty to educate the returning soldiers, and the rapid expansion of clinical psychology resulted in an increase in faculty positions for Jewish psychologists, many of whom became prominent contributors in clinical, experimental, social, and other areas of the field. Many Jewish psychologists worked to combat antisemitism and racial prejudice and to promote civil rights. Responses to the Holocaust included the classic study of the authoritarian personality (Adorno, Frenkel-Brunswik, Levinson, and Sanford 1950) and research by Stanley Milgram (1933–1984) on obedience to authority. In the case of *Brown v. Board of Education,* Isidor Chein (1912–1981) coauthored the *amicus curiae* statement on the psychological effects of segregation; signatories included Jerome Bruner (b. 1915), Else Frenkel-Brunswik, Daniel Katz, Otto Klineberg, and David Krech (1909–1977; formerly Isadore Krechevsky).

By 1969, Jews were highly represented among psychology faculty in universities and colleges in the United States (Steinberg 1974), especially in clinical, experimental, and social psychology. During the postwar period, many Jewish psychologists have been among the most eminent contributors not only to these areas, but to all areas of the discipline. Examples include Abraham Maslow (humanistic psychology); Jerome Bruner, Herbert Simon, and Elizabeth Loftus (cognitive psychology); Erik Erikson and Lawrence Kohlberg (developmental psychology); and Michael Posner (neuropsychology). Throughout their history, Jewish psychologists in the United States have represented a diversity of generations, national origins, orientations to Jewish ethnicity and to Judaism, and degrees of assimilation or resistance to assimilation. Their professional activities, research interests, and theoretical preferences have reflected this diversity.

Nicole B. Barenbaum

References and Further Reading

Adorno, Theodor W., Else Frenkel-Brunswik, Daniel J. Levinson, and R. Nevitt Sanford. 1950. *The Authoritarian Personality: Studies in Prejudice.* New York: Harper.

Feuer, Lewis S. 1982. "The Stages in the Social History of Jewish Professors in American Colleges and Universities." *American Jewish History* 71: 432–465.

Heinze, Andrew R. 2004. *Jews and the American Soul: Human Nature in the Twentieth Century.* Princeton, NJ: Princeton University Press.

Hollinger, David A. 1996. *Science, Jews, and Secular Culture: Studies in Mid-Twentieth-Century American Intellectual History.* Princeton, NJ: Princeton University Press.

Samelson, Franz. 1978. "From 'Race Psychology' to 'Studies in Prejudice': Some Observations on the Thematic Reversal in Social Psychology." *Journal of the History of the Behavioral Sciences* 14: 265–278.

Steinberg, Stephen. 1974. *The Academic Melting Pot: Catholics and Jews in American Higher Education.* New York: McGraw-Hill.

Winston, Andrew S. 1996. "'As His Name Indicates': R. S. Woodworth's Letters of Reference and Employment for Jewish Psychologists in the 1930s." *Journal of the History of the Behavioral Sciences* 32: 30–43.

Winston, Andrew S. 1998. "'The Defects of His Race': E. G. Boring and Antisemitism in American Psychology, 1923–1953." *History of Psychology* 1: 27–51.

Jews in the Development of American Psychoanalysis: The First Fifty Years

Though psychoanalysis was born in Vienna in the final years of the nineteenth century, during the first decades of the next century its center of gravity shifted to the United States. In the 1930s events in Europe accelerated the spread of Freud's ideas in America and led to the establishment of New York as the new center of the psychoanalytic movement. The culture of Europe at the turn of the century was also decisive in fostering and consolidating the Jewish identity of the psychoanalytic movement. The antisemitic climate in Central Europe discouraged the absorption of psychoanalysis into the mainstream of intellectual and social life, and had the effect of concentrating, to Freud's dismay, the new field's ethnic associations.

The forced emigration of numerous Jewish analysts from Europe in the first half of the twentieth century brought many to the United States, which ensured that the development of psychoanalysis here would continue to be influenced by Jewish thinkers. Furthermore, some of the forces that had made psychoanalysis in Europe attractive to Jews were also found in the United States. Few university appointments were open to Jews; so a profession that shared much of the social and financial prestige of medicine but could be practiced independently of unwelcoming institutions, had great appeal. Given all of these circumstances, it is not surprising that most of the great contributors to the establishment of psychoanalysis in America (1908–1958) were Jews, and that the Jewish influence on psychoanalysis remains very strong even today.

Psychoanalysis came to America out of a Jewish milieu. Founded by Freud, a Viennese Jew, it was subsequently nurtured and developed by Freud with his mostly Jewish students and followers and their mostly Jewish patients. The Jewish pedigree of psychoanalysis was a sensitive issue for Freud, who feared that the new field would never be given its due if it were seen only as a "Jewish" science. "Rest assured," he wrote to his early disciple Karl Abraham, also a Viennese Jew, "if my name was Uberhuber, in spite of everything my innovations would have met with far less resistance" (Abraham and Freud 1965). He made an effort to enlist Christian followers such as Oskar Pfister, a Protestant minister, and C. G. Jung, both of whom were early converts to psychoanalysis. Nonetheless, Andrew Heinze, an American historian and Judaic scholar, places Freud in the tradition of rabbinic moralists like Israel Salanter and Schneur Zalman, in the way that they looked to the family for universal laws of psychological conduct and morality. So the Jewishness of psychoanalysis—and of psychoanalysts—was from the beginning a complicated issue.

Abraham Arden Brill was the first practicing American psychoanalyst. Born in 1875 in Kanzcuga, a small village in Eastern Galicia not far from the birthplace of Freud's father, he came to the United States alone at fourteen with two dollars in his pocket, determined to make a place for himself in society. Brill shared Freud's wish to keep psychoanalysis from being seen as Jewish, but for different reasons. He intentionally distanced himself from his provincial Orthodox roots in his efforts to integrate himself fully into what he saw as American culture. He achieved the foothold he needed by putting himself through medical school at Columbia University and training as a psychiatrist at New York's Central Islip State Hospital. Brill learned about psychoanalysis at Eugen Bleuler and C. G. Jung's Burgholzli Clinic in Zurich, and visited Freud in Vienna. As soon as he returned to the United States in 1908, after he had traveled to Vienna and had a brief analysis with Freud, he established a psychoanalytic practice.

Brill was Freud's first English translator, and the founder in 1911 of the first American psychoanalytic society, the New York Psychoanalytic Society. "Psychoanalysis was unknown in this country until I introduced it in 1908," he wrote in 1938. "[Psychoanalytic] terminology, some of which I was the first to coin into English, can now be found in all standard English dictionaries. Words like *abreaction, transference, repression, displacement* and *unconscious,* which I introduced as Freudian concepts, have been adopted and used to give new meaning, new values to our knowledge of normal and abnormal behavior" (Brill 1938).

Brill strove throughout his life to bind psychoanalysis with psychiatry and establish it as a medical specialty. As a financially and socially ambitious Jew in America, he wanted to consolidate his own access to medical prestige; he also believed that the new field would be more likely to survive as a medical specialty. Therefore he stubbornly opposed Freud's acceptance of lay analysis, the practice of psychoanalysis by nonphysicians, and he succeeded in building his own preference for medical exclusivity into the young American psychoanalytic institutions, where it was to leave a bitter and haunting legacy.

However Brill tried to assimilate himself into American gentile society, his Jewish identity permeated his work. He saw a parallel between Judaism, which preached control of the emotions, and psychoanalysis, in which superego and ego (roughly conscience and reason) were set up in opposition to the biological passions: Brill in a public lecture in 1937 said, "The old rabbis preached, 'He who conquers his primitive feelings is as strong as one who can conquer a city'" (Heinze 2004). Politically, Brill would likely have been less forceful in his campaign to restrict the practice of psychoanalysis to physicians if he had been more confident of his own place in society. His New World struggle with his Old World Jewishness left an indelible mark on American psychoanalysis.

Freud recognized Brill's contribution to psychoanalysis in America. He wrote in the preface of the 1932 edition of the *Interpretation of Dreams:* "If psychoanalysis now plays a role in American intellectual life, or if it does so in the future a large part of this result will have to be attributed to this and other activities of Dr. Brill's." Ever fearful, however, lest psychoanalysis be marginalized as a "Jewish science," Freud supported James Jackson Putnam, a Boston gentile, as first president of the American Psychoanalytic Association over Brill, and Horace Frink, another non-Jew, as president of the New York Psychoanalytic Society, which Brill himself had founded.

But Freud's hope that gentiles would lead American psychoanalysis was never realized. Putnam founded the Boston Psychoanalytic Society, the second American society and a very influential one, in 1914, but his cofounder, Isidor Coriat (1875–1943), was a Sephardic Jew, a member of the American Jewish Historical Society, and married to a rabbi's daughter. The Boston society became home to many refugee analysts after the war, notably two influential couples (Helena and Felix Deutsch, and Edward and Grete Bibring) and Hans Sachs, the first training analyst at the Berlin Institute and the editor of *Imago.*

Meanwhile, Brill's New York Psychoanalytic Society and Institute (NYPI) maintained its preeminence and its Jewish leadership. In 1937–1938 Bertram Lewin, born in Texas but trained in Berlin, was president. During his term Walter Langer, a gentile analyst training in Vienna, came back to New York seeking help in getting the remaining Jewish psychoanalysts out of Europe. Lewin refused this help on the grounds that there were already too many psychoanalysts in the country, and certainly too many in New York (Langer and Gifford 1978).

In 1938, however, Lawrence Kubie succeeded Lewin as president. Kubie was a German Jew, and, with another psychoanalyst from a wealthy German Jewish New York family, Bettina Warburg, he organized the Rescue Committee of the NYPI, which provided passports, money, and jobs for almost all of the Jewish psychoanalysts in Europe who were at risk.

On September 23, 1939—Yom Kippur—Freud died, after having asked his doctor, Max Shur, to administer the lethal dose of morphine that would release him from his losing battle with cancer. After his death, centrifugal tendencies in the analytic movement became more apparent. The organizational harmony, such as it was, of the 1930s was followed by the schisms of the forties, also initiated mostly by Jewish analysts. Sandor Rado, a Hungarian Jew who had been director of training at the Berlin Institute, came to New York to take the same position at the New

York Psychoanalytic. In 1942 Rado, who shared with Brill the wish for a close connection with the medical establishment, left the NYPI to start a new institute affiliated with the medical school of Columbia University. There he promoted a modification of classical Freudian theory and practice that he called Adaptational Psychoanalysis. The second schism began almost at the same time, when Karen Horney, whose book *The Neurotic Personality of Our Time* had views on sexuality and women that departed from Freud, lost her faculty position at the NYPI. When she resigned in protest against no longer being permitted to teach beginning candidates, but only advanced students, Erich Fromm and William Silverberg (Jews), and Clara Thompson (a gentile) went with her, and together they founded the Association for the Advancement of Psychoanalysis. This group also subsequently split over the question of lay analysis; Fromm and Thompson started the William Alanson White Institute, which trained nonphysicians, and William Silverberg founded the Institute of the Flower Fifth Avenue Hospital, associated with New York Medical College, which trained only physicians.

Theodore Reik came to study at the New York Psychoanalytic in 1938. He was a student of Freud's, a nonphysician, and in fact had been the subject of Freud's paper "The Problem of Lay Analysis," with which nonmedical psychoanalysts had unsuccessfully argued for their legitimacy against Brill. But Brill had prevailed in the United States, and Reik left the NYPI because his lack of a medical degree meant that he could never be a training analyst there. He founded the National Psychological Association for Psychoanalysis in 1948, a prestigious institute for the training of lay analysts. Reik clashed with Brill also on account of his unapologetic pride in his Jewish heritage and its spiritual and ethical values; he felt that Ernest Jones, Freud's biographer, did not adequately understand the place of Freud's Jewishness in his personality and his work.

New York in the late forties became home to a group of prominent Jewish women, refugee analysts. Edith Jacobson made an outstanding contribution to what has come to be known as Object Relations theory in her monograph *The Self and the Object World*. She was imprisoned in Berlin by the Nazis for two and a half years for shielding a patient who was a Jewish Communist. Annie Reich and Elizabeth Gero Heyman convinced the Gestapo to release Jacobson, who had diabetes, because she was ill. This group also included the noted child analyst Berta Bornstein; Mar-

garet Mahler, who formulated a seminal theory of separation and individuation in early childhood; and Annie Reich, who was an early student of narcissism and related phenomena.

Jews figured prominently in West Coast psychoanalysis also. Ernst Simmel organized the first psychoanalytic study group in Los Angeles in 1934. In Europe he and Otto Fenichel had belonged to the group of Jewish analysts who came to be known as the Freudian Left (Jacoby 1983). Other members of the group, which included Jacobson, eventually emigrated to New York. But Simmel went to California. Fenichel joined him there later, arriving in 1938 in Los Angeles, where he published his great 1945 work, *The Psychoanalytic Theory of Neurosis.*

In 1944 Ernst Simmel organized a conference on antisemitism in San Francisco, in which Otto Fenichel participated. The proceedings were published as *Anti-Semitism: A Social Disease* (1946) and offered a psychoanalytic critique of prejudice. Fenichel proposed that the Jew occupies a special place in the mind of the antisemite; the Jew is the authority that oppresses him and the "primal instincts that he harbors within himself." The conference was an attempt to use psychoanalysis to account for the malignancy of antisemitism, a subject that continues to concern psychoanalysts. In 1951, Rudolph Loewenstein published *Christians and Jews: A Psychoanalytic Study* on the subject.

Elsewhere in the country, other Jewish analysts were directing the course of events. The key figure in San Francisco was Siegfried Bernfeld. Bernfeld was not a physician. He was an outspoken advocate for lay analysis and for less rigid and constricting techniques of psychoanalytic training. In Chicago, Bruno Bettelheim established the Orthogenic School at the University of Chicago, a therapeutic school based on psychoanalytic principles. He wrote about his concentration camp experiences and published several other psychoanalytically related volumes of broad popular and professional appeal.

Roy Grinker Sr. from Chicago was one of Freud's last analysands. Before the war Grinker psychoanalyzed Rabbi Joshua Liebman, who subsequently wrote *Peace of Mind* (1946), a great work that popularized Freudian depth psychology. Two Jewish women also did a great deal to popularize psychoanalysis after World War II; one was Lucy Freeman with her book *Fight against Fears* (1951), and the other was Joanne Greenberg, author of *I Never Promised You a Rose Garden* (1964).

By the end of World War II, the center of psychoanalysis had shifted from Vienna to New York and Boston. This was the heyday of psychoanalysis in the United States, partly thanks to a vogue for the psychoanalytic treatment of "shell shock," which brought analysis into the public eye. Grinker contributed to this awareness, having done notable work treating soldiers who returned emotionally ill from combat.

A new generation of American-born Jewish analysts came to prominence during this Golden Age. In New York, this included Charles Brenner, who came from Boston; Martin Wang, who emigrated from Germany via Italy; and native New Yorkers Jacob Arlow and David Beres. These four founded an influential postgraduate study group and, in combination and as individuals, made important contributions to the classical psychoanalytic literature. One of these, Brenner's *Elementary Textbook of Psychoanalysis,* is perhaps the most widely read introduction to psychoanalysis ever published.

In Los Angeles this later generation included Ralph Greenson, the model for Leo Rosten's novel *Captain Newman, M.D.,* and the movie that was made from it with Gregory Peck. Greenson wrote extensively about psychoanalytic technique. Another was Leo Rangell, who wrote extensively on psychoanalytic theory, and who has the distinction of having been president of both the American and International Psychoanalytic Associations. Rangell, in his nineties, remains an important voice in American psychoanalysis.

Although no data are available about the actual numbers of Jewish versus gentile psychoanalysts, during its developing years in this country the Jewish influence has been enormous. How things will develop remains to be seen as the lay analysis issue is resolved and as sociopolitical questions about psychoanalytic theory come into dispute. Why were American Jews so interested in becoming psychoanalysts? During the first part of the twentieth century there were two American industries with a preponderance of Jews: movies and psychoanalysis (Gabler 1990). These were new enterprises that offered opportunities for advancement, recognition, and financial success to the cohort of first- and second-generation American Jews. Psychoanalysis probably has an appeal also based on its emphasis on interpretation and exegesis that were central to Jewish tradition and scholarship. But in the final analysis the main determinant might have been the identification of these Americans with the charismatic Jew and first psychoanalyst—Sigmund Freud.

Arnold Richards

References and Further Reading

Abraham, Hilde C., and Ernst I. Freud, eds. 1965. *A Psycho-Analytic Dialogue: The Letters of Sigmund Freud and Karl Abraham, 1907–1926.* London: Hogarth.

Brill, A. A. 1938. "Introduction." In *The Basic Writings of Sigmund Freud,* edited and translated by A. A. Brill, 3–32. New York: Modern Library.

Fenichel, Otto. 1945. *The Psychoanalytic Theory of Neurosis.* New York: W. W. Norton.

Gabler, N. 1990. *An Empire of Their Own: How the Jews Invented Hollywood.* New York: Random House.

Heinze, Andrew. 2004. *Jews and the American Soul: Human Nature in the Twentieth Century.* Princeton, NJ: Princeton University Press.

Jacobson, Edith. 1964. *The Self and the Object World.* New York: International Universities Press.

Jacoby, R. 1983. *The Repression of Psychoanalysis.* Chicago: University of Chicago Press.

Langer, W. C., and S. Gifford. 1978. "An American Analyst in Vienna during the Anschluss, 1936–38." *Journal of the History of the Behavioral Sciences* 14: 27–54.

Jewish Emigrés of the Frankfurt School

Critical theory may have been an outgrowth of German philosophy, but it was actually born in the United States. The Institute for Social Research was founded in 1923 in Frankfurt, and under its first director, Carl Grünberg, many of its early members—Henryk Grossman, Fritz Sternberg, Felix Weill, and others—contributed to the study of political economy, imperialism, and the history of the labor movement. Max Horkheimer, who became the new director in 1930, changed this orientation. Three years later, however, he was forced to flee Nazi Germany for Switzerland and, in 1934, he moved the Institute to Columbia University. It was therefore in the United States that Horkheimer's inner circle—all of whom were Jewish or, in the case of Theodor W. Adorno, part Jewish—produced the major works of "critical theory" usually associated with the "Frankfurt School." Among the most important were Leo Lowenthal, who joined the Institute in 1926; Adorno, who began to participate in 1928, but only became an official member ten years later; Erich Fromm, who started his nine-year collaboration in 1930; Herbert Marcuse, who joined in 1933; and Walter Benjamin, who never officially became a member.

Walter Benjamin had the most remarkable career of any thinker associated with the Institute. He was completely unknown in the United States until the preeminent political theorist Hannah Arendt edited a collection of his essays, *Illuminations* (1969). He thereafter became celebrated as an iconoclastic thinker involved with investigating and meshing traditions as diverse as Jewish messianism, the Baroque, Modernism, and Marxism. With the new popularity of the radically subjective postmodern movement during the 1980s, however, his fame reached extraordinary proportions: a library of secondary works has appeared and almost every volume of Benjamin's *Selected Writings* has become an academic best-seller. His critique of progress and optimistic illusions, his attempt to reconstruct theory through the assimilation of seemingly mutually exclusive traditions, his skepticism concerning traditional foundations and universal claims, and his preoccupation with subjectivity produced a transformation of the entire critical project. Benjamin's work spoke directly to many on the Left who, following the collapse of the social and cultural movements associated with the 1960s, felt they were living in an age of "ruins." Above all, however, his inability to decide whether to emigrate to Israel or the United States and his subsequent tragic death in 1940, while attempting to flee the Nazi invasion of France, put a particularly dramatic stamp on the experience of exile.

Exile marked the work of the Institute. Horkheimer, in fact, only coined the term *critical theory* in 1937, after having fled to the United States. His seminal essay on the subject, "Traditional and Critical Theory," treated it as an approach qualitatively different from "vulgar" materialism—i.e., positivism or behaviorism—and metaphysical idealism. Critical theory should be equated with neither a system nor a fixed set of proscriptions. It should instead be understood as a method of liberation, a cluster of themes or concerns, that would express an explicit interest in the abolition of social injustice and the psychological, cultural, and political reasons why the proletarian revolution failed following the events of 1917 in Russia. With the publication of "Authority and the Family" (1934), for example, Horkheimer sought to analyze how a patriarchal familial structure inhibited the development of revolutionary consciousness among workers. "The Jews and Europe" (1938) insisted that confronting bigotry called for confronting economic exploitation, or, as Horkheimer put it, "he who wishes to speak of anti-Semitism must also speak of capitalism." Works like these set the stage for a new mode of "dialectical" thinking that went beyond the economic interests of classes and elites as well as the institutional dynamics of the state.

Reactionary sexual mores, mass culture, the division of labor, and the need to grasp the universal through the particular would prove essential themes for the Institute. Deeper issues mired in the anthropology of human existence became issues for critical theory. Indeed, the need for a response to them turned critical theory into an ongoing threat to the stultifying dogma and collectivism of "actually existing socialism." Critical theory leveled an attack on all ideological and institutional forms of oppression. Its general objective was to foster critical reflection, a capacity for fantasy, and new forms of political action in an increasingly bureaucratized world.

Most members of the Institute remained suspicious of the different ways in which supposedly neutral formulations of science veiled repressive social interests. That is why they employed a methodological approach indebted to both the critique of ideology (*Ideologiekritik*) that emerged with German idealism and the sociology of knowledge that derived from Karl Marx. Ideals of freedom and liberation provided the basis for their critique of the existing order. In the United States, however, the character of this engagement changed dramatically from that of the early days. The most compelling reasons were connected with the failure of the proletarian revolution and the increasingly stark reality of totalitarianism.

Major scholars associated with the Institute—albeit often at the fringes—added much to an understanding of the ideological forces behind the new totalitarian phenomenon and its structure. Its emergence in Germany was analyzed in works as diverse as the enormously popular study of the psychological appeal underlying totalitarianism, *Escape from Freedom* (1941) by Erich Fromm, and the classic examination of German film in the Weimar Republic by Siegfried Kracauer—who was close to Adorno and Benjamin—*From Caligari to Hitler* (1947). In a more social scientific vein, Otto Kirchheimer contributed *Political Justice* (1961), and Franz Neumann *Behemoth* (1942), the first significant work that analyzed the structure of the Nazi state. Horkheimer edited a five-volume work, *Studies in Prejudice* (1949), for the American Jewish Committee, while Adorno led a team of researchers in producing the classic *The Authoritarian Personality* (1950). In the context of the United States, both looking backward to the 1930s and forward to McCarthyism, it is also useful to consider *Prophets of Deceit: A Study of the Techniques of the American Agitator* (1948) by Leo Lowenthal and Norbert Guterman, as well as Lowenthal's work on American antisemitism, *Images of Prejudice* (1945).

Following the Hitler–Stalin pact, which unleashed World War II, the proletarian revolution ceased to serve as the ultimate aim of the critical enterprise. As a consequence, the working class lost its standing as the revolutionary subject of history, and many no longer saw its interests as sufficient for generating a critique of the status quo. A new phase in the development of critical theory began with the completion of *Dialectic of Enlightenment* (1944), including a sensational last chapter "Elements of Anti-Semitism," in 1947. Horkheimer and Adorno, its authors, called into question the old belief in progress, science, and the benefits of modernity. They insisted that, by privileging mathematical reason, the Enlightenment assaulted not only reactionary forms of religious dogma, but also, whether intentionally or unintentionally, the more progressive normative ways of thinking. Scientific rationality divorced from ethical concerns was indeed seen as culminating in the number tattooed on the arm of the concentration camp inmate.

Dialectic of Enlightenment offers less the vision of a better world emerging from the Enlightenment than one increasingly defined by the "commodity form" and bureaucratic rationality, in which the individual is stripped of conscience and spontaneity. Stalinism on the left, Nazism on the right, and an increasingly bureaucratic and robotic mass society emerging in the United States: mass society, the horror of war, and—perhaps above all—the concentration camp universe inspired this book. The new reality demanded a significant revision in the more traditional understandings of critical and radical theory.

Socialism had proved a nightmare, Nazism was even worse, and liberalism had seemingly become anachronistic. For Horkheimer and Adorno, the possibility of revolutionary transformation faded in the face of an apparently seamless bureaucratic order buttressed by a culture industry intent on eliminating subjectivity and any genuinely

critical opposition to the status quo. This development is what required a rethinking of the usually positive view regarding the Enlightenment. It was therefore the bohemian intellectual, who challenged society in its entirety, rather than the political revolutionary who held out whatever emancipatory hope still existed. Thus, for the proponents of critical theory, it had become necessary to supplement the dialectical framework of Hegel and Marx with the more individualist tenets of Schopenhauer and Nietzsche in combating the collectivist strains in advanced industrial society.

To put it another way, it was now incumbent on a genuinely critical theory to recognize the ways in which civilization in general, and modernity in particular, were flawed from the beginning. The critical theory of society would require a more directly anthropological form of inquiry. It had become necessary to highlight not the needs of some class-bound and collectivist revolutionary subject, but the ways in which individual subjectivity might resist the conformity generated by an increasingly administered and culturally barbaric universe. Political resistance made way for a philosophico-aesthetic assertion of subjectivity in the two great works by Theodor Adorno, *Negative Dialectics* (1966) and *Aesthetic Theory* (1970), and the philosophico-religious concerns of Max Horkheimer in his *Longing for the Totally Other* (1970).

Theodor Adorno was probably the most talented proponent of this new turn in critical theory. His interests extended from musicology and literary analysis to sociology, metapsychology, and philosophy. The only real disciple of Benjamin, the inventor of "negative dialectics," Adorno's works evidence a rare standard of intellectual brilliance. They include extraordinary studies on modern music, a masterpiece that transformed aesthetic theory, and *Minima Moralia: Reflections of a Damaged Life* (1947).

Adorno's work exemplifies the abstruse style employed by so many critical theorists. The heritage of dialectical philosophy surely had an impact; the complex use of complex concepts often demanded a complex style. Especially in the ideologically charged context of the war and its aftermath, however, members of the Institute also self-consciously employed an Aesopian form of writing. As exiles living in the United States, it only made sense for them to hide their indebtedness to Marx by substituting the highly abstract language of Hegel. But there is also a theoretical justification for their abstruse style. The famous analysis of the culture industry developed in *Dialectic of Enlightenment,* written while its authors were living in Los Angeles, implied that popularity would necessarily neutralize whatever critical or emancipatory messages a work might retain. Nevertheless, there was nothing ambivalent about the willingness of Erich Fromm—or Herbert Marcuse—to engage the public in a radical fashion.

Fromm was surely the most lucid stylist to emerge from the Institute. He was also the most popular and arguably the most loyal to its original purpose insofar as he always sought to link theory with the practical demands of social change and individual transformation. Fromm grew up Orthodox, and he studied with leading rabbis: his dissertation dealt with the Jewish Diaspora and another of his early works with the Sabbath. The psychoanalytic institute he founded in Berlin with his first wife, Frieda Reichmann, soon became known as the *Torah-peutikum.* His interest in the psychological appeal and ethical impulse provided by religion, in any event, never fully disappeared.

Erich Fromm was initially one of the most influential members of the Institute and a close friend of Horkheimer. His concern was with how psychological attitudes mediated the relation between the individual and society. Even during the 1920s, he was intent on linking Freud with Marx. For this reason, when Adorno first insisted on developing an anthropological critique of civilization from the standpoint of Freud's instinct theory, he clashed with Fromm. The dazzling newcomer won the battle. Fromm divorced himself from the Institute by 1940, and he proceeded to write a number of best-sellers, including *Escape from Freedom.* Quickly enough, his former colleagues condemned him for the "superficial" quality of his writings, even while his influence soared among left-wing intellectuals and a broader public from the 1950s to the 1970s.

Herbert Marcuse, while in the United States, not only worked with the Office of Strategic Services as an expert on West European politics, but also wrote papers on totalitarianism and in 1958 published a highly respected study entitled *Soviet Marxism.* In spite of his penchant for utopian thought, so prominent in *Eros and Civilization* (1955), Marcuse also remained faithful to the original practical impulse of critical theory. His most influential work, *One-Dimensional Man* (1964), actually anticipated the seminal role of the new social movements and a radical cultural politics in responding to the bureaucracy, commodification, and conformism of advanced industrial so-

ciety. Pessimism concerning the future of a society in which all radical alternatives were being absorbed, and in which all ideological contradictions were being flattened out, combined with a utopian vision built on the radical humanism of the young Marx, on the play principle of Schiller, and on the metapsychology of Freud. This tension, indeed, permeated all of Marcuse's writings.

The popularity of Fromm and Marcuse in the United States contrasted strikingly with a virtually total ignorance of the work produced by the rest of the Frankfurt School. The legend that critical theory inspired the movement of the 1960s is, certainly in America, misleading; its major works were translated only in the 1970s. During that decade, journals like *Telos* and *New German Critique* helped in publicizing its ideas and the works of its most important representatives. The emphasis on alienation, the domination of nature, the regressive components of progress, the mutability of human nature, and the stultifying effects of the culture industry and advanced industrial society made the enterprise relevant for young intellectuals who had come of age through "the movement" of the 1960s.

Max Horkheimer and Theodor Adorno, however, were appalled by what they had helped inspire. Following their return to Germany, the former became rector and the latter, somewhat later, a dean at the University of Frankfurt. Neither showed much of an inclination for Zionism, and Horkheimer in particular was critical of the Eichmann trial and various policies undertaken by Israel. Still, it is ironic that these new stalwarts of the establishment should have anticipated the movement's concern with a "cultural revolution" and the transformation of everyday life demanded by so many of their students. These themes were as real for many activists of the 1960s, both in Europe and the United States, as the quest for racial justice and the anti-imperialist opposition to the Vietnam War. Nevertheless, they lost their salience in the general malaise that followed the collapse of the movement and the emergence of a neoconservative assault on what has been called the adversary culture.

A new set of academic radicals embraced instead the "deconstructive" and radically subjectivist elements in the thinking of Adorno and Benjamin: their emphasis on the fragmentary character of reality, the illusion of progress, the substitution of experimental culture for political resistance. All this fit the time in which radicalism retreated from the streets into the university. Critical theory of this new deconstructive, or poststructuralist, sort invaded the most prestigious journals and disciplines ranging from anthropology and film to religion, linguistics, and political science. Elements of it have, indeed, become features of the very society that the Frankfurt School ostensibly wished to challenge.

But that time, too, is passing. If it is to remain relevant, especially in the United States, critical theory must begin taming its metaphysical excesses, mitigating its subjectivism, and affirming its repressed political character. These concerns inform much of the work undertaken by Jürgen Habermas, the brilliant student of Horkheimer and Adorno, who came to maturity in the aftermath of World War II. Of particular interest, in this vein, is his *Philosophical Discourse of Modernity: Twelve Lectures* (1985). Habermas was never in exile: he experienced the impact of totalitarianism directly in his youth, and it left him with a profound respect for the liberal political legacy, the "public sphere," and the repressed possibilities of "communicative action." Habermas has also gained a large academic following in the United States. Nevertheless, his work provides an important beginning for resurrecting the critical undertaking.

Economic globalization and political reaction, in any event, are creating a new set of issues for a new generation of critical theorists. It is becoming increasingly necessary for a new generation of thinkers to reconstruct the practical impulse of the critical project, its repressed political purpose, and its speculative legacy for the present. Critical theory is "Jewish" insofar as it is an expression of the modern diaspora and part of that secular Jewish tradition—concerned with social justice, toleration, and the abolition of suffering—that extends over Mendelssohn and Heine to Marx, Kafka, and Einstein. Such a tradition cannot remain immune from criticism. Remaining honest to the tradition of critical theory thus calls for confronting it from the critical standpoint. In the need to support this claim, whatever the other differences between them, all of its major representatives would assuredly—today—find themselves in agreement.

Stephen Eric Bronner

References and Further Reading

Bronner, Stephen Eric. 2002. *Of Critical Theory and Its Theorists*, 2nd ed. New York: Routledge.

Buck-Morss, Susan. 1977. *The Origin of Negative Dialectics: Theodor W. Adorno, Walter Benjamin, and the Frankfurt Institute.* New York: Free Press.

Held, David. 1980. *An Introduction to Critical Theory: Horkheimer to Habermas.* Berkeley: University of California Press.

Jay, Martin. 1973. *The Dialectical Imagination: A History of the Frankfurt School and the Institute of Social Research, 1923–1950.* Berkeley: University of California Press.

Kellner, Douglas. 1989. *Critical Theory, Marxism and Modernity.* Cambridge, UK: Polity Press.

Tarr, Zoltan, 1985. *The Frankfurt School: The Critical Theories of Max Horkheimer and Theodor Adorno.* New York: Random House.

Wiggershaus, Rolf. 1994. *The Frankfurt School: Its History, Theories, and Political Significance,* translated by Michael Robertson. Cambridge, UK: Polity Press.

American Jews in Economics

Many of the most prominent American economists, past and present, are Jewish. Indeed, more than half of all American Nobel Prize winners in economics have been Jewish (that is, at least one parent was Jewish). The Nobel Prize in economics was initiated in 1969, and the first American recipient was Paul Samuelson, in 1970. Various aspects of the profession attracted Jews. Some were motivated by the wish to improve the economy, and therefore social well-being, by focusing on economic policy. Some found the rigor of economic theory intellectually appealing. Those with mathematical skills derived additional intellectual satisfaction from studying economics. But no particular theory or school of economics is more associated with Jewish economists than with others. Their interests, their views on theory and on the application of theory to policies, have all been diverse.

There is no specific element of Jewish culture or religion that drew so many Jews to economics. Indeed, many prominent economists are non-Jews. The foremost economist of the twentieth century was the Englishman John Maynard Keynes, who was not Jewish. Among American economists, however, many would agree that Paul Samuelson has been the outstanding member of their profession in the past century. He and Milton Friedman are the two most influential American Jewish economists of recent decades.

Paul A. Samuelson (b. 1915)

Paul Samuelson received his BA at the University of Chicago in 1935 and his PhD at Harvard in 1941, after being elected to the distinguished Society of Fellows there (1937–1940). Since 1940 he has been a professor at Massachusetts Institute of Technology (MIT). It is his presence there that has attracted so many notable scholars to MIT's department of economics.

Samuelson's enormous influence on economic thinking and economic policy is attributable to his many papers and books written for fellow economists; to his role as an economic adviser and consultant; and to the impact of his textbook, *Economics,* on millions of students. First published in 1948, and translated into many languages, it is now co-authored with Professor William Nordhaus of Yale University and is in its eighteenth edition.

In presenting the Nobel Prize, Assar Lindbeck, the Swedish economist, stated, "more than any other contemporary economist, [Samuelson] has contributed to raising the general analytical and methodological level in economic science" (Bank of Sweden n.d.).

His work has influenced thinking in numerous fields of economics. Unlike many other economists, Samuelson has not specialized. He has written on consumer behavior, international trade, price theory, growth theory and various other aspects of macroeconomics, financial analysis, and the history of economic thought. As a macroeconomist, he can be characterized as a neo-Keynesian. That his early book *Foundations of Economic Analysis* (1947), though highly mathematical, was reissued as a paperback in 1965 testifies to the value of his professional work.

Samuelson's most prestigious advisory role was to John F. Kennedy, as U.S. senator, presidential candidate, and president-elect, for whom he wrote a report on the state of the American economy. He was also a consultant to the U.S. Treasury Department, the Bureau of the Budget, and the Council of Economic Advisers. Lawrence Summers, Harvard president until 2006 and former secretary of the treasury, is his nephew, and Kenneth Arrow, a Nobel Laureate in economics, is his sister-in-law's brother.

Milton Friedman (1912–2006)

Milton Friedman was awarded a scholarship to Rutgers University, where he earned his BA in 1932. There he was introduced to economics by Arthur Burns. Friedman did graduate work at the University of Chicago and Columbia University, where he received his PhD in 1946, after spending two years at the Treasury Department in Washington. He joined the economics faculty at the University of Chicago in 1946 and also became associated with the National Bureau of Economic Research, where Burns was Director of Research.

Like Samuelson, Milton Friedman has had a significant impact on both economic theory and policy. He was the leading monetarist in the United States, focusing on monetary policy and the quantity of money as an influence on economic activity and a tool for maintaining economic growth and stability. In 1959, he published *A Program for Monetary Stability,* calling for constant growth of the money supply and rejecting countercyclical monetary policy. He has also argued that the Federal Reserve's countercyclical policies have often caused instability, and that "the Fed" should be subject to a rule regarding money supply growth. In general, Friedman opposed the popular Keynesian view that favored discretionary monetary and fiscal policy. Among his many books is the widely circulated *A Monetary History of the United States* (1963), written with Anna J. Schwartz.

The Monetarist school is, however, less influential in the early twenty-first century than it was twenty to thirty years earlier. The Federal Reserve no longer targets the money supply in conducting its monetary policy, although the European Central Bank does.

Friedman was awarded the Nobel Prize in 1976 "for his achievements in the fields of consumption analysis, monetary history and theory, and for his demonstration of the complexity of stabilization policy" (Bank of Sweden n.d.).

Other Economists of Recent Decades
Arthur F. Burns (1904–1987)

Arthur Burns was born in Austria and emigrated to the United States in 1914. He received his PhD at Columbia University in 1944, after teaching at Rutgers University from 1927 to 1944. Then he was a professor at Columbia for twenty years. He was chairman of the Council of Economic Advisers from 1953 to 1956. Upon his return to Columbia, he was appointed president of the National Bureau of Economic Research, a position he held for ten years.

In 1969, Burns became economic counselor to newly elected President Richard M. Nixon, and in 1970, when William McChesney Martin's term as chairman of the Federal Reserve Board ended, Nixon appointed Burns to succeed him. Burns held that position until 1978.

In 1981, President Ronald Reagan appointed him ambassador to Germany, a position he held for three years. He then joined the American Enterprise Institute. Burns was better known for the prominent offices he held, both private and public, than for his academic work. He did, however, publish several books. The best known is *Measuring Business Cycles* (1946), co-authored with Wesley Clair Mitchell.

Wassily Leontief (1906–1999)

Wassily Leontief was born in St. Petersburg, the son of a professor of economics. He studied at the University of Leningrad and, after receiving a degree in learned economics (1925), went to the University of Berlin, where he earned his PhD. After three years at the Institute for World Economics at the University of Kiel and a year in China as advisor to the Ministry of Railroads, he moved to New York City and joined the National Bureau of Economic Research in 1931. Leontief became an instructor in the economics department at Harvard University in 1932, assistant professor in 1933, and finally, professor in 1946. From 1953 to 1975, he held the Henry Lee Chair of Political Economy. Although Leontief was very much an empirical economist, he was also an esteemed professor of economic theory. He spent his final years at New York University.

Leontief is best known for initiating and developing input–output analysis, which he began while at the Kiel Institute, if not earlier. It is concerned with the interdependence in production among industries. As Assar Lindbeck put it when Leontief was awarded the Nobel Prize in 1973, "in order to produce steel we need not only labor but also coal and thousands of other intermediary products, or 'inputs,' in the production process. But to produce the necessary coal and other inputs we require, in turn, steel and other intermediary products in addition to labor" (Bank of Sweden n.d.). Leontief worked on this both theoretically and empirically. It has had practical applications, for example, in judging the effects of disarmament in the United States after World War II and in estimating the effects of changes in oil prices. He began to construct an input–out-

put table for the U.S. economy in the midthirties and published the first edition of *The Structure of the American Economy, 1919–1939* in 1941. Over time, technological advances in computing made the calculations easier.

Franco Modigliani (1918–2003)

Franco Modigliani was born in Rome and studied at the University of Rome. In 1938, after the Italian racial laws came into effect, he left for Paris. In 1939, just before the outbreak of World War II, he moved to New York. The New School for Social Research in New York, the American university most willing to hire Jewish refugees fleeing from Nazism, awarded him a fellowship. Later he was associated with a number of colleges and universities until, in 1960, he went to MIT as a visiting professor. After a short break, he returned to MIT, remaining for the rest of his career.

Modigliani's research focused on the process of saving, monetary policy, and financial markets. Over the years he worked and published on household saving and its relation to overall economic activity: the life-cycle hypothesis. It was these contributions and his theorems on the value of a firm (done in collaboration with Merton Miller, another Jewish Nobel Laureate) that earned him his Nobel Prize in 1985.

Robert Solow (b. 1924)

Robert Solow was awarded a scholarship to Harvard University in 1940, but left in early 1943 to join the U.S. Army, serving in North Africa and Italy. In 1945 he returned to Harvard, where he took Leontief's class in theory. He became Leontief's research assistant, working on empirical aspects of input–output. After a year at Columbia, he joined the MIT economics department, with an office next to that of Paul Samuelson, with whom he had daily conversations. His work, which involves growth theory and many other aspects of macroeconomics, has appeared not only in books and professional journals, but also in popular periodicals such as *The New York Review of Books*. In 1987 he was awarded the Nobel Prize mainly for his theoretical and empirical contributions on economic growth.

Early Economists
Frank W. Taussig (1859–1940)

Frank W. Taussig received his BA and PhD at Harvard, where he became a professor. He was strongly influenced by the writings of English economists John Stuart Mill and Alfred Marshall. His two-volume *Principles of Economics* (1911) was widely used. He edited the *Quarterly Journal of Economics* from 1896 to 1936. A classical economist, Taussig contributed to the field of international trade. President Woodrow Wilson appointed him chairman of the newly created Tariff Commission, and he helped formulate the commercial policy clauses of the Versailles Treaty.

Edwin R. A. Seligman (1861–1939)

After receiving his PhD from Columbia University, Edwin Seligman was appointed to its faculty, where he remained until he retired in 1931. His field was public finance and he was an expert on taxation. An advocate of progressive taxation, he served as an advisor in a number of countries, as an expert on a League of Nations Committee, and as a special adviser to the Ways and Means Committee of the U.S. House of Representatives. He was one of the founders of the American Economic Association and editor in chief of the *Encyclopedia of the Social Sciences* (1930–1935).

Simon Kuznets (1901–1985)

Simon Kuznets was born in Russia and came to the United States in 1922. Having started his university studies in Russia, he completed his BSc, MA, and PhD at Columbia University. There he met Wesley C. Mitchell, founder of the National Bureau of Economic Research, with which Kuznets was associated for many years. He was at the same time a professor at the University of Pennsylvania (1931–1954), Johns Hopkins University (1954–1960), and Harvard University (1960–1971).

Kuznets was an empiricist who worked on collecting and organizing the national income accounts of the United States and analyzing business cycles. In his later years he also published on development economics. His work in developing measures of consumption, saving, and investment—components of national income—dating back to 1869, supported the revolution in economic thinking that followed the publication of Keynes's *The General Theory of Employment, Interest and Money* (1936).

Kuznets was awarded the Nobel Prize in economics in 1971. In presenting it, Swedish economist Bertil Ohlin—who later also received the Nobel Prize—observed, "To put it briefly, his empirically-based scholarly work has led to a new and more profound insight into the economic and so-

cial structure and the process of change and development" (Bank of Sweden n.d.).

Jacob Viner (1892–1970)

Jacob Viner was born in Montreal, Canada, and earned his BA at McGill University in 1914. He did his graduate work at Harvard University, writing his dissertation on international trade under Taussig. Viner began his teaching career at the University of Chicago, but during World War I left for government service in Washington. Returning in 1919, he became a full professor in 1925. Along with Frank Knight, he founded the so-called Chicago School, which stresses reliance on free markets and opposes government intervention in the economy.

Viner edited the *Journal of Political Economy* for eighteen years and published two books in the international field in 1923–1924. His magnum opus, *Studies in the Theory of International Trade,* appeared in 1937. He also wrote on the history of economic thought, including the relationships between theology and economics in the period before Adam Smith. During the Great Depression, Viner returned to Washington as an assistant secretary of the treasury, where he advocated government spending and budget deficits as means to restore the economy.

Ironically, he was a critic of John Maynard Keynes on analytical grounds, although they agreed on policy prescriptions. His November 1936 article, "Mr. Keynes and the Causes of Unemployment" (*Quarterly Journal of Economics*), characterized Keynes's *General Theory of Employment, Interest and Money* as "an outstanding intellectual achievement" but also contained some criticisms. Keynes's well-known response in the same journal in February 1937 accepted Viner's objection to his "definition and treatment" of the concept of involuntary unemployment. But he was "prepared to debate" Viner about hoarding and liquidity preference and their effects on interest rates.

In 1946, Viner moved to Princeton University. He published several books and numerous articles both before and after his retirement in 1960. A number of these articles were on the history of economic thought, including, in 1963, "The Economist in History" (*American Economic Review*).

Fritz Machlup (1902–1983)

Fritz Machlup was born in Wiener Neustadt, Austria, and studied at the University of Vienna under Ludwig von

Mises and Friedrich Hayek. His dissertation on the gold-exchange standard was published in 1925 in Austria. He worked in his father's cardboard manufacturing company from 1922 to 1932, but maintained contacts with economists and wrote two books during that period.

Machlup came to the United States as a Rockefeller Fellow in 1933 and visited Columbia, Harvard, Chicago, and Stanford universities, meeting many American economists. He taught at several American universities from 1935 to 1941. During World War II, while teaching at American University, Machlup was a consultant to the U.S. Department of Labor on postwar problems and wrote numerous papers on international economic issues.

In 1947 he became a professor of political economy at Johns Hopkins University. Over the next few years, he was a visiting professor at the University of California at Los Angeles and two universities in Japan. In those years Machlup published on balance of payments problems but also began to study the concept of knowledge. That led to several articles, including *The Production and Distribution of Knowledge in the United States* (1962), *Education and Economic Growth* (1970), and the three-volume *Information through the Printed Word: The Dissemination of Scholarly, Scientific, and Intellectual Knowledge* (1978). In the early 1980s he published three volumes of a projected ten-volume study entitled *Knowledge: Its Creation, Distribution, and Economic Significance.*

In 1960 Machlup was appointed Walker Professor of International Finance and director of the International Finance Section at Princeton University, where he remained until 1971. He continued to spend time at other universities in New York City, Osaka, and Melbourne. Beginning in 1963, Machlup formed and chaired a group of economists specializing in international monetary problems that met periodically at various locations, including Bellagio, from which the group took its name. It was concerned with current and potential policy problems in the international monetary system. In 1977 and 1978, he published *A History of Thought on Economic Integration* and *Methodology of Economics and Other Social Sciences.*

Abba P. Lerner (1903–1982)

Abba Lerner was born in Russia, grew up in London, and engaged in various other activities before enrolling at the London School of Economics in 1929. There he performed brilliantly, began publishing articles in economic journals in 1932, and, with others, established a new journal, *Review of Economic Studies.* He spent some time at Cambridge University, where he became acquainted with Keynes. He is said to be one of the first economists to fully grasp the significance of Keynes's *General Theory* and to promulgate the "Keynesian Revolution." Before that, he published a number of journal articles on international trade theory.

Lerner emigrated to the United States in 1937, moving from one university to another over his career. He published on socialist economics, though his views were not doctrinaire. Later he developed the concept of functional finance, which was concerned with government policies aimed at full employment and price stability. In 1944 he published the widely read *The Economics of Control.*

There have been many other prominent American Jewish economists: Alan Greenspan, Alan Blinder, Otto Eckstein, Jacob Frenkel, Albert Hirschman, Leon Keyserling, Paul Krugman, Arthur Okun, Herbert Stein, Robert R. Nathan, and Nobel Laureates Leonid Kantorovich, Herbert Simon, Lawrence Klein, Harry Markowitz, Merton Miller, Gary Becker, Robert Fogel, John Harsanyi, Reinhard Selten, Robert Merton, Myron Scholes, George Akerlof, Joseph Stiglitz, and Daniel Kahneman. Among these, Greenspan has been chairman of both the Council of Economic Advisers and the Federal Reserve; Okun and Stein also chaired the Council of Economic Advisers; Albert Hirschman, a professor at Princeton, has written several outstanding books; Jacob Frenkel has been both a professor and governor of the Bank of Israel.

Discrimination

In the decades before World War II, there was widespread discrimination against Jews at universities, corporations, banks, and in some parts of the federal government. There were very few Jewish professors at Ivy League universities. Notably, none of the economists discussed above was at Yale University. There were also few Jewish faculty members at the large state universities. Even the University of Chicago, at which there were some Jewish professors, practiced antisemitism. Harvard also had a quota on the admission of Jewish students (Samuelson 2002).

It is uncertain if Harvard's failure to offer Paul Samuelson tenure when he was considering the offer from MIT was due to antisemitism—or, solely to antisemitism. According to Joseph Schumpeter's biographer, Richard

Swedberg, the Harvard economics faculty let Samuelson go because "he was just too brilliant for them!" (Swedberg 1991). Stanley Fischer—former professor at MIT, former deputy managing director of the International Monetary Fund, and now governor of the Bank of Israel—has written: "It is hard to believe that even the Harvard faculty of 1940 would have been unable to find room for an economist of Samuelson's already recognized stature unless a non-academic reason or reasons stood in the way. Among those reasons were anti-Semitism, his then brashness, and his brilliance" (Eatwell 1987).

Some prominent economists were also known to be antisemitic. John Maynard Keynes made a few remarks critical of Jews. In 1926, after returning from Berlin, Keynes described Germany "as under the 'ugly thumbs' of its 'impure Jews,' who had 'sublimated immortality into compound interest'"—"his most prejudiced utterance on the subject." Keynes's biographer Robert Skidelsky notes that "[s]tereotyping of Jews was common in Keynes's circle, and the stereotypes were usually unfavorable," adding that "Keynes's letters are mercifully free from personal abuse" (Skidelsky 1994).

The big change came after World War II. In recent decades, Jewish economists have not only been admitted to institutions that earlier practiced discrimination, but many of them have reached pinnacles at Harvard, Princeton, and other universities, as well as at the Federal Reserve System, the Treasury Department, the International Monetary Fund, the World Bank, major commercial banks, and brokerage houses.

Robert Solomon

References and Further Reading

Bank of Sweden Prize in Economic Sciences in Memory of Alfred Nobel. No date. Available at: http://nobelprize.org/economics. Accessed March 14, 2007.

Blaug, Mark, ed. 1986. *Who's Who in Economics*, 2nd ed. Cambridge, MA: MIT Press.

Blaug, Mark. 1998. *Great Economists since Keynes*, 2nd ed. Northampton, MA: Edward Elgar.

Eatwell, John, Murray Milgate, and Peter Newman, eds. 1987. *The New Palgrave Dictionary of Economics*. New York: Stockton Press.

Jewish Contribution to World Civilization. No date. "Jewish Economists." Available at: http://www.jinfo.org. Accessed March 14, 2007.

New School for Social Research. No date. "The History of Economic Thought." Available at: http://cepa.new-school.edu/het/profiles/htm. Accessed March 14, 2007.

Samuelson, Paul A. 2002. "Pastiches from an Earlier Politically Incorrect Academic Age." In *Editing Economics: Essays in Honour of Mark Perlman*, edited by Hank Lim, Ungsuh K. Park, and Geoffrey C. Harcourt, 47–55. New York: Routledge.

Skidelsky, Robert. 1994. "John Maynard Keynes." In *The Economist as Savior, 1920–1937*. Vol. 2. New York: Penguin.

Swedberg, Richard. 1991. *Schumpeter: A Biography*. Princeton, NJ: Princeton University Press.

Hannah Arendt (1906–1975)

Political Theorist

The most influential political theorist in the history of American Jewry, Hannah Arendt focused contemporary thought—particularly in scholarly circles—on the experience of exile. Her most important book, *The Origins of Totalitarianism*, tapped her talent for grand historical generalization in confronting the worst horrors of twentieth-century tyranny. Her magnum opus was published in 1951, the year she secured American citizenship; thereafter she devoted herself, while teaching at Princeton, Chicago, the New School for Social Research, and elsewhere, to applying classical thought and German philosophy to a post-totalitarian age.

Arendt was born in Hanover, Germany; her parents were secular, middle-class, and assimilated Jews. She studied theology and philosophy at the universities of Marburg, Heidelberg, and Freiburg; in 1929, the year that she briefly married a Jewish psychologist named Günther Stern, Arendt also completed and published a doctoral dissertation on St. Augustine. In the waning moments of the Weimar Republic, she became a political activist and, beginning in 1933, helped German Zionists publicize the plight of the victims of National Socialism. Arrested by the Gestapo in that year, Arendt managed to escape to Paris, and from there helped relocate German Jewish children to Palestine. In 1940 she married an ex-Communist and a gentile, Heinrich Blücher, but both were interned in southern France, along with other stateless Germans later that year. From the camp at Gurs, Arendt again succeeded in escaping. She joined her husband, and the pair arrived in the United States in May 1941. She broke out of emigré circles, however, and affiliated with the New York intelligentsia

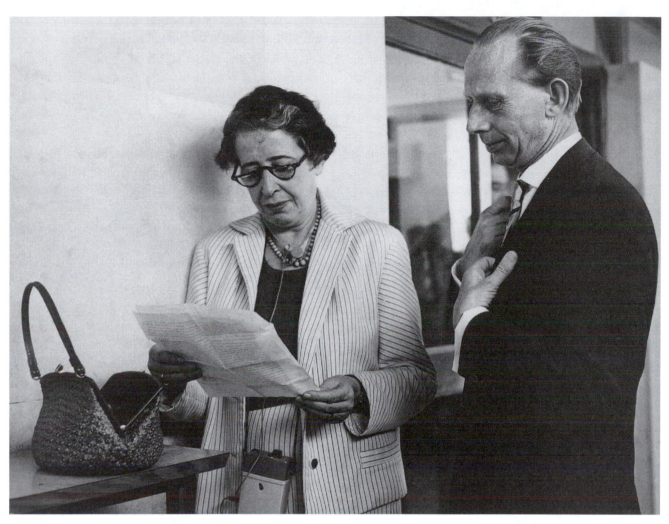

Hannah Arendt, political theorist. (Library of Congress)

(nearly all of whom were also Jewish). Drawing on her own experience with Nazism, Arendt published *The Origins of Totalitarianism* in 1951 and immediately became an intellectual celebrity.

No book resonated more powerfully in tracking the historical shocks registered by the unprecedented despotisms of Hitler and Stalin or in measuring how grievously damaged the membranes of Western civilization had become. Arendt calculated the depths of racism in the politics of Central and Western Europe by the end of the nineteenth century. By then imperialist governments had also experimented chillingly with the possibilities of cruelty and mass murder. The third section of her book exposed the operations of "radical evil." She argued that the extermination camps of the Nazi SS (*Schutzstaffel*) were designed to make life itself superfluous, to make discontinuous the very idea of what it has meant to be human. *The*

Origins of Totalitarianism constituted a cartography of nihilism, tracing how Nazism in particular had realized what medieval artists had only imagined as hell.

Written in the immediate aftermath of World War II, Arendt's masterpiece adumbrated a pessimism that almost anticipated a third world war. *The Origins of Totalitarianism* was widely interpreted as an icicle of the Cold War, since she insisted on the parallels between Nazi Germany and Stalin's Russia—despite their obvious ideological conflicts and the eruption of the barbaric warfare between the two powers from 1941 to 1945. This isomorphism was especially criticized, in part because the primary sources on Soviet totalitarianism were very scarce; nor could Arendt read Russian. When documentation on Stalin's rule became much more available after 1991, however, Arendt's astringent portrayal of his autocracy was largely confirmed. Her own experience as a refugee endowed with special poignancy the emphasis in her book on the plight of the Jews, who suffered the most from the collapse of the Enlightenment ideals of universal human rights that nation-states were pledged to protect. Arendt's pivotal insight that the Third Reich had been conducting two wars—one against its military foes, the other against the Jewish people itself—has since become a staple of the history of the Holocaust. More than any other scholar, Arendt made compelling the notion of totalitarianism as a distinctive exercise of power that sought to achieve lethal fantasies of domination and revenge.

In behalf of the Zionist movement in the Weimar era, Arendt had studied the antisemitic ideology. She had welcomed the birth of the Jewish state but broke with Zionism shortly thereafter, and generally regarded any sort of nationalism with distaste. Her criticism of Israel had hardened by 1961, when the *New Yorker* sent her to Jerusalem to cover the trial of the SS lieutenant-colonel who had organized the transportation of Jews to the camps. The resulting articles ignited a storm of controversy that never quite subsided. *Eichmann in Jerusalem: A Report on the Banality of Evil* (1963) offered a political and psychological portrait that emphasized genocide as the consequence of duty—not fanaticism. Arendt acknowledged that in 1962 Israel was right to have hanged Adolf Eichmann. But she doubted that he was only the latest in the line of antisemitic murderers. He was hateful, but he was not a hater. Eichmann had perpetrated crimes against humanity and against Jewry, she argued, not because he was a sadist, or a bigot, or a madman, but because he handled his bureaucratic responsibilities with an eerie thoughtlessness: Eichmann had failed to think through what he was doing. Such a conclusion was widely disputed, and at least in tone the phrase *banality of evil* repudiated her earlier *radical evil*.

But the short-circuiting of thought that she attributed to Eichmann inspired Arendt to return, in the final phase of her career, to the love of philosophical reasoning that had punctuated her earliest writings. *On Revolution* (1963) and *Crises of the Republic* (1972) especially sought to connect theory and action and to show historical possibilities latent in revolutionary upheavals. Especially fruitful for political thought and practice was her striking claim that revolutions often generated popular councils, which privilege participation and freedom and downplay efforts to solve "the social question" of material necessity. Yet the later books lacked the impact of the studies that

the challenge of Nazism had generated. Unaffiliated with the feminist movement that had emerged in intellectual and academic life by the 1970s, uninterested in the category of gender as an instrument to expose the operations of power, Arendt had become by the end of her life even more singular as a thinker; she was a representative only of herself.

Blücher died in 1970; and five years later, a life ennobled by speculative audacity and enriched by love ended with a heart attack in New York City.

Stephen J. Whitfield

References and Further Reading

Arendt, Hannah. 1951. *The Origins of Totalitarianism*. New York: Harcourt Brace.

Baehr, Peter, ed. 2000. *The Portable Hannah Arendt*. New York: Penguin.

Whitfield, Stephen J. 1980. *Into the Dark: Hannah Arendt and Totalitarianism*. Philadelphia: Temple University Press.

Young-Bruehl, Elisabeth. 1982. *Hannah Arendt: For Love of the World*. New Haven, CT: Yale University Press.

Franz Boas (1858–1942)

Founder of Modern American Anthropology

Franz Boas was among the leading scientists and public intellectuals on the issues of race, language, and culture in the early twentieth century. In a long and productive career, he undertook pioneering research in Baffinland and on the Northwest Coast, published tirelessly on the crucial questions of the day, and trained the seminal generation of American anthropologists. His work was indebted to German and German Jewish intellectual traditions.

Franz Boas was born and raised in Westphalia, Germany, the son of assimilated middle-class Jewish parents who prized the memory of the 1848 revolution and adhered to the Enlightenment values of German Jewish culture. Drawn at an early age to the natural sciences, Boas initially studied physics, completing a dissertation on the color of seawater in 1881. His fascination with knowledge and perception of the physical world soon drew him to geography and an extended expedition to Baffinland (1883–1884), where he hoped to study the relationship

Franz Boas, the "Father of American Anthropology." (Library of Congress)

between people and their surroundings. Upon his return to Germany, he grew dissatisfied with geography's environmental determinism. An apprenticeship under Adolf Bastian, Germany's leading ethnologist and the founding director of Berlin's Royal Ethnographic Museum, led Boas to anthropology. In 1886, Boas completed a habilitation, qualifying him for a German university position. But prospects for an academic career were dim, not least because of increasing antisemitism. In 1887, he decided to emigrate to the United States.

Settling in New York, Boas worked for a time as an editor for the journal *Science* before securing his first academic position, a lecturership at Clark University, where he trained the first American PhD in anthropology. After being fired in the infamous faculty revolt of 1892, Boas worked on ethnographic exhibits for the Chicago World's Fair. A period of professional instability ensued, ending in 1895 with his appointment as curator at the American Mu-

seum of Natural History in New York. In the interim he had received several grants to undertake fieldwork on the Northwest Coast. In 1896, he was also hired as lecturer in anthropology at Columbia University, where he was promoted to full professor in 1899. Boas held the position until his retirement in 1936.

During his decades at Columbia, Boas shaped American anthropology in his intellectual image, bestowing on it the classic four-field approach comprised of ethnology, linguistics, archaeology, and physical anthropology. For much of his tenure, he was the discipline's undisputed leader, centrally involved in all professional matters, from the editing of key journals to organizational governance. Most importantly, Boas trained the seminal generation of American anthropologists. Early in his tenure, his PhD students included Alfred Kroeber, Robert Lowie, and Edward Sapir. After World War I, Margaret Mead, Ruth Benedict, and Melville Herskovits studied under him. As Boas's students went out to found influential departments of anthropology, they transmitted his vision to the rest of the country. By the 1930s, the Boasian approach not only dominated the discipline, but was also reshaping American thought on race and cultural difference.

Boas's specific intellectual contributions are difficult to pin down. A product of the dominant currents of late nineteenth-century German scholarship, he was a staunch empiricist, wary of the facile generalizations and premature classifications he associated with the reigning ideas of sociocultural evolutionism. As a consequence, he has long been viewed as more of a critic of previous models than as a theory-builder. Central to this stance was his disaggregation of race, language, and culture in the classification of human groups. In contrast to the dominant classifications of the late nineteenth century, which conflated racial, linguistic, and cultural groupings, as in the latter-day deployment of the category "Aryan" for example, Boas insisted on their independence. Organizing ethnographic maps based on linguistic features thus produced different groupings than those organized by ethnological artifacts. Underlying this position was Boas's constant emphasis on diffusion, the process by which human features, be they material or intellectual, traveled from one group to another, complicating any attempt at isolated descriptions. The history of any group, along with its interactions with other groups, thus was central to understanding any phenomenon the anthropologist might observe in the field.

Indeed, the reconstruction of such histories was anthropology's principal object.

This stance yielded massive empirical projects, and they were often mobilized to debunk such classifications as those organized by a category like race. In this respect, Boas's famous study of immigrants was seminal. He demonstrated that the core assumption of racial stability was not borne out by immigrants to the United States and their American-born children, who, he concluded, showed significant variance from their parents, particularly in regard to weight and height. This essentially negative finding—which privileged an amorphous set of environmental factors over the supposed continuity of racial types—was in line with Boas's other critical strategies in regard to the question of race. He continuously emphasized that groups' supposed differences in the averages of particular features (cranial size, for example) were negligible in light of the enormous variation found within groups. Along with his stress on the constant diffusion of racial traits, which made the clear demarcation of racial groups inherently impossible, Boas thus presented an effective deconstruction of the very concept of race. Minimally, he always insisted that race played an utterly insignificant role in determining human behavior.

This was in contrast to his assessment of the roles of language and culture in human existence. In particular, Boas privileged language, which he regarded not only as the defining human characteristic, but also as the most promising variable in the reconstruction of historical relationships. Boas contributed extensively to the study of indigenous languages, particularly those of the Northwest Coast. But his greatest achievement was the multivolume *Handbook of American Indian Languages,* which enlisted numerous collaborators (many of them Boas's students) in the creation of the most comprehensive description of indigenous languages produced prior to World War II.

In regard to culture, too, Boas was a tireless empiricist, collecting—with the help of key informants—myths, stories, recipes, and anything else that might be used by present and future anthropologists to reconstruct the histories of Native American groups. Boas, who was moved by a strong sense of the impending disappearance of many indigenous traits, initially conceived of culture in a traditional humanistic sense. Myths, in this context, were the Native American equivalents of European literature and needed to be treated with analogous philological care. By the 1930s, Boas expanded that purview, influenced in large part by the pioneering work of Sapir, Mead, and Benedict. For them, cultures were more than assemblages of texts and artifacts; they were patterns that organized humanity's collective experiences. The result was the modern anthropological concept of culture, the most enduring legacy of Boasian anthropology. Defined by "historicity, plurality, behavioral determinism, integration, and relativism" (Stocking 1968), it allowed an alternative interpretation to the classic anthropological question: Why do human groups do what they do? Prior to the codification of the modern culture concept, the standard answer was because of their race. After its anthropological generation and gradual dissemination into America's public sphere, it became because of their culture.

How relevant was Boas's Jewish background to his thought? According to his students and early biographical treatments, not very much. Instead, they followed mid-twentieth-century conventions in painting him as a wholly impartial scientist, committed to nothing but the truth. Boas might well have agreed with this assessment. While he never denied his Jewishness, he was a resolutely secular man who, in a complicated stance vis-à-vis his chosen profession, regarded tribal affiliations as essentially primitive obstacles to a truly universalist future.

More recent assessments essentially agree with this characterization. But they no longer see Boas's stance as evidence for the irrelevance of his background. Writing in a general mode, a number of scholars have pointed to the crucial presence of secular Jews among American anthropology's pioneering generation (Lowie, Sapir, Herskovits, Alexander Goldenweiser, Alexander Lesser, Leslie Spier, Paul Radin, Ruth Bunzel, and Ruth Landes, among others). More focused scholarship, meanwhile, has gone beyond arguments linking Jewish difference to anthropology's commitments to social justice and the rights of marginalized populations.

In Boas's case, the legacy of German Jewish emancipation is now widely seen as particularly relevant. This goes far beyond his liberal cosmopolitanism and social democratic leanings. It also includes the scholarly tradition of *Völkerpsychologie* (psychology of peoples), a discipline pioneered in mid-nineteenth-century Germany by Jewish scholars Moritz Lazarus and Heymann Steinthal. Seminal public figures in the German Reform movement, they had a direct influence on Boas, who adapted their emphasis on the empirical study of the *Volksgeist* (the genius of a people) and made it the building block of his philologically oriented anthropology. Lazarus and Steinthal mobilized the concept to defend the accomplishments of German Jewish emancipation, stressing, especially in the face of growing antisemitism, that while Jews' biological heritage might render them racial outsiders, the plasticity of their *Geist* gave them the mental capabilities to fully integrate into German society.

This ascendancy of mind over matter, along with the assimilationist agenda of Jewish integration that it safeguarded, fully characterized Boas's work as well. It underwrote all his published remarks on Jews, which, while not systematic, could be found throughout his career and particularly toward the end of his life in his impassioned struggle against National Socialism. In these remarks, he continuously pointed to Jews' ability and desire to adapt to their respective cultural environments. This vision also organized his much more voluminous writings on Native Americans and African Americans. These groups possessed all the intellectual agility that Jews had mobilized in their move from the ghetto to the German salon. Ultimately, that trajectory was Boas's model for the future of American minorities. What held them back were the racist walls that encircled them. To break those down was the goal of Boas's transplanted German Jewish project.

Matti Bunzl

References and Further Reading

Boas, Franz. 1928. *Anthropology and Modern Life*. New York: W. W. Norton.

Boas, Franz. 1940. *Race, Language and Culture*. New York: Macmillan.

Bunzl, Matti. 2003. "*Völkerpsychologie* and German-Jewish Emancipation." In *German Anthropology in the Age of Empire*, edited by Glenn Penny and Matti Bunzl, 47–85. Ann Arbor: University of Michigan Press.

Cole, Douglas. 1999. *Franz Boas: The Early Years, 1858–1906*. Seattle: University of Washington Press.

Frank, Gelya. 1997. "Jews, Multiculturalism, and Boasian Anthropology." *American Anthropologist* 99: 731–745.

Stocking, George. 1968. *Race, Culture, and Evolution: Essays in the History of Anthropology*. Chicago: University of Chicago Press.

Horace Kallen (1882–1974)

Social Thinker

Horace Meyer Kallen introduced the idea of "cultural pluralism" to the American public as part of his endeavor to reconceive the national culture. Since his day, various notions of cultural pluralism have been recurrent and contentious issues in American political, social, and intellectual life. Kallen was born in Berenstadt, Silesia, Germany, son of an Orthodox rabbi who brought Horace to this country when he was five years old. Although Kallen broke from his father's religious beliefs, he retained a deep attachment to what he termed Hebraism, a secular version of Judaism. Kallen was redefining Hebraism throughout his life. His intellectual and emotional relationship with his father resembled his relationship with the other major figures who shaped his outlook—William James, George Santayana, and Barrett Wendell, three professors at Harvard, where he received his PhD in philosophy in 1908. With these men he developed a deep emotional and intellectual connection, at the same time finding the need to

Horace Kallen, social scientist. (American Jewish Archives)

strongly assert his personal independence. This was much like his broader social disposition, impelled by both the wish to belong and the urge to be different.

From James, he took his fundamental philosophic orientation of Pragmatism and ontological pluralism. However, Kallen did not share James's receptiveness to religious experience, whose intellectual mischief and social detriment, as Kallen saw it, outweighed any benefit it might provide. Kallen relished Santayana's critique of the liberal Protestantism that pervaded Harvard of his day, but he could not sympathize with Santayana's more radical alienation from American life. Kallen greatly admired Barrett Wendell's attempt to conceptualize American culture; however, Kallen could not accept Wendell's notion that the life-spring of the nation had been American Protestantism.

Kallen's struggle with his father's and his mentors' ideas found its way into the most influential work of his career, his two-part essay "Democracy versus the Melting Pot" (Kallen 1915). This essay was widely discussed at the time, and some of the repercussions of that discussion are still with us. Kallen highlighted the ethnic substructure of the American nation and urged that all ethnic groups be placed on a par with the Anglo-Saxon white Protestant component, which at the time was clearly predominant. This, he argued, would liberate previously repressed forces of cultural creativity and enrichment. He rejected the prevailing metaphor of the melting pot, which was used to describe the favored program for the absorption of immigrants. The pragmatic meaning of that metaphor, Kallen argued, was the complete assimilation of the immigrant into a uniform society. As an alternative, he offered the metaphor of the orchestra, which allowed for both diversity and harmony. Overarching and uniting the diverse cultural forces were to be the ideals of the American Enlightenment, the political structure of the Constitution, and (somewhat inconsistently) a shared English language.

While earlier Kallen had taken up the rigid forms of racial science, as of 1915, Kallen's notions of ethnicity rested on racial thinking that was flexible, compassionate, and even fraternal. It involved no ranking of the races, no inevitable conflict between them, and no unequivocal fixity of racial traits. Kallen was a Lamarckian. He believed that acquired characteristics could be inherited, and for him that meant that history (and Jewish history in particular) could be carried into the present by biology. He thought that this was the most advanced, enlightened, and rigorous science

of his day. Later critics who attacked him as an "essentialist" did not read him closely or extensively enough. Kallen did not see ethnicity and assimilation as polar opposites, but rather as processes dependent on each other. In later years, under the influence of Boasian anthropology, he gave up the racial supports for ethnicity, but then sought various other underpinnings for the ethnic bond. In Kallen's scheme, Enlightenment ideals and the ethnic bond provided two kinds of belonging, and at the same time ethnicity granted the basis of a right to be different.

Kallen's proposal quickly became entangled in the cultural conflicts of the pre–World War I era and the debates surrounding America's entry into the war. Among the leading proponents of intervention were upper-class people of Anglo-Saxon background and members of "our First Families," while some of the strongest supporters of neutrality could be found among more recent immigrants. Kallen's notions were denounced by Theodore Roosevelt and championed by some midwestern opponents of American entry, as well as some of the young literary intellectuals rebelling against what Santayana had dubbed the Genteel Tradition. Kallen was an assistant professor of philosophy at the University of Wisconsin on a one-year renewable contract when he published this essay. It made him many friends but also powerful enemies. Although before America's entry into World War I, Kallen had advocated a neutrality policy, when the country joined the conflict, he supported the war effort.

At the end of the war, Kallen's contract at Wisconsin was not renewed, but with the financial support of Jewish philanthropists he found a place in the recently established New School for Social Research. It became his academic base for the rest of his career. During the early days of the school, its eminent faculty divided between those who believed that it must become a research center (something akin to what would now be called a think tank) and those who saw it as an innovative school of adult education. Kallen, a talented lecturer and a fiery speaker, sided with the second group, and they ultimately prevailed.

Beyond the walls of the school, he was usually less successful. In the prewar era, Kallen was seen as an up-and-coming intellectual riding the crest of various waves of the future. In the postwar era, Kallen found himself pushed to the sidelines of the endeavors that had been his primary concerns. He had been an active Zionist since his student days, for Zionism had been a central component of his secular Judaism. It is not surprising that Kallen, as a pluralist, was for a while attracted to various kinds of Zionist binationalism that proposed programs of Jewish–Arab parity and rapprochement. However, in light of Arab unresponsiveness and rejection of the proposals at that time, he set aside binationalism as a form of utopianism. During the early 1920s, in the conflict between Louis Brandeis and Chaim Weizmann for control of the American Zionist movement, Kallen sided with Brandeis's losing faction. Nonetheless, Kallen remained a Zionist for the rest of his life, but was kept far from the circle of leadership.

In 1924, Kallen gathered most of his previously printed essays on what he now called cultural pluralism and published them in a book, *Culture and Democracy in the United States.* The essays that had aroused a flurry of excitement in 1915 were now met with indifference and even disdain. The great onrush of immigration, which had buoyed up Kallen's notions of ethnicity, had been stemmed. Moreover, prewar German American culture, which had appeared as a model for many other ethnic groups, had been deemed treasonous during the war and was forcefully suppressed. It was not until after World War II that Kallen would find a renewed public interest in his notions of cultural pluralism.

Kallen continued to write on public issues, but now, much to his regret, he did so primarily from the sidelines. He took little interest in academic philosophy. As he saw it, philosophy must work in the midst of things and with the pressing issues of the day. This approach encouraged a scattering of intellectual focus, and much of Kallen's writing came to resemble a kind of philosophical journalism. Early in his career, Kallen had developed a meta-Freudian perspective, which suggested that the clash of the Pleasure Principle with the Reality Principle was a central juncture of human experience. Most people and most thinkers, Kallen believed, adopted compensatory devices (this was Adler's version) to cope with such existential frustration. (For Kallen, Jewish messianism was a compensatory device to deal with historic defeat and oppression.) Such illusional paths might be avoided, Kallen believed, by sticking closely to the methods of science. However, he never explained exactly what that meant.

One of the issues that concerned Kallen throughout his career was finding an effectual Jewish education that could carry the abundance and profundity of Hebraism to the new generations of American Jews. He despaired of the various proposals advanced by educators and ultimately placed his hopes in a program of secular Jewish day schools. In the 1920s, Kallen chose to take on the great shibboleth of the era, individualism, and give it philosophic bearing. It was his bad luck that, when this work was finally published, the Great Depression had struck and the advantages Kallen had attributed to individualism seemed particularly irrelevant.

Throughout the social upheavals of the 1930s, Kallen advocated social programs that would maintain a realm for individual initiative and individuality amid the calls for various kinds of collectivism. He championed the cause of consumer cooperation, although his critics argued that such palliatives were unsuited to the great social dislocations of the era. Yet, for Kallen, consumer cooperatives provided something like an economic analogue of the relationship he envisaged between the individual and the collective in his idealized ethnic groups. One belonged but maintained one's difference.

After World War II, with the growth of the civil rights movement and African American self-assertiveness, and with a renewal of large-scale immigration (this time primarily from Asia and Latin America), many rediscovered Kallen's notions of cultural pluralism. However, the scholars and activists who reexamined Kallen's earliest statements found them laced with what seemed to be a repugnant racialism. The new advocates of cultural pluralism went about reinventing it without Kallen.

Kallen continued to write into his nineties. Although he never regained the acclaim of his early career, his energy and personal optimism did not falter to the very end. Yet perhaps there was something too willed in his cheerfulness. It seemed as if he intended to prove, *ad hominem,* that a robust secularity could yield a happy ending. Though he scorned Hegel and hegelisms ("word magic"), it would not be unfair to say that Kallen ultimately proposed a dialectical resolution of the conflict of the Pleasure Principle and the Reality Principle in something like a *L'Chaim* Principle.

Samuel Haber

References and Further Reading
Kallen, Horace Meyer. 1915. "Democracy versus the Melting Pot." *The Nation* (February 18 and 25).
Kallen, Horace Meyer. 1933. *Individualism: An American Way of Life.* New York. Liveright.

Kallen, Horace Meyer. 1956. *Cultural Pluralism and the American Idea: An Essay on Social Philosophy.* Philadelphia: University of Pennsylvania Press.

Kallen, Horace Meyer. 1998. [orig. 1924]. *Culture and Democracy in the United States,* with a new introduction by Stephen J. Whitfield. New Brunswick, NJ: Transaction Publishers.

Konvitz, Milton Ridvas. 2000. "Horace M. Kallen." In *Nine American Jewish Thinkers,* edited by Milton R. Konvitz. New Brunswick, NJ: Transaction Publishers.

Schmidt, Sarah. 1995. *Horace Kallen: Prophet of American Zionism.* Brooklyn, NY: Carlson Publishers.

Sollors, Werner. 1986. "A Critique of Pure Pluralism." In *Reconstructing American Literary History,* edited by Sacvan Berkovitch, 250–279. Cambridge, MA: Belknap/Harvard University Press.

Paul Lazarsfeld (1901–1976)

Social Scientist

Paul Lazarsfeld changed the social sciences. Born in Vienna in 1901, he studied mathematics and social science at the University of Vienna. Going to America in 1933, he worked in several applied settings and was professor at Columbia University until his death in 1976. He worked with many talented persons, which makes his unique contribution harder to specify, but his collaborators consistently acknowledge his importance.

He wrote little about Jewish foundations of his work, but many elements can be identified. His mother was personally close to the leading Socialists in Vienna, influencing his early socialist-related research, which was conducted outside a university because the Austrian universities were antisemitic. Migrating to the United States when Hitler came to power, Lazarsfeld's wartime work sought to assess propaganda, the media, and their effects, all embedded in a cultural context that he would discuss as all encompassing, yet still joke about ironically. (For instance, he would adapt slogans, such as "In the USSR, the revolution succeeded, so they need engineers, but in America, it failed so we need sociologists.") Lazarsfeld illustrated the itinerant Jew qua marginal man who had the confidence and talent to link with many competing subgroups and subcultures, to draw upon and combine the best of each—and to seek to pass this on to others. For instance, in the 1930s he sought to collaborate with T. W. Adorno and

other quasi-Marxist cultural critics of the mass media while he simultaneously conducted research with Frank Stanton of the Columbia Broadcasting System. Lazarsfeld sought to draw out the best of each of these and create a new amalgam. And he did, brilliantly and repeatedly. His impact was in four areas: in personal research, on research institutes, in refocusing social science, and in encouraging the interpretation of postindustrial society.

In his personal research and related consulting work, Lazarsfeld helped launch new fields and approaches. Market research, before him, was anecdotal and casual. He showed how to do large empirical surveys of consumers, which today define market research. Voting behavior before Lazarsfeld was studied with "ecological" methods; he developed surveys of individual voters to measure their policy views and personal friendships, and to chart other processes that influenced them, but that had not previously been assessed. His books *The People's Choice* (1944) and *Voting* (1954) are the foundations of contemporary political behavior studies.

Lazarsfeld refined survey methods for mass communications. Before him many believed that radio and newspapers had huge impacts and manipulated individuals directly. These "mass society" arguments held sway with most intellectuals and commercial firms. He demonstrated instead how media effects were generally more limited and operated differently. In politics, marketing products, and mass communication, he showed that direct messages were seldom accepted; the key impacts were indirect, often via "opinion leaders" who would talk with their friends, thus selectively accepting, or rejecting, news, advertisements, and political messages. Such processes constituted a "two-step flow of communication"—first through the media, second through the personal contact—which he documented with detailed analyses of neighbors discussing politics, women choosing new fashions, and doctors prescribing new drugs (Katz and Lazarsfeld 1955).

Lazarsfeld considerably strengthened social science methodology by developing new techniques and writing about how to use older methods more self-consciously. Although his PhD was in mathematics, most of his methodological work was written in very clear, simple language, and aimed to change the ways that social scientists thought and did research. He succeeded. For instance, to sort out distinct effects of media content, personal discussions, and other factors, he developed the panel study, in which a panel of persons was re-interviewed several times to moni-tor change, such as during a political or advertising cam-paign. To analyze the effects of several variables, he showed how multicausal analysis was necessary. But he continually sought to transcend the simple, linear models (such as in ordinary least-squares regression) by showing how to study and measure interaction effects (of a third variable shifting the effect of X on Y) or contextual effects (like Marx's analysis of low salaries causing more worker dis-content in larger than in smaller factories). His method-ological treatise *The Language of Social Research* became popular in America as a practician's guide and was trans-formed into a more theoretical-philosophical work with Raymond Boudon (Boudon 1965, 1993). Unhappy that most history of social science was written in a narrowly theoretical way, he helped develop the history of empirical social research as a subfield, which could strengthen more general histories of social science.

These rich intellectual contributions did not come from an isolated scholar, but were by-products of a vigor-ously active series of projects. He created the Bureau of Ap-plied Social Research at Columbia, and lectured and wrote about the importance of such research institutes as settings for conducting social research. They could collect data, house staff to interpret and analyze data, and, by joining practical policy concerns with basic university research, foster a climate for joining empirical and theoretical work in a practical context.

The third contribution is the hardest to specify but perhaps the most important: he transformed social sci-ence. Sociology, economics, and political science in the 1930s had theoretical traditions and empirical traditions, but they seldom joined. The grand theories of social sci-ence were European. Public opinion, basic values, political support, confidence in government, even the Gross Na-tional Product, were unmeasured concepts in 1930. In America, Pitirim Sorokin and Talcott Parsons continued this European tradition at Harvard. Distinctly American work was problem-oriented and empirical. The main tra-ditional center of social science was the University of Chicago, ranked number one in many surveys in the 1920s and 1930s. Its leaders in sociology, Robert Park and Ernest Burgess, barely joined their empirical work with European theories. Sociology changed at Columbia in the 1940s and 1950s, when Paul Lazarsfeld, through his collaboration with Robert Merton and talented students, set a new tone

in their work and many publications. They seriously joined ideas from the European theories with empirical work to create a new amalgam: "middle-range theories" were codi-fied and tested in fourfold contingency tables. Previously disparate activities were joined that give far more analyti-cal power to the result.

Students from Columbia became professors at other leading universities, and in the 1960s the social sciences changed, irrevocably. In economics, econometric work in-creasingly joined abstract theory, encouraged by the Na-tional Bureau of Economic Research, which brought many academics to its New York headquarters. Political science went through an analogous revolution, led by the behav-iorism of Robert Dahl and Gabriel Almond at Yale, the po-litical behavior work of V. O. Key at Harvard, and the Michigan voting tradition of Philip Converse and others.

Lazarsfeld was a leading consultant to the Ford Foun-dation, which substantially funded such developments in the 1950s and 1960s in the United States and internation-ally. Lazarsfeld and Merton proposed to Ford a new center, which became the Center for the Advanced Study of the Behavioral Sciences in Palo Alto, fostering such ap-proaches. In Europe, the European Consortium for Politi-cal Research (ECPR) was launched by Stein Rokkan, who collaborated with Columbia-trained Seymour Martin Lipset. The ECPR included a few young Turks in the 1960s; by the 1980s, it was the establishment. International pro-fessional groups like the International Sociological Associ-ation and its Research Committees, the International Political Science Association, and others brought social sci-entists the world over in contact with analogous develop-ments. The tone and focus of the social sciences obviously shifted.

Columbia sociologists, led by Lazarsfeld and Merton, helped create modern sociology through a continuous dia-logue, albeit often latent, with Marxist themes and con-cepts. This holds in many areas, if we examine their shifts from past topics chosen for study (dress shoppers in De-catur, Illinois, rather than unemployed workers), or the shift from a top-down focus in organizations to bottom-up cooptation. Core concepts were invented or redefined (e.g., from the proletariat to student activist, from politics as part of production to part of consumption).

Lazarsfeld's contribution may be framed with the con-cept of postindustrial society, first by identifying sources for the concept in subfields of Columbia sociologists after the 1930s. The gradually resulting framework generated a paradigm shift away from Marxist-inspired thinking, but this shift was largely "unannounced," as elements of Marx continued even in many Columbia studies. The big bang built on smaller "revolutions" in subparadigms, like organization theory and mass media; together they generated a deeper overall change.

More generally, Lazarsfeld and the Columbia armory of ideas have an elective affinity with postindustrial society in ways that were not recognized or scarcely mentioned in earlier years. This is in good part because the concept of Post-Industrial Society itself crystalized only *after* the most vibrant years of Lazarsfeld and Merton. The label Post-Industrial Society is from Daniel Bell. Overlapping ideas were elaborated by Lipset, Ronald Inglehart, and Terry Nichols Clark's writings on the New Political Culture.

The Columbia synthesis built on elements of American society that distinctly differed from Europe with its peasantry, class, work, and party-defined patriarchal, authoritarian social structure. Instead the new was driven by consumption, not production; by the household, not the job; by leisure, not work. Thus voting was not seen as explained by men and fathers working on an assembly line, but by women, mothers chatting with neighbors about whom to vote for while listening to soap operas. They made decisions for political candidates following rules like those for buying Campbell's soup and, later, Mary Kay cosmetics.

Terry Nichols Clark

References and Further Reading

Boudon, Raymond, and Paul Lazarsfeld. 1965. *Le vocabulaire des sciences sociales* (*Vocabulary of the Social Sciences*). 3 Vols. Paris: Mouton.

Boudon, Raymond. 1993. *Paul F. Lazarsfeld: On Social Research and Its Language*. Chicago: University of Chicago Press.

Clark, Terry Nichols. 1996. "Clientelism and Universalism: Columbia Sociology under Merton and Lazarsfeld." *The Tocqueville Review* 17,2: 183–205.

Clark, Terry Nichols. 1998. "Paul Lazarsfeld and the Columbia Sociology Machine." In *Paul Lazarsfeld (1901–1976): La sociologie de Vienne à New York*, edited by Jacques Lautman and Bernard-Pierre Lecuyer, 289–360. Paris: Éditions L'Harmattan.

Clark, Terry Nichols. 2002. "Changing Visions about the Post-Industrial Society." In *Advances in Sociological Knowledge*, edited by Nikolai Genov, 46–83. Paris: International Social Science Council.

Katz, Elihu, and Paul Lazarsfeld. 1955. *Personal Influence: The Part Played by People in the Flow of Mass Communications*. Glencoe, IL: Free Press.

Lautman, Jacques, and Bernard-Pierre Lecuyer. 1998. "Paul Lazarsfeld (1901–1976)." In *La sociologie de Vienne à New York*, edited by Jacques Lautman and Bernard-Pierre Lecuyer. Paris: Éditions L'Harmattan.

Shils, Edward. 1961. "The Calling of Sociology." In *Theories of Society*, edited by Talcott Parsons, Edward Shils, Kaspar D. Naegele, and Jesse R. Pitts. Vol. 2, 1405–1451. New York: Free Press.

Simonson, Peter, and Gabriel Weimann. 2002. "Critical Research at Columbia." In *Canonic Texts in Media Studies*, edited by Elihu Katz, John Durham Peters, and Tamar Liebes. Cambridge, UK: Polity Press.

Max Lerner (1902–1992)

Newspaper Columnist and Intellectual

A prominent newspaper columnist and academic, Max Lerner was a leading American Jewish intellectual, a champion of liberal causes who became more conservative in his later years. The author of numerous widely read essays and books, his magnum opus was *America as a Civilization* (1957).

"Few men have the gift you possess to think profoundly and speak softly," wrote Justice Hugo Black in 1943 after hearing a radio talk by Max Lerner (Lakoff 1998). Idolized by liberals like Black who followed his writings, speeches, and broadcasts, and feared by conservatives—he delighted in crossing swords with them and was proud to have made President Richard Nixon's enemies list—he had an especially devoted following among Jews. For many of them he was a preeminent champion and guide on the issues of the time. Although a self-described secular Jew and very much an assimilationist, twice married to non-Jewish women and preoccupied with themes of general American interest, he never sought to deny or marginalize his ethnic identity to ingratiate himself. One of the organizers of a 1942 rally in Madison Square Garden called to draw attention to the Nazi persecution of Jews, he was an outspoken critic of antisemitism and all other forms of racism at a time when other prominent figures of Jewish origin, notably Walter Lippmann, thought silence on such matters the better part of valor. When the State of Israel came into being and became embroiled with neighboring enemies, Lerner was one of its most passionate public defenders, though he urged Israelis to make territorial compromises for the sake of peace.

Lerner was the last of four children born in a *shtetl* near Minsk, then in Byelorussia. The family name was adopted, originally having been Ranes. His parents, like many other Jews trapped in the pogrom-plagued Pale of Settlement, decided to emigrate to America—the "promised land" to most East European Jews at the time, Lerner would later remark. His father, Benyumin, went first, in 1902, leaving the first three children in the care of his wife Basha, then pregnant with Max. By 1907, when his father had earned enough money to pay for their passage, the rest of the family was brought over. They went first to Bayonne, New Jersey, and, after failing at running a boardinghouse in the Catskills, settled in New Haven, Connecticut, where they owned a small dairy business. Young Max rose early to drive a horse-drawn cart through the city streets and deliver the milk.

A precocious student, he earned a scholarship to Yale awarded to the boy with the best record in the Hillhouse High School graduating class. In college he compiled an impressive academic record, majoring in English literature. It was at Yale too that he first felt the sting of antisemitism. Warned at graduation by a sympathetic professor that because he was a Jew he could not hope to acquire a prominent teaching appointment in that field, Lerner decided reluctantly to go to Yale Law School instead. Within a year he left to do graduate work in economics and politics at the newly founded Brookings Graduate School in Washington, D.C.

After earning his doctorate at Brookings, Lerner was appointed managing editor of the *Encyclopaedia of the Social Sciences.* When that project was completed, he embarked on a career as a college teacher. His first posts were at Sarah Lawrence, Williams, and Harvard. In 1949, a year after Brandeis University was founded, he was appointed to hold its first endowed chair, later serving as dean of the social sciences. He also offered a popular adult class at the New School in New York and went on to teach, after retiring from Brandeis, at United States International University in California and Notre Dame. An inspiring teacher, he had many devoted students, including, at Williams, the future Pulitzer Prize winner James MacGregor Burns, and, at Brandeis, Martin Peretz, who followed in his footsteps by

becoming both a university lecturer and editor in chief of *The New Republic.*

As early as the mid-1930s, when he began to write for *The New Republic* and then became political editor of *The Nation,* Lerner was drawn to political journalism. For the rest of his life, he was torn between the active life of a media commentator and the reflective life of a scholar and teacher, managing to pursue both vocations more successfully than anyone else of his generation. In 1943, after a brief stint in a wartime agency in Washington, he left Williams to become chief editorial writer for the new and experimental New York daily *PM* (which at first disdained all advertising so as to be free from corporate influence). When *PM* folded in 1948, he moved briefly to its short-lived successor *The Star,* and then became the leading political columnist of the liberal *New York Post,* a niche he filled for the remaining four decades of his life.

In the 1950s and 1960s he was a centrist liberal, defending John F. Kennedy's New Frontier and Lyndon Johnson's Great Society and containment in foreign policy and attacking the New Left and the counterculture as expressions of an "infantile leftism." By the late 1970s, he had become more conservative, blaming the McGovern wing of the Democratic Party for highjacking traditional liberalism and turning it into an amalgam of anti-Americanism and naïve adulation of Third World revolutionaries and terrorists, coupled with advocacy of preferential quotas and political correctness in the universities. He agreed with neoconservatives that America should adopt a "tough-minded" foreign policy in defense of liberty, and domestic reforms to end welfare dependency and free the economy from overregulation, and that it should experiment with tax cuts to stimulate economic growth. In November 1980, to the shock of many of his readers, he announced he had voted for Ronald Reagan. He continued to write his column, but as its old readership died off or turned away, he became a much less prominent commentator than previously.

While some of Lerner's voluminous literary output, especially his compilations of newspaper columns, soon became dated, much of it remains worth reading both for style and substance. His essays comparing American presidents, collected by Robert Schmuhl as *Wounded Titans,* remain of considerable historical interest. His kaleidoscopic *America as a Civilization* (1957; reissued 1987) was among the first major efforts to recognize the American impact on the world as a civilization in its own right rather than merely an offshoot of Euro-British civilization. Legal scholars continue to study his edition of *The Mind and Faith of Justice Holmes,* his seminal 1933 *Yale Law Journal* essay on "The Supreme Court and American Capitalism," and his other essays on jurisprudence, collected by Robert Cummings in *Nine Scorpions in a Bottle.* Students of the history of political thought are fortunate to have his sparkling introductory essays to editions of the writings of Thorstein Veblen and Machiavelli (collected with others by Schmuhl in *The Magisterial Imagination*). And his final book, *Wrestling with the Angel,* an account of his struggle with aging and cancer, is a poignant testament to human tenacity and to his own love of life and thought.

Lerner was married first to Anita Marburg, a Brookings classmate with whom he had three daughters, and then, following their divorce in 1940, to Edna Albers, a former student he had taught at Sarah Lawrence, with whom he had three sons.

Sanford Lakoff

References and Further Reading

Lakoff, Sanford. 1998. *Max Lerner: Pilgrim in the Promised Land.* Chicago: University of Chicago Press.

Robert Merton (1910–2003)

Sociologist

Robert King Merton was an eminent professor at Columbia University and founder of the discipline of the sociology of science. He was born to a poor Jewish immigrant family in South Philadelphia and showed intellectual promise at an early age. Winning a scholarship to Temple, he quickly became the protégé of leading faculty members there, who groomed him for an academic career. At the age of nineteen, he legally changed his name from Meyer Schkolnick to Robert King Merton, which doubtlessly eased his way into academic life. At that time, quotas limiting entry of Jews into colleges and universities as students and as faculty were a fact of life of American higher education. Merton clearly aspired to the intellectual life that academia made possible. Taking up this new name suggests

the strength of his academic aspirations and something of his lack of attachment to his Jewish origins. It also proved advantageous later when he joined the battle against racial thinking in American scholarship. An Anglo-Saxon name made it less likely that his arguments would be discounted as personal pleading. A review blasting the work of an influential Harvard scholar that had been based on racial categories would probably have had a different impact if its authors, Robert King Merton and M. F. Ashley Montagu, had signed it with their birth names, Meyer Schkolnick and Israel Ehrenberg.

Merton won a graduate fellowship to the sociology department at Harvard in 1931 and at first worked closely with its chairman, Pitirim A. Sorokin. But his intellectual allegiance soon shifted to a younger man, Talcott Parsons, who was bringing intellectual excitement to the department by introducing into a somewhat parochial American setting the provocative and largely unfamiliar work of the leading European sociologists. At the same time, Parsons was challenging the chairman as to the direction that the department should take. In this precarious situation, Merton adroitly chose an outsider, George Sarton, to be his dissertation director. Sarton was a historian of science, who was a member of no department and drew no regular salary, but who nonetheless occupied a position of prestige on the Harvard campus. Merton remained on relatively good terms with all three.

He wrote his dissertation on the growth of science in seventeenth-century England. This work became the source of what later was famously called the Merton Thesis. It underscored the importance of Protestantism for the development of science. This seemed to be a transference, in a modified form, of Max Weber's *Protestant Ethic and the Spirit of Capitalism* (which Parsons had recently translated) into the realm of science. However, if the dissertation drew from Weber and Parsons, it also drew from Marx. Merton later recalled that he was "a dedicated socialist" in the early years of the Great Depression. Many young people who came of age in that era readily concluded that the existing economic system could not work. A Marxist perspective, taken with various levels of attachment and different kinds of qualifications, seemed to make sense to many intellectuals. In his dissertation, Merton argued that, while some of the impetus for the growth of science in seventeenth-century England arose from Protestant belief, the direction that science and technology took was in great measure influenced by economic developments.

Merton received his doctorate in 1936 and served as instructor and tutor in the Harvard sociology department for the next three years. He then took up his first permanent position at Tulane, where he rose rapidly to the rank of full professor and became chairman of the department. In 1941 he moved to Columbia, where he spent the rest of his scholarly life as a much honored teacher and scholar. However, even before he established himself at Columbia, he had made his colleagues take notice with an outburst of scholarly energy that gave rise to a series of auspicious scholarly papers on a diversity of sociological topics, some of them still read and reprinted today. Yet beneath this diversity is a subtext that unifies most of them. This subtext is an implicit argument for an open and accepting society, and at the same time the assumption by the author of an identity of opposition to things as they are. (Lionel Trilling, Merton's colleague and friend, would call such an identity "the opposing self" [Trilling 1955].)

This dual subtext is evident in the two papers on the ethos of science that presaged much of Merton's later work. In these articles (Merton 1938a, 1942) he outlines four principles that inform the ethos of working scientists. He later called these norms because, he claimed, they were enforced by the scientists themselves. Nonetheless, they clearly reflected Merton's ideals as well. The first two norms, universalism and disinterestedness, signified the absence of local and ethnic prejudice as well as the avoidance of selfish bias. Merton translated these further into a demand for "careers open to talent." The second two norms, organized skepticism and communism (he later called this communalism), suggested a type of contrarianism, the taking up of a position contrary to prevailing opinions. His unblushing use of the term *communism* pointed to the cooperative and synergistic aspects of scientific endeavors, but it also indicated a view, only briefly held, that existing property relations placed fetters on scientific productivity. Undoubtedly, the ethos that Merton found in science, acceptance based on merit and a disposition antithetical to the status quo, were sentiments that he actively embraced at this time.

While at Columbia, Merton published a textbook (revised and enlarged twice) that was widely used in sociology departments across the country. This text not only pro-vided students with the rudiments of the discipline, but also advanced a program for bringing sociology closer to the physical sciences. The purpose of this program was to give the findings of sociology something like the validity and effectiveness that were generally accorded to the discoveries of science. The growing subdiscipline of the sociology of knowledge, which interpreted knowledge as a social construction, threatened to undermine the cogency of sociology itself. The physical sciences, however, seemed impervious to the acids of this kind of relativism, and to the extent that sociology could be made scientific it might develop a similar autonomy and invulnerability.

The most likely methodology for bringing sociology closer to the physical sciences, Merton believed, was functional and structural analysis. However, behind functional analysis, as it was commonly employed, stood the metaphor of the organism. Merton wished to free his functional analysis from direct dependence on any such metaphor by sublimating it through abstraction. Merton's functional analysis became an orientation that focused on the complex interrelation of events, "the practice of interpreting data by establishing their consequences for larger structures in which they are implicated" (Merton 1949). While most forms of functionalism were accused of containing an inherent conservative proclivity, Merton insisted that his functional analysis would avoid any tacit bias in favor of the status quo. It would emphasize social dysfunctions as well as functions, functional substitutes and equivalents as well as functional needs; most important, it would not overlook the significance of sheer power in society.

If Merton's functional analysis was an enhanced version of Parsons's, his structural analysis was a discriminating and enriched version of Marx's class analysis. Class, Merton believed, was too loose and ambiguous a category to be useful in illuminating the workings of society. It must be resolved, amplified, and made pluralist by such notions as status, group, and role. Nonetheless, as Merton himself explained, he owed to Marx the basic notion that social position in large part influenced social vision and behavior, and upon that principle most structural analysis rests.

At this stage in the development of sociological theory, Merton urged, practitioners should avoid any attempts to create grand theories or total systems. It would be more effective to develop small sets of empirically verified theorems, "theories of the middle range" (Merton 1957). Using functional and structural analysis, this kind of theory and its verifying research might be consolidated and codified to yield broad and reliable theoretic gains. Merton also urged only a restricted use of the great founding social theorists of the discipline. Their works might be sifted for suggestions that could be empirically tested, but one must not be distracted by their imposing imaginative visions, which eluded adequate evidence and proof. At the head of all three editions of his textbook, Merton placed the superscript, "A science which hesitates to forget its founders is lost." Such unmindfulness of precursors may have had a personal dimension as well. Surely Merton did not want to be bound by the past, but rather to bind the past to the present and future.

Merton's long teaching career at Columbia helped shape his outlook and style. Unlike Harvard, where Parsons at one point had tried to bring Merton onto the faculty, Columbia had a diverse graduate student enrollment, drawing some of its scholars from the lower reaches of society. Many of these students supported their studies with part-time work as cabbies, hotel workers, and temporary teachers. There were also many Jewish students. New York had the largest population of Jews of any city in the world. After World War II, when restrictive Jewish quotas were gradually eliminated at Columbia, Jewish students rushed to its gates. All this made for an exciting, strenuous, and somewhat contentious graduate student body. The secular Jewish intellectual life of New York was dominated by many varieties of socialism. Merton's textbooks often seemed to be addressing students with socialist backgrounds. In each edition, Merton presented a long discussion of the points of agreement of functional analysis with dialectical materialism in order to demonstrate that, like the physical sciences, functional analysis is ideologically neutral. Merton's sociology may have had the latent function of providing a way station for young socialists on their way to a broader and more acceptable American social vision.

Merton's later work indicates an important shift in emphasis. From an earlier determination to make sociology more scientific, he turned toward an effort to understand the work of the physical sciences in sociological terms. Perhaps he believed that, once one understood how science worked, the uses of that knowledge would become readily available for sociology. However, his notions of the norms of science also shifted. In his later work, Merton began to explore the notion of intellectual "property rights" as an integral part of the institution and ethics of science. Moreover, instead of the somewhat instrumentalist approach to the late nineteenth-century founders of the discipline, he began to write about his sense of affinity with them. In addition, Merton's public remarks about his own forebears became more explicit. Previously, in a 1961 *New Yorker* profile, he was described as resembling a stereotypical minister and his father as an Eastern European, with a "ripe Slavic accent." However, in a 1994 address to the American Council of Learned Societies, Merton announced that he was born Meyer Schkolnick, that his mother and father were Jewish immigrants, and that he grew up in the South Philadelphia immigrant ghetto, described somewhat nostalgically.

Perhaps the most striking expression of the continuity and change in Merton's outlook over the course of his career can be seen in his response to the radicalism of the 1960s and 1970s. Within the discipline of sociology, this radicalism took the form of a relatively short-lived neo-Marxism. Merton had long considered Marxism, as a system, to be a defunct form of utopianism and seemed surprised at its sudden recrudescence. He responded, for the most part, by casting his debate with the younger sociologists in terms of an argument about epistemology and the sociology of knowledge. To the accusation that his form of sociology was "a social construction" reflecting the bias of privileged scholars, Merton replied that sociologists had created a neutral body of autonomous knowledge with radical possibilities. The profession of sociology, like the profession of science, still provided a basis for organized skepticism and for a form of oppositional identity. But to the radical accusation, which he himself had made a quarter of a century earlier, that the prevailing academic sociologist overlooked the role of sheer power in society, he gave no reply.

Samuel Haber

References and Further Reading
Merton, Robert King. 1938a. "Science and the Social Order." *Philosophy of Science* 5 (July): 321–337.
Merton, Robert King. 1938b, 1970. *Science and Technology in Seventeenth Century England*. Bruges, Belgium: The St. Catherine Press. (1938)/With new Preface (1970). New York: H. Fertig.

Merton, Robert King. 1942. "A Note on Science and Democracy." *Journal of Legal and Political Sociology* 1 (October): 115–126.

Merton, Robert King. 1949, 1957, 1968. *Social Theory and Social Structure*. New York: Free Press. (1949)./Revised and enlarged ed. (1957)./Enlarged ed. (1968).

Merton, Robert King. 1973. *The Sociology of Science.* Chicago: University of Chicago Press.

Merton, Robert King. 1994. *A Life of Learning.* New York: American Council of Learned Societies.

Trilling, Lionel. 1955. *The Opposing Self.* New York: Viking.

American Jews in Science

American Jews in the Physical Sciences

To pose the question of Jews' role in, or impact on, any creative occupation—science, art, or literature—is, in itself a controversial issue. If science were an objective and impersonal reflection of physical reality, this article would have no *raison d'être*. In fact, many Jewish scientists, Albert Einstein the best known among them, have been averse to any association between their Jewishness and their scientific pursuit. Some scientists consider the topic of "Jews in science" prejudicial; others deem it as nonsensical as that of green-eyed men in science. In their view, there cannot be anything specifically Jewish in scientific endeavor. Science is viewed as an activity devoid of cultural traits traceable to any country, religion, or ethnicity. This remains a strong belief both among the public and among practicing natural scientists in spite of the findings of historians of science, who, since the 1960s, have discerned social, cultural, religious, and other "external" influences on science.

The effect of Jews on science has a long history of conflicting claims. Antisemites have blamed Jews for contaminating what would otherwise have been "pure science" with Jewish ideas. In some countries, this claim has led to discrimination against Jews, the dismissal of Jews, and their emigration. Conversely, others have expressed pride in "Jewish geniuses" like Einstein and looked for the roots of their success in Jewish cultural and educational values. Some have asserted that Jewish marital practices tend to breed geniuses, in contradistinction to the Catholic custom of celibacy for the clergy, who for many centuries were the most important contingent among the intellectuals. A recent work surveys the current issues and opinions in the literature on Jews in world science (Deichmann and Charpa 2004).

Science as an Instrument of Secularization

Until recent decades, American Jews chose science, where meritocracy was expected to reign supreme, as a refuge from discrimination. As early as the 1940s, Robert Merton's codification of the scientific ethos ("a complex of values and norms which is held to be binding on the man of science") reassured them of an even playing field. The young Jewish sociologist, who had changed his name, Meyer Schkolnick, to the English-sounding Robert Merton, attributed to science four norms: universalism, disinterestedness, communism, and organized skepticism. (By communism, Merton meant the "belief in the 'common ownership' of the results of science" [Hollinger 1996].) Universalism was particularly appealing to American Jews, many of whom had foreign names and spoke with "strange" accents. Prodded by Georges Gurvitch, a Jewish refugee from Nazi-occupied France, Merton also linked democracy and science, largely in reaction to the Nazification of science in Germany and, to a lesser degree, to the growing use of political arguments in science in the Soviet Union in the 1930s (Hollinger 1996).

Some Jews saw science as a tool to reshape American society to become more open and more secular. They wanted the meritocratic norm to transcend science, to be applied throughout American society. Thus science offered not only a meritocratic refuge from prejudice, as had formerly been the case in other countries, but was now construed as a politically progressive activity, appealing to the largely left-leaning American Jewish population in the middle of the twentieth century. Science also exhibited a particular ideological pull on Jews, a group then abandoning religious practice faster and more radically than most other denominations in the United States. The entry of Jews into the universities and, more specifically, into the scientific profession triggered a trend that some scholars would later call de-Christianization, and that was accompanied by rapid de-Judaization of the Jews themselves.

In Europe, Jewish identity underwent major metamorphoses in the nineteenth and twentieth centuries that were important in making science, particularly the physical sciences, a strong magnet for Jews. The massive immigration of Jews from the Russian Empire and its successor states in the early twentieth century brought these metamorphoses to American shores, where part of the new Americans' intellectual heritage became the concept of the secular Jew. This concept, which had gained popularity in Eastern Europe, and particularly in the Russian Empire, eliminated the religious—and thus normative—dimension of Judaism and retained only the components of lineage and culture. The secular Jewish identity thus took on a sociocultural coloration: it could be applied only to those who had consciously rejected Judaism while preserving linguistic (Yiddish and, later, Hebrew) and cultural traits. The identity that took shape was channeled into a diversity of political options, often inspired by nationalism and socialism. The concept of the secular Jew, which overtly negated the traditional Jewish perspective, would become the cornerstone of Zionism and of the Bund, as well as of the Soviet definition of Jewish nationality. Jewish secularism as an expression of ethnicity found no long-term support in American society and has experienced a decline since the 1950s.

A striking example of the vacuum left by Judaism was the plea that young Jews in Riga, Latvia, made to Vladimir Jabotinsky (1880–1940), a Russian author and Zionist leader, in 1923: "Our life is dull and our hearts are empty, for there is no God in our midst; give us a God, sir, worthy of dedication and sacrifice, and you will see what we can do" (Schechtman 1961). Zionism offered one such God; Bolshevism offered another. Prior to the 1960s, the physical sciences also figured prominently as a substitute for Judaism and an alternative to it.

The idea of progress, particularly the positivist idea of progress from the theological to the scientific level of consciousness, found enthusiastic response among Eastern European Jews. The deterministic image of science, grounded in Newtonian physics, survived remarkably well the ascendance of the concepts of relativity and uncertainty, introduced in the course of the scientific revolution associated with the names of Albert Einstein and Werner Heisenberg in the early twentieth century. The deterministic image of science could be conveniently held up as a challenge to religion. Throughout the latter part of the nineteenth and much of the twentieth century, science as the antipode of religion had a strong impact on the public around the world. American Jews were in the forefront of the struggle for this kind of scientific progress.

Scientific Training

There were practically no scientists, or even university graduates, among the Jewish immigrants to the United States until the 1930s. The severe restrictions on university admission that the czarist authorities had imposed on the country's Jews made it highly improbable to find scientists among those who fled the Russian Empire. It was only among those escaping from National Socialism later in the century that significant numbers of scientists could be found.

Young American Jews began to enter universities in significant numbers at about the same time as new scientific careers were opening in academia and, to a lesser degree, in the private sector. While in Europe, emancipation of the Jews roughly coincided with the emergence of science as a profession in the late nineteenth century; in the United States it was the mass immigration of Jews from Eastern Europe that coincided with the somewhat later beginnings of professional science in America. In other words, the professionalization of science was taking place at the same time as Jews were entering general society in their respective countries (Rabkin and Robinson 1994).

American Jews embraced the physical sciences with particular enthusiasm and success. Mertonian universalism held the promise of full acceptance, and the vanguard physical sciences appeared more transnational than the traditional botany or zoology. Several European Jews were, by the beginning of World War I, well known as proponents of the New Physics. Pushed to the margins of mainstream traditional physics, they found themselves on the forefront of a scientific revolution that was reshaping their discipline. Young Jews entering American universities were aware of the prominence achieved by Jewish scientists in Europe, mostly in Germany. Their example showed how the physical sciences could help Jews transcend parochialism and discrimination, and make universally recognized contributions to science. It would appear that the hope of universalism, rather than ethnic pride, was in play.

Orthodox Jewish Scientists

Paradoxically, it was during the rebellious sixties that Orthodox Jewish scientists began to make a mark in America's physical sciences. Several factors account for the growing presence of observant Jews in physics. One is the implantation of a new kind of Jewish Orthodoxy on American soil. Developed since the 1850s, this trend, associated with its founder, Rabbi Samson Raphael Hirsch, stressed the integration of Judaism with modern culture, including science. This emphasis distinguished it from the Orthodoxy of Eastern and Central Europe that shunned modernity altogether. The new trends of Orthodoxy migrated to America both before and after World War II. The German Orthodox in exile took over a decade to produce a first crop of Orthodox scientists, many of them forming the Association of Orthodox Jewish Scientists in New York in 1947. It has tackled both the theological aspects of research results as well as the applications of science to the elucidation of Jewish law (Carmell and Domb 1976).

Another factor that facilitated the entry of Jews into the physical sciences was the increasing tolerance on America's campuses. The opening of kosher cafeterias and accommodation to Sabbath observance were signs of growing cultural diversity rather than measures taken specifically for American Jews. Although before the 1960s, most Jews tried to downplay their Jewishness, to change their names, and to appear paragons of universalism, it became increasingly acceptable for observant, and otherwise conspicuous, Jews to join the faculties of major American universities.

The sixties were also a period of unprecedented expansion of American physics and its consolidation as the center of the world scientific community. The nuclear arms race, the increased emphasis on American science education in reaction to the launch of Sputnik by the Soviet Union in 1957, the superpower competition in space exploration, and other elements of the Cold War boosted the physical sciences, creating many openings for qualified researchers in the United States. During this particularly propitious time to embark on a career in the physical sciences, Jews, including many Orthodox Jews, were among the new recruits. They were joining the center of world science that was undergoing rapid growth, a situation that resembled the entry of Jews in the scientific profession in the latter third of the nineteenth and the first third of the twentieth century in Germany.

While the universalistic ethos had drawn German Jews to science, the physical sciences offered an additional refuge to observant Jews in the United States. They needed relatively little familiarity with the ambient culture, which was indispensable for those interested in becoming historians, philosophers, or anthropologists. Indeed, Judaic scholars often distrusted the humanities and the social sciences and discouraged Orthodox Jews from studying them seriously (Levi 1983). By contrast, they held physical science to be an objective search for truth, devoid of cultural influences, which could thus be reconciled with the scientist's personal practice of Judaism.

Current Situation

Since the 1960s prominent Jewish physicists have also become outspoken about the impact of Jewish culture on their scientific work. Judaism and Talmudic study came to be praised in the acceptance speeches of Jewish Nobel laureates. Indeed, the Jews are clearly overrepresented among America's religious groups in terms of the ratio between their share among the Nobel Prize winners and their percentage in faculties. This disproportion is particularly pronounced in the physical sciences (more than three to one), and the first American to earn a Nobel Prize in physics was a Jew, Albert A. Michelson.

In the early twenty-first century American Jews perceive themselves mostly as part of the country's mainstream. They are no longer "outsiders" as defined by sociologist Thorstein Veblen, who ascribed Jews' success in the sciences to their socially marginal status. Today science is no longer seen as an avenue to social mobility. While Jewish scientists in the sixties came from poor and lower-middle-class backgrounds, becoming a scientist today entails an economic sacrifice for many American Jews. This may explain the apparent decline in the percentage of Jews in the physical sciences. Another factor is the change of emphasis from the physical sciences to the life sciences that accompanied the end of the Cold War.

Yakov M. Rabkin

References and Further Reading

Carmell, Aryeh, and Cyril Domb, eds. 1976. *Challenge: Torah Views on Science and Its Problems.* New York: Feldheim.

Deichmann, Ute, and Ulrich Charpa. 2004. "Jews in the Sciences—Sciences and the Jews—The Nineteenth and Twentieth Centuries." *Simon Dubnow Institute Yearbook* 3: 1–11.

Hollinger, David A. 1996. *Science, Jews, and Secular Culture.* Princeton, NJ: Princeton University Press.

Levi, Leo. 1983. *Torah and Science.* New York: Feldheim.

Rabkin, Yakov M., and Ira Robinson. 1994. *The Interaction of Scientific and Jewish Cultures in Modern Times.* Lewiston, NY: Edwin Mellen Press.

Schechtman, Joseph B. 1961. *The Jabotinsky Story.* New York: Thomas Yoseloff.

Albert Einstein (1879–1955)

Renowned Theoretical Physicist

Albert Einstein is known for the development of the special and general theories of relativity and for numerous contributions to quantum theory. He utilized his fame to work for such causes as pacifism, Zionism, antifascism, civil liberties, socialism, world government, and banning nuclear weapons.

Born to south German Jewish parents who moved to Munich when he was one, Einstein was brought up in a well-to-do, secular home. He nevertheless developed

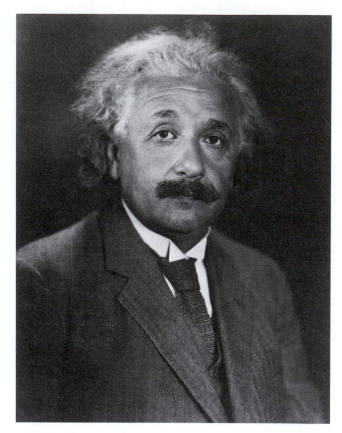

Albert Einstein, physicist, one of the greatest scientists of all time. (Library of Congress)

strong religious feelings as a child, fostered by private Jewish religious instruction and Catholic instruction at his primary school. His exposure to antisemitism and his resistance to rote learning contributed to an early sense of social isolation. Except for his sister Maja and other relatives, he rarely played with other children, developing his visual and motor skills through slow, methodical play with construction sets and other toys. His mother Pauline fostered an interest in music that led to a lifelong involvement with the violin and later the piano. Introduced at about age ten to popular scientific literature by a much older student, he abruptly dropped his attachment to religion, but kept his sense of wonder at the cosmos and his desire to understand its structure. In a private secondary school he did well in mathematics and developed a love of classical, German, and later, world literature that endured for the rest of his life.

The family electro-technical business was managed financially by his father Hermann and technically by his uncle Jakob, an engineer who fostered Einstein's interest in mathematics and later challenged him with technical problems. While initially prospering, the medium-sized firm's business dwindled in the face of competition from Germany's major electrical enterprises, and in 1894 the two brothers moved the firm from Munich to northern Italy where prospects seemed better. But within a couple of years the firm collapsed, and, although Hermann continued on a smaller scale, he was still in debt when he died in 1902.

Young Albert combined a lifelong fascination with technology and an equally strong abhorrence of its commercial exploitation. Originally destined to take over the business, it became clear to him that such a course was incompatible with his nature. Left behind in Munich to finish his secondary education, he abruptly left school in 1895 to join his parents in Italy. Fearing military service, he renounced German citizenship in 1896, remaining stateless until granted Swiss citizenship in 1901. He also declared himself "without religious affiliation," a practice he continued throughout his life. He completed secondary school in Switzerland, where the educational philosophy was markedly more sympathetic to him than that of his German schools, and he retained a lifelong affection for Swiss democracy.

In 1896 Einstein entered the Swiss Federal Polytechnic (ETH) in Zurich, studying physics and mathematics for four years in preparation for a teaching career. There he met several lifelong friends and his future first wife, fellow physics student Mileva Marić. His independent if not arrogant attitude earned him the dislike of some of his teachers, notably his initially well-disposed physics professor, in whose laboratory Einstein spent most of his time. Upon graduation in 1900, he was the only one of his small cohort of fellow students not to receive an assistantship at the ETH. Efforts to find a physics position elsewhere proved fruitless, and Einstein felt that antisemitism played a role.

He lived from hand to mouth for two years, unable to marry his pregnant fiancée. In 1902, a school friend's father persuaded the head of the Swiss Patent Office to give Einstein a job, and he married Marić in 1903, but no trace of their first child, born the previous year, has been found. The couple later had two sons: Hans Albert became a hydraulic engineer and moved to the United States. Eduard developed schizophrenia during adolescence and ended up in a Swiss mental institution. Einstein began an affair with his cousin Elsa in 1912, and his wife left him in 1914 soon after his move to Berlin, where Elsa lived. He married her in 1919 shortly after his first wife agreed to a divorce.

Einstein published his first paper in 1901. While at the Patent Office (1902–1909) he produced a steady stream of papers, culminating in 1905, his *annus mirabilis* (year of wonders), during which he produced five papers that heralded the birth of modern physics: two provided strong evidence for the kinetic-molecular theory of matter at a time when it was still being questioned and developed the first quantitative theory of a stochastic (random) process. Two others developed what is now called the special theory of relativity, the result of a ten-year-long attempt to resolve the conflict between Newtonian mechanics and Maxwell's electrodynamics, especially as applied to the optics of moving bodies. To do so, he had to replace Newton's kinematics (theory of space, time, and motion), based on the concept of absolute time, with a new kinematics based on the relativity of simultaneity. One of the most important consequences is the possibility of interconverting quantities of mass and quantities of energy, now expressed in one of the most famous formulas in physics: $E = mc^2$.

But the developments of 1905 proved to be only a way station in his search for a deeper understanding of the structure of the cosmos. Attempting in 1907 to fit gravitation into the framework of the special theory, Einstein soon convinced himself that this could not be done. Because of what he came to regard as the most essential feature of gravitation—the equality of gravitational and inertial mass—his theory of relativity would have to be further generalized. He embarked on the quest for this generalization, which culminated in 1915 when he formulated the final version of the general theory of relativity. All previous physical theories were based on the existence of fixed, given space–time structures, providing the kinematic stage on which the dynamic dramas of matter and radiation were enacted. The special theory drastically renovated the stage, but left it fixed and given. In the general theory, the stage becomes part of the play and itself changes in the course of the drama. To revert from the metaphor, in general relativity there is no fixed kinematic background—no kinematics independent of dynamics. Einstein considered this insight to be his greatest contribution to physics.

The fifth 1905 paper was the only one that Einstein characterized as revolutionary. It argued for the first time that the existence of the quantum of action h, which Max Planck had introduced in 1900, required the replacement of both classical (prequantum) mechanics and electromagnetism (including light) by new, quantum theories. He introduced the idea of the light quantum in 1905 and developed the idea in the face of the skepticism and opposition of most physicists until it won general acceptance two decades later. Over the course of these two decades, Einstein contributed mightily to the development of quantum theory in many other ways. But he was never satisfied that the new quantum mechanics developed in the 1920s—or the new quantum field theory developed in the 1930s–1950s—provided a complete explanation of the quantum phenomena that he had first brought to light.

He hoped that some further generalization of the general theory of relativity would be found that would include the electromagnetic field—the only other fundamental field known when he started his search for a unified field theory—and would also explain the quantum phenomena without recourse to the paradoxical features he saw in quantum mechanics. Although his quest for a satisfactory unified field theory started in the 1920s, and he developed and rejected many unsatisfactory ones, it remained uncompleted at his death in 1955.

By 1909 the renown of Einstein's work brought him his first academic job, an assistant professorship at a Swiss university. Thereafter he rose rapidly to a full professorship in 1911, and in 1914 he became a member of the Prussian Academy of Sciences, moving to Berlin, where he remained until the Nazis took power in 1933. He began to manifest an interest in politics during World War I, which broke out soon after his move to Berlin. He was horrified to find himself at the center of German militarism as a wave of patriotism and jingoism swept over Europe, including most of its intellectuals. Most of his German colleagues proclaimed their allegiance to the fatherland as it invaded Belgium in the name of German culture, and he became active in efforts to counter their jingoism and end the war.

After the war, he actively advocated the pacifist cause, both in Germany and abroad, until the Nazis' takeover. He then advocated armed resistance to fascist aggression, especially during the Spanish Civil War (1936–1939), arguing the impracticality of preaching pacifism while Hitler was waging war in Spain and preparing for another world war. In 1932, before the Nazis took power, Einstein had agreed to spend a half year at the new Institute for Advanced Study in Princeton, New Jersey, and he left Germany for the United States. The Nazis would confiscate his bank account and his property, which they could "legally" do because he was a German citizen—his citizenship having been automatically granted during the Weimar years. Einstein became an American citizen in 1940, and during World War II (1939–1945) he vigorously supported the Allied cause. His famous letter to President Franklin D. Roosevelt warned against the dangers of German development of an atomic bomb, but otherwise he took no part in the atomic bomb project. With the onset of the Cold War between the United States and the Soviet Union, he refused to support either side, vigorously warning against the dangers of growing American militarism, with its attendant threats of preventive wars abroad and the abrogation of civil liberties at home. He felt that only universal disarmament and the ceding of all military power to a world government could end the threat to civilization posed by the growing destructive power—particularly the H-bomb—being developed in the arms race.

The treatment of East European Jews who came to Germany after World War I in search of higher education, as well as his contacts with the Jewish masses during his 1921 tour of the United States with Zionist leader Chaim Weizmann, made him a staunch advocate of the Zionist project as a means of giving a sense of cohesion and self-worth to Jewish people everywhere. As Arab resistance developed to the Jewish colonization project in Palestine (then under British mandate), he advocated the creation of a binational state. After settling in Princeton, New Jersey in 1933, he spoke out vigorously against Nazi persecution of the Jewish people and warned Americans of the dangers of German aggression. The head of the new Institute for Advanced Study at Princeton, of which Einstein was the major luminary, tried to silence him, but Einstein threatened to resign and continued to speak out on issues of the day.

The failure of the Allied powers to help Jewish victims of persecution before World War II, to halt the horrors of the Holocaust during the war, or to allow its survivors to emigrate to Palestine after the war led him to endorse the creation of the State of Israel. However, he remained a critical supporter, urging neutrality in the Cold War and making its treatment of its Arab minority a key test of its democratic bona fides. After the death of Weizmann in 1952, Einstein was offered the presidency of Israel in a gesture that both sides knew to be symbolic.

During the Red Scare in 1950s Cold-War America, Einstein stood like a bulwark in defense of civil liberties, urging intellectuals to resist any assault on constitutionally guaranteed freedoms of speech and action, protesting against many encroachments on these rights, and defending those who exercised them in the face of governmental pressures. He chose this moment to publicly advocate a socialist solution to the economic difficulties he felt to be inextricably bound to the capitalist system of production for profit, which fostered excessive individualism and greed. But, with the example of the Soviet Union before him, he warned of the dangers of a collective economy that did not provide strict guarantees of individual freedom.

John Stachel

References and Further Reading

Einstein, Albert. 1954. *Ideas and Opinions.* New York: Crown.

Hoffmann, Banesh, and Helen Dukas. 1972. *Albert Einstein: Creator and Rebel.* New York: Viking.

Jerome, Fred. 2002. *The Einstein File: J. Edgar Hoover's Secret War against the World's Most Famous Scientist.* New York: St. Martin's Press.

Pais, Abraham. 1982. *"Subtle Is the Lord . . . ": The Science and the Life of Albert Einstein.* Oxford, UK: Clarendon Press and New York: Oxford University Press.

Stachel, John. 2002. "Einstein's Jewish Identity." In John Stachel, *Einstein from "B" to "Z,"* 57–83. Boston, Berlin, and Basel: Birkhäuser.

Sayen, Jamie. 1985. *Einstein in America.* New York: Crown.

American Jews and the Ideology of Modern Science

Over the course of two centuries, American Jews have embraced science in various ways, associating ideas such as universalism, objectivity, and freedom of thought with a scientific ethos and tying that ethos to their religious views. Many Reform Jews in the nineteenth and twentieth centuries found the ideology of science to be entirely consonant with their Jewish faith. By contrast, secular Jews in the twentieth century have often used science to bludgeon traditional religion. Some of the latter have been among the most influential popularizers of science, and their works have been prominent in American popular culture.

Science plays a key role in the modern world far beyond its practical efficacy; people of widely different backgrounds have embraced science as an ideology or an ethos to guide their thinking or bolster their beliefs. At least since the Enlightenment, thinkers from various traditions have used science to support liberalism, democracy, freedom of thought, cosmopolitanism, and objectivity. Jewish intellectuals have often drawn on science to promote or reinforce a universalistic perspective associated with broader cultural agendas they have adopted.

Although the American Jewish population was never higher than 3.9 percent, 40 percent of Nobel Prizes awarded U.S. citizens in the physical and biological sciences have gone to someone of Jewish or half-Jewish ancestry (Hollinger 2002). As early as 1919, the sociologist Thorstein Veblen noticed the disproportionate involvement of Jews in science and sought to explain it as intrinsic to the Jewish intellectual experience. He claimed that Jewish intellectuals, having abandoned their religious beliefs and having adopted a wholly skeptical frame of mind, were alienated from the dominant culture and thus exhibited a liberated and detached mode of thinking strongly conducive to theoretical scientific work.

The historian David Hollinger has disagreed, pointing out that Jews have been prominent in all aspects of American culture and society, from business to entertainment to law. Indeed, the high percentage of Jewish Nobel Laureates and Jewish faculty in elite universities is comparable to Jews' elite rankings in other professions. Hollinger's thesis, in which class and family professional background help explain the differentials in accomplishments, suggests that other ideological commitments that have been associated with science—such as cosmopolitanism and universalism—may have played a role in Jews' interest in scientific fields.

Jews' engagement with modern science began during the Enlightenment, when physicians and philosophers left the ghettos and the relatively insular world of Talmudic thought and encountered the intellectual world of eighteenth-century Europe. Science and scientific ideas proved a safe arena in which Jewish intellectuals could engage with gentile philosophy, without threatening their Jewish identity. Moses Mendelssohn, renowned as an Enlightenment philosopher as much as a Jewish scholar, asserted that Judaism was both a natural religion—with rationally deducible and universally applicable doctrines—and a particular religion—derived from the Laws given to the Jews on Mt. Sinai. Judaism, in other words, was a particular manifestation of religion, which promoted a universal ethical doctrine that was rationally accessible to anyone.

Reform Judaism grew out of these ideas. The three foundational principles of Reform were all closely allied to the sciences and to classical Enlightenment ideology: reason, progress, and universalism. In America, Reform flourished in German Jewish communities during the second half of the nineteenth century and was codified in the 1885 Pittsburgh platform, which announced Judaism's complete consonance with science and biblical criticism.

Reform Jews embraced science in much the same way that liberal Protestants did; they found ways to utilize scientific ideas in their theology. Evolution is a good example. Although there was great skepticism about evolution in the first decade and a half after the publication of Darwin's *Origin of Species* (1859), both liberal Jews and liberal Christians eventually found ways to tame it. Both groups initially found it problematic because of its materialistic implications, but gradually both came to accept it in a teleological form, in which a divine hand guided evolutionary change. Liberal religious thinkers, however, often went further, embracing evolution as a central framework for describing change not only in the biological world, but in all human history. Religion became imbued with a progressive evolutionary vision.

The overall Jewish response to evolution, however, suggests that there were significant differences with the Christian tradition taken as a whole. Reform and traditional Jews both seemed less concerned about the implications of modern science than did the spectrum of conservative-to-liberal Christians. Even many traditional Jews accepted it and found ways of using evolution as an ideological support in religious arguments. Since questions about the role of ritual and law were of great import to traditionalists, it should not be surprising that evolutionary arguments were put into the service of orthodoxy. Some Conservatives marshaled evidence showing that Jewish rituals were scientifically and medically efficacious and increased the fitness of the group in medically demonstrable ways. Hence, in the hands of some Jews the evolutionary doctrine of survival of the fittest ended up as a pillar for conservative Jewish thought.

Science played an even more important role among secular Jews. In the twentieth century, a great number of Jews became proponents of a starkly secular social order, one in which traditional religious forms were discarded for a universalistic and nontheistic humanism. Although many, perhaps most, secular Jews remained unaffiliated,

some came to be involved with specific humanist organizations. Ethical Culture, one of these groups, spawned by Felix Adler, the son of a prominent Reform rabbi at Temple Emanu-El in New York, welcomed both Jews and gentiles into a faith focused on ethical concerns. Other secularists found their way to the humanist movement in the Unitarian church. Still others, toward the end of the century, declared themselves secular humanists and adopted often aggressively antireligious rhetoric. Rabbi Sherwin Wine drew inspiration from the broader humanist movement when he founded the Society for Humanistic Judaism (1969) for people who identified with the Jewish historical and cultural experience but who were no longer able to accept a theistic metaphysic.

It was not until the coming of age of a generation of secular Jews in the middle of the twentieth century that the ideology of science came to be integrated with the promotion of secularism. In contrast to the nineteenth-century Reform view that saw Judaism itself as a framework within which Enlightenment values could flourish, the ideals of these twentieth-century Jews were starkly secular. To these thinkers, Judaism was particularistic and narrow, whereas science was broad and universal. This twin promotion of science and secularism was especially strong among the children and grandchildren of East European immigrants. These humanists argued that the ideology of science should be an essential part of the modern worldview, in part because it provided knowledge and control, but also because it promoted critical thinking, ethical conduct, and liberal democratic values.

Four late twentieth-century figures stand out as cultural spokesmen for the scientific humanist position: Paul Kurtz, Isaac Asimov, Carl Sagan, and Stephen Jay Gould. All were of Jewish descent, and all espoused a deep and abiding love of the ethos of science and felt passionately about its importance to the modern world. Though they had slightly different ideas about the proper place of religion, their ideas about science and its role in the world were very similar.

Paul Kurtz played a singular role in the American humanist movement, transforming it from a small movement of liberal ministers and academics into an important media force by promoting the humanist agenda aggressively and widely in print, on television, and with publicity events. He built a successful publishing house, Prometheus Press, and edited three popular journals—*The Humanist,*

Skeptical Inquirer, and *Free Inquiry*—that defended science against superstition and attacked dogmatic religion, especially Christian fundamentalism.

Asimov, Sagan, and Gould were among the most well-known popularizers of science in the late twentieth century. Asimov and Sagan wrote extensively on science, its ethical dimensions, and its importance for the modern world. Sagan's television series *Cosmos* (1980) was translated into many languages and was viewed around the world, and his science fiction novel *Contact* (1985) was posthumously released as a major motion picture. Through both fiction and nonfiction, Sagan and Asimov argued that citizens of a democratic and technically sophisticated society should know and embrace science and the scientific worldview. They prophesied great dangers to a culture that ignored the skeptical frame of mind and the universal perspective of science and that failed to reject dogma.

The paleontologist Stephen Jay Gould wrote extensively during his lifetime about the proper uses of science. His sensitivity to history and his ability to turn episodes in the history of science into moral stories appealed to readers of *Natural History Magazine* for over twenty-five years. Taking a softer line on religion than many humanists, Gould argued that religion and science were *both* important magisteria of knowledge, but they had to be kept separate. He termed this idea Non-Overlapping Magisteria (NOMA) and discussed it in his popular book *Rocks of Ages* (1999). The strict limits he placed on acceptable religious belief made it clear, however, that in many realms, science was the greater authority.

Historian Naomi Cohen noted that the secularizing influence of the law in the United States is much indebted both to Jewish lawyers and to lawsuits initiated by Jewish plaintiffs. The American Civil Liberties Union, with its strong Jewish presence, was one of the primary conduits of this secularist interpretation, and helped to promote the principle of separation of church and state as a pillar of American constitutional law. Similarly, Jews who found themselves in a position to promote the connection between science and secularism did so. The historical experience of religious discrimination against Jews goes far to explain why so many Jews have strongly embraced the ideology of secularism. It also helps to explain the importance that so many Jews have placed on depicting science as a neutral territory, where objectivity and rational reasoning can prevail over prejudice. Although scholars of science now debate how accurate this picture of scientific neutrality is, in many cases—and clearly in Jewish intellectual history—the ideology of scientific universalism has played a dominant role.

Stephen P. Weldon

References and Further Reading

Feiner, Shmuel. 2002. "Seductive Science and the Emergence of the Secular Jewish Intellectual." *Science in Context* 15: 121–135.

Hollinger, David A. 1996. *Science, Jews, and Secular Culture.* Princeton, NJ: Princeton University Press.

Hollinger, David A. 2002. "Why Are Jews Preeminent in Science and Scholarship? The Veblen Thesis Reconsidered." *Aleph* 2: 145–163.

Swetlitz, Marc. 1999. "American Jewish Responses to Darwin and Evolutionary Theory, 1860–1890." In *Disseminating Darwinism,* edited by R. L. Numbers and J. Stenhouse. Cambridge, UK: Cambridge University Press.

Weldon, Stephen P. 2004. "Humanism: Secular Humanism in the United States." In *New Dictionary of the History of Ideas.* New York: Scribner's.

American Jews and Education

Jewish Education in America

The story of Jewish education in the United States is about the triumph of American-style models over European imports. From the outset, American Jews took their cues about how to educate their children from their Protestant neighbors. Although between 1840 and 1924 immigrants transplanted educational institutions from Europe, these generally lasted one generation, evolving into, or giving way to, unmistakably American alternatives.

In the colonial and early federal periods, general education was often tied to religious instruction. The pervasive religious content of both public and private schools dissuaded Jews from enrolling their children. Following the general custom, some well-to-do families engaged private tutors for their children. Most, however, relied on the *kehillah* (the synagogue community) to provide education for their young. In New York, K. K. Shearith Israel dedicated its Minhat Areb School in 1731, but it probably did not open until the *hazzan* (cantor-reader), David Mendez Machado, arrived in 1737. Machado's duties included operating the school and teaching Hebrew. Families with means were expected to pay for the hazzan's services, while children of the poor were taught gratis. A similar arrangement likely prevailed in the decades prior to the Revolutionary War in Newport, Rhode Island.

By 1755, Shearith Israel's school had expanded to include general studies. But the kehillah's ability to sustain a full education program was dependent on parental interest as well as on the hazzan's expertise. At times, a separate schoolmaster was hired, although qualified teachers were not easy to find. The Polonies Talmud Torah, a Hebrew school established in 1803 by Shearith Israel, was plagued by low attendance and operated only intermittently before the 1840s, when it was converted into a supplementary school. An attempt in 1808 to transform the school into a tuition-driven community school with a limited number of scholarship students won state funding, but it failed after its popular schoolmaster Emanuel Nuñes Carvalho (1771–1817) left.

By the early nineteenth century, many Christian congregations had opened free schools for the children of their impoverished members. After 1801 the Charleston kehillah, influenced by this approach, offered education for the needy through its Society for the Relief of Orphans and Indigent Children. For the Southern well-to-do, private academies and home tutoring were the norm. Among the private academies that catered to Jewish children was Carvalho's school in Charleston (1811–1814), where Hebrew, as well as Latin, French, English, and Spanish were taught. Carvalho wrote what is believed to be the first Hebrew textbook authored by a Jew in the United States, *Mafteah*

Leshon Ivrith (Key to the Hebrew Language, 1815). It was intended for secondary schools and universities.

By the second quarter of the nineteenth century, public education was making rapid gains, despite resistance from working-class parents who feared the loss of income from their school-age children, and from Catholics who objected to the Protestant cast of the public schools. The Central European Jewish immigrants shared many of the Catholics' concerns. Readings from the King James Bible, the recitation of prayers, the singing of Christian hymns, and instruction from textbooks reflecting a triumphalist Protestant perspective rendered the schools unacceptable.

As a result, in the 1840s and 1850s tuition-supported coeducational Jewish day schools, often associated with synagogues, proliferated. Among the most successful were Cincinnati's Talmud Yeladim Institute, associated with K. K. B'nai Yeshurun synagogue (today the Isaac M. Wise Temple), and Dr. Max Lilienthal's private day school in New York City. Typically, Hebrew instruction in these schools was limited to one or two hours per day. Younger students were taught to read Hebrew mechanically from the *siddur* (prayer book), while older ones mastered simple Bible translations. Catechisms were employed for instruction in religion and biblical history. Boys were also prepared for their bar mitzvahs. The general studies curriculum approximated that in other private schools.

By the 1860s and 1870s, however, the vast majority of day schools had closed or become supplementary schools. As Jews and others fought successfully to remove overt Christian content from the public schools in many cities, public education became a more palatable option. Even as Catholics established an extensive network of parochial schools, Jews were loath to separate themselves from other Americans. Jewish immigrants saw in the public schools the most promising avenue for upward mobility.

With few exceptions, religious education became supplementary to the public schools. In this, Jews were heavily influenced by the Protestant Sunday school movement. Indeed, the earliest Jewish Sunday school was established in 1838 by Rebecca Gratz (1781–1869) and the Female Hebrew Benevolent Society in Philadelphia, the birthplace of the American Sunday School Union (ASSU). Although she borrowed liberally from the Protestant Union, even bowdlerizing their textbooks, Gratz received encouragement and assistance from Mikveh Israel's rabbi, Isaac Leeser (1806-1868). Although the school was open to all, Gratz

was especially interested in attracting the children of poor Central European immigrants. Parents who could afford tuition paid two dollars, but no student was turned away for lack of funds.

The growth of the Sunday school revolutionized the role of women in Jewish education. Unlike previous Jewish school models, most Jewish Sunday schools were operated almost entirely by women, frequently as volunteers. Two female teachers at the Hebrew Sunday School in Philadelphia, Simha Peixotto and Rachel Peixotto Pyke, wrote two of the earliest Jewish Sunday school primers. As in the ASSU schools, catechisms, hymns, and Bible reading anchored the curriculum. Over the next quarter century, Jewish Sunday and Sabbath schools spread quickly, and they were opened even in many traditional congregations. In 1886 a Hebrew Sabbath School Union (HSSU) was formed. The HSSU published a unified curriculum and educational pamphlets, but its reach was limited because many of the larger schools, fearing a loss of autonomy, refused to join. The Union was eventually incorporated into the Union of American Hebrew Congregations (UAHC).

In opening her Sunday school, Gratz was motivated in part by fears that immigrant Jewish children would fall prey to evangelical Christian missionaries at Philadelphia's Central High School. Indeed, Jews' resolve to counter extensive missionary activities fueled other educational initiatives in the mid-nineteenth century, including the Hebrew Free School movement in New York. The first Free School, an all-day school, was opened in 1866 with three hundred students and six teachers. Subsequently, five supplementary afternoon schools were opened. At their height, New York's Jewish Free Schools enrolled over a thousand students. However, attrition rates were high, with the average pupil remaining one year.

As Eastern European Jews began to arrive in greater numbers in the 1860s and 1870s, two European-style educational models also gained ground: the *heder* and the Talmud Torah. The heder—typically a one-room school conducted out of a storefront synagogue, private apartment, attic, or cellar—was operated by a single teacher who was compensated by the parents. Many offered little more than bar mitzvah training. The Talmud Torah, which served the children of the poor, provided a somewhat higher quality of education because its activities were at least nominally supervised by a lay board representing the funders. Typically, it operated on weekday afternoons after public school hours and on Sundays. Among the best was the Machazikai Talmud Torah, on the Lower East Side of New York, founded in 1857 by Pesach Rosenthal. Not only were children able to attend gratis, but they were also provided with free clothing and a pair of shoes.

In the late nineteenth century, influenced by the Russian *haskalah* (Enlightenment), a new model of Jewish education developed in Eastern Europe: the *heder metukkan* (improved Jewish school). These schools taught Hebrew as a spoken language and imbued students with a sense of Jewish nationalism. Although the traditional curriculum was retained, the heder metukkan added Hebrew literature and secular subjects, which were taught in Russian. By the turn of the century, a few American Talmud Torahs began to reflect the impact of the heder metukkan. Under the influence of educators like Hillel Malachowsky (1860–1943), Abraham Friedland (1891–1939), and Louis Hurwich (1886–1967), a handful of schools in New York, Boston, Chicago, Detroit, Indianapolis, and Minneapolis introduced the Hebraic, nationalistic curriculum.

Among the greatest innovators was Dr. Samson Benderly (1876–1944). A native of Safed, Palestine, he arrived in Baltimore in 1898 to study medicine, eventually abandoning that career for Jewish education. As superintendent of the Hebrew Free School in Baltimore, Benderly pioneered an American-style Talmud Torah that incorporated both the Hebrew language emphasis of the heder metukkan and concern for students' hygiene and stamina. Recognizing that his pupils arrived after a full day at public school, Benderly added recreational activities to his school program and honed students' language skills through games, songs, and conversation. Many of the teachers he employed were women, whom he prepared through a "college department" that combined evening classes with on-the-job training in the afternoons. Benderly's school won many admirers, but also had detractors, especially among the parent body, who objected to Modern Hebrew instruction because it was the Holy Tongue. Others were simply interested in having their children learn rudimentary synagogue skills and prepare for bar mitzvah.

As Benderly and others experimented with a Hebraic model of Jewish education, Yiddish benevolent and political organizations created Yiddish-speaking schools. The Poale Zion in 1910 pioneered the Yiddish folk schools, the oldest network of Yiddishist schools. Unlike the Talmud Torahs, religious instruction was not included in the school

Dr. Samson Benderly, superintendent of the Hebrew Free School in Baltimore. (American Jewish Archives)

program. The emphasis was on Jewish culture—Yiddish and Hebrew language, literature, folk music, Zionism, Jewish history—and socialist ideology. Later in the decade, other ideological groups—the Sholem Aleichem Folk Institute and the Workmen's Circle—founded Yiddish socialist school networks. Although the Workmen's Circle was originally staunchly anti-Zionist, over time it became reconciled to teaching Jewish culture and Hebrew language alongside Yiddish. As all of these schools became more Jewish and less radical, they also became more Americanized.

In 1910, Dr. Judah Magnes, chairman of the New York Kehillah, invited Benderly to organize and direct the first Bureau of Jewish Education (BJE). Funded through a $50,000 gift from philanthropist Jacob Schiff and $25,000 from Professor Morris Loeb's New York Foundation, the BJE was charged with organizing and improving standards in the city's Jewish schools. Recognizing that the funds were insufficient for a complete overhaul of the Jewish educational system, Benderly resolved to use the money "as a lever for the study and improvement of primary Jewish education in New York City" (Winter 1966). Benderly worked with the eight largest Talmud Torahs to standardize curricula, improve pedagogical methods, and professionalize Jewish teaching through an established salary scale and a board of license. Scholarship money was provided to defray the tuition of indigent children. The BJE also operated laboratory schools for girls, where Benderly experimented with new techniques and curricula. New textbooks and teachers' guides were published, as well as a magazine for parents.

Another priority was enlisting talented young people to make their careers in Jewish education. In this effort Benderly collaborated with Rabbi Mordecai Kaplan (1881–1983), head of the Jewish Theological Seminary's (JTS) newly inaugurated Teachers Institute (TI). Both men viewed the Jewish school as an agent of American acculturation as well as of Jewish cultural renewal. Both were dedicated progressives and admirers of the educational philosophy of John Dewey and the behaviorist educational psychology of Edward Thorndike. Among those trained for careers in teaching, an elite group of young men and a few women, nicknamed the Benderly Boys, was selected for future leadership positions. The brightest were encouraged to do doctoral work at the Teachers College of Columbia University, where they were exposed to Dewey, Thorndike, and educational philosopher William Heard Kilpatrick. Many of these Benderly protégés went on to direct bureaus, Talmud Torah associations, Hebrew teacher colleges, and other Jewish educational organizations, spreading Benderly's vision across the country.

After the Kehillah fell apart during World War I, the BJE became an independent organization supported by New York's Federation of Jewish Philanthropies. The resulting cut in its budget severely curtailed its activities, and the BJE never realized Benderly's dream of a communal system of Jewish education. It was Benderly Boy Alexander Dushkin (1890–1976) who created the first truly transpartisan, central educational agency. As director of the BJE of Chicago from 1923 to 1934, Dushkin was the first to bring congregational schools under the bureau's aegis. In 1939, Dushkin was appointed executive director of the newly formed Jewish Education Committee of New York, successor to the BJE, which provided educational services and grants for educational experimentation to a wide range of schools, including Jewish community center schools, Yiddish schools, Jewish day schools, and congregational schools while continuing to subsidize larger communal Talmud Torahs.

In the postwar era, many bureaus adopted the New York model. By the 1960s there were thirty-four central Jewish education agencies across North America. These bureaus were coordinated and supported on a national level by the American Association of Jewish Education (AAJE, 1939), known today as the Jewish Education Service of North America. Originally, the AAJE membership consisted of individual laypeople and professionals, but in 1965 it was reorganized as an umbrella body for educational organizations, congregational bodies, and denominational commissions.

One reason for the bureau's shift was the decline of community Talmud Torahs and the concurrent ascendancy of congregational schools. By the 1930s, the population in weekday congregational schools outnumbered that in the Talmud Torahs. The decline of the Talmud Torahs accelerated in the aftermath of World War II. The immediate factor that favored the congregational school was the demographic shift of Jews away from urban enclaves to more upscale, less dense neighborhoods and suburbs. Outside of work, the public school, and local civic activities, social segregation along religious lines was mostly taken for granted by Jew and gentile alike. Many of these Jews eagerly built synagogue centers, housing social, recreational, educational, as well as religious facilities. Taking a cue from the habits of their Protestant neighbors, they embraced the synagogue as a socially acceptable form of Jewish fellowship, a token of middle-class status, and accepted congregationally based religious education as normative. Thus, congregational education became dominant because of Protestantization. Outwardly, Jews were adopting religiously based forms of Jewish identity, even as the content of American Jewish culture was essentially ethnic.

Benderly, Kaplan, and their students favored community models of Jewish education, seeing them as laboratories where an Americanized Jewish culture could emerge. Because their conception of Judaism was largely ethnic and national, they viewed denominationalism as divisive. They failed to appreciate that America was more hospitable to religious pluralism than to cultural pluralism and that, in the absence of a state church, denominationalism was a hallmark of American religious life. Benderly and Kaplan also feared that congregational schools would reduce the intensity of Jewish education. These fears were well-founded. In the immediate postwar era, over half of all congregational schools were Sunday schools. Under the leadership of another Benderly disciple, Director of Religious Education Emanuel Gamoran (1895–1962), the UAHC's Commission on Jewish Education (CJE) encouraged Reform temples to intensify their educational programs. Although some introduced voluntary weekday Hebrew programs, most resisted the change. The Conservative movement's Commission on Jewish Education launched a similar effort in the middle to late 1940s with better results. By 1950, seventy-five Conservative congregations had converted their Sunday schools into two- or three-day-a-week schools. Nevertheless, congregational schools averaged one-third fewer teaching hours per week than the community Talmud Torahs, which were typically five-day-a-week schools.

Theoretically, the curriculum of the Conservative weekday congregational school and the community Talmud Torah was similar. In practice, however, the reduction in teaching hours in the congregational school rendered Hebrew fluency an unrealistic goal. Gamoran's religious school curriculum encouraged Reform schools to move away from the direct teaching of morals and ethics and to focus instead on Biblical stories, history, Hebrew, holidays and ceremonies, and music.

Gamoran's CJE had a great impact on textbook publishing. During his tenure (1923–1958), Gamoran edited a graded series of textbooks, many of which circulated well beyond Reform educational settings. In the postwar era, the textbook industry expanded. The Conservative movement's commission published its own line of textbooks, and trade publishers like Behrman House, Ktav Publishing House and, more recently, Tora Aura captured an increasingly large share of the market.

The 1940s and 1950s also witnessed the phenomenal expansion of day schools. Earlier in the twentieth century, day schools and *yeshivot* attracted a minuscule percentage of the student population, especially outside New York City. In 1935 there were only seventeen schools with a combined enrollment of about 4,500 students (Schiff 1966). In the late 1930s, the day school movement began to gain momentum. Alongside the traditional yeshivot, which were characterized by gender segregation, Yiddish or English language instruction of Judaic studies, Talmud-centered education for boys, and the relegation of general studies to the middle or late afternoon, other day school models gained in popularity. These included the coeducational Modern Orthodox day schools, where general and Judaic studies were placed on an equal footing and the primary language of Judaic instruction was Hebrew, and the progressive Jewish academy, where the general studies program was designed to rival the best private schools and the integration of Jewish and American culture became a primary goal. By the mid-1950s day school enrollment topped 40,000 and climbed higher in subsequent decades (Schiff 1966). Many schools were organized with the assistance of Torah U'Mesorah, the Orthodox day school network.

Scholars have offered various explanations for the growth of the day school movement. Initially, the impact of the Holocaust was decisive. In the 1940s and 1950s, many day school students were children of immigrants who had fled Nazi Europe or who were Holocaust survivors. In addition, the shock of the Holocaust may have strengthened the resolve of some American-born Orthodox Jews to preserve their religious and cultural heritage, even at the price of abandoning the public school. After 1960, the replacement of the melting pot ethos with cultural pluralism, and later with multiculturalism, along with the disenchantment of many Americans with public education made day schools more palatable to a wider swath of Jews. Some were also persuaded by the gloomy assessments of the effectiveness of supplementary school education in the 1970s and 1980s. As concerns about Jewish continuity became more pronounced, many hoped day schools would stem the rising rate of intermarriage. Notably, the growth of day schools has its analogue in the growth of Christian all-day academies, many of which are affiliated with evangelical denominations.

By 2000, almost 200,000 children, 40 percent of the entire Jewish school population, were receiving a day school education. The vast majority of these schools were affiliated with various streams within Orthodoxy; Orthodox and Hasidic schools accounted for 80 percent of day school enrollment. However, the percentage of non-Orthodox schools was rising steadily. The Conservative movement officially embraced day school education in the 1950s, with the first Solomon Schechter day school established in 1956 in Queens, New York. In 2000, there were sixty-three Conservative-affiliated schools. The Reform movement, which was most reticent about embracing day schools, reevaluated its position in the 1960s. By 2000, the Progressive Association of Reform Day Schools had twenty day school affiliates in the United States and Canada

(Schick 2000). In recent years community day schools have also been on the rise. In 2004, Ravsak, the Jewish Community Day School Network, boasted ninety member schools serving 25,000 students.

Another educational innovation that grew markedly in the 1940s and 1950s was educational camping. The Jewish camping movement began in the 1890s and was connected to the fresh air movement, which was designed to improve the health of poor, urban children. In subsequent decades, overnight camps catering to a wealthier population also opened, some with (nominal) religious or cultural content. In 1919 Benderly disciple Albert Schoolman (1894–1980), director of the Central Jewish Institute (CJI), a progressive Manhattan Talmud Torah, established the first truly educational Jewish summer camp. Concerned that over the summer break his students forgot much of what they had learned, Schoolman decided to open a summer version of the CJI, where vacation would be combined with study. A permanent facility was eventually built in Port Jervis, New York. The nonprofit camp was an early and successful experiment in Jewish experiential education. Jewish cultural content was embedded in the camp's regular activities. Campers experienced Jewish life through religious services, festive Shabbat observances, Keren Ami activities, arts and crafts, and the performance arts. Schoolman, with two couples, opened a similar camp for more affluent children, Camp Modin, in 1922. The Yiddishists and the Zionists also established educational camps in the 1920s and 1930s. Among the most well-known were Camp Boiberik (Sholem Aleichem Folk Institute, 1922), Camp Yehupets (Workmen's Circle, 1923), Camp Kinderwelt (Jewish National Workers Alliance, 1925), Camp Kvutza (Young Poale Zion–Habonim, 1933), Camp Moshava (Bnei Akiva, 1937), Camp Young Judaea (Hadassah, 1938), and Camp Betar (B'rith Joseph Trumpeldor, 1940).

The Hebrew-speaking camp marked an important development in overnight camping. Samson Benderly first introduced this at Camp Achvah in 1926. The financial pressures of the Great Depression forced Benderly to reconceive Achvah as a Jewish culture camp in 1932. However, his experiment inspired the Hanoar Haivri Organization to found Camp Massad, a religious Zionist Hebrew-speaking camp, in 1941. Speaking Hebrew also became important in the Conservative movement's Ramah camps, which were founded by JTS's TI for leadership

training. The first Ramah Camp, in Conover, Wisconsin, opened in 1947. Unlike Massad, Ramah incorporated formal classes into its program. Leadership training was also the primary motivation for the founding of the Brandeis Camp Institute, in Amherst, New Hampshire (1941), and the first UAHC camp in Oconomowoc, Wisconsin (1951).

By the 1960s many acknowledged that educational camping was one of the most effective forms of Jewish education. And the camps proved to be an important breeding ground for a younger generation of educators. Today, tuition costs can be prohibitive (Sales and Saxe 2004), and affluent youth have other summertime options, including overseas travel, sports clinics, and college preparatory programs. Currently, only 4 percent of Jewish youth attend Jewish summer camps.

By the early 1970s, Jewish education was in crisis. Supplementary school enrollments were plummeting, largely as a result of declining birthrates. More disturbing, recent studies suggested that supplementary education had little positive impact on Jewish identity formation. Guided by their own positive camp experiences and the countercultural spirit of the times, the younger generation of educators counseled that supplementary schools emphasize affective learning and enculturation rather than academic subjects. The Coalition for Alternatives in Jewish Education (CAJE), established 1973, grew out of this movement. CAJE was transdenominational, reflecting many younger educators' antiestablishment bent. CAJE members sought to eliminate sexist educational materials and encourage family education.

Since the 1980s, informal educational travel options have mushroomed. A number of organizations offer teen educational summer travel packages to Israel and Europe. In 1988, the annual March of the Living pilgrimage was organized to promote Holocaust awareness, Zionism, and Jewish identity. Each year, thousands of students tour the remnants of the Nazi death camps and Israel, in a trip that coincides with Yom Ha-Shoah (Holocaust Remembrance Day) and Yom Ha'atzmaut (Israel Independence Day). In the late 1990s, philanthropists Michael Steinhardt and Edgar Bronfman started the Birthright Israel program, which offers a ten-day, all-expenses-paid trip to Israel to any Jewish college student who has not previously participated in a peer educational trip.

In the 1980s and 1990s, as the organized community's fears about Jewish continuity increased, there were new efforts to revitalize conventional Jewish education. Community leaders and educators made their peace with the inherent limitations of supplementary education, even as they embraced day schools. One of the most important changes of the past few decades has been the increasing involvement of local Jewish Federations and private donors in promoting Jewish education. Although historically, Federations avoided allocations to Jewish day schools, they have changed their policies. Foundations like Avi Chai and the Jewish Education Fund have poured money into day school initiatives, while funders like the Mandel Associated Foundation and the Nathan Cummings Foundation have supported new experiments in congregational education. The Wexner Foundation, Boston Hebrew College, and philanthropist Florence Melton have undertaken initiatives in adult education. The importance of foundations and Federations in conceptualizing and funding educational initiatives has weakened the central educational agencies. Some have disbanded, while others have become service agencies of local federations.

Jonathan B. Krasner

References and Further Reading

Ashton, Diane. 1997. *Rebecca Gratz: Women and Judaism in Antebellum America.* Detroit, MI: Wayne State University Press.

Dushkin, Alexander. 1918. *Jewish Education in New York City.* New York: Board of Jewish Education of Greater New York.

Gartner, Lloyd. 1976. "Temples of Liberty Unpolluted: American Jews and Public Schools, 1840–1875." In *A Bicentennial Festschrift for Jacob Rader Marcus,* edited by Bertram W. Korn. New York, NY: Ktav Publishing House.

Goren, Arthur. 1970. *New York Jews and the Quest for Community: The Kehillah Experiment, 1908–1922.* New York: Columbia University Press.

Kaufman, David. 1997. "Jewish Education as a Civilization: A History of the Teachers Institute." In *Tradition Renewed: A History of the Jewish Theological Seminary,* edited by Jack Wertheimer. New York: The Seminary.

Pilch, Judah, ed. 1969. *A History of Jewish Education in America.* New York: National Curriculum Research Institute of the American Association for Jewish Education.

Sales, Amy L., and Leonard Saxe. 2004. *How Goodly Are Thy Tents: Summer Camps as Jewish Socializing Experiences.* Hanover, NH: University Press of New England/ Brandeis University Press.

Schick, Marvin. 2000. *A Census of Jewish Day Schools in the United States.* New York: Avi Chai.

Schiff, Alvin. 1966. *The Jewish Day School in America.* New York: Jewish Education Committee Press.

Wertheimer, Jack. 1999. "Jewish Education in the United States: Recent Trends and Issues." In *American Jewish Year Book 1999,* edited by David Singer, 3–115. New York: American Jewish Committee.

Winter, Nathan. 1966. *Jewish Education in a Pluralistic Society: Samson Benderly and Jewish Education in the United States.* New York: New York University Press.

Brandeis University

The founding of Brandeis University in 1948 by members of the American Jewish community followed the American tradition of colleges and universities established by various denominational groups. Harvard and Yale began as Congregationalist schools; Brown was Baptist; Swarthmore, Quaker; and Princeton, Presbyterian. Named for Associate Supreme Court Justice Louis Dembitz Brandeis (1856–1941) and established in part to provide educational opportunities for Jews who suffered discrimination due to the anti-Jewish quotas widespread in academe at the time of its founding, Brandeis has become one of the preeminent small, liberal arts research universities in America. It is a member of the Association of American Universities, which represents the leading research universities in the United States and Canada.

Beginning in the mid-nineteenth century, Jewish leaders put forward various proposals "for the establishment of Jewish institutions of higher learning where Jewish studies would predominate" (Goldstein 1951), anticipating the establishment of Hebrew Union College in 1875, the Jewish Theological Seminary in 1886, and Rabbi Isaac Elchanan Theological Seminary in 1897. Brandeis University's founders, however, had a different vision, one that reflected an increasingly prevalent assimilationist view. The establishment of Brandeis signified American Jewry's growing affluence, confidence, and acculturation after World War II, along with its attendant ethnic assertiveness and expanded philanthropic objectives. Brandeis was not only a new institution in the roster of Jewish philanthropies, but a new kind of institution. Though possessing a clear character based on Jewish values, Brandeis was not to be a Jewish university, focused on the study of religious texts, existing exclusively for the benefit of Jews, or representing any one movement within Judaism. Brandeis would be established on broad foundations, representing the increasingly secular American Jewish community as a whole. At a time when most Ivy League schools were male only, and many colleges and universities had admission quotas for Jews and other minority groups, Brandeis would be nonsectarian and open to men and women on the basis of merit alone, without reference to race, religion, ethnicity, or national origin (Goldstein 1951).

Early in 1946, C. Ruggles Smith, general counsel of Middlesex University in Waltham, Massachusetts, approached Rabbi Israel Goldstein with a proposal to turn Middlesex University over to a new board of trustees. Rabbi Goldstein was past president of the Synagogue Council of America, founded in 1926 to provide congregationally affiliated Jews with a common voice in interfaith activities, and a representative of the Albert Einstein Foundation for Higher Learning, the organizational and fund-raising arm for the entity that became Brandeis University. Middlesex University, the former Middlesex College of Medicine and Surgery—before that, the Worcester Medical Institution, founded in 1849, and revived in 1914—operated on the principles of freedom and equality, maintaining a racially, religiously, and ethnically diverse student body. However, lack of accreditation by the American Medical Association and declining enrollments during World War II doomed the university.

In February 1946, Rabbi Goldstein was elected president of the board of trustees of Middlesex University; he was succeeded by George Alpert, a railroad executive, who served from 1947 to 1954 as the first board chair of the newly renamed Brandeis University. In May 1948, Dr. Abram Sachar, one of the organizers of the B'nai B'rith Hillel Foundation, whose many writings include the popular one-volume *History of the Jews*, became the first president of Brandeis University. In October, classes began with 107 students and 13 faculty members.

Since then, Brandeis University has grown to become an institution of some 450 faculty members serving approximately 3,100 undergraduate and 1,200 graduate students. It has had seven presidents: Abram L. Sachar, who served until 1968 and subsequently as chancellor and then chancellor emeritus until his death in 1993; noted attorney and former ambassador Morris B. Abram, who stepped down in 1970 to run for the U.S. Senate from New York; Charles I. Schottland, commissioner of Social Security in

the Eisenhower administration and the first dean of the Heller School for Social Policy and Management at Brandeis, who served as interim president from 1970 to 1972; Marver H. Bernstein, former dean of the Woodrow Wilson School at Princeton, who served from 1972 to 1983; biologist and former president of the University of New Hampshire Evelyn E. Handler, who served from 1983 to 1991; Samuel O. Thier, a physician and former president of the Institute of Medicine of the National Academy of Sciences, who served from 1991 to 1994, when he became president of the Massachusetts General Hospital; and Jehuda Reinharz, the Richard Koret Professor of Modern Jewish History, an alumnus, and former Brandeis provost, appointed in 1994.

Brandeis has undergone great physical change, maturing from a campus with one brick building, a stable, and a castle, to one of the finest repositories of the International style of architecture in the country *and* a castle. From its first master plan by internationally renowned architect Eero Saarinen (1910-1961), through subsequent plans by other practitioners of modernism, "the Brandeis campus can be seen as a microcosm of the history of the Modern Movement in architecture" (Bernstein 1998).

Nonsectarianism

Although Brandeis has always been nonsectarian in its admission of students and the employment of faculty and staff, its historic description as a "Jewish-sponsored, nonsectarian" university masked a complex self-image. Members of the extended Brandeis community of alumni and friends have often asked how Jewish this non-Jewish university should be.

In the late 1940s and early 1950s, when virtually all members of the entering classes were Jews, Brandeis worried about the public's perception of the institution's commitment to nonsectarianism and a quota-free admissions policy. President Sachar struggled, as did his successors, to dispel the notion that an educational institution founded *by* Jews must be meant exclusively or even primarily *for* Jews. He made a determined effort to emphasize Brandeis's ethnic and religious diversity. The lineup of the university's football team made it clear, he said, that Brandeis was not a parochial school. "There were Goldfaders and Steins and Shapiros, but there were also Baldaccis and Hemingways and Napolis" (Sachar 1976).

In 1953, when the trustees debated the establishment of a single interfaith chapel on campus, board chair George Alpert argued that Brandeis was intended to be nonsectarian "not only in the classroom, the laboratory, and the athletic field, but in the chapel as well." The proposed interfaith chapel would symbolize the institution's nonsectarian spirit of equality and parity (Minutes 1953). In the end, and partly in response to religious sensitivities, separate Jewish, Catholic, and Protestant chapels were constructed. Nearly fifty years later in 1998, space was set aside on campus for a prayer room to accommodate the needs of Brandeis's growing Muslim student population, the latest indication of the university's diverse and nonsectarian nature. Today, slightly over half of Brandeis undergraduates identify themselves as Jews.

Brandeis is determined to be nonsectarian and simultaneously Jewish, not in a sectarian sense, but by virtue of its service to the Jewish community and by having a character based on Jewish values of education, tolerance, social justice, and the life of the mind. Thus, while Brandeis admits students without regard to religion and offers no religious instruction, its academic calendar is tied to the Jewish religious calendar, and it has a number of programs designed specifically to serve the broader Jewish community. Occasionally, differing perceptions of what it means to be both Jewish and nonsectarian have created misunderstandings, if not tension. In the late 1980s, a report by the board of trustees called for the introduction of pork and shellfish dishes in the one dining hall that had always been nonkosher. This produced a furor, eliciting a flood of letters, almost equally divided for and against the change, from alumni and individual members of the campus and Jewish communities. The reaction was a measure of both the campus and the larger Jewish community's expectations for Brandeis, expectations that have always been as diverse as the American Jewish community itself. Those approving of the change applauded Brandeis's commitment to nonsectarianism, while those opposed argued that, as an institution, Brandeis should respect Jewish religious tradition.

Today, Brandeis students are drawn from more than a hundred countries and represent more than a dozen different faiths. As a nonsectarian university that takes pride in its Jewish identity and is open to students, teachers, and staff of every nationality, religion, and political orientation, Brandeis affirms America's heritage of cultural, ethnic, and religious diversity, equal access to opportunity, and freedom of expression.

Social Justice

Perhaps more than any other academic institution in America, Brandeis honors a commitment to social justice, marked by a tradition of social activism by its members. Founded in the aftermath of World War II, the university took form as an institution in which human values and social concerns were of vital importance. The original faculty, some of whom, such as Alexander Altmann and Nahum Glatzer, were refugees from Nazi Germany, did much to shape this character.

At a time when the costly lessons of complicity through silence were all too apparent, many Brandeis professors worked to make a difference both in the classroom and in society at large. Former First Lady Eleanor Roosevelt served on the board of trustees from 1953 until her death in 1962 and, beginning in 1959, also taught a seminar on nongovernmental agencies of the United Nations. Other members of the early faculty included Irving Howe, socialist literary critic and editor of *Dissent*; Philip Rahv, founder of *Partisan Review*; political scientist Lawrence Fuchs, first head of the Peace Corps in the Philippines and executive director of the U.S. Select Commission on Immigration; sociologist Irving Zola, who founded a self-help center in Boston for individuals with disabilities; and anthropologist and political activist Robert Manners.

In 1968, Brandeis faculty members donated their own funds to establish the Transitional Year Program (TYP), a one-year program of classroom instruction designed to prepare educationally disadvantaged students for college. The program, an outgrowth of the civil rights movement of the 1960s and long since supported by university funds, has enabled an ethnically diverse group of hundreds of young people to earn a college degree. Nearly two hundred TYP graduates have received a Brandeis degree, while others have pursued their educations at other American colleges and universities. Although the program has had its detractors in the administration—presidents Abram and Bernstein were firm critics of the program—more recent president Handler and current president Reinharz have given it their full support. TYP remains the longest running program of its kind in America.

Thirty years after the launch of TYP, Brandeis began its participation in the Posse Foundation program, the brainchild of Deborah Bial, a Brandeis alumna. The nationwide program, which annually recruits ten student leaders from inner city public high schools to form multiethnic teams, is rooted in the belief that a small group of students, a "posse," can serve as a catalyst to help ensure the personal and academic achievement of all members of the group. The Posse students at Brandeis are fully supported by the university and graduate at or above the 90-percent graduation rate of participants in the program nationwide.

The university's spirit of *tikkun olam* (putting the world aright) has inspired generations of Brandeis students to social activism. Chapters of the student division of Americans for Democratic Action, the nation's oldest liberal lobbying group (founded in 1947), and the National Association for the Advancement of Colored People (founded in 1909) were formed on campus in the 1950s. In the 1960s, individual Brandeis students, faculty, and alumni worked in the South to register black voters and to demonstrate against segregation.

In January 1969, a tumultuous period at many universities following the assassination of Dr. Martin Luther King Jr., members of the Brandeis Afro-American Organization occupied a campus building and presented a list of ten, nonnegotiable demands, including the creation of an autonomous black studies department, in which members would have control over the hiring and firing of faculty and the appointment of a chairman selected by a committee of students. Eighty-five Brandeis faculty members signed a letter published in the *New York Times*, denouncing the demands, which they called "a specific program for racial segregation and discrimination" (January 19, 1969). Yet, while the administration and some faculty members denounced the takeover strategy as antithetical to the practice of open discourse that must characterize a university, as well as a clear threat to faculty control over academic affairs, many faculty members supported the students' demands. With the campus deeply divided on the issue, and lacking any agreements except amnesty for the sit-in, the building occupation ended after eleven days; however, in subsequent negotiations involving faculty, students, and administrators, the university acknowledged the "deeply felt and unfulfilled needs" of many black students. This resulted in the establishment, under faculty resolution, of the Department of African and Afro-American Studies, an ac-

tion that was already being implemented before the takeover; the appointment of two black professors in the departments of English and American civilization; the hiring of a black assistant director of admissions; and the creation of Martin Luther King scholarships, originally for disadvantaged black students, but later opened to all students who demonstrate financial need, academic achievement, and a record of community service. Then president Morris Abram regarded the outcome as a triumph for the university in that the dispute had been resolved without relinquishing faculty control over academic affairs or establishing an exclusionary precedent.

Protests against the war in Vietnam took place at Brandeis as early as 1965. For two weeks in December 1968, Brandeis students joined the growing sanctuary movement by giving refuge in a campus building to an AWOL soldier until his peaceful surrender to authorities. In 1970, following President Richard M. Nixon's decision to attack enemy sanctuaries on the Cambodian–Vietnam border, there were calls on campuses across the country for nationwide demonstrations. Some Brandeis students established themselves as the National Strike Information Center, collecting news of strike activities and publishing frequent newsletters to inform participating schools, the media, and the public of strike activities throughout the country.

The 1960s also witnessed student activism of another kind at Brandeis with the establishment of the student-run Waltham Group, a volunteer service organization through which hundreds of students participate in noncredit social and educational outreach programs, responding to the needs of children, the elderly, and others in greater Boston.

In the 1980s, Brandeis students and faculty were active in the antiapartheid movement, urging the university to divest from South Africa. A student–faculty advisory committee on shareholder responsibility worked to educate the campus community about the complexities of the divestment issue while attempting to persuade the board of trustees to remove from the university's endowment portfolio holdings in companies doing business in South Africa, a position ultimately adopted in May 1987 and rescinded following apartheid's demise.

The commitment to social justice was institutionalized at Brandeis as early as 1959 with the establishment of the university's first professional school, the Florence Heller Graduate School for Advanced Studies in Social

Welfare, renamed the Heller School for Social Policy and Management in 2001. Its mission is to promote public health and social justice for vulnerable populations, especially those lacking the capacity or resources to secure their own well-being.

The university's commitment to social justice is also found in the International Center for Ethics, Justice, and Public Life. Established in 1998, the Center develops responses to conflict and injustice by offering innovative approaches to coexistence, strengthening the work of international courts, and encouraging ethical practices in civic and professional life.

Service to the Jewish Community

From the beginning, Brandeis accepted a special mission in the area of Judaic studies. For its founders, Brandeis, though not a Jewish university, would bring to American higher education a cultural perspective reflecting Jewish traditions of scholarship and community service, along with a commitment to social justice personified by the university's namesake, Louis Dembitz Brandeis. Throughout its history, Brandeis has enjoyed a relationship with the American Jewish community marked by particularism, but not parochialism. In many ways, Brandeis is a microcosm of American Jewry, defining its mission of service to the American Jewish community broadly and without reference to the different streams of Jewish religious expression or communal interest. At the same time, Brandeis views its overall mission as that of a nonsectarian research university dedicated to the advancement of the humanities, arts, and sciences and the transmission of new knowledge.

Some of the special programs, centers, and institutes created at Brandeis that benefit the Jewish community are new and innovative; others, like the Philip W. Lown School, are decades old. The Lown School's Department of Near Eastern and Judaic Studies, established at a time when Judaic studies were largely ignored in American higher education, has educated more Judaic studies scholars and is more comprehensive than any other department or program of Judaic studies outside Israel. The Association for Jewish Studies was established at Brandeis in 1970 and was housed on the campus until 2003. Its first president was Leon Jick, a Judaica scholar who had come to Brandeis in 1966 to direct the newly established Lown Center for Contemporary Jewish Studies. The Hornstein

Program in Jewish Communal Service, founded in 1969, offers an interdisciplinary graduate program that combines organizational behavior, modern and classical Judaic studies, and studies in contemporary Jewish life. It has placed hundreds of its graduates in leadership positions in Jewish organizations around the world. The Cohen Center for Modern Jewish Studies, established in 1980, conducts research on topics of special relevance to the Jewish community, such as Jewish family life, intermarriage and assimilation, Jewish education and identity, adolescent development, and relations between Israel and the world's Jewish communities.

Among the newer programs and centers are the Tauber Institute for the Study of European Jewry, established in 1980; the Hadassah-Brandeis Institute, founded in 1997 by Hadassah, the Women's Zionist Organization of America, Inc.; the Fisher-Bernstein Institute for Leadership Development in Jewish Philanthropy, established in 1997, and the Institute for Informal Jewish Education, founded in 1999. These programs are designed to help shape and fulfill the national agenda of the American Jewish community, educate and inform communal professionals and lay leaders, and bring research to bear on some of the thorniest issues facing the Jewish community, such as Jewish identity, intermarriage, and Israel–Diaspora relations. One of the newest initiatives is the Mandel Center for Studies in Jewish Education, founded in 2004, which conducts studies of teaching and learning in Jewish education and develops model programs for Jewish educators.

Brandeis is also a major site for research on and interdisciplinary study of Israel and the modern Middle East. The Crown Center for Middle East Studies, officially opened in 2005, is committed to balanced and nonideological treatment of the full range of issues confronting the states of the greater, modern Middle East. Brandeis has ties with institutions and scholars in Israel, Turkey, Egypt, Jordan, Syria, Iran, and Morocco.

Academic Excellence

From the first, Brandeis set out to build a small, excellent, liberal arts college within a major research university, with a commitment to both undergraduate and graduate education and with close personal attention from senior faculty. Brandeis has also consistently sought to make a difference in the ideals and values it imparts to its students.

To compete with far larger and older institutions, Brandeis has tried to set itself apart by developing academic programs designed to fill a particular niche.

The scholars who composed the early faculty at Brandeis were obtained by "aggressive recruitment of younger men [and women] whose scholarship has been indicated but not fully demonstrated" (Sachar 1976). Others, like Ludwig Lewisohn, *Nation* magazine editor and professor of literature, had reached the age of retirement and were forced out of other universities despite their continued desire to teach. Still others, like Saul Cohen, who became a professor of chemistry and the first dean of faculty, "had sought out Brandeis after encountering anti-Semitic hiring discrimination at other universities" (Gliedman 1988).

The early result was a faculty that contained an astonishing number of distinguished scholars: Max Lerner in American civilization; Abraham Maslow in psychology; Frank Manuel in European history; Irving Howe, the editor of *Dissent*, and Albert Guérard in the humanities; Nahum Glatzer and Alexander Altmann in Jewish studies; Lewis Coser in sociology; and Erwin Bodky, a student of Richard Strauss, in music. Even the athletics department had its celebrity: professional football star Benny Friedman became Brandeis University's first athletic director.

The early core of influential scholars soon recruited and attracted others: Simon Rawidowicz, Nahum Sarna, and Benjamin Halpern joined the faculty in Near Eastern and Judaic studies (NEJS); today, MacArthur Award winner Bernadette Brooten is a member of the NEJS faculty. In the other humanities and social sciences, outstanding scholars—such as Herbert Marcuse, Robert Preyer, Philip Rieff, J. V. Cunningham, Walter Laqueur, John Roche, Lawrence Fuchs, I. Milton Sacks, Claude Vigee, Marie Syrkin, and Maurice Stein—joined the faculty; today's history faculty includes Jacqueline Jones, another MacArthur Award winner. Saul Cohen was joined in the sciences by Sidney Golden and Orrie Friedman in chemistry, Albert Kelner in biology, Herman Epstein in biophysics, and Ricardo Morant and Richard Held in experimental psychology, and then by biochemists Robert Abeles, William Jencks, Nathan Kaplan, and Martin Kamen, by physicists David Falkoff, Eugene Gross, Silvan Schweber, Max Chretien, and Jack Goldstein, and by mathematicians Oscar Goldman, Arnold Shapiro, Maurice Auslander, and Edgar Brown. Today four Howard Hughes Medical Institute investigators, six members of the National Academy of Sciences, and seven fellows of the American Association for the Advancement of Science are counted among the science faculty, and the Department of Biology includes Gina Turrigiano, another MacArthur Award winner.

From the beginning, Brandeis regarded the creative arts as part of its academic curriculum, which was unusual among universities at the time (Sachar 1976). It attracted Irving Fine and Leonard Bernstein in music, and painter Mitchell Siporin, sculptor Peter Grippe, and art historian Leo Bronstein in fine arts. In theater arts, it attracted set designer Howard Bay, playwright John Matthews, and, later, scholar Martin Halpern and acting teacher Charles Werner Moore. At its inaugural commencement in 1952, Brandeis staged its first Festival of the Creative Arts, a four-day event that saw the world premiere of Bernstein's one-act opera, *Trouble in Tahiti;* the first American staging of Brecht's *Threepenny Opera,* adapted by Mark Blitzstein; a performance of a Stravinsky ballet by Merce Cunningham's dance troupe; and appearances by Lotte Lenya, Aaron Copland, and jazz critic Nat Hentoff. Today, the Festival of the Arts continues as an annual event, and the university's office of the arts coordinates activities among the academic departments in creative arts, as well as the Spingold Theater Center, Slosberg Music Center, and the Rose Art Museum. The Rose, built in 1961, began acquiring its collection under the directorship of Sam Hunter and today houses one of the finest collections of modern and contemporary American art in New England (Hauptman 1999).

In 1951, the Commonwealth of Massachusetts authorized Brandeis to confer graduate and professional degrees. Established in 1953, the Graduate School of Arts and Sciences was formally inaugurated on January 14, 1954. Initially, the university created one graduate program in each of its four schools: sciences, creative arts, social sciences, and humanities. Chemistry offered a master of science degree; music, a master of fine arts degree; psychology, a doctoral degree; and Near Eastern and Judaic Studies, a master of arts and a doctoral degree. Brandeis awarded the first master's degrees in 1954, the first doctorate in 1957. Today more than thirty departments offer postbaccalaureate degrees.

Only thirteen years after its establishment in 1948 and in the shortest time in Phi Beta Kappa history, Brandeis received authorization to establish a Phi Beta Kappa chapter. Following three years of scrutiny, the committee on qualifications of the united chapters of Phi Beta Kappa reported on "the university's remarkable achievement in creating in ten years' time—only three student generations—a full-fledged institution capable of providing undergraduate instruction comparable to that offered by other American universities of the first rank" (Pasternack 1988).

Excellence in the sciences has long been a hallmark of Brandeis. Today, approximately one hundred faculty members teach and do research in the sciences, and between two hundred fifty and three hundred graduate students take part in nine graduate programs. A gift in 1972 permitted the establishment of the Rosenstiel Basic Medical Sciences Research Center, "a research center unlike any other in the United States . . . [whose mission is] to bring together in one facility world-class scientists from a wide range of disciplines but with a common focus, the application of the tools of structural biology, genetics, and immunology to basic research questions with immediate and long-term impact on human health" (Brandeis University n.d.). Structural biology was virtually invented at the center by such researchers as Donald Caspar, Carolyn Cohen, Susan Lowey, and David DeRosier, most of whom had worked in the famous Cavendish Laboratory at England's Cambridge University, studying with James Watson and Francis Crick, who, along with Rosalind Franklin, cracked the DNA code. In 1975, another interdisciplinary center, the Henry and Lois Foster Biomedical Research Laboratories, was built to provide additional facilities for basic research in biology, biochemistry, and other biomedical areas.

The year 1994 saw the completion of the Benjamin and Mae Volen National Center for Complex Systems, formed to study the brain and human intelligence. The center, composed of faculty members who specialize in artificial intelligence, cognitive science, linguistics, and a wide range of topics in neuroscience, houses an interdisciplinary group with the ability to perform scientific analysis of the brain from the cellular and molecular to the cognitive and computational levels.

A number of other innovations have contributed to Brandeis's reputation for academic excellence. In 1958, Lawrence and Mae Wien established the Wien International Scholarship Program to further international understanding among nations, to provide foreign students with an opportunity to study in the United States, and to enrich the intellectual and cultural life of the Brandeis campus.

What sets the Wien program apart is that its scholars must demonstrate a commitment to their community, their country, and the world at large *before* applying to Brandeis. In 1996, the Slifka scholarship program, open to Arab and Jewish Israelis with a demonstrated commitment to coexistence, was launched.

In 1986, Brandeis inaugurated a program for students planning careers in international business. To fill a niche between disciplines and the curricula of business schools and schools of international relations, the Lemberg Program offered a two-year master's program and a five-year combined BA/MA option for qualified Brandeis undergraduates. This program grew to become the Graduate School of International Economics and Finance, renamed the International Business School in 2003.

A short list of Brandeis's most prominent alumni includes Thomas L. Friedman, foreign affairs columnist for the *New York Times;* Roderick MacKinnon, 2003 Nobel Laureate in chemistry; Judith Shapiro, president of Barnard College; novelist Ha Jin, National Book Award recipient and author of *Waiting, The Crazed,* and *War Trash;* Otis Johnson, mayor of Savannah, Georgia; Robert Gallucci, dean of the Georgetown University School of Foreign Service; CBS correspondent Robert Simon; CNN analyst Bill Schneider; Thomas Glynn, deputy secretary of labor under former secretary of labor, and now Brandeis professor, Robert Reich; Gary Tinterow, curator of the department of nineteenth-century, modern, and contemporary art at the Metropolitan Museum of Art; Adam Weinberg, director of the Whitney Museum of Modern Art; Shen Tong, leader at the 1989 pro-democracy demonstrations in Tiananmen Square, Beijing; Eli Segal, former Americorps head; Ellen Goodman, president of Tootsie Roll Industries; and Jehuda Reinharz, president of Brandeis University and a leading scholar of modern Jewish history.

Clifford D. Hauptman and John R. Hose

References and Further Reading
Bernstein, Gerald S., ed. 1998. *Building a Campus: An Architectural Celebration of Brandeis University's 50th Anniversary.* Waltham, MA: Brandeis University Press.
Brandeis University. No date. "Rosenstiel Basic Medical Sciences Research Center, Mission Statement." Available at: http://www.rose.brandeis.edu/rose_mission.html. Accessed June 18, 2004.

Fischer, David Hackett. 1998. "The Brandeis Idea: Variations on an American Theme." *Brandeis Review* 19,1 and 2: 26–29.

Gliedman, John. 1988. "From Haven to 'Host': The Origins of Brandeis University." Senior essay in history. New Haven, CT: Timothy Dwight College, Yale University.

Goldstein, Israel. 1951. *Brandeis University.* New York: Bloch Publishing Company.

Hauptman, Cliff. 1999. "The Collection at the Rose: An American Beauty." *Brandeis Review* 20,1: 30–35.

Minutes. 1953. Executive Committee of the Board of Trustees, Brandeis University. March 20.

Pasternack, Susan, ed. 1988. *From the Beginning: A Picture History of the First Four Decades of Brandeis University.* Waltham, MA: Brandeis University.

Sachar, Abram. 1976. *A Host at Last.* Boston: Little, Brown and Company.

Jewish History and American Jewish Historians

Salo Baron (1895–1989)

Dean of Jewish Historians

Salo (Shalom) Wittmayer Baron was one of the dominant figures in Jewish historiography for much of the twentieth century. Called the dean of Jewish historians, he was the first witness at the 1961 trial of Adolph Eichmann in Jerusalem, where he provided historical context for the prosecution. Baron's career was emblematic of the early migration of Jewish studies from Europe to the United States, a process accelerated by World War I and the postwar dislocations. When Baron emigrated to America, Jewish history was not part of the curriculum of the secular universities, and the field was dominated by theologians and philologists. Baron did not believe that mastery of Talmudic literature was a prerequisite for all historical scholarship. Instead he argued that Jewish history had to be separated from apologetics, filiopietism, or providential design. Students needed to master modern historiography, not rabbinic literature.

Born in Tarnow (Galicia), Baron earned three doctorates from the University of Vienna—philosophy (1917), political science (1922), and law (1923)—and received rabbinic ordination from the Jewish Theological Seminary of Vienna in 1920. He taught at the Jewish Teachers College of Vienna until 1926, when he joined the faculty of

Jewish historian Salo Baron. Baron was the first witness in the 1961 trial of Adolph Eichmann in Jerusalem, where he provided historical context for the prosecution. (American Jewish Archives)

Stephen S. Wise's Jewish Institute of Religion (JIR) in New York City.

During his tenure at the JIR, Baron began to develop his critique of contemporary Jewish historiography. In "Ghetto and Emancipation" (1928), he used the term *lachrymose conception* of Jewish history for the first time and challenged scholars to reassess the impact of modernization on Jewish life. In other publications, Baron called for integrating Jewish history into general world historiography, arguing that this would make it possible to see the Jewish experience as something more than centuries of persecution. This anti-lachrymose crusade characterized much of his professional writing.

In 1930, Baron was appointed to the Miller Chair at Columbia University, only the second university chair in Jewish studies in the United States and the first devoted to Jewish history. Baron argued that the Miller Chair should be located in Columbia's history department, where the faculty were devotees of the "new" history (already two decades old), which accorded social, economic, and religious factors equal stature to politics. This emphasis, which Baron also embraced, enabled him to help shape the academic study of Jewish history in the United States for a generation.

By the 1930s Baron's historical methodology followed three basic principles: a rejection of the lachrymose conception of Jewish history; an emphasis on the relationship between social, political, and religious forces in Jewish history; and his belief that the evolution of Jewish history was the product of the interaction of Jewish and gentile societies.

In 1937, Columbia University Press published his three-volume *Social and Religious History of the Jews*, which covered all of Jewish history from biblical origins until the modern age. Baron's study was among the earliest academic works to give religion equal credence with social forces, while at the same time divorcing the evolution of Jewish history from providential design. It was also one of the earliest works in Jewish studies to be published by a secular university press.

Although it was not his passion, Baron published a number of essays on American Jewish history. During World War II he came to understand that the war had placed American Jews at the forefront of world Jewry, with "all the challenges and responsibilities which it entails." Over the next decade he wrote several articles demonstrat-

ing his appreciation of the significance of American Jewish history, which, when compared to Europe, seemed the proof-text of his anti-lachrymose vision. Baron served as president of the American Jewish Historical Society in 1952 and again in 1954, during the American Jewish Tercentenary. *Steeled by Adversity,* his collected essays on American Jewish history, was published in 1971.

After his retirement from Columbia in 1963, he dedicated himself to expanding his *Social and Religious History.* He completed eighteen volumes, bringing the story to the end of the Middle Ages. His wife, Jeannette, was instrumental in his work, and after her death in 1985 Baron ceased to publish. Although a monumental achievement, *Social and Religious History of the Jews* was criticized for lacking a focus and for making sweeping generalizations.

Frederic Krome

References and Further Reading
Baron, Salo. 1928. "Ghetto and Emancipation: Shall We Revise the Traditional Views?" *Menorah Journal* 14 (June): 515-526.
Gurock, Jeffrey. 1998. "Jacob Rader Marcus, Salo Baron, and the Public's Need to Know American Jewish History." *American Jewish Archives Journal* 50,1 and 2: 22–27.
Liberles, Robert. 1995. *Salo Wittmayer Baron: Architect of Jewish History.* New York: New York University Press.
Ritterband, Paul, and Harold S. Wechsler. 1994. *Jewish Learning in American Universities: The First Century.* Bloomington: Indiana University Press.

Jacob Rader Marcus (1896–1995)

Founding Director of the American Jewish Archives

Jacob Rader Marcus was the first academically trained historian of the Jewish people born in the United States and the first to devote his scholarly energies full-time to American Jewish history. Marcus published hundreds of books, journals, and essays on the history of the American Jew. As a faculty member at Hebrew Union College (HUC) in Cincinnati for seventy-five years, Marcus's ideas influenced generations of rabbis. He enlisted his students' help in building the American Jewish Archives (AJA) into one of the world's largest research centers dedicated solely to the study of American Jewish history. His scholarly contribu-

Jacob Rader Marcus, Jewish historian, professor, and founding director of the American Jewish Archives. (American Jewish Archives)

tions, coupled with his influential role as a mentor, earned him the honorific title dean of American Jewish historians.

Born in New Haven, Pennsylvania, on March 5, 1896, Marcus's interest in Jewish scholarship emerged while attending religious school at Wheeling, West Virginia's Eoff Street Reform Congregation, whose rabbi, Harry Levi, was an ordinee of HUC in Cincinnati. Levi was impressed by the young Marcus's intellect and encouraged him to study for the rabbinate. In 1911, Marcus began his rabbinical training at HUC. With the exception of two years of military service during World War I and his years of graduate study in Europe, Marcus spent the remainder of his long life at HUC in Cincinnati.

Upon his ordination in 1920, Marcus was appointed to the HUC faculty by its president, the distinguished Jewish theologian Kaufmann Kohler. Initially, Marcus taught courses in biblical history and general Jewish history. Recognizing that his academic training was not adequate for

his professorial role at HUC, Marcus traveled to Berlin in 1922 to pursue doctoral studies with the noted Jewish historian, Ismar Elbogen. The University of Berlin awarded Marcus a PhD in 1925, and in 1926 he resumed his faculty duties at HUC.

Prior to the Holocaust, the great centers of Jewish life were located in Europe. Consequently, scant attention had been paid to the history of American Jewry. Marcus was among the first to recognize the growing importance of American Jewish history. In the early 1940s, Marcus began to apply modern critical methodology to the writing of American Jewish history. In 1941, he began teaching at HUC what was probably the first required university-level course in American Jewish history.

In 1946, Marcus recommended to Reform Judaism's rabbinical association, the Central Conference of American Rabbis (CCAR), that American synagogues begin a systematic effort to preserve congregational records and documents relating to Jewish communal life. Recognizing the scholarly value in having a centralized institution to preserve and catalogue these documents, Marcus advocated the establishment of an American Jewish Archives. In 1947, Marcus—with the support of his friend and classmate, Nelson Glueck, the newly elected president of HUC—convinced HUC's board of governors to establish the AJA, a semi-autonomous national institution with its own building and staff, on the school's Cincinnati campus. Marcus became the AJA's founding director and led the institution until his death in 1995. Under his leadership, the AJA grew into one of the world's largest and most significant catalogued collections of archival material documenting the history of Jewish life in North America.

Marcus launched the AJA's semiannual periodical in 1948, wherein he promised to provide "at least one article of scientific calibre" in each issue, as well as a listing of the important documents that the AJA was acquiring (Zola 2004). For nearly forty-seven years he edited this bulletin, which quickly evolved into a major academic publication. Today, the *American Jewish Archives Journal,* with a circulation of more than 4,000, is one of only two scholarly journals devoted exclusively to publication of articles on the entire scope of American Jewish history. In 1956, Marcus founded a central repository for the preservation of American Jewish journals and bulletins: the American Jewish Periodical Center.

From the 1940s on, Marcus devoted practically all of his energy to retrieving and reconstructing the American Jewish past. He authored or edited nearly three hundred articles and books. Marcus was particularly interested in publishing documentary histories. "The fact scrubbed clean," Marcus insisted, "is more eternal than perfumed and rouged words" (Zafren and Peck 1978). This perspective not only fueled Marcus's interest in establishing an American Jewish Archives but inspired him to publish volumes of documents and to make the source material widely available. Convinced that historical interpretations were inevitably transitory, Marcus maintained that the documents he published would never become dated. In fact, many of his best-known works are documentary histories: *The Jew in the Medieval World* (1938), *Memoirs of American Jews* (1955), *The American Jewish Woman: A Documentary History* (1981), and *The Jew in the American World* (1996).

Marcus also published important reference works aimed at facilitating historical research: *To Count a People: American Jewish Population Data, 1585–1984* (1990) and *The Concise Dictionary of American Jewish Biography* (1994). His multivolume historical narratives—like *The Colonial American Jew, 1492–1776* (1970) and his four-volume magnum opus, *United States Jewry, 1776–1985* (1989–1993)—were encyclopedic outgrowths of Marcus's mastery of the vast reservoir of primary source material he had assembled. Critics repeatedly stressed that Marcus's historical writings were characterized by a "faithful adherence to the facts, a critical evaluation of the data, and a complete avoidance of apologetics" (Falk 1994).

Although deeply devoted to his scholarly pursuits, Marcus never lost touch with the active rabbinate. He advised hundreds of rabbis on a wide range of issues. He was intensely involved in the affairs of the CCAR and, from 1949 to 1951, served as its president, the first HUC faculty member elected to that office since Isaac Mayer Wise founded the rabbinical organization in 1889. In 1978, the CCAR named Marcus its honorary president. The title, Marcus acknowledged, was "the greatest honor that a rabbi can receive in the [Reform] movement" (Zola 2004).

Marcus's role in the CCAR provided him with a valuable platform to enlist rabbinic support for the field of American Jewish history and the AJA. Each year, he wrote to his students asking them to contribute monies from their discretionary funds to support his work and, equally important, to be on the lookout for primary source materials that deserved to be preserved in the AJA. His love for his subject was infectious; he inspired many rabbinic students to complete important research projects in American Jewish history. A select group of his students went on to earn doctorates and become major scholars in the field. The growth of scholarly research in American Jewish history, as well as the AJA's burgeoning collection, owes much to Marcus's role as a beau ideal for a large number of HUC rabbinic alumni.

Marcus's professional career was an alloy of two elements: Marcus the rabbi and Marcus the scholar. A religious perspective informed his concept of history; a secular critical historian would not have written about the past in the way he did. Toward the end of his life, Marcus embraced this tension; he made no apologies for it. The historian, he noted, could not "jump out of his skin." He insisted that he was "devoted to the critical method" of scholarship, but simultaneously declared himself a loyal partisan: "I like Jews," he wrote. "I am convinced that they are an unusually gifted lot" (Zola 2004). Marcus consciously sought to maintain a balance between what he called a "pardonable filiopietism" and "the desire to create a new American historiography which will more truly reflect the growth of the American people" (Zola 2004).

Marcus occupied a number of leadership positions. For many years, he served on the board of directors of the Jewish Publication Society of America, where he chaired the influential Publications Committee (1949–1954). This post provided him with the opportunity to influence the direction of Jewish book publishing in the United States. Marcus also played a prominent role in the American Jewish Historical Society, serving as president from 1955 to 1958.

Marcus frequently asserted that the annihilation of European Jewry beckoned the American Jewish community to become a great spiritual center for the Jewish people. To fulfill their destiny, Marcus emphasized, American Jews needed to create a vibrant and autochthonous culture. He asserted that the moral lessons of its religious heritage were the source of Jewish survival—what the historian Simon Dubnow called Judaism's "living soul" (Zola 2004). Like many of the European Jewish historians he admired, Marcus believed that civilizations and nations may rise and fall, but as long as Jews clung to their ethical legacy they would never be completely obliterated. Again following Dubnow, Marcus insisted that the Jewish experience transcended territorial boundaries and the history of the land of Israel. The Jewish people's presence in all parts of the world—a phenomenon that Marcus called omniterritoriality—was a key factor in its indestructibility.

Marcus married Antoinette Brody on December 31, 1925. They had one daughter, Merle, who perished in a fire in 1965. Marcus died on November 15, 1995, in Cincinnati, four months shy of his one hundredth birthday.

Gary P. Zola

References and Further Reading

1998. *The American Jewish Archives Journal* 50,1 and 2.

Chyet, Stanley F. 1958. "Jacob Rader Marcus–A Biographical Sketch." In *Essays in American Jewish History to Commemorate the Tenth Anniversary of the Founding of the American Jewish Archives under the Direction of Jacob Rader Marcus,* 1–22. Cincinnati, OH: American Jewish Archives.

Falk, Randall M. 1994. *Bright Eminence: The Life and Thought of Jacob Rader Marcus.* Malibu, CA: Joseph Simon Publishers/Pangloss Press.

Zafren, Herbert C., and Abraham J. Peck, comps. 1978. *The Writings of Jacob Rader Marcus: A Bibliographic Record.* Cincinnati, OH: American Jewish Archives.

Zola, Gary Phillip, ed. 2004. *The Dynamics of American Jewish History: Jacob Rader Marcus's Essays on American Jewry.* Hanover, NH: University Press of New England.

Bertram W. Korn (1918–1979)

Historian of American Jewry

Bertram Wallace Korn was one of the first American-born scholars to use a modern critical methodology in studying the history of American Jewry. Korn's research focused primarily on Jewish life in the South during the antebellum and Civil War periods. Through his prodigious scholarship, his work as the rabbi of a large and historic metropolitan congregation, and his distinguished career as a military chaplain, Korn emerged as one of the most prominent Reform rabbis and highly regarded American Jewish historians during the post–World War II years.

Korn was born in Philadelphia on October 6, 1918, to Manuel and Blanche (Bergman) Korn. Korn reminisced about the fact that his American-born parents were nonob-

Bertram Korn, rabbi, military chaplain, and historian of American Jewry. (American Jewish Archives)

servant Jews whose identification with Jewish life was cultural, not religious. They never fully understood their son's childhood ambition to become a rabbi. Not until matriculating at the Hebrew Union College (HUC) in 1936 did Korn find a community of like-minded individuals who shared his interests in a liberal Jewish approach to religious life. He received his baccalaureate degree from the University of Cincinnati in 1939 and his rabbinic ordination from HUC–Cincinnati in 1943. To meet chaplaincy needs for the U.S. military during World War II, HUC ordained Korn and his fellow graduates five months ahead of schedule. The newly ordained rabbi moved to Mobile, Alabama, where he served Congregation Shaari Shomayim (1943–1944), until he received a commission as captain in the U.S. Navy. After his discharge in 1946, Korn transferred to the Naval Reserves and began graduate studies at HUC under the tutelage of the distinguished American Jewish historian, Jacob Rader Marcus.

Upon receiving his Doctor of Hebrew Letters degree (1949), Korn became the rabbi of Reform Congregation Keneseth Israel in Philadelphia, a pulpit he occupied for the remainder of his life. While ministering to this large congregation, Korn continued to pursue his interest in the history of American Jewry. Influenced by Marcus's approach, Korn's historical analyses were built on a bounty of data harvested from his prodigious research. Like Marcus, Korn believed that historical interpretations continually evolve, but the documentary infrastructure on which the historian constructs an analysis will remain a useful tool for future generations of scholars. All of Korn's historical writings reflect a deep commitment to this ideology.

His first volume, *American Jewry and the Civil War* (1951), based on his doctoral dissertation, sought to provide a group biography of American Jews on both sides of the war. Korn argued that "[p]ersonal background and environment, rather than Jewish teachings, determined their views; their version of Judaism was cut to fit the pattern of the conclusions which they reached independently."

During the year he spent as rabbi in Mobile, Korn conducted comprehensive research on the history of the Jews in the South, particularly during the antebellum period. He later published *The Early Jews of New Orleans* (1969) and *The Jews of Mobile, Alabama* (1970).

Korn produced an impressive number of carefully researched, groundbreaking studies. In *The American Reaction to the Mortara Case: 1858–1859* (1957), Korn demonstrated that Jews and non-Jews throughout the United States joined in vigorously condemning the Vatican's actions in the affair, which, from an American perspective, were viewed as the embodiment of religious intolerance. His monograph *Jews and Negro Slavery in the Old South, 1789–1865* (1961) was a pioneering analysis of the different attitudes American Jews held toward slavery. Korn's extensive documentation makes it a valuable tool for researchers to the present day.

Korn served as an adjunct faculty member for several institutions, including the HUC–Jewish Institute of Religion in New York, Gratz College, and the Reconstructionist Rabbinical College in Philadelphia. From 1959 to 1961, Korn was president of the American Jewish Historical Society. Founded in 1892, it is the oldest national ethnic historical organization in the United States. Numerous colleges and universities conferred honorary doctorates on Korn in recognition of his seminal contributions to the field of American Jewish history.

In addition to his rabbinical and scholarly activities, Korn had a distinguished career in the Naval Reserve. In 1975, Korn was promoted to the rank of rear admiral—the first rabbi in American history to achieve flag rank. He received the Legion of Merit, the Navy's highest award, upon his retirement from the Chaplaincy Corps in 1978.

Korn married Rita Rosenfeld in 1951. Their son, Benyamin, was the longtime editor of the *Jewish Exponent* (Philadelphia). A second marriage to Rita Packman Dogole, in 1971, also ended in divorce. Korn died on December 11, 1979. In accordance with his instructions, he was buried in Arlington National Cemetery.

Gary P. Zola

References and Further Reading

Olitzky, Kerry M., Malcolm H. Stern, and Lance J. Sussman, eds. 1993. *Reform Judaism in America: A Biographical Dictionary and Sourcebook*. Westport, CT: Greenwood Press.

Raphael, Marc Lee. 1980. "Necrology: Bertram Wallace Korn (1918–1979)." *American Jewish History* (June): 506–508.

YIVO Institute for Jewish Research in the United States

YIVO is the acronym for *Yidisher visnshaftlekher institut* (Yiddish Scientific Institute), the leading institution for scholarship on the history and culture of Yiddish-speaking Jews and their descendants in Eastern Europe and the United States. From its founding in 1925 until 1940, when its headquarters were in Vilna (then Wilno, Poland, and now Vilnius, Lithuania), YIVO's American Section was its largest and most significant branch. From 1940 to the present, YIVO has been located in New York, where it houses one of the world's largest collections on East European and American Jewish history.

YIVO was founded in 1925 as the first center for scholarship in and about the Yiddish language, then spoken by approximately 11 million East European Jews and their emigrant communities throughout the world. It sought to coordinate research, collect relevant materials, train young scholars, and standardize Yiddish, which was often denigrated as inferior to Hebrew or other European languages. In the late nineteenth century, concerns over the erosion of traditional Jewish society led to efforts to document the Jewish past, while in the wake of World War I Yiddish-speaking Jews sought to show that they constituted a distinct group with its own language and culture, which was thereby deserving of national rights. YIVO's founders hoped to foster the development of Yiddish and raise its status in order to make it a suitable vehicle for modern Jewish culture—and to bolster their fight for Jewish rights in the Diaspora.

In February 1925 Nokhem Shtif, a Russian Jewish linguist then living in Berlin, sought support for such an institute from leading American Yiddish cultural figures, including Chaim Zhitlowsky as well as activists in Berlin and Vilna. In October 1925, when the institute opened, supporters in New York led by the historian Jacob Shatzky established the *Amopteyl* (short for *Amerikaner opteyl* [American Section]). Although Vilna became YIVO's headquarters, the American Section was the most important of its numerous branches throughout the world.

During the period between the World Wars, several of YIVO's leading scholars resided in New York, including Shatzky, folklorist Y. L. Cahan, and Leibush Lehrer, who became head of one of the institute's four research divisions, the Psychological-Pedagogical Section. The Amopteyl published important scholarly works as well as the journals *Der pinkes* (*The Record Book,* 1927–1929) and *Yorbukh fun amopteyl* (*American Section Yearbook,* 1938–1939). Moreover, the section became crucial to YIVO's fund-raising efforts, with American sources contributing as much as two-thirds of the institute's total budget. YIVO founded support groups in American cities with significant Yiddish-speaking populations, sent representatives on fund-raising campaigns throughout the United States, and solicited donations from organizations such as the American Joint Distribution Committee.

In January 1940 YIVO's New York branch, then located on Lafayette Street, was designated its headquarters for the duration of World War II. In 1942 YIVO moved to its own building at 531–535 West 123rd Street. With the capture of Vilna by the Nazis in 1941, German troops forced YIVO workers to select the institute's most valuable objects to be sent to Frankfurt, and the rest was to be destroyed. At the war's end New York became the permanent headquarters under the leadership of Max Weinreich, one of YIVO's founders, who escaped from Vilna and led the institute until his death in 1969. In July 1947 part of YIVO's collections were recovered near Frankfurt and brought to New York, along with materials rescued by workers in Vilna. In 1955 YIVO moved to a former Vander-

bilt mansion at 1048 Fifth Avenue and changed its English name from the Yiddish Scientific Institute to the YIVO Institute for Jewish Research.

During World War II, YIVO became one of the first American organizations to document the fate of European Jewry, publishing a brochure on the Warsaw Ghetto Uprising in 1944. It published Weinreich's study, *Hitler's Professors,* immediately after the war (1946). YIVO also turned its attention to American themes, sponsoring an autobiography contest for American Jewish immigrants (1942) and the two-volume *Geshikhte fun der yidisher arbeter bavegung in di fareynikte shtatn* (*History of the Jewish Labor Movement in the United States,* 1943–1945). While continuing the institute's Yiddish-language journal *YIVO bleter* (*YIVO Pages*) (established 1931) and creating *Yidishe shprakh* (*Yiddish Language,* 1941–1986), it reached an Anglophone audience with the *YIVO Annual of Jewish Social Science* (1946–1996). In the 1950s, the acquisition of records from the American Jewish Committee and the Hebrew Immigrant Aid Society (HIAS) made the YIVO Archives a major center for the study of American Jewish history.

As the number of native Yiddish speakers declined in the United States, YIVO aided students of Yiddish by publishing standard reference works such as the textbook *College Yiddish* (1949) and the *Modern English–Yiddish Yiddish–English Dictionary* (1968) by Uriel Weinreich, the son of Max; Nokhem Stutchkoff's *Oytser fun der yidisher shprakh* (*Thesaurus of the Yiddish Language,* 1950); and Max Weinreich's *Geshikhte fun der yidisher shprakh* (*The History of the Yiddish Language,* 1973). In 1959 Uriel Weinreich began work on the *Language and Culture Atlas of Ashkenazic Jewry,* but the first volumes were not published until 1992. In 1968 YIVO founded the Uriel Weinreich Program in Yiddish Language, Literature, and Culture, an intensive language course, and the Max Weinrcich Center for Advanced Jewish Studies, a graduate teaching component. The institute played an important role in the revival of *klezmer* (East European Jewish folk) music by creating the Max and Frieda Weinstein Archive of Recorded Sound (1982) and the Yiddish Folk Arts Program, popularly known as KlezKamp (1984).

In the late 1980s YIVO learned that much of its prewar collection that had survived the Nazis and that was believed to have been destroyed during the Stalin era had instead been hidden in Vilna. In 1995–1996, the archival portion of these materials was brought to New York for processing and duplication. In 1991 Project Judaica, a joint venture of YIVO, the Jewish Theological Seminary of America, and the Russian State University of the Humanities in Moscow, became the first academic program in Jewish studies in the former Soviet Union.

YIVO's collections continued to expand, most notably with the acquisition of the Bund Archives of the Jewish Labor Movement in 1992. By this time, space constraints in YIVO's Fifth Avenue headquarters led to the creation of the Center for Jewish History, a facility jointly housing several Jewish research organizations. In 1999 YIVO relocated to the center's new building at 15 West Sixteenth Street. There it continues to hold public programs and to support scholarly work in Yiddish studies, today conducted primarily in English. YIVO's collections of over 350,000 volumes and 10,000 linear feet of archival material, the largest extant on the Yiddish language and its speakers, continue to attract researchers from around the globe.

Cecile Esther Kuznitz

References and Further Reading

Baker, Zachary M. 1995. "Die Amerikanisierung der jiddischen Wissenschaft (The Americanization of Yiddish Scholarship)." *Judaica* 4 (December): 222–236.

Dawidowicz, Lucy S. 1989. *From That Place and Time: A Memoir, 1938–1947*. New York: W. W. Norton.

Fishman, Joshua A. 1980. "Yivo in amerike (YIVO in America)." *YIVO bleter* 46: 98–101.

Miron, Dan. 1990. "Between Science and Faith: Sixty Years of the YIVO Institute." *YIVO Annual* 19: 1–15.

Soyer, Daniel. 1999. "Documenting Immigrant Lives at an Immigrant Institution: Yivo's Autobiography Contest of 1942." *Jewish Social Studies* 6,3 (Spring/Summer): 218–243.

The American Jewish Archives

The American Jewish Archives (AJA), an internationally known research center for the study of American Jewish history, was founded in 1947 by historian Jacob Rader Marcus (1896–1995) on the Cincinnati campus of the Hebrew Union College–Jewish Institute of Religion (HUC–JIR). Marcus established the AJA in the aftermath of the Holocaust, when American Jews inherited the primary responsibility of preserving the continuity of Jewish life and learning for future generations. The AJA functions as a semi-autonomous organization to collect, preserve, and make available for research materials on the history of Jews and Jewish communities in the Western hemisphere, primarily in the United States. The AJA construes the term *history* in its broadest aspect to embrace data of a political, economic, social, cultural, and religious nature.

In its collections, the AJA assembles data describing the American Jew, both as a Jew and as an American. The AJA possesses one of the largest and most diverse collections of source materials found anywhere documenting the history of the Jewish community of a country. Important accessions to the collection are listed annually in *The American Jewish Archives Journal* and in the *National Union Catalogue of Manuscript Collections*.

The AJA began with a small assortment of congregational and societal minute books and a few collections of private papers. By the dawn of the twenty-first century, it contained more than 12,000 linear feet of manuscripts and archival records. The collection includes the papers of famous Reform rabbis such as Isaac Mayer Wise, David Philipson, and Max Heller; scholars and authors Trude Weiss-Rosmarin, Horace M. Kallen, Annie Nathan Meyer, and Maurice Samuel; scientists and physicians Selman A. Waksman and Robert C. Rothenberg; lawyers and civil servants Anna M. Kross, Samuel Dickstein, and Fanny E. Holtzmann; philanthropists and Jewish communal leaders Louis Marshall, Jacob Schiff, Felix Warburg, among many others.

The holdings also include documents and letters of prominent colonial and Civil War–era Jews such as Aaron Lopez, Raphael J. Moses, Judah P. Benjamin, and the Gratz and Franks families. In its collections are the records of B'nai B'rith lodges, women's synagogue auxiliaries, and organizations such as the American Jewish Alternatives to Zionism, the Intercollegiate Menorah Association, the World Union for Progressive Judaism, and the Association of Hillel and Jewish Campus Professionals. The records of the New York office of the World Jewish Congress form one of the AJA's largest archival holdings.

In 1998, the AJA was designated as the official repository of the historical records of the Union for Reform Judaism (formerly the Union of American Hebrew Congregations). These materials complement the records of the HUC, the JIR, the combined HUC–JIR, and the Central Conference of American Rabbis (CCAR).

The AJA's collection holds many different types and formats of material: manuscripts and typescripts, photographs, film and video recordings, indices, publications, and programs. It also holds nearprint items—all the ephemeral material in the vast zone between letters and books: throwaways, news releases, broadsides, mimeographed announcements and advertisements, newspaper and magazine clippings, and brochures. The audiotape holdings consist of over 6,500 cassettes of oral histories, lectures, religious services, and music. A photograph collection of over 20,000 images is used by scholars, publishers, and filmmakers to illustrate books, articles, movies, and television programs. A nearly thousand-item film and video collection contains broadcast and private footage from numerous organizations and individuals. Indices have been made of nineteenth-century magazines like *Sinai, American Hebrew, Israel's Herold, Occident, Deborah,* and *Menorah Monthly.* One of the AJA's most important publications is the *American Jewish Archives Journal* (established 1948), which appears semiannually. The institution has also published monographs, including Malcolm H. Stern's *Americans of Jewish Descent* (1960), a milestone in the study of American Jewish genealogy, updated and revised in 1991 as *First American Jewish Families: 600 Genealogies, 1654–1988.* An online version of Stern's classic text, as well as a roster of the AJA's manuscript holdings, is available on the institution's website, www.AmericanJewishArchives.org.

Closely associated with the American Jewish Archives is the American Jewish Periodical Center, founded by Marcus in 1956, which microfilms all American Jewish serials to 1925 and selected periodicals after that date.

Marcus directed the AJA from its founding in 1947 until his death in 1995, when the institution was renamed the Jacob Rader Marcus Center of the American Jewish Archives. Gary P. Zola became the second director of the AJA in 1998.

Gary P. Zola

References and Further Reading

Chyet, Stanley F. 1972. *The American Jewish Archives.* Cincinnati, OH: American Jewish Archives.

Marcus, Jacob Rader. 1948. "Program of the American Jewish Archives." *American Jewish Archives* 1,1: 2–5.

Proffitt, Kevin. 1985. "The American Jewish Archives: Documenting and Preserving the American Jewish Experience." *Ethnic Forum: Journal of Ethnic Studies and Ethnic Bibliography* 5,1 and 2: 20–29.

List of Contributors

Roger I. Abrams, Northeastern University School of Law

Edward A. Abramson, University of Hull

Edward Alexander, University of Washington

Michael Alexander, Temple University

Donald Altschiller, Boston University

Glenn C. Altschuler, Cornell University

Peter M. Ascoli, Spertus College

Matthew Baigell, Professor Emeritus, Rutgers University

Neil Baldwin, Montclair State University

Nicole B. Barenbaum, University of the South

Yehudit Barsky, American Jewish Committee

Samantha Baskind, Cleveland State University

Aviva Ben-Ur, University of Massachusetts, Amherst

Linda J. Borish, Western Michigan University

Harold Brackman, Simon Wiesenthal Center

Stephen Eric Bronner, Rutgers University

Vincent Brook, University of California at Los Angeles and University of Southern California

Phil Brown, Brown University

Matti Bunzl, University of Illinois, Urbana–Champaign

Kathleen Shine Cain, Merrimack College

Jerome A. Chanes, Cohen Center for Modern Jewish Studies, Brandeis University

Barry R. Chiswick, University of Illinois at Chicago

Carmel U. Chiswick, University of Illinois at Chicago

Terry Nichols Clark, University of Chicago

Naomi W. Cohen, Professor Emerita, City University of New York and Jewish Theological Seminary of America

Richard M. Cook, University of Missouri, Saint Louis

Irving Cutler, Chicago State University

Jeremy Dauber, Columbia University

Etan Diamond, Independent scholar, Toronto

Seymour Drescher, University of Pittsburgh

Ellen Eisenberg, Willamette University

Lawrence J. Epstein, Suffolk County Community College

Candace Falk, University of California, Berkeley

Henry D. Fetter, Independent scholar, Los Angeles

Eva Fogelman, Generations of the Holocaust and Related Traumas, Training Institute for Mental Health, New York City

Abraham H. Foxman, Anti-Defamation League

Murray Friedman, Temple University

John George, University of Central Oklahoma

Benjamin Ginsberg, Johns Hopkins University

Stephen J. Goldfarb, Independent scholar, Atlanta

Karla Goldman, Jewish Women's Archive

Calvin Goldscheider, Brown University

Gil Graff, Bureau of Jewish Education of Greater Los Angeles

Henry A. Green, University of Miami

Lawrence Grossman, American Jewish Committee

Jeffrey S. Gurock, Yeshiva University

Samuel Haber, University of California, Berkeley

Clifford D. Hauptman, Brandeis University

Milly Heyd, Hebrew University

John R. Hose, Brandeis University

Bette Howland, MacArthur Fellow

Jack Jacobs, John Jay College, City University of New York

Frederic Cople Jaher, University of Illinois, Urbana-Champaign

Richard D. Kahlenberg, The Century Foundation

Ava F. Kahn, California Studies Center

Mark Kligman, Hebrew Union College–Jewish Institute of Religion

Gerd Korman, Cornell University

Michael P. Kramer, Bar-Ilan University

Jonathan B. Krasner, Hebrew Union College

Ori Kritz, University of Oklahoma

Frederic Krome, Hebrew Union College

David Z. Kushner, University of Florida

Donald Kuspit, State University of New York, Stony Brook

Cecile Esther Kuznitz, Bard College

Sanford Lakoff, University of California, San Diego

Elaine Leeder, Sonoma State University

Michael Levy, University of Wisconsin, Stout

Kenneth Libo, Hunter College

Edward T. Linenthal, Indiana University

Larry M. Logue, Mississippi College

Sarah S. Malino, Guilford College

Gail Malmgreen, New York University

Rafael Medoff, David S. Wyman Institute for Holocaust Studies

Ralph Melnick, Independent scholar

Ross Melnick, Museum of the Moving Image

David Mesher, San Jose State University

Robert Michael, University of Massachusetts, Dartmouth

Tony Michels, University of Wisconsin, Madison

Deborah Dash Moore, University of Michigan

Ewa Morawska, University of Essex

Ira Nadel, University of British Columbia

Stanley Nadel, University of Portland

Allan Nadler, Drew University

Edna Nahshon, Jewish Theological Seminary of America

Stephen H. Norwood, University of Oklahoma

Ranen Omer-Sherman, University of Miami

Annelise Orleck, Dartmouth College

Fraser M. Ottanelli, University of South Florida

Terry Otten, Wittenberg University

Grace Palladino, Samuel Gompers Papers, University of Maryland

Robert D. Parmet, York College, City University of New York

William Pencak, Pennsylvania State University

Mark Perlman, University of Pittsburgh

Eunice G. Pollack, University of North Texas

Yakov M. Rabkin, Université de Montréal

Arnold Richards, Former chairman of the board, now board member of YIVO

Robert A. Rockaway, Tel-Aviv University

Leonard Rogoff, Jewish Heritage Foundation of North Carolina

Jonathan Rosenbaum, Gratz College

Stephen J. Sass, Jewish Historical Society of Southern California

David M. Schiller, University of Georgia

Edward S. Shapiro, Seton Hall University

Mark Shechner, State University of New York, Buffalo

Renée Rose Shield, Brown University

Debra Shostak, The College of Wooster

Ben Siegel, California State Polytechnic University, Pomona

Steven H. Silver, Independent scholar

Robert Sklar, New York University

June Sochen, Northeastern Illinois University

Robert Solomon, Brookings Institution

Ori Z. Soltes, Georgetown University

Gerald Sorin, State University of New York at New Paltz

Sandra Spingarn, Stein Yeshiva of Lincoln Park

John Stachel, Boston University

Jacob J. Staub, Reconstructionist Rabbinical College

Christopher M. Sterba, State University of New York, Oneonta

Lance J. Sussman, Reform Congregation Keneseth Israel

Stephen E. Tabachnick, University of Memphis

Elizabeth Hayes Turner, University of North Texas

Gus Tyler, *Forward*

Melvin I. Urofsky, Virginia Commonwealth University

Alan M. Wald, University of Michigan

Donald Weber, Mount Holyoke College

Stephen P. Weldon, University of Oklahoma

Stephen J. Whitfield, Brandeis University

George R. Wilkes, Cambridge University

Hana Wirth-Nesher, Tel-Aviv University

David S. Wyman, University of Massachusetts, Amherst

Gary P. Zola, Hebrew Union College

Index

A. T. Stewart, 395
Aaronson, Boris, 453
Abbandando, Frank, 352
Abbott, Lyman, 528
Abel, Elie, 273
Abie the Agent, 470–471 (illustration)
Abie's Irish Rose, 464–475
Abolitionist movement
    antisemitism in, 321–322, 420
    Jews in, 30, 34, 76, 112, 143, 147, 322,
    420–421
Abortion, 100, 341
Abraham, Karl, 710
Abraham, Pearl, 546, 552–553
Abraham & Straus, 395, 397–398
Abraham Lincoln Brigade, 328, 426
Abram, Morris B., 756–758
Abramowitz, Bessie. See Hillman, Bessie
    Abramowitz
Abramowitz, Bina, 453
Abramowitz, Herman, 71
Abramson, Herb, 670
Abramson, Jesse, 520
Abzug, Bella, 310
Academic Coalition for Jewish Bioethics,
    91
Achille Lauro, Palestinian terrorist attack
    on, 258
Adams, Henry, 172, 626
Adams, John, 21, 541
Addams, Jane, 309, 528
ADL. See Anti-Defamation League
Adler, Celia, 453
Adler, Cyrus, 31, 84, 141–143, 184–185,
    240

Adler, Felix, 77, 343
Adler, Jacob P., 450–452, 454, 554
Adler, Max, 136, 406
Adler, Sarah, 454
Adler, Stella, 453–454
Admirals, Jewish, 137, 332
Adomian, Lan, 328
Adorno, Theodor W., 709, 713–717, 730
The Adventures of Augie March, 560
Affirmative action, 200, 274, 300, 304–306,
    430, 432–435
Afghanistan, 447
AFL-CIO, 255, 366–367, 390–392
African American history, Jewish scholars
    of, 427
After the Fall, 588–589
Agricultural Adjustment Administration
    (AAA), 339, 345
Agricultural colonies, American Jewish,
    34, 42, 162–164, 268, 565
Agudath ha-Rabbanim. See Union of
    Orthodox Rabbis of the United
    States and Canada
Agudath Israel, 73, 220, 434, 439
Aguilar, Grace, 541–542
Ahad Ha-am, 80, 90, 93
Akerlof, George, 721
Akzin, Benjamin, 212
Alabama, 146, 191, 324, 346, 422, 424–426,
    428, 431, 521
    See also Birmingham; Mobile; Selma
Alaska gold rush, 153
Alcott, Amy, 526
Alexenberg, Mel, 638
Algren, Nelson, 139

Ali, Muhammad, 129, 522
Allen, Gracie, 484–485
Allen, James, 424, 427
Allen, Maury, 521
Allen, Mel, 521
Allen, Steve, 702
Allen, Woody, 390, 465, 475, 483, 488–489,
    491–493, 547
Allen Street (Lower East Side), 116–117
Allied War Crimes Declaration, 220
Allport, Gordon, 185
Almond, Gabriel, 731
Alpert, George, 756–757
Alpert, Rebecca, 94
Al-Qa'ida, 446
Alsace (Alsatia), 25, 27, 146, 158, 481
Alter, Victor, 367, 374
Alterman, Nathan, 216
Altman, Edith, 644–645
Altman's, 395
Altmann, Alexander, 757, 760
Amalgamated Clothing and Textile
    Workers Union (ACTWU), 362
Amalgamated Clothing Workers of
    America (ACWA), 119, 235,
    252–253, 284, 308, 370–371, 374,
    382–383
The Amboy Dukes, 125
America First Committee, 520
American Association of Jewish Education
    (AAJE), 752
American Basketball League (ABL),
    516–517
American Broadcasting Company (ABC),
    474, 522

American Civil Liberties Union (ACLU), 139, 249–250, 280, 340, 747
American Conference of Cantors, 668
American Council for Judaism, 79, 148, 207
American Emergency Committee for Zionist Affairs, 220
American Enterprise Institute, 719
American Federation of Labor (AFL), 251, 253, 255, 285, 316, 339, 360, 365–370, 372, 377, 388–389
American Federation of Teachers (AFT), 284, 390, 392
American Football League (1930s), 519
American Football League (1960s), 519
American Friends of the Hebrew University, 143, 343
American Friends of Yad Vashem, 226
American Gathering of Jewish Holocaust Survivors, 225
American Hebrew, 31, 41, 52, 142, 172, 272, 525–526, 541, 544, 771
American Historical Association resolution on Atlantic slave trade, 199
American Israel Public Affairs Committee (AIPAC), 280
American Israelite, 31, 76, 272–273, 541
American Jewish Archives, 764–766, 770–771
American Jewish Commission on the Holocaust, 344
American Jewish Committee (AJC), 33–34, 54, 100, 139, 141–143, 179, 184, 204, 206–207, 220, 222, 238–242, 248–251, 254, 274, 279, 282, 300–301, 304, 343, 399, 407, 410, 427–428, 433–435, 444–446, 715, 769
American Jewish Congress (AJCongress), 54, 100, 126, 129, 139, 143, 188, 220, 222, 238–241, 248–253, 279, 282, 295, 327, 373, 409–410, 427–428, 433, 444–445, 615
American Jewish Historical Society, 31, 141–142, 711, 764, 766, 768
American Jewish Publication Society, 111
American Jewish Press Association (AJPA), 273
American Jewish Relief Committee, 240
American Jewish World Service, 94
American Labor Party (ALP), 253, 289, 365–366, 372
American League for a Free Palestine, 211
American Muslim Council, 443–444, 446
American Muslim Mission, 444
American Nazi Party, 189, 191, 193, 238
American Pastoral, 604–605
American Psychoanalytic Association, 226, 711

American Psychological Association, 707–708
American Revolution, 2, 9–15, 17–19, 22, 157, 188, 193, 343, 415, 539, 544, 708, 749
American Sephardi Federation, 8
American Society of Muslims (ASM), 444
American Sunday School Union (ASSU), 750
American University, 721
American Zionist Emergency Council, 212
Americans for a Safe Israel, 273
Americans for Democratic Action, 367, 758
Americans for Peace Now, 94
Amherst College, 625
Am Olam (Eternal People), 162–163, 268, 270, 451, 565
Amsterdam, Morey, 140
Amsterdam, 10, 17, 39, 54, 404, 413, 537, 594
Anarchism, 212, 266, 270, 297–300, 308, 311–314, 360, 372, 381–383, 564–565, 569, 594, 614, 623
Anderson, Sherwood, 173, 622, 630
Andros, Edmund, 11
Anglo–Saxon Federation of America, 182
Annie Hall, 465, 489, 491–492
Annihilation camps. See Death camps
Anti-Defamation League (ADL), 126, 129–130, 134, 139, 179, 184, 188, 192, 196, 199, 225–226, 238, 242–251, 259, 279, 295, 303, 356, 383, 399, 427–428, 433–434, 444–445, 518, 557, 654
Antin, Mary, 120, 547
Antisemitism, 8, 32–34, 37, 40–41, 45, 50–54, 62, 65, 73, 78–79, 117, 136, 139–140, 151, 156, 159–160, 162, 203–204, 208–209, 211, 216–219, 223–224, 226, 230, 232, 238–249, 258–259, 271, 278, 280, 282–283, 287–288, 291, 293–295, 297, 306–308, 311–313, 326–328, 332, 343–345, 350, 355, 370–371, 373, 390, 409–410, 423–424, 435–438, 461–462, 464, 471, 473–474, 477, 481–483, 485–486, 495–496, 499, 513–514, 532, 544, 592, 611–612, 619, 642, 651, 653, 685, 695, 705, 707–710, 712, 722, 724–725, 732, 739, 742
    African American, 136, 189–190, 192, 194–202, 245–246, 257, 281–282, 303–304, 392, 411, 419, 422–423, 426, 429–431, 442, 444–445
    and American literature, 169–175, 509, 540, 555–556, 559, 570, 581–582,

    587, 592, 602, 604, 609–610, 612–613
    and appointment of Louis Brandeis to Supreme Court, 336–337
    and Leo Frank case, 175–180, 425, 582
    and Populism, 278
    and Slansky trial, 294
    and Southern Baptist Convention, 148
    and Supreme Court, 336–337, 340
    and United Nations, 245–246, 310, 389
    Arab and Muslim, 7, 54, 238–239, 241, 244, 246–247, 258, 282, 442–443, 520
    Catholic, 32–33, 111, 123, 151–152, 187–189, 218, 244, 281, 355, 424, 516, 530, 542–543, 768
    desecration of Jewish cemeteries, 11, 187
    desecration of synagogues, 187–188, 322
    during Civil War, 30, 321–325, 420
    exclusion of Jews from hotels and resorts, 128, 171, 188, 245, 332, 424, 469, 482, 486, 520
    exclusion of Jews from private clubs, 130, 133, 147–148, 159–160, 242, 482, 486, 518, 520
    Henry Ford's, 180–186, 189, 243, 353
    in American colleges and universities, 60, 64–65, 78, 148, 185, 195–199, 243–246, 250, 279–280, 282, 305–306, 332, 344, 353, 379, 424, 430, 486, 513, 516, 518, 530, 559, 573, 577, 708–710, 721, 733–734, 736, 755–756, 760
    in antislavery movement, 321–322, 420
    in Christian textbooks, 242, 750
    in colonial America, 11–14, 537
    in czarist Russia, 33, 36–38, 41–43, 64, 136, 162, 182, 188–189, 203, 212, 239–240, 263–264, 268, 286, 308, 311, 315, 326, 359–360, 378, 409–410, 424, 436, 450, 457, 514, 544, 565, 578, 683, 740
    in employment, 62, 64–65, 78, 242–244, 250, 278–279, 282, 332, 343, 346, 353, 402, 404, 424, 486, 513, 530, 708, 721
    in European universities, 16, 38, 378, 725, 727, 730, 740, 743
    in feminist movement, 310
    in film, 243, 465, 581–582
    in France, 204, 238, 247, 257
    in housing, 78, 124, 128, 136, 138, 159, 165, 243–244, 279, 332, 390, 424
    in Japan, 258
    in labor movement, 255, 373
    in Poland, 37, 64, 100, 220, 222, 239, 327, 466, 592

in Revolutionary and early national
period, 15, 22–23
in Romania, 38, 64, 128, 239, 327
in Scottsboro trial, 425–426
in South, 14, 130, 146–149, 157,
175–180, 323–325, 398, 400–403,
420, 423, 425, 441, 582
in South America, 2, 11, 128, 241, 537
in sports, 427, 513–520, 522–523, 526,
529–532
in U.S. military, 243, 331–333, 410
Irish American, 33, 123, 187–189, 218,
344, 390, 424, 491, 514
Middletown studies on, 159
Nazi (German), 49, 189, 218, 240–241,
282, 288, 312, 318, 327, 333, 373,
388–389, 465, 486, 513–515, 519,
570, 592, 610, 612, 643, 650, 732
of American Red Cross, 410
on American extreme Right, 136,
189–195, 257, 259, 355
on Internet, 246, 259
Soviet, 47, 49, 195, 233, 241, 245, 287,
294, 389, 556
Swiss, 32
violent outbreaks in Boston, 187–189,
218, 424
violent outbreaks in New York, 123,
187–189, 200–202, 218, 424,
430–431
See also Concentration camps; Death
camps; Deicide accusation;
Expulsions of Jews; Farrakhan, Louis;
Ford, Henry; Hitler, Adolf; Nazis and
Nazism; Nation of Islam; Pogroms;
Protocols of the Elders of Zion
Antwerp, Belgium, 39, 389, 525
as diamond center, 404–405
Hasidic communities in 97, 101
Appel, Anna, 453
Aptheker, Herbert, 294, 427
Arab massacres of Jews in Palestine
(1929), 208, 271, 273, 287
Arab slave trade, 198
Aramaic, 1–3, 665
Arbayter Fraynd, 265, 298, 564, 594, 614
Arcel, Ray, 515
Arendt, Hannah, 216, 597, 622, 625, 714,
722–723 (photo), 724
Argentina, 39, 86, 131, 459
Arizona
Goldwater family of, 395
"secret Jews" in, 7
Tucson, 577
Arkansas, 367, 379, 383, 401
Jewish agricultural colony in, 162–163
Arlen, Harold, 457, 698
Arlow, Jacob, 713
Armageddon, 612
Armenia, 48, 275

Armory Show, 656
Armstrong, Louis, 129, 696–699
Army Air Corps, 331, 656
Arnold, Matthew, 90, 631–632
Arnold, Reuben R., 177
Arnovich, Morrie, 517
Arrow, Kenneth, 718
Artef Theater, 454
Aryan Nations, 189, 194
Asch, Sholem, 270, 452, 454, 554
(photo)–557
Asimov, Isaac, 507, 510–512, 746–747
The Assistant, 578–580
Associated Jewish Charities, 407
Association for Jewish Studies, 759
Association for Relief and Protection of
Jewish Immigrants, 142
Association of Orthodox Jewish Scientists,
741
Association of Reform Zionists of
America, 80, 441
Atlanta, Georgia, 145, 147–149, 379, 395,
398–399, 402–403, 422–423, 436
and Leo Frank case, 175–180, 243, 403,
582
The Temple in, 147, 403
Atlanta University, 403
Attell, Abe, 514
Auerbach, Red, 516
Auschwitz-Birkenau, 100, 192, 223–227,
229–230, 257, 493, 589, 659
Austria-Hungary, 32, 36–37, 39, 97, 261,
378, 427, 495, 599
Autoemancipation, 38

Baal Shem Tov, 97
Babel, Isaac, 625, 631–632
Bacharach, Burt, 673
Baer, Max, 514–515 (photo)
Bak, Samuel, 226, 646
Bakke v. Regents, University of California,
430, 433
Baldwin, James, 301, 303, 419, 597
Balfour Declaration, 78, 205–206, 240,
288, 316, 326, 373, 440, 615
Balkan Jews, 6
Baltimore Orioles, 532
Baltimore, Maryland, 16, 28, 32, 72, 75–76,
113, 143, 145, 147–148, 225, 272, 359,
419, 422, 532, 611, 637, 673, 699,
751
Yiddish press in, 266
Yiddish theater in, 454
Banking, Jews in, 28, 39, 44, 132, 181, 408,
410
antisemitic fantasies about Jews in,
181–182, 199, 423
discrimination against Jews in, 64, 121
Baptists, 11, 22, 130, 148, 331, 419–420,
436, 438, 755

Bar mitzvah, 19, 85, 105, 109, 155, 166,
274, 343–343, 482, 491, 513, 558,
585, 659, 750–751
Barbados, 11, 14
Barbary states and pirates, 22, 540
Barbie, Klaus, 257
Bard College, 559
Barenboim, Daniel, 139
Baron de Hirsch Fund, 34, 117, 148, 409
Baron, Salo, 274, 301, 763–764
Baruch, Bernard, 326
Baseball, 351, 399, 474, 485, 491, 503,
517–518, 520–522, 529–535
and Jewish High Holidays, 529–532
and literature, 577
and women, 524, 528
bats as weapons, 355
desegregation of, 427, 520–522
Basketball
men's, 468, 513, 515–519, 522, 525, 528,
531
women's, 468, 522–525, 527–528
Baskin, Joseph, 252
Basle program, 204, 207
Bat mitzvah, 84, 90, 96, 106, 108–109, 274,
549
Batman, 471
Battle Cry, 611–612
Battle of the Bulge, 239
Battleship *Maine,* 238
Baum, Phil, 230
Bavaria, 27–28, 31, 112, 135, 150, 155, 193,
396
Bay, Howard, 760
Beastie Boys, 677
Beatles, 672–674
Beats, 522
Becker, Gary, 721
Begin, Menachem, 130, 212, 215
Begley, Louis, 226
Beichman, Arnold, 188
Bell, Daniel, 301, 304, 732
Bellow, Saul, 139, 301, 546, 557–563, 622,
624–625
Belmont, August, 28
Ben David, Mordechai, 680
Ben-Ami, Jacob, 453
Ben-Ami, Yitshaq, 210
Benderly Boys, 752
Benderly, Samson, 751–754
Benedict, Ruth, 725
Ben-Gurion, David, 207–208, 216, 241,
294
Ben-Horin, Eliahu, 210
Benjamin, Judah, 128, 146, 321, 323–324,
345, 419, 770
Benjamin, Richard, 465
Benjamin, Walter, 714–716
Bennett, Harry, 185
Bennington College, 693

Benny, Jack, 140, 475, 478, 483, 485
    (photo)–486
Bentley, Elizabeth, 292
Ben-Zion, 641–642
Berenson, Bernard, 173, 527
Berenson, Senda, 525, 527–529
Beres, David, 713
Berg, Alan, 194, 257
Berg, Cherney, 475
Berg, Gertrude, 475 (photo), 483,
    488–489, 496
Berg, Moe, 517
Bergen-Belsen, 100, 224–227
Bergdorf Goodman, 395, 398
Berger, Victor, 34, 284, 315
Bergson group, 210–212, 220, 222
Berkman, Alexander, 299
Berkowitz, Henry, 142–143
Berle, Milton, 483, 487–488
Berlin, Germany, 31, 39, 99, 230, 239, 253,
    258, 439, 459, 462–463, 519, 526,
    573, 612, 631, 641, 666, 675, 691,
    704–705, 711–712, 716, 719, 722,
    743–744, 765, 769
Berlin, Irving, 50, 457, 463, 496, 683
    (photo)–686, 698
Berman, Shelley, 140, 488
Bermuda Conference on Refugees,
    221–222, 241
Bernfeld, Siegfried, 712
Bernshteyn, Tsvi Hirsh, 262
Bernstein, Julius, 254
Bernstein, Leonard, 457, 686–690, 699, 760
Bernstein, Marver, 756–757
Berry, Chuck, 670, 672, 674
Berryman, John, 559
Besht. See Baal Shem Tov
Bessarabia, 239, 364, 424
Bessie, Alvah, 464
Betar youth movement, 208, 212
Beth Elohim (Charleston, SC), 2, 10, 75,
    107, 147
Bettelheim, Aaron S., 422
Bettelheim, Bruno, 712
Bezmozgis, David, 546–549
Bialik, Haim Nachman, 216
Biberman, Herbert, 464
Bierce, Ambrose, 171
Bikel, Theodore, 680
Bilbo, Theodore, 148
Billboard, 671
Biltmore Conference, 207
Binder, Abraham, 668
Bintel Brief, 270
Birmingham, Stephen, 2, 29
Birmingham, AL, 147, 402–403
Birthright Israel, 441, 754
Bitburg controversy (1985), 227, 239
Black Hundreds, 182
Black Legion, 190

Black, Hugo, 346, 732
Black, Jay (David Blatt), 674
Black, John, 177, 180
Blackstone Memorial, 436
Blackstone, William, 436
Blatt, Sol, 148
Blaustein, David, 117
Blaustein, Jacob, 241
Bleuler, Eugen, 710
Blinder, Alan, 721
Blitzer, Wolf, 227
Blitzstein, Marc, 691–693, 760
Bloch, Emanuel, 291
Bloch, Ernest, 668, 693–696
Bloch, Sam, 225
Blood libel and ritual murder accusations,
    170, 174, 187, 436
  by Arabs, 244, 246, 258
  Beilis affair, 182, 578
  Damascus, 32, 111, 281, 543
  Franz Kafka and, 471
  Tisza Eszlar, 450
Bloom, Allan, 563
Bloom, Hyman, 641
Bloomenfeld, Isidore, 352
Bloomingdale's, 398
Blue Hill Avenue (Boston), 165
Blues, 496, 507, 670–671, 674, 678, 680,
    691–692, 698
Blumenthal, Nissan, 666
Blumenthal, W. Michael, 279
Blyden, Edward Wilmot, 421
B'nai B'rith, 30–31, 34, 44, 54, 112, 129,
    135, 139, 148, 153, 164, 179,
    184–185, 213, 216, 220, 243, 324,
    399, 419, 442, 557, 770
B'nai B'rith Hillel Foundation, 216, 756
Board of Delegates of American
    Congregations, 33–34
Board of Delegates of American Israelites,
    112, 141, 281, 322
Board of Deputies of British Jews, 281
Boarders, 16, 30, 116, 151, 385, 467, 496,
    733
Boas, Franz, 709, 724–725 (photo),
    726–727
Bodenheim, Maxwell, 139
Bodky, Erwin, 760
Bohemia (central Europe), 24, 31, 75, 135,
    541
Bohemia (counterculture), 120, 527
Bohrod, Aaron, 139
Bolshevik Revolution, 19, 270, 316, 326,
    361, 365, 372–373, 385, 410, 555,
    569, 628, 714
Bond, Julian, 403
Bondi, August, 34, 421 (photo)
The Book of Lights, 592
Bookbinder, Hyman, 242
Boone, Daniel, 146

Boone, Pat, 672
Boorstin, Daniel, 179
Bordeaux, France, 415
Bornstein, Berta, 712
Boro Park, Brooklyn, 53, 97–98, 101–102
Borowitz, Eugene, 80
Borscht Belt, 475, 486–487, 489, 507–508
Bosnia, 444–445
Boston Braves, 518
Boston Celtics, 516
Boston Red Sox, 427
Boston Symphony Orchestra, 688–689,
    694, 702
Boston University, 559, 628
  School of Medicine, 511
Boston, Massachusetts, 28, 41, 47–49, 52,
    116, 144, 165, 193, 210, 237, 239,
    247, 254, 298, 335–336, 343,
    350–351, 361, 376, 382, 395, 427,
    439, 454, 538, 559, 569, 628,
    653–654, 682, 687–689, 702, 751,
    755, 757–758
  antisemitic riots in, 187–189, 424
  English-language Jewish press in,
    274–275
  Hasidim in, 98, 103–104
  psychoanalysis in, 711, 713
  sports in, 427, 516, 518, 520, 525, 527
  Yiddish press in, 264, 266, 270, 615
  Zionism in, 204
Botwin, Naftali, 328
Bouton, Jim, 521
Bovshover, Joseph, 563–565
Bowery district, 450–453, 683–684
Bowling, 524
Boxer Rebellion, 239
Boxing, 129, 513–515, 517–518, 520–522
Boycott of German goods, 221 (photo),
    236, 238–239, 249, 253, 355, 366,
    519, 526
Brackman, Harold, 192, 257
Braddock, Jimmy, 515
Braham, Randolph, 226
Brandeis, Louis, 249, 361, 759
  and Supreme Court, 30, 205, 277,
    335–336 (photo), 337–338,
    342–348, 361, 755
  and Zionism, 33, 148, 204–205,
    (photo), 206–208, 214–215, 288,
    342, 344, 347, 729
  as advisor to Franklin D. Roosevelt,
    277
  as advisor to Woodrow Wilson, 288,
    336
Brandeis University, 49, 216, 271, 519, 577,
    622, 630, 733, 755–762
Brandel, Max, 472
Braslavsky, Abba, 265
Brasol, Boris, 182–183
Brazil, 2, 11, 131, 412–417, 459, 537, 675

Bread Givers, 550
Bremen, Germany, 39, 46
Brenner, Charles, 713
Breton, André, 656
Breyer, Stephen G., 335, 341 (photo)–342, 345–346
Brice, Fanny, 455, 465, 483–484, 495–497, 502
Bridget Loves Bernie, 475–478
Brighton Beach, 47–48, 501, 567
Brill, Abraham Arden, 710
British East India Company, 10
British Foreign Office, unwillingness to rescue Jews, 220–221
British White Paper (1939), 220, 241
Broadcasters, sports, 521–522
Broadway theater, 51, 211, 453–460, 462–464, 486, 489, 497, 501–502, 506–507, 555, 561, 583–584, 587–588, 665, 674, 685–686, 688–689, 692, 696, 698
Brodsky, Joseph, 425
Broken Glass, 589
Bronfman, Edgar, 754
Bronstein, Leo, 760
Bronx, NY, 121, 215, 225, 285, 291, 301, 428, 453–454, 473, 475–476, 491, 496, 516, 529, 534, 555, 621, 625, 658, 661–662, 673, 685
Brookline, MA, 103–104, 165
Brooklyn, NY, 53, 71–72, 121–126, 175, 179, 200–202, 225, 238, 301, 303, 310, 359, 391, 430, 440, 453, 465, 477–478, 491, 508, 534, 547, 555, 566, 584–586, 588, 592, 622, 624, 637, 652, 654, 657, 672–674, 676, 680
  Bensonhurst, 6
  East New York, 123, 126
  Hasidic Jews in, 97, 99–102, 104–105, 200–202, 430, 553
  Mizrahi Jews in, 6–7, 669
  organized crime in, 352, 354
  Soviet Jews in, 47
  sports in, 427, 516–517, 519, 531, 534
  Yiddish theater in, 454
  See also Brownsville; Ocean Hill-Brownsville experiment and conflict; Williamsburg
Brooklyn Atlantics, 517
Brooklyn Boy, 584–586
Brooklyn Bridge, 122
Brooklyn Bridge, 477–478
Brooklyn College, 225, 440, 622
Brooklyn Dodgers
  baseball, 427, 531, 534
  football, 519
Brooklyn Jewels, 516
Brooks, Albert, 489
Brooks, David, 306

Brooks, Mel, 456 (photo), 465, 475, 483, 488–489
Brookwood Labor College, 381
Brooten, Bernadette, 760
Brown v. Board of Education, 130, 245, 255, 338, 403, 709
Brown, H. Rap, 429
Brown, Harold, 279
Brown, Irving, 253
Brown, John, 34, 322, 420–421, 569
Browning, Robert, 571
Brownsville, 122–123 (photo)–127, 301, 303, 305–306, 359, 391, 430–431, 516, 599, 624
  antisemitic violence in, 123
  crime, 124–125, 352
  libraries, 125
  population, 124–126
  settlement house, 652
  synagogues, 123, 126
  yeshivas, 71
  Yiddish theater in, 124
Bruce, Lenny, 484, 488–489
Brundage, Avery, 520
Bruner, Jerome, 709
Bryant, William Cullen, 169
Bryn Mawr College, 376
Bryn Mawr Summer School for Women Workers in Industry, 381
Buber, Martin, 301
Buchalter, Louis "Lepke," 125, 349, 351–352, 353 (photo)–354, 356–357
Buchanan, James, 33
Bucharest, Rumania, 462, 562
Buchenwald, 232, 317, 643
Buckley, Jr., William, 304
Budapest, 24, 43, 223, 462–463, 498
Bukharan Jews, 48, 669
Bukhner, Y. K., 262
Bukiet, Melvin Jules, 546
Bulgaria, 222
Buloff, Joseph, 453
Bund, Jewish (Labor) Workers', 235, 237, 253, 285, 316, 362, 365–367, 370–371, 374, 380, 389, 514, 652, 740, 770
Bunzel, Ruth, 726
Bureau of Applied Social Research, 731
Bureau of Jewish Education (BJE), 133, 751–752
Bureau of the Budget, 718
Burgess, Ernest, 731
Burgholzli Clinic, 711
Burial practices, 6, 10, 13–14, 32, 44–45, 118, 132, 135, 146, 229, 562, 642, 658
Burke, Edmund, 286
Burns, Arthur, 718–719
Burns, George, 475, 478, 483–485

Burns, James MacGregor, 733
Burstein, Pesach, 454
Busch, Isidore, 419
Busch, Wilhelm, 469
Bush, George H. W., 279, 434
Bush, George W., 279, 283
Butler, Benjamin, 324
Butler, Richard, 194
Buttons, Red, 486
Byers, Louis, 191
Byzantium, 1, 638

Cabinet, Jewish members of U.S., 219, 222, 273, 279, 281, 344, 346, 718
Cacek, P. D., 509
Caesar, Sid, 475, 483, 486, 488–489, 491
Cafe Royal, 120, 453
Cahan, Abraham, 51, 116, 119, 264–268, 269 (photo)–271, 274, 285, 360, 375, 455, 465, 547, 555–556, 561–562, 615
Cahan, Y. L., 760
Cain, 170, 189, 654, 692
Cain, James M., 583
The Caine Mutiny, 615–617
Caldwell, Janet Taylor, 190
California Gold Rush, 28, 150, 152
Call It Sleep, 125, 546, 548, 568, 584, 598–600
Calverton, V. F., 632
Cambridge University, 83, 301, 379, 721, 761
Camp David Agreement, 319
Camp, Walter, 518
Campanella, Roy, 521
Canada, 13, 27, 29, 39, 70, 79, 91, 97, 101, 142, 149, 153, 225, 254, 256, 311, 359, 363, 382, 505, 548, 555, 558, 561, 583, 720, 753, 755
Cantor, Eddie, 455, 463, 484–486, 502, 506
Cantor, 68, 84, 87–88, 106, 109, 116, 450, 455, 457, 502–503, 539, 552, 641, 665–669, 680–681, 683, 749
Cantorial Conference of America, 668
Capone, Al, 137, 351–352, 356, 566
Cardozo, Benjamin, 2–3, 288, 335–337 (photo), 338, 343–348
Carew, Rod, 521
Caribbean and West Indies, 2, 91, 121, 127–128, 414–415
  blacks from, 200–202, 377, 421
  Jews in, 10, 13, 22, 91, 145, 414–416, 537
  slavery in, 411, 413–418
Carigal, (Raphael) Hayyim Isaac, 2, 538–539
Carlebach, Shlomo, 669, 680
Carmichael, Stokely (Kwame Touré), 429
Carnegie, Andrew, 408
Carnera, Primo, 514

Carr, Carol, 509

Carter, Jimmy, 139, 225, 228–229, 256, 279, 319, 339

Carto, Willis, 190–192, 257

Carvalho, Emanuel Nuñes, 749

Casals, Rosie, 526

Castle Garden, 30, 40

Castro, Fidel, 129, 302

Cather, Willa, 173

Catskills, 457, 467–469, 473, 682, 733

Celler, Emanuel, 222

Center for Jewish History, 770

Center for the Advanced Study of the Behavioral Sciences, 731

Central Conference of American Rabbis (CCAR), 74, 76–81, 142, 184, 434, 441, 667, 765–766, 770

Central Jewish Institute (CJI), 754

Central Relief Committee for Galveston Storm Sufferers, 45

Cézanne, Paul, 649, 652

Chagall, Marc, 556, 640, 642, 652–653, 705

Chanukah, 166, 312–313

Chaplin, Charlie, 471, 486, 492, 499

Charles, Ray, 671, 673

Charleston, SC
    and American Revolution, 14–15
    black community of, 698
    Jews in, 10–11, 14–16, 21, 35, 145–147, 151, 157–159, 401, 539–541, 543, 573, 749
    slavery in, 415, 418
    synagogue in, 2, 16, 19, 75, 107, 146–147, 158

Chaucer, Geoffrey, 170

Cheder. See Heder

Chemical warfare threat to Israel, 258

Chesler, Phyllis, 309–310

Chess, Leonard, 670–671

Chess, Phil, 670

Chicago, Judy, 636–637, 647

Chicago, 91, 116, 134–140, 165–166, 185, 210, 225, 231–233, 238, 289, 298, 308–309, 339, 349, 355, 371, 373, 382, 399, 406, 420, 428, 461, 470, 494–495, 515, 558–560, 562, 565, 582–583, 595, 670–671, 689, 695, 699–700, 708, 751
    antisemitism in, 136, 138–139, 344
    as one of largest Jewish cities, 42, 134, 136
    crime in, 349–352, 355
    East European Jews in, 42, 132, 134, 136, 139
    English-language Jewish press in, 275
    German Jews in, 29–30, 33, 35, 134–135, 139
    Hasidim in, 98
    impact of Chicago fire, 135

Jewish organizations and institutions in, 135–139, 184, 243, 254, 256, 309, 407, 582, 752
    Lawndale, 137–138, 595, 699
    Maxwell Street area, 136–138, 165, 344, 699
    psychoanalysis in, 712
    Sephardim in, 5, 136
    Soviet Jewish emigrés in, 47–49
    sports in, 351, 517–519, 524, 526
    Yiddish press in, 262, 264, 266
    Yiddish theater in, 137, 450, 454
    Zionism in, 138–139, 213

Chicago Bears, 519

Chicago Cardinals, 519

Chicago Cubs, 518, 529

Chicago Hebrew Institute (CHI), 524

Chicago School [of Economics], 720

Chicago Symphony Orchestra, 139

Chicago White Sox, 351, 530

Chicago World's Fair. See Columbian Exposition

Chickamauga, Battle of, 323

Child, Lydia Maria, 169

China, 121, 275, 317–319, 392, 406, 456, 529, 639, 678, 719

Chipmunks, 521

Chmielnicki massacres, 609–610

The Chosen, 590–592

Choynski, Joe, 514

Christian Front, 186–188, 190, 244, 255, 424

Christian Identity, 189

Christian missions targeting Jews, 272, 438, 541, 750

Christian Mobilizers, 187

Christian Nationalist Crusade, 190

Chrystie Street (Lower East Side), 116, 119, 269

Church of England, 11

The Church of the Creator. See The World Church of the Creator

Churchill, Winston, 207, 483

Cigarmakers' International Union (CMIU), 29, 369

Cincinnati, Ohio, 146, 163, 421, 544, 565, 670, 750, 767, 770
    German Jews in, 27, 31, 57, 117, 542
    Holocaust survivors in, 224
    Reform Judaism in, 31, 57, 75–77, 79, 83, 109, 113, 147, 159, 272, 541, 764–765, 767

Cincinnati Reds, 351

Circumcision, 51, 68, 77, 113, 128, 136, 171, 329, 471, 578, 602, 605

Citrine, Walter, 253

City College of New York (CCNY), 60, 90, 225–226, 287, 290, 317, 343, 462, 491, 516, 519, 566, 621, 624, 626, 675, 696

City University of New York (CUNY), 226, 535, 622–623, 625

Civil Rights Act of 1964, 245, 255, 303, 428, 432

Civil rights movement, 86, 148, 400, 403, 476, 660, 674, 680, 729, 757
    Jewish involvement in, 35, 80, 130, 149, 192, 226, 238–240, 242, 244–245, 250–252, 254–255, 278, 280, 282, 289, 309, 367, 391, 393, 422, 424–428, 432–433, 709, 758
    March on Washington (1941), 432
    March on Washington (1963), 239, 255, 391
    murder of civil rights workers, 428

Civil War, 28, 30, 34, 43–44, 75, 77, 110, 112, 128, 135, 141, 143, 146, 175, 272, 278, 321–326, 396, 399, 401–402, 408, 418, 421–422, 426, 543, 569, 573, 613, 626, 695, 767–768, 770
    antisemitism during, 30, 322–325, 420
    Jews in Confederate army, 146, 321–325
    Jews in Union army, 238–239, 321–325, 420, 542

Clara de Hirsch Home, 117

Clark University, 708, 725

Clarke, Arthur C., 510

Cleveland, 309, 350–351, 376, 382, 471, 474, 519, 672, 689, 694
    Yiddish theater in, 454

Cleveland Conference, 69, 76, 111–113

Cleveland Indians, 518, 530

Cleveland Institute of Music, 694

Clinton, Bill, 228 (photo), 279, 341–342, 346, 393

Clinton, DeWitt, 20

Clinton, George, 21

Coalition for Alternatives in Jewish Education (CAJE), 754

Coalition of Labor Union Women, 377

Coalition on the Environment and Jewish Life, 94

Cohen, Andy, 517

Cohen, Benjamin, 277, 338

Cohen, Elliot, 274, 288, 301–302, 305–306, 631

Cohen, Gerson, 87

Cohen, Haskell, 516

Cohen, Henry, 45–46

Cohen, Hermann, 439

Cohen, Isadore, 362–364

Cohen, Marilyn, 639, 648

Cohen, Mickey, 353

Cohen, Mortimer J., 355

Cohen, Myron, 488

Cohen, Philip "Little Farfel," 125

Cohen, Richard, 196, 198

Cohen, Saul, 760–761

Cohen, Yankev, 262
Cohen Brothers, 401, 403
Cohn, Fania, 377
Cohn, Harry, 461
Cohn, Jack, 461
Cohn, Linda, 526
Cohn, Michael, 299, 564
Cohn, Roy, 291
Cohn-Bendit, Daniel, 483
Cohon, Samuel S., 79
Cold War, 79, 126, 253, 256, 258, 304, 328,
    365, 465, 483, 571, 578, 612, 630,
    637, 690, 741–742, 744
  and *Commentary*, 301–302
  and Hannah Arendt, 723
  and Henry Kissinger, 318–319
  and Rosenberg case, 290, 297
Cole, G. D. H., 379
Cole, Lester, 464
Cole, Nat King, 670
Columbia Broadcasting System (CBS),
    137, 474, 496, 505, 521, 586, 730,
    761
Columbia College, 19, 21
Columbia Pictures, 133, 461
Columbia University, 35, 90, 226, 281, 287,
    301, 337, 390, 457, 496, 519, 553,
    573, 575, 593, 617, 697, 713,
    718–721, 752
  and anti-Jewish quotas, 60, 280, 736
  and Franz Boas, 725
  and Lionel Trilling, 631
  and Meyer Schapiro, 652–654
  and Paul Lazarsfeld, 730–732
  and Robert Merton, 734–736
  and Salo Baron, 764
  antisemitic speeches and article at,
    195–196, 198
  law school, 340
  medical school, 280, 710, 712
  radical student movements at, 287, 300
Columbian Exposition, 138, 708, 725
Columbians [neo-Nazi], 427
Columbus, Christopher, 127, 412, 502,
    547
Comedians, 450, 452, 469–470, 483–492,
    506, 561
Comic strips, 469–474
Commentary, 215, 274, 300–306, 621, 650
Commission on Jewish Education (CJE),
    753
Committee for a Jewish Army of Stateless
    and Palestinian Jews, 210, 220, 222
Committee for Industrial Organization
    (CIO), 365–366, 372, 381–383
Committee on Army and Navy Religious
    Activities (CANRA), 331
Committee on Jewish Law and Standards,
    86–88, 166
Commons, John, 378–380

Communism and Anti-Communism, 34,
    47, 79, 119, 125, 139, 182, 193, 217,
    244–245, 252–254, 283–285,
    287–289, 290–297, 299–302, 318,
    328–329, 338, 355, 364–368, 372,
    374, 388–390, 392, 400, 454,
    463–465, 499, 556, 562, 564, 566,
    569, 571, 593, 600, 604, 611–612,
    615, 618, 625–631, 663, 692, 712,
    722
Communist Party (CP), 34, 119, 236, 284,
    287–288, 292–295, 328, 338, 361,
    364, 424–425, 463–465, 483, 556,
    569, 571, 611, 622, 626, 628–629,
    631, 692
Concentration camps, 100, 218, 224–227,
    232, 256, 317, 472–473, 588–589,
    613, 636, 643–644, 675, 712, 715
Conference of Presidents of Major Jewish
    Organizations, 91
Conference on Jewish National Claims
    Against Germany, 389
Confirmation, 109, 373, 666
Congress of Industrial Organizations
    (CIO), 125, 339, 366, 370–373
Congress of Racial Equality (CORE), 255,
    390
Congressional Black Caucus, 421
Congressional Medal of Honor, Jews
    awarded, 323, 332–333
Conley, Jim, 176–177, 179–180, 243
Constitutional Convention (1787), 18
Converse, Philip, 731
Conversion
  forced from Judaism to Christianity, 2,
    4, 37–38, 127, 343, 413, 420
  forced from Judaism to Islam, 7
  Judaism to Christianity, 3, 10, 14, 23,
    148, 408, 436, 438, 492, 538, 571,
    704–705, 708
  Christianity to Judaism, 6, 8, 17–18,
    55, 61, 88, 113, 129, 171, 483, 506,
    544
Conversos. See New Christians
Coolidge, Calvin, 185, 288–289, 470
Cooper, Abraham, 258
Cooper, Sybil Koff, 526
Coordinating Committee of Jewish
    Organizations Concerned with
    Discrimination in the War
    Industries, 432
Copeland, Lillian, 523, 526
Copland, Aaron, 688, 691, 696, 698–699,
    760
Coplon, Judith, 292
Coriat, Isidor, 711
Cornell University, 175, 215, 340, 379, 702
Cosell, Howard, 521–522
Coser, Lewis, 622, 670
Costello, Frank, 351

Coughlin, Charles, 174, 186–188 (photo),
    190, 218, 244, 355, 424, 530
Council of Economic Advisers, 718, 721
Council of National Defense, 327, 368
Counter Reformation, 18
Country clubs, 157, 166, 186
  exclusion of Jews from, 148, 159–160,
    482, 520
  Jewish, 482, 520, 526
Country Joe and the Fish, 675
Crane, Stephen, 271
Crommelin, John, 191
Cromwell, Dean, 519–520
Crosby, Bing, 670, 686
Crosby, Norm, 489
Cross, Leach, 514
Crossfire, 465
Crossing Delancey, 465
Crown Heights, Brooklyn, 97–99, 102,
    200–202, 430, 553
Crown Heights Riot, 200–202, 430–431
The Crucible, 587–588
Crumb, Robert, 473–474
Cruse, Harold, 429
Crypto Jews, 7–8, 155, 413
Crystal, Billy, 490
Cuban Jews, 129–131
Cukor, George, 463
cummings, e. e., 173, 692
Cunningham, J.V., 760
Cuomo, Mario, 201
Curaçao, 91, 414–415
Curran, Edward Lodge, 188
Curtis, Tony, 506
Curtiz, Michael, 463
Cushing, Richard Cardinal, 189
Cyprus refugee camps, 612
Czars of Russia
  Alexander II, 37, 359
  Alexander III, 38
  Nicholas I, 37
  Nicholas II, 38, 41
Czechoslovakia, 224, 294, 388, 459, 466

Dachau, 232
Dadaism, 655, 658
Dafni, Reuven, 355–356
Dahl, Robert, 731
Dahlberg, Edward, 288
Dali, Salvador, 656
Dalitz, Moe, 349, 351, 356
Dallas, Texas, 148, 395, 398, 402, 678, 701
Dangerfield, Rodney, 483, 489
Dangling Man, 559
Daniel, Dan, 520
Dann, Jack, 507, 509
Danning, Harry, 517
Dartmouth College, 353, 519, 521
Darwin, Charles, 746
Das Volk, 215

David, Larry, 480, 490
Davidson, Avram, 507–508
Davis, David Brion, 195, 197, 199
Davis, Jefferson, 146, 324
Davis, John, 288
Davis, Jr., Sammy, 129, 506–507
Davita's Harp, 592–593
Dawidowicz, Lucy, 295
Daytshmerish, 263–265, 452
DC Comics, 472
De Leon, David, 323
de Sola Pool, David, 4, 274
Dearborn Independent, 182–183, 185, 189,
    241, 243, 353
Death camps, 100, 192, 206, 223–227,
    229–230, 256–257, 317, 333, 383,
    458, 466, 493, 560, 588–589, 612,
    636, 640, 643, 659, 705, 723, 754
Death of a Salesman, 584, 586–587
Debs, Eugene V., 284–285, 315, 372, 376,
    379, 386
Declaration of Independence, 20
Decter, Midge, 305
Defenders of the Christian Faith, 190, 218,
    355
DeFunis v. Odegaard, 430, 433
Deicide accusation, 12, 36, 148, 169–170,
    245, 400, 419, 436, 518
    and Second Vatican Council, 437
    at Howard University, 198
    at Kean College, 198
    in Arab and Muslim worlds, 246
    in Ben-Hur, 173
    in film, 243–244
    in rap music, 257
DeKooning, Willem, 651
Delany, Martin R., 421
DeLeon, Daniel, 284–285, 315, 615
DeLeon, Mordecai, 146
del Rey, Lester, 507
DeMille, Cecil B., 243–244
Democratic Party, 33, 237, 262, 304, 346,
    360, 372–373, 377, 386, 733
    Jewish voters and, 223, 277–281,
        288–289, 431
Denver, CO, 104, 194, 212, 257, 399, 436,
    565
Department stores, 28, 144, 154, 385,
    395–403, 423, 428, 531
Der Fraynd (Russia), 261
Der Fraynd (Workmen's Circle), 236–237
Der Morgn Zhurnal, 119, 360, 502, 595
Der Tog, 188, 360, 663
Dershowitz, Alan, 53
Detroit, MI, 12, 181–182, 185–186, 255,
    289, 350–352, 355–356, 429, 751
    Hasidim in, 98, 103
    Yiddish theater in, 454
Detroit Tigers, 517–518, 529–530, 532
Dewey, John, 53, 84, 390, 393, 617, 752

Deutscher, Isaac, 631
Dewey, Thomas E., 356
Dharma and Greg, 477, 480
Diamond business, 105, 404–405 (photo),
    406, 594, 678
Diamond, David, 682
Diamond, Neil, 672
The Diary of Anne Frank [book, play, film],
    224, 232–233, 465
The Dick Van Dyke Show, 475
Dickens, Charles, 543–544
Dickinson, Emily, 170, 624
Dickstein, Morris, 546, 567
Dickstein, Samuel, 770
die Deborah, 31–32 (illustration), 771
Dies Committee, 328
Dietrich, Sepp, 239
Dinkins, David N., 200–202, 431
Displaced Persons and Displaced Persons
    camps, 212, 215–216, 224–225,
    227, 241, 254, 256, 367, 374, 390,
    612
Dissent, 288, 622, 757, 760
Divorce, 58, 86, 96, 109, 117, 270, 307,
    439–440, 497, 532, 575, 577, 582,
    588, 622, 639, 734, 743, 768
Doctors' Plot, 294
Doctorow, E. L., 296
Dolin, Nate, 518
Donne, John, 647
Dorchester (neighborhood of Boston),
    104, 187–188
Dorsey, Hugh M., 177–180
Dos Passos, John, 173, 569
Dostoevsky, Fyodor, 630
Douglas, Kirk, 224
Douglas, William O., 295
Douglass, Frederick, 421–422, 427
Dove, Arthur, 637
Drachman, Bernard, 69
Dreiser, Theodore 174, 574–575, 624
Drescher, Fran, 479
Drescher, Seymour, 7, 199
Dreyfus Affair, 204, 238
Dreyfuss, Barney, 518
Dreyfuss, Richard, 465, 582
The Drifters, 673
Driving Miss Daisy, 149
Dropsie College, 141–143
Dropsie, Moses Aaron, 141–142
Dry goods, Jews in, 27–28, 128, 135, 146,
    148, 155, 396, 399–401, 558
Drysdale, Don, 518, 532
Dubin's Lives, 579
Dubinsky, David, 252–254, 284, 287, 289,
    361, 365–366 (photo), 367,
    383–384
Dubnow, Simon, 766–767
DuBois, W.E.B., 419
Duchamp, Marcel, 656

Duke, David, 245
Duke University, 149
Dulles, Allen, 193
Dulles, John Foster, 193
Dumas, Alexandre, 543
DuMont, Allen, 474
Duran, Khalid, 446
Durham, North Carolina, 148, 401
Dutch Antilles, 414
"Dutch Mob" of 1860s–1870s, 29
Dutch Reformed Church, 11
Dutch West India Company, 11, 414, 537
Dyer, Isadore, 43, 45
Dyer, Leon, 43
Dylan, Bob, 672, 674–675, 681
Dymov, Osip, 452

Earth Day, 305
East Broadway, 117–118, 120, 316
East Harlem, 515
East River, 556
"Easter Parade," 686
Eastman, Monk, 29, 349–350, 352
Eban, Abba, 130, 274, 441
EC Comics, 472
Eckart, Dietrich, 184
Eckstein, Otto, 721
Edelshtat, David, 298–299, 564–566
Eden, Anthony, 221–222
Ederle, Gertrude, 525
Edgeworth, Maria, 541
Edison, Thomas A., 460
Edlin, William, 267
The Education of H*Y*M*A*N
    K*A*P*L*A*N, 596–597
Educational Alliance, 35, 117, 120, 524,
    663
Egg creams, 125
Egypt, 7, 214, 258, 317, 319, 356, 374,
    759
    ancient, 420, 611
    antisemitism in, 244, 442
    Exodus from, 419, 421–422, 659, 678
    harboring of Nazi war criminals, 239
Egyptian Jews, 7
Ehrlich, Arnold B., 90
Eichmann, Adolph, 224, 245, 256, 625,
    689–690, 716, 724, 763
Eichmann in Jerusalem, 622, 724, 763
Eilberg, Amy, 109
Einhorn, David, 31, 34, 69, 76–77,
    112–114, 143, 147, 419
Einsatzgruppen, 49, 220
Einstein, Albert, 34–35, 385, 387, 695, 717,
    739–740, 742 (photo)–745
Eisendrath, Maurice N., 79–80
Eisenhower, Dwight D., 193, 244–245, 279,
    294–296, 597, 756
Eisenhower, Milton, 193
Eisenstein, Ira, 91, 144

Eisner, Will, 471, 473
El Al airlines, 617
    flights to Miami, 130, 441
    terrorist attacks on, 247, 258
Eliot, Charles, 409
Eliot, T. S., 458, 483, 567, 597, 621, 626, 628, 632
Ellenson, David, 81
Ellenson, Jacqueline Koch, 81
Ellington, Duke, 696–699
Elliot, Cass, 674
Ellis Island, 5, 30, 40
Ellison, Harlan, 507–508
Ely, Richard T., 378–379
Emancipation of Jews, 91–93, 162, 203, 215, 407, 645–646, 689, 740, 764
    and Napoleon, 6–7, 203, 395–396
    in German states and Germany, 26, 78, 726–727
    in United States, 19
Emancipation of Russian serfs, 37
Emancipation Proclamation, 322
Emanuel, Rahm, 139
Emmanuel, David, 146
Emergency Committee to Save the Jewish People of Europe, 210, 222
Emerson, Ralph Waldo, 170, 544, 564, 571, 582, 624
Englander, Nathan, 546
Enlightenment, European, 11, 17–18, 312, 652, 715, 724, 745–746
Entebbe rescue, 619
Epidemics, 14
    cholera (Poland 1869), 37
    flu (1918), 499
    yellow fever (Galveston), 43
Epstein, Benjamin, 245
Epstein, Brian, 674
Epstein, Charlotte, 523 (photo), 525–526
Epstein, Jason, 306
Epstein, Julius J., 463
Epstein, Mike, 517
Epstein, Morris, 473
Epstein, Philip G., 463
Equality League of Self Supporting Women, 386–387
Erlich, Henryk, 367
Ernst, Max, 656
Estrin, Brokha, 201
Ethical Culture, 74, 77, 343, 370, 691, 746
Ethiopia, 421, 426
    Jews from, 8, 227, 509
Evian Conference, 218
Exiles and refugees from Nazi Germany and Nazi-occupied countries, Jewish, 35, 148, 167, 210–211, 218–219, 221–224, 253, 278, 332, 385, 388–389, 491, 515, 577, 640–641, 711–715, 719, 722–723, 740–741, 757

Exodus
    film, 465
    novel, 465, 611–613
Expulsions of Jews
    from Baltic seacoast, 412
    from Brazil, 2, 11, 414, 537
    from England, 412
    from France, 412
    from Habsburg Netherlands, 412
    from Italy, 412
    from Portugal, 404, 412–413
    from areas of Russian Empire, 37–38, 409
    from Spain (1492), 3–4, 128, 238, 404, 412–414, 426, 610

Fair Employment Practices laws, 239, 254–255, 424, 426, 432
The Family Moskat, 608–610
Famine
    Irish potato, 180
    Lithuania (1867–1869), 37
Fanon, Franz, 429
Fard, W. D., 192, 444
Farmer, James, 255
Farrakhan, Louis, 136, 192, 194, 196–199, 245, 257, 429–430, 444–445
Farrell, James T., 173
Farrell, Perry (Bernstein, Peretz), 678
Fast, Howard, 294
Faulkner, William, 173, 560, 609, 622
Federal Bureau of Investigation (FBI), 190–191, 193–194, 259, 290, 293, 296, 352, 354, 356, 446, 692
Federal Reserve Board, 718–719, 721
Federal Reserve System, 181, 199, 722
Federated Department Stores, 400
Federation of American Zionists (FAZ), 33, 142, 204–206, 342
Federation of Jewish Agencies (FJA), 144
Federation of Jewish Charities (FJC), 143–144
Federation of Jewish Philanthropies, 50, 142, 301, 399, 752
Federation of Latin American Sephardim, 131
Federation of Reconstructionist Congregations, 91
Fehr, Donald, 535
Feigenbaum, Benjamin, 360–361
Fein, Dopey Benny, 117, 349–350
Fein, Leonard, 274
Feingold, Gustave, 708–709
Feldstein, Al, 472
Female Hebrew Benevolent Society, 141, 750
Fenichel, Otto, 712
Fernberger, Samuel, 708
Fiddler on the Roof, 202, 459, 497
Fiedler, Jay, 519

Fiedler, Leslie, 301
Filene, Edward, 28
Filene brothers, 361, 395
Filene's, 361
Fillmore, Millard, 345
Fine, Irving, 760
Fine, Larry, 487 (photo)
Fineberg, S. Andhil, 295
Finger, Bill, 471
Finkelstein, Louis, 85
Firestone, Reuven, 446
Firestone, Shulamith, 309–310
First Temple, 610, 688
First Zionist Congress, Basle. See Zionist Congresses
Fischel, Harry, 121
Fischer, Stanley, 721–722
Fisher, Carl, 128
Fisher, Eddie, 672
Fitzgerald, F. Scott, 173, 351
The Fixer, 578–580
Flack, Audrey, 643
A Flag is Born, 211
Flegenheimer, Arthur. See Schultz, Dutch
Fleischer, Nat, 521
Flood, Curt, 522
Florida, 99, 127–131, 145–146, 148–149, 161, 219, 225, 227, 256, 342, 356, 403, 419, 440–441, 493, 518, 606. *See also* Miami; Miami Beach
Foer, Jonathan Safran, 546
Fogel, Robert, 721
Fogelman, Eva, 225–227
Folk music, 559, 668–669, 680–682, 751
    American, 428, 665, 674, 678, 681
    Israeli, 680–681
    Yiddish, 449–450, 680–681, 769
Folk-rock music, 74, 81, 674, 677, 681
Foner, Philip, 427
Football, 128, 518–522, 528, 534, 756, 760
Foote, Henry S., 324–325
Forcible baptism of Jewish children, 32–33, 151–152, 281, 413, 420, 542, 768
Ford Foundation, 303, 305, 391, 429, 693, 731
Ford Motor Company, 181, 185
Ford, Gerald, 279, 317 (photo), 317
Ford, Henry, 180–187, 243, 353
    admired by Hitler, 184
    and *Protocols of the Elders of Zion*, 180, 182–185, 241, 243, 353
    awarded medal by Nazi government, 186 (photo)
Forster, Arnold, 245
Forster, E. M., 631–632
Fortas, Abe, 335, 339–340, 344–347
Forvarts. See *Forverts*
Forverts, 119–120, 126, 129, 139, 184, 252, 268–271, 274, 284–287, 293, 316,

326, 360, 363, 375, 424, 428, 546, 555–557, 594–595, 608, 615
Forward [English–language], 274–275, 472
Forward [Yiddish–language]. See *Forverts*
Fox, William, 461, 504–505
Foxman, Abraham, 196, 225, 445
France, 10, 21, 23, 26, 214, 218, 225, 389, 413, 459, 491, 523, 557, 562, 571, 575, 693
   antisemitism in, 204, 238, 247, 257
   emancipation of Jews in, 18–19
   expulsion of Jews from, 412
   German invasion and conquest of (1940), 219, 253, 389, 640, 714, 722, 740
   intermarriage in, 18
   Jewish immigrants from, 131, 150, 740
   Jewish soldiers killed in, 239
   Jews in, 16, 20, 174, 328, 332, 540, 555
   Napoleonic, 317–318
   Vichy, 18
Franco-Prussian War, 262
Frank v. Magnum, 178
Frank, Anne, 224, 231–233, 465, 604
Frank, Jerome, 277
Frank, Leo, 33, 147, 175–180, 243, 403, 425, 582
Frankel, Zechariah, 82–83
Frankfurt, Germany, 112, 388, 407, 588, 693, 713, 716, 769
Frankfurt School, 35, 713–717
Frankfurter, Felix
   and *Brown v. Board of Education,* 339
   and Jewishness, 343–344
   and Rosenberg case, 297
   and Sacco-Vanzetti case, 338
   and Supreme Court, 297, 335, 337–339, 345–347
   and Zionism, 205, 344
   as advisor to Franklin D. Roosevelt, 219, 277, 338
Franklin Simon, 398
Franklin, Aretha, 671
Franklin, Benjamin, 19–20
Fraternities, Jewish, 519
   exclusion of Jews from, 242
Frazier, Walt, 521
Frederic, Harold, 172
Free Speech Movement, 302
Freed, Alan, 672
Freed, Isadore, 668
Freedman, Andrew, 518
Freedom Schools, 391
Freedom Summer (1964), 403
Freehof, Solomon, 79, 331
Freier Arbayter Shtimme, 119, 270, 299, 360, 544–546
Freiheit, 284, 571
French and Indian War, 10, 12

Frenkel, Jacob, 721
Frenkel-Brunswik, Else, 709
Freud, Sigmund, 174, 309, 492, 561, 576, 591, 631, 710–713, 716, 729
Frick, Henry Clay, 299
Friedan, Betty, 309–310
Friedland, Abraham, 751
Friedman, Benny, 518–519, 760
Friedman, Debbie, 668, 681
Friedman, Milton, 717–718
Friedman, Mordechai Shlomo, 98
Frieman, Israel, 98
Friends, 477, 479–480
Frink, Horace, 711
Fromm, Erich, 35, 712–714, 716
Fuchs, Daniel, 288, 566–568
Fuchs, Emil, 518
Fuchs, Klaus, 292
Fuchs, Lawrence, 757, 760
Fulton Fish Market, 687
Fundamentalist Christians, 148, 422, 436, 438, 674, 747
Funny Girl, 465, 497
Furnishing merchants, 400

Gadhafi, Muammar, 198
Gadol, Moise, 5
Gaines, Max, 471–472
Galicia, 39, 116, 595, 599, 710, 763
   Hasidim from, 100, 102
   pogroms in, 239, 327
   poverty of, 37–38
Galveston, Texas, 42–47, 514
Galveston Plan, 46, 148, 409
Gambino, Carlo, 351
Gamoran, Emanuel, 78, 753
Gangsters, Jewish, 29, 125, 129, 137, 349–359, 372, 470, 566
Garfunkel, Art, 674–675
Garland, Hamlin, 271
Garland, Judy, 129
Gates, Jr., Henry Louis, denounced by Leonard Jeffries, 196
Gaynor, William Jay, 5
Gebiner, Benjamin, 252
Geffen, David, 675–676, 678
Gelbart, Larry, 475, 488
Gellert, Hugo, 657
General Order No. 11, 30, 324–325
Generals, Jewish, 323, 332
Genovese, Vito, 351
Gentleman's Agreement, 465
George, Henry, 284
George Washington University, 246
Georgetown University, 761
   students' antisemitism, 516
Gephardt, Richard A., 445–446
German Americans (non-Jewish), 28, 33–34, 186, 190, 218, 244, 263, 265, 355, 389, 420–421, 514, 729

Germany, 39, 135, 155, 184, 191, 214, 216, 326, 368, 378, 388, 395, 410, 555, 614, 722, 724–727, 741–744
   emancipation of Jews in, 26, 78, 726–727
   Jewish immigration from, 16, 24–36, 43, 49, 59, 63, 68, 75–76, 110, 150, 155, 160, 175, 243, 298, 316–317, 323, 396, 399, 455, 461, 481, 503, 644, 675, 708, 713, 725, 727, 744
   Judaism in, 31, 74–76, 82, 111–113
   Nazi, 35, 174, 186, 190, 206, 208–209, 218–222, 230, 238–239, 243–244, 252, 256, 274, 278, 287, 295, 312–313, 316–317, 328–330, 333, 355, 366, 374, 388–389, 466, 482, 491, 514–515, 571, 577, 619, 640–641, 644, 649, 692, 713–714, 723, 740, 744, 757
   post–World War II, 191, 224, 238, 241, 247, 254, 256–257, 301, 374, 379, 459, 520, 647, 714, 719
   See also Berlin; Hamburg; Exiles and refugees from Nazi Germany and Nazi–occupied countries; Hitler, Adolf; Hitler-Stalin Pact; Holocaust; Nazis and Nazism
German-American Bund, 186, 190, 218, 244, 355
Gershwin, George, 457–459, 463, 696–699
Gershwin, Ira, 456, 458–459, 463, 696, 698
Gestapo, 186, 253, 472, 712, 722
Gettysburg, Battle of, 135, 323
Ghetto, Eastern European Jewish, 11, 16–17, 19, 26, 48, 50, 85, 108, 159, 163, 167, 172, 174, 213, 215, 229, 270, 297, 357, 409, 460, 464, 500, 514, 569–571, 585, 594, 612, 619, 624, 640–642, 694, 727, 745, 764
   ghetto defense in Eastern Europe, 188, 514
   Lodz, 225
   London, 51
   Lower East Side, 116–121
   Maxwell Street (Chicago), 136–138, 165, 344, 699
   south Philadelphia, 736
   Warsaw, 99, 188, 224, 254, 458, 556, 612
Giacometti, Alberto, 656–657
Giancana, Sam, 356
Giddings, Franklin, 90
The Gift of Asher Lev, 592
Gillman, Sid, 519
Gimbel, Adam, 28, 396
Gimbel, Jacob, 144
Gimbel's, 395, 397–398
Ginsburg, Ruth Bader, 335, 340–341 (photo), 342, 345–347
Gitlow, Benjamin, 284
Giuliani, Rudy, 200, 202, 431

Glantz, Leib, 668
Glaser, Joseph B., 80
Glatzer, Nahum, 757, 760
Glazer, Nathan, 300–304, 306
Glickman, Daniel, 273, 279
Glickman, Marty, 519, 522
The Glory, 615, 618–619
Gluck, Pearl, 546
Glueck, Nelson, 79, 109, 765
"God Bless America," 50, 685
God's Grace, 579, 581
Goddard College, 582–583
Goebbels, Josef, 244, 388, 604
Goell, Milton, 124–125
Goering, Hermann Wilhelm, 186, 258, 617
Gold, Ben, 284, 364–365
Gold, H. L., 507
Gold, Harry, 290–292
Gold, Herbert, 560, 562
Gold, Mike, 117, 288, 568–571
Goldberg, Arthur, 137, 335, 339–341, 344–347, 534
Goldberg, J. J., 275
Goldberg, Marshall, 519
Goldberg, Molly, 475 (photo), 496–497
Goldberg, Rube, 470–471
The Goldbergs, 474–476, 478, 496–497
Golden, Harry, 179
Goldenson, Leonard, 474
Goldenweiser, Alexander, 726
Goldfaden, Abraham, 449–450, 453
Goldfarb, Abraham, 669
Goldfinger, Arnon, 454
Goldin, Irene, 328
Goldman, Charley, 515
Goldman, Emma, 212, 298–299, 308–311 (photo), 313–313, 326, 381–383
Goldman, Henry, 398
Goldman, Marcus, 28
Goldman, Maurice, 187
Goldman, Solomon, 138
Goldman, William, 455
Goldman, Sachs & Co, 398
Goldmark, Joseph, 30
Goldschmidt, Neil, 279
Goldsmith's of Memphis, 395, 402
Goldstein, Israel, 756
Goldstein, Jennie, 453–454
Goldstein, Lisa, 510
Goldstein, Martin "Bugsy," 352, 357
Goldstein, Neil, 250
Goldstein, Rebecca, 552–553
Goldwyn, Samuel, 461, 505
Golem, 469, 474, 508, 510
Golf, 130, 469, 520
   women's, 522–523, 526
Golub, Leon, 635, 643
Golubok, Leon, 450
Golubok, Myron, 450
Gompers, Samuel, 29, 327, 360, 367–370

Goodbye Columbus, 166, 601–605
Goodman, Allegra, 546, 552–553
Goodman, Benny, 137, 139, 699–702
Goodman, Morris L., 132
Goodman, Paul, 302
Gorbachev, Mikhail, 47
Gordin, Jacob, 451–452
Gordon, Aaron David, 213
Gordon, Sid, 518
Gordon, Waxey, 351, 353, 357
Gorfinkel, Jordan, 474
Gormé, Edie, 672
Gottheil, Richard, 33
Gottlieb, Adolph, 636
Gottlieb, Eddie, 516, 521
Gottschalk, Alfred, 80, 226
Gould, Elliott, 465
Gould, Stephen Jay, 746–747
Graham, Bill (Wolfgang Grajonca), 675
Graham, Billy, 438
Graham, Frank, 148
Grand Street, 116
Grand Theater, 452
Grandees, 2–3
Grange, Red, 519
Granit, Arthur, 124–125
Grant, Ulysses S., 30, 324–325
Grateful Dead, 675
Gratz, Rebecca, 31–32, 111, 141–142, 541, 750
Gratz College, 141–142, 144, 768
Graziosi, Anthony, 201
Great Depression, 60, 64, 124, 129, 159, 186, 190, 206, 217, 231, 236, 244, 287–290, 309, 336, 345, 355, 365, 372, 400, 402, 406, 426, 463, 473, 485, 490, 503, 505, 528–529, 534, 559, 566, 569–570, 586, 588, 601, 628–630, 662–663, 685, 701, 720, 729, 734, 754
Great War. See World War I
Greece, 116, 132, 459, 612
Greek Jews, 1, 4–5, 116, 132
Greeks (non–Jewish), 4–5, 51, 364, 545, 692
Green, Shawn, 517
Green, William, 253
Greenberg, Clement, 301, 628, 649–650
Greenberg, Eliezer, 622
Greenberg, Hank, 427, 517–518, 529–530 (photo), 531–532
Greenberg, Hayim, 215, 288
Greenberg, Irving, 230
Greenberg, Jack, 196
Greenberg, Joanne, 712
Greene, Shecky, 489
Greenebaum, Gary, 445
Greenglass, David, 290–293, 296
Greenglass, Ruth, 290–292
Greenson, Ralph, 713

Greenspan, Alan, 721
Greenwich Village, 375, 377, 465, 529, 555, 621, 626, 674
Gregory the Great, Pope, 189
Griffith, D. W., 502
Grinker, Roy Sr, 712–713
Grippe, Peter, 760
Gropper, William, 640–643, 657
Gross, Aaron, 364
Gross, Chaim, 660
Gross, Milt, 470–471
Gross, Milton, 521
Grossinger, Jennie, 468
Grossinger's, 468 (photo)
Grossman, Henryk, 713
Grove, Andrew, 226
Groves, Leslie, 292
Gruen, Victor, 167
Grünberg, Carl, 713
Grunge music, 670
Gulf War, 258
Gun-running to Israel, late 1940s, 130, 207, 355–356, 515
Gurvitch, George, 739
Guterman, Norbert, 715
Guthrie, Woody, 674, 682
Gutow, Steve, 94
Guttman, Adolph, 667
Guys and Dolls, 457
Guzik, Jake, 137, 356
Gymnastics, 30, 524–525, 527–528

Habermas, Jürgen, 717
Hacker, Andrew, 305
Hackett, Buddy, 484, 489
Hadassah, 33, 129, 139, 148, 166, 205–206, 208, 273, 397, 435, 459, 571, 754, 759
Haganah, 355–356
Haifa, 407, 689
The Haj, 613
Halberstam, Bentzion, 102
Halberstam, Shlomo, 102
Hale, Matt, 194
Halevi, Yehudah, 594
Haley, Bill, 672
Halivni, David Weiss, 226
Hall, Stanley, 708
Halpern, Benjamin, 760
Hamas, 258, 443, 445
Hamburg, Germany, 39, 75, 408, 666
Hamilton, Alexander, 19, 589, 653
Hammerstein I, Oscar, 501
Hammerstein II, Oscar, 399, 456–459
Hanafi Muslim attack on B'nai Brith building, Washington DC, 442
Handball, 467–468
Handler, Evelyn E., 756–757
Hapgood, Hutchins, 120, 173–174
Hapgood, Powers, 383
Har Sinai (Baltimore), 75–76, 113, 147

Harburg, E. Y. (Yip), 455–457
Harby, Isaac, 75, 147, 539–540, 543
Harkavy, Alexander, 40, 266
Harlem, 192, 426, 428–429, 506, 517, 599–600, 671, 697, 702
Harlem Globetrotters, 517
Harriman, Averell, 366
Harriman, Edward, 408
Harrington, Michael, 304
Harris, David, 242
Harsanyi, John, 721
Hart Schaffner & Marx, 135, 137, 371
Hart, Lorenz, 457–458
Harte, Bret, 171
Hartog, Marion, 542
Harvard Law School, 53, 335–338, 341, 343–344
Harvard Medical School, Jewish quota at, 280
Harvard University (and College), 52, 117, 196, 281, 317–318, 336, 353, 457, 538, 553, 569, 594, 653–654, 687–688, 707–708, 718–722, 727–728, 731, 733–736, 755
   Jewish quota at, 185, 344, 353, 721
   Jewish Studies program, 103
   Semitics Museum, 409
   sending of delegate to Nazified Heidelberg University, 239
Hashomer Hatzair, 440
Hasidim, 39, 73, 78, 97–106, 200–202, 232, 430–431, 439, 489, 492–493, 553–554, 556, 566, 606, 609–610, 638, 646, 669, 753
   and Holocaust, 97–98, 100–102
   Belz, 97, 101–102, 105
   Bobov, 97, 102, 105
   Boyaner, 98, 102
   Ger, 97
   in Catskills, 469
   in clothing trade, 105
   in computer industry, 105
   in diamond trade, 105, 405
   in novels of Chaim Potok, 590–592
   Lubavitch, 97–102, 105, 200–202, 405
   music of, 669, 680–682
   Satmar, 97–98, 100–103, 105, 405
   Skverer, 103–104
   Vizhnitz, 97
   women, 104–105
Haskalah, 24–25, 39, 263, 615, 652, 751
Hatikvah, 78, 684
Havazelet, Ehud, 546
Hawn, Goldie, 465
Hawthorne, Nathaniel, 171, 543, 624
Hayek, Friedrich, 721
Haymarket Affair, 270, 298, 308, 565–566, 594
Hazzan, 16, 20–21, 29, 75, 111, 132, 141, 272, 539, 665–666, 668–669, 749

Hearst, William Randolph and Hearst press, 185, 469
The Heartbreak Kid, 465
Heavy metal music, 670, 676
Hebrew Actors' Union, 452
Hebrew Committee of National Liberation, 211
Hebrew Emigrant Aid Society (HEAS), 40–41
Hebrew Hip Hop, 678–679
Hebrew Immigrant Aid Society (HIAS), 42, 47–48, 128, 139, 769
Hebrew Orphan Asylum, 117
Hebrew Orphan Society
   Lower East Side, 117
   San Francisco, 150
Hebrew Sabbath School Union (HSSU), 750
Hebrew Settlement House (Brownsville), 652
Hebrew Sheltering and Immigrant Aid Society, 40
Hebrew Sheltering and Immigrant Aid Society, Oriental Bureau, 5
Hebrew Technical Institute
   for boys, 117
   for girls, 524
Hebrew Union College (HUC) and Hebrew Union College–Jewish Institute of Religion (HUC-JIR), 31, 74, 77, 79–80, 83, 109, 113, 133–134, 147, 159, 226, 446, 668, 755, 764, 766–768, 770
Hebrew Union Veterans Association (HUVA), 238–239
Hebrew University, 143, 343, 380
Hebrew Veterans of the War With Spain (HVWS), 239
Hebron, 2, 538, 639, 703
Hecht, Ben, 139, 210–211, 463, 562
Heder, 70, 268, 314, 375, 385, 558, 594, 614, 750–751
Heine, Heinrich, 455, 545, 571, 594, 717
Heine, Maurice, 450
Heinlein, Robert A., 510
Heisenberg, Werner, 740
Held, Adolph, 253, 255
Heldman, Gladys, 526
Heldman, Julie, 526
Helfman, Max, 668
Heller, Joseph, 598
Heller, Max, 770
Hellman, Lillian, 233, 463, 692
Hemingway, Ernest, 173, 232, 560
Henderson the Rain King, 560
Henry Street Settlement, 35, 117
Henry, O., 173
Hentoff, Nat, 197, 760
Hep! Hep! riots, 26
Herberg, Will, 216

Hersey, John, 224
Hershfield, Harry, 470–471
Hershman, Mordecai, 668
Herskovits, Melville, 427, 559, 725–726
Herut USA, 212
Herzl, Theodore, 172, 203–204 (illustration), 205, 212, 273, 509, 705
Herzog, 558, 560–561
Heschel, Abraham Joshua, 226, 437
Heschel, Abraham Joshua (Kapitshinitzer Rebbe), 98
Heschel, Moshe, 98
Hester Street, 465
Heyman, Elizabeth Gero, 712
Hezbollah, 246, 443
Hibbat Zion (Love of Zion), 203–204
Hidden Child Foundation, 226
Hier, Marvin, 256–257
Hill, James, 408
Hillel (campus), 81, 134, 195. See also B'nai B'rith Hillel Foundation
Hilliard, Earl, 431
Hillman, Bessie Abramowitz, 308, 373
Hillman, Sidney, 139, 284, 289, 308, 370–371 (photo), 372–374
Hillquit, Morris, 265, 284, 286–287, 315
Himmelfarb, Milton, 242, 303
Hip hop, 670, 677–679
Hirsch, Emil, 136, 407
Hirsch, Samson Raphael, 741
Hirsch, Samuel, 113
Hirschbein, Peretz, 452
Hirschman, Albert, 721
Hirshberg, Al, 520
Hiss, Alger, 292, 301
Histadrut, 130, 208–209, 213, 373–374, 383, 441
Hitler, Adolf, 171, 174, 190–191, 195, 206–208, 211, 218–219, 221, 238–239, 244, 251–252, 257–258, 294, 318, 328, 355, 373, 388, 463, 471, 482, 486, 493, 509, 515, 531, 557, 587, 610, 625, 631, 640–641, 646, 695, 714, 723, 730, 744, 769
   and Henry Ford, 180, 184, 186
   Hitler youth, 184
   Jewish boxers' opposition to, 514–515
   portrayed by Moe Howard, 486
Hitler-Stalin Pact, 372, 379, 454, 593, 715
Hizballah. See Hezbollah
Hoenlein, Malcolm, 446
Hoff, Max "Boo Boo," 349, 351, 355, 357
Hoffman, Dustin, 465, 587
Hoffman, Eva, 546
Hoffman, Michael, 192
Holdheim, Samuel, 113
Holly, James T., 421
Hollywood Anti-Nazi League, 463
Hollywood Ten, 464

Holm, Eleanor, 525
Holman, Nat, 515–516, 519
Holmes, Jr., Oliver Wendell, 337–338, 470, 734
  and Leo Frank case, 178
  relationship with Louis Brandeis, 336
Holmes, Oliver Wendell, 170
Holocaust, 54–55, 87, 121, 130, 189, 207, 215–216, 240–241, 254–255, 258, 301, 312, 355, 371, 373, 383, 385, 404, 412, 426, 429, 437–439, 598, 621, 709, 724
  and art, 224, 635–637, 640–647, 654, 658–660
  and comics, 473
  and film, 466, 492
  and music, 561, 678, 689–690, 703
  and television, 477, 676
  denial of, 191–192, 229, 244, 257
  education and commemoration, 131, 216, 224–233, 246, 251, 256–259, 301, 383, 466, 754
  impact on Hasidim, 97–102
  inadequate response to, 169, 207, 217–224, 278, 306, 344, 744
  Jewish resistance during, 188, 216, 224, 254–255, 328, 458, 556, 612, 641, 769
  literature, 224–225, 465, 508–509, 546, 561, 563, 580, 588–589, 602, 604, 608, 610–613
  minimization/justification, 429
  refugees, survivors, and survivors' children, 72, 127, 136, 201, 210–212, 216, 224–227, 244, 254–257, 333, 367, 374, 466, 472–473, 546, 561, 593, 612–613, 643, 659–660, 753, 765, 770
Holtzman, Ken, 517–518
Holzman, Elijah M., 542
Homage to Blenholt, 566–568
Homosexuals and Lesbians, 278, 438, 479–480, 497, 555, 688, 691
  Judaism and, 74, 81, 88, 90, 93, 96, 110, 134
  Leonard Jeffries and, 196
  Nazis and, 230
Hook, Sidney, 53, 288
Hooper, Frank, 177–178, 189
Hoover, Herbert, 337
Hoover, J. Edgar, 207, 290, 293, 296, 692
The Hope, 615, 618
Horkheimer, Max, 35, 713–717
Horn, Dara, 546
Horn, Milton, 139
Horner, Henry (governor), 139
Horney, Karen, 712
Horowitz, Barbara Ostfeld, 109
Horowitz, Eugene, 709
Horowitz, Levi Yitzchok, 104
Horowitz, Moshe (playwright), 450–451

Horowitz, Moshe (rabbi), 104
Horowitz, Pinchas, 104
Horowitz, Ruth, 709
Horowitz, Vladimir, 691
Horwitz, Phineas, 323
Houdini, Harry, 498 (photo)–499, 585
Houghton, Harris Ayres, 183
House Un-American Activities Committee (HUAC), 192, 364, 464, 556, 588
Howard University, 698, 709
  antisemitic speeches at, 196–197
  cancellation of David Brion Davis's lecture, 197
Howard, Moe, 486–487 (photo)
Howe, Irving, 262, 288, 301, 449, 545–546, 548–549, 560, 566, 568, 598, 607, 609–610, 621–623, 650, 684, 696, 757, 760
Howe, Julia Ward, 169
Howells, William Dean, 172
Hruska, Roman, 348
Hughes, Charles Evans, 178
Hughes, Sarah, 526
Hull, Cordell, 221
Hull House, 524, 699
The Human Stain, 604–605
Humboldt's Gift, 561–562
Hungary, 37, 49, 113, 322, 461, 498, 569
  Holocaust in, 223
  Holocaust survivors from, 224–226
Hunter College, 60, 622, 625
Hurst, Fannie, 550
Hurwich, Louis, 751
Hurwitz, Henry, 631
Hutchins, Robert M., 558
Hyams, Henry, 146
Hyneman, Rebecca Gumpert, 543–544

I Am the Clay, 592
I Married a Communist, 604–605
Iberia, 308, 451, 453, 587, 615
Ibsen, Henrik, 308, 451, 453, 587, 615
Illowy, Bernard, 147
Immigration restriction, 33–34, 41–42, 46, 52, 64, 71, 78, 124, 154, 217–219, 222, 239, 244, 262, 272, 282, 286, 315–316, 373, 708
In the Beginning, 592
Incident at Vichy, 588
Independent Social Democratic Party (USPD) of Germany, 388
Independent Socialist League, 622
Indies (record companies), 670–672, 678
Inglehart, Ronald, 732
Inquisition, 1–3, 8, 13–14, 128, 172, 238, 327, 343, 404, 413, 417, 424
Institute for Advanced Study, Princeton, NJ, 35, 39, 744
Institute for Historical Review, 191–192, 257

Institute for Social Research, 713
Institute for Southern Jewish Life, 149
International Association of Machinists, 534
International Brigades, 328–329
International Confederation of Free Trade Unions (ICFTU), 367, 388–389
International Conference on Antisemitism, Paris (1983), 257
International Conference on Feminism and Orthodoxy, 110
International Conference on Terrorism, Los Angeles (1986), 258
International Federation of Trade Unions, 368
International Fur and Leather Workers' Union, 365
International Fur Workers' Union, 313, 362–365
The International Jew, 183–186, 353
International Jewish Sports Hall of Fame, 526
International Labor Defense (ILD), 424–425
International Ladies' Garment Workers' Union (ILGWU), 119, 125, 235, 252–254, 284, 287, 308, 313, 359–362, 365–367, 371–372, 374–377, 381–383, 386, 398, 597
International Monetary Fund (IMF), 722
International Political Science Association, 731
International Psychoanalytic Association, 631, 713
International Sociological Association, 731
International Workingmen's Association, 29, 368–369
Iran, 258, 442–443, 759
  Jews in/from, 1–2, 6–8, 48, 134, 405, 639, 669
Iraq, 258, 300, 319, 328, 442, 447, 493, 618
  Jews from, 669
Irene Kaufmann Settlement House, 524
Irgun Zvai Leumi, 211–212, 220
Irish Americans, 85, 116, 122–123, 351, 387, 390, 420–421, 423, 464, 475, 478, 486, 489, 673, 684–685
  and antisemitism, 187–189, 344, 424, 491, 514
  and Mortara affair, 33
  in comics, 470
  relations with African Americans, 420–421, 423
Irvin, Monte, 521
Irving, David, 192
Irving, Washington, 541
Isaacs, Samuel, 69
Isaacs, Stan, 521
Islamic Action Front, 446

Islamic Jihad, 443, 445
Islamic Supreme Council of America
    (ISCA), 446
Israel, state of, 1, 7, 47, 53–54, 58, 61–62,
    73, 79, 86–87, 93, 97–98, 100–101,
    127, 130–131, 134, 140, 144, 148,
    195, 198, 200, 203–204, 207–208,
    212–216, 224–226, 228–229,
    231–233, 237–242, 244–248, 251,
    255–256, 258–259, 273–275, 277,
    279–283, 289, 294, 301, 305–306,
    317, 319, 328, 344, 355–356,
    366–367, 374, 405, 429, 431,
    437–446, 454, 459, 465, 483,
    509–510, 513, 515, 520, 522, 553,
    557, 562, 582, 598, 600, 602, 605,
    611–613, 617–619, 623, 625, 630,
    639, 642–643, 648, 661, 668–669,
    676–677, 680–682, 689–690, 703,
    705, 714, 716, 724, 732–733, 744,
    754, 759, 761
Israel Academy of Music, 705
Israel Bonds, 353, 441
Israel Defense Forces (IDF), 355
Israel Independence Day, 754
Israel Museum, 654, 658, 660
Israel Philharmonic Orchestra, 689
Israel's War of Independence, 208, 210,
    356, 515
Italian Americans, 85, 349–354, 390, 423,
    426, 460, 473, 476, 478, 482, 486,
    577, 580, 612, 646, 672, 684, 692
    in garment industry, 362, 376, 385
Italian racial laws, 719
Ivanhoe, 541

Jabotinsky, Vladimir, 207–209 (photo),
    210–212, 740
Jachman, Isadore S., 332 (photo)
Jackson, Jesse, 198, 257, 281, 430
Jackson, Reggie, 518
Jacobs, Mike, 515
Jacobson, Edith, 712
Jacobson, Edmund, 708
Jacobson, Israel, 665–666
Jaffe, Rona, 552
Jamaica, 414–415
James, Henry, 172, 571, 602, 624, 629–630
James, William, 52, 90, 172, 708, 727
Jamestown (colonial), 145, 199
Janowski, Max, 668, 682
Jastrow, Joseph, 707–708
Javits, Jacob, 318, 340
Jay and the Americans, 674
Jazz, 658, 675, 678, 680, 682, 690–692, 760
    and Al Jolson, 502–503
    and Benny Goodman, 699–702
    and George Gershwin, 696–698
    bebop, 701–702
The Jazz Singer, 464, 496, 499, 502–503

Jefferson, Thomas, 19–20, 22, 542
The Jeffersonian, 178
Jeffries, Jim, 514
Jeffries, Leonard, 195–196
Jerusalem, 22, 86, 152, 171, 225, 445, 452,
    509–510, 517, 541, 548, 562, 605,
    611, 618, 639, 643, 648, 654, 658,
    665, 689, 759
    AJCongress office, 251
    Conference on Jewish Solidarity with
        Israel, 258
    Eichmann trial, 622, 724, 763
    Hasidim in, 100
    HUC-JIR campus, 79–80, 442
    Simon Wiesenthal Center office, 256
    World Gathering of Holocaust
        Survivors, 225, 227
Jessel, George, 486, 502
Jewish Agency, 206, 208, 214, 373
Jewish Agricultural Society, 129, 273, 467
Jewish Community Centers (JCC), 65,
    133, 138–139, 167, 403, 524, 553,
    654, 752
Jewish Council for Public Affairs, 94, 432,
    444
Jewish Daily Forward. See Forverts
Jewish Defense League (JDL), 676
Jewish Division of New York Public
    Library, 142–143
Jewish Documentation Center, Austria,
    256
Jewish Education Fund, 755
Jewish Federations, 54, 149, 167, 251,
    273–275, 755
    Atlanta, 179
    Boston, 144
    Chicago, 139
    Los Angeles, 133, 483
    Philadelphia, 144
    South Florida, 129, 131
Jewish Frontier, 215–216
Jewish hospitals, 30, 32, 35, 54, 112, 118,
    126, 135, 137, 212, 409
Jewish Labor Bund. See Bund, Jewish
Jewish Labor Committee (JLC), 126, 220,
    236–237, 249, 251–256, 288, 295,
    366
Jewish Legion, 213, 239
Jewish Music Forum, 668
Jewish Orthodox Feminist Alliance, 110
Jewish Publication Society, 31, 142–143,
    766
Jewish Reconstructionist Federation (JRF),
    90–91, 96
Jewish Spectator, 274
Jewish Telegraphic Agency (JTA), 232,
    273–274
Jewish Territorial Organization, 46
Jewish Theological Seminary (JTSA), 2–3,
    69–71, 77, 83–90, 109, 133–134,

141–143, 226, 301, 310, 344, 409,
    668–669, 752, 754–755, 763, 770
The Jewish Veteran, 239
Jewish Veterans of the Wars of the
    Republic, 239
Jewish War Veterans of the United States
    of America (JWV), 129, 238
    (illustration), 239–240, 252, 295
Jewish Welfare Board (JWB), 79, 326,
    331–332, 343, 524
Jews Without Money, 568–570
Jick, Leon, 759
John Birch Society, 189–191, 193, 245
John Paul II, Pope, 437
John Reed Club, 626, 628, 663
Johns Hopkins University, 84, 379, 708,
    720–721
Johnson, Hall, 698
Johnson, Jack, 514
Johnson, Lyndon B., 279, 302, 339–340,
    344, 346, 432, 485, 733
Johnstown, PA, 157–158, 160–161, 672
Joint Distribution Committee, 6, 32, 204,
    326, 373, 407, 555, 769
Joint Emergency Committee on European
    Jewish Affairs (JEC), 220, 222
Jolson, Al, 455, 463, 491, 499–500 (photo),
    501–503, 506–507, 697
Jonas, B. F., 148
Jones, Bobby, 526
Jones, Ernest, 712
Jones, James, 173
Jordan Marsh, 395
Joseph, Jacob, 70
The Joys of Yiddish, 598
Judaea, 471
Judah Maccabee, 542
Judah, Samuel B. H., 539–540
Judeo-Arabic, 1
Judeo-Farsi, 1
Judeo-Greek, 1
Judith, 313, 544
Juedisch-Theologisches Seminar, 82
Juilliard School, 583, 658, 695, 698, 702
Jung, C. G., 710–711

Kafka, Franz, 459, 473, 549, 627–628, 630,
    650, 717
Kahane, Meir, 274, 676
Kahn, Julius, 154, 326
Kahn, Roger, 427, 521
Kahn, Tobi, 637
Kahneman, Daniel, 721
Kaiser, Alois, 666
Kalb, Marty, 635, 644
Kalich, Bertha, 452, 494 (photo)–495
Kallen, Horace, 52, 214–215, 287–288,
    572, 727–729, 770
Kane, Bob, 471
Kantor, Mickey, 279

Kantorovich, Leonid, 721
Kaplan, Israel, 90
Kaplan, Kivie, 80, 280
Kaplan, Mordecai, 54, 71, 79, 84–85, 90
  (photo)–91, 93–95, 109, 216,
  440–441, 752
Karpeles, Leopold, 323
Kastner, Rudolf, 100
Katchor, Ben, 474, 541
Katz, Daniel, 709
Katz, Hyman, 327
Katz, Michael, 636
Katz, Moshe, 298
Katznelson, Berl, 216
Kaufman, Andy, 490
Kaufman, Irving, 291, 293, 295–296
Kaufman, George S., 459
Kaufman, Morris, 363–364
Kaufman, Murray "The K," 672
Kauvar, Charles, 71
Kaye, Danny, 486
Kazakhstan, 48
Kazin, Alfred, 122, 301, 560, 623–624
  (photo), 625
Kean College, antisemitism at, 196–198
Keaton, Buster, 486, 492
Kemble, Fanny, 541
Kemp, Maida Springer
Kempner, Harris, 44–45
Kempner, Isaac, 45–46
Kennedy, John F., 245, 302, 339, 346, 366,
  432, 492, 507, 637, 689, 718, 733
Kennedy, Robert, 346
Kent, Roman, 225
Kent State, killings at (1970), 662
Kern, Jerome, 456–457, 459, 501, 698
Kerouac, Jack, 522
Kessler, David, 450, 452–453, 555
Kestenberg, Judith, 225
Kestenberg, Milton, 225
Key, V. O., 731
Keynes, John Maynard, 379, 717, 720–722
Keyserling, Leon, 721
KGB, 191, 593
Kharkov, 697
Kheyder. See Heder
Khrushchev, Nikita, 702
Kiev, 37, 46, 49, 212, 271, 425, 565, 625,
  660
  Beilis trial, 182
  pogroms in, 37–38
Kilpatrick, William Heard, 752
Kilson, Martin, 304
King, Alan, 486, 488
King, Billie Jean, 526
King, Jr., Martin Luther, 198, 226, 280, 391
  (photo), 429–430, 758
King, Phil, 518
The King of Kings, 243
Kirby, Jack, 471

Kirchheimer, Otto, 714
Kirkpatrick, Jeane, 274, 306
Kirshner, Don, 673
Kiryas Joel, NY, 98, 100–101
Kishinev pogrom, 38, 239–240, 271, 424,
  428, 514
KISS, 676
Kissinger, Henry, 35, 279, 304, 316–317
  (photo), 318–319, 618
Klaidman, Kitty, 635
Klein, Gerda Weissmann, 226
Klein, Lawrence, 721
Klein, Philip Hillel, 70
Kleindeutschland (Little Germany), 29
Kleinman, Morris, 351
Klezmer music, 679–682, 684, 769
Klineberg, Otto, 709
Klinghoffer, Leon, 258
Klutznick, Philip, 139, 279
Knefler, Frederick, 323
Knesset, 214
Know Nothing Movement, 420
Koch, Ed, 431
Koffka, Kurt, 709
Kohler, Kaufmann, 31, 77, 540, 542, 765
Kohs, Samuel, 708
Kohut, Alexander, 31
Komar, Vitaly, 640, 648–649
Kominsky-Crumb, Aline, 473
Kook, Hillel (Peter H. Bergson), 209–210,
  212
Kooper, Al, 673, 675
Korean War, 292–293, 301, 500, 503, 592,
  675
Korn, Bertram W., 143, 415, 418, 767
  (photo)–768
Kornbluth, C. M., 507
Kosinski, Jerzy, 226
Kotler, Aaron, 104
Koufax, Sandy, 517–518, 531 (photo)–533
Koussevitzky, David, 668
Koussevitzky, Moshe, 668
Koussevitzky, Serge, 688–689, 695
Krants, Philip, 265–267
Krauskopf, Joseph, 142–143
Krech, David, 709
Kristallnacht, 196, 198, 218, 589, 641, 644
Kristol, Irving, 300–301, 304
Kronish, Leon, 130, 440–442
Kropotkin, Peter, 213, 297–299
Kross, Anna M., 770
Krugman, Paul, 721
Krystal, Henry, 226
Ku Klux Klan, 46, 128, 130, 147, 159, 174,
  179, 189–190, 192–193, 243–244,
  257, 288, 353, 401, 422, 426–427,
  437
Kuhn, Fritz, 186, 244
Kuhn, Loeb, 181, 184, 408, 410
Kurtz, Paul, 746

Kurtzman, Harvey, 472–473
Kuznets, Simon, 720

La America, 5, 119
La Follette, Robert, 288, 370
Labor Non-Partisan League, 372
Labor Party (Israel), 93, 213–214
Ladino (Judeo–Spanish), 5
  language, 1, 3–4, 8, 131, 538
  press, 5, 119, 272
  songs, 682
Laemmle, Carl, 461
Laffite, Jean, 43
Lahr, Bert, 455, 484
Landau, Jacob, 273
Landers, Ann (Eppie Lederer), 139
Landes, Ruth, 726
Landesman, Alter, 124–125
Landis, Kenesaw Mountain, 518
Landsmanshaftn, 42, 59–60, 118, 137, 139,
  225, 236, 248, 360, 363
Lane, Burton, 456
Langer, William, 222
Langston, John Mercer, 422
Lansky, Meyer, 29, 129, 349, 351–356
Lantos, Tom, 225
Laqueur, Walter, 304, 760
The Larry Sanders Show, 477, 490
Lasker, Morris, 44–45
Lasky, Jesse L., 461
Lassallean socialism, 29
Lateiner, Joseph, 450–452
Laurents, Arthur, 689
Lawrence, Steve, 672
Lawson, John Howard, 463–464, 569
Lazarus, Emma, 2, 51, 272, 336–337,
  544–545, 571–572 (photo), 573
Lazarus, Moritz, 726–727
Leadership Conference on Civil Rights
  (LCCR), 433
League of Nations, 241, 288, 720
Lebedeff, Aaron, 453
Lebowitz, Israel, 121
Lee, Newt, 176–177
Lee, Stan, 471–472
Leeser, Isaac, 31–32, 69 (photo), 76,
  110–112, 141–143, 147, 272, 541,
  543, 750
Lehman, Herbert, 361
Lehrer, Leibush, 769
Leiber, Jerry, 673
Leibowitz, Samuel, 425–426 (photo)
Leisler, Jacob, 11
Leivick, H., 452
Lemlich, Clara, 361
Lenin, V. I., 287, 372–373
Leonard, Benny, 482, 515
Leonard, Jackie, 140
Leontief, Wassily, 719
Lerner, Abba P., 721

Lerner, Alan Jay, 457
Lerner, Max, 732–734, 760
Lerner, Michael, 274
Lesser, Alexander, 726
Letting Go, 602
Levantine Jews, 3–5, 22
Levenson, Sam, 488
Levi, Edward, 279
Levi, Primo, 493, 613, 659
Levien, Sonya, 463
Levin, Meyer, 137, 139, 231 (photo)–233, 273
Levine, Abraham, 352
Levine, Jack, 635, 654–655, 660
Levine, Sam "Red," 352
Levinsky, Kingfish, 514
Levinthal, Bernard, 70, 142–143
Levison, Stanley, 280
Levitt, Joy, 94
Levitt, William, 165–166
Levy, Alton, 426
Levy, Louis Edward, 142
Levy, Marv, 519
Levy, Moses, 145
Levy, Richard N., 81
Lewandowski, Louis, 666
Lewin, Kurt, 709
Lewis, Jerry, 483–484, 486–487, 506
Lewis, John L., 372–373
Lewis, Monk, 542
Lewis, Roman, 298–299
Lewis, Sinclair, 173, 570
Lewisohn, Irene, 386
Lewisohn, Ludwig, 216, 562, 573–577, 760
Leyden, Tom, 259
Liberal Party, 365–367
Liberty Lobby, 189–190, 192, 245
Libya, 198, 258, 442
Lieberman, Joseph, 279
Lieblich, Irene, 226
Liebling, A. J., 521
Liebman, Charles, 87
Liebman, Joshua, 712
Liebold, Ernest Gustav, 181–183, 185
Life sciences, 261, 267, 728, 741–742, 760
Likud party, 215
Likud USA, 212
Lilienthal, Augusta, 34
Lilienthal, Max, 25, 31, 75, 750
Lilienthal, Meta, 34
Lilith, 275
Lincoln, Abraham, 30, 77, 321–325, 360, 377, 398, 507
Lindbergh, Charles, 186
Lindsay, John, 303, 306, 366–367, 392, 429, 431
Lingg, Louis, 565
Lipchitz, Jacques, 640
Lipset, Seymour Martin, 731–732
Lipsky, Louis, 206

Lipsky, Seth, 275
Lipstadt, Deborah, 192
Lipton, Seymour, 642–643
Liptzin, Keni, 450
Literacy
    rate of Jewish immigrants, 262–263, 541
    requirement for immigrants, 35, 42
Lithuania, 24, 37–38, 70, 90, 97, 142, 253, 263, 266, 268, 299, 370–371, 375, 386, 412, 499, 527, 614, 646, 652, 654, 768
Little Odessa, 47, 548
Little Richard, 670–672, 674
Little Rock, AR, 99, 148–149
Litvak, Anatole, 463–464
Liveright, Horace, 575
Livingston, Sigmund, 139, 184, 243
Lloyd, Harold, 486
Locke, John, 14
Lodz (Poland), 37, 225, 365, 595, 608
Loeb, Albert, 406
Loeb, James, 428
Loesser, Frank, 457
Loew, Marcus, 461, 504–505
Loew's Inc., 124, 461
Loewenstein, Rudolph, 712
Loftus, Elizabeth, 709
Logemann, Jane, 638
London, Jack, 378
London, Meyer, 236, 284, 286, 313–314 (photo), 315–316
London, England, 10, 16, 26, 46, 54, 145, 150–151, 171, 189, 209–211, 343, 368, 408, 450, 459, 462, 483, 534, 544, 557, 583, 588–589, 594, 613–614, 659, 676, 692, 695, 721
    anti-Jewish riots in, 11
    Hasidim in, 97, 101
    Jewish anarchist press in, 265, 298, 564
    Jewish ghetto, 51
    rabbinate, 54
    Zionist meetings in, 206
London School of Economics, 596, 721
Long, Breckinridge, 219, 222
Long Island, NY, 165, 296, 673, 676–677, 685
Long Island University, 516, 519
Long is the Road, 224
Longfellow, Henry Wadsworth, 169, 470, 544
Longyear, Barry, 510
Lopez, Aaron, 13–14, 418, 770
Lord & Taylor, 395
Lord, Alice, 525
Los Alamos laboratories, 155, 290–291, 296
Los Angeles, 132–134, 152, 154, 192, 210, 225, 258–259, 353, 355–356, 445, 460, 482–483, 505–507, 568, 597,

656, 670, 673, 676, 678, 681, 698–699, 701, 703, 716
    Hasidim in, 98, 101
    HUC-JIR branch, 79–80, 133–134, 446
    ILGWU in, 381, 383
    Jewish Labor Committee in, 254
    Jewish press in, 270
    Museum of Tolerance, 259
    psychoanalysis in, 712–713
    Sephardim in, 5, 8
    Simon Wiesenthal Center headquarters, 256
    Soviet Jewish émigrés in, 47–49, 134
    University of Judaism, 86, 134
    Watts riot, 429
    Yiddish theater in, 452 (illustration), 454
Los Angeles Dodgers, 517–518, 531–532
Los Angeles Rams, 519
Louis, Joe, 515
Louis, Morris, 637
Louisiana, 128, 146–148, 162, 321–322, 345, 401, 419, 423
Louisville, KY, 32, 146, 398
    Louis Brandeis and, 148, 335, 342, 345
Lovers of Zion (*Hovevei Zion*), 152, 203–204
Lovestone, Jay, 253, 284
The Lovin' Spoonful, 674
Low Company, 566–568
Lowell, A. Lawrence, 336, 344, 646
Lowell, James Russell, 170
Lowenthal, Leo, 713, 715
Lower East Side, 29, 42, 48, 54, 70, 115 (photo)–116, 121–124, 286, 290, 293–294, 297, 315, 343, 349, 368, 461–463, 465, 470, 481, 514–515, 521, 534, 546, 550, 556, 566, 569, 575, 599–600, 683, 685, 699
    anarchism, 297–298
    boundaries of, 115
    cafés, 120
    crime in, 117, 349–350
    garment industry and unions, 116–120, 252, 376
    Hasidim, 98
    housing in, 116, 120–121
    Jewish population, 115–116, 262, 349
    rent strike, 376
    Sephardim, 4–5, 116
    settlement house movement, 117–118, 184, 409, 518
    socialism, 206, 286, 313–316
    synagogues and Jewish institutions, 115, 117–119, 121, 751
    Yiddish press, 115, 117, 119, 121, 262–271
    Yiddish theater, 115, 119, 121, 450, 494
Loyalists in American Revolution, 12, 14

Lubin, Sigmund, 460
Lubitsch, Ernst, 463
Lublin, Poland, 494, 659
Luciano, Charley "Lucky," 125, 351–352
Luckman, Sid, 518–519
Lueger, Karl, 171
Luftwaffe, 186
Lumet, Sidney, 465
Luria, Isaac, 636, 642
Lusitania, sinking of, 182, 482, 486
Lutheranism and Lutherans, 14, 19, 22, 33, 44, 667
Lux, Lilian, 454
Luxembourg, 389
Luxemburg, Rosa, 306
Lynd, Helen, 158–159
Lynd, Robert, 158–159

Maas, Samuel, 43
Maccabiah games, 520, 525–526
Macdonald, Dwight, 597, 622, 628
Machado, David Mendez, 749
Machlup, Fritz, 720–721
Mack, Julian, 205–206, 240
Macy, Rowland Hussey, 396–397
Macy's, 28, 395–398, 400
Mad About You, 477, 479–480
Mad Magazine, 472–473
Madison, James, 19, 22
Madole, James, 193
"The Magic Barrel," 578, 580, 693
Magnes, Judah, 184, 363, 751
Magnin, Isaac, 396, 398
Mahler, Margaret, 712
Mailer, Norman, 302
Maimonides, Moses, 53, 654
Maimonides College, 112, 141–142
Maione, Harry "Happy," 352
Majdanek, 230, 257
Major League Baseball Players Association, 533–534
Malachowsky, Hillel, 751
Malamud, Bernard, 301, 546, 560, 562, 577–578 (photo), 579–581, 693
Maltz, Albert, 464
Mamas and the Papas, 674
Mamet, David, 139, 581–584
Man Ray (Emmanuel Radnitzky), 640, 655–656 (photo), 657–658
Mandel, Marvin, 148
Mandelbaum, Frederika "Marm," 29
Manhattan Bridge, 124
Manhattan College, 516
Manhattan Project, 290–292
Mann, Alonzo, 179
Mann, Erika, 388
Mann, Klaus, 388
Mann, Thomas, 388, 576, 630
Manuel, Frank, 760
Mapai party, 213–214

March (February) 1917 Revolution in Russia, 19, 410
March on the Pentagon (1967), 302
Marciano, Rocky, 515
Marcus, Jacob Rader, 274, 301, 418, 764–765 (photo), 766–768, 770–771
Marcus, Mickey, 618
Marcuse, Herbert, 35, 302, 714, 716, 760
Margolis, Moses Sebulun, 70
Margoshes, Samuel, 187
Margulies, Donald, 454, 584–586
Marinov, Jacob, 470
Marjorie Morningstar
  film, 465, 616
  novel, 465, 615–616
Markovitz, Harry, 721
Marks, Leon, 323
Marshall, George, 193
Marshall, John, 346
Marshall, Louis, 30, 33, 42, 184–185, 240–242, 278, 282, 410, 428, 770
Marshall, Thurgood, 347
Martin, Billy, 518
Martin, Dean, 487, 507
Martin, Tony, 197, 429
Martin, William McChesney, 719
Marvel Comics, 472, 676
Marx Brothers, 462, 481 (photo)–483, 486
Marx, Chico (Leonard), 462, 481–482, 486
Marx, David, 422
Marx, Groucho (Julius), 462, 481–483, 486, 492, 684
Marx, Harpo (Adolph), 462, 481–484, 486
Marx, Herbert (Zeppo), 481
Marx, Karl, 30, 285, 309, 368, 378, 380, 470, 651, 714–717, 731–732, 734–735
Marx, Milton (Gummo), 462, 481–482
Marxism, 264, 378, 380, 608, 622, 626–627, 629, 631, 714, 716, 736
Mary Tyler Moore Show, 476, 497
Maryland, 23, 113, 148, 419, 611
  and religious tests for office, 18–19, 22, 146
Masculinity, Jews and, 513–515, 519
Mashadi Jews, 7
Maslow, Abraham, 709, 760
Maslow, Will, 250
Massachusetts, 187, 273, 379, 525, 527, 675, 688
  in colonial, Revolutionary, and early national periods, 11, 13–14, 18, 22
  Lawrence, 379, 687
  Newton, 48
  Provincetown, 569
  Socialist Party of, 383
  Soviet Jewish émigrés in, 48
  See also Boston; Brandeis University; Brookline; Harvard University;

National Yiddish Book Center; Smith College
Massachusetts Institute of Technology (MIT), 718–719, 721–722
The Masses, 569
Masters, Edgar Lee, 575
Mather, Increase, 538
Mattapan, 165, 187–189, 687
Matthews, Robert, 189, 194
Mauritania, 259
Maus, 473
Mauthausen, 256, 588
May, Elaine, 465, 488–489
May Laws, 37, 136
Mayer, Louis B., 461
Mayer, Nathan, 542, 544
Mays, Willie, 521
Mazursky, Paul, 465
McCalden, David, 192
McCarthy, Joseph, 245, 291–292, 301, 340, 367, 472, 605, 630
McCarthyism, 244–245, 301, 587, 715, 744
McClellan, John, 367
McCollum v. Board of Education, 244
McCoy, Rhody, 430
McDonald, Country Joe, 675
McGill University, 583, 720
McGraw, John J., 517
McGuffey Reader, 181
McKinley, William, 181, 299
McKinney, Cynthia, 281, 431
McLaren, Malcolm, 676
McLuhan, Marshall, 630
McReynolds, James Clark, 336
McVeigh, Timothy, 189, 191, 194, 259
Mead, Margaret, 725–726
Meaney, Helen, 525
Meany, George, 253, 390
Meed, Benjamin, 225
Meenes, Max, 709
Meir, Golda (Golda Meyerson), 130, 212–213 (photo), 214–216, 319, 441, 618
Melamed, S. M., 355
Melamid, Alexander, 640, 648–649
The Melting Pot, 51–52
Melton, Florence, 755
Melville, Herman, 171, 617, 624, 629
Memphis, TN, 145–146, 148, 339, 344, 395, 402, 415, 671
Mencken, H. L., 174, 191, 575
Mendelssohn, Moses, 53, 717, 745
Mendes, Henry P., 69, 184
Menken, Adah Isaacs, 543–544
Menorah Journal, 53, 91, 215, 274, 288, 301, 570, 631
Menshevism, 370–371, 380
Merchant, Larry, 521
The Merchant of Venice, 181, 540, 564
Mereminsky, Israel, 374

Meretz, 273
Merman, Ethel, **686, 698**
Mermelstein, Mel, **192, 257**
Merril, Judith, **507**
Merton, Robert (Meyer Schkolnick),
 731–732, 734–737, 739–740
Merzbacher, Leo, **31, 75**
Messianism, false, **39, 342, 610**
Messinger, Ruth, **94**
Messner, Edward, **670**
Messner, Ida, **670**
Messner, Leo, **670**
Methodists, **14, 331, 573–574**
Metro-Goldwyn-Mayer, **133, 461**
Metternich, Klemens von, **317**
Metzger, Tom, **257**
Meyer, Annie Nathan, **2–3, 770**
Meyer-Bernstein, Gerda, **644**
Miami Beach, FL, **127–131, 440–442, 555**
Miami Dolphins, **128**
Miami, FL, **127–131, 149, 225, 227, 403,
 441, 518, 680**
Michel, Ernest, **225**
Michelbacher, Maximilian, **146**
Michelson, Albert A., **742**
Michigan, **180, 182, 187–188, 376, 382,
 731.** *See also* Detroit
Midler, Bette, **465, 497**
Midstream, **215, 273**
Mikhalesco, Mikhel, **453**
Mikva, Abner, **139**
Mikveh Israel (Philadelphia), **2, 10, 12, 17,
 20, 31, 54, 68, 76, 83, 107, 111,
 140–142, 272, 750**
Mila 18, **224, 458, 612–613**
Miles, Nelson, **238**
Milgram, Stanley, **709**
Military chaplains, Jewish, **768**
 Civil War, **112, 324**
 Korean War, **592**
 World War II, **330–331, 767**
Miller, Albert, **363**
Miller, Arthur, **582, 584, 586–587 (photo),
 588–590**
Miller, Frieda, **376–377**
Miller, Louis, **265**
Miller, Marvin, **533 (photo)–535**
Miller, Merton, **719**
"Million Man March," **257**
 distribution of antisemitic tracts at,
 199
Milwaukee, **498, 503**
 Goldie Mabovitch (Meir) in, **212–213**
 Hasidim in, **98, 104**
 labor organizing in, **382**
 socialism in, **34, 284, 378**
 Yiddish press, **265**
Milwaukee Brewers, **518**
Minkoff, Isaiah, **253**
Minneapolis, MN, **167, 352, 355, 503, 751**

Minnesota, **46, 163, 352, 476, 503, 532, 674**
Minsk, **48–49, 657, 733**
Mints, Moyshe, **265**
Mintz, Leo, **672**
Minutemen, **355**
Mirvis, Tova, **546**
Mississippi, **147–149, 324, 391, 401, 403,
 423, 464**
Mississippi Delta, **145**
Mitchell, Margaret, **611**
Mitchell, Samuel, **708**
Mitchell, Wesley C., **719–720**
Mitla Pass, **611, 613**
Mix, Ron, **518–519**
Mizrachi, **71, 90, 205**
Mizrachi Organization of America, **142**
Mizrahi Jews, **1, 6–8**
Mobile, AL, **27, 146, 301, 666, 767–768**
Modern Language Association, **631**
Modigliani, Franco, **719**
Mogulesco, Sigmund, **450, 452**
Moise, Abraham, **75**
Moise, Penina, **147, 541, 543**
Moldavian folk music, **682**
Molotov-von Ribbontrop Pact. See
 Hitler–Stalin Pact
Moment, **274**
Monday Night Football, **521**
Monis, Judah, **538, 541**
Monroe, James, **539–540**
Monroe, Marilyn, **129, 588**
Monsey, NY, **98**
Montagu, Ashley (Israel Ehrenberg), **734**
Montreal, Canada, **29, 97, 101, 311, 382,
 558, 561, 583, 720**
Montgomery, AL, **148, 226**
 bus boycott, **660**
Moore v. Dempsey, **178**
Moore, Charles Werner, **760**
Morais, Sabato, **69, 83, 141–143**
Morgan, J. P., **28, 408, 410**
Morgenstern, Julian, **79**
Morgenthau, Jr., Henry, **211, 219, 222, 277**
Morgenthau, Sr., Henry, **288**
Morocco, **8, 33, 128, 442, 669, 759**
Morrow, Bruce "Cousin Brucie," **672**
Morse, Josiah, **708**
Mortara affair, **32–33, 151–152, 281, 542,
 768**
Moscow, **37–38, 48–49, 251, 287, 364, 482,
 555, 565, 702, 770**
Moscow Trials, **215, 287, 626, 628**
Moses, **20, 83, 170, 419, 422, 470, 503, 593,
 641, 704–705**
Moses, Raphael J., **770**
Moskowitz, Belle, **289**
Moskowitz, Sam, **507**
Moss, Celia, **542**
Moss, Richard, **533**
Mossad, **509**

Most, Johann, **298, 308**
Mother, image of Jewish, **476, 488, 496,
 508, 584, 603, 702**
Moynihan, Daniel Patrick, **306**
Mr. Sammler's Planet, **561**
Muchnick, Isadore, **427**
Muhammad, Elijah, **192, 198, 444**
Muhammad, Khalid, **195–199**
Muhammad, Warith Deen, **192, 442,
 444–445**
Mumford, Lewis, **288**
Muncie, IN, **157–161**
Muni, Paul (Muni Weisenfreund), **137, 453**
Münsterberg, Hugo, **707–708**
Muravchik, Emanuel, **254**
Murder, Inc., **125, 352–354, 356–357**
Musar Movement, **90**
Muscular Christianity movement, **513**
Museum of Jewish Heritage, New York,
 225
Museum of the Diaspora, Tel Aviv, **226**
Museum of the Southern Jewish
 Experience, 149
Muslim American Society (MAS), **444**
Muslim Americans, **442–446**
Muslim Public Affairs Council (MPAC), **444**
Mussolini, Benito, **328, 426**
My Fair Lady, **457–458**
My Life as a Man, **603**
My Name is Asher Lev, **591**
Myer, Buddy, **517**
Myers, Abraham, **323**
Mysell, Hyman, **453**

Naismith, James, **525, 527**
The Nanny, **477, 479–480**
Napoleon Bonaparte, **318, 543**
 and Jewish emancipation, **6–7, 203,
 395–396**
 defeat of, **317**
Napoleon III, **189**
Napoleonic wars, **317, 395**
Nasser, Gamal Abdel, **244**
Nathan, Robert R., **721**
Nathan, Syd, **670–671**
Nation of Islam (NOI), **136, 189–190, 192,
 194–199, 245, 257, 411, 429–430,
 442, 444–445**
National Alliance, **189, 193, 259**
National Association for the Advancement
 of Colored People (NAACP), **126,
 249–250, 252, 255, 280, 282, 367,
 403, 424, 428, 434, 758**
National Association of Jewish Holocaust
 Survivors, 225
National Basketball Association (NBA),
 516–517
National Book Award, **761**
 Saul Bellow's, **557, 560–561**
 Irving Howe's, **623**

Bernard Malamud's, 577–578
Isaac Bashevis Singer's, 606
National Broadcasting Company (NBC),
474, 477, 496, 505, 586, 701
National Bureau of Economic Research,
718–720
National Civic Federation, 367
National Collegiate Athletic Association
(NCAA), 516
National Conference of Christians and
Jews (NCCJ), 437
National Council of Jewish Women, 32,
35, 54, 117, 129, 138, 148, 153–154,
184, 309, 433, 435
National Council of Synagogues, 91
National Education Association (NEA),
390, 392
National Federation of Temple Sisterhoods
(NFTS), 78, 108
National Federation of Temple Youth
(NFTY), 79
National Football League (NFL), 519, 534
National Football League Players
Association, 534
National Invitation Tournament, 516
National Jewish Community Relations
Advisory Council (NJCRAC), 279,
432–434, 524
National Negro Convention (1853), 421
National Organization for Women
(NOW), 309–310
National Pencil Factory, 175, 178–179
National Psychological Association for
Psychoanalysis, 712
National Recovery Administration (NRA),
387
National Renaissance Party, 193
National Review, 304
National Socialist White Peoples Party, 193
National Yiddish Book Center, 273
National Youth Alliance (NYA), 191
Nativism, 159–160, 183, 216–217, 219,
278, 322, 327, 371, 420–421, 423,
499, 707–708
The Natural, 577
Nazi war criminals, 220, 227, 241,
256–257, 259, 588
and statute of limitations, 239, 256–257
as winners of the Cold War, 256
in Arab lands, 239
paroles of, 239
U.S. leniency toward, 256
West German leniency toward,
238–239, 256
Nazis and Nazism (German), 35, 49, 79, 97,
99–100, 103, 148, 167, 173, 186, 188,
190–192, 206, 209–211, 216–223,
225–230, 236, 238–239, 241,
243–244, 246, 251–254, 256–257,
259, 278, 282, 287–288, 295,

312–313, 316–317, 327–330,
332–333, 366, 385, 388–389, 458,
463–466, 473, 486, 489, 493, 509,
514–515, 519–520, 526, 556, 560,
570–571, 576–577, 588–589, 593,
610, 612, 617, 621. 636, 645, 649,
675, 704, 712–715, 719, 722–724,
727, 732, 740, 744, 753–754, 757, 769
American film depictions of, 464, 486
and Albert Einstein, 744
and science, 740
Nazi party, Germany, 180–181, 184
Nazi oppression of women, 389
Nazi propaganda in United States, 389
Nazi-Soviet Pact. *See* Hitler–Stalin Pact
Neiman-Marcus, 398, 402
Nelson, Lemrick, 201
Neoconservatives, 275, 278, 300–306, 392,
557, 716, 733
Netanyahu, Benzion, 209–212
Netanyahu, Jonathan, 615, 618
Netherlands, 413–415
exclusion of Jews, 412
German conquest of, 389
Jews in, 9–11, 26, 404
Neturei Karta, 100
Neuman, Alfred E., 472
Neumann, Franz, 35, 714
Neumark, Devorah, 639
Neustein, Joshua, 226
New Amsterdam, 2, 9–11, 15, 128
New Christians (Conversos), 1, 8,
127–128, 238, 343, 413–417
New Deal, 277–280, 289, 313, 336–339,
345–346, 371–372, 385, 387
New Jersey, 140, 224, 246, 275, 601, 661,
673, 733, 744
in colonial and early national periods,
18–19
crime in, 351, 356
Jewish agricultural colonies in,
162–164
Jewish anarchism in, 297
Jewish immigrants to, 164
Orthodox Jews in, 167
Soviet Jewish émigrés in, 48
yeshiva in, 104
See also Newark, NJ; Roth, Philip
New Leader, 295, 389, 557
New Left, 255, 289, 302, 305, 483,
622–623, 630, 733
New Masses, 569–570, 652, 692
New Mexico, 7, 155–156, 291
New Netherland, 11
New Odessa colony, 162–163
New Orleans, 43–44, 131, 146, 321, 398,
418
and jazz, 699–700
in Civil War, 146, 321, 324–325
Jews in, 147–148, 321, 324–325, 768

New School for Social Research, 35, 622,
692, 719, 722, 728, 733
New Spain, 155
New Square, NY, 98, 103
New York, state of, 35, 71, 75, 100, 103,
106, 239, 280, 285, 287–289,
308–309, 339, 372, 376–377,
384–385, 387, 441, 541, 553, 559,
618, 756
Albany, 107
Assembly, 125, 287, 315, 360, 540
Civil War regiment, 322–323
Court of Appeals, 288, 337
executions in, 293
in Revolutionary and early national
periods, 18–19
Jewish Board of Guardians, 125
Jews in Nassau county, 165
Mamaroneck, 616
Port Jervis, 754
Poughkeepsie, 564
Senate, 287
Supreme Court, 337, 343
Utica, 541
women's suffrage movement in,
386–387
Woodstock, 675
See also Catskills; New York City;
Syracuse
New York Association for New Americans,
48
New York City, 5–6, 20, 27, 40, 46, 54, 60,
71–72, 75, 77–80, 83, 90–91, 110,
126, 132–133, 141–143, 146, 148,
152, 163, 172, 175, 181, 210, 215,
221–223, 233, 236, 243–244,
270–272, 274–275, 288, 291, 300,
306, 317, 327, 338, 340, 366–367,
371, 374, 387, 389, 401, 415, 420,
422, 425–426, 429, 439–440, 462,
476–478, 482, 489, 493, 496–498,
500–501, 503–504, 508, 538–541,
544, 547, 550, 552–553, 556, 559,
561, 564, 573–575, 577, 580,
582–583, 586–589, 596–597, 600,
608, 617–618, 621–626, 628, 631,
635, 637, 652, 675, 683–689,
691–692, 694–697, 699, 701–703,
719, 721–725, 731, 733, 741,
749–753, 764, 768–769
antisemitism in, 23, 45, 60, 171–172,
174, 187–189, 424, 426
anarchism in, 120, 297–299, 382,
563–566, 594–595
and comics, 469–470, 472–474
artists and art scene, 635–636, 640–642,
646, 650–651, 654–657, 659–660,
662–663
Board of Aldermen, 253
Broadway theater, 455–460, 463

New York City *(continued)*
Bronx, 121, 215, 285, 291, 301, 428,
453–454, 473, 475–476, 491, 496,
516, 529, 534, 555, 621, 625, 658,
661–662, 673, 685
Central Asian Jews in, 48
Chinatown, 684
crime, 29, 286, 315, 349–357
department stores, 28, 395–400
diamond business, 105, 404–406
East Harlem, 515
fur industry and workers, 362–365, 521
garment industry and unions, 29, 40,
105, 116, 119–121, 123, 269, 297,
308, 313, 342, 345, 354, 356,
359–363, 365–366, 370, 372,
375–377, 381, 383–386, 563–564,
594–595, 615, 657
German Jews in, 27–34, 41, 75, 150,
171, 175, 181, 362, 395–396, 408,
555, 571
Hasidim in, 97–106, 200–202
in colonial, Revolutionary, and early
national periods, 2, 10–12, 14, 16,
20–21, 23, 26, 107
Jewish music in, 667, 680, 682
Jewish organizations and institutions
in, 32, 41, 118, 125, 225–227, 235,
237–238, 240, 247, 252–254, 256,
301, 524, 752, 770
Jewish population of, 3, 12, 15, 28,
42–43, 45, 59, 63, 89, 115, 120, 124,
130, 136, 167, 229, 291, 294, 332,
351, 736
libraries, 125, 142–143, 201, 561
psychoanalysis in, 710–713
rock and punk music in, 672–673,
675–678
Sephardim in, 5–7, 51, 181, 336, 571
settlement houses in, 35, 409, 518
socialism in, 119–120, 125, 284–287,
313–316, 326, 360, 365, 376, 615
Soviet Jewish émigrés in, 47–50
sports in, 514–522, 524–526, 529–532,
534–535
synagogues and temples in, 2, 7, 16, 19,
21–22, 31, 70–71, 75, 107, 113, 181,
209, 224–225, 317, 669, 746, 749
teachers' unionism in, 255, 303,
390–393
transplants in Miami/Miami Beach,
127–129
World's Fair (1939), 239
Yiddish press, 102, 119, 129, 188,
261–268, 272, 316, 360, 379,
564–566, 594–595, 615
Yiddish theater, 119, 124, 449–455,
494–495, 554–555
Yorkville, 355, 389, 482
Zionism in, 204–205, 208–209

See also Brooklyn; Brownsville; City
College of New York; Columbia
University; Harlem; Jewish
Theological Seminary; Lower East
Side; New York University; Ocean
Hill–Brownsville experiment and
conflict; Williamsburg; Yeshiva
University
New York City Symphony, **689**
New York Giants
baseball, 517–518
football, 519, 522
New York Jets, **522**
New York Kehillah, **184**, 363, 751
New York Medical College, **712**
New York Philharmonic, **686, 688–689,**
695
New York Post, **188,** 521, 733
New York Psychoanalytic Society, **711**
New York Psychoanalytic Society and
Institute (NYPI), **711–712**
The New York Review of Books, **302,** 306
New York University (NYU), **53,** 287, 491,
516, 519, 521, 529, 534–535, 559,
569, 626, 719
New York University College of Medicine,
709
New York University Law School, **315,** 521
New York Yankees, **518,** 521, 529–530, 532
New Yorker, 473, 482, **685**
and A. J. Liebling, 521
and Hannah Arendt, 724
and Isaac Bashevis Singer, 606
and Leo Rosten, 596–597
and Norman Podhoretz, 301
and Robert Merton, 736
and Saul Bellow, 557
New Zionist Organization of America
(NZOA), **209–212**
Newark, NJ
and ILGWU, 359
and Jewish anti–Nazi resistance, 355
and organized crime, 350–351,
355–356
and Philip Roth, 586, 601
and Yiddish press, 266
and Yiddish theater, 454
race riot, 429
Newman, Barnett, **636–637, 642, 646–647,**
650
Newman, Harry, **519**
Newman, Louis I., **209**
Newman, Paul, **583**
Newman, Pauline, **308, 374–378, 386–387**
Newport, Rhode Island
and slave trade, 13, 415, 418
during American Revolution, 13–14
Jews in, 2, 9–11, 13–14, 19–20, 145,
169, 538–539, 544, 749
Sephardim in, 2

synagogue in, 2, 10, 13, 16, 19–20, 107,
538, 544
Nichols, Anne, **475**
Nichols, Mike, **488–489**
Niger, Shmuel, **288**
Night, 225
Night school and Jews, 117, 120, 402, 569,
580, 596
Nitzberg, Irving, 352
Nixon, Richard M., 279, **317–319,** 346,
348, 438, 483, 507, 603, 617, 619,
719, 732, 758
Noah, Mordecai, 2–3, 272, **539–541,**
543–544
Nobel laureates, American Jewish, 134,
226, 228, 247, 274, 449, 557, 562,
717–721, 741–742, 745
North Carolina, 81, 148, 259
and religious tests for office, 18–20, 146
antisemitic terrorism, 403
Greensboro, 81, 148, 157–159
Jews in, 148, 157–159, 401
North End of Boston, 42, 342, 527
Northwest Ordinance, 18–19
Northwestern University, 339, 557–559
Northwestern Law School, 344
Norwood, Stephen H., 199
Nostra Aetate, 242, **245,** 437, 440
Nuchi, Natan, **645**
Nuremberg trials, 256
Nussbaum, Perry, **403**
Nyro, Laura, **675–676**

Oakland, CA, **152,** 154, 569, 702
Object Relations theory, **712**
*The Occident and American Jewish
Advocate,* 31, 76, 111, 141, 272–273,
541, 543, 771
Ocean Hill-Brownsville experiment and
conflict, 126, 255, 303, **305–306,**
391, **430–431**
Ochs, Adolph, 31, **243**
O'Connell, William Cardinal, **189**
O'Connor, Sandra Day, **346**
Odessa, 38, 48, 162, 666
pogrom in, 38
O'Dwyer, William, **124**
Oglethorpe, James, **14**
Ohlin, Bertil, **720**
Ohrbach's, **398**
O'Keefe, Georgia, **637**
Oklahoma! **457–458**
Oklahoma City bombing, Murrah Federal
Building (1995), **191, 194, 246, 259**
Oklahoma City National Memorial, **230**
Okun, Arthur, **721**
Old Men at Midnight, **593**
The Old Religion, **582**
Olitski, Jules, **650**
Oliver, Revilo P., **193**

Olsen, Tillie, **551**

Olympic games, **523, 525–526**
    Amsterdam (1928), 526
    Antwerp (1920), 525
    Berlin (1936), 230, 239, 253, 519–520, 526
    Los Angeles (1932), 525–526
    Mexico City (1968), 526
    Munich (1972), 483, 520, 522
    Paris (1924), 523 (photo), 525

Oppenheim, Moritz, **639**

Oppenheimer, J. Robert, **292**

Oransky, Howard, **644**

Orchard Street, **121**

The Order, **189, 194, 257, 259**

Orgen, Jacob "Little Augie," **354, 356**

The Origins of Totalitarianism, **722–723**

Ormandy, Eugene, **689**

Ornitz, Samuel, **288, 464**

Orphanages, Jewish, **32, 35, 118, 136, 150**

ORT, **139, 433**

Orthodox Union. See Union of Orthodox
    Jewish Congregations of America

Orwell, George, **175, 510, 632**

Oslo Accords, **444**

Osterman, Rosanna Dyer, **43–44**

Otis, James, **14**

Ottoman Empire, **412**
    and Damascus ritual murder case, 32
    Sephardim from, 1, 3–4

Outcault, R. F., **469**

Ozick, Cynthia, **551–552, 560, 606–607**

Paige, Satchel, **521**

Pale of Settlement, **36–38, 78, 97, 162, 326, 503, 565, 683, 687, 733**

Palestine, Mandatory, **78–79, 90, 93, 130, 144, 203, 203, 205–216, 220, 232, 249, 254–255, 327, 342–343, 367, 373–374, 385, 387, 407, 410, 525, 555, 571, 575, 577, 612, 689, 744**
    Arab riots and massacres in, 208, 273, 287
    Hasidim in, 97, 100, 104
    Jewish immigration to, and
        curtailment of, 206, 208–211, 213, 218, 220–221, 232, 239, 241, 404, 577, 722, 744
    partition of, 241, 244, 642
    See also Yishuv

Palestine, pre-Mandatory, **2, 171–172, 203–205, 213, 215, 238–239, 271, 288, 316, 326–327, 342, 397, 540, 543–544, 555–556, 572, 615, 703, 751**
    Jewish agricultural settlements in, 162, 203–204
    Jewish immigration to, 39, 45, 52, 213, 268
    See also Yishuv

Palestine Symphony Orchestra, **689**

Palestinian terrorists' murder of Israeli
    Olympic athletes, **520, 522**

Paley, Grace, **551, 560**

Paley, Johann, **267**

Paley, William, **137, 474**

Palmer raids and Red Scare, **35, 182, 299, 308, 313, 338**

Pan-American Federation of Labor, **368**

Panken, Jacob, **360–361**

Paramount Pictures, **133, 461, 505**

Parent, Gail, **552**

Paris, Harold, **643**

Paris Commune, **566**

Paris, France, **232–233, 251, 256–257, 388–389, 455, 457, 462, 501, 544, 555, 559–560, 562, 575–576, 592, 631, 655–658, 675, 693, 705, 719, 722**

Paris Peace Conference (1919), **205, 240, 368**

Park, Robert, **262, 276, 731**

Parks, Rosa, **660**

Parsons, Albert, **298**

Parsons, Talcott, **731, 734–736**

Partisan Review, **288, 301, 557, 609, 621, 625–628, 630, 652, 757**

Passover, **68, 95, 112, 150–153, 163, 187, 345, 373, 424, 454, 636, 689**

Patinkin, Mandy, **139–140, 682**

Patler, John, **193**

Patterson, Floyd, **521**

Paulding, James Kirke, **541**

Pearl Harbor, **190, 237, 330, 372, 515, 529, 612**

Pearson, Drew, **190**

Peck, Gregory, **713**

Peddlers, Jewish, **10, 22, 27–30, 37, 41–42, 44, 63, 117, 121, 135–136, 139, 146–148, 321–322, 324, 344, 360, 395–396, 400–401, 418–419, 422, 527, 621, 658**

Pekar, Harvey, **474**

Pekelis, Alexander, **249–250**

Peleg, Ephraim, **226**

Pelley, William Dudley, **355**

Pennsylvania, **10–14, 18–20, 22, 27, 143, 157–158, 160, 297, 366, 503, 672, 765.** *See also* Johnstown;
    Philadelphia; Pittsburgh

Pennsylvania State University, **353**

People's Council for Democracy and
    Peace, **326**

Peretz, I. L., **554–555, 606–608**

Peretz, Martin, **733**

Perkins, Frances, **376, 385**

Perlman, Selig, **378–381**

Perlow, Jacob, **98**

Pershing, John, **239**

Petegorsky, David, **250**

Peter, Paul and Mary, **681**

Pfeffer, Leo, **250**

Pfister, Oskar, **710**

Phagan, Mary, **176–180**

Philadelphia, **163, 171, 210, 380, 420, 429, 431, 460, 494, 496, 505, 539, 543, 565, 655, 657, 672, 688–689, 691, 708**
    antisemitism in, 23
    during American Revolution, 13–14
    English-language Jewish press, 768
    Jewish organizations and, 248, 254, 615
    Jewish schools and institutions in, 91, 112, 141–144, 750, 768
    Jewish women in, 141–142
    Jews in, 10–13, 15–16, 20, 26, 28, 31, 42, 54, 76–77, 91, 111, 116, 140–145, 147, 160, 272, 298, 349, 428, 524, 541, 734, 736
    Main Line, 165
    organized crime, 350–351, 355, 357
    organized labor, 359, 376
    "Philadelphia Group," 142–143
    radical groups, 298–299
    sports, 516–517, 519–520
    synagogues and temples, 2, 10, 17, 19, 31, 54, 68, 76, 83, 103, 107, 111–113, 140–143, 767
    Wanamaker's, 400
    Yiddish press, 264, 266
    Yiddish theater, 450, 454
    Zionism in, 142–144, 204

Philadelphia Eagles, **519**

Philadelphia Orchestra, **691, 694**

Philadelphia Phillies, **517**

Philadelphia Warriors, **516**

Philanthropy, Jewish, **2, 6, 32, 41–47, 50, 53, 117–118, 129, 136, 139, 142, 144, 152, 184, 238, 240, 301, 356, 386, 395, 397–400, 406–410, 418, 422–424, 499, 524, 728, 751–752, 754–755, 759, 770**

Philippines campaigns, **239**

Phillips, Jonas B., **539–540**

Phillips, Michelle, **674**

Phillips, Philip, **146**

Phillips, William, **625–628, 630**

Philipson, David, **542, 770**

Photography, **636, 647, 656–657**

Physics, **267, 724, 740–744, 760**

Picon, Molly, **453, 494–495**

Pierce, Franklin, **345**

Pierce, William, **189, 191, 193–194, 259**

Piersall, Jimmy, **520**

Pike, Lipman "Lip," **517**

Pinchik, Pierre, **668**

Ping pong, **520**

Pinner, Moritz, **419**

Pins and Needles, **366**

Pinsker, Leo, **38**

Pinski, David, 452, 574
Pinto, Isaac, 538
Pioneer Women, 213
Pioneers of Liberty, 266, 298–299, 565
Pipp, Edwin. G. (E. G.), 182–183
Pitkin Avenue (Brownsville), 122, 124–125
Pittsburgh, 12, 81, 99, 103, 206, 224, 254, 266, 299, 395, 524, 671
Pittsburgh Pirates, 518, 530
Pittsburgh Platform, 69, 77–78, 83, 142, 746
Pius IX, Pope, 281, 437
Pius XII, Pope, 437
Planck, Max, 743
PM, 188, 733
Poalei-Zion, 205, 208, 213
Podhoretz, Norman, 274, 300–305, 616
Podoloff, Maurice, 516
Poe, Edgar Allan, 564, 624
Pogroms
    in Russia and Eastern Europe, 32–33, 37–39, 41, 45, 49, 51, 59, 128, 130, 136, 162, 195, 203, 212, 239–240, 263–264, 268, 271, 286–287, 315, 327, 359, 378, 409, 424, 428–429, 436, 450, 457, 473, 544, 565, 576, 609–610, 683, 733
    in Germany, 218–219, 389
    in Morocco, 33
    Jewish self-defense, 188, 514
    See also Arab massacres of Jews in Palestine (1929); Kishinev; *Kristallnacht*
Poland, 37, 50, 255, 308, 420, 461, 495, 515, 554, 576, 594, 624, 768
    and Hasidim, 99
    and Pale of Settlement, 36
    annihilation of Jews in, 100, 220, 222, 466
    International Brigade from, 328
    Jewish Bund in, 253, 365
    Jewish immigration from, 26, 49, 132, 150–151, 224, 263, 322, 385, 483, 566, 611, 669
    Jewish migration to, 24, 412
    Jews in, 136, 385, 439, 497, 592, 606
    Nazi invasion and conquest of, 99, 253, 330, 366
    pogroms in, 37, 239, 327
    post-Six Day War antisemitic campaigns, 328
    yeshivas of, 24
    Yiddish film in, 495
    Yiddish in, 608
    Zionism in, 71
    See also Antisemitism; Lodz; Lublin; Warsaw
Polansky, Esther, 363
Polizzi, Big Al, 351
Pollack, Ben, 700

Pollack, Eunice G., 199
Pollock, Jackson, 649, 651
Polner, Murray, 275
Polo Grounds, 517
Pomus, Doc, 673
Ponce de León, Juan, 127
Pontiac's War, 12
Pop Art, 640, 658–659
Popular Front, 372, 463, 626, 628–629
Porgy and Bess, 457, 507, 696, 698
Porter, Cole, 457, 698
Porter, Katherine Anne, 173
Portland, OR, 7, 150–154, 164, 396, 446, 501, 695
Portnoy's Complaint, 492, 601–605
Portugal, 10, 247
    and New Christians (conversos), 8, 343, 581
    and reconquest of Brazil, 2, 11, 537
    and Sephardim, 1–3, 10, 14, 43, 111, 343, 669
    and slave trade, 412–417
    crypto Jews in, 8
    expulsion of Jews from, 404, 412
    forced conversion of Jews, 413
    Inquisition in, 2–3, 13–14, 404, 413
Potofsky, Jacob, 139, 374
Potok, Chaim, 590 (photo)–594
Pound, Ezra, 174–175, 622
Pournelle, Jerry, 509
Povich, Shirley, 427, 519–521
Powderly, Terrence, 45
Powell, Adam Clayton Jr., 424
Poznanski, Gustavus, 75
Prago, Albert, 329
Prague, 24, 43, 91, 294, 335, 342, 462, 473, 547, 666
Prejudice, study of, 185, 242, 707–709, 712, 714–715
Prenner, Isidore, 298
Presbyterian church and Presbyterians, 44, 438, 456, 541, 755
Presley, Elvis, 670, 672–673
Preyer, Robert, 760
Priesand, Sally, 80, 109, 310
Princeton University, 353, 457, 518, 552, 559, 622, 652, 662, 721–722, 755–756
Progressive Association of Reform Day Schools, 753
Prohibition, 349, 351
    repeal of, 357, 700
Proletarian literature and poetry, 565–566, 569–571, 594–595, 614–615, 627–629
The Promise, 591–592
Proskauer, Joseph, 207, 222
Protocols of the Elders of Zion, 38, 180, 182–185, 187, 189, 190, 195, 241, 243–244, 246–247, 258–259, 429,

443. *See also,* Ford, Henry; Nation of Islam
Prussia, 26, 135, 147, 263, 463, 708
Prussian Academy of Sciences, 744
Psychoanalysis and Jews, 35, 459, 472, 552, 576, 710–713, 716
Psychology and Jews, 267, 372, 707–710, 760
The Public Interest, 300, 304
Pulitzer, Joseph, 469
Pulitzer Prize, 233, 459, 470, 473, 577–578, 581, 583–584, 587, 616, 733
Punk rock, 670, 676–678
Purim, 158, 481, 483, 538
Puritans, 11, 170, 538
Purple Gang, 352
Pushcart vendors, 117, 120, 124, 136, 484

QB VII, 611, 613
Quakers, 11–12, 22, 157, 420, 755
Quebec Act, 12, 15
Queens, N.Y., 165, 201, 390, 674, 678, 753
    Central Asian Jews in, 48
    Forest Hills, 48, 200, 673, 677
    Orthodox neighborhoods, 680
    Rego Park, 473

Rabbinical Council of America (RCA), 72–73, 439–440
Rabin, Yitzhak, 130, 319, 441
Rabinowitz, Dorothy, 305
Rachlis, Arnold, 94
Radcliffe College, 594
Radin, Paul, 726
Radner, Gilda, 465, 490
Rado, Sandor, 711–712
Raevsky, Charles, 264
Rafaeli, Alexander, 210
Ragpickers, 474
Rahv, Philip, 288, 301, 626–630, 757
Ramah camps, 86, 754
Rand, Archie, 474, 637–638
Rand, Otto, 576
Rangell, Leo, 713
Raphaelson, Samson, 463, 502
Raphall, Morris J., 69, 420
Rattner, Abraham, 640, 642
Ravelstein, 563
Rawidowicz, Simon, 760
Reagan, Ronald, 225, 274, 278–279, 282, 305, 346–347, 392, 589, 719, 733
    Bitburg visit, 227, 239
Reconstructionist Rabbinical Association, 90–91, 96
Reconstructionist Rabbinical College, 90–92, 94–96, 109, 144, 768
Red Army, 374
Red Hook district, Brooklyn, 588

Reform Zionists of America (ARZA), 80, 441
Reformation, Protestant, 18
Reformed Society of Israelites, 75, 147, 540
Refugees, Jewish, in World War I, 326–327
Refugees from Nazi-occupied Europe. See Exiles and Refugees from Nazi Germany and Nazi-occupied Europe
Regner, Sidney, 79
Rehnquist Supreme Court, 342, 434
Reich, Annie, 712
Reich, Robert, 279, 761
Reich, Steve, 682, 702–704
Reichmann, Frieda, 716
Reik, Theodore, 712
Reiner, Carl, 465, 475, 478, 488–489
Reiner, Fritz, 139, 688–689
Reines, Isaac Jacob, 90
Reinhardt, Elaine Rosenthal, 525
Reinhardt, Max, 453, 555
Reinharz, Jehuda, 756–757, 761
Reles, Abe, 125, 352, 354
Religious Coalition for Reproductive Choice, 91
Rembrandt van Rijn, 638–639, 661
Republican Party (post-1854), 159, 200, 236, 280, 315–316, 340, 346, 355, 367, 373, 422, 431, 470
  and Henry Ford, 182
  and Israel, 281
  and Jews, 30, 137, 278–279, 287–288, 337, 347, 360, 420
  and Revisionist Zionists, 210–211
Rescue of Jews during Holocaust and efforts to frustrate it, 209–211, 217–223, 230, 241, 244, 254, 366, 387, 466, 508, 705, 711
Resnick, Mike, 508–509
Ressler, Susan, 639, 647
Revel, Bernard, 70, 72
Revisionist Zionism, 207–212, 216
Revolutions of 1848, 30, 43, 151, 419, 724
Rhineland, 24, 30, 388
Rhoda, 476–477, 480
Rhythm & Blues, 670–673
Rice, Abraham, 68, 147
Rich's, 148, 398–399, 402–403
Richmond, Virginia, 76, 323
  antisemitism in, 324
  defense of Jews in, 325
  Jews in, 16, 111, 145–147, 401, 415, 422
  synagogues and temples, 2, 19, 111, 146
Ricker, Frances, 525
Rickey, Branch, 427
Rickles, Don, 483, 489
Rickover, Hyman, 137
Rieff, Philip, 760
Riga, Latvia, 25, 99, 548, 564, 740

Riggin, Aileen, 525
Riis, Jacob, 116
Rintel, Ruth, 226
The Rise of David Levinsky, 51, 270–271, 455
Riskin, Robert, 463
Rivers, Joan, 483, 486, 489–490
Rivers, Larry, 658–659
Rizzo, Frank, 431
Roan, Leonard Strickland, 176–178
Roanoke Island, 145
Roback, A. A., 708
Robbins, Jerome, 459, 688–689
Robbins, Trina, 473
Robeson, Paul, 518
Robinson, Edward G. (Emanuel Goldenberg), 462
Robinson, Jackie, 427, 521–522, 530
Roche, John, 760
Rockefeller, John D., 28, 128
Rockefeller, Nelson, 318, 339
Rockwell, George Lincoln, 193
Rodeph Shalom (Philadelphia), 140, 142–143
Rodgers, Richard, 399, 456–459, 698
Roe v. Wade, 341
Romanesky, Marilyn, 526
Romania, 24, 83, 462, 562, 705
  and Holocaust, 223–224
  and Yiddish publications, 261
  antisemitism and pogroms in, 38, 128, 239, 327
  birth of Yiddish theater in, 449
  Hasidim in, 100
  Jewish immigration from, 36, 38–39, 128, 224, 401, 425, 516, 529, 569
  Rumanian quarter, Lower East Side, 116
Romaniote Jews, 1, 8
Roosevelt, Eleanor, 377, 384 (photo)–385, 387, 757
Roosevelt, Franklin D., 174–175, 338, 347, 366, 373–374, 376–377, 387, 432, 576, 662, 744
  and Holocaust, 207, 211, 218–223, 241, 278
  and Jewish advisors, 219, 277–278, 338, 372, 384–385
  and Jews' political alignment, 277–281, 345, 372
Roosevelt, Theodore, 45, 52, 239, 279, 336, 378, 470, 728
Rose, Alex, 366
Rose, Ernestine, 307 (photo)–308, 322, 420
Rose Bowl, 519
Rosen, Al, 518
Rosen, Goody, 517
Rosenbach, Abraham S., 142
Rosenbaum, Thane, 546

Rosenbaum, Yankel, 201
Rosenberg case, 290–297, 301, 338
Rosenberg, Ethel, 290–297
Rosenberg, Harold, 288, 650–652
Rosenberg, Julius, 290–297
Rosenblatt, Yossele, 668
Rosenbloom, Slapsie Maxie, 514
Rosenfeld, Isaac, 139, 548, 558
Rosenfeld, Monroe, 684
Rosenfeld, Morris, 265, 363, 564, 594–595
Rosenman, Samuel, 219, 277
Rosenman, Yehuda, 242
Rosensaft, Josef (Yosel), 224–225
Rosensaft, Menachem, 226–227
Rosenthal, Elaine, 523, 526
Rosenwald, Julius, 185
  acts against antisemitism, 138, 184
  and ILGWU, 361
  and Jewish Federation, 139
  and Sears, Roebuck, 28, 136, 398, 406 (photo)–407
  and Zionism, 407
  as philanthropist, 35, 136–138, 398, 406–407, 423–424, 428
Rosenwald schools, 407, 424, 428
Rosenzweig, Franz, 301
Rosenzweig, Saul, 709
Rosh Hashanah, 72, 75, 137, 152, 344, 506, 529–530, 538, 668–669
Rosove, John, 446
Ross, Barney, 137, 515
Ross, Edward A., 378–379
Rosser, Luther Z., 177–178
Rosten, Leo, 139, 595–596 (photo), 597–598, 713
Roth, Cecil, 274
Roth, Henry, 125, 288, 546, 568, 584, 598–599 (photo), 600–601, 625
Roth, Philip, 166, 301, 492, 509, 546, 548, 560, 562, 586, 601 (photo)–606, 686
Rothafel, Samuel "Roxy," 503–504 (photo), 597–598, 713
Rothenberg, Robert C., 770
Rothko, Mark, 636–637, 642, 650
Rothkopf, Louis, 351
Rothschild, Jacob, 403
Rothstein, Arnold, 29, 117, 351–352, 354, 356
Rotterdam, 39
Roxbury (section of Boston), 103, 166, 187–189, 654
Royal African Company, 414
Rubin, Robert, 279
Rubinow, I. M., 120
Rudahl, Sharon, 473
Rumania. See Romania
Rumshinsky, Joseph, 454
Russell, Bill, 516
Russell, Henry, 539

Russian Empire, 20, 410
  anarchism in, 297–298
  and Yiddish press, 119, 261–262
  antisemitism in, 33, 37–38, 41–43, 64,
    136, 182, 189, 240, 308, 311, 326,
    359–360, 378, 409–410, 424, 578,
    740
  conscription of Jews, 37, 43
  Hasidim in, 78, 97, 99
  Jewish Bund in, 235, 253, 285, 362, 365,
    370–371, 380, 514, 652, 740, 770
  Jewish immigration from, 26, 34,
    36–43, 45–46, 62–64, 107, 116,
    120–121, 128, 132, 136, 145, 147,
    150, 162, 235, 238, 253, 261–264,
    268–269, 271, 285–286, 298, 308,
    311, 314–315, 322, 326, 352, 359,
    361, 371, 375, 381, 390, 409,
    422–423, 425, 451, 453, 457, 461,
    463, 470, 483, 491, 495, 514, 516,
    519, 521, 558–559, 563–566, 625,
    628, 639, 657, 662, 683–684, 687,
    696, 707, 740
  Jewish self-defense in, 188, 514
  Jews in, 16, 37, 70, 78, 163, 171–172,
    212, 215, 263, 268, 313–314, 370,
    378, 381, 407, 409, 439, 459, 492,
    555, 563, 565, 614, 641
  Pale of Settlement, 36, 78, 97, 503, 565,
    683, 687
  pogroms in, 33, 37–38, 41, 136, 162,
    188, 203, 212, 239–240, 263–264,
    268, 286, 315, 359, 378, 409, 436,
    450, 457, 514, 544, 565, 683
  socialism in, 39, 78, 265, 268, 371, 614
  U.S. policy toward, 33
  White emigrés from, 182–183
  Zionism in, 39, 203, 208, 214, 740
Russian Orthodox Church, 19, 36, 38, 380
Russian Progressive Labor Association,
  298
Russian revolution of 1905, 235, 261, 285
Russian Yiddish Opera Company, 450
Russo-American treaty of 1832, 240
Russo-Japanese War, 408, 410
Russo-Turkish War, 262
Rutgers University, 353, 661, 718
  and Partisan Review, 627–628
  Law School, 340
Ruth, Babe (George Herman), 529
Ruthenia, 100
Rwanda, genocide in, 258–259
Ryskind, Morrie, 459, 463

Saarinen, Eero, 756
Sabbatai Zevi, 39, 342, 610
Sabbath, Adolph J., 139
Sacco-Vanzetti case, 338, 381–383, 646,
  692–693
Sachar, Abram, 756

Sachs, Hans, 711
Sachs, Joseph, 28
Sacks, I. Milton, 760
Sadat, Anwar, 618
Safam, 681
Sagan, Carl, 746–747
Sahl, Mort, 488
Salanter, Israel, 710
Sales, Soupy, 488
Salomon, Edward, 323
Saltonstall, Leverett, 187–188
Salvador, Francis, 10, 14, 146
Samuel, Maurice, 215–216, 770
Samuels, Diane, 638
Samuelson, Paul, 717–719, 721–722
San Diego, CA, 99, 150, 152
San Diego Chargers, 519
San Francisco, 28, 132, 191, 241, 253,
  274–275, 301, 341, 399, 461, 470,
  503, 544, 569, 571, 675, 694,
  702–703
  antisemitism and, 514, 712
  Jewish community in, 150–154, 666,
    695
  labor organizing in, 382
  psychoanalysis in, 712
  Yiddish press in, 266
San Francisco Conservatory of Music, 694
San Jose, CA, 152
Sand, George, 542
Sandler, Adam, 490
Sanger, Isaac, 396, 398
Sanger, Margaret, 125, 528
Sanger Brothers, 398, 402
Santa Fe, NM, 7, 155–156, 399
Santa Fe Trail, 155
Santayana, George, 527, 727–728
São Tomé, 412–413
Saperstein, Abe, 517
Sapiro, Aaron, 185
Sarasohn, Kasriel Tsvi, 263–264, 266–267
Sarasohn, Yehezl, 263–264, 266–267
Sarna, Nahum, 760
Sarnoff, David, 474
Sarton, George, 734
Sartre, Jean-Paul, 651
Sasso, Sandy, 109
Satan in Goray, 608–609
Satz, Ludwig, 453
Saudi Arabia, 250, 282
  and ritual murder accusation, 244
  and slavery, 198
Savannah, Georgia, 2–3, 10–11, 14, 19,
  145–146, 325, 418, 761
Saypol, Irving, 291–292
Schakowsky, Jan, 139
Schapiro, Meyer, 650, 652–654
Schayes, Dolph, 516
Schechter, Mathilda, 108
Schechter, Solomon, 83–84, 87, 142

Schechtmann, Joseph, 210, 212
Schenck, Joseph, 461
Schenck, Nicholas, 461
Schiff, Jacob, 33, 35, 42, 46, 117, 181, 184,
  240, 407–408 (photo), 409–410,
  422, 428, 751, 770
Schiff, Mortimer, 428
Schildkraut, Rudolph, 453, 555
Schindler, Alexander M., 80
Schindler, Oskar, 466
Schindler's List, 466 (photo)
Schlemiel, 480, 547
  Alfred E. Neuman as, 472
  Jerry Lewis as, 484
  Seinfeld characters as, 479
  Woody Allen playing, 489, 491–492
Schlesinger, Benjamin, 360–361, 366
Schlesinger, James R., 319
Schlesinger, Sigmund, 666
Schlimazl, 479
Schlossberg, Joseph, 373
Schmeling, Max, 514–515
Schneeberger, Henry W., 69
Schneerson, Joseph Isaac, 99
Schneerson, Menachem Mendel, 98
  (photo)–100, 102, 105, 201–202
Schneider, Benno, 454
Schneiderman, Rose, 308–309, 375, 377,
  383–384 (photo), 385–388
Schoenberg, Arnold, 699, 704–706
Schoenbrun, David, 273
Scholem, Gershom, 301
Scholes, Myron, 721
Schoolman, Albert, 754
Schorr, Daniel, 273
Schottland, Charles I., 756
Schultz, Dutch (Arthur Flegenheimer), 29,
  351, 356, 470
Schulweis, Harold, 94
Schumpeter, Joseph, 721
Schwalb, Susan, 638
Schwartz, Delmore, 561, 622, 677
Schwartz, Maurice, 453–454
Schwarz, Sid, 94
Schwimmer, Rosika, 182
Science fiction, 507–512, 583, 747
Scooler, Zvi, 453
Scott, Harry, 177, 180
Scott, Walter, 541
Scottsboro Boys, 424–425 (photo), 426
Sears, Roebuck & Co., 28, 136, 184, 361,
  398, 406–407, 428
Seattle, WA, 150, 153–154, 703
  East European Jews in, 153
  labor organizing in, 382
  Sephardim in, 5, 153, 669
  Soviet Jews in, 50
  Zionism in, 154
Second Avenue, New York, 120, 316
  and Yiddish theater, 453, 495, 697

Second Temple, destruction of, 412, 452, 539, 639, 665
Second Vatican Council, 242, 245, 437, 440. *See also Nostra Aetate*
The Secret Relationship Between Blacks and Jews, 192, 195–198, 429
Securities and Exchange Commission (SEC), 277, 339, 345
Sedgwick, Catherine, 541
Sedran, Barney, 515–516
Sedway, Moe, 356
Seeger, Pete, 674, 681
Seeligson, Michael, 43
Seforim, Mendele Mocher, 607
Segal, George (sculptor), 643–644, 659–660 (photo), 661–662
Seinfeld, 477–478 (photo), 479–480, 490
Seinfeld, Jerry, 480, 483–484, 490
Seitz, Peter, 533
Seixas, Gershom, 16, 20–21, 539
Seixas, Moses, 539
Seize the Day, 547, 560
Selig, Bud, 518
Seligman, Edwin R. A., 720
Selma, AL, 226, 391
Selten, Reinhard, 721
Semitics Museum, Harvard University, 409
Sender, Toni, 388–390
Sephardic Jews, 1–10, 26, 31, 51, 68, 75–76, 83, 107, 110–111, 116, 119, 127–128, 130–132, 136, 141, 143, 145, 147–148, 150–151, 153–154, 157–158, 184, 274, 284, 336, 343, 487, 537, 540, 571–572, 665, 669, 682, 703, 711
Settlement houses, 35, 51, 70, 117, 154, 184, 373, 386, 409, 515, 522–524, 528, 569, 652, 654, 699. *See also* Hebrew Settlement House; Henry Street Settlement; Hull House; Irene Kaufmann Settlement House; Young Women's Union
Seward, William, 33
Shabazz, Malik, 196, 198
Shahn, Ben, 635, 646, 660
Shakespeare, William, 540, 544, 564, 576
Shakow, David, 709
Shalom, Yitzhak, 6
Shanker, Albert, 390–391 (photo), 392–393, 430
Shapiro, Jake "Gurrah," 354, 356–357
Shapiro, Sam, 139
Shapiro, Saul, 87
Sharansky, Natan, 144
Sharpton, Al, 281
Shatzky, Jacob, 769
Shavuoth. See Shevuot
Shearith Israel (New York), 2–4, 7–9, 16–17, 20–21, 184, 343, 539, 749
Shecter, Leonard, 521

Sheingold, Joseph, 453
Shelley v. Kramer, 244, 428
Shelley, Mary, 539
Shelton, Robert, 192
Sheridan, Art, 671
Sherman, Allan, 140
Sherman, Allie, 519
Sherry, Larry, 517
Sherry, Norm, 531
Shevuot, 270, 578
Shiplacoff, Abraham, 125
Shlemiel. See Schlemiel
Shoah Foundation, 225, 259, 466
Sholem Aleichem, 316, 459, 508, 567, 607–608
Sholem Aleichem Folk Institute, 751, 754
Show Boat, 455, 457
Shteyngart, Gary, 545–548
Shtif, Nokhem, 769
Shulman, Irving, 125
Shuster, Joe, 471–472
Shwartz, Susan, 509
Sidis, Boris, 707
Siegel, Benjamin "Bugsy," 349, 351, 353–354, 356
Siegel, Jerry, 471–472
Siegman, Henry, 250
Silver Shirts, 190, 218, 355
Silver, Abba Hillel, 207–208, 211–212
Silver, Joan Micklin, 465
Silverberg, William, 712
Silvers, Phil, 484, 488
Simmel, Ernst, 712
Simmons, W. J., 189
Simmons, William, 239
Simon Wiesenthal Center, 256–259
    Museum of Tolerance, 134, 259
Simon, Danny, 475
Simon, Herbert (economist), 721
Simon, Herbert (psychologist), 709
Simon, Leonard, 355
Simon, Neil, 475, 488
Simon, Paul, 674–675
Sinai (Suez) campaign, 1956, 7, 214
Sinatra, Frank, 129, 507, 670, 701
Sinclair, Upton, 575
Singer, Isaac Bashevis, 129, 226, 270, 274, 449, 465, 606–607 (photo), 608–610 (illustration), 611, 659, 663
Siodmak, Robert, 463
Siporin, Mitchell, 760
Six Day War, 7, 80, 87, 101, 129, 214, 242, 245, 282, 304, 306, 319, 328, 344, 429, 441, 557, 562, 600, 618, 643, 680
Skokie, IL, 136, 138, 165
Skulnik, Menasha, 453, 492
Slaiman, Donald, 255
Slansky trial, 294

Slaton, John, 176, 178, 243
Slave labor in Soviet Union, 389
Slomovitz, Philip, 350
Slovakia, 24, 635–636
Smiley, Allen, 355–356
Smith, Adam, 720
Smith, Al, 288–289, 376, 437
Smith, Benjamin, 194
Smith, Bessie, 697
Smith, Bradley, 257
Smith, Gerald L. K., 186
Smith, Kate, 685
Smith, Orlando J., 181
Smith, Red, 521
Smith College, 309, 525, 527–528
Smithsonian Institution, 84, 142
Sobell, Morton, 291–293
Social Democratic Party (SPD) of Germany, 388
Socialism, 39, 42, 53, 59–60, 90, 216, 232, 270–271, 283–290, 297–299, 302, 304, 307–308, 313–316, 364–369, 371–373, 375, 378–381, 386–390, 392, 409, 470, 474, 551, 564–566, 568, 595, 614–615, 621–625, 629, 640, 661, 691, 714–715, 721, 730, 734, 736, 740, 742, 745, 751, 757
    and agrarian colonies, 162
    and Bund, 285, 316, 365–366, 371, 374, 652
    and Jewish Labor Committee, 255
    and Jewish press, 119, 139, 264–270, 274–275, 284–285, 360, 375, 564, 594, 614–615
    and Jews, 19–20, 34, 41, 119–120, 284–289, 314, 751
    and Turnverein, 30, 34
    and United Hebrew Trades, 284, 286
    and Workmen's Circle, 125, 235–236, 286, 299, 360, 751
    and Zionism, 120, 205, 208–209, 212–216, 373–374, 440, 551
    in Milwaukee, 34, 284, 378
    Lassallean, 29
Socialist Labor Party, 34, 265, 284–285, 315, 615
Socialist Party, 34, 285, 313, 315–316, 363–365, 372, 376, 379, 383, 386
    and German Socialist Federation, 34
    and Jewish Labor Committee, 253
    and Jewish Socialist Federation, 236
    and Jews, 284–289
    and Workmen's Circle, 236–237, 284–285
    and World War I, 236, 286, 316, 326, 364, 410
    in New York State Assembly, 125
    post–World War I split, 34, 364
    Women's National Committee, 34
Society for Humanistic Judaism, 746

Society for the Advancement of Judaism, 90–91, 96
Sokolsky, George E., 693
Solis-Cohen, Solomon, 142
Solomon, Benjamin, 332
Solomon, Charles "King," 349, 351–352
Solomon, Clara, 325
Solomon, Elias L., 71
Solomon, Hannah, 32, 35
Solomon Schechter schools, 86, 131, 753
Solomons, David, 171
Solotaroff, Hillel, 298
Soloveitchik, Joseph Dov, 72, 437–440
Solow, Robert, 719
Solti, George, 139
Sombart, Werner, 411–412
Sondheim, Stephen, 457–458, 689
Sonneschein, Rosa, 308–309
South Africa, 174, 197, 231, 246, 459, 675, 758
   Jews in, 39, 134, 404
South Carolina, 10, 12, 14, 18–19, 75, 146, 148, 157, 401, 415, 573
South Sea Company, 415
Southern Baptist Convention, 148
Southern Jewish Historical Society, 149
South Pacific, 458, 674
South Philadelphia Hebrew Association, 516
Southern Poverty Law Center, 257, 259
Southern Tenant Farmers Union, 383
Soviet Union, 19, 191, 217, 227, 236, 271, 287–288, 293, 301–302, 304–305, 318–319, 367, 372–374, 392, 398, 547, 549, 556, 569–571, 593, 615, 617–618, 626, 629, 675, 702, 716, 723, 740–741, 744–745
   antisemitism and oppression of Jews in, 49, 87, 99, 144, 233, 241, 245, 251, 255, 275, 282, 287, 294, 389, 548, 556, 681
   collapse of, 283, 648
   during Holocaust, 220
   espionage and, 290–292, 294–297
   German invasion of, 220, 692
   Holocaust survivors from, 224
   Jewish immigration from, 47–50, 58, 131, 134, 138, 144, 344, 546–548, 640, 648
   slave labor in, 389
Soyer, Isaac, 640, 662
Soyer, Moses, 640, 662
Soyer, Raphael, 635, 660, 662–663 (photo), 664
Spain, 1–2, 8, 10, 14, 116, 172, 389, 540
   Civil War in, 232, 313, 327–329, 366, 744
   Expulsion of Jews, 3–4, 128, 238, 404, 412–414, 426, 610
   Inquisition, 1–2, 7, 14, 128, 172, 238, 404, 413, 417, 424

pogroms of 1391, 2
war with United States (1898), 238–239
See also Sephardic Jews
Spanish-American War, 238–239
Spector, Phil, 673
Speakeasies, 351, 700
SPHAs, 516
Spider-Man, 471
Spiegel, Marcus, 322, 325
Spiegelman, Art, 473, 546
Spielberg, Steven, 225, 259, 465–466 (photo)
Spier, Leslie, 726
Spingarn, Arthur, 424
Spingarn, Joel, 424, 428
The Spirit, 473
Spitz, Mark, 520, 532
Sportswriting and Jews, 427, 513, 516, 519–521
Springer, Maida, 377
Springfield College, 525
St. Louis Cardinals, 517
St. Louis, MO, 316, 401, 521
   Jewish institutions, 524
   Jews in, 27–28, 146, 309, 419–420, 550
   Yiddish theater in, 454
St. Louis, 219
St. Petersburg, Russia, 37–38, 49, 410, 558, 696, 719
Stalin, Joseph, 195, 287–288, 293–294, 364, 366, 483, 557, 610, 626, 631. 723, 769
   and Erlich-Alter affair, 367
   and purges, 49
   pact with Hitler, 372, 454, 715
   See also, Moscow Trials; slave labor in Soviet Union; Soviet Union
Stalinism and Stalinists, 233, 287, 313, 569, 573, 593, 621, 715. See also Communism and Anti-Communism
Stalingrad, 458
Staller, Max, 298
Stamp Act, 12–14
Stanford University, 267, 341, 553, 622, 708, 721
Stanton, Frank, 730
Stark, Abe, 124
Stark, Albert "Dolly," 518
Stark, Edward, 666
Stasi, 191
State University of New York, Stony Brook, 625
Statue of Liberty, 2, 51, 545
Steamship transportation, 39–40, 46, 128, 150, 153
Steele, Julian, 424
Steffens, Lincoln, 173
Stein, Herbert, 721
Stein, Joseph, 459

Stein, Maurice, 760
Steinhardt, Michael, 754
Steinhem, Gloria, 473
Steinthal, Heymann, 726–727
Stern College, 109
Stern, David, 516
Stern, Horace, 143
Stern, Steve, 149, 546
Stern's, 395
Sternberg, Fritz, 713
Stevenson, Adlai, 339
Stewart, Jon, 490
Stickball, 517
Stiglitz, Joseph, 721
Still, Peter, 419
Stiller, Ben, 490
Stiller, Jerry, 479, 489–490
Stillman's gym, 515
Stirling, S. M., 509
Stoller, Mike, 673
Stoller, Sam, 519
Stollman, Areyeh Lev, 546
Stone, I. F., 274, 295
Stone, Richard, 127, 130, 148
Stone, Steve, 517
Stoop ball, 517
Strasser, Adolph, 29, 34, 369
Straus, Isidor, 35
Straus, Lazarus, 28, 396
Straus, Nathan, 238, 397–398
Straus, Oscar, 30, 33, 240, 279
Strauss, Harry, 352, 357
Strauss, Leo, 35
Strauss, Levi, 28, 150
Strauss, Lewis, 279
Streisand, Barbra, 455, 465, 497, 672, 682
Strikes, 264, 266, 286, 298, 315, 367, 369, 386
   and Sephardim, 5
   and Workmen's Circle, 235
   auto, 382
   bakers', 264, 365
   baseball players', 533–534
   cigar makers', 369
   Fulton Bag, 180
   furriers', 362–365
   garment, 137, 287, 297, 308, 342, 360–361, 366, 371, 376, 382, 386, 615
   Great Upheaval, 264
   Homestead, 299
   hospital, 126
   miners', 402
   rent, 125, 376
   Republic Steel, 232
   Revisionists' opposition to, 209
   rubber workers', 382
   teachers', 303–305, 390–392, 430–431
   Yiddish writers', 267
Strochlitz, Sigmund, 225

Strum, James, **474**

Strunsky, Anna, **378**

Student Nonviolent Coordinating Committee (SNCC), **255**

Stutchkoff, Nokhem, **769**

Stuyvesant High School, **390**

Stuyvesant, Peter, **11, 537–538**

Suburbs, Jews in, **62, 72, 108, 131, 136, 138–140, 165–167, 297, 351, 357, 395, 429, 475, 478, 488, 513, 520, 532, 616, 623, 674, 752**
   and Soviet Jewish émigrés, **47–49**
   antisemitism in, **165**
   Conservative Judaism in, **72, 85–86, 88–89, 138**
   Hasidim in, **98, 100, 104**
   Orthodox Judaism in, **72, 166–167**
   Reform Judaism in, **72, 79, 138**
   Sabbath driving and, **89, 166**
   satirized, **166, 602**
   shopping malls, **167, 401**
   sociological studies of, **85, 88, 166**
   Workmen's Circle in, **237**

Sudan, **230**
   Jews from, **8**
   slavery in, **259**

Sue, Eugene, **542**

Suicide bombings against Israelis, **247, 258, 444–446**

Sukkot, **92 (photo), 137**

Sulzberger, Cyrus L., **172**

Sulzberger, Mayer, **142, 240**

Sulzer, Salomon, **666**

Summer camps, Jewish, **79, 86, 133, 137, 208, 236–237, 457, 519, 680–682, 754**

Summer in Williamsburg, **566–567**

Summers, Lawrence, **279, 281, 718**

Super Bowl, **519**

Superman, **471–472**

Surrealists, **642, 651, 656–658**

Sutro, Abraham, **111**

Swartz, Maud, **377, 387**

Sweeney, Frances, **188**

Swerling, Jo, **463**

Swimming, **467, 482, 520, 522–526, 532**

Switzerland, **52, 139, 214, 268, 459, 693, 713, 743**
   and antisemitism, **32**
   Zionist congresses in, **183, 203–204**

Synagogue and temple bombings, **259**
   in Florida, **130, 403**
   in Istanbul, **247**
   in South, **403**

Synagogue Council of America, **73, 331, 756**

Syracuse, NY, **667**
   largely Jewish Civil War company from, **322–323**
   Women's Rights Convention (1852), **308**

Syracuse Nationals, **516**

Syracuse University, **516, 677**

Syria, **116, 214, 244, 319, 669, 759**
   antisemitism in, **32, 111, 244, 258, 442**

Syrian Jews, **6–7, 32, 116, 669**

Syrkin, Marie, **214–215, 288**

Syrkin, Nachman, **214–215, 288**

Szell, George, **689**

Szold, Benjamin, **422**

Szold, Henrietta, **33, 148, 205, 272, 571**

Taft, Philip, **379**

Taft, William Howard, **243, 336, 338, 398, 410**

Taft-Hartley Act, **365**

Tageblat, **119, 263–267, 595**

Tajikistan, **48**

Talmud Torahs, **2, 6, 20, 71, 378, 440, 749–754**

Tanenbaum, Marc, **242**

Tannenbaum, Frank, **427**

Tappan, Arthur, **420**

Tappan, Lewis, **420**

Taubman, Craig, **681**

Taussig, Frank W., **719–720**

Taxi, **476–477**

Taylor, Elizabeth, **129, 257, 490**

Taylor, George, **534**

Teitelbaum, Joel Moshe, **100–101, 105**

Teitelbaum, Moshe, **101**

Tel Aviv, **127, 213, 226, 459, 689**

Temple University, **144, 734**

The Tenants, **579, 581**

Tenn, William, **509**

Tennis, **468, 520, 522, 524, 526**

Terkel, Studs, **139**

Teutsch, David, **96**

Texas, **340, 606, 701**
   Galveston and Galveston Plan, **42–47, 148, 409, 514**
   Jewish stores in **398, 401–402**
   Jews in and from, **175, 398, 526, 678, 711**
   "secret Jews" in, **7**
   See also Dallas; Galveston; Neiman-Marcus

Thier, Samuel O., **756**

Thomas, Norman, **236–237**

Thompson, Dorothy, **218**

Thorndike, Edward, **752**

Three Cities, **555**

Three Stooges, The, **483, 486–487 (photo)**

Tikkun, **274, 679**

Tin Pan Alley, **455, 672–673, 683–686, 697**

Tisha B'Av, **610, 688**

Tlas, Mustafa, **244, 258**

Tobin, Maurice, **188**

Toblinsky, Joseph, **349**

Todd, Michael, **140**

Tolkin, Mel, **475**

Tolstoy, Leo, **451, 630**

Tomashefsky, Boris, **450–453**

Tomashefsky, Paysach, **450**

Topfer, Rudolph, **469**

Tormé, Mel, **139**

Touro, Judah, **2, 418**

Touro College, **133**

Touro Synagogue (Jeshuat Israel), **2, 13, 107**

Track and field, **519–520, 522–524, 526**

Trade Union Educational League (TUEL), **364**

Transylvania, **24**

Treaty of Brest–Litovsk, **326**

Treblinka, **230, 705**

Triangle Fire, **376, 385, 473**

Trilling, Diana, **288, 301, 631**

Trilling, Lionel, **274, 288, 625, 630–631 (photo), 632–633, 735**

Trotsky, Leon, **302, 557, 621–623, 626, 628, 630**

Truman, Harry S, **207, 280, 294, 367, 377**

Tuberculosis, **40, 566**
   and Workmen's Circle sanatorium, **236**
   in Brownsville, **124**
   in garment industry, **361**

Tucker, Benjamin, **564**

Tucker, Sam, **351**

Tucker, Sophie, **494–497**

Turkish Jews, **6, 8, 116, 132, 669**

Turkus, Burton, **354**

Turner, Big Joe, **671, 673**

Turner, Frederick Jackson, **378**

Turner, Nat, **198, 419**

The Turner Diaries, **189, 191, 194, 259**

Turnverein, **30, 34**

Tuska, Simon, **146**

Tuskegee Institute, **423, 428**

Twain, Mark, **171–172, 578, 629**

Twentieth Century Fox, **461**

Twerski, Michel, **104**

Twerski, Mordechai, **104**

Twerski, Yaakov Israel, **104**

Twersky, Dovid, **103**

Twersky, Isadore, **103**

Twersky, Meir, **103**

Twersky, Nahum, **103**

Tyler, John, **396**

Ukraine, **24, 666**
   Hasidim in, **103**
   Jewish agricultural colonies in, **407**
   Jewish immigrants from, **38–39, 47–48, 212, 516, 628, 641, 658, 660, 666, 697**
   pogroms in, **38, 212, 239, 268, 287, 327**
   See also Kiev; Odessa

U.S. Constitution, **18, 26, 342, 347, 728**
   Article VI, **18, 20, 22**

U.S. Constitution (continued)
Bill of Rights, 18–19, 100, 246, 250,
283, 337, 380, 434, 464
Fourteenth Amendment, 380
Eighteenth Amendment, 351
Nineteenth Amendment, 309
U.S. Department of Commerce and Labor,
46
U.S. Department of Justice, 187, 341, 410
U.S. Department of Labor, 368, 377, 721
U.S. Department of State, 99
and Balfour Declaration, 205
and Israel, 207, 280, 319
response to Nazism and Holocaust,
218–224, 253
U.S. Department of the Treasury, 718, 722
and Holocaust, 211, 219, 222
U.S. Department of War, 223, 331, 338
U.S. Revisionists, 208–210, 212
U.S. Sanitary Commission, 323
U.S. Supreme Court, 190, 246, 250, 328,
335–348, 464, 734
U.S. Tariff Commission, 720
U.S. Women's Bureau, 377
Uhry, Albert, 149
Ulmer, Edgar G., 465
"Uncle Jake" awards, 275
Underground comics of 1960s, 472–473
Underground Railroad, 419
Uniate Church, 36
Union for Reform Judaism, 74, 81, 132,
143, 281, 445, 770
Union of American Hebrew
Congregations, 31, 44, 77–81,
112–113, 147, 184, 253, 281, 295,
433–435, 441, 750, 753–754, 770
Union of Needletrades, Industrial, and
Textile Employees (UNITE), 362
Union of Orthodox Jewish Congregations
of America (OU), 7, 69, 71, 73, 184,
433–435
Union of Orthodox Rabbis of the United
States and Canada (UOR), 70–71,
73, 91, 142
Union of Soviet Socialist Republics
(USSR). See Soviet Union
Unitarians, 22–23, 74, 147, 169, 420, 436,
746
United Artists, 461
United Auto Workers union, 252, 255, 382,
622
United Cloth Hat and Cap Makers' Union,
386
United Federation of Teachers (UFT), 126,
303, 390–392, 430
United Garment Workers (UGW),
371–372
United Hatters, Cap and Millinery
Workers International Union, 366
United Hebrew Charities, 32, 41, 144, 399

United Hebrew Relief Associations, 32,
135
United Hebrew Trades, 29, 119, 121, 125,
252, 265, 271, 284–286, 298, 313,
362–363, 370, 453
United Jewish Appeal (UJA), 208,
224–225, 353, 356
United Jewish Communities, 91, 149
United Jewish Organizations (UJO), 101
United Mine Workers Union, 372,
382–383
United Nations, 207, 241, 244–245, 255,
274, 292, 310, 339, 377, 388, 430,
642, 689, 757
United Nations Conferences on Women
(1975, 1980, 1985), 310
United Nations Economic and Social
Council, 388
United Nations Partition of Palestine, 241,
244, 642
United Spanish War Veterans, 239
United States Holocaust Memorial
Council, 225, 228–230
United States Holocaust Memorial
Museum, 228–231, 246, 659
United Steelworkers of America, 339, 433,
534
United Steelworkers v. Weber, 433
United Synagogue of America, 84, 87, 142
United Synagogue of Conservative
Judaism, 84, 88–89, 143
United Zionists-Revisionists of America,
212
Universal studios, 133, 461
Université de Paris, 99
University in Exile, 35
University of Arkansas, 379
University of Berlin, 99, 439, 719, 765
University of California, Berkeley, 300,
302, 470, 695
University of California, Davis, 433
University of California, Los Angeles
(UCLA), 721
antisemitism at, 195
University of Chicago, 35, 136, 232,
557–559, 563, 594, 596, 712, 718,
720–722, 731
University of Cincinnati, 531, 767
University of Denver, 445
University of Frankfurt, 716
University of Ghana, 703
University of Heidelberg, 239, 457, 722
University of Illinois, Champaign-Urbana,
193, 390, 502
University of Judaism, 86, 134
University of Kiel, 719
University of Leningrad, 719
University of Louisville, 345
University of Miami, 131
University of Michigan, 434–435, 519, 586

University of Minnesota, 559
University of North Carolina, 148, 157
University of Notre Dame, 190, 733
University of Pennsylvania, 144, 380, 691,
708, 720
University of Pittsburgh, 199, 519
University of Rome, 719
University of South Carolina, 708
University of Southern California, 225,
526
University of Texas, 606
University of Vienna, 720, 730, 763
University of Virginia, 678
University of Washington, 433
University of Wisconsin, 52, 378–380, 559,
574, 708, 728
University Settlement, 518
Untermeyer, Louis, 274
Uprising of the 20,000, 308, 360–361, 376,
386
Urban League, 126, 424, 428
Uris, Leon, 224, 611–613
Uzbekistan, 48

Van Buren, Martin, 32–33
Van Doren, Carl, 575
Van Doren, Mark, 575
Van Gogh, Vincent, 652–653
Vance, Dazzy, 534
Vapnyar, Lara, 546–548
Vatican, 654
and Damascus blood libel, 33, 111
and Holocaust, 437
and Israel, 438
and Mortara affair, 33, 281, 768
and Nazis, 241
and Second Vatican Council, 242, 245,
437, 440
Vaudeville, 451, 460–462, 475, 481–484,
486–487, 490, 494–495, 498–499,
501, 503, 505–506, 589, 598,
684–685, 697
Vaynshteyn, Bernard, 265
Veblen, Thorstein, 380–381, 734, 742, 745
Venona Project, 296–297
Versailles conference and treaty, 205, 240,
248, 327, 720
The Victim, 559
Vienna, 29, 37, 39, 47, 171–172, 174, 256,
258, 337, 455, 462–463, 465, 576,
704, 730
Jewish Theological Seminary of, 763
music in, 666, 690
psychoanalysis in, 710–711, 713
Vietnam War, 80, 238, 255, 278, 289, 300,
302, 304, 318, 328, 339, 455, 458,
622, 662, 674, 716, 758
A View from the Bridge, 588
Vigee, Claude, 760
Villard, Oswald, 565

Vilna, 299, 594, 652–653
    Jews from, 70, 299
    Jews in, 70, 227, 268, 608, 614, 769
    killing of Jews in, 214, 646
    YIVO in, 768–769
Viner, Jacob, 720
Vinson, Fred, 339
Virginia, 17–19, 76, 111, 197, 443, 611,
    678. *See also* Richmond
Virginia Act for Religious Freedom, 18,
    146
Virginia Military Institute (VMI), 341
Viteles, Morris, 709
Vladeck, Baruch Charney, 252–253
Volleyball, 524
von Mises, Ludwig, 720–721
von Sternberg, Josef, 463
von Stroheim, Erich, 463
Voting Rights Act of 1965, 245, 428, 432

Wage Earners League for Woman Suffrage,
    387
Wagner, Robert, 376
Wagner Act, 277, 345
Wagner-Rogers Bill, 218–219
Waksman, Selman A., 770
Wald, Lillian, 35, 117–118, 287, 409
Waldman, Leibele, 668
Walker, David, 421
The Wall, 224
Wallace, George, 191
Wallace, Lew, 173
Walling, William English, 378–379
Wanamaker's, 399–400
Wang, Martin, 713
War and Remembrance, 615–616
War of 1812, 75
War Refugee Board, 211, 222–223, 241
Warburg, Daniel, 418
Warburg, Eugene, 418
Warburg, Felix, 278, 361, 428, 770
Warburg, Paul M., 181
Warner Brothers, 133, 461, 464, 502
Warner, Harry, 461, 464, 502
Warner, Jack, 502
Warner, Sam, 502
Warren, Earl, 339–340, 346
Warren Court, 339–340, 347
Warsaw, 606, 699, 704–705
    annihilation of Jews of, 705
    German bombing of, 609
    Jews in, 24, 37, 99, 136, 172, 439, 461,
        515, 554–555, 594, 608
    pogrom in, 37
    Yiddish press in, 274
    Yiddish theater in, 494
Warsaw Ghetto Uprising, 188, 224, 254,
    458, 556, 612, 641, 769
Warshow, Robert, 295, 301
Washington Heights, 35

Washington Redskins, 519, 521
Washington, Booker T., 407, 421, 423,
    428
Washington, George, 19–20, 26, 539, 618,
    659
Washington, DC, 30, 33, 80, 91, 99,
    209–210, 220, 222–223, 225,
    228–229, 239, 242, 246, 252, 255,
    324, 338–340, 363, 377, 387, 395,
    442–443, 499, 553, 596–597, 619,
    654, 659, 662–663, 674, 718, 720,
    733
Washington University, 309
Waterloo, battle of, 317
Watson, Tom, 147, 178–180
The Way We Were, 497
We Will Never Die pageant, 210, 220
Webb, Beatrice, 379–380
Webb, Del, 356
Webb, Sidney, 379–380
Weber, Max (artist), 640–642, 645, 657
Weber, Max (sociologist), 734
Wechsler, David, 709
Weill, Claudia, 465
Weill, Felix, 713
Weill, Kurt, 455, 692
Weimar Republic, 388, 555, 714, 722, 724,
    744
Weinberg, Chaim, 298
Weinberg, Shaike, 230
Weiner, Lazare, 668
Weinreich, Max, 769
Weinreich, Uriel, 769
Weinstein, Joyce Ellen, 635
Weintraub, Phil, 517
Weisberg, Joseph, 274
Weisberg, Ruth, 643
Weiss-Rosmarin, Trude, 274, 770
Weizmann, Chaim, 205–206 (photo), 207,
    215, 342, 380, 575, 729, 744
Welch, Jr., Robert H. W., 193
Welles, Orson, 257, 692
Wellesley College, 197, 527, 594
Wendell, Barrett, 52, 727
Wertham, Fredric, 472
Wertheimer, Max, 709
Wesley, John, 14
West End of Boston, 104
West India Company. See Dutch West
    India Company
West Side Story, 457, 686, 689
Westphalia, 31, 111, 724
WEVD radio station, 254, 389
Wexler, Jerry, 670–672
Wharton, Edith, 173, 624
When She Was Good, 602–603
White Aryan Resistance (WAR), 257
"White Christmas," 685–686
White Citizens Councils, 400
White, Theodore, 273

Whitman, Walt, 54, 170, 543–544, 564,
    571, 624, 629–630, 691, 694–695
Whittier, John Greenleaf, 169
Wickersham, George, 336
Wiesel, Elie, 129, 225–228 (photo), 247
Wiesenthal, Simon, 256–257, 259
Wildenberg, Harry L., 472
Wilder, Billy, 463
Wilder, Gene, 465
Wilder, Thornton, 570
Wilderness, Battle of, 323
Wilkins, Roy, 255
Wilkinson, Bill, 192–193
Will and Grace, 477, 480
William Alanson White Institute, 712
Williams, Roger, 13
Williams, Tennessee, 582
Williams College, 457–458, 733
Williamsburg, Brooklyn, 124
    Daniel Fuchs trilogy, 566–568
    Hasidim in, 97–98, 100–101
    Orthodox yeshiva in, 71
    Soviet Jews in, 48
Williamsburg Bridge, 124
Wilson, Edmund, 173, 559, 621, 625, 632
Wilson, James Q., 306
Wilson, Woodrow, 213, 720
    and antisemitism, 185, 243
    and Balfour Declaration, 205, 288
    and Louis Brandeis, 205, 288, 336, 345
    and Federal Reserve system, 181
    and football, 518
    and immigration, 42
    and League of Nations, 288
    and World War I, 326
Winchell, Walter, 427
Winchevsky, Morris, 267, 564, 614–615
The Winds of War, 616
Wine, Sherwin, 746
Winrod, Gerald B., 190, 355
Wisconsin, 34, 213, 367, 381, 461, 498,
    754. *See also* Milwaukee
Wise, Isaac Mayer, 31–32, 34, 69, 75–76
    (photo), 77, 80, 107, 111–113, 147,
    272, 399, 420, 436, 540–544, 667,
    766, 770
Wise, Stephen S., 33, 78–79, 205–207, 220,
    222, 248–249 (photo), 250, 252,
    271, 282, 288, 343, 370, 374, 436,
    440–441, 576
Wish, Harvey, 427
Wisse, Ruth, 560, 609
Wittfogel, Karl-August, 35
Wolf, Simon, 30, 33, 42, 324, 422
Wolfe, Thomas, 173, 630
Wolff, Milton, 328
Wolfson, Harry Austryn, 274, 288
Wolfson, Mitchell, 128
Wollheim, Norbert, 225
Women's Emergency Brigade, UAW, 382

Women's Rabbinic Network, 80
Women's suffrage movement, 78, 309, 527, 550
    Jewish women in, 34, 308, 376, 386–387
Women's Swimming Association (WSA), 525–526
Women's Trade Union League (WTUL), 308, 363, 375–377, 384–387
Wood, Grant, 639
Workers Party, 621
Workers Party of the United States, 236
Workers' Education, 379, 381, 389
Workman, Charley, 353, 356
Workmen's Circle (Arbeter Ring), 119, 125, 129, 139, 235–238, 252–254, 267, 284–286, 299, 360, 363, 453, 467, 595, 751, 754
Works Progress Administration (WPA), 452 (illustration), 559, 654
World Church of the Creator, 189, 194
World Federation of Diamond Bourses, 405
World Jewish Congress, 241, 249, 390, 770
World Labor Athletic Carnival, 253
World of Our Fathers, 29, 545, 622–623, 684
World Series, 521, 530
    (1919), 351
    (1934), 517–518
    (1935), 518
    (1940), 529
    (1945), 529
    (1959), 517
    (1963), 532
    (1965), 532
    (1966), 532
World Union for Progressive Judaism, 91, 770
World War I, 32, 35, 38, 40, 42–43, 45–46, 49, 52, 60, 64, 71, 78, 108, 118, 124, 128, 153, 181, 200, 204, 215, 239–240, 243, 248–249, 273–274, 280, 284, 297, 299, 308–309, 313, 317–318, 338, 342, 349–351, 362–363, 368, 370, 372, 385, 387–388, 398, 400, 402, 406–407, 409, 428, 436, 439, 452–453, 463, 482, 499, 505, 526, 555–556, 569, 574, 592, 661, 667, 685, 708, 720, 725, 728, 741, 744, 752, 763, 768–769
    American Jews and, 326–327
    and Jewish Legion, 213, 239
    and Socialist Party, 236, 286, 316
    and split in anarchist movement, 299
    Jewish soldiers in, 239, 243, 326, 765
World War II, 5, 49, 54, 60, 64–65, 71–73, 78–79, 83, 85, 90, 97, 106, 108–109, 121, 127, 129–130, 132–134,
        136–138, 148, 154–158, 160–161, 165, 190–191, 201, 206, 209, 215–217, 232, 236–241, 243–244, 249, 251, 280, 290, 295–296, 300, 309, 313, 318, 328, 339–340, 344, 349, 357, 362, 366–367, 371–372, 374, 377, 385, 388–389, 400, 404, 424, 426–428, 432, 436–437, 441, 461, 463–466, 469, 476, 483, 488, 494, 503, 506, 513, 517–521, 529, 534, 555–557, 561, 595, 597–598, 615–616, 618, 627–628, 630, 640, 643, 646, 651, 656–658, 667, 670, 680, 707–709, 712–713, 715, 717, 719, 721–723, 726, 729, 736, 741, 744, 752, 755–757, 764, 767, 769
    Albert Einstein during, 744
    American Jewish soldiers in, 237, 239, 328–334, 521, 529, 611–612, 618–619, 658
    and America's response to the Holocaust, 169, 207, 217–224, 278, 744
    antisemitic riots in Boston and New York, 187–189, 218, 424
    in literature and drama, 559, 588, 593, 598, 611–612, 615–616
    Jewish chaplains in, 330–331, 767
World Zionist Congresses. See Zionist Congresses
World Zionist Organization, 206, 209, 212, 575
Wouk, Herman, 562, 615–619
Wright, Frank Lloyd, 233
Wright, Richard, 419
Wright, Wade, 425

X, Malcolm, 192, 194, 196, 429–430

Y. L. Perets Fareyn, 268
Yablokoff, Herman, 453
Yale Law School, 339, 344, 733
Yale College and Yale University, 13, 16, 195, 197, 301, 457, 564, 583, 606, 702, 718, 721, 731, 733, 755
Yanofsky, Zal, 674
Yanovsky, Shoel (Saul), 266, 299
Yates, Sidney, 139
Yates, W. R., 510
Yeats, W. B., 632
Yemeni Jews, 6–8, 669
Yentl, 465, 497
Yeshiva University, 70, 109, 133, 142–143, 439, 604, 617, 668
Yeshivas, 6, 24, 70–71, 76, 78, 90, 100–105, 112, 136, 226, 309, 370, 439–440, 469, 592, 753
Yezierska, Anzia, 547–548, 550–551, 575
Yiddish Art Theater, 453–454
Yiddish cinema, 454, 465, 495, 680

Yiddish literature, 37, 39, 119, 555–557, 564, 606–611, 614–615, 622, 663
Yiddish poetry, 363, 563–566, 594–595, 622–623
Yiddish press, 102, 115, 117, 119–121, 126, 129, 136, 139, 184, 187–188, 252, 261–274, 284–287, 293, 298–300, 314, 316, 326, 350, 360, 363, 375, 379, 424, 426, 428, 470, 472–473, 502–503, 546, 555–557, 564–565, 571, 594–595, 606, 608, 614–615, 622, 663
Yiddish theater, 42, 115, 119, 121, 124, 136–137, 237, 449–455, 457, 459, 462, 473, 492, 494–495, 554–555, 574–575, 680, 697
Yishuv, 78–79, 93, 144, 203–210, 232, 407, 615
YIVO, 139, 768–770
Yockey, Francis Parker, 190–192
Yoffie, Eric H., 81
Yom Ha'atzmaut. See Israel Independence Day
Yom Ha–Shoah. See Holocaust Remembrance Day
Yom Kippur, 43, 135, 155, 298, 305, 311, 322, 343–344, 529–530, 532, 552, 641, 643, 700, 705, 711
Yom Kippur War, 72, 152, 212, 214, 245, 317, 319, 344, 429, 506, 529–530, 617–618, 661, 668–669, 676
Yorkville, 355, 389, 482
Young Israel Movement, 71
Young Men's Hebrew Association (YMHA), 32, 515, 522, 524
Young Women's Hebrew Association (YWHA), 522, 524–526
Young Women's Hebrew Athletic League, 524
Young Women's Union, 524
Young, Andrew, 430
Young, Dick, 521
Youngman, Henny, 489, 508
Your Show of Shows, 475, 488
Yugoslavia, 259
Yulee, David L., 127–128, 146, 419

Zacharie, Isachar, 323
Zalman, Schneur, 99, 105, 710
Zangwill, Israel, 51–52, 272, 500, 541
Zaslofsky, Max, 516
Zelig, Big Jack, 350
Zelig, 493, 547
Zelikovitsh, Getsl, 267
Zeyfert, Moyshe, 267
Zeyfert, Shomer, 267
Zhitlovsky, Chaim. *See* Zhitlowsky, Chaim
Zhitlowsky, Chaim, 288, 769
Ziegfield, Florenz, 502, 697
Ziegfield Follies, 495–496, 502, 697

Zim, Paul, **681**

Zim, Sol, **681**

Zimiles, Murray, **644**

Zimmerman, Charles, 252 (**photo**),
254–255

Zimmerman, Harold, **654**

Zionism, 7, 33, 39, 51–53, 71, 73, 75,
78–80, 90, 93, 100–102, 120,
128–130, 132, 134, 137–139,
142–144, 148, 154, 157, 184, 187,
195, 203–206, 208, 212–216, 220,
232–233, 237, 241–242, 248–250,
253–255, 266, 271, 273–275, 288,
309–310, 316, 326–327, 333,
342–344, 347, 355, 367, 372–374,
389, 410, 421, 436, 439–442, 446,
493, 514–515, 541, 544, 551,
571–573, 575–577, 591, 594, 600,
605, 619, 705, 716, 722, 724,
728–729, 740, 742, 744, 751, 754,
759
Labor, 208–209, 213–216, 235, 252,
288, 373, 385, 441
opposition to, 33, 71, 73, 78–79,
100–101, 113, 142, 144, 148, 154,
183, 195, 235, 237, 240–241,
244–246, 248, 253–254, 275, 294,
304, 310, 312, 367, 370, 389, 407,
437, 442, 751, 770
Revisionist, 207–212, 216

Zionist Congresses, **204**
(1897), 33, 183, 203–204, 309
(1900), 594
(1903), 705
(1905), 705

Zionist Organization of America (ZOA),
129–130, 139, 184, 206–207, 212,
343, 446, 577

Zola, Gary P., **771**

Zola, Irving, **757**

Zubrin, Robert, **510**

Zuckerman Bound, **604**

Zukor, Adolph, **461–462**

Zurich, **711, 743**

Zuroff, Ephraim, 257, 259

Zussmann, Raymond, 332–333 (**photo**)

Zwillman, Abner "Longy," 349, 351–357

Reference